P9-EGD-181

HUGO BLACK

HUGO BLACK

A BIOGRAPHY

ROGER K. NEWMAN

A Cornelia & Michael Bessie Book

PANTHEON BOOKS

New York

Copyright © 1994 by Roger K. Newman

All rights reserved
under International and Pan-American Copyright Conventions.
Published in the United States by Pantheon Books,
a division of Random House, Inc., New York, and simultaneously in
Canada by Random House of Canada Limited, Toronto.

Permissions acknowledgments appear on pages 711–12.

Library of Congress Cataloging-in-Publication Data

Newman, Roger K.
    Hugo Black : a biography / Roger K. Newman.
        p.   cm.
    "A Cornelia & Michael Bessie book."
    Includes bibliographical references and index.
    ISBN 0-679-43180-2
    1. Black, Hugo, LaFayette, 1886–1971.   2. Judges—United States—Biography.
I. Title.
KF8745.B55N49   1994
347.73'2634—dc20
[B]
[347.3073534]
[B]   94-10233

Designed by Michael Mendelsohn of MM Design 2000, Inc.

Manufactured in the United States of America
First Edition
9   8   7   6   5   4   3   2   1

To my parents,
Sydney and Shirley Newman

CONTENTS

"If a single man plant himself on his convictions and then abide, the huge world will come round to him."

—Ralph Waldo Emerson

THE FUNERAL

THE GLORY AND THE POMP, the pageantry and the ceremony were there. It was a state funeral in everything but name. President Richard M. Nixon, conferring fullest honors on the senior Associate Justice of the United States Supreme Court, had ordered flags lowered on all local federal installations. Much of official Washington was present; for a blip of time the business of government stalled.

Scattered throughout the Washington Cathedral were hundreds of notables whose paths had crossed with those of the deceased. He had been in high public office for forty-five years, longer than anyone else on the current American scene, and a mélange of governmental, legal and journalistic personalities came to pay tribute to one of the leading figures of the era. From the New Deal, now graying with age, were Thomas Corcoran and Benjamin V. Cohen, Joseph L. Rauh, Jr., and James Rowe, as well as many other prominent lawyers who got their start then. Margaret Truman represented her father, former president Harry Truman. Another former president, Lyndon Johnson, and his wife Lady Bird were out of the country; otherwise they would have attended. A large congressional delegation came. Columnist Joseph Alsop came; a faithful scion of the northeastern aristocracy whose lineage could not have been more different from the deceased's southern, rural roots and still be in the same country, Alsop looked up to him as "the best that America can produce."

Hugo LaFayette Black had touched them all, just as he had struck a deep chord in the American psyche. Throughout his long life he had consistently shown an unaffected dignity that one could escape only at the price of denying one's own humanity. Hundreds of others came simply to pay their

respects, unknown except as the backbone of the country, the people for
whom the deceased had labored, to give them a better life, to expand their
rights. There were his law clerks, his second family. A bus took nearly all
of the forty-seven surviving clerks, and their wives, to the cathedral. They
had served him with rare devotion and most of them loved him, for he was
an easy man to love. They were naturally expected. But also attending were
General William C. Westmoreland, army chief of staff and an architect of
the war in Vietnam that Black so despised; Deputy Attorney General Richard
Kleindienst and Solicitor General Erwin Griswold, who presented the government's cases to the tribunal on which he played such a conspicuous part;
Secretary of Health, Education and Welfare Elliott Richardson; Attorney
General John N. Mitchell; and, most surprisingly of all, President Nixon.

The entire Supreme Court had worked on the funeral, as if work could
lessen the mourning. It was a time of unparalleled emotion for the justices.
The two most respected of their number, the institution's pillars and the
dearest of friends, Black and John Marshall Harlan, popularly called liberal
and conservative, although those terms were singularly inapt here, had recently retired; and Harlan was suffering from cancer. The present chief
justice, Warren E. Burger, called the deceased "a rare and remarkable man."
The prior occupant of the post, Earl Warren, had said, "A great man has
passed away." Little else could be added.

One thousand persons attended the brief and simple services, homey like
the man himself. At the door pocket-size, Government Printing Office–
issued copies of the Constitution were free for the taking; several copies were
in Black's suit pocket. Members of the Supreme Court police force carried
the coffin into the cathedral. Past and present justices served as honorary
pallbearers, walking slowly behind the coffin under the high gothic arches.
Only Harlan was not present: his doctor ordered him not to attend. Looking
shattered was William O. Douglas, the colleague to whom Justice Black was
ideologically closest over a full generation. The pine knots, the markings
on the wood, and the joinery on the corners and sides of the coffin showed
clearly as it sat on a perch of royal purple velour. "I got him what he wanted,"
the deceased's daughter Josephine said. "We knew what statement my father
wanted to make." The coffin's stark simplicity looked strangely out of place
in the magnificent cathedral, a last dissent by the boy from the Clay County,
Alabama, hill country.

The service was almost ecumenical. The organ intoned "Swing Low,

Sweet Chariot" and "In the Garden," two of his favorite hymns, and the congregation sang "Rock of Ages." The dean of the cathedral, the Reverend Francis B. Sayre, Jr., read the deceased's favorite biblical passage, from I Corinthians 13. Then he recited the Twenty-third Psalm and led the assemblage in the One Hundred Twenty-first: "I will lift up mine eyes unto the hills; from whence cometh my help." As the military held the flag over the coffin, Unitarian minister the Reverend Duncan Howlett read passages from the classics that lined Black's study and from some of his most stirring and eloquent opinions, and talked about the personal qualities that drew a throng so disparate that their admiration for him was one of the few things they could agree on.

Each person had to acknowledge that Hugo Black had stubbornly defended old freedoms while boldly pioneering their extension during a particularly turbulent time in American history. Gentle yet combative, courtly yet tenacious in argument, he praised the sincerity of antagonists. He was steeped in learning but spoke as simply as a front-porch philosopher, offering volumes of homespun liberalism, as plain as it was pure, alternately seducing and frustrating opponents in the process. Above all, he was the driving force behind the constitutional revolution that transformed the nation. "No Justice in our history had a greater impact on our law or on our constitutional jurisprudence," his colleague William J. Brennan, Jr., later wrote. His impact on the country was greater than that of most presidents.

The Constitution meant the same thing from its inception, Hugo Black insisted. He read the Bill of Rights in a liberating spirit. It was his bible on social ethics and a testament of liberty, and he worshiped it without apology. Yet he sang of himself in the words of an old ballad, "I Am a Dirty Rebel." To many of his fellow southerners he was a pariah, a traitor. But he had a serene faith in the ultimate goodness of people. All would be fine if only they would follow the Constitution's guidelines for democracy, the procedures it mandated, the human dignity it ensured. It represented the Republic's best hope for security. Hold to its values of freedom, and Americans could always solve their problems, the noble would ultimately triumph, right would conquer evil. He set the climate for the Supreme Court's decisions, he put the issues on the table. Rarely did he win individual battles over doctrine; almost always did he win the war.

Part of the reason he was being so deeply mourned was his open and passionate love affair with the Constitution and with America. He cherished this "sweet land of liberty," silently bearing the mountains of calumny that came his way. He proudly called himself a patriot. For he had confidence in the good sense of a free people, the Blue and the Gray going forward together, under the Stars and Stripes, the children of the Flag advancing to the march of inevitable progress while retaining timeless human decencies.

The family followed the flag-draped coffin out of the cathedral as the bell tolled eighty-five times, one for each year of the deceased's life. At Arlington National Cemetery a military honor guard lined the route as the coffin was taken to the grave site. The Reverend Howlett repeated the scripture, this time saying, "And the greatest of these is Love." Three cannon shots rang out as a salute. The military, which held the flag throughout the ceremony, now meticulously folded it and handed it to the widow, Elizabeth. She arose to accept it and called on Frank Dillingham, the son-in-law of Justice Harlan, to read a message from him. "Give him our love," she called out. A breeze ruffled the trees and a bugler played the haunting notes of taps.

Hugo Black was buried next to his first wife, Josephine, under a huge oak tree on one of Arlington National Cemetery's highest hills, overlooking the Washington where he spent forty-five years, first as a senator from Alabama and for thirty-four years on the Supreme Court he revered. After a lifetime of achievement on behalf of his fellow citizens, the great man— whose accomplishments ranked him with Franklin D. Roosevelt and Martin Luther King, Jr., among contemporaries, and on the bench with "the great Chief Justice" John Marshall in the early nineteenth century and, in the early twentieth, Oliver Wendell Holmes, Jr., and Louis D. Brandeis—was laid to rest.

Caught in the web of memories, every person present had his or her own favorite Hugo Black story, action or passage. Common to all recollections was the man's character—an inexorable drive that rested uneasily under a relaxed exterior, and a surface simplicity that cut through pretense and baffled sophistication. So ardent were his views as prosecutor, trial lawyer, senator and justice, and so forcefully did he present them, that strife seemed to follow him everywhere. The appropriateness of his stunning feats will be debated as long as democratic self-government survives under the Constitution. That is how it should be. But there can be no argument that the road to those views started in Clay County.

I

THE EARLY YEARS

CHAPTER 1

THE HILL COUNTRY

"I'M JUST A CLAY COUNTY HILLBILLY," Hugo Black liked to say. It usually got a chuckle. But those who had been there smiled knowingly. Clay County, Alabama, lies sixty miles east of Birmingham and thirty miles west of the Georgia state line. On one side is the Tallapoosa River, on the other the Talladega National Forest, alongside a range of mountains. The lush verdant countryside contrasts with the unyielding red clay soil in the small coves of cleared land. Isolation has always been the dominant impression. Early settlers earned a scant living, existing on their own resources, as frontier people always did. Survival was precarious.

One of those who did not survive was Mary Ardella (Little Della) Black. She died on February 22, 1886, two days after her second birthday. Her parents, William LaFayette Black and Martha Ardella Toland Black, of the tiny hamlet of Harlan, and their six other children trundled up to nearby Mount Ararat Cemetery to bury her. Graveside rites were necessarily brief: a storm was sweeping the area and her mother was carrying another child, whose birth was imminent. At home over the next few days the children huddled together; part of the roof of their house had been blown off and carried a short distance. The pains began to rack their mother. The oldest son, Robert Lee, hurried to Hackneyville, about eight miles away, to get Dr. John J. Harlan, a cousin. Dr. Harlan arrived in his buggy and that night, February 27, 1886, a blustery, rainy Saturday, a boy was born.

His name was entered in the family Bible as LaFayette Hugo Black, incongruously Gallic for the Alabama backcountry. LaFayette was his father's middle name, and Hugo was suggested by his oldest sister, Leora, who had been reading the French novelist Victor Hugo when he was born and persuaded her parents not to call him Hugh, which had often been used in the family. But just as almost everybody in Clay County called William LaFayette Black Faet, so the baby was known as Hugo.[1]

Dissent—the right to dissent—was in Hugo Black's blood. Tolands had lived for centuries in New Town Stewart, in County Tyrone, near Londonderry in north Ireland, mainly as farmers and Protestants with strong social consciences. The American Revolution had inspired one of their tribe, Robert Emmet, to become active in the United Irish organization in the 1790s, promoting parliamentary reform and the full civil and political rights of Catholics. Another member was his cousin Elihu (Hugh) Toland. For his activities against the Crown, Toland was sentenced to be beheaded. But before the sentence could be executed, he fled the country. His Masonic brethren put him in a box and bribed the captain of a ship at Londonderry to allow him to remain in the vessel's cargo area until he reached American shores. Because of the Emmet relation the family was under siege. (Emmet was hanged in 1803 after participating in the murder of the Irish chief justice.) Toland's wife and children boarded the same ship, and did not know he was on it until arriving at Charleston, South Carolina, in 1797.

Other Tolands had landed there earlier, a cousin John in 1787 apparently being the first. After fighting at the end of the American Revolution, John settled in the Laurens District of South Carolina, near Newberry, in the western part of the state, where he raised a large family. To this virgin area also came Hugh with his wife and seven children, of which Hugh, Jr., was the oldest. In time Hugh, Jr., met Mary (Mollie) Langston, and they were married in 1812. Their second son, James, was born in 1816. By early adulthood he had become a skilled craftsman, mechanic and maker of household furniture. From his mother's sister, who had recently moved to Tallapoosa County, Alabama, where her husband, the Reverend James Harlan, became pastor of a church, James heard that land was cheap and plentiful. He moved there in the spring of 1846. Soon he married Mildred Street, whose family owned more property than any other in the county and was the only considerable slave-holding family in the section. James and Mildred shortly left for South Carolina, where their first child, Martha Ardella (called Della by everyone), was born in 1848. There she attended an academy: this marked her as a girl of privilege in the antebellum South. He returned to Alabama, where he had already bought land and acquired some slaves to work it. But in 1859, after Della came back, her mother died, and until her father remarried the next year, she assumed many of the responsibilities for her two younger brothers.[2]

The Civil War cast a large shadow over many southern families even as it instilled pride. One of those families was that of George Walker Black and his wife, Jane Vernon. George and Jane arrived in Alabama in 1835 from north Georgia, where their people had lived for several generations and where Jane had taught school. They wanted to marry, but his parents objected because he was only eighteen. So George and Jane eloped, rode to Alabama on one horse, and were married. On a farm at Goldville, just within the Tallapoosa County line, they raised eight children. A few miles away, at Bluff Springs, was Toland's 1,600-acre farm; and he probably bought some merchandise at the cabin store Black owned. Three months after the shots at Fort Sumter, George Black's son Columbus (Clum) enlisted in the Confederate army. Before he left, he and Della Toland agreed to marry when he returned. He fought with General Robert E. Lee all the way to Gettysburg. Going up the hill during Pickett's Charge, Clum was shot. He threw up his hands, flung his gun away and said, "Oh Lordy, Oh Lordy," then dropped, dead at nineteen. (An informal family history notes, "wounded in shoulder, never heard of since.")

After the war, Clum's younger brother William LaFayette tried to win Della. He had been smitten with her before. On the day they were baptized together, at the age of thirteen, he proposed to her; she turned him down. Faet was a lad of admirable determination. During winters when farmwork was not pressing, he walked six miles to a crude country school. The war had so stirred his enthusiasm that he left home in 1862 at the age of fourteen to volunteer for the Confederacy. He went to Atlanta, where the authorities held him and notified his father, who insisted that Faet be sent home. Two years later, with ranks thinned and the cause increasingly desperate, he was judged old enough to fight. He served as a private in an Alabama regiment, which was captured in southwest Georgia in April 1865 and imprisoned in Mississippi. There Negroes guarded it and "Old Frank," one of the guards, said to the boys, "Close up dar white man, the bottom rail is on top now." The unit was paroled the next month. Back home Faet wooed Della. His persistence along with his more obvious qualities—his native intelligence and his desire for self-improvement—overcame her doubts (and likely family objections), and they were married in December 1868.

They settled in nearby Harlan, named after Della's cousin Dr. John

Harlan. Faet's independent streak soon showed. The rest of his family moved to Crossville, Alabama, in De Kalb County near Fort Payne, 125 miles north—but Faet stayed put. Like his father, he farmed. Several sharecroppers lived in cabins on his 320 acres, land so poor that he prophesied that they would all starve to death. He established a little crossroads store where he was also the local money lender; and like his mother, he taught school. To give his property a post office address he became postmaster (for one dollar a year). He built a home of wood and logs, with a clapboard roof made from timber on the farm. In the spool bed that Della's father made eight children were born, five boys and three girls, starting with Robert Lee (known as Lee) in 1870 and ending with Hugo in 1886. The privy and a barn were behind the house. A stock of animals provided food and labor.

But educational opportunities in the country were severely limited. In the county seat of Ashland, however, the schools were being reorganized and improved, and in December 1889 the family moved there. Faet had saved money to buy a half interest in a general store on the courthouse square. All the children went to school except for Hugo who was too young. He was also directly exposed to political ferment. "Before I could articulate my syllables distinctly I recall how angry people could make me by saying: 'You are a Populist, a third party-ite.' My reply in those days, Clay County people tell me, was: 'I am *not* a tird party—I a democat.' "[3]

"Democrat" and "Populist" were indeed battle cries in Clay County in the early 1890s. Under the crop lien system that ruled farmers' lives, supply merchants such as Faet Black advanced—at interest rates of up to 75 percent—the required seed, fertilizer, and equipment, and sold food, clothes and other goods on credit, in exchange for a lien on the crops. The price of commodities nearly doubled as a result and land became harder to obtain. Families became scant of clothes and short of food. Angry farmers looked to politics for relief.

Units of the rapidly expanding Farmers Alliance were organized and agrarianism evolved into populism. Populists wanted a chance at a better life, not to be saddled to a merchant's account books, and proposed a broad program of national governmental involvement in the economy. During the 1892 gubernatorial campaign, the People's Party of Alabama was formed in Ashland. Its guiding spirit was twenty-two-year-old Joseph C. Manning, the "Clay County Evangel," whose oratorical flourishes wove a spell of urgency around any subject he touched. Populists held monthly meetings (Manning along with a Negro delegate from the county attended the Omaha national convention), opened a state-certified school, even held a primary to run a candidate against the Democrats in the general election.

And the party won every county office against a Democratic Party split by discord and scandal. Only the Populist candidate for Congress, Martin W. Whatley, lost. He collected evidence of ballot-stuffing and presented it to Congress, staying in Washington for ten months, but the Republicans who controlled Congress claimed it was fictitious and refused to seat him. The *People's Party Advocate* (published in Ashland) could barely contain its outrage against the Democrats: "We still insist that the people are entitled to the good times promised or the bosses are entitled to the belt as the most distinguished liars in the universe." Enemies were both political and economic. "The grand mission of the People's party is to avert the evil which the money power has injected in the nation. It seeks to do this through peaceful means—through reason, education and the ballot box."

Such agitated rhetoric typified the populist mentality. Populists relied much on bashing scapegoats and searching for panaceas. They paraded a list of horribles in language that conveyed a sense of (barely) smothered violence. To their plutocratic oppressors they charged an overwhelming brutality and conspiracy. Populists reduced all conflict to only two sides; they saw no middle ground, no compromise. One single reform could transform the world overnight, although just which miraculous remedy was never agreed upon. Heroes and villains were brought into stark relief. It was a great but basically simple struggle the populists were engaged in, and if the evils and deceptions that beset them were exposed, the future would be theirs.

In "the free state of Clay" Populists opened 1894 in high spirits. But a new state law kept many of them from being registered as voters. And except for Joe Manning, who won by a whisker, the Populists lost all local contests. In 1896 the Democrats won 10 of 16 races, even if by narrow margins; in 1898, all but one.[4] Populism in Clay County had a short, mercurial life. Its effects, however, were much more long-lasting.

*   *   *

Ashland College was the reason the Black family moved to Ashland. "The people of Clay County," Hugo noted, "took much pride in the fact or at least the belief that their county turned out more school teachers than any other county in the state." The school's plans were as impressive as its name. Its secondary department offered instruction in some twenty subjects at a time when there were no free high schools in Alabama; a degree pretty much assured admission to the University of Alabama or a job as a teacher. But it was no more than a country high school: it had no library, study facilities or laboratories, and supplies were rudimentary. "It was heated with a wood stove in the winter," said one student. "The furnishings were as good as in most of our homes. The school was rough but it didn't lack anything that was important." What it had above all lies at the heart of any educational institution—able teachers who cared.

Hugo was forever enraptured by his first and "most beloved" teacher, Lizzie Patterson. He always remembered her in the auditorium, her small figure dancing with energy, cheerfully leading the students in exercise. In the classroom, her ruler at hand, Miss Lizzie brooked no nonsense. "She guided me like a mother," Hugo recalled. He finished four *McGuffey's Readers* in one year. A class in Greek and Roman history taught by Hiram M. Evans led to a lifetime romance with the classics. Something about their timeless simplicity and the lessons they provided caught Hugo's mind. Evans had long been a teacher and, until the Populists swept him out of office, Clay County probate judge. His sons carried on both interests: one, Cecil, was a college president (and first mentor to Lyndon B. Johnson), while Hiram W., the youngest child and five years older than Hugo, becamse the Imperial Wizard of the Ku Klux Klan. In front of the students "Professor" Evans, ever stately looking, paced silently for what seemed an eternity before he banged his cane on the table and proclaimed: "Young gentlemen and young ladies, if you can't say something good about a man, don't say it!"

When not in school or reading, Hugo spent much time with another student, Barney Whatley. A bright, lively and sweet lad four months older than Hugo, Barney came from a farm family so poor that he didn't wear shoes until he was thirteen. He walked barefoot for miles to go to school. His father, Martin Whatley, took him to many of the same rallies Hugo attended. Barney quit school after the eighth grade to work as a clerk-bookkeeper in Faet's store to support his family after his father deserted it. "Things were so desperate then," he said. "They worked so hard just to survive in Ashland that if you worked that hard someplace else, you had to do well in the world." Barney did. He and Hugo were dear, lifelong friends.[5]

Before moving to Ashland, Faet had bought a house in town, paying cash. Four years later, he purchased another one, recently built by Della's cousin Dr. Aaron Harlan, and the family lived in it for many years. Both houses were modest frame dwellings with five rooms—a parlor and a kitchen, and bedrooms for the boys, the girls and the parents; each room had a fireplace. A water well was on the back porch and there was space to keep a horse, a cow and chickens. Honeysuckle vines covered the front porch and flowers surrounded small cedar trees on each side of the front walk. The school was across the street, Faet's store on the town square two blocks away, and churches also close by.

The store—Black and Manning—was a focal point of town life. Faet's partner, Henry Manning, had made it "a small empire based on fifty-dollar liens, attachments of cattle and tools, and frequent lawsuits." But in 1891 he died. Faet bought his half share and was now the sole owner of the largest store in the county. He sold everything from cradles to coffins—dry goods and notions, shoes, clothing, drugs, phoenix flour, meat and lard, and hardware. His stock grew to reach upward of $15,000, a considerable amount for a rural area in the late nineteenth century and ten times larger than that of the only other store in town. Hugo accurately called him "the most prosperous merchant in the county. I am confident that at the time of his death he owned more property than any other person" there. He owned several Ashland buildings and homes and nearby farms in addition to the store and, for a while, the Ashland Hotel; traded some horses and mules; and continued, as in the country, to be a money lender—so much so that one old-timer said, "Faet had a credit business which dealt in general merchandise."[6]

He appreciated learning and prided himself that he could educate his children. "He had a hunger for knowledge, sought it avidly," said Della's nephew Harlan Martin. "Only good books, no trash, were in his library." They included the complete works of Shakespeare, Martin Luther and John Bunyan ("many religious books"), as well as Blackstone's eighteenth-century classic *Commentaries on the Law of England*. The Bible and Bunyan's *Pilgrim's Progress* were the two best-read books in the house. (The best-thumbed volume, *Burpee's Seed Catalogue*, was a necessity.) Faet even subscribed to the *Montgomery Advertiser* and the *Atlanta Constitution*, one of the handful of people in Clay County to do so.

Faet had always been involved in politics and civic affairs. As far back as 1877 he had been a justice of the peace; the next year he was an election inspector. He soon lost a creditable race for county tax assessor. In 1894 he was elected an Ashland councilman, and he served as a member of the Ashland College Board of Trustees; later he was active in the movements to establish a town charter and to gain a railroad line. He was an engaging fellow who "always had a good word for anyone he ran into," Harlan Martin recalled. He often waited before collecting on his loans, as politically sensitive (but by no means all) creditors did. Considering his location, he was something of a dashing bon vivant too. "W. L. Black, a leading merchant and enterprising citizen of Ashland, takes in the exposition at Atlanta this week," ran a typical newspaper notice. "With a comely form and faultless approach, he will be the Beau Brummel of Clay while he stays with the comers and goers in the Gate City."

He was a natural "insider," part of the local power structure, yet some of his actions were often those of an outsider. One Sunday the family brought the preacher home from church for dinner. He sat with Faet and Hugo on the porch while the meal was being prepared. Down the street walked a man who belonged to no church. Although he was known as a "worldly" man (probably because he had traveled to a couple of nearby counties), many people in town regarded him as a "sinner" because of his lack of affiliation. But Faet, a "free thinker" of sorts, insisted that a man's soul was his own business, nobody else's; and not the least embarrassed by the pastor's presence, greeted the man, engaged him in conversation at the front gate and urged that he also stay for dinner.[7]

Few other people in Ashland could get away with such behavior. Everyone spoke of his intelligence, his industriousness, and his thrift—when he was sober. For Faet was a drunkard. When bootleggers came to town, he went on periodic binges. He was even sweeter when under the influence. People greeted him as he staggered down the street. Then he would dry out. To young Hugo, seeing his father totter around town, sobriety became essential. Drinking led to loss of self-respect and to social disgrace. He determined to control his own mind and body.

Della was suffering from Little Della's death when he was born. "Grief fills the room up of my absent child," Shakespeare wrote. This set up a barrier that filtered emotional communication and that Hugo never completely overcame. Childhood friends considered him "likeable but somewhat remote at times." Della pampered him; he reciprocated. Because of a lack of space in the other bedrooms he slept in his parents' room until he was twelve. When Faet was gone on one of his carousals, Hugo stayed up nights trying to comfort Della. "Hugo wanted to please everybody no end," his sister Daisy said. But sometime during his childhood, as Faet's drinking grew more pronounced, this changed. Hugo withdrew slightly. He didn't play with his friends as much and spent more time by himself, reading. In books he found sanctuary from the turmoil amidst love around him. "Hugo didn't talk about his family much, mainly about his mother but not the others," said his chum Clarence Pruet, who was the half brother of the husband of

Hugo's oldest sister, Ora. "And I thought it was strange because I knew just what was going on there."

Della kept the family together. Every day she did the bookkeeping in the store and every night she devoutly read Scriptures. Faet provided well, but comfort in Clay County—and no family was more comfortable—still meant much physical labor. Della did not like housekeeping, even though she sto-ically went about it. She was a frail woman, and years of labor finally took their toll. Emotional and superstitious, she took to her bed for a while. Ora inter-rupted her education to relieve her, to serve in effect as mother, cooking and washing for the family. When Ora became a teacher and moved to the country to operate a school with her husband, Della hired two Negro women to take her place. Della personified perfection to Hugo his whole life. Faet's drinking tightened the bonds between them. Her love was steady, reliable, uncon-ditional, a source of energy and power. He always believed he was her favorite child. "A man who has been the indisputable favorite of his mother," wrote Freud, "keeps for life the feeling of a conqueror, that confidence that often induces real success." As Hugo noted, "I was the family pet."[8]

He had in full measure much of what is traditionally associated with the South—the unfailing courtesy, hospitality, and graciousness of manner; the strong feeling of kinship and distinction between family and non-family; the sense of attachment to home and roots. Hugo was equally true to his "other South" heritage. He loved his region for its virtues yet dissented from its prevailing views while trying to overlook them. The Civil War he could not ignore. As a child he was taught the southern version of its history and meaning. In 1900 his brother Lee published a book, *The Deserter*. The story started with a man "who had fought like a hero with blind unquestioning faith," but who suddenly realized "that his country was wrong." He deserted, turned his back "upon the blood-soaked battle fields of Virginia" and went southward, to his home. Late in life Hugo recalled that several deserters in the federal army and other people, at least some of whom opposed the war, hid out in Clay County. "In my judgment their position was sound at that time although I am not at all certain that I would have done that had I been old enough to go to the war. My action probably would have been like that of my father"—running away from home to try to join the army.

To his children, however, Hugo said he would have joined the Union army. "The Free State of Winston," a county in northwest Alabama that remained loyal to the Union, evoked his admiration. The Civil War, he thought, was "tragic," the most disastrous of all American wars. "I have felt for a long time," he wrote in 1959, "that the war which we of the South called 'the war between the States' was a wholly unnecessary one. . . . A wiser leadership in the South would have been honest with the people and would have let them know that, brave as they were, there was practically no possibility of their winning a military or political victory." Nevertheless, Hugo was proud that every generation of his American ancestors had fought in a war. But Clay County's remoteness immunized him from the travail of Reconstruction as well as from much of the sentimentality that swept the South after the Civil War and continued into the twentieth century. Ashland newspapers hardly ever mentioned the war or its aftermath. Not one reunion of Confederate soldiers was ever held in the county during Hugo's youth. There was no town square statue of Johnny Reb, gun in hand, perpetuating the Confederate legend, none of the myths and symbols designed to overcome defeat and the Lost Cause. [9]

While very little in any way happened in this very small, very slow place, Hugo read. "One of my earliest memories is lying on the floor while reading or on the front porch with a book propped underneath" or "somewhere in the shade of trees in the woods" nearby. "Always had his head in a book," Clarence Pruet said. "Never saw him do a hard day's work, just read, read, read." Stretched out on the porch for hours without moving, he read *The Wandering Jew* when he was eleven. "The Bible was the only book my mother read to me," he recalled. "She made me study it." He read a set of Sir Walter Scott's novels, as well as his poem *Lady of the Lake,* the *Nick Carter* detective and the *Fred Fearnot* series, King Bradys, much of Dickens, Victor Hugo and "loads of history. It was a favorite subject in our home, much of it of course being the history of the South." Hugo enjoyed John Esten Cooke's stories defending the plantation literary legend. "I was steeped in southern books." And "Frank Merriwell's stories left me with a great admiration for a clean sportsman, whether the game played was baseball or the serious activities of life."

There was also play—horseback riding, baseball, croquet, pitching horseshoes or silver dollars at a hole in the ground, checkers and dominoes, swimming in the creeks, fishing, hiking and enjoying the occasional traveling circuses. Hugo could play most instruments by ear, * and he liked to sing

---

* When he was eighty-three, one of his grandchildren said, "If you hadn't been born fifty years too soon, you might have been the Johnny Cash of this era" (ESB to Ethel and JMH, 12/27/69, JMH papers). References for sources follow the Epilogue.

country songs. And, of course, there was young romance; but, alas, no record survives. This is not to say that recreational activities were abundant. "Sometimes we would pitch pennies on the cracks of the wood and call it crack-a-too," recalled Barney Whatley, "or we would just run after one another, because there was nothing else to do." Hugo also wandered in and about Ashland, visiting many relatives. He especially liked going to the farm of his grandfather James Toland. There he learned much family lore and could also play with cousins who lived nearby. Usually he managed the games: the older boys allowed him to be the leader.

For spending money Hugo did odd jobs such as chopping wood, riding a mule to the mill for farmers and selling old novels cheaply; but he really enjoyed working after school as a printer's devil for Ashland's two weekly newspapers. He also acted as a sort of roving reporter for the *Ashland Standard,* writing the "locals" columns. His first story, as he recalled it, was: "Bill Jones has been seen on the streets of Ashland. Bill is looking fine." At the age of fifteen he found himself practically managing and editing the *People's Party Advocate* because the owner was often ill and unable to work much. This job thoroughly imbued Hugo with populist doctrine.[10]

Racial relations in Ashland and Clay County were ordinarily placid. Negroes made up slightly less than 10 percent of the county's population of 15,000, according to the 1890 census, and "stayed in their place." One day an elderly Negro who worked for Faet told Hugo to offer "Uncle Dan" some food. Hugo filled a plate and started to take it to the back steps when Della made him bring Uncle Dan into the kitchen to eat. In their quiet way she and Faet insisted that all people be treated equally. The murder of Eli Sims, then, disturbed them greatly. A friendly young Negro, Sims was swimming in the same creek with some white boys one day in August 1896 when one of the whites, Jim White, ordered him to leave. Sims talked back; White went home to get his gun, came back, and, while sitting on his horse, shot and killed Sims, who was standing next to his own horse. White was indicted for murder but acquitted. Almost everyone in Ashland conceded he was guilty, but White's father had been both state representative and county sheriff, and witnesses were bribed.

The whole matter deeply troubled the Black family. It was not too long since Eli had pushed Hugo about in his wheelbarrow; and when he called on Hugo at home, as a friend he came through the front door. Faet did not approve of White's release and frequently discussed the subject at dinner with the family. This was simply a matter of right and wrong, he felt; race did not enter. "If one murderer can escape, none of us will be safe," Faet said. After two more murders, White was finally sent to prison. People around Ashland said that he was "just a bad man," and because the case was so clear-cut, Hugo developed a tendency to apply that label to anyone who mistreated Negroes.

Hugo spent much time in Faet's store or on the square listening to townsfolk discuss trials at the courthouse. These animated conversations captivated him, and from the time he was about six years old, Hugo attended almost every session of court held. County court met for only one afternoon monthly, and circuit court for only two weeks every six months, with the more important cases held over for the late summer meeting, after the crops had been laid by and jurors would be available. These sessions provided a fount of stories that Hugo repeatedly told. One of his favorites was about the sharecropper who was charged with stealing the landlord's mule. The evidence against him was so overwhelming that he did not even testify in his own defense, and the jury took only five minutes to decide the case. The foreman handed the verdict to the clerk. The clerk put on his glasses, took the paper, unfolded it, cleared his throat, and said, "We the jury find the defendant not guilty, provided that he return the mule." "There is no such verdict in the law," the judge declared, bringing his gavel down sharply. "The defendant is either guilty or not guilty." He ordered the jury to return with a lawful verdict. Five minutes later, they were back in the courtroom. The clerk announced, "We the jury find the defendant not guilty. He can keep the mule."

Hugo found the trials fascinating. Sitting in the back row of the half-filled courtroom, trying to look inconspicuous and sympathizing with the underdogs, he listened to the lawyers ask questions and argue. "Then I would figure out how I would have done it, how I could have improved on what they did." During recesses, he asked "what next?" while imagining himself a great lawyer. The prominence of Della's brother Thomas Orlando Toland as a lawyer in California had already become family legend. Hugo and Barney Whatley usually attended these sessions together ("the best entertainment we had," Barney called them), and decided that they were going to be lawyers. Even before he reached his teens, Hugo announced his decision to the family.

Politics absorbed him. Hugo attended practically all the public speeches in Ashland. During elections, he stayed at the polls until the last vote was counted—once, at the age of ten, until seven o'clock the next morning. A bright child with an active imagination stimulated by reading could well imagine himself as a candidate. *McGuffey's Readers* emphasized heroic lives. Hugo's childhood dreams and ambitions were those of a frontier boy who has all the world to conquer. "I expected to go to Congress, become a governor, and probably a senator," even president, he hoped at one fanciful moment. "All of this fling into politics, however, was to occur only after I had been successful as a lawyer."[11]

As the 1890s closed with Faet's health declining, the focus of family life shifted toward the children. Lee took over the store; Faet tried to collect all debts owed him so Lee could increase the stock. Throughout the decade Lee was deeply involved in community affairs. But he was not alone in the new family pantheon. Pelham went into law practice with A. S. Stockdale, long a Democratic stalwart and now chairman of the party's county executive committee, who took Orlando with him to the Democratic state convention in 1900. The next generation stood poised at the center of the local power structure. Its number was less by one. A typhoid fever epidemic struck the area in 1895 and Vernon, seventeen, died. Hugo had idolized him. Faet's drinking had deprived Hugo of a male role model: now Hugo turned to Pelham. He could have looked to his other brothers, but Lee drank with Faet at the store; and Orlando, small and intense, was away at medical school. Family tradition holds that Pelham studied for the Alabama bar in the woods and received the highest grade anyone had ever gotten up to then. When he was admitted to the bar in early 1900, Hugo proudly noted in the *People's Party Advocate*, "Pelham is a brilliant, energetic young man and we expect him to rise rapidly in the legal profession."

Faet's death in September 1900 was not surprising. For more than a year he had been sick, and "conversed freely with his family concerning his prospect for eternity," or so the Baptist minister wrote in an obituary. Finally his liver gave out. All the businesses in town were closed during the funeral. Faet had no will, and when his estate was added up, it came to $27,856.06— a remarkable sum considering where and when he made it and that he started with nothing. It was the largest in the county. Two thirds of it were in notes and accounts past due, which he had not attempted to collect. To the end, while resolutely looking after himself, Faet was, as the preacher said, "a friend to the needy."

One day in late 1901 the new, young co-principal of Ashland College, Professor Turnipseed, punished Hugo's sister Daisy for whispering at her desk. He ordered her to stand in a corner of the room on one leg. This struck Hugo as humiliating, so he went home, across the street, to report it to his mother. Tell the teacher to let Daisy come home, she said; and Hugo did that. The professor then announced he was going to "whip" Hugo. Hugo was in his seat when Turnipseed came over with a switch and started to hit him. Hugo grabbed it and broke it into pieces. "You sure had the 'grit' to attack a so much larger man," a classmate wrote him many years later. "Your sister ran out toward you and was much worried over the fight." Turnipseed asked Professor Yarbrough, his co-principal, to bring another switch and to hold Hugo. Both of them tried to whip Hugo, but he broke all their switches, and the other refused to get more switches. By now Della had come to the school, and the whipping stopped. After the family talked it over, Hugo never again attended Ashland College. It was his first questioning of authority, his first dissent, his first experience acting as a defense lawyer, protecting himself and his sister from unjust punishment, and he met it with defiance.[12]

A high school dropout, and not yet sixteen years old, Hugo drove people in a buggy to Goodwater, twenty miles away, to catch the Central of Georgia train. Or he drove a team of mules pulling a wagon twenty-four miles in the other direction, to Talladega, to get supplies for the store. The trip took over a day each way, and he spent "many nights" sleeping at the "wagon yard," curled up on the floor of the wagon under blankets he carried with him. He got paid one dollar a day. This unexciting routine was interrupted in June 1902. His brother Pelham was riding home in the family wagon from a weekend dance in "wet" Talladega County when he fell asleep and took the wrong road. The wheels of the wagon got stuck in a pond, and the horse bucked and threw Pelham. He was on his haunches when found, drowned. Around Ashland the word quickly spread that Pelham had been on a drinking spree. The loss of "this genius who was taken off the earth so young" (the feeling that Hugo later conveyed to his children) reinforced his hatred of alcohol. But he still had to find something to do. In January 1903 he took the semiannual statewide test to become a third-level teacher (the lowest of three levels). When the list of those who received licenses was published the next month, his name was not among them. Hugo had failed.

The family concluded that he should go away to college the next year.

Hugo had his heart set on studying law, but Della was eager that he should follow in the steps of Orlando, by now "a physician of promise" in Wilsonville, Alabama. Orlando, probably hoping that Hugo would join him in practice, offered to pay for his medical education. There was also, in Birmingham, a medical school closer to home than the law school at the University of Alabama in Tuscaloosa, sixty miles farther west—no small consideration for a seventeen-year-old. Hugo reluctantly yielded to the others' insistence.

The Birmingham Medical College accepted him despite his age and his lack of a college degree. Hugo found a room close to the school for $8 a month and a nearby place to eat for $15 a month. Wanting to finish the three-year course in two years, he persuaded the school's administrators to allow him to take the first two years in one. A "life of practical seclusion" was the result. He took time out only for Sunday school and church. From 8 A.M. to 4 P.M., Monday through Saturday, with only four unscheduled hours the whole time, he attended lectures or clinics; until 6 P.M. he was in the laboratory, dissecting cadavers. He passed both the first- and second-year examinations satisfactorily and, thereafter, regarded himself as somewhat of a medical authority, freely giving advice to family, friends and even physicians.

Even though the smells around medical school affected his sensitive nose and dismembering corpses in the lab upset him, he spent the summer assisting Orlando. The sight of blood flowing, however, unnerved Hugo (he once ran from a woman having a nosebleed). And he brooded about the death of a woman in labor whose baby was twisted and also died: Orlando had tried to save the woman's life. Soon Orlando told him that while Hugo could make a good doctor, he doubted if Hugo would ever be happy as a doctor and suggested he go to law school instead. He just could not get interested in medicine, Hugo said to Della's disappointment; the pull of the remembrances of all those fascinating trials he had attended was just too strong. He went home and arranged to go to the University of Alabama.[13]

* * *

Tuscaloosa, where Hugo arrived in early September 1904, was an old southern town with an enveloping air of graciousness. He wished to enter the sophomore class on the basis of his Ashland College and medical school courses. But the admissions office required an examination (which he didn't want to take) for admission with advanced standing, and the university president would not waive the rule. Hugo entered the law school.* It was a stepchild of the university: its forty-three students in his first year were not assured of rooms in the barracks or board in the dining room, both of which were available to other students. Dean William S. Thorington liked to tell the story of the judge who protested that a bar committee had admitted to practice a young man "so notably stupid, utterly without learning or the ability to learn" as to be obviously without qualifications. Committee members had claimed that they could hardly refuse him admission:

> We asked him what an easement is, and he said he didn't know, and that was correct. And then, we asked him, What is the rule in Shelley's case?, and he said, "writing poetry," and that was incorrect. And then we asked him what an incorporeal hereditament is and he said he didn't know— and that was correct; so two-thirds of his answers were right and we figure he is entitled to a license.

But the two faculty members were capable and devoted to teaching future lawyers. Thorington had been a justice of the Supreme Court of Alabama. His words seemed to come from far behind his thick handlebar mustache. "One had to want to learn to be able to stay awake, particularly on hot summer afternoons while Judge Thorington was giving his lectures," Hugo recalled. "Humor was not his chief asset." The other professor was Ormond Somerville, a shy, kindly scholar who had also taught Latin and English at the university. He prepared thoroughly for his classes and spoke carefully. Whereas Thorington was "serious, unimaginative and therefore a trifle dull," Somerville, "while equally serious, had a twinkle in his eyes that bespoke a sense of dry humor, and he taught us the driest subjects with enough imagination to give them life and sparkle."

Courses for the two-year program were prescribed. Leading cases and the Alabama code were their principal sources. The text Hugo remembered longest was Walker's *Introduction to American Law*, then in its eleventh edition. "Our country," Walker had written in the 1835 original edition, reprinted now, "claims the transcendent merit of having made the first grand

* The law school's admission requirements, in the university's catalog, stated: "Any person of good moral character is at liberty to matriculate. . . . Graduates of universities, colleges, state normal schools, accredited high schools, or academies are admitted without exception. Other candidates for a degree, before being admitted, must pass such examination in English, United States history, and General History, as shall satisfy the Faculty. . . ." As Hugo had not been graduated from any institution nor taken any examination, he was apparently admitted in violation of the regulations.

experiment of limiting delegated power by written constitutions." Law, Hugo was taught, is a system of formalistic rules: the judge applies deductive reasoning to the case at hand; he has no discretion; the entire process is mechanical. Both professors used the lecture method of teaching rather than the new Socratic case system of analyzing appellate court decisions and posing hypothetical situations to supplement the real ones in the books. They interrupted recitations of seemingly immutable legal principles to ask questions that ended, in Thorington's case, "If so, why so, and if not, why not?"[14]

Although Hugo spent much of his time in the library, other activities also kept him busy. He assisted a lawyer preparing for trials, and he greatly enjoyed the weekly meetings of the Kent Club, a debating society run by the law students. One debate, during his first year, "was of much interest," noted *The Crimson White,* the student newspaper, "because of its interesting subject—woman—an enigma that the grave lawyers could not solve. The discussion was 'Resolved, That Co-Education is destroying College Spirit.' " Mssrs. Scrivner and Black were of the affirmative opinion; however, Mssrs. Wiley and Ward defeated their erroneous arguments. It was then rightly decided conclusively that co-education should exist—and rightly this when they give their financial as well as moral support."

Realizing his scanty background, Hugo enrolled in courses in history and political economy and in literature, as law school regulations permitted. Thomas C. McCorvey, a southerner of the old school, was the sole professor in the School (Department) of History and Political Economy. In his two-part course, "Principles of Economics" and "Political and Constitutional History of the United States," Hugo learned some (undoubtedly classical) economics and had his first systematic exposure to American history. McCorvey also introduced Hugo to the writings of Thomas Jefferson, which had recently appeared in multivolume editions. Jefferson's idealism appealed to the youngster from the hills, and he quickly became Hugo's leading historical hero. Charles H. Barnwell, a Harvard Ph.D. in English, taught a course in rhetoric, American literature and English composition. Students were required to write at least one short essay weekly and to discuss it with him. Hugo prepared his version of Orpheus and Eurydice. This stimulated his nascent interest in Greece and the Greek way of life. "And whether he ever knew it or not, Dr. Barnwell succeeded in teaching me a more practical lesson—that the best way to tell any story is to tell it as simply as possible, in the simplest words possible, and in the shortest way possible."

Tuscaloosa offered Hugo his first glimpse of a more refined life-style. He enjoyed the amenities. On one visit home he persuaded his sister-in-law

Hattie to replace her wooden-handle steel table forks and knives with silver-painted tableware. He smoked cigars some. And he started to play tennis. . . . The inscriptions in his law school yearbooks best capture Hugo's essence at this time. Following tradition, the *Corolla* poked fun, sometimes cruelly, at students. Hugo was popular, serving as secretary of his class the first year and secretary and treasurer the second year, it noted. The class roll the first year stated, "I am one of those souls that will use the devil himself with courtesy." And the next year, alongside the picture of a slightly apprehensive young man wearing a cap and gown, was written, "This fellow seems to possess but one idea, and that is a wrong one."

He had the right ideas in his classes, never receiving any grade lower than A. In May 1906 he was awarded his LL.B. degree with highest honors as one of seven members of his class who had obtained an average of 95 or more in all his courses. And he was elected to Phi Beta Kappa. Several times later Somerville took great pleasure in telling people in Hugo's presence, "I won't say whether Black was my best student or not. I will say he learned the most of any of my students." Somerville then paused and smiled. "He had the most to learn."[15]

Hugo returned to Ashland upon graduation in June 1906. He moved into the old family home with Lee and his ever-expanding brood, paying $6 monthly for board. Della had died on February 17, 1905. "She was never as congenial after Faet's death," said her nephew Harlan Martin, keeping to herself and staying home even more, reading the Bible with even greater piety. Then she caught pneumonia to which she succumbed. Since she would have wanted it, Hugo joined the Baptist church; soon he was its clerk and the Sunday school teacher and organist. He had grandiose plans. Eventually he wished to practice law in New York City for the simple reason it was the nation's largest city, but only after a political career in Alabama. It was, he later realized, a "thoroughly impossible" dream, if with any reflection he wanted it at all.

For an office he rented two rooms over a grocery store on the southeast corner of the square. He had a very good collection of law books—Faet's old Blackstone and Pelham's books, those he had spent most of his extra money on in law school, and others local lawyers had given him—and he added to them by buying volumes of past cases and subscribing to current legal reports. It was the best law library in Ashland. At the street entrance to the office hung a seven-dollar painted sign: HUGO L. BLACK, ATTORNEY AND COUNSELOR AT LAW. Upstairs he waited for business. But litigants did not appear. Hugo began to study English, history and other subjects he had not taken in Tuscaloosa. He bought textbooks on grammar, rhetoric, writing and history, and followed their suggestions by writing to law school friends "letters that must have sounded more like stilted essays than chatty comments on daily happenings," he recalled. On visits to his sister Daisy in the country he frequently went into the woods by the creek and practiced speaking alone. Soon "I had learned far more about writing simple English and talking on my feet than I had ever known before."

Barney Whatley, who had moved to Birmingham and was collecting bills for a hardware company while studying law at night, kept after Hugo to move there. "I can throw you some of this collecting business and I have a lot of friends," he said. "Together this will give you enough to get started. By the time I get admitted to the bar, we'll form a partnership." Hugo hesitated. Instead of practicing law in Ashland, he prepared "private reports" at 50 cents each for large insurance companies for the Atlanta-based Retail Credit Corporation. He also collected old accounts still owed to Faet's estate. To pass time he strolled across the square to Jordan's drugstore to buy six nickel cigars for a quarter, making a separate trip to pick up each one. He made an overture to a Birmingham law firm but its partners rejected him in favor of another neophyte.

This leisurely activity stopped on the night of February 12, 1907, when a fire destroyed both the building in which he had his office and the adjoining one, where Lee had the store. "Hugo was an object of pity," said Hillary Carwile, a contemporary who later served in the state legislature. "He sat down and looked at the ashes which were all that remained." Another Ashland lawyer let him share his office, the only other suitable space left in town, while John J. Haynes, the county solicitor, continued to tutor him. Haynes's strength as a lawyer in Ashland and later as an assistant attorney general of Alabama was in cross-examination, and he took Hugo under his wing, spending many hours teaching him the fine points of the art, recalled Haynes's daughter Annie Haynes Moore. But Hugo had only one case in which he could apply his newly learned knowledge.

His income from pure legal business during this year did not reach even $150, and most of that came from collecting fees due Faet's estate. On May 16, 1907, he posted the required $1,000 bond with the county tax commissioner to run for office, but he had not yet even voted. He was going nowhere fast. "Col. H. L. Black, one of the leading young lawyers of east Alabama, has decided to leave Ashland and locate in Birmingham," the *Ashland Standard* noted in late August 1907.

Later Hugo joked that he was "not too unhappy," indeed it was "rather a relief when the office burned down": it gave him "an incentive for moving on to Birmingham." Or "The best way to get something moving is to put a fire under it." With a smile he said, "You have never heard such mourning as when I left Ashland. They told me, 'You're just throwing away a brilliant career.' After due consideration, I concluded to throw it away." But at the time it was a courageous step. "Friends offered to help him out," his brother Lee recalled, "but he refused, saying 'I can go on alone.'" With less than $10 in his pocket, walking part of the way to save train fare, Hugo Black left for Birmingham.[16]

CHAPTER 2

BIRMINGHAM

Hugo arrived in Birmingham the same year the United States Steel Corporation took over the Tennessee Coal, Iron and Railroad Company, and began to dominate the city. It was a rough, grimy, crime-ridden place, "Bad Birmingham, the murder capital of the world," where coal and iron rested near the surface and could be extracted easily. Raw and roistering, as coarse as Ashland was crude, Birmingham was booming. Contrasts abounded. Founded only in 1871, Birmingham was a New South city without an Old South past; a mining city in the heart of the South, just ninety miles from the cradle of the Confederacy. Its small cadre of nouveau riche industrialists, a self-appointed elite of common origins who ran it, were confident that they were the reincarnation of Old South aristocracy. They called for progress while glorifying that long-ago era when "darkies" dotted the shining fields and fragile belles in white dresses danced on moonlit verandas. All the while, they did their best to ignore the fact that most of the profits earned from the mines were going up to the East. The dependency of this colonial relationship did not disturb them. Life was comfortable in their Big Houses on the South Side.

It could never be for the miners and blast furnace workers who toiled in the pits for sixty or seventy hours a week. They sought relief in taverns and brothels. Also thriving were the churches, progressive on many social issues but determined to keep parishioners from the temptation of liquor and other vices. Churchmen were politically active; by 1908 they had pressured the city into passing ordinances prohibiting many Sabbath amusements as well as sports, hunting and card playing—even dominoes were forbidden on Sunday. And Jim Crow was thriving. Laws defining the Negro's "place" and status from before birth to after death mushroomed across the South at the turn of the century. Some southerners viewed this "permanent system" of legal segregation as a "return to sanity." Others, in words that would gain currency in Nazi Germany, called it the "final settlement." Birmingham, which was 43 percent Negro according to the 1900 census, made sure it would not be outdone. The city passed a law that did not omit much: in "any room, hall, theatre, picture house, auditorium, yard, court, ball park, or other indoor or outdoor place," the races must be "distinctly separated . . . by well defined physical barriers."

Hugo's first need was a place to sleep. While in medical school he had become very good friends with Woodson Duke, a fellow Clay Countian who was now working as a collector in a furniture store. Woodson, his brother Brooks and David J. Davis, a north Alabama country boy who had worked his way through Andover Academy in Massachusetts and, recently, the Yale Law School, were boarding at a home on Fifth Avenue North, between Twentieth and Twenty-first streets. They paid $20 a month each to share a small room with two double beds. Hugo joined them for the same rate. Because he couldn't afford to have his trousers professionally pressed, he did it by putting them between the mattress and the springs.

He found an office on the second floor of a downtown building four blocks from the courthouse. After no clients came to him in a month, he rented desk space for $7 a month, cash in advance, in a building across from the courthouse filled with lawyers. "There I picked up some stray practice," Hugo recalled. "Have been pretty busy since I came back but have not made so much," he told his brother Lee in his first known surviving letter, which he signed "H. L. Black." "This panic seems to have struck Birmingham with a full force and there is not much money floating around. Hope it soon improves, however, and believe it will." That took a while. At times he had trouble scraping together enough money for a meal. He kept the connection he had made in Ashland, checking on applicants for the Atlanta insurance company at 50 cents per investigation. Soon he was earning $50 a month while meeting many of the applicants and their friends. For a time this was his only source of income and he looked upon it as a life saver.

One day an unshaven farmer in overalls walked into the office asking for a lawyer. He had a controversy over the ownership of a sow. Two years earlier a small female shoat had wandered into his barnyard; he fed and kept it until now. Another man, however, claimed to recognize the sow by a mark on her, and demanded her return. Hugo's client assured him there was no such mark, so Hugo thought that was the single issue involved. But there was also a question as to who owned the litter of pigs that the sow had given birth to in the client's backyard. Hugo found to his dismay that under the vague common law doctrine the owner of a sow was also recognized as the owner of her pigs.

Upon arriving at the town, some distance outside Birmingham, for the trial before a notary public ex officio justice of the peace, Hugo saw many large men squatting, with guns in their hands or alongside them. They were friends of the adversary, witnesses who would support his identification of the sow. This was the type of matter that brought out loyalty in men, and one witness after another offered strong proof of the adversary's ownership of the sow. Hugo tried to persuade the judge to give at least half of the sow's offspring to his client, whose ownership of the reported father of the pigs no one questioned. Awarding all the pigs to the claimant would remove them from their hog father who, likely with their mother, had watched over them, Hugo told the justice of the peace who heard the case in the commissary of the coal company where he worked. The judge awarded the mother sow to the adversary and, to Hugo's satisfaction, divided the pigs equally between the litigants. Two months later, the client came to Hugo's office again. A coal mine under his home and farmland had cracked the topsoil. Hugo settled the case and earned himself a fee of $250. On that strength he moved into another office in the same building and shared it with another lawyer, with each paying $15 rent monthly. And when Woodson Duke referred some collection cases to him, which he won in the lower courts, Hugo "no longer worried about making a living" and thought he was "well on my way to success as a Birmingham lawyer."[1]

Building up a law practice is a difficult task, especially for one who, like Hugo, wanted to do it on his own. He met as many people as he could from the day he reached Birmingham. "This was largely responsible for most of the cases I got in the first instance." Lodge and church memberships helped. He had long wanted to join the Masons, and by special arrangement with the Ashland lodge his application for membership went in early, before he reached twenty-one, when he was initiated into the order. The night before he left Ashland to go to Birmingham, he joined the Knights of Pythias.

Immediately he began to visit local lodges to determine which one he should transfer to. He joined the Jefferson Valley Lodge where he met Herman Beck.

Herman Beck was a Jewish Birmingham merchant, an owner of a candy and grocery company, and an established community leader. Twenty years older than Hugo, he was serving as grand vice chancellor and was slated to become state grand chancellor in a few months. He took an instant liking to Hugo. Become my secretary, he urged Hugo, and I'll pay you the grand chancellor's full salary of $100 per month, which will help you through a lean period in your law practice. Hugo accepted the offer and met many people as they traveled around the state; Beck's influence soon made Hugo one of the chancellors of their local lodge. They also spent holidays together, fishing, hunting and picnicking. Beck gave him advice and helped him further financially, and Hugo frequently stayed with the childless Becks, sometimes for weeks at a time. They "became almost as close as father and son, a relationship that continued to his death," Hugo wrote. More than sixty years later he said, "Herman Beck was one of the best people ever to do, the best friend I ever had."

On his first Sunday in Birmingham, his second day there, Hugo went to the First Baptist Church and its all-male Sunday school (Baraca) class. Soon he was elected class president and then its teacher. In 1910 he started lecturing to the same group of hundreds of men week after week. Many of them worked in the mines. One of the few Birmingham lawyers who dared risk his career to take their cases was Frank S. White. An old friend of Alabama governor Braxton Bragg Comer, whose 1906 campaign he ran, White was a deacon in the church where he met Hugo. Miners, most of whom were Negroes, had recently gone on strike when their already low wages were cut even further. Tennessee Coal and Iron (TCI), under pressure from New York bankers who wanted to increase their own profits, moved to smash the strike. Miners fired in the air as a train filled with replacement workers approached a mine, then shot at another train. The violence continued for two months in the summer of 1908, with someone killed daily. Comer ordered the National Guard to evict miners from tent colonies set up on privately leased land and to arrest them as vagrants. White asked Hugo to help him. Black hurried about arranging bail for the miners who were arrested and got them out of jail. Soon he was representing the miners' union and the carpenters' union in court. Word about him got around Birmingham's small community of reformers, and soon Hugo began to serve on the advisory board of the newly formed Carrie Tuggle Institute, a school and orphanage established by Negro fraternal institutions with strong white financial support.[2]

Bonner Miller, whose single-room office Hugo shared, was a shy man. He wanted someone else to try his cases for him. So when a case requiring his appearance came to him from his native Wilcox County, in the southern part of the state, he asked Hugo to take it. Leasing convicts to industrial companies and cities as laborers was a common practice in Alabama and throughout the South. It was an inhumane system that combined, in the words of Julia Tutwiler, the grande dame of Alabama reform, "all of the evils of slavery without one of its ameliorating features." Many whites believed it was the most effective punishment for the Negro vagrant. Birmingham shackled its vagrants in a chain gang and worked them ten hours daily, cleaning and repairing city streets. Convicts were worked in swamps and forests, often kept on the verge of starvation, and flogged for the slightest violation; the annual death rate ran between 10 and 20 percent. The "chief inducement" for the system, the president of TCI admitted, was the "certainty of a supply for our manufacturing operations."

Willie Norton, a Negro convict, had been kept prisoner for twenty-two days after his sentence had legally ended, laboring in a mine owned by the Sloss-Sheffield Steel and Iron Company. He sued for damages and the case was set before Judge A. O. Lane. Hugo met the white-haired Lane several times; they were members of the same Knights of Pythias lodge. Opposing Hugo was William I. Grubb, perhaps the leading corporate lawyer in Birmingham and soon to be appointed a federal district judge. Hugo spent "weeks" preparing for the trial. A good pleader had tactics galore that could get a meritorious case dismissed, delay it until the statute of limitations ran out, or prevent issue from being "joined" by raising immaterial matters. Many cases were lost without the jury's hearing any evidence because most lawyers did not know how to plead, and Grubb had a bagful of tricks.

Hugo's knowledge was purely theoretical, since this was his first jury case in Birmingham, but he had thoroughly studied how he could plead to raise the issues. His written complaint charged false imprisonment, to which the defense would usually plead "not guilty," the equivalent of a general denial. Grubb made the customary motion that the case be dismissed. Both he and Lane were surprised when Hugo jumped to his feet with a vigorous demurrer—that is, to plead "So what?" For a day and a half Grubb filed so-called special pleas. To each one Hugo demurred; to each motion he countered effectively. Grubb moved again for dismissal and entered more pleas. Hugo wrote his demurrers. Lane read them, looked at Grubb, smiled, and laughed as he said, "Well, they didn't work, did they, Billy? I don't think you are going to be able to scare this young fellow or talk him out of it. Let's get down to the case."

"I recognized his ability," Lane said later. "I started out deliberately to trip him up in a case. I would fire questions at him with the thought that they would floor him. But every time I did he landed on his feet like a cat, and came right back at me." The all-white jury awarded Willie Norton $150 damages, "not because . . . of your eloquence," its foreman told Hugo many years later, "but because we believed the young fellow should have justice even if he was a colored fellow." On appeal the Alabama Supreme Court upheld the verdict in May 1909. Hugo and Bonner Miller split half of the damages, $37.50 each. It was not much of a fee, but Hugo was proud of it as a moral victory of sorts. And he had impressed two major figures in the Birmingham political-legal establishment.

Grubb offered him a position with his firm, Tillman, Grubb, Bradley and Morrow, which represented United States Steel. Even though the offer held out the prospect of a secure financial future, an appreciative Hugo turned it down—he wanted a different type of client. But, still, few of any type came. "Things were pretty rough for a while," he recalled. He considered moving to New York City ("all the best lawyers were there and I wanted to be the best"), the Oklahoma Territory or even California, where he could join his uncle Orlando Toland. Later he did not like to talk about this period. But then he became active in an anti–ambulance chasing campaign directed against insurance claim agents who secured releases for pitifully small amounts from injured workers. And matters brightened considerably when Barney Whatley apprenticed under Hugo. When Barney joined the bar, Hugo moved out of Bonner Miller's office so he and Barney could become partners. Theirs was a general practice, making petty collections and representing small businesses, injured workers, the carpenters' union and virtually anyone who came through the door. Soon they did well enough to move into a new building only a block from the courthouse.

One day a Negro woman walked into the office. Whatley asked if he could help her. "No, not you," she said. "I want the mean-looking one." Out came Hugo with that scowl he wore at work. "He was a sharp dude, all business during the day," Barney recalled, "but afterwards it was a different story. Then he had a great sense of humor and was a practical joker." Many of his jokes stung, however; rarely did Hugo turn the humor on himself.

Faet's alcoholism had cheated him out of part of his childhood and of a normal family life. He was belatedly angry and he showed it. The mere mention of certain "fighting words" often led to blows. He was allowing himself to experience long-hidden emotions. In the midst of this Barney was diagnosed as having tuberculosis. On his doctors' suggestion he moved to Colorado, and sold his interest in the firm to Hugo's roommate David J. Davis.[3]

* * *

In 1910 Birmingham reorganized its government, with a three-member city commission replacing the mayor-alderman system. Judge Lane stepped down from the bench to become one of the new commissioners, in charge of the police and legal departments. Early in April 1911, he told Hugo that he planned to consolidate the duties of five city recorders (police court judges or magistrates) into one position, to which he wanted to appoint Hugo; the salary would be $125 a month. Hugo protested, saying that he wished to continue his law practice, which he could not do while doing the work of five men at the same time. Lane persisted. Hugo could start the recorder's work early enough to finish it before nine-thirty each morning, when the state courts in which he practiced began their day. Hugo asked for time to think it over. The following day he told Lane he did not want the job. Lane argued that if Hugo took it, he would release him from it as soon as he felt Hugo had received all the advantage from it he could. That persuaded Hugo. "I have talked with a young lawyer for whom I can vouch," Lane told the press. "He is quick, enterprising and smart. He can fill the recorder's bench well."

At ten o'clock the next morning, April 11, Judge Black stepped behind the bench in what one reporter called the "dingy, dank, dark and dirty backroom in the city hall that is mistermed a courtroom." In morning and afternoon sessions, totaling two and one half hours, he tried fifty-five cases. He announced that hereafter court would convene at eight-thirty. "There will be no afternoon session . . . and I shall utilize this time with my practice. The firm of Black and Davis will continue to serve its clientage with no interference between my duties at the recorder's court and my private business." After banging the gavel the morning following, he said, "There shall be no delay in the matter of summoning witnesses. I shall require absolute punctuality and the best of order." Before ten-thirty he had decided thirty cases.

So it continued for over half a year. Hugo submitted his resignation.

"But Judge Lane asked me to stay on longer so we could prove convincingly that one court could handle all the police cases." He agreed to remain in office another six months. His spirits lifted when a visiting student of police administration, Dr. A. S. Orne, said late in 1911 that he had "visited practically every police court" in the country and that Hugo was "on the road to a greater degree of perfection as a police court judge than I have ever seen. . . . Judge Black," he continued, "has one of the most analytical minds of which I have known, he comes nearer dealing out real justice than any police court judge I have ever seen. I told him the other day that I expected big things of him and told him that there was plenty of room for him at the top of his profession."

At about the same time Hugo struck up a friendship with Charles H. Mandy, a reporter for the *Birmingham Age-Herald,* whom he met in one of the fraternal lodges. Mandy soon switched to the police court beat. His colorfully written articles pointed out the exact shade of the defendant's skin ("octoroon" or "gamboge colored") and reproduced the culprit's remarks in demeaning dialect. Hugo, however, was presented as stern, even severe, but with common foibles; decisive, competent and eloquent, friendly, accommodating, not without a sense of humor, and "not to be outdone in politeness." He did not fit the prototype of a judge. Twenty-five years old, five foot nine and a half, and wiry at 125 pounds, he regularly circulated around the city and exercised the prime requirement of the job—quick common sense judgment—in a manner that was quick indeed. It was not unusual for him to handle up to 130 cases in a four-hour morning session.

The spectators had to listen carefully to hear him. Black rarely spoke in a higher than ordinary tone. "His face is as immobile as the Egyptian Sphinx and no one can tell from his expression what is passing in his mind as he listens to testimony," Mandy wrote. "Then like a bolt from a clear sky he eases out '90 and 100 days' in a low well-modulated voice." Defendants were mostly Negroes arrested for drinking, using dope or shooting craps, thievery or vagrancy, fighting or marital disturbances. On Monday mornings, after rowdy weekends during which police regularly raided saloons and gambling dens, the caseload was especially heavy and the odor stifling. Black ascended the bench one such Monday, took off his coat, rolled up his sleeves and spit on his hands. Common sense and humane sympathies prevailed in his courtroom. When three men were charged with smoking opium, and one of them had lung trouble, Black jailed and fined two of them, and allowed the sick man to leave town. He lowered from $25 to $5 the fine of a white man whom he had scolded for arriving in court late, as soon as the man explained that he lived with his elderly mother and was her sole support.

Race played no role in Black's decisions. Mose Roden, a Negro, was charged with carrying a rusty gun, a concealed weapon. Black tried the gun, found it unworkable and dismissed the case (and gave Mose back the gun). He demanded to hear all the facts when a Negro furnace worker was accused of severely beating a white man, a collector for a secondhand furniture store. The collector, Hugo's questioning revealed, wanted to repossess the man's furniture. Pointing out that his wife was ill and bedridden, the Negro begged the white man not to disturb her. Only when the collector ordered a moving crew to take the furniture did the Negro strike him. Hugo asked to see the worker's hands. They bore calluses like shoe soles. The worker said he had already paid $94 for $50 worth of furniture, the difference representing interest. "You get back home to your sick wife," Hugo told him, "and if I hear of you paying any more on the furniture I'm going to put you in jail— not for beating this man, but for—well, for contempt of court." And to the bruised and bandaged collector he said, "You'd better go back to the furniture and your doctor; and if I hear of you bothering this Negro again I'm going to put you in jail for—well, for a long, long time."[4]

The matter of Birmingham's prohibition law came before Judge Black. In his first written opinion he held that the city's excise commission would be violating the state's prohibition law by revoking the license of wholesalers selling to illegal liquor dealers. This meant that "there will be no law governing the sale of liquor until the excise commission grants licenses," said a surprised Birmingham police commissioner, George H. Bodecker. The city, however, continued its raids and Hugo continued meting out stiff penalties, such as a $500 fine and ninety days to an offender working from a parked car. Thirty years later, he recalled a drunken old Negro who was dragged into court three times. The first time Black fined him $2, whereupon the drunk borrowed the money from Hugo, paid the fine, and went on his way. The next time Hugo doubled the fine and again found himself paying it. The third time Hugo must have run out of money, because he sentenced the fellow to jail.

Since moving to Birmingham, Hugo had been questioning his father's conservative creed. No single dramatic episode or event started this. He just "got to thinking." Living in an environment in which economic injustice was rampant certainly sped the process, as one case showed. A Negro was arrested for not repaying $50 to a loan shark quickly enough. The rate of interest charged was 300 percent for the first year, 240 percent for the second. On the bench Hugo took a pencil and paper and deduced that the interest paid was well in excess of the Negro's salary. Hugo glared at him and at the loan shark's agent. "You can go," Hugo told the prisoner. "You don't owe this man anything." The agent looked bewildered and waited for some explanation why the Negro was released. This, after all, was not the usual course of events in Birmingham courtrooms at the time. Turning to the agent, Hugo said, "The Negro needs no punishment. He's been punished enough."

By now Black had gained wide local visibility, largely because of Charles Mandy's articles. These portrayed "the young disciple of Blackstone" receiving "his morning callers, the majority being of the $90 and 30 day variety," asking them skillful questions ("those flashes of quick thought that . . . so often startled the court officials"), and then making eloquent remarks. Hugo often used words that certainly he did not learn in Ashland. The testimony in one case led him to examine the defendant's "spotulated" hands in order to determine character traits. Noticing the "conical" formation of the "phalanges," he applied the "indisputable rules of palmistry" in accordance with the "science of chirognomy." Mandy showed Hugo enjoying himself while doing his job, once singing the tune he heard the night before. "Everybody's doing it, doing it, doing it," and then, as he handed out fines, "Everybody's getting it, getting it, getting it." Black was good copy and Mandy wrote about him almost daily. They also lunched and attended various evening functions together. Mandy, Hugo said later, "gave me my start in politics."

In October 1912 Black resigned. "It has been valuable experience and afforded me a broad insight into human nature," he said. He had been able to observe at first hand the seamiest side of a rapidly expanding industrial city. But he felt he had seen enough of poor people and his law practice was growing. As he closed the docket on his last day with the remark that his duties were over, the bailiff approached Hugo and placed him under arrest. Startled, Black asked what the charge was. "Abandonment," the clerk said. The new judge ordered Hugo arraigned. He pleaded "not guilty" and took his seat. The judge said that the police chief would substantiate the charge. The chief then came forward and presented Hugo with a gold watch "in token of our appreciation and as a mark of the high esteem in which you are held by the police department and the many friends in the city hall. . . . We wish you every success, and some day expect to see you in a much higher judicial position than that you have so ably filled."[5]

. . . .

Black returned to private practice full-time. He had enjoyed a taste of the spotlight, heady stuff for a twenty-six-year-old. Because of a hyperthyroid condition he had energy to spare. He did not sleep much or well, and his mind kept racing from one task to another. He moved around the city, often on horseback, joining almost every organization he could except those that did not allow dual membership or those, such as the "elite" Kiwanis Club, which would not accept him because of his background; and he regretted that he could not enter these. Members noticed his self-confidence and his humor when he addressed groups. "Gentlemen," he told a Men and Religion Forward Movement banquet, "judges and ministers may not always have been honest men."

> I know of two instances to the contrary—Dr. L. D. Patterson, here, and myself, were once thieves. Yes, thieves in the worst sense of the word, but we were cured of stealing in rather an odd way. We had a special fondness for eggs and many a broken-hearted hen owes her heart-break to our thievery. Thus we held forth for some time and all went merrily—even the eggs we stole—until one fatal day on which we robbed the henhouse of Dr. Patterson's mother. We secured eggs all right—but not all right eggs.
>
> The hen had been over them too long, but shells hold odors close within and we knew nothing. We boiled the eggs—we always liked them best that way (boiled not spoiled) and with great gusto and a few grains of salt, proceeded with our egg-fest. Shall I go on? Ah, nux vomica—perhaps I may as well leave the rest to your imagination.
>
> At any rate for ten years thereafter I could not be induced to eat eggs no matter how they were prepared or obscured. I put the hard boiled eggs back in the nest so Mrs. Patterson wouldn't know the difference—but would you think it? She actually found out that some one had been tampering with those tissue builders. Some women are wonderful.

From such occasions came new friends for Hugo and new clients for the firm of Black and Davis. David J. mainly handled the office work, especially the real estate part, while Hugo tried nearly all the court cases, which dealt largely with personal injuries and contracts. The arrangement satisfied him completely. He enjoyed everything about the practice—drafting pleadings and contracts, research, writing briefs and, above all, trying cases. In the Masonic Lodge he met the owner of a lumber company whom the Louisville & Nashville Railroad had overcharged when shipping freight. Demanding payment, Hugo asked that the court seize all the typewriters in the L & N freight office. "They paid us quick," the lumberman recalled.

Hugo was becoming especially adept at examining witnesses. His devout belief in the jury system began during these years. He preferred to submit his cases to juries composed of plain citizens rather than to judges who often reflected the viewpoint of the employers whom they formerly represented. Alabama law required that in some cases juries had to hear evidence as to punishment even when a defendant pleaded guilty. This put a premium on a lawyer's persuasive powers. In Birmingham's small legal community—the city had fewer than two hundred lawyers—Hugo was winning acclaim for his "rapid fire grasp of minor points and enlarging on them on cross-examination."

In 1913 Davis suddenly told Hugo that he wanted to dissolve the partnership. Hugo "attracted more business," was "a better lawyer," and was thus "worth more to the firm," Davis said. This greatly surprised Hugo, for they had "never had any kind of friction." They had been dividing their income evenly, which bothered David J.'s conscience as he "had long before promised himself that he would never be in a partnership where he brought in less income than any other member"; and he was adamant about it. Hugo went out on his own. Soon he was earning $7,500 yearly. With some of this money he bought law books; the rest he saved as a nest egg for a future run for public office.

It was at this time that Hugo's personality adopted a new trait: he became a survivor. A naturally resilient temperament and a highly self-directed nature enabled him to overcome the struggle against circumstances. Having lost both of his parents and been deprived of a normal family life, he needed and developed strong relationships with mentors—indeed, Herman Beck had become a proxy parent. The anger in him subsided somewhat. "It took me a long time," Hugo later admitted, "to realize that soft words were nearly always more persuasive than invective and adjectives."

His reputation for winning lawsuits brought him more cases. Other lawyers approached him about forming new partnerships or joining their firms. He rejected another offer to become a partner in Tillman, Bradley and Morrow, Judge Grubb's old firm and the largest in the state. When Hugh Morrow proffered it, Hugo wondered if he could be "wholly happy" defending clients such as the street car company in serious personal injury and death cases. He did not want to be a "defendants' lawyer." He also said that he was seriously thinking about runnning for Jefferson County solicitor (or district attorney).[6]

....

Politics was never far from Hugo's mind. In 1913 he represented the Hobson-Starnes Coal Company. One of its principals was Richmond Pearson Hobson, the hero of the sinking of the *Maine* during the Spanish-American War who parlayed that fame into a seat in Congress from Alabama in 1906. This company and the Zurich Insurance Company of Switzerland were the only two corporations Hugo represented during his more than twenty-five years of law practice. He never recalled Hobson-Starnes because he represented it for a political motive: Hobson, an ardent prohibitionist, was preparing to run for the Senate in 1914 against Birmingham congressman Oscar W. Underwood; and to admit that this was the real reason would have been too blatant. Hugo always believed so strongly in what he was doing that he had a hard time admitting that things really might not have been as he liked to think they were.

He talked about running for solicitor with a few close friends—Davis, Lane, Beck and the small nucleus of liberals in Birmingham. He could afford to run and had many friends who could help. With the help of William E. Fort, a criminal court judge in whose campaign for the bench he had been active, Black announced his candidacy in September 1913:

> No office within the gift of the people of this county is of greater importance to their well-being than the office of County Solicitor. The people of this county have the right to demand a firm, vigorous and efficient administration of the laws against crime. . . . If elected I will devote my time and energy to the prosecution of crime, and during my canvass for this office will make no allegiance which could embarrass me in the discharge of my duties.[7]

Over the next eight months, except for the time his practice demanded, Hugo campaigned full time. In a new Model T Ford he drove around the county, or he rode on horseback. He saw people at lodges, picnics, basket suppers, baseball games. One whole afternoon he spent pitching horseshoes in a western precinct, and received every vote there but ten. He learned to shake every hand, look a person in the eye and keep walking. Some sections he visited several times, just dropping into stores and other gathering places to talk, really to listen. He asked people to tell him what they expected of a county prosecutor. Generations later, candidates would hire pollsters to take the public pulse and tailor their campaigns to it. Hugo did this himself. He found that people opposed professional gambling and bootlegging, as he did, and "were tired of having hundreds of Negroes arrested for shooting craps on pay day and crowding the jails with these petty offenders. I promised to clear the jail of these prisoners and the docket of long-standing cases. I promised, too, that I would carry out to the fullest my repeated belief that 'it is as much the duty of the prosecuting attorney to protect the innocent as it is to convict the guilty.' "

After a few months he put what the people told him in newspaper advertisements, but first he identified himself further to the masses. It was a homespun technique, direct and simple, one that still remains effective. A picture of Hugo, young and earnest-looking, appeared in the press daily, and below it, "This is your next solicitor" or "The gamblers are against this man for solicitor." Soon his name was added and the words changed to "Hugo Black will make a good solicitor—ask the judges" or "ask the voters." This "crime suppressor," when elected, would be at the courthouse busily prosecuting criminals, citizens were told. For he had learned that "delay is the greatest criminal lawyer."

Since 1898, while the crime rate spiraled, the solicitor had been Harrington P. Heflin. This brother of United States senator J. Thomas Heflin seemed to give the impression that he should be reelected just because he held the job. Also running were Zebulon T. Rudulph, a political neophyte supported by the city's establishment, and F. D. McArthur, who was backed by organized labor. These candidates placed large, solemn ads, filling many newspaper columns. In sharp contrast stood Hugo's small appeals with their brisk, catchy slogans. He emphasized that he was without his opponents' means ("I have not sought the indorsement of any newspaper, monied interest or lawless element"), and that his friends were not "a few capitalists or ring politicians" but hundreds of men in every walk of life. A candidate, he felt, should make it appear that he is running for office at the request of his friends. So he started his own draft. An informal Young Men's Club for Hugo Black for Solicitor was formed; members signed a petition stating their intention to vote for him. This was quickly expanded to include influential politicians and other prominent persons. Eventually more than two thousand names were on the rolls of the Hugo Black Club.

That the majority of voters opposed Heflin no one doubted. The problem was which candidate could beat him. Hugo, Davis and Barney Whatley, who returned from Colorado for the campaign, decided to distribute small strips of colored pasteboard about the size of a theater ticket. On both sides were printed: "Black or Heflin: Which?" These cards "covered Jefferson County like the dew," Hugo later wrote. He was convinced that they persuaded people to vote for him. The other candidates quickly copied his tactic while complaining about it, but it was too late. In the primary on

April 8, 1914, Black received 6,843 votes; Heflin, 4,572; Rudulph, 3,286; and McArthur, 1,875.

The Democratic primary then being equivalent to election in the South, Hugo resumed his practice full time. Soon he found a new partner, William H. Sadler. A graduate of the University of Virginia, "refined, and proud of it," said his son, Sadler "liked gentlemen. He found Black a pretty rough type, very country in his manners." As soon as the partnership ended, Hugo began to make a serious study of the role of the county prosecutor's office in the American governmental scheme. He read books on county government, on the prosecutor's duties and on the sociological roots of crime. And he visited several large northern and midwestern cities, to meet district attorneys to discuss methods of criminal prosecutions.

Election day came. "Only seven years after the young hillbilly from Clay County arrived, almost a total stranger in Jefferson, Alabama's most populous county," Hugo wrote more than fifty years later with still a little wonderment, "he was elected its Prosecuting Attorney by the people." The press praised him. He announced the appointment of two assistant solicitors—William S. Welch, who was a few years older than he and did not support him in the campaign, and Walter J. Brower, a close friend just three years out of law school—and got down to work.[8]

CHAPTER 3

PROSECUTOR

W E, THE JURY, find the defendant guilty as charged," read the court clerk at the end of Black's first trial. It was a common refrain that opening week. He and his assistants obtained eleven convictions of capital offenses and one acquittal, and six cases were continued. Despite this auspicious beginning, he believed that the solicitor's purview should be expanded, at least in the pretrial stage. Black prepared bills for the state legislature, urging that his office be allowed to employ detectives to secure additional information, and to summon witnesses to appear before him when serious crimes had been committed. The next month the grand jury, prodding the legislature, made these recommendations and also called for the appointment of an emergency judge for the criminal court. A third judge would speed up cases by giving each prosecutor a court in which to try cases, Black wrote the governor, as well as save the state money by cutting the jail population to a minimum. Facing Black and the judges was a docket of staggering proportions: 3,268 cases, including ninety-two for capital offenses such as murder, violent robbery and rape.

The fee system caused the clogging. Under state law sheriffs, constables, jailers and court officers received not salaries but fees based on the number of arrests and court proceedings in which they participated and the number of legal notices that they served. This resulted in tidy incomes for these officials. Negro "spotters" were used to spy out craps games on payday for the deputies to raid. Workers were arrested wholesale and kept in jail as long as possible. Indeed, one of Black's first cases had been pending ten years. In 1912 voters approved an amendment to the state constitution to put the beneficiaries of the fee system in the county on a straight salary basis; but this did not take effect for several years.

Hugo toured the jail immediately after taking office and found despicable conditions: up to nine men living in one small cell, and seventy-five prisoners in the basement without any light, fresh air or sanitation, all "huddled together as dogs, not as human beings." To be sure that they were served adequate food—sheriffs spent less than 10 cents of the 30 cents' daily food allowance, pocketing the remainder—Hugo frequently ate meals there. Some prisoners he found languishing for months without indictments or even charges brought against them; their records were lost. And one man— "nobody knew how long he had been in there, nobody knew what he was there for, he was just there," Hugo said. He released these prisoners on the spot, scheduled trials for others and offered to all the opportunity to plead guilty (sometimes he advised the court to fine them one cent); first offenders were given light jail sentences. But after examining the record in each instance, he refused to prosecute five hundred cases cluttering the docket.

The result was talk of impeachment. He had promised convictions but turned prisoners loose instead, critics charged. But "what was wanted from them," as Black later said, "was not expiation of offenses against society, but the fees that could be wrung from their pitiful wages." By May only 142 prisoners were in the jail awaiting trial, down from 376. This number swelled as more Negroes were arrested but could not afford bail and the criminal courts adjourned from June to October. At Black's suggestion summer court sessions were scheduled, and extra judges from around the state were temporarily assigned to sit in Birmingham. He renewed his plea for the state legislature to act. It passed a bill providing for the appointment of another judge and appropriating funds for detectives and clerical help for the solicitor. When there were indications that the governor might veto the bill, Black wrote him a public letter, noting the length of the backlog and the necessity for speedy justice. "Time is the best criminal lawyer." The governor signed the bill. Within a year the docket was almost completely up to date.[1]

Few people favored prohibition more than Black. In July 1915 Alabama became a dry state. Also enacted, to take effect after he became solicitor, was a law banning liquor advertising in any form within the state. Most newspapers in Jefferson County announced they would follow the law. The *Birmingham News,* however, stated it would continue to allow such advertisements and would even test the law's constitutionality. "There will be a prosecution in every case where there has been a violation," Black warned. The *News* retreated after he told its publisher that he would arrest "all [persons] responsible, from the publisher on down" and, further, enjoin the paper's publication.

Soon a Birmingham news agent sought an injunction to prevent a news-stand operator from selling newspapers and magazines containing liquor advertisements. In March 1915 a city court judge denied the petition, noting that no statute prohibiting the circulation of newspapers with such ads was in force. Black immediately stated that he would enforce the prohibition statute and filed two suits. One was against a businessman who advertised liquor on an outside wall of his building; the anti-advertising law was held valid and in full operation. The other suit was against the newsstand operator, who continued to sell the same papers, including the *Cincinnati Inquirer*, which ran two advertisements for whiskey on the day Black went to court. The same judge, John H. Miller, denied the petition, holding that news-papers published in other states are articles of interstate commerce, he wrote, and thus the state government has no authority to interfere. On appeal the Alabama Supreme Court unanimously reversed, holding that the law was a proper exercise of the state's power to regulate in the public welfare, and entered an order granting the injunction. Disregarded was the fact that the law apparently conflicted with the federal statute.

Brewery interests naturally opposed the prohibition law. Often it was very difficult to convict a person for selling or possessing beer without proof beyond a reasonable doubt by a chemical analysis that the beer contained enough alcohol to be intoxicating. As a result the "near beer" business quickly sprang up and flourished. Alabama countered by making illegal any liquid that looked like, tasted like, smelled like or foamed like beer. The brewers hired Forney Johnston to challenge the constitutionality of this law.

If a hereditary nobility had ever been legal in Alabama, Johnston would have been born into a lifetime peerage. His grandfather was a renowned Confederate general, and his father served as governor and United States senator. Seven years older than Hugo, he took time away from representing large corporations to act as Oscar Underwood's campaign manager in his victorious 1914 Senate race. Hugo considered him "the best Establishment lawyer," defending the claims and privileges of the Alabama Bourbons. *

---

* Populists called his post-Reconstruction establishment Bourbons, without knowing the origins of the term. Of the Bourbon kings of France—Henry IV, Louis XIII–XV and Charles

Inheritance fated them to be enemies. Johnston often let his feelings get the best of him. "Cut out the rhetoric and get down to facts," a judge once told him. Behind his back Hugo and friends called him "phony Johnston."

Johnston filed suit in federal court to prevent Black from prosecuting for the sale, transportation or possession of "near beer." The beer provisions of the Alabama law, he contended, violated the due process clause of the Fourteenth Amendment of the United States Constitution (". . . nor shall any State deprive any person of life, liberty, or property, without due process of law"). Black countered that the case raised nothing but factual questions that the statute answered, that it was constitutional, and that the federal court lacked jurisdiction to prohibit his actions. They argued the matter at length before Judge Grubb, who dismissed Johnston's petition for an injunction. More important, for the first time Black was forced to think seriously about the meaning of due process and about the power of the government to pass laws that might infringe upon citizens' rights, liberties and property.

The brewers, however, were undeterred. They distributed a concotion called ambrosia, a cereal beverage attested to be nonalcoholic, nonintoxicating and not an imitation of beer. Fehr's Ambrosia was manufactured in New Jersey; when it reached Birmingham, the sheriff seized a carload of seventy-nine barrels on Black's orders. Johnston challenged this action in court. On several occasions Black postponed the scheduled hearing; he was satisfied with the status quo of the stuff not being sold. The judge set a final date. But no lawyer appeared for the government. Black was found, and he said he did not have any interest in the proceeding. The judge, dismissing the case, said he would rule that the ambrosia should be released for want of prosecution.

"I object to that," Black said. "This disposal of this particular hearing does not mean that ambrosia will be sold in Birmingham."

"Such braggadocio statements are too puerile for us," replied Johnston.

"Order in court, gentlemen," interjected the judge.

"Well, there will be no ambrosia sold. I'll tell you that now," Black said as he walked away.

Johnston now went to federal court, which granted a temporary injunction restraining Black from seizing or interfering with the ambrosia's storage. "We surely will fight the final injunction to the last notch," Black

---

X—it has been said that they "learned nothing and forgot nothing," certainly an apt description of Birmingham's rulers.

said. He had the manufacturer's agent arrested. Anyone possessing or selling
ambrosia could be arrested the moment it left the company's hands, according
to Black. Soon the judge made the temporary injunction permanent. Still,
Black convicted a man for selling "Brother Wiser." He did not dispute the
claims that the beverage contained no alcohol, was harmless and was not a
malt brew. To him the whole issue was clear: "It looks like beer and that is
clearly a violation of the law."[2]

In mid-1915 Black noticed that the steel town of Bessemer, outside Birmingham, was producing an inordinately high number of confessions. He
had been hearing reports of ruthless treatment of prisoners by the local
police for several years, and he had seen some evidence of this when representing Negro laborers in his practice. Even though his jurisdiction over
the matter was unclear and he did not stand to reap any foreseeable political
gain, the horror stories that kept circulating were just too great to bear. He
asked the grand jury to investigate. A few liberal friends and a small number
of Negroes who had by now recognized his evenhandedness helped to supply
him with many witnesses and much information.

The tone the grand jury's report should take presented something of a
dilemma. If Black made it a racial issue only, he would probably accomplish
nothing constructive and might leave the situation worse than it had been
before. But if it were treated as a problem of basic human decency, with
little or no reference to the Negro factor, he could perhaps marshal the
necessary support of prominent citizens who might otherwise be indifferent
or oppose any action at all; his evidence would have to be overwhelming.
Black drafted the report and submitted it to the criminal court judges; the
grand jury approved. When published on September 17, 1915, it was a
scorcher:

> We find that, according to their own statements, Officers Maddox and
> Houston have repeatedly been guilty of the practice of the "third degree"
> in a manner so cruel that it would bring discredit and shame upon the
> most uncivilized and barbarous community. We find that a uniform practice
> has been made of taking helpless prisoners, in the late hours of the night,
> into a secluded room in the presence of these two officers, and others whose
> names we have not been able to obtain, and there beat them until they
> were red with their own blood, in an effort to obtain confessions. We find
> that this cowardly practice, in which four big officers with pistols safely
> strapped on their bodies, would thus take advantage of ignorance and

helplessness, has been continuously in operation for a number of years. A leather strap with a buckle on one end and a big flap on the other was invented for the purpose of assisting officers in this heinous practice, contrary to the letter and spirit of the constitution of the United States, the constitution of Alabama, the universal sympathy of the human heart. . . .

The Bessemer police had assumed, as those who use the third degree always have, that the victims were guilty. Here their innocence was apparent. Only the officers committed offenses, and the grand jury recommended that they, and a third officer, who was habitually drunk, be dismissed at once. The report concluded on broader grounds. A man does not

> forfeit his right to be treated as a human being by reason of the fact that he is charged with, or an officer suspects that he is guilty of a crime. Instead of being ready and waiting to strike a prisoner in his custody, an officer should protect him. The "third degree" methods are not protected by law, by custom, nor by conscience. . . . Such practices are dishonorable, tyrannical, and despotic, and such rights must not be surrendered to any officer or set of officers, so long as human life is held sacred and human liberty and human safety of paramount importance.

The Bessemer aldermen roundly criticized the grand jury and the Birmingham papers for headlining its report. Black called for an investigation of the police department. "Thorough publicity is the best corrective," he said. "The truth and the whole truth is the mightiest factor in human life." Bessemer decided to initiate a probe—an open one in order to accommodate Black who would not cooperate otherwise. He remained in the background, furnishing evidence for the Bessemer solicitor and promising protection for witnesses. The chairman of the Bessemer council's police committee resigned, and four officers who "strung" a Negro to a door were indicted for assault with intent to murder. Quickly the scandal died down, but not before the *Birmingham Age-Herald* minimized its significance, saying "matters have been exaggerated. . . . Conditions such as are prevalent in every other city have been brought to light." Black took satisfaction that brutal police interrogations and coerced confessions in Jefferson County did lessen, at least while he was solicitor.

Hugo Black disregarded race as much as a public official in Birmingham at the time could. An assistant whom he inherited from the previous solicitor convicted a Negro whom Black later discovered to be innocent. Black immediately wrote the governor, explaining the mistake and asking for a pardon. The governor took no action. Twice more Black repeated the request, with still no results. Finally he telegraphed the governor, stating that if the Negro was not released within twenty-four hours, he would issue a statement to the press along with a list of all the gamblers the governor had found time to pardon. The Negro was quickly pardoned.

Guilt was Black's criterion in deciding whom to prosecute. Several times he brought murder charges against white men for killing Negroes, and he tried the cases himself. Gus Goolsby, the seventeen-year-old son of a poor widow, was unable to pay the fine for violating a Pinckney City ordinance. Sentenced to jail, he was walking there when he escaped from the clutches of the town marshal, Albert Box, and started running. Eight eyewitnesses testified that Box deliberately fired his gun at Goolsby but missed. Goolsby stopped, turned around and made a face at the officer. Another shot, with both hands steadying the pistol, killed Goolsby instantly. Box immediately turned on his heel and walked calmly to a saloon for a drink. "This did appear to me to be a very bad killing," Black recalled, "because the victim was only a boy and it was thought he had done no more than be engaged in some kind of small gambling game." At trial Box claimed that first he fired in the air and then, as he stumbled over a ditch, the gun discharged again. On cross-examination, however, he admitted that he had been in several shooting contests and had shot chicken's heads off at ten paces. Black told the jury this was a coldblooded, premeditated murder. Box was convicted and given a twenty-five-year sentence; but the jurors could not bring themselves to impose capital punishment, as Black had asked, upon a white policeman, the son of a former circuit court judge, who had shot a Negro youth.

Capital punishment did not faze Black. He did not spend much time pondering its morality. A small class of crimes, especially brutal murders, demanded it, he believed. He was a prosecutor with a job to do and wanted punishment to serve as an effective deterrent. Killing another person showed contempt both for the law and for human life. Birmingham newspapers carried articles announcing hangings, and Black and his staff had no compunction in asking for the death penalty.[3]

Black's reputation spread outside Birmingham. The small town of Girard, Alabama, across the Chattahoochee River from Columbus, Georgia, has always been, as one later Alabama governor put it, "a pretty wild place."

According to Black, "some people decided to make Girard the leading bootleg center of the United States," or at least of the Southeast. Several local attempts to control its liquor traffic had failed. Alabama Attorney General William Logan Martin undertook to enforce the state's prohibition law. Black's performance as solicitor and in two recent cases before the state supreme court in which they worked together had impressed Martin, and he asked Hugo to prosecute liquor violations in Girard. State officials, acting on a tip, found buildings honeycombed with false walls and trapdoors, hiding thousands of gallons of the contraband. Another cache was discovered in the river, attached by rope to the Alabama shore. Six known ringleaders were indicted, but they skipped town. When they failed to appear for trial, Black received court permission to destroy the liquor on the grounds that the six were fugitives from justice, in contempt of court and therefore had no legal standing.

Appealing to the southern love of grand gestures, Black dramatically ordered the destruction. Thirty men worked for three days emptying more than half a million dollars' worth of whiskey and beer—46 barrels of whiskey and 108 barrels of beer in all—into Girard's streets. Guards had to be placed along the stream in order to give the stuff a chance to float down the hill to the river without interruption. Black presided triumphantly over the pungent stream, standing on the sidewalk in shirtsleeves and wearing a hard straw hat as hundreds looked on and photographers took pictures ("the man of the hour," the Birmingham News called him in a front-page shot). The bootleggers were soon caught, and he convicted the first three tried (two others were fined $2,500 each and their Negro hauler $300) as well as a host of local officials. "We convicted everybody that remained behind to stand trial," Black later said, "and those that we did not convict ran away from the county." On appeal the state supreme court held that the seizure was justifiable. The discovery of illegal goods, the court noted, "cured" the "defect" of no warrant.

Hugo was in the middle of his crusade at Girard when he received a telegram that his friend Barney Whatley had killed his own father. Since leaving Birmingham for Colorado for health reasons, Barney had done well. He settled in Breckinridge, and in 1914 he was elected district attorney in the area. His family lived together except for his father, who had drifted away and lost contact over the past decade. But one day the senior Whatley suddenly appeared. That night, Barney said later, "my father fell into the worst fit of anger I have ever seen." The next day, while standing on the veranda with Barney and his sister, who was holding her baby, Martin Whatley reached for a shotgun. Barney thought his sister was going to be shot. He got a revolver and fired. His father died instantly.

In court the following day Hugo explained the incident to the judge and asked for a recess. It was granted and he left immediately for Colorado. Barney had already surrendered to the sheriff and resigned as district attorney. Hugo and a local lawyer represented Barney before a judge whose animus against him was apparent. The local lawyer handled the pretrial motions and the opening phase of the trial, and examined witnesses. Hugo made what one newspaper called "an eloquent address" to the jury. Forty-four counts of the judge's forty-five-count charge to the jury detailed how Barney could be found guilty; the remaining count was "If you find him not guilty, vote not guilty." Which is what the jury found. Upon hearing the verdict, Barney rushed up and hugged Hugo. "He came when I needed him," Barney later said on those very rare occasions when he mentioned the matter. To Hugo it was simply something one does for a dear friend.[4]

*   *   *

Late in 1916, the Alabama legislature passed a law effective the next January, consolidating all existing county and circuit courts (which generally covered several counties) and solicitors' offices. A specific exception, however, was made for the Jefferson County solicitor. Black was left without a court to prosecute in. He had quickly lost confidence in the present Birmingham circuit solicitor, Joseph R. Tate, because of Tate's racial attitude and incompetence. Before the court consolidation bill became law, Tate moved to assume control of the solicitor's office by naming three assistants whom Black considered amiable hacks. Both solicitors appeared in court when the first case under the new arrangement came up. Tate said he was not ready for trial and asked for an extension; Hugo said he was ready to proceed. After lengthy argument, the judge ruled that Black was the chief criminal prosecutor of the county, but that the circuit solicitor could assist him; another judge soon held the same.

Tate immediately appealed to the Alabama Supreme Court, asserting he had the right to appoint all deputy solicitors, including Black's. That court decided that both Black and Tate were correct: until Hugo's term expired, Jefferson County could have two prosecutors who could prosecute in the circuit court and appoint assistants, but Hugo was not required to have any and those that he did have would be paid from county funds; all would be subject to the orders of both solicitors. It was an obviously un-workable arrangement.

Forney Johnston, who was counsel to the county treasurer, advised that only Tate's assistants could be paid from county funds. Black went to court. The county court upheld him, but the treasurer refused to honor the warrants for the salaries. The board did not appeal and Black became counsel for the board. Since Tate refused to handle his few circuit court cases, Black asked the state auditor to deduct $25 per day from the salaries of Tate and his three assistants. The grand jury demanded that Tate discharge them lest the next grand jury oust him from office for "gross and willful abuse" of his discretion. The assistants refused to resign. The matter went before the Alabama Supreme Court again which in early July 1917 handed down a "Solomon-like" opinion. "No one could have anticipated" it, Hugo believed to the end of his life. The court affirmed that he was indeed the county's chief prosecutor and sustained his power to appoint assistants, but added that the county must not pay salaries for his assistants and that he must use Tate's assistants before any others.

Black announced his resignation effective August 1, 1917. Not wanting to be solicitor in name only, he wrote the governor, "I do not feel that I can perform the duties of my office satisfactorily to the people and in accord with my own conscience with these assistants." He always said thereafter that this was the worst political turmoil in his life. Even his political op-ponents had to admit that conditions had greatly improved. As of the end of June only ninety-seven prisoners were in the county jail, the food bill was down to $1,000 a month, and there were 608 cases on the docket. Walker Percy, corporation lawyer, civic leader and chairman of a committee to investigate the salaries of public officials, had been asked how much he thought the solicitor should be paid. "It depends upon what solicitor you have in mind," he replied. "Our present one would be cheap at $25,000 a year."

As solicitor, Black conceived of the office as being as much concerned with clean and efficient government as with the more dramatic and headline-grabbing work of prosecuting crimes. The job strengthened his growing belief that the cause of crime was rooted in the social fabric of the community. His liberalism, he later explained, was the result of experience and study. As a police court judge he had delved into hundreds of case histories of individuals and families "gone wrong": it was a virtual laboratory to observe the seamiest side of life in a city like Birmingham. After serving as prosecutor, he concluded that crime sprang from poverty, economic injustices and the social diseases and frustrations that were their by-products. Government had to address itself to those problems.

Public attention focused on Black. Rumors circulated that he was planning to run for "every office in the state from constable to governor." The local papers, regardless of political viewpoint, vied with each other in heaping praise on him. Zealousness, energy, vigor and efficiency marked his service, they all agreed. Hugo did not realize the degree to which people outside the confines of Jefferson County had watched his fight for good government. Letters from all over Alabama poured in. The most poignant letter came from Adele Fort, a poet and the wife of Judge William E. Fort. Saying that her husband felt awkward about complimenting anyone to his face, Mrs. Fort explained how "he so frequently rejoices in your fearless qualities—a thing which especially appeals to a man weary of the sight of graft. We feel that this [Hugo's resignation] is an undeniable loss to our county and one not easy to fill."[5]

*   *   *

Europe was at war during Black's solicitorship. A proponent of Secretary of State William Jennings Bryan's peace program, and a pacifist at heart, Black believed the war was unnecessary; but once Congress declared war on April 6, 1917, he wanted to do his part to "make the world safe for democracy." He discussed with Judge Fort the advisability of resigning as solicitor and volunteering for the army. Fort noted that at the age of thirty-one Hugo was exempt from the draft; that his work as solicitor was an essential activity of wartime as well as of peacetime; that he was, after a fashion, conducting a minor war for democracy in his own county; and that he was somewhat honor bound to carry out the mandate the people had entrusted to him. So Black decided to continue as solicitor.

Shortly after resigning, he volunteered for the army. He took an officers' training course in Birmingham and was accepted to continue training at Fort Oglethorpe, Georgia. There he spent three hard months, often riding bareback on old army horses. Although he wanted the infantry, he was assigned to the artillery and was commissioned a captain in the 81st Field Artillery. He quickly became the adjutant to Colonel William T. Littebrandt and helped him reorganize the unit. In late 1917 Hugo was transferred to Camp Tremont, California. He visited some of his mother's family, the Tolands, in Los Angeles and San Francisco on a short leave in April. Her brother Orlando offered him a future partnership in his Los Angeles law firm which Hugo agreed to consider when the war ended. Soon he was sent to Fort Sill,

Oklahoma, where he took another three-month course, in the artillery "school of fire." In time this unit was sent to the port of embarkation on the Atlantic coast on the way to Europe. Littebrandt informed him he was to serve as major; his superior planned to make him a colonel. Hugo arranged for another few days' leave in late October 1918 to return to Birmingham to dispose of some matters; he looked over his will—long ago he had named Herman Beck as sole executor—and bid good-bye to his friends.

While home he received an order by telegram from Washington to report back to Fort Sill to help train another brigade. It "appeared to have knocked all the joy out of his promotion," wrote a friend who saw him that day. The War Department had denied Littebrandt's plea to go to the battle front. Hugo was then assigned to a new field artillery brigade, which Littebrandt would command. Little could he know that the sole reason Hugo was eager for overseas duty was that he feared in postwar politics it might be held against him if he were not a member of the Veterans of Foreign Wars.

After the armistice on November 11, 1918, Hugo went to Los Angeles to speak with his uncle Orlando Toland. Orlando had left Alabama for California in the mid-1870s and become a lawyer mixing progressive politics with a lucrative corporate practice. In 1910 he ran as the Democratic candidate for lieutenant governor. Republican Hiram Johnson won a close election; later Orlando claimed, with a good deal of truth, that "a good part of Johnson's platform had been pirated right from [him]." He would "ease out" if Hugo joined his firm, he said. Hugo rejected the offer; he had already established a political base in Birmingham.

"Captain Black has resumed practice and has opened his office on the ninth floor of the First National Bank Building," noted the *Birmingham Age-Herald* at the end of 1918. For a short time he practiced alone. Then he formed a series of partnerships that ended quickly. He was the youngest lawyer listed among the "leading lawyers of today" included in a two-volume description of Birmingham's outstanding citizens. His practice was the same type he had before becoming solicitor: almost exclusively he represented individuals, largely injured workers. Most of his cases, as a result, were against the corporations that ruled Birmingham. On the basis of his first three postwar months alone, Hugo bought a new car.[6]

*   *   *

Hugo's toughness in the courtroom was a shield for his innate sympathy and tenderness, and hid a deep romantic streak. In his off hours he was "just as good at foolishness as at the heavy stuff," said his close buddy Albert Lee

Smith. He shared a country house with Borden Burr, already a successful corporate lawyer, and vacationed with his assistant Walter Brower; with both fellow country boys he had contests as to who could take more women to bed. Hugo met Smith, a Birmingham native, the son of a former president of Howard College and a rising insurance man, at the First Baptist Church as soon as he came to Birmingham, and they spent much of their spare time together. One New Year's Eve they went to New York, took in the town wearing white suits and hats, and stayed in a hotel penthouse.

Back home, "we drove around on horses to see girls," Smith recalled. On Sundays, before evening church socials, they often rode the trolley around Highland Avenue and the South Side, stopping to eat ice cream at each shop where the girls would call them Tweedledum and Tweedledee. Or they would go to the Birmingham Country Club where Hugo, leaning back in a big club chair, took his time dramatically smoking his weekly cigar. He and Hugh Locke, also a young politically ambitious lawyer, sometimes staged mock trials. Twice Hugo met Zelda Sayre of Montgomery, who soon married the young novelist Scott Fitzgerald. Hugo remembered her as "the raciest woman I ever met." "We called ourselves the ladies' delight because the girls enjoyed themselves when we were there," Smith said.

Many young Birmingham women considered the dashing, courtly Hugo, with his trim, relaxed exterior hiding a driven interior, quite a "catch." He had dated a woman in Herman Beck's family before going into the army. They planned to marry when he returned but her parents, Orthodox Jews, forbade it. Then he put his career first. "Hugo was having too much fun to get married," recalled Smith. He had been so involved with many women that a cousin, Eugenia (Jenny) Toland, who had moved to Birmingham, later jokingly threatened to blackmail him and harm his political career. "Now, Hugo," she would say, "if you don't do this, I'll tell some things you wouldn't want others to know." But, as Smith noted, "he didn't meet the right girl."

One day on Niazuma Avenue in the heart of Birmingham's fashionable South Side, around the corner from his apartment, Hugo noticed a strikingly attractive young woman standing at the door of the imposing family home, wearing a bathing suit and talking to a friend. Another time he saw her walking uphill, struggling to keep an especially long skirt from hitting the ground. He determined to find out who she was. It turned out she was Josephine Foster. They both belonged to the Southern Club, and at one of its formal dances he met her, now wearing the blue uniform, flowing red-lined cape and stiff-brimmed sailor hat of a navy yeomanette.

....

Josephine came from a proper and respected family. Her maternal grand-father, Josiah Patterson, was a Civil War hero and congressman from Memphis; his son Malcolm, her uncle, was a former Tennessee governor; and her paternal grandfather once owned much of Bullock County, Alabama, and had been its largest slaveholder. Her father, Sterling J. Foster, born just after the end of the Civil War, was an independent-thinking Presbyterian minister. Unusually well educated and widely traveled, he epitomized the stage presentation of a southern gentleman, with a twinkle in his eye and a wonderful voice, a proudly unreconstructed member of the fading aristocracy. In 1909 the South Highland Presbyterian Church in Birmingham dismissed him as minister because he would not swear that the whale swallowed Jonah and three days later spewed him up alive. "He had enormous enthusiasms when things went well and sick headaches when they went badly," recalled his younger daughter Virginia. "Mother said it was like living in an elevator, always going up or down." With part of his large inheritance he bought an insurance company. It was an unlikely choice: a "gentleman" did not lower himself to ask for or to accept money. Not long after he bought the company, he lost it. Soon he became an insurance salesman; quickly he lost the job. A sucker for con men, he lost $100,000 in bad investments, including graphite mines in Clay County.

In her quiet way Josephine was also a rebel. She was of the first generation of southern women who did not view the existing order as one of the eternal verities. She accepted many of the prerogatives of pure white southern womanhood—she came out at a Junior League ball—but saw through the false society that established them. After one year, she left Sweet Briar College in Virginia, then as much a finishing school as a college. Soon, caught up in the patriotic fervor of World War One, she became a yeomanette in the Naval Intelligence bureau there, looking up names on suspicious cablegrams. Throughout, even though she "never said very much and never seemed to make any effort," she was courted constantly.

Hers was a subtle rebellion, charged with a questing aesthetic sense and affected by the problems that beset upper-middle-class southern women. Her father unabashedly favored her over her older brother and younger sister. Familial discord was concealed from outsiders, individual feelings often repressed, and outlets for self-expression by women limited but expanding: the suffrage and temperance movements were riding high. These group activities did not suit Josephine's strong but subdued streak of individualism. She went to many teas dressed to the hilt and said she enjoyed herself. But she felt unfulfilled, with no sense of direction or purpose to her life. "The Negro slaves had been emancipated," historian Anne Firor Scott has written, "but women were still providing men with creature comforts and bolstering their egos." In his own family Dr. Foster was trying to keep intact the old order of the woman as "queen of the home" who obeys her husband and submits to him and to God.

Southern women were slowly coming down from the pedestal and gaining self-esteem, and Josephine was comfortable with anyone, regardless of position. The phrase "a lady to the manner born" fit her to a magnolia. But her smooth surface camouflaged deep problems. As a child she pointed to the stars one night and said, "I'm going to join the angels up there too." Even then she suffered from melancholia; later generations called it depression. She worked hard to be as relaxed and lovely as she was. As she got older, the effort took its toll.

At the Southern Club dance Josephine's escort scarcely saw her the rest of the evening, because "Hugo had her behind a palm." Thereafter, Hugo pursued her relentlessly. "He assumed that I was fated to marry him and that everybody else was out of the picture," Josephine later said. "He was like an irresistible force; he just kept coming at me"—without once writing her a love letter. Her friends warned that she would be betraying her class (her "natural friends," her mother called them) if she married this "crude, common man." Several times she changed her mind. Hugo's being thirteen years older than Josephine disturbed Dr. Foster, as did his workingman's law practice; but with a father who was a failure in so many ways perhaps she was looking for a successful "father figure." As the story goes, Dr. Foster wanted to know more about this fellow Black. He went to his good friend and neighbor—Forney Johnston. "Tell me about this Black," he said. "Why, that Bolshevik!" replied Johnston. Dr. Foster took to calling Hugo "that young Bolshevik" while noting his exemplary manners.

Hugo and Josephine were married on February 23, 1921. He had told the Fosters he had to have either a big wedding, with his political friends there because he was planning to run for office, or a small one. The Fosters were unable to afford a large one, and fewer than a dozen people attended the ceremony in the parlor of their home. The press called it "an event of conspicuous social interest in Birmingham and throughout the state." Albert

Lee Smith and Hugh Locke unexpectedly showed up and drove the newlyweds to the train to leave on their honeymoon. Hugo and Josephine appeared "scared," sitting "bolt upright, like two sticks, in the back seat of my car," Smith recalled. "They looked so stiff and stern, like a judge on the bench ready to pronounce a sentence." He stopped the car, got out and found a piece of mistletoe. Back in the car he turned around and said, "Hugo, now kiss your bride." With that done, they continued to the station.

Hugo rarely talked about his courtship of Josephine. But to a cousin he said, "We Blacks always marry above ourselves." And late in life he told his granddaughter, "If you're going to go far in politics, you have to marry the right woman."[7]

CHAPTER 4

TRIAL LAWYER

T HE NEXT SEVERAL YEARS saw Black become enormously successful. He practiced almost exclusively in the personal injury field, adamantly refusing to work for corporations, rejecting even Albert Lee Smith's offer to represent his insurance company. He would not sacrifice his convictions. "I have no sympathy with the idea . . . that this is 'just the lawyer's opinion,' " Black said later. "If the lawyer does not believe the principles he asserts for his client are true and righteous, then I assert the lawyer is not an honest man." To Black there was a difference between what the lawyer felt in his heart and his argument, what he proffered on behalf of the client. Nevertheless he served as local counsel for a Swiss insurance company—but on his own terms, demanding, and receiving, complete discretion as to which cases he would try and which he would settle.

His partner throughout these years was Crampton Harris. A gifted but lazy graduate of Emory and the Harvard Law School, and two years younger than Hugo, he had known Black for several years. Hugh Morrow suggested that they hook up and, after a three-month trial period, they became partners on November 1, 1919. Several junior lawyers worked for them, as did three secretaries who kept busy transcribing from five Dictaphone machines in a ninth-floor corner suite in the First National Bank Building commanding a sweeping view of Birmingham. Hugo was the business getter. "He had lots of energy, lots of drive, and he knew everybody," Harris said. "They wanted him to handle their cases. He was in court almost every day. I was more the office lawyer and drafted most of the pleadings and the contracts, and we shared writing briefs." This suited Harris, who was pompous and elitist and

54

had a powerful mind. From the beginning their minds meshed. "We never separated with a disagreement as to what the law was," Harris remembered. "Hugo had an uncanny ability to pick out the right theory in a case. He could make a jury cry or a supreme court sit up and take notice. He was the best all-around lawyer I ever met, and an ideal partner."

In the courtroom he was nearly unbeatable. Hugo had a way with juries. Cocky, sure that he could persuade any juror, he was satisfied only if he won 90 percent of his cases. He bluffed and gambled, making jurors think that there was much information on the sometimes blank paper he waved in front of them. He used facial expressions—a smirk, grimace or raised eyebrow, a tense or eager look—or he assumed a certain posture or adopted an inflection of his marvelously adaptable voice. "Hugo's timing was exquisite," said Harris, "like that of a fine Shakespearean actor reading his lines." His "honey-smooth mildness of voice and manner . . . ," a friend wrote, "almost wholly masks the strength and firmness behind it and leads all who oppose him to underestimate him—once." By then his calculated stabs had hit the heart.

To Hugo the courtroom was virtually his. The judge presided, but Hugo staged a presentation designed to create an impression on the jury. He had only a bare platform with which to work, no backdrop or props, no effects to create illusions, no opportunity for retakes; and the search for truth curtailed his imagination. The courtroom was his theater. "That's my turf," he once said. He moved around confidently and purposely, never at random. Jurors felt that he could be believed when he suggested something. His eyes took in all and his face was passive with just the hint of a smile, as he probed for weaknesses he could exploit. But he stopped short of being harsh or caustic or too imposing. Rather, he struck a pose of confident humility. The verdict belonged to the jury alone. "Look 'em in the eye but give 'em room," he said. He tried to make jurors feel not that he was a great showman, but that he just had a great case.

It all came naturally. Many years later, Hugo took an aptitude test under another name. The result: he was best suited to be an actor. His adversaries would not have been surprised. Nor was he—he always said that if he couldn't be a lawyer, he wanted to be an actor. During trial, he was usually feisty and contentious. He deliberately skirted the limits, provoking foes and infuriating judges who often threatened to, but never did, charge him with contempt of court. ("If you're not threatened at least once during a case, you're not doing your job," he said.) He kept his outward calm. When Hugo, Jr., was in law school, his father gave this advice:

Forswear adjectives for your moot court ordeal. Be sure to keep a well-modulated voice. If necessary to think momentarily in order to answer a question, take time to think. *Do not get excited.* Think up all the answers in advance that you possibly can. The only way to do this is to analyze the case and know the points involved. Do not laugh; that is ordinarily the way many people reveal an inward excitement. Do not be too emphatic and do not be dogmatic at all.

It was commonsense guidance, heeded by few lawyers, but articles of faith with Hugo. "On one occasion a young lawyer in Birmingham made a personal attack on me," he recalled, "and I killed him with kindness. . . . The best lawyer is a perfect master of himself."[1]

Cross-examination was his forte. It perfectly suited what Harris called his "triple-decker mind": Hugo could listen to a witness, anticipate the remarks and set a trap to catch the witness on what he was about to say—all at the same time. Many lawyers came to watch him perform, to learn from him, in often packed courtrooms. Those who remember him in court agreed that he was the best trial lawyer they ever saw and certainly the best cross-examiner. He seized every point and followed through, using the examining style that best fit the circumstances. Sometimes, recalled John Gillon, "he would turn his head, close his eyes and nod his head and slowly say, 'I see.' Even though the answer might have been insignificant. That was his way of saying it was significant."

Hugo let a witness who prided himself on his cleverness play to the audience. Then he moved with deliberate pace to discredit the gentleman's remarks. "He would start off so friendly that the witness on the other side would think he was being a witness for Hugo," said Carter Monasco, who later served as a congressman. "He would gain the witness's confidence and then tear right into him. The fellow was at his mercy. It was almost scary." Regardless of the character of the witness, Hugo was a master at "spotlighting testimony": the attention of the jurors is focused on the important point which, above all others, will remain on their minds when they retire to the jury room to deliberate. He reduced every case to a single, holy issue.[2]

Like all great trial lawyers, Hugo took great pride in his ability to litigate *anything.* He saw, even more than before, the power of a trial judge in admitting evidence, in tailoring his charge to the jury in order not to be reversed on appeal and in taking the case from the jury. But the cases he enjoyed the most and upon which he built his reputation involved negligence and personal injuries, torts—noncriminal wrongs—from which large damages can often be collected.

Mary Miniard, a white woman, boarded a train in Chicago with her husband and baby to return home to Birmingham. A Negro woman immediately cursed her, partly undressed in front of her, jumped over the baby, stood on the seat and swung from the hat rack (sometimes while singing). The woman "seemed to be mad at the person she was with, and everybody," Miniard later said. Eventually, the conductor came, telling her only that they would reach the Mason-Dixon line. There, one witness testified, "they took the negroes right on off, which they had to do anyhow," and transferred them to the "Jim Crow car." Miniard, who remained in her car, didn't sleep that night. After she arrived home, she retained Black. He sued the railroad, charging the conductor with "gross and wanton negligence."

From the beginning of the trial in October 1919 Black used "nigger," "nigger woman" and "crazy nigger" with regularity. So did the other lawyer, LeRoy Percy, who came from a literary family and had only recently entered practice. The jury awarded Black's client $2,900. His reason in asking for that amount was simple. Whenever he represented an individual against a large corporation, he always brought suit in Alabama courts. State court judges usually allowed juries to determine the issues in a case; and juries usually favor the individual. Federal judges, on the other hand, were much more likely to set aside a verdict for the plaintiff or to direct one against him on the grounds that the case for the corporation was so clear that the jury could not rule for the plaintiff; and Birmingham federal judge Grubb was the former lawyer for the United States Steel Corporation. At that time a corporation incorporated in another state could remove the case to federal court if the controversy involved $3,000 or more, so Black sued for less in state court.

But the Alabama Supreme Court did what it could to protect the purses of corporations in the state's stratified society. It even went as far as to declare a lawyer's referring during trial to Birmingham's elegant South Side, in hope of winning the jury's sympathy, as an automatic ground for mistrial. The judges were very adept at finding reasons to reverse juries when they wished. In Mary Miniard's case they found that "the question of defendant's management of the crazy woman was one of judgment and discretion," which the conductor "exercised in good faith"; and remanded the matter for a new trial.

In court Percy continually referred to Hugo as "Ego," a rather common allusion by Birmingham lawyers. Percy went back to his office and told his experienced partner some of his remarks about Hugo. The partner asked, "Has the jury come in?" When Percy said it had not, the partner suggested that he wait before commenting any further. Hugo had upped his request to $2,999.99 and the jury awarded every penny he had asked for. The "strange verdict," as Hugo sarcastically called it years later, cured Percy of his approach thereafter. (They became good friends.) The supreme court, however, was still not satisfied, holding that the judge charged the jury incorrectly. Another trial was ordered. This time Black won that amount.[3]

John Ellenburg's case also showed Black's persistence. A switchman for the Birmingham Belt Railroad Company, Ellenburg was standing on the footboard across the front of an engine arranging a train, including several cars of grain moving in interstate commerce, when the engine malfunctioned. It was fixed, and as the train approached the yard, a collision with an automobile on the street seemed imminent. Although no accident occurred, to escape danger Ellenburg fell under the engine and lost a leg. It was a tough case and even Ego wished he had never taken it. He tried to settle with the company, but its attorney, John R. C. Cocke, refused. Every time Black spoke in court, Cocke laughed and cackled and whistled, saying "what a silly case" he had: it was all part of an attempt to keep Black from presenting as much of his case as possible. "Hugo just sat there, lips pressed together, putting his fingers together at the tips like he did when he was holding himself in, kinda looking at the ceiling." Then came his closing argument to the jury. Black called Ellenburg up to the witness stand. Slowly the former worker made his way on crutches, his left pant leg empty to the hip. His wife and little children were sitting in the gallery where the jury could easily see them.

Black turned to the jury. "Gentlemen, we have all been treated to a grand performance. Mr. Cocke's a comic genius. But the line between the comic and what the poets call sadistic is a slim one. Maybe Mr. Cocke knows the difference. But look here, gentlemen, look here." And he pulled Ellenburg's empty pant leg. "That's not funny to me. Not funny at all. But did you hear Mr. Cocke? He laughed and cackled all over this courtroom." After helping to seat Ellenberg, Black now read to the jury from actuarial and mortality tables and argued that it had the right to consider Ellenburg's life expectancy and his loss of income because of the injury. He asked for $14,500 in addition to damages for mental and physical pain and suffering. "Go out there and teach Mr. Cocke that losing a leg . . . is not something to whistle or sing about—it's a matter for justice. Teach Mr. Cocke and his client what it means to chew off a man's leg for profit." Tears were in Black's eyes. They were tears of joy, observed Cocke, because Hugo would be getting half of what the jury would award. "That's right," said the judge, standing up. "So you ought to figure out what the plaintiff is entitled to and double it." The jury returned a verdict for $20,000.

On appeal the Alabama Supreme Court held that the action should have been brought under Alabama's workers' compensation statute. The matter went back to trial: the trial judge awarded Ellenburg $4,500, $15 weekly for three hundred weeks. The state's highest court once again reversed, but the court was sharply divided, with the dissenting opinion strongly upholding Black's position. He applied for another rehearing. The dissent was now adopted as the court's opinion, the trial judge's award to Ellenburg was affirmed, and he got his money.

John Millonas injured his eye at work as a sheeter. When he couldn't reach a satisfactory settlement with the insurance company providing coverage for his employer, he sued his employer. He refused to drop the suit as ordered, and was promptly fired. At trial his employer's lawyer "boasted about having a man discharged and run out of Alabama," the court reporter noted. Black persuaded the jury to award Millonas $25,000. The defendant appealed to the Alabama Supreme Court, charging that "plaintiff's counsel persisted for the obvious purpose of engendering passion and prejudice against the defendant in the minds of the jury." "Passion and not reason dictated the amount of the award," the court concluded in lowering the award to $6,000. The judges threw a bouquet to Hugo by noting his "strong and passionate appeal to the jury on behalf of the preservation of human rights and condemnation of oppression," which were not involved in the case. "Indeed, counsel for appellant demonstrated, upon submission of this cause in oral argument, his ability to eloquently present the cause in the most forcible manner."

Indeed, keeping the supreme court from reducing his verdicts was a big problem for Black. "Courts must deal with such cases in a practical rather than in a sentimental and sympathetic way," the judges said in lowering from $50,000 to $30,000 an award he obtained for an injured railroad worker who spent a year and a half in bed and was crippled for life. "We cannot avoid the suspicion that the jury in this case has been rather too liberal with the money of the defendant" was their comment after a fifteen-year-old girl was granted $10,000 for a sprained arm and dubious internal injuries. But the court upheld other, usually lower, amounts. "We would have a good

month's work until the supreme court got finished with us in one day," said
Crampton Harris.[4]

Hugo worked at a headlong pace. From 1919 to 1925 his firm handled 108
cases in Alabama appellate courts alone, an average of fifteen a year, in
addition to a full calendar of trials and federal court cases. "He was intense
on everything, tight-geared," Harris said. "There was nothing aloof about
him." He was "meticulously honest" in dealing with a client. Until the
client paid, he was "on pins and needles," calling long distance if necessary
to demand payment. With Harris he "always dealt with perfect candor.
Every six months or so we talked about what wasn't going right. Hugo never
offered an explanation or an excuse if he felt he did something wrong. He
took responsibility."

Preparation was a fetish. "Hugo felt he would let down the client unless
he knew everything about a case so that nothing would surprise him," Harris
said. Most week nights he spent in the office or the law library (or at lodge
meetings). He collected as much information as possible, studied books on
the subject, spoke to potential witnesses. Hugo wielded hard-won facts as
nimbly and deftly as a surgeon wields a scalpel. First he built a solid foundation of fact, which juries need and want before anything else. Then he
could construct and apply his emotional appeal. He implored each juror to
use not only his five senses but also horse sense and common sense. "Black
played on the art of ingratiating himself with the jury," said Leigh Clark,
later an outstanding defendant's lawyer. "He would court the jury throughout. He could turn something which would be against him for him. He just
had a winning way about him."

And he did it all with a flair that was not forgotten. "Lawyer Black!
Lawyer Black!" said a woman who worked in the building where he had
his office. "He was *some* lawyer! And was he a strutter! He'd strut into his
office and sling dat hat of his'n on the chair, den he'd strut on into his back
office. Why, that man would strut all over that cote-house! That man was
a *strutter!*"[5]

Most of his cases came on referral from other lawyers. "The reaction of
people to the knowledge that a lawyer gets large verdicts is the one that
sends clients to the lawyer's door," Hugo later wrote. "That is chiefly the
reason I had a large law practice. Not merely laymen but other lawyers will

hire the big-verdict lawyer." Among them was Francis Hare, who eventually succeeded him as Birmingham's leading plaintiff's lawyer. Once they tried a case together. Hugo got a $20,000 verdict. "How come you didn't cry?" Hare asked afterward. "Hugo Black doesn't cry for less than $25,000," Hugo answered.

"Black was the first lawyer in Alabama to represent plaintiffs who provided scholarship and a detailed preparation of the facts, and knew the law," Hare said. "He was a vicious adversary, a strong-willed scholar who could argue with anyone, one of the great lions of the law." Nevertheless, Hare felt Hugo's emotions carried him away: "He took liberties in his closing arguments." Much harsher were those lawyers who flaunted their self-proclaimed superiority (usually because they represented corporations) or couldn't bring themselves to respect his ability (or his causes). White Gibson (who at one point represented unions) reflected the attitude of some in the "country club gold bar," as Hugo called defendant's lawyers. "Black was the only lawyer in Birmingham who couldn't be trusted to carry out an agreement in court," he said. "You had to be there to check on him. He would do anything to achieve an objective." Other defendants' lawyers similarly disparaged Hugo, but never to his face, as merely a "damage suit lawyer." But he was friendly with many who opposed him bitterly.*

When an adversary played fairly, Hugo reciprocated. He represented a little girl who was seriously injured when a coal delivery truck jumped the curb on a steep hill on her way home from school. The day before the case was set, the insurer's lawyer notified the trucking company's lawyer (and Hugo's friend), Frank Spain, that the insurer had just that day been declared bankrupt. At trial, after Hugo made out his case, Spain put the driver on the stand. He testified that he was coming down the hill at a reasonable speed when his brakes gave way. During cross-examination, Hugo moved his chair from counsel's table up to the feet of the driver. As Spain recalled it, the dialogue went like this:

---

* Borden Burr represented railroads, public utilities and large corporations. After his death in 1952, Hugo recalled their friendship of half a century, how Burr's early practice frequently brought him to the Ashland courthouse.

> I distinctly remember how admiringly I watched him try cases there. He was from the beginning aggressive and alert to protect his clients' interests. . . . Years later he and I tried many cases against one another. In no one of them did I ever win a single point by default. He was an intense and earnest partisan on his client's side. He was a courtroom scrapper but an honest one. . . . Despite our many tense and wordy conflicts over cases, I am happy that Borden and I could go directly from court to golf course and have a grand time together. [HLB to A. Leo Oberdorfer 12/16/52.]

"Mose, you say you were driving twenty miles an hour."

"Yes, sir."

"You weren't driving thirty miles an hour?"

"No, sir."

"Now, Mose, come right down to it, you don't know how fast you were driving?"

"No, sir, Boss."

Hugo had laid the predicate for punitive damages. During a brief recess before their closing arguments, Spain told him: "I'm checking it to you on principle. That jury will give you any damages you ask. You can bankrupt [the coal company owner] who did all he could do to protect your client. He could not foresee his insurer would bankrupt. Can you in good conscience ask this jury for any more than doctor and hospital bills?" "I don't want to break your man," Hugo replied. "Just give me a judgment for the amount of the insurance." He explained the situation to the girl's parents, then told the jury: "Here are the doctor's bills and here are the hospital's bills and we ask for a verdict for that amount—$15,000." He received it.[6]

Much of Black's public personality was forged in the courtroom over the years. He reveled in its thrust and parry. With his plain-spoken eloquence, his silken-tongued spontaneity, his talent for saying the same thing in several ways, as if he were wound up, each time seemingly more convincingly than the time before, he overwhelmed his adversary. He was persistent and con-tentious to the point that one virtually had to be exposed to it in order to believe it; yet he fought his battles with a gentlemanliness notable even in the South. Despite his stubbornness in his pursuit of principle ("he never gave anyone the remote idea he would ever give up on a case," a contemporary said), he easily controlled himself when necessary. Hobart Grooms, later a federal district judge, remembered facing Black in a case filed by an owner of a house against a plumbing company that had cut off the water. The house caught on fire and burned down. "Black was quiet for a while. Then he said, 'Could I ask questions?' And he did. He asked questions which he knew would be sustained. He then leaned back and let the reaction take its course. It did, as he knew it would, and he won a good-sized verdict."

The jurors did not seem to mind, and aside from the judges they were the ones who counted. Most jurors were working people. His instinctive identification with them was obvious. He never talked down to them. He could translate relatively complex matters into terms that the average juror could understand and, equally important, relate to. Indeed, he was readily familiar to many of these jurors. Because of his organization memberships, he had a wide acquaintance. "I didn't draw a jury that I didn't know at least one person," he said; "you can't pick a jury without his friends," other lawyers commonly lamented. Opposing, especially corporate, lawyers were left at a distinct disadvantage. If the judge allowed a claim of Hugo's to go to the jury, he invariably won. Adversaries charged he could poison a jury. The saying among Birmingham lawyers was "If you don't watch out, Hugo will get in the jury box with you every time."[7]

*   *   *

In November 1923 federal agents uncovered a huge, "vicious, lawless" whiskey ring in Mobile. More than ten thousand quarts stored at the customhouse and valued at over $100,000 were seized. A federal grand jury indicted 117 persons, including several Democratic high office holders, the former chief of police and county sheriff among them, and charged them with conspiring to bribe the local United States attorney, Aubrey Boyles. When they contended that he conspired to bribe them, he asked to be temporarily relieved of duty.[8]

The Department of Justice, under the direction of assistant attorney general Mable Walker Willebrandt, searched for a special assistant to replace Boyles. She was "straight as a string" and "wanted to do her job," recalled Alabama Attorney General Harwell Davis, but she was unable to find a prominent enough Republican in overwhelmingly Democratic Alabama. Davis suggested Black, telling Willebrandt about his vigorous prosecution of prohibition violators as Jefferson County solicitor and in the Girard trials. Black accepted her offer but, he later claimed, insisted on not being paid. He went to Washington to meet with her and also with Attorney General Harlan Fiske Stone, who demanded that Black receive a salary for his services, which he did. Later Willebrandt listed her reasons for her choice: "incorruptible courage, studiousness, resourcefulness and fairness."

"Mobile citizenship stands for law enforcement," Black told the jury as the trial opened. "The only real soldier in time of peace is the man who walks in obedience to law." Immediately he obtained some convictions. It seemed odd, he observed, that apparently no state official "had had his nostrils offended" by whatever was "rotten" in Mobile, although the smell had reached "even to Washington." Twenty-one attorneys represented the defendants. Since they might question the validity of the original indictments because one of the jurors had been replaced, the grand jury at Black's request returned a new, sweeping general indictment, which reduced the number of defendants to seventy-two. (He dropped an attempt to indict presiding federal judge Robert Ervin, before the case would be tried, after he found that Ervin had taken a few drinks on hunting and fishing trips.) Black decided to concentrate on the "big fish."

One of the biggest fish was Frank Boykin, a wealthy wheeler-dealer of a businessman who later served in Congress. Even though his motto was "Everything's made for love," as a colleague said, "I don't think Frank knew right from wrong." (Franklin Roosevelt once told him, "Frank, one of these days you'll come down here and ask me to move the Treasury Building to Alabama." No, Boykin replied, "Just move the money down to Alabama and that'll be sufficient.") Black charged that Boykin was closely associated in bootleg operations with Mal Dougherty, brother of former attorney general Harry M. Dougherty, who had recently been forced to resign in scandal. The defense offered to pay Dougherty's expenses to testify; the judge took the request under advisement.

Boykin's lawyer had in his possession a telegram that would probably have persuaded the jury not to convict, but for technical reasons it was not admissible as evidence. Black demanded the telegram. The defense raised every apparent subterfuge and objection. Goaded, as the defense wished, he said, "I offer the telegram in evidence, Your Honor, sight unseen, and demand that counsel produce it." The judge called a recess and said, "I'll see counsel in chambers." He demanded that the telegram be produced. Back in the courtroom, defense counsel confidently reached into his brief-case. The telegram was gone. A long and desperate search began. No luck. After a while Boykin, grinning, said aloud, "I ate it."

Soon Black dropped the conspiracy charges against Boykin and six others on grounds of insufficient evidence, but said they might be tried for violations of the prohibition law. Tensions ran high in the courtroom. Two of the defendants engaged in a "fistic encounter," and all persons entering were searched for concealed weapons. In a "holiday-like atmosphere" the jury convicted eleven people, including five of the "Big Six," whom Black disclosed to be connected with an underworld syndicate in Chicago and Detroit. Thirty-three of the remaining defendants were acquitted.

Another factor was at work. "The Klan 'Klunked' onto the scene to give Black what support it could . . . ," Boykin's nephew wrote. "The grand jury was well stacked with Klansmen as were the trial juries." Black referred to Negro witnesses as "niggers." He "endeavored to convict the defendant by attempting to prove that he was a Catholic," recalled Harry H. Smith, a defense lawyer whom the Klan burned in effigy for denouncing it at the trial. "Those liquor cases in Mobile—our boys were on that jury and we were able to convict," said James Esdale, the head of the Alabama Ku Klux Klan. The Mobile rum trial was daily front-page news throughout Alabama in April and May 1924. Black became known across the state as a staunch upholder of prohibition.[9]

*   *   *

Since his days as solicitor, Black had remained involved in the movement to eradicate the convict lease system. He was one of a handful of lawyers in Alabama who represented convict miners. This led to what he called one of his "most memorable" cases, involving a convict who had been killed in an unsafe mine. As Black told the story:

> The judge was a friend of the coal miner and couldn't bring himself to believe that the mine was as unsafe as I described it. I was persistent. Finally, the judge said that he would not affirm the decision unless I agreed to have a former safety inspector for U.S. Steel that was an acquaintance of his, inspect the mine. I had no choice, so I agreed. When the safety inspector had completed the inspection of the mine, he contacted the judge and told him he was ready to report. The judge said he wanted the report deferred until both he and counsel could hear it together. The judge called me and we met to hear the report. The judge opened the meeting by addressing the inspector and said he had some questions to ask. The inspector interrupted and said, "Judge, I thought you were a friend of mine!" The judge said, "I am!" At which point the inspector exclaimed, "Judge, that mine was the damnest, unsafest place I have ever seen in my entire life!" Needless to say, I won my case!

Black served as president of the Alabama League to Abolish the Convict Lease, which he had been instrumental in founding, and in 1923–24 of its successor, the Alabama Prison Reform Association. But not until 1928 was this barbarian practice, so common in the South since the Civil War, ended. Alabama was the last state to do so. Governor William W. Brandon was a partner in the procrastination. In 1923 he proposed that the state operate certain coal mines, using convicts as miners, and sell the coal to the operators from whom the mines had been leased. Such action would be "striking at the wage scale of the free miner," Black wrote Brandon. Convicts would lose the right to sue in state courts in case of injury or death due to the operator's negligence. "Taking away from an injured convict his right to recovery is so cruel and inhuman that I do not believe you, as their representative, will tolerate it."

The state had leased a Negro convict named Henry Lewis to a mining company to work in its coal mines. Because of the company's negligence, he was injured in an accident. Black was Lewis's lawyer and he won a $4,000 judgment against the company in state court. Four months later the company declared bankruptcy. In federal court Black filed a claim against its estate for the amount. The referee in bankruptcy held that under the Bankruptcy Act the only kinds of claims the estate was required to pay were those involving debts owed to anyone with whom the company had made a contract; and federal district judge Grubb and, in November 1923, the Fifth Circuit Court of Appeals agreed. Since the debt owed Lewis was not based on any kind of contract, he did not have to be paid.

This injustice outraged Black. He decided to appeal the case to the United States Supreme Court, his first contact with that body. But his appeal was not the traditional one, in which the lawyer files papers and waits for the response. Black made an appointment in Washington with the Court's clerk and asked that the case be considered as a pauper's proceeding, with the Court assuming the cost. Even though the existing law provided that the Supreme Court should hear indigent cases, it had resisted doing so out of a concern over its mounting workload. Indeed, in 1925 Congress passed the Judiciary Act, giving the justices almost total control over their docket. The Court clerk thus denied Black's request. Few precedents existed for such a course, and exceptions to the formalities of presentation were rarely permitted; this case did not fit within those exceptions. Black pressed his point. The clerk allowed only that he could speak to Justice Edward T. Sanford, who oversaw the Fifth Circuit and who also happened to write most of the Court's opinions in bankruptcy cases.

In researching his case, Black had found an opinion written by Sanford, while serving as a federal district judge, which accorded with his position and had been upheld on appeal. In addition, other appellate decisions interpreting the Bankruptcy Act conflicted with the decision in the case, leaving that area of the law, admittedly small, in some disarray. Black pointed these matters out to Sanford. "He agreed to try to get three of his colleagues to go along with him and have my case heard," Black recalled, and suggested that Hugo also speak to Chief Justice William Howard Taft. "Why should we take this type of case?" Taft asked. "This has never been done before." "Just for that reason you should do it," Black replied. The justices agreed to hear the case, and the Court paid the costs involved in its preparation.

On January 29, 1925, for the first and only time as a lawyer, Black appeared before the United States Supreme Court. Counsel for the other side, the respondent trustee in bankruptcy, did not show up. Less than two months later, in a three-page opinion written by Sanford, the Court ruled unanimously in Black's favor; Lewis received his $4,000. This set a precedent for indigent cases: for the first time a poor man was entitled to his day in the highest court in the land at government expense.[10]

*   *   *

Family life was conventional for a young, successful professional man. Hugo and Josephine had two sons, Hugo, Jr., and Sterling, within four years. After living for two years with her parents, they bought a French provincial house on nearby Altamont Road overlooking Birmingham. On the baby grand piano in the living room Josephine played Chopin preludes—while Hugo, even in his off-key way, sang folk songs and country tunes better than he could play the piano. They had live-in help, which was new to Hugo but the norm for Josephine's class. Appropriately for one of the city's leading lawyers and his Junior League wife, they joined the Birmingham Country Club; he and Albert Lee Smith now called themselves the "visitors' delight." Hugo and Josephine both played golf and tennis, but he preferred the latter's brisk clip.

In court he was aggressive, wary and combative; in social settings his natural charm, warmth and compassion shone. Hugo fused opposites and yet he could instinctively drop one end of the equation for the other. With Josephine the surface image masked the reality. She was quietly rebelling against the society in which she had been reared: the man she married was one proof of this. Yet she still put stock in symbols. Even though status and family lineage did not mean much to her, Hugo filled out an application for her to join the Daughters of the American Revolution. But she never did mail it and kept it.

The library in their home was large, for Hugo read widely. He especially enjoyed history, biography and poetry, noted Crampton Harris. "He talked much about the classics." They gave him a perspective on the vagaries of life, a renewed belief that there are really no new plots, resulting in even greater confidence when trying a case. He devoured nearly everything by and about Jefferson. "Before I was married, he was quoting Jefferson to me all the time," recalled Virginia Durr, Josephine's sister, who married Clifford Durr in 1926. Hugo drew from his readings in his weekly Sunday school class at the First Baptist Church. He awoke before dawn to prepare the lectures that gave him wide local visibility; as many as one thousand men attended. "He was a good, alert, concise teacher," said one of the class members, "and used illustrations from the Bible to make his point. He was a Bible scholar." He tied the mundane—"Black spoke of no drinking or womanizing; he didn't want that," another member said—with the theoretical, and made his interpretations with the same passionate conviction that he used to sway juries. "Religion," Hugo told the students,

> is a vital part of the warp and woof of our national existence. Its glowing burning truths inspired the hearts of American pioneers. Its sacred precepts established our home life; shaped our infant institutions and nourished a spirit of equality and democracy. The voice of Roger Williams and his followers played no small part in impressing the principles and policies that molded our institutions and crystallized our sentiments into [a] written Constitution and laws. The Bible penetrated the trackless forests with the pioneers and strengthened the sturdy character of our early settlers. In the name of Religion and Freedom of Religion laws were resisted to cross a tempestuous ocean to an unknown land. Our country has grown great, wealthy and prosperous beyond the wildest dreams of avarice, under a government instituted by readers and lovers of the Bible.
>
> Today, there are those who say that no longer do we need religion; no longer is the Bible essential. Like an ungrateful and overgrown child, we are urged by some to renounce the old-time religion to which many attribute the stability of our institutions and therefore the cause of our greatness. With the pride and boastfulness of the Prodigal Son, we are asked to leave the safety of our Father's House to wander in search of Happiness and glory into distant lands and other climes. The laymen of the church can contribute to the furtherance of religious zeal and devotion [and] to the departure of our people from their old ideals.

He admonished his listeners to keep faith, remain optimistic, and work hard, for then they could reap the inevitable rewards of the Promised Land. And they left his sessions ready to go out and "do good."[11]

Life was enjoyable. The period he spent practicing law was his "happiest time," Black later said. His trial court work was the "most fun" he ever had known. He taught a course on business law at the Birmingham School of Law in 1921. Newspapers solicited his opinion on matters of local importance. His noble and inspiring language increased his demand as a speaker. In 1924 he spoke at a banquet honoring *Birmingham News* publisher Victor Hanson for his contributions to and support of education in Alabama.

Black noted he owed no allegiance to the *News* and often disagreed with its politics.

> But there are those whose vision is not dimmed, who can look far out into the world and see everywhere suffering humanity, hear the call to which their heart is attuned and heed the plea to come and help. It is for that reason that I champion this resolution [honoring Hanson]. Philosophers and statesmen have said in all ages that the only keys that will unlock the doors of progress are universal education and knowledge. . . .
>
> I rise to second this motion in the name of every man, woman and child in this state that believes in the cause of education. I second that motion in the name of the boys and girls who are now in the schools of Alabama by reason of his effort. I second it in the names of those who are to go there in the future by reason of his effort. I second it in the name of those citizens who I believe, influenced by his generous example, will cease to contemplate themselves in their own mirrors and to ponder over their own greatness in making money, and will instead turn that money loose like Victor Hanson is doing to unshackle the minds of Alabama boys and girls and place them on the way to educational freedom and progress.

And he prospered. Juries in Birmingham—the railroad crossroads and industrial center of the South—were more sympathetic than otherwise to workers injured on the job or in accidents. Black was the city's first lawyer with a lucrative personal injury practice. His income rose quickly after the war. In 1923, his tax returns show, he made $32,000; in 1924, $44,000; and in 1925, over $65,000. For the first half of 1925 he and Harris grossed $8,500 monthly, of which Hugo received, depending upon the client, either 60 percent or two thirds. That year, he always claimed, he had as large an income as any lawyer in Alabama. With Smith, and sometimes other friends, he bought several parcels of property. Hugo's total worth probably reached $250,000 by 1925. He refused several judgeships. "I had been asked to be a judge on a number of occasions in Alabama on the trial judge level, and on the Supreme Court of the state," he said many years later. "It had not appealed to me." Also, the latter position paid only $7,500 and he couldn't afford the drop in income.

In 1925 he was elected vice president of the Birmingham Bar Association, with the expectancy that he would become its president the next year. Some corporate lawyers might have "hated him because he licked them," as Harris said, but they recognized his ability. The name partners in the firm which represented the Alabama Power Company all privately "admitted on separate occasions that they regarded Black as one of the ablest lawyers in the state." Other Birmingham lawyers thought he was better trying a case, because "he was more comfortable—it fit his talents better"—than handling one on appeal, although "he was mighty good at that. Of course, so many judges had different views from his." Despite their clashes, Forney Johnston felt Black "was just a superb lawyer, the top trial lawyer and the outstanding negligence lawyer in the state by far," said his son Joseph Johnston. "He would have been a very wealthy man today because these lawyers make a million dollars a case, and he had them all the time and never lost any."

The idea of a long and prosperous career at the bar was not fully satisfying. The political bug had bitten Hugo Black long before. Even though he did not talk much about politics with or show any political ambitions to many friends, the only question was when would he run for which office. Once he told Albert Lee Smith, "I want to go to the Senate"; and he confided the same thing to his former partner David J. Davis.[12] But how could this political unknown, without any visible support, win a statewide election?

CHAPTER 5

THE PARISH HOUSE
MURDER

Bᴸᴀᴄᴋ ᴡᴀꜱ ᴛᴀᴋɪɴɢ his annual monthlong vacation, visiting Barney Whatley in Colorado in August 1921, when his partner Crampton Harris tele-
phoned excitedly. A Methodist minister named Stephenson had killed Father
James E. Coyle on August 11, a day or two earlier. Hugo was greatly surprised,
because he inferred Harris meant the Reverend H. M. Stephenson of the
West End Church, one of Birmingham's most prominent pastors. Both
Coyle's Catholic friends and Stephenson's friends were on the way to the
office to ask Black to be their lawyer. Alabama law allowed for the appointment of a special prosecutor under certain circumstances. He never wanted
to send men to the gallows merely for pay, Hugo said, and therefore, would
not accept the appointment. But, "Are you sure that this is Brother Stephenson?" Harris replied that all he knew was that it was a Methodist
preacher by that name. Feeling that "if a man like the Stephenson I knew
had done a killing, there must have been some extenuating circumstances,"
Black agreed to defend the minister. He told Harris to arrange to have the
trial set for a date shortly after he returned from Colorado in early September.

So goes the story Black told twenty-five years later. Like so many of his
recollections, its broad outline was true enough, plausible without further
investigation and certainly a good veil for what really happened. But what
he omitted gives this case its significance.

The minister, Harris had in fact told him, was the Reverend Edwin R.
Stephenson. They saw him almost every day. Virtually every person who
entered his "church," the Jefferson County Courthouse, recognized Roscoe
Stephenson. The friendly, smiling, fast-talking former barber, carrying his
cane, dressed in black and with his thick handlebar mustache turned up at

71

the corners, spent every day there on the lookout for young couples (white and Negro alike) seeking the marriage bureau, helping them obtain a license and offering to perform the ceremony. Over the previous two years alone, the "marrying parson" claimed he had wed 1,140 couples, about half of them in the courthouse. Father Coyle had been the head of Birmingham's sizable Catholic community since 1904. For nearly thirty years Saint Paul's Church, with its twin spires and tolling bell, had been a city landmark. On the day he was killed, he had officiated at the marriage of Stephenson's eighteen-year-old daughter, Ruth, to a middle-aged, dark-skinned Puerto Rican paperhanger, Pedro Gussman, whom she had met at Saint Paul's several years before. A few hours later, Stephenson went to see Coyle, who was sitting in a swing on the porch of the rectory, reading his breviary.

Stephenson had long been having trouble with the literarily inclined Ruth. She had run away from home twice over the past eight months and was found with the help of the Birmingham police; once she escaped from a train on which she was riding with her mother, only to be discovered at a Catholic hospital the next day. As a parent, the Reverend Stephenson was no model of Christian forgiveness. He had whipped Ruth the winter before for staying out after nine-thirty one evening, locked her in her room without food or water for three days at another time, and on a doctor's advice, filled out papers to send her to the asylum for the insane in Tuscaloosa. (But after visiting the place, not even Stephenson could send her.) "Roscoe," a relative said, "came from the old school of strictness, the very old school."

On August 11 Ruth disappeared again. She went with Gussman to nearby Bessemer to get a marriage license, not wanting to obtain one at the Birmingham courthouse, where her father would see her. When Stephenson couldn't find her, he asked Birmingham police chief Thomas J. Shirley "to watch the trains. He thought the Catholics were going to spirit her away, and have her." He went to the sheriff's office to obtain a warrant to search Saint Paul's, its rectory, the West End convent and the house of Fred Bender. He was her "godfather" whom she had recently met at a Catholic church. Ruth had told her father the previous April that she had joined the Church, after flirting with the idea for several years, because it was "the only true, the only way by which I could save my soul." But no judge was in the courthouse to grant a warrant to Stephenson. He went back home to talk to his wife, picked up his gun and left, a man possessed.

He walked to Saint Paul's Church. It was about six-thirty and he found Father Coyle sitting on the rectory's porch. This was the first time these two men of the cloth had met, although they had once spoken over the telephone when Ruth ran away. Coyle now invited Stephenson to come in, Stephenson later recounted. He explained she had left again and asked if he could help find her. "Did you know that your daughter was a Catholic and has been for some time? When a person is a Catholic, they are one forever?" Stephenson replied he didn't know. "When your girl has become a Catholic, it should not concern you," Coyle continued. "You would not have jurisdiction over her anymore. When your girl becomes married she isn't yours anymore. You talk about this underage affair."

"Well, my girl isn't married," Stephenson said.

"Your girl is a Catholic and she is married, for I married her this evening."

"To whom?" Stephenson asked.

"To Pedro Gussman, a Catholic."

Just the Friday night before, Ruth had told her parents that she had never expected to marry (even though Gussman had already proposed and she had accepted, and he had mentioned to Father Coyle that he expected to get married). There had been no obvious courting, but the Stephensons had met him: he had hung paper at their house a month earlier. Mrs. Stephenson looked upon him "as a servant, half Greek." She "could hardly understand his English."

"You have married her to that nigger! You have treated me dirtier than a dog," Stephenson told Coyle. "You have acted like a dirty, low-down yellow dog." Coyle warned him not to repeat that. "You are a dirty dog," said Stephenson. "You have ruined my home. That man is a nigger." Coyle hit Stephenson and said he was "an heretical son of a bitch." He hit him again, knocking him against a post, kicked him, pulled him up, and stepped back and put his hand in his pocket. To Stephenson this meant Coyle was trying to get a pistol. Stephenson got his own gun out and fired "two or three times. I didn't fire after he fell."

Stephenson looked down at Coyle's body for a few seconds, turned and walked toward the courthouse. His belt was swinging and hanging down between his knee and his ankle. "I want you to put me in jail," he told the deputy sheriff. "I am in trouble." He admitted he shot the priest but otherwise didn't want to talk. An hour later, the assistant coroner discovered "a knot on his head." The county physician "found him in rather a nervous, excited condition," with "something like a split bird egg" on his head, "just a little elevation on the scalp. I gave him bromide."

....

The murder took place in "the American hot bed of anti-Catholic fanati-
cism," as the *Nation* reported. Few public figures could or wanted to fight
for elemental decencies. (A grand total of two ministers spoke publicly about
the murder.)[1] Nor did the press help much. The *Birmingham News* and the
Birmingham Age-Herald both "deplored" the "unfortunate tragedy" that "profoundly shocked" the city, and hoped that Stephenson would receive a fair
trial. But their editors wrote not one word about the religious animosity
that made Birmingham what a local editor later called "a cesspool of racial
and religious hatred." This silence stood in sharp contrast to the blanket
coverage all the papers gave to almost every aspect of the murder.

Even in this heated atmosphere, the Stephensons' hatred stood out.
Stephenson often expressed a wish that the "whole Catholic institution was
in hell," Ruth noted, and that Coyle was "one of humanity's biggest enemies.
I have heard my mother say many a time that she would like to see a bomb
put under St. Paul's." Stephenson's friends, fellow members of fraternal
organizations, often warned her about changing religions. Stephenson had
a robe of one of these groups at home and once Ruth wore it. The organization
was the Ku Klux Klan, which arranged for his defense and quickly raised
money for it at specially held meetings throughout the state. Of the lawyers
named to represent Stephenson—Black and Harris, John C. Arnold and
Fred Fite (who practiced together), and Thomas E. McCullough—all except
Hugo were then members of the Klan.

Heading the prosecution was the county solicitor, and Black's former
antagonist, Joseph Tate. He directed the coroner's inquest and brought the
matter before the grand jury. Ruth, the first person questioned, testified
about her parents, their religious beliefs and how they tried to control hers.
But even though the grand jury almost always follows the prosecutor's lead,
it refused to return an indictment at its first hearing. "Murder fans" packed
the courthouse for a preliminary hearing the next day. Ruth assailed her
parents again. Judge H. B. Abernathy ordered Stephenson, dressed in the
clerical garb that he would wear whenever he appeared in court, held without
bond to await the grand jury action.

The grand jury finally returned an indictment against the Reverend
Stephenson for murder in the second degree ("with malice aforethought . . .
but without premeditation or deliberation"), which would spare him the
death penalty. Bond, fixed at $10,000, was waived in order to speed the
trial. Black took charge of the defense strategy. The newspapers reported

that Stephenson would plead "not guilty by reason of insanity": his mind
was temporarily deranged by reports that the Catholic Church influenced
Ruth to join it and to marry a member. Her father's trial, "the most sen-
sational episode in the history of Birmingham," was set for October 3,
apparently before Judge Abernathy, eccentric and very conservative.

Then the powers that be switched the date to October 17 and assigned
the case to Judge Fort, Black's old friend, who was currently on vacation
but would soon be returning. "The arraignment, the setting, the docketing
and the drawing of the jury for the week had all been attended to by other
officials in my absence," Fort wrote in 1937.

> I would have fain avoided this case on account of the notoriety, and danger
> of the trial judge's being misunderstood by many persons, no matter which
> way the case should turn. But as I knew neither man involved, and could
> hear the testimony with an open mind, there seemed to be no reason why
> I should not try any case placed on my side of the docket. . . . At the time
> the case was tried there was no association between [Black and me] other
> than the casual friendliness of members of the legal profession. I did not
> know that Hugo L. Black was the defendant's counsel in this case until
> the morning of the trial.

*   *   *

"A little of the spirit of the guillotine during the French revolution, when
women knitted and watched human beings beheaded, seemed to prevail
[over] the room," a Birmingham reporter noted as the trial opened. Hundreds
were turned away only to jam the hallway; newspapers throughout the nation
and the wire services sent reporters. A total of 187 witnesses (110 for the
defense) were called to testify; among them were Ruth for the prosecution
and Gussman for the defense. But even though she had sent a message that
she expected to appear after a subpoena had been returned to the court
marked "not found," she was not among them. Only eighty witnesses answered the bailiff's call, thirty for the state and fifty for the defense.

At noon Black announced, "The defense is ready." In the afternoon a
jury, composed largely of relatively young men, mainly laborers and office
workers, was chosen and sworn. Assistant solicitor John H. McCoy read the
indictment of murder. (He and another assistant, John Morrow, handled
almost the entire trial.) Black entered the pleas of "not guilty" and "not
guilty by reason of insanity."

After presenting only five witnesses and taking barely two and a half
hours, the prosecution closed its case. McCoy's announcement "The state

rests" stunned the courtroom. All the state had established was that Stephenson had killed Coyle. Questions of motive had not been brought up
and the defense had only vaguely hinted at them in cross-examination.
Apparently the prosecution was holding back the rest of its witnesses for
rebuttal, when it planned to make its principal points. If so, it would be a
strange way to convict. To three of the five prosecution witnesses Black's
last question was "You are a Catholic, aren't you?"

"Yes, sir," each witness answered.

"That's all," Black said. *

Black called forty-four witnesses to the stand. All admitted that there was
something wrong with Stephenson's behavior, but not that he was "insane"
on the day of the murder. Some attributed it to his being nervous, excited
or agitated. Several said he was "abnormal." The judge, interpreting this as
having a direct bearing upon Stephenson's sanity, ruled that he could see
no distinction between an "abnormal mind" and an "unsound mind," and
continued to admit evidence tending to show that the defendant was not
normal at the time. It was also brought out that Stephenson said he acted
in self-defense, which accounted for the knot on his head, his broken belt
and the pains in his body.

Many witnesses had known Stephenson over the years, and their testimony was aimed to establish that his reputation had been good in the
communities in which he had lived. What also came through was Stephenson's checkered career. Even though he had been ordained in 1892, he never
had a church of his own except for one short period. He supported his family
by being a barber until a few years before, when he became the "marrying
parson."

The prosecution tried to show that this was not a minister of sterling
character: that Stephenson shot a fellow barber a few years earlier; that he
embezzled $400 from the barbers' union while serving as its secretary, was
expelled from it and then acted as a scab; that other barbers in Birmingham
would not believe him even on oath; that he was forced to leave the Methodist

---

* Black "asked several witnesses as to their relationship to one another and whether or not
they were Catholics," Judge Fort later wrote. "These questions were not objected to, but
were allowed under the law to throw any legitimate light on the membership of the witness
in the same church as the deceased, and in the same church with other witnesses for the
State. It has always been the law that membership in the same church with another may
be called to the attention of the jury on cross-examination, for the purpose of showing any
relation or bias which such membership may tend to show."

Episcopal Church South and to join the Methodist Episcopal Church (commonly called the Northern Methodist), because the presiding elder in the southern church demanded his license, since he was conducting himself in a manner that disgraced the ministry; and that the church considered expelling him from the ministry. (Not brought up, because it was immaterial, was Stephenson's participation in a lynching of a Negro who asaulted a white girl in Cedartown, Georgia, in 1902, when Ruth was born.)

Whenever the prosecution mentioned one of these allegations, Black raised an objection. Invariably the judge sustained it. "I don't think that ought to be brought in" was his typically soft-spoken but firm response. It was a rare moment when he did not favor Black. One time the prosecution objected to a question Black asked a witness. Judge Fort thereupon asked him three questions, which he answered, and then said, "I will allow that question." Black also objected whenever a witness was queried about the Catholic Church. After one such question, he jumped up, saying, "We object to that, trying a man for his feelings toward the whole church—I don't care." And similarly: "A man might not like the Catholic Church, but may like some of its members." Those were Black's feelings; but he used every possible opportunity to show that a witness was a Catholic. He made certain to ask a witness who mentioned Joe Maggeo, a barber and formerly the union treasurer, "He is an Italian, isn't he?"

If Black didn't receive an answer to his satisfaction, he would preface the next question, "Do you mean that no human being . . ." To make a point while examining a witness, he filled the courtroom with overstatements, broad, virtually all-inclusive remarks, rhetorical extravagance and exaggeration not without a touch of sarcasm—all of which he made with an undeniable certainty that no one in his right mind could or would conceivably question. Ruth would not just be "going abroad with some friends," as she wrote before the trial, but it would be "for an indefinite period and a long number of years" (or so Black told the judge), and this was simply "a fact . . . about to be put into effect, forever taking [Stephenson's] daughter away from him." Such comments had several purposes—to keep the opposing lawyer offtrack, to goad him so as to draw a reaction that Black could turn to his advantage, or to undermine the credibility of a witness. The cumulative effect could be telling on the jury.

A cross-examiner can go about his task of breaking down a witness and obtaining his desired information in different ways. He can "go for the jugular" and concentrate on the essence of the direct testimony. He can demonstrate that the witness has told untruths which cumulatively undermine his credibility. His approach must fit the witness's mood. Occasionally resorting to irrelevancies and asking inconsequential questions can make the witness feel more confident, all the better before unleashing a series of questions that slowly makes him bleed. To discredit a recalcitrant witness, a roundabout method is sometimes needed, holding one's ammunition until the appropriate moment. Black cross-examined B. G. Lackey, a barber whom Stephenson had known since 1906:

> Q. . . . When you got on the stand was the first time you had ever discussed his character with any human being. That is correct, isn't it?
> A. Yes, sir.
>   . . .
> Q. You like Mr. Stephenson, don't you?
> A. No.
> Q. Are your feelings good, or bad, toward him?
> A. Personally, neutral.
> Q. You are neutral, too. Who have you discussed this neutrality business with?
> A. Not anyone.
> Q. Did you tell Mr. Morrow your feelings were neutral?
> A. He did not ask me.
>   . . .
> Q. You all talked about what you were going to testify, didn't you, Lackey, just a little on the side; you all discussed whether your feelings were good, or bad, didn't you?
> A. (No answer)

Six times Lackey would not answer Black's question whether or not his feelings toward Stephenson were bitter.

> Q. You said you knew.
> A. Yes, sir, I know it.
> Q. They are; that is right, isn't it?
> A. Yes, sir.
> Q. You used to work for him, didn't you?
> A. Yes, sir.
> Q. At Talladega, Alabama?
> A. Yes, sir.

Q. And he fired you, didn't he?
A. Yes, sir.

"That's all," Black said.

He made other points. Fundamental constitutional issues were rarely raised in Alabama then. Only matters of procedure and evidence were generally raised during trials. This was not because of any aversion to constitutional concerns, but simply because hardly anyone thought of them. But even before he put Stephenson on the stand, while he was questioning the assistant county coroner, Black said, "Wasn't any lawyer there" with him in the jail. No lawyer represented Stephenson at any time before he appeared in court. Black continued the theme when examining Stephenson:

Q. Did [Tate] tell you that, under the laws of this country, a man was required to have a lawyer represent him, . . . or suggest or intimate . . . anything like that?
A. No, sir.
   . . .
Q. Did Mr. Tate advise you that whatever you said would be used against you?
A. No, sir.
Q. Did he make any suggestion that he was wanting to get a statement from you to use against you?
A. He said it was necessary for me to make some statement.

"The defendant," Black said, "doesn't have to talk and ought to have been advised by the Solicitor and the coroner he should not talk, and the fact he has not talked should not only not be held against him, but it is his constitutional right not to talk, and a right that should not be invaded by anybody."

The two most prominent witnesses were police chief Shirley and Stephenson himself. On cross-examination the prosecution grilled Shirley in an attempt to show prejudice and undue interest in Stephenson's plight. Black's repeated objections ("no evidence on earth except Mr. Morrow's repeated insinuations"), sustained by the court, prevented the prosecution from getting far.

As Stephenson unfolded the murder through Black's guiding questions, his body quivered and trembled and he broke down and cried three times. He talked in such a low voice that both lawyers asked that he speak louder. Even in their imaginations, those in the audience could feel the horror of seeing a man die. The prosecution asked Stephenson to demonstrate the positions of his and Coyle's bodies at the time. He wouldn't, and the prosecution did not press the point.

Black had prepped Stephenson well—admit nothing, be evasive and equivocal, don't answer if you can't turn the question to your advantage. The examination continued. Stephenson noted that he was standing when he shot Coyle. The prosecutor paused.

Q. Is Pedro Gussman a negro?
A. Yes, sir, I knew him when I seen him.
Q. I say is Pedro Gussman a negro?
A. I looked upon him as such.
Q. You say he is a negro.

The witness hesitated.

A. I say I look upon him as such.
Q. I asked whether or not you know he is a negro?

   MR. BLACK: We object to that. That is as far as a man could tell. He could not trace his lineage; very difficult to trace some of them.

The Court sustained the objection.

Q. You told Father Coyle he was a negro, didn't you?
A. That is what I said yesterday evening, I believe in the question I asked.
Q. Sir?
A. I looked upon him as such.
Q. I asked if you told Father Coyle he was a negro?
A. That is what I said.
Q. How is that?
A. Yes, sir.
Q. You told him something like this, didn't you, "you have married my daughter to a negro"?
A. That is not the exact words.

Q. What were the exact words you used?

A. I said yesterday evening, "You have ruined my home. That man is a negro."

Black had had a battery of floodlights installed in the courtroom, and at one point during Stephenson's testimony he suddenly switched them on. They were trained on Gussman, sitting in the courtroom. The jury's eyes were averted. "I want you to look at that man," Black said. Turning to Stephenson, he asked, "Were you aware that Gussman was a Puerto Rican?"

"You can call him a Puerto Rican," the minister said, "but to me he's a nigger."

"The trial was a sort of Hollywood spectacle—culminating in an amazing scene under Kleig lights when the Reverend Stephenson was testifying," an observer later wrote. "Mr. Gussman was called to attend under the blazing lights; the stage was all set for the climax, and it came quickly."[2]

Near the end of his examination of Stephenson, just as the defendant tearfully finished graphically describing the murder, Black paused and asked that the courtroom blinds be drawn. The lights were also dimmed. No objection was heard from the prosecutor. The judge did not say anything. Black turned to the bailiff. "Call Pedro Gussman in."

The jury leaned forward. Stephenson stared at the door. Gussman re-entered the courtroom and walked to the railing that separated the spectators from the people involved in the trial. "Evidently he didn't understand what was wanted of him but he seemed perfectly willing to do as told," a reporter wrote.

"Is that Pedro Gussman?" Black said.

"Yes, sir," Gussman replied. The jury looked straight at him. "Is this the Pedro Gussman you referred to?" Black asked Stephenson, still in the witness chair. "Yes," he answered. Mrs. Stephenson, sitting behind relatives, pulled at a handkerchief she held in her hand. After a moment Gussman turned as if to walk out. "Let him come around further, Judge, so we can see him," one juror said to Black. "Bring him closer to the jury and let them see his eyes," Hugo said of the man whom he had called "a negro, a dago, or a Porto Rican." The bailiff escorted the astonished Gussman in front of the jury box.

Black had the floodlights turned on. While Gussman had been out of the room, they had been rearranged to focus on the spot where he was now standing. And with the blinds closed, his dusky complexion was accentuated. "His eyes grew wider, his dark skin seemed to pale. His heavy coal black hair was combed straight back; his features showed amazement more than ever." For a moment he just stood there without speaking. "He seemed little concerned with the trial." The jury glared at him. Linked in their minds were two characters and two images—a weeping father and the swarthy bridegroom.

"That will do," Black said, and Gussman was returned to the witness room. "I just wanted the jury to see that man."

The enmity between Black and Tate, evident throughout the trial, peaked toward the close. (Hugo was friendly with the other prosecutors and jested with them in court despite occasional slashing repartees.) Tate put Gussman on the stand "to prove he wasn't a negro." But, as Black pointed out, the prosecutor "did not ask if there was any negro blood in him." In an unusual move Tate was the state's witness on rebuttal. Without a question being asked, he began, "I want to say." Black interrupted: "We object to any statement voluntarily; just want the questions propounded so we can object," which he did repeatedly. His objections reached the point that when the next witness was asked a question, he said, "Wait a minute. I would like to have the court instruct her not to answer the questions until I object."

After the state closed its case, Tate put on the stand a new witness who allegedly saw Stephenson shoot Coyle. Black objected strenuously: "The law contemplates that the state shall put on its evidence and the defendant shall then put on its evidence. It never has contemplated that a supposed eyewitness to a murder, or alleged eyewitness to a murder, could be held back until the defendant puts on his evidence and then bring him in. It isn't fair, and not proper and not according to the law." Nevertheless, four times Tate asked the witness questions in violation of this elementary principle. Each time Black objected, and the judge affirmed his objections.[3] One of the assistant prosecutors testified that he had first obtained information as to the witness before the trial started; the other said it was on the third day of the trial, which was now in its fifth day. And this was despite the state's having two months to prepare its case. Yet Tate told the court he had "never heard of this man until I went up and was in the office, after we had closed [our case]."

·   ·   ·

Before the judge called the court to order the next morning, Ruth unexpectedly appeared in the courtroom. After hesitating, she kissed her parents without saying one word and took a seat. Soon the testimony was completed. The jury then visited the murder scene where wire was inserted in a bullet hole in the rectory wall to check Stephenson's story that he was not yet completely upright when he shot Coyle. They returned to court to hear the lawyers make their closing arguments to the jury.

Silence prevailed when Black rose. He tried to be fair in his conduct, he said, and did not appeal to any passion or prejudice, or complain because the solicitor had done so. "There should be no halo of glory around the prosecutors' heads" because they had prosecuted the case, as they seemed to think from their arguments. The burden of proof rested with them and they had not met it. Nor should the jury be interested in the eyes of the world. "Return a fair verdict without any fear that Birmingham might receive a black eye," Black said. "I admit that there are certain localities where a verdict of guilty from this jury would be looked upon with favor but these eyes have nothing to do with the evidence in the case."

He accused the state of injecting prejudice into the trial at the beginning by proving that Father Coyle was a Catholic.

> Because a man becomes a priest does not mean that he is divine. He has no more right to protection than a Protestant minister. Who believes Ruth Stephenson has not been proselytized? A child of a Methodist does not suddenly depart from her religion unless someone has planted in her mind the seeds of influence. They say she was locked up in Fred Bender's home from the inside. I do not care how she was locked. It has been said, "Stone walls do not a prison make." There is no such thing as imprisonment of the human will by influence, vice and persuasion. When you find a girl who has been reared well persuaded from her parents by some cause or person, that cause or person is wrong.

These were code words to a jury in a southern, Protestant city like Birmingham in the 1920s. To make his meaning transparently clear, Black read from the official Ku Klux Klan prayer. The prayer began, "Our Father and our God. We, as klansmen, acknowledge our dependence upon Thee . . ." and continued, "Harmonize our souls with the sacred principles and purposes of our noble Order that we may keep our sacred oath inviolate."[4]

Prosecution witnesses who were Catholic were "Siamese twins," "brothers of falsehood as well as faith," who gave perjured testimony, Black charged. He attacked Gussman's background, saying there were twenty mulattoes to every Negro in Puerto Rico. If "Gussman were of proud Castillian descent," as the state contended, "he has descended a long way." Stephenson shot

Coyle in an "uncontrollable impulse" while temporarily insane over Ruth's behavior. Mrs. Stephenson wept as Black described the empty house she and her husband would return to without their daughter; several times Stephenson put his handkerchief to his eyes. Spectators were in tears as Black concluded:

> If the eyes of the world are upon the verdict of this jury, I would write that verdict in words that cannot be misunderstood, that the homes of the people in Birmingham cannot be touched. If that brings disgrace, God hasten the disgrace.

For the prosecution John Morrow, pointing his finger repeatedly at the gum-chewing Stephenson, assailed him as a "cold-blooded murderer. . . . He says he has no prejudice against the Catholics, but who on this jury believes that statement? . . . The eyes of the entire country are turned upon this Birmingham jury. They want to see whether a southern jury will free a murderer because of prejudice." Morrow waved his hand toward Saint Paul's Church, which was visible through the window. "When you render your verdict, gentlemen, be fair and just to those people. Do not try to persecute them by crucifying one of their priests in this courtroom."

Tate then spoke. All the state had to do was to prove the death, that it happened in Jefferson County, show the means of the killing and that it took place before the accused had been indicted, he said. Then the burden of proof shifted to the defense. "If you go into the jury room, and kick out the evidence, gentlemen of the jury, and then render a verdict of not guilty, you will have all the narrow-minded, fuzzy-necked people come and pat you on the back, but for the remainder of your lives you will have your conscience to prick and sting you."

Judge Fort charged the jury, instructing them on the law of murder as applied to the case and on the law governing all phases of self-defense. He warned against allowing any prejudice or passion to sway them from pursuit of the truth. The jurors were handed the pistol with which Stephenson shot the priest and the suspenders he was wearing at the time. The minister scanned their faces as they filed out. They picked up their hats before going to a nearby hotel for supper. Then they returned to deliberate.

"The first thing we did when we began to go into the case," the jury foreman said later, "was to read several selections from the Bible. I don't know what passages they were, but they were excerpts from the words of Jesus. Those were read by one of our number, a fervent Christian" who carried a small Bible in his pocket throughout the trial. "This same man then prayed earnestly for wisdom and guidance in the task ahead." The others joined him. On bended knees, they asked for divine counsel before deciding the fate of one minister of God who took the life of another.

The jury took only one vote. It was unanimous: "not guilty by reason of self-defense," changed from the insanity plea the defense had entered. "We did what we thought was the right thing," the foreman said. The evidence, not the eloquent speeches of the lawyers, was decisive. "We were worried . . . by our desire to give justice." After being out less than two hours, they called Judge Fort at home at ten o'clock to say that they had reached a decision. He came to court, the defense lawyers were summoned, but the prosecutors could not be located. Stephenson was brought from the jail. His wife took a seat beside him in the dimly lit courtroom. Only a few dozen other people were present. They had been hanging around the courthouse, smoking cigarettes, laughing and joking. Now they were still. Stephenson bowed his head and waited.

The foreman handed the verdict to the clerk who read it to the court. "We, the jury, find the defendant not guilty." Stephenson brushed a tear from his eyes, embraced his wife and smiled widely. His lips quivered—he seemed to be saying a prayer. The audience broke into cheers. The judge gaveled for silence and spoke to the jury. "I believe you have done your best. There will be many opinions, but no one can properly criticize the honest verdict of twelve honest men." They left the jury box and filed by Stephenson, who heartily but silently shook hands with each one. "God bless you, sir!" he said to them collectively. He extended his hand to Hugo. With tears running down his cheeks and in a trembling voice, he said, "I'll never forget. As long as I live, I shall live to show the world that your fight was right." He went to Judge Fort and thanked him for the "fair way" in which he had presided. "I am a broken-hearted man, judge," he said, "but I am going to try to live so that no man on the jury will ever be sorry for their verdict. I pray God that I may be worthy. I have only love in my heart for every person in Birmingham. I am going to remember them in all my prayers."

Stephenson started to walk out of the courtroom. Suddenly he turned to see if anyone was alongside. No one was. "I'm not used to walking by myself," he said with a smile. A deputy sheriff drove him and his wife home.

. . . .

Working for one of its own behind the scenes was the Ku Klux Klan. The Klan was well represented at the trial. Not only were all the defense lawyers except Black members at the time, so too was Judge Fort;* and police chief Shirley was a long-time member and national officer. Through Hugo's partner Harris, the head of the Alabama Klan, James Esdale, secured Hugo as Stephenson's lawyer. Then Esdale "set up the trial," he said. About two weeks ahead of time the jury venire, the list from which jurors are drawn, was sent out to the local Klan units to check for members. The majority of jurors were Klansmen, and the foreman was a field organizer for the Klan chapter in Ensley, in the western part of Birmingham. Members in the courtroom used hand gestures to the jury during the trial. And Hugo likewise gave jurors the Klan's signature.[5]

"Hugo didn't have much trouble winning that verdict," Esdale said many years later. The prosecutors' incompetence and attitude helped. Black had long known Tate's ineptitude; even later, he was considered by common consent "a second rate lawyer at best." "It is my unconfirmed suspicion," recalled a reporter covering the trial, "that the prosecution did not really want to convict Stephenson and deliberately held back the eyewitnesses until their testimony was no longer valid."[6] Then there was Ruth. Even though Black would have subjected her to a withering cross-examination, the prosecution called her to testify, "and then refused to put me on the stand and made no explanations."

Black played upon local prejudice, as critics later correctly charged. "He was not beyond exploiting an emotional feeling based on race if that helped his client," Hugo, Jr., wrote. But he was only doing what a lawyer must do. The adversary system demands that a defense lawyer work for his client's acquittal. As the Alabama Bar Association code of ethics at the time rather grandiloquently put it, an attorney

"owes his entire devotion to the interest of the client, warm zeal in the maintenance and defense of his cause, and the exertion of the utmost skill and ability," to the end, that nothing may be taken or withheld from him save by the rules of law, legally applied. No sacrifice or peril, even to the

* One evening the next June, reporter Ray Sprigle noted in 1937, Fort

presided over a Klan meeting, and the next morning he took his place on the bench to preside at the trial of a vicious group which had flogged Dr. Dowling, Health Officer of the City of Birmingham, because of the latter's aggressive action against dairies producing inferior milk. The trial was a joke, in that the floggers were Klansmen, who were winking and grinning during the trial at attorneys for the defense, all of this being necessarily known to Fort.

loss of life itself, can absolve from the fearless discharge of this duty. Nevertheless, it is steadfastly to be borne in mind that the great trust is to be performed within and not without the bounds of the law which creates it. The attorney's office does not destroy man's accountability to the Creator, or loosen the duty of obedience to law, and the obligation to his neighbor; and it does not permit, much less demand, violation of law, or any manner of fraud or chicanery, for the client's sake.[7]

Black gave to Stephenson's defense his professional devotion. The circumstances of the case made him uncomfortable. He disliked the Catholic Church as an institution—how it solicited money from often poor parishioners, its demand that they unquestioningly obey a higher order, its owning so much property. He treated prosecution witnesses not just as adversaries but virtually as mortal enemies, as a comparison with other transcripts of his trials during these years shows. His questions likewise had even more of a sting. Perhaps he was on edge because Josephine was pregnant again, after suffering a miscarriage a few months earlier. Or perhaps he was trying harder because it was not the type of case he would have taken on his own, but one he felt that he must.

The Klan's power was rising in Alabama, and especially in Birmingham. Floggings were regular occurrences. Hugo abhorred violence, and his mild case of anti-institutional Catholicism would not permit him to defend an admitted murderer. But he was an ambitious politician, and not only Harris but some of his closest friends and professional associates were Klan members. He could rationalize that accepting this case, despite its stench, might at a minimum neutralize one of the most vocal elements of the community in the future. And it could also redound to his great advantage.*

Ruth did not contact her parents after the trial. In a letter to a newspaper— her favorite form of communication—she wrote that "there has been absolutely no reconciliation. I am very sorry for them in their trouble, but only they are responsible for what has happened. I have forgiven them all their unjust treatment, punishment and censure of me, but it will be years

* Another indication of the Klan's power at the time is that no public record of the trial survives, only the grand jury proceedings, the most secret part of the criminal process. And only one of the several copies of the transcript of the trial, as transcribed by the official court stenographer, exists. There is no record of the case in the Jefferson County criminal courts. Records of all other cases tried in 1921 remain. But that of *State v. Stephenson*, #1123-21, was apparently destroyed, long ago and almost certainly by the Klan.

before I can forget. There shall be no reconciliation." Soon she became completely estranged. She became ill, and in 1932 she died. She was thirty.

With his newfound fame Stephenson traveled throughout the state, addressing Klan rallies. He occupied a position of honor as a martyr to the cause. Then he went back to plying his trade as the "marrying parson" at the courthouse, buttonholing couples as he opened the door obsequiously and charging them one dollar; and on Saturdays he barbered. During World War Two, couples seeking his services lined up outside his gloomy, ghostly house. "Roscoe had no bitterness about the murder," a relative recalled, "but he didn't look back at it either." In later years "he never talked about the trial," his second wife said. "It just made him too nervous. He was a nice looking, lively old devil. He certainly was." He died in 1956 at the age of eighty-six.

"On several occasions after he went to Washington, Black, on visits back to Birmingham came around to the *News* and chatted with the editorial writers," remembered J. Fisher Rothermel, who reported the trial. "At one such visit, I was moved to ask Black if he remembered the appearance of Gussman at the trial. Black gave me a quick but, I think, somewhat hard look, and said he had forgotten all about the incident. Maybe he would like to forget it. Maybe it is, to him, only one of those things that a politically ambitious young attorney has to do."[8]

CHAPTER 6

THE HOODED
ORDER

T HE AFTERMATH of World War One saw a wave of nativism and xenophobia surging over the country. It was a time of reaction against prewar progressivism and the idealism of the war as a great crusade for democracy. In the South a new Ku Klux Klan, organized in 1915, grew spectacularly in the early 1920s. The Klan offered an easy answer. It extolled older and simpler virtues, and allowed mankind's base instincts free rein. In Birmingham and other cities it served a psychological purpose for laborers and steel and mill workers who had uprooted themselves from farms and rural areas, and found themselves tossed about as strangers in the hurly-burly of urban industrialism. The Klan provided these newcomers an opportunity to believe in something larger than themselves by giving them a sense of belonging. Its mysteries and secrecies, elaborate rituals and mystic ceremonies, rich pageantries and exotic titles, indeed bizarre nomenclature—all gave meaning and added excitement to an otherwise humdrum existence.

Five million men across the country donned the white hood and gown. "The Klan is as absolutely American as chewing-gum, crooked district attorneys, or Chatauquas" offering popular lectures and entertainment, observed H. L. Mencken. Klansmen saw themselves as protectors of a traditional American morality threatened by immigration, urbanization and mobility. Change was their enemy, fear of change their rallying cry. The Klan was dedicated to the supremacy of the Caucasian race, its version of "one hundred per cent Americanism" ("to make America safe for Americans," as all prospective members were told) and a radically fundamentalist interpretation of Protestantism. "The real indictment against the Roman Church," wrote Imperial Wizard Hiram Evans, "is that it is . . . actually and actively alien, un-American and usually anti-American. . . . America was Protestant from birth" and "must remain Protestant, if the Nordic stock is to finish its destiny. . . . We admit that this is intolerant; we deny that it is either bigoted or unjust."[1]

Alabama, and especially Birmingham, was fertile territory for the Klan. Its white population was overwhelmingly of native-born and pure Anglo-Saxon stock. The True Americans, a secret society whose motto was "No Catholics in Public Office," had made its impact felt in Birmingham's 1917 municipal elections when its candidate was chosen president of the city commission. Its devotees were largely working-class whites of limited education and fundamentalist Protestant background who competed with Negroes for industrial jobs. All city workers were Protestants by 1920, except for two policemen; soon all workers were. Vigilance committees threatened to boycott businesses that continued to employ Catholics. Baptist Hospital did not admit Catholics for a period. As the murder trial of the Reverend Stephenson had shown, passions in Birmingham ran high when Catholics were involved.

Imperial Wizard (Colonel) William J. Simmons, the founder of the modern Klan, sent a trusted assistant, Jonathan Frost, to Birmingham to enlist members at a 1916 reunion of Confederate veterans. After enrolling a number and collecting their initiation fees, Frost absconded with the funds. As solicitor, Black promptly convicted him.[2]

Birmingham's Robert E. Lee Klan No. 1 had only a few hundred members in 1920 when James Esdale joined as Kleagle (recruiter). A small-time Birmingham lawyer with a largely criminal practice, and a contemporary of Black's, whose economic bent he shared, he quickly built the membership up to several thousand. Soon he was chosen Cyclops (leader of the local Klan unit), and in 1923 he was made Grand Dragon of the Realm of Alabama. It was a militant, hierarchical organization. "There was no democracy in the Klan," Esdale said. He ran the show.

In the early 1920s the Klan controlled Birmingham. White-robed men and cross burnings; whippings and lashings; floggings and abductions; tarrings, featherings and brandings; flashing lights into parked cars, closing dance halls and beating people in the name of morality—all were common sights in the Magic City. Klansmen paraded openly through town, cradling shotguns or rifles and peering like white, pointy-headed owls from under their sheets, with only their shoes visible. White sheets also hid license plates on cars; masks covered the drivers' faces. People were regularly beaten for such violations of the Klan's moral code as friendly relations with Negroes. They were urged to patronize only those shops whose windows displayed T.W.K. (Trade With a Klansman) signs.

Lawlessness was the order of the day—or rather the Klan sought to maintain law and order by its own lights. Klansmen appeared uninvited at funerals. Individuals took the law into their own hands, sometimes acting as the police; uniformed officers did not investigate. Juries dominated by the Klan "routinely" acquitted members or sympathizers of "a variety of crimes, the only requirement being that the victim must have been (a) Negro, (b) Catholic, (c) an immigrant, (d) or an idle boozer. (That the Klan was itself shot through with secret boozers was something else.) Anyway, they were KLANSMEN, and everybody knew that the hood and the sheet, for one night at least, made even the boozers the avenging angels of the Lord." In this atmosphere the "rule of lash and mask" reigned, suffusing the air like a pollen of fear.

The Invisible Empire drew from all levels of society—men who worked with their hands and behind desks, middle-class businessmen and devout churchgoers alike. "We had the best people in the state," Esdale said without exaggeration. Bank presidents and physicians joined; "nearly all the preachers belonged to it," Black noted. Most of the important city and county officials as well as many members of the sheriff and police departments were on the Klan rolls. Jefferson County sheriff and former Birmingham police chief Thomas Shirley was a member of the Imperial Kloncilium, the national Klan's supreme judicial body and executive council.[3]

On September 13, 1923, Black joined the Klan. He had already paid his $10 initiation fee (Klectoken). He was one of 1,500 "aliens" (the noninitiates) who were "naturalized" that day by 5,000 Alabama Klansmen as well as 7,500 visiting members from a half dozen southern states. Some 25,000 people and a host of national Klan officials from Atlanta witnessed the ceremony in Birmingham's Edgewood Park. The *Birmingham News* described the proceedings:

> Promptly at 9 o'clock [P.M.] the hooded knights began the first preparations for the naturalization ceremonies by lighting the large flaming crosses, which added a peculiar and awe-inspiring atmosphere to the entire surroundings. Following this, hundreds of the knights began taking their places

around the field. Then came the candidates formed in double ranks and eight abreast in a large circle.

Soon the entire procession began to move and the circles moved clockwise and stopped before each of the three stations situated at intervals of 450 feet, where a portion of the obligation was received. At the close of the march the entire assembly was marched in front of the imperial wizard where the final touches of the ceremony were given. At this point the famous band of the Chattanooga Klan struck up "America" and was followed by the drum and bugle corps of the same organization.

Hugo had placed his left hand over his heart, palm downward in a fascistlike salute, raised his right straight to heaven, and repeated the Klan oath. He was now able to engage in all the practices of Klankraft.

It was a decision he did not make lightly. When he was first approached, "somewhere around 1920," he pleaded lack of time. He deliberated almost a year before joining. Many of his friends and clients, and most other lawyers with similar practices, were members; symptomatically, Crampton Harris would shortly replace Walter Brower as Exalted Cyclops, as Brower soon became Grand Titan, head of a Province of a group of counties. Peer pressure was becoming increasingly difficult to resist. More important, Hugo could not ignore the Klan's rapid growth. In July 1923, a Klan official claimed to represent 50,000 men in the state; the number of sympathizers was much higher. Estimates of membership in its five Klaverns in the Birmingham area ranged from 15,000 to 20,000. The Lee Klan No. 1 alone numbered 10,000 on its rolls and was the largest and "perhaps the most powerful klavern in the Southeast," a historian wrote.

The Klan's popularity came at a moment when secret fraternal orders reached their peak, just before the advent of such competing attractions as the cheap motorcar, the radio and, especially, talking movies. Black shared its platform, such as it was—for prohibition, the "common people" and the rights of organized labor, and against corporations, immigration and what was viewed as Catholic intolerance. But how could he join a group that had other tenets he always found odious in the extreme? "Simply as a piece of political behavior . . . ," Max Lerner explained.

> For the Klan had not inconsiderable roots, although twisted ones, in the mass mind. Its superpatriotism fitted the anti-radical mood after the war; its law-enforcement plank went strong in the period of Prohibition racketeering; in regions of economic distress its nativism seemed an insurance against the competition of immigrant behavior; amid the decay of religious

faith its mystical religionism had an appeal; its attitude toward the Negroes was integral to the Southern psychosis of "white supremacy." . . . The common people had been captured by the Klan, for it buttressed them against problems they could not understand with principles that seemed eternal. The Klan assumed, moreover, a radical attitude on many specific issues which appealed to the progressives. Like the fascist movement in Germany, it combined a spurious radicalism with terrorism. Those who leaned toward the first were often able to shut their eyes to the second.

But Black could not have had any illusions about the group he joined. Illegal Klan activities were part of daily life in Birmingham. Hugo had nothing to do with these. At one Konklave a resolution to whip a fellow was being debated. Black said, "This is a law-abiding organization and if you whip him, I leave the Klan." The resolution passed. "Consider me no longer a member," Hugo said. He put on his hat and walked out, but still remained a member. This episode, however, (apparently) stood apart. Black's political and economic sympathies lay with rank-and-file Klansmen. Without this well-disciplined bloc of voters, he well knew, no candidate could hope to get elected to any office in Alabama in the foreseeable future. The Klan offered Black a ready-made base for political advancement. It was a vehicle he had to ride, to whatever destination would be his.

As a card-carrying Klansman he was characteristically idiosyncratic in other ways. In early 1924, the Klan tried to have a well-regarded high school principal, Chester Bandman, discharged simply because he was Jewish. (While "the Jew is a more complex problem" than the Catholic, Hiram Evans had written, combined they constituted "the permanently unassimilable alien.") Hugo had known and liked Bandman, who was also a lawyer, for years. He persuaded the Klan to abandon its attempt. The next year, however, it was renewed (as the Klan also sought, ultimately unsuccessfully, to take control of the board of education). Hugo determined to use his influence within the greater community to help his friend. As the movement to oust Bandman climaxed, he spoke at a luncheon of the Civitan Club. If Bandman were not wanted in his present position, Hugo said, he would be happy to have the "best principal in the city" transferred to his children's future school; the club passed a resolution protesting the attempted dismissal. Bandman's job was saved but, saying "everything just got too much," he soon left Birmingham for Pittsburgh.[4]

. . . .

Black was active in every group he joined. The Klan was no exception. His standard response—"I went to a couple of meetings and spoke about liberty"—was invariably accepted at face value without further investigation. Sometimes, to make his answer more plausible, he added that he agreed to be the "speaker of the evening," as if he were addressing a business group. That is true, but sharply incomplete. He did more—much more.

He marched in parades, and attended and spoke at meetings around the state. Dressed in full Klan regalia, he addressed a local Klavern in Greensboro, seventy-five miles southwest of Birmingham and attended meetings in Tuscaloosa. Not even the small village of West Blocton, thirty miles from Birmingham, was ignored. Hugo spoke at a Konklave there. A Klan hood and mask with his name written in it was found forty years later in a trunk filled with other Klan ornaments in an old Clay County Klan gathering place. Perhaps it was from the time he returned to Lineville, six miles from Ashland. The daughter of John Haynes, one of his first mentors, recalled: "Once as a little girl I ran into the house and a closet door was open. A white Klan uniform fell on me. I didn't recognize what it was so I asked my mother. She said, 'Oh, that's Mr. Black's costume. He's going to wear it in a play Saturday night.'"

As a speaker Black had already gained local renown. In a power struggle Hiram Evans, a roly-poly, politically minded Dallas dentist of dubious credentials, had wrested control of the national Klan from William Simmons, who then began promulgating a rival fraternal order, known as the Knights of the Flaming Sword. Simmons soon put Black's talents to good use. On September 22, 1924—just eleven days after Hugo's son Sterling was born— he went to Toledo, Ohio, with Simmons and a few other former Klan leaders. There, before three hundred persons meeting at a church, Simmons outlined the principles of his new organization, calling it a "white, protestant, gentile, eleemosynary institution" that would not promote any discrimination. Introduced as "Mr. Blackburn," Black also spoke to the crowd.[5]

But the highlight of his Klankraft was initiating new members into the Invisible Empire. This job falls to the Kladd of each Klavern. The Lee Klan letterhead listed Hugo Black as an officer.

In a stately ritual the initates pledged their allegiance to the United States, its Constitution and flag, the Klan and its members, and the Christian creed. Crossed swords lay on the Bible on the altar. Black read the oath from the Kloran ritual book:

I swear that I will most zealously and valiantly shield and preserve by any and all justifiable means and methods . . . white supremacy.

I most solemnly vow and most positively swear that I will never yield to bribe, flattery, passion, punishment, persecution, persuasion, nor any enticements whatever coming or offered to me from any person or persons, male or female, for the purpose of obtaining a secret or secret information of the Ku Klux Klan. I will die rather than divulge same, so help me God. Amen.

All to which I have sworn to by this oath, I will seal with my blood, be thou my witness Almightly God. Amen.

As the participants moved slowly before him, Black and other officers engaged in extended liturgylike colloquies. "Worthy aliens from the world of selfishness and fraternal alienation prompted by unselfish motive," he told the assembled,

desire the honor of citizenship in the Invisible Empire and the fellowship of klansmen. . . . The distinguishing marks of a klansman are . . . spiritual; namely a chivalric head, a compassionate heart, a prudent tongue and a courageous will. All devoted to our country, our klan, our homes and each other . . . oh, Faithful Klexter! And these men claim the marks. [A traitor] would be immediately banished from the Invisible Empire without fear or favor, conscience would tenaciously torment him, remorse would repeatedly revile him, and direful things would befall him. . . .

Faithful Klexter: A Klansman speaketh the truth in and from his heart. A lying scoundrel may wrap his disgraceful frame within the sacred folds of a klansman's robe and deceive the very elect, but only a klansman possesses a klansman's heart and a klansman's soul.

Sirs: The portal of the Invisible Empire is being opened for you. Your righteous prayer has been answered and you have found favor in the sight of the Exalted Cyclops and his klansmen assembled. Follow me and be prudent!

[I am] the Kladd of the klan with a party, whom the eye of the unknown and seen and doth constantly observe.

Faithful Klaliff: THESE ARE MEN, as the Invisible Empire and a time like this demands; men of strong minds, great hearts, true faith and ready hands. Worthy aliens know and vouched for by klansmen in klonklave assembled, and by order of his Excellency, I, the Kladd of the klan, am their guide to the sacred altar.

Your Excellency, Sir [the Exalted Cyclops], pursuant to your orders, I present to you these alien aspirants, men of dependable character and courage, who aspire to the noble life and the high honor of citizenship in the Invisible Empire. The aliens in our midst from the world of selfishness and fraternal alienation, forsake the past and are now ready and willing to bind themselves to the Invisible Empire, Knights of the Ku Klux Klan.[6]

Although Black did not advertise his Klan involvement, neither did he keep it completely secret. Close friends, of course, knew. But at dinner in Ashville in 1923, where he was trying a case, he admitted his membership. He acknowledged it to fellow Birmingham lawyer Borden Burr while playing golf. In Ashland "everybody" in his family knew it. "I'm doing the right thing even though I don't like the Klan," Hugo told his sister Ora, said her daughter Helen Garrett Byrnes. To his cousin Pauline Clayton he said he was an officer. But otherwise, he kept mum about his activities. To those close to him later in life, his Klan activities remained nearly as enshrouded in mystery as they were when they took place. "He didn't talk about that much," said Hugo, Jr.; "only very indirectly," recalled a friend, television reporter Martin Agronsky. "That hardly ever came up," noted Frances Lamb, his secretary for his last fourteen years. It was the classical skeleton in the closet; only Black had the key to open the door, and on the rare occasions he tried to use it, it didn't fit—it couldn't. He suffered guilt and pangs of conscience as he outgrew regional prejudices and provincialisms. To the few writers who had enough guts to ask him about the Klan, he gave different answers as he sometimes reinvented, and always attempted to rationalize, a critical part of his past.

- He told one student that a Klan recruiter continually circulated in his office building and sold memberships for $10, keeping $6 for himself. "I paid him to get him off my back as much as anything else."

   You know how it is with all these clubs down there, with a man in public life. They keep after you—and keep after you. It's always something to join or contribute to. The Odd Fellows kept after me for five years. The Klan kept after me, and kept after me, so I finally gave them the $10.

- He told another inquirer:

   An old law partner got me to join. Practically everyone joined. The preachers, etc., were all for it. The name Klan is magic down there. Thad Stevens and his Reconstruction have never been forgotten. I said I'll pay an initiation fee, sign up, but not be initiated. I went to three or four meetings. Then I joined the Moose. The speeches I made I could have made . . . to the A.C.L.U., and they'd have liked it. Whether I'd join if I had to do it again, I'm not sure.

• He told the *New York Times* in 1967 for his obituary:

The Klan in those days was not what it became later. There were a few extremists in it, but most of the people were the cream of Birmingham's middle-class. It was a fraternal organization, really. It wasn't anti-Catholic, anti-Jewish, or anti-Negro. In fact, it was a Jew, my closest friend, Herman Beck, who asked me to join, said they needed good people in the Klan. He couldn't be in it, of course, but he wanted to keep down the few extremists. . . .*

Anyway, the only reason I didn't join before I did was that I was too busy with other organizations, Knights of Pythias, Odd Fellows, others. But before I finally agreed to join, on the night I was supposed to join, I got up first and spoke and told 'em I was against hate, I liked Negroes, I liked Jews, I liked Catholics, and that if I saw any illegality goin' on I wouldn't worry about any secrecy, I'd turn 'em in to the grand jury. Well, when I finished they cheered and they said to me that's what you're obligated to do under our rules. And they were right, that's what the rules said, anything illegal, no secrecy.

[He leaned back in his chair and had a boyish grin.] You want to know the main reason I joined the Klan? I was trying a lot of cases against corporations, jury cases, and I found that all the corporation lawyers were in the Klan. A lot of the jurors were too, so I figured I'd better be even up. [He chuckled.] I haven't told that before, but that's how it was. People think it was politics, but it wasn't politics.

• He told an interviewer late in life: "At that time, I was joining every organization in sight! . . . In my part of Alabama, the Klan was not engaged in unlawful activities. . . . The general feeling in the community was that if responsible citizens didn't join the Klan, it would soon become dominated by the less responsible members. My membership in the Klan was passive."

* This story has some truth to it. In 1926, when Alabama attorney general Harwell Davis was running for Congress, James Esdale offered to make him a member of the Klan on the spot; its support would assure his election. Davis took the proposition to Beck, who listened and then gave him $50 for the initiation fee, saying, "I'm donating it to your campaign fund. . . . I'll tell you like I told Hugo Black, whom I worked with. The Klan is nothing in the world but an organization to get office, and we had better use it to get the best men in office we could. If it lasts, we want some level-headed fellows on the inside to keep it from hurting the Jews too bad." Davis did not join the Klan, and was defeated by less than two hundred votes (Davis int., UAB OHP, 10–11).

- He told a reporter shortly after he was confirmed for the Supreme Court: "The Klan was, in effect, the underground Democratic Party in Alabama. It was revived as a force to counteract the corporations. All candidates for public office trooped around and spoke at Klan halls. The corporations tried to get their lawyers admitted, but they were blackballed. The leading department store owner in Birmingham [Louis Pizitz], who was Jewish, asked me to join. I was signed up by the Chief Justice of Alabama [John C. Anderson], the fellow who wrote the dissenting opinion in the *Scottsboro* case."

- He told a friend the first month he sat on the Court: "When I joined the Klan it was not anti-Catholic or anti-Jewish. With other progressive Democrats, I went in to prevent it from falling into the hands of machine politicians. We succeeded and I quit when I saw the Klan was going in the wrong direction."

- He told a Supreme Court law clerk: "The Klan was the liberal wing of the Democratic Party in Alabama." He paused. "By that I mean anti-railroad and against the corporations." As, earlier, he had told an interviewer: In Alabama the Klan had been a "representative of the down-trodden," a "hang-over from populism."

- He told this writer: "Herman Beck, one of my best friends ever, said I should join the Klan. Nobody went after the Klan in Alabama. I'm not willing to agree in retrospect that joining was the best thing in the world to do. But," he quickly added, almost defensively, leaning forward for emphasis, "the best people in Alabama joined it."

On one of the rare occasions Black talked about the Klan at home, he said: "I wanted to know as many possible jurors as I could. I was joining everything then. It was just another group and they were always after me. After a while I left." He gave the impression that it was "really insignificant," Sterling Black recalled. "But for a while whenever he mentioned it he also referred to the rabbi in Birmingham [Morris Newfield] and said how friendly they were. There was a period when it seemed that the rabbi and the Klan went together." Josephine never spoke about the Klan to the children, and "she tried to be frank about him." Black did not allude to the Klan to his Senate staff, even though his chief assistant, his nephew Hollis, had also been a member and had asked friends to join.

But to Supreme Court law clerks, perhaps as a form of expiation, Black showed no hesitation in discussing the Klan. As time went on, he brought it up himself and exhibited less defensiveness. ("Even the rabbi was a member then," he told one early clerk who was Jewish.) Usually, he would go down the list of organizations he joined and compare the Klan ("a working man's club") to someone's membership in the Kiwanis or the Rotary. "He gave the impression it was a mistake," even conceding, "it was stupid." Once he said that he was "particularly active but didn't say what he did, just that many people joined and it was politically valuable." "There was a political need to join," he admitted.[7]

Hugo was, as he said, an inveterate "jiner." Getting out and meeting people, he felt, was the best way for a lawyer to acquire new clients; it is conceivable that becoming acquainted with possible jurors was among the reasons he joined the Klan. He was already a member of many fraternal orders—among them the Knights of Pythias (he was State Grand Chancellor in 1921, he recruited one thousand new members for his lodge, and he served as Supreme Representative to the Supreme Lodge); Masons—the Blue Lodge and the Scottish and York Rite Masons (he joined the Zamora Temple in 1909 and became a lodge officer and, ultimately, a 33rd-degree mason); Odd Fellows; Woodmen of the World; Redmen; Eagles; Shriners; Dokies; Civitan Club (founded in Birmingham in 1917; he was president of the Mother Club in 1922); Moose (which he later regretted joining, and joined only because its head came to his office and asked him; "I couldn't turn him down"); Pretorians (from which he bought insurance, "pretty cheap too," he recalled); and the American Legion (as was Josephine, also a veteran). "I made friends in all these organizations. I would have joined the B'nai B'Rith [or Knights of Columbus, changing the group to match what he felt was the inquirer's religious affiliation], if they would've let me in." Certainly he hoped to expand his circle of friends in the Klan.*

But there were other, more compelling considerations. The Klan controlled the voting machinery in practically every county in Alabama. By 1923 government in Jefferson County had become virtually a wholly owned subsidiary of the Invisible Empire. Klansmen accounted for 15,000 of Bir-

---

* "Black says that by joining all these societies and orders he kept himself politically free. For their number was so great that he never felt the slightest political debt to any one" (Rodell, "Black"). In 1937 he told his New Deal friend Tom Corcoran, "I was running for office and looking for position and like every young man, I joined every organization that might help me in some way" (draft of Corcoran to HLB, marked "not sent," Lash papers).

mingham's 32,000 registered voters—nearly half. It was simply a fact of
Alabama politics that no candidate could be elected without the hooded
order's support or, at the minimum, its non-opposition. *

Many years later, while relaxing between sets of tennis, a friend, Marilew
Kogan, asked Black, " 'Why did you join the Klan? You never believed in
what they were doing.' I put it to him bluntly so he had to answer," she
recalled. "A look of contrition came over his face and he almost appeared
to be in real physical pain. He put his head down and shook it from side to
side. Finally he said, 'It was a mistake. But I had to do it. I just had to.' "
"I would have joined any group if it helped me get votes," he told another
friend.

The same question arose shortly before, in early 1958, while lunching
with a group of law clerks. After the usual small talk about cases, one clerk
suddenly asked, "Mr. Justice, why did you join the Klan?" "There was complete silence," another clerk recalled. "It was eerie. We just stared straight
ahead. Those few seconds seemed like hours. Then Black laughed and
drawled, 'Why, son, if you wanted to be elected to the Senate in Alabama
in the 1920s, you'd join the Klan too.' "[8]

* One public official who was not a member was George Huddleston, Birmingham's contrary
curmudgeonly congressman. Almost alone among Alabama politicians, he opposed it. "His
life was threatened by Klan leaders," his daughter wrote, "and steel workers and coal
miners—including Klansmen—volunteered to serve as his bodyguards at political rallies"
(Nancy Huddleston Packer, In My Father's House: Tales of an Uncomfortable Man [Santa
Barbara, Calif., 1988], 76).

CHAPTER 7

TO THE SENATE

A SMALL GROUP OF KLANSMEN, all lawyers who had their offices in the same Birmingham building, often gathered after work for some political talk—Esdale, Black, Crampton Harris, Judge Fort, who had resigned from the bench and joined Hugo in practice, sometimes others. Their idea was to promote Black's candidacy, but for what office? In the spring of 1925 he returned to Ashland on one of his regular visits. "I am going to run for governor but you cannot tell anybody," he told his sister Daisy. He bought a new car for the campaign. A few weeks later he came back and said, "I'm running for senator."

In May 1925 Senator Oscar W. Underwood announced that he had bought a Virginia mansion. He did not need his lieutenants to tell him that he was in political trouble at home because of his strong denunciation of the Klan at the Democratic National Convention the previous year: "It is either the Ku Klux Klan or the United States of America. Both cannot survive. Between the two, I choose my country." His removal from public life stood at the top of the Alabama Klan's priority list. "I am not very much disposed to get into another fight, and am rather inclined to retire," he wrote a friend. Rumors circulated that Underwood would move to his new home and not stand for reelection in 1926. Moreover, his health was not good; Black thought it dictated his retirement. Regardless of Underwood's plans, Hugo was running. To make it appear he was being drafted, a group of friends placed newspaper ads urging that Black enter the race.

Underwood's statement set off a flurry of political activity. Former governor Thomas E. Kilby, of Anniston, a reform-minded industrialist, who had indicated through an associate several months earlier that he would

101

oppose Underwood, made those plans definite on June 6, 1925. Later that day, a spokesman for Black stated:

> Friends of Hugo Black want it understood, definitely and unequivocally, that he will be a candidate for this position. In due course, Judge Black will announce his candidacy upon a progressive platform that will appeal to the forward-thinking citizenship of Alabama, and will be in line with the ideals exemplified by his private and public life.

Other candidates soon joined the fray. John H. Bankhead 2d, of Jasper, a lawyer who ran and represented coal mining companies, and whose father served in Congress from 1886 until his death in 1920, including two terms in the Senate, declared. Lycurgus Breckenridge Musgrove (thankfully called Breck), also of Jasper, a leader and "sugar boy" of the Anti-Saloon League and a wealthy coal operator, perhaps the richest man in the state, said that he would run. James J. Mayfield, of Tuscaloosa, a former state supreme court justice and strong Underwood supporter, also disclosed his intention. So did J. Sanford Mullins, an Alexander City lawyer, spellbinding orator and former secretary to Senator Tom Heflin, wet—the only avowed wet in the field—and a Klansman.[1]

Immediately, pundits made Bankhead and Kilby the leading contenders. Kilby, Bankhead, Musgrove, and Mayfield were all affluent men, but only Bankhead and Mayfield were truly representatives of the Big Mules*—the Birmingham-based utilities, iron, railroad and coal interests—and of the Black Belt planters (so named because of the color of the lush soil across the south center of Alabama and where Negroes constituted the main labor force), who viewed the state as their private fiefdom. Indeed, their strong support led Bankhead to run. Musgrove and Kilby, the two richest candidates, were independent characters not beholden to any group.

By the time Underwood stated on July 1, 1925, that he would retire at the end of his term, Black had already begun to shape his campaign. Jim Esdale admired him enormously as a lawyer and also simply liked him (much more

---

* Bibb Graves would soon so aptly label Alabama business and industrial leaders during his campaign for governor; he had seen many wagons loaded with hay pulled by little mules while the big mules, tied to the back, crunched away at the load. If elected, he vowed, he would "hitch the big mules to the wagon" and make them shoulder a heavier portion of the tax burden (John Temple Graves II, " 'I Promised 'em Pie,' " [publication unknown], 1/19/35, John Temple Graves papers, BPL).

than Hugo reciprocated). "Hugo and I were like brothers, saw one another every day in court," the Grand Dragon recalled. "He was like a monkey on a tree, jumped from one law firm to another, got a few clients, took them to the next firm, got a few clients there, moved on. Hugo was—what is the word I'm looking for?—an opportunist. In the '26 campaign Hugo didn't ask for Klan support. It was just understood. He was the only Klansman [who stayed] in the race." Gratefully, Black followed Esdale's advice. "Give me a letter of resignation and I'll keep it in my safe against the day when you'll need to say you're not a Klan member." In this way he would be protected from criticism from anti-Klan forces. So on the Grand Dragon's letterhead on July 9 he wrote to the Lee Klan's Kligrapp (secretary): "Dear Sir Klansman: Beg to tend you herewith my resignation as a member of the Ku Klux Klan, effective from this date on. Yours, I.T.S.U.B., Hugo L. Black." The initials stood for "In the Sacred, Unfailing Bond."

Hugo gradually wound down his law practice in order to campaign. By the fall he had stopped completely, except for a very occasional appeal that involved a large sum or an issue or client that would help him politically. One problem remained. As vice president of the Birmingham Bar Association, he was scheduled to become its next president, just as the campaign would be warming up. Many corporate lawyers thought he would be hurt politically if, against custom, he were denied the post; and a small clique determined to flout the tradition and elect one of their own. Black decided not to take any chances. He wanted his name removed from consideration, Crampton Harris told the group, because he would not have enough time to give to the post's duties. Harris and Hugo's old partner David J. Davis played major roles in the campaign. Davis became the official campaign manager, lending a non-Klan cover, and Harris, now Exalted Cyclops of Birmingham's Lee Klan and feeling "closer than ever" to Hugo, was finance chairman. "I went around and got money"—from Klaverns. Hugo went on the hustings.[2]

Within a few months Black bought another car. He used one for the northern part of the state, the other for the southern part—and eventually wore out both. After returning to Birmingham for short stays (sometimes not "long enough to catch my breath," he told Herman Beck), he rode the train back to where he left the car, worked the countryside and then drove to the center of the nearest town. His first stop, in secret, was the local Klavern to meet the faithful. Then he took the robes off to meet the natives. "Every place

I went," Bankhead soon discovered, "Hugo Black had been there before me. And he had them."

He had them mainly because of the Grand Dragon.* Esdale was campaign manager in everything but name. Shortly after Hugo announced his candidacy, they determined their strategy. Rarely did they deviate from it thereafter. They examined the list of Klaverns to determine the ones at which Black would speak. At first Esdale chauffeured Hugo around and introduced him; then another Klansman took over the driving. Hugo eventually talked at nearly all 148 Klaverns. Throughout, Esdale sent out information about the campaign in a weekly bulletin. Many years later he told an interviewer about "the psychology of that race. I arranged for Hugo to go to Klaverns all over the state, making talks on Catholicism. What kinds of talks? Well, just the history of the church and what we know about it. Not to talk on politics. Hugo could make the best anti-Catholic speech you ever heard." If anyone asked about the Klan, he advised Hugo to say, " 'That reminds me of a story,' and keep talking until you get out of there."†

This plan continued until nearly six months before the primary. By the end of February 1926, Hugo had toured fifty-seven of Alabama's sixty-seven counties. With the formal opening of the campaign the next month, the Klan receded into the background. Instead, Hugo started going to every courthouse in the state, with his cousin Harlan Martin driving him. Esdale in his continuing newsletters encouraged Klansmen to attend. At each appearance "there'd be 40 or 50 of our boys sprinkled around the crowd," he later explained, "and when the man next to one of them would ask who's that, well, he'd be told about Hugo by the Klansman. Because, you see, Hugo wasn't known about the state except for those liquor cases in Mobile. . . ."

Until the primary in August Black traveled continually. He visited each county at least twice, some as often as twenty-five times. He went into every town and village on the map. The vote of a citizen who lived down a branch head, he knew, counted as much as any other, and because the candidate

---

* An unaffiliated Klan unit was formed in the Woodlawn section of Birmingham. It was a radical and rival group whose head, as Black put it (int.), "said that I was soft on nigras and Jews. I said I'm soft only to the extent that they are citizens, told 'em I believe all citizens have rights, that rights are the glory of citizenship. It kept them quiet."

† In January 1926, the middle of the campaign, Black told a former Birmingham friend, "I am accused by *the opposition* of being a candidate of the Ku Klux Klan. This will further show that I am not amenable to Catholic influences" (to Mary C. Pittman, 1/18/26; originally emphasized).

made the effort to see him, that chap and his family might well never forget it. Some of these places no other statewide candidate had ever visited, and sometimes Hugo almost didn't get there himself. Even during the campaign, he liked to tell the story of trying to get to Andalusia, a small town in south Alabama. He asked a boy for directions. "Andalusia or Montgomery—which way is which?" The boy didn't know.

"You don't know much, do you?" Hugo said.

"No," the boy answered. "But I ain't lost."

Wherever, like a political trick-or-treater, he could find a voter, Black went. He spoke from pickup truck beds, even from a tree stump, or while people were fishing, in plain words they could understand. And he gradually lost his voice and fifteen pounds, and almost ruined his feet.

His routine varied little. He always went to the town square to meet people and walked up and down, shaking hands. Supporters often held signs reading HUGO BLACK, THE CANDIDATE OF THE MASSES or MEET HUGO BLACK AT DREW'S STORE. But when he went to the small north Alabama town of Vina, he went alone. He stepped out of his roadster dressed all in white— linen suit, necktie and shoes. "He just stood there by his car, completely at ease, as an audience of about a hundred circled around him," wrote Carl Elliott who later served in Congress. Hugo spoke of the promise of rural electrification to light homes and make fertilizer for the fields. "His speaking style was more conversational than any I'd heard, but he knew exactly what he was doing, working the crowd with care, every sentence with a strategy to it. When he was done, I felt I'd seen a smart man, a real smart man. Almost a scientist."

After such talks, Hugo made certain to see local editors and politicians. Next stop was the general store. Hugo introduced himself and struck up a conversation. The country people were polite but reserved, but soon realized he shared their background and idiom. He talked about education, working conditions, family concerns. As always, he made his points succinctly; thirty minutes was the longest he spoke in any setting. And he asked questions: Should there be federal aid to education? to the University of Alabama? What are the major problems of teachers? of steel workers? Are long hours taking a toll on family life? And he listened. The campaign, he said later, was "the best education I ever had." Voters felt he was taking them into his confidence. His desire to eradicate their hand-to-mouth way of life was evident. And he left a slew of campaign cards people could give to their friends.[3]

....

Alabama had never seen anything like it. Candidates were customarily members of the established ruling class, elitists who *stood* for office. How lucky,
their manner virtually exclaimed, that the populace had such obviously
superior persons to vote for. Once they were elected, their mere presence
would grace the legislative chambers, and the populace would be even further
blessed. The result was government by gentlemen. Hugo threatened this
entire tradition. Here was a commoner, a brash upstart, poaching upon the
exclusive preserves of the "best men." He was zestfully crisscrossing the state,
presenting himself as a young Lochinvar running against the "interests." He
was the tribune of the little people, with their individual, but similar, problems. For the first time in a generation in Alabama a candidate truly *cared*.
Once Black drove north of Birmingham ostensibly to meet a brickyard owner.
After they chatted amiably for a few minutes, Hugo spent over an hour with
the plant's fifty employees. In Talladega, Bankhead had called on only the
probate judge, admittedly the most important figure in each county under
Alabama's county-seat form of government. Black shook hands with every
person in the courthouse, including the probate judge. By dealing with voters
as equal partners in the democratic process, Black widened the gap between
himself and the other candidates in the public perception.

The matter of his age arose often. All the other candidates were at least
a decade older and tried to paint the forty-year-old Hugo as inexperienced
with the affairs of state. Thomas Kilby dismissed him as simply "too
youthful." In Huntsville one day Hugo came to the law office of John Sparkman, who was running his campaign in the county, sat down in the rocking
chair, put his hands to his face and said, "I hope you don't mind if I just
sit here and rock. I am tired and a little discouraged. Everybody is telling
me I am too young to be a senator." If someone in a crowd said that a senator
should be "an older man," Hugo answered, "I'm not that much younger
than they are"; or he'd mention some high official younger than he or that
also the Founding Fathers were young and that he would be able to "give
the best years of my life" to public service.

To Hugo the most effective campaigning was shaking hands and looking
the person in the eye. He was easily approachable and always friendly. But
his cloak of amiability kept his innermost thoughts and desires to himself.
An unspoken dignity permeated his bearing, holding off any undue familiarity. This separation worked to his advantage: although all could tell that
he was one of the "plain people," he was obviously different enough to be

respected as a leader. The "grass-roots mind" has "a disposition to find heroes—kind of a yearning after some person who while being common clay has risen to the overarching achievement usually possible only in private dreams."

Hugo had the true politician's gift of making each person feel he was his best friend. Many of these people he persuaded to hang his posters and distribute his cards—and for the rest of his life he remembered who did so. (Forty years later, a Birmingham reporter, Clarke Stallworth, came to see him. "Where are you from, son?" Thomaston in Marengo County was the answer. Hugo leaned back and thought for a moment. "Aren't there a lot of Stallworths from Monroe . . . and Conecuh?" he asked, referring to nearby counties. Thomaston, he mused, and then turned, unlocked a cabinet, took out a well-worn looseleaf notebook and thumbed through it. It was his 1926 campaign book, with a page for every Alabama town. On the page for Thomaston was the name of the reporter's great-aunt in her own handwriting. The number 75 was next to it, which meant that Hugo gave her that many campaign posters to put up for him.) He often slept at the home of one of these newly made friends; if not, he tried to stay at the best (sometimes the only) hotel in town, remaining in the lobby until the last person left, and to eat at the finest restaurant. In one small county seat he asked a man on the street to suggest the best place to dine. Told that "there's no good place around here," Hugo ate only soup that day.

He was folksy if without much humor, but he had his formal side. Perhaps to make himself look physically bigger, he usually campaigned in a white double-breasted suit, kept the jacket buttoned and wore a long-sleeve shirt even on broiling summer days. Women flocked to him even though he did not make any particular effort to attract them. He was by far the youngest candidate to run for major office in Alabama since they had been granted the right to vote in 1920, and they found his charm especially alluring.[4]

In late March, Black formally launched his campaign with a speech in Ashland. He had long ago learned that poetry—cadence, rhythm, imagery, sweep—makes for an effective speech. It reminds us that words have the power to make even a deadbeat's heart surge. Most of Clay County seemingly came to hear him. "The times cry aloud for men in public office who have not lost the common touch," Black said. Large institutions had forced the people to find "to their grief as did the anxious father of old that 'the voice is Jacob's voice, but the hands are the hands of Esau.' " He outlined his platform: he endorsed prohibition ("the day of whiskey is doomed"), veterans' benefits, better roads and the protection of cooperative farm marketing, and he urged the private development of Muscle Shoals to produce cheap fertilizer (not electric power). Immigration received much attention: "The shuffling feet of myriads of immigrants fill my heart with dread. The melting pot idea is dangerous to our national inheritance. . . . Immigration must be stopped for a while completely. Only desirable immigrants should ever again be admitted. We should welcome them, but our welcome should not be given until we have cleaned house and Americanized all the foreigners within our gates."

He denounced power trusts, concentrated wealth, higher tariffs, cliques in government and "organized money," which "perverts public sentiment." In appealing to the victims of these evils, he concentrated on the opponent he felt would be his strongest, John Bankhead: "I am not now, and have never been, a railroad, power company or corporation lawyer. I am not a millionaire. I am not a coal operator. My father was not a United States Senator. My father was a farmer." That was not the case, but Hugo was getting "all hepped up" (in Clay County parlance):

> Shall the cup of hope be dashed untasted from the lips of all who have not the boast of ancestral office holders, or sufficient money to hire writers to sing their praises? . . . I see a religion of love for mankind filling the hearts of our people. It is true now, and I believe it will be true hereafter, that the humblest son of the humblest citizen, born in the humblest surroundings, can lift his eyes in confidence toward the star of hope. So may it ever be! and when the mothers of Alabama look down into the sleepy little face of their baby, and sing to it the sweet lullaby of love, may that music always have within it the triumphant note and spirit of belief that her child can wear the spurs that his manhood and courage and bravery can win. Such is the spirit of life. Such is the spirit of America.

It was vintage populism delivered with a revivalist spirit. . . . The night before, the Klan held a rally at the Ashland courthouse.

Issues took a back seat to allegations and accusations. In the grand tradition of southern politics personalities became magnified. This put Bankhead and Kilby at a disadvantage. Bankhead disliked compaigning, and Kilby conveyed the impression that he was above it. Black tailored the dialogue by ignoring some topics and escalating others with inflated rhetoric. He talked about how politicians were allied with industrialists, an unmistakable reference to Bankhead, and stressed that Kilby exploited his pipe and sword shop employees by paying them unusually low wages. His rivals lost whatever initial advantage they may have had as the contest fell back to the localism, the "friends and neighbors" approach, which long typified Alabama politics. Candidates built their own coterie of supporters from the ground up. And Hugo had made 'friends' all over the state with his intensive personal canvassing.

He was hardly known in Anniston, Kilby's home town. Only a handful of people showed up at his first official appearance even though his campaign workers in this Klan stronghold had hung posters announcing his arrival. The *Anniston Star,* whose publisher managed Kilby's campaign, refused to print Black's statements; at first it did not even mention his name. Hugo felt that people in the area used the *Star* instead of the Bible as a guide for daily living. He had to do something to gain publicity. In the courthouse facing the square he said that the next time he was in town he would talk about the *Star.* To great cheers he continued, "If Kilby had given as much time to the state government when he was Governor as he does to his shops, then the state wouldn't be in such bad shape." Kilby showed up unexpectedly to declare that Black had "no right to come into my home town to solicit votes." Kilby, Hugo calmly replied, had "no right to say who could or could not speak in a public building in a public square in Anniston." Several *Star* reporters appeared. Hugo received the coverage he wanted.

The press had anointed Kilby and Bankhead, both dull and cautious, the leading candidates. Black's candidacy stood somewhat apart. Seasoned politicians minimized it, deeming him a political nonentity. Until the race heated up, the other candidates generally ignored Black. Kilby and Bankhead set up a series of joint debates. Sounding like two empty bags berating each other, they swapped political insults and harmed their chances. Black's supporters hired a mule-drawn dray to parade outside the hall during one debate, carrying signs that read on both sides: BANKHEAD SAYS KILBY WON'T DO. KILBY SAYS BANKHEAD WON'T DO. BOTH ARE RIGHT. VOTE FOR HUGO BLACK. In the next day's papers Hugo's tactic drowned whatever Kilby and Bankhead said.

Black then complained to the Democratic State Executive Committee that the other candidates were spending more than $1 million each, while he was staying within the $10,000 legal limit, and demanded a federal investigation. "The question," he told an agreeing audience, "is whether public office shall be sold to the highest bidder; whether the road to the

United States Senate shall be paved with gold." Striking at what he called Black's "poor country boy" pose, Bankhead said that Hugo owned property worth $250,000; Hugo offered to sell it for half that amount. He and Kilby both attacked Black, charging that he was a "damage suit lawyer" who demanded half the damages his poor and crippled clients won, and that he was "warming up" to "secret orders."

They made a mistake. The campaign was turning into a name-calling contest, and words were Black's game. He was a master counterpuncher and aimed at his opponents as if he were cross-examining a witness in court: he knew his answers in advance. He had as much right to respresent his clients— "the injured and the broken, the widows and the orphans of men killed beneath the wheels of trains or buried in the falls of rock down in the mines of coal and iron"—as Bankhead had to represent corporations. When Bank- head noted that the majority of the Birmingham Bar Association opposed Black in refusing him its presidency, Hugo said, "When could a bunch of lawyers agree on anything?" He admitted that he was a "jiner": "I joined the Masons and the Knights of Pythias the first meeting after I became twenty-one years of age, and I'm glad of it." These matters were effectively diffused.

With attention now focused on him, Black took the offensive. He had assailed Bankhead in his Ashland speech and never let up. The "imperialist" Bankhead family made one of his most inviting targets. "If John Bankhead got into the Senate, with William already in Congress, the Bankheads would take over the United States Government," he told one crowd. "Do you want that?" "No!" the throng roared. They sought "a line of royal succession," he told receptive workers in industrial Bessemer. Black's strategy was personal but not overly so—he never questioned Bankhead's honesty (indeed they had once opposed each other in court)—and it was part of the political game. "I had no bitterness in my heart," Bankhead said later, "because I had no justification for it. Hugo Black had treated me just as I tried to treat him, with fairness."

Hugo continued on the attack, directing his heaviest ammunition at Bankhead. During a coal strike, Bankhead served as a guard against miners, he charged. False, cried John's brother Will: John used a sawed-off shotgun to kill a labor man. Black denounced Bankhead as the tool of the vested interests, the "candidate of the Alabama Power Company." His opponents claimed that they were running because their friends insisted on it. Not Hugo anymore: "I am running, not because my friends are forcing me, but because I want the job."[5]

....

Hugo was distancing himself from his opponents and the press's antagonism was helping. To publishers and other community leaders his yearning to give "the common people," as one paper put it, "the sympathetic representation which they deserve" smacked of class warfare; and his vision of "the sunlight of justice to all and special favor to none" directly threatened the status quo from which the leaders profited. He opposed the Big Mules with a special fervor, and his meat-and-potatoes taste appealed to the proletariat. And he was the Klan's candidate: to a good many people that was reason enough to resist him.

Publishers, who mainly favored Bankhead, did everything they could to keep Black's groundswell of popular support from erupting. The *Tuscaloosa News*, located in a major center of Klan activity, carried a half-page cartoon picturing him as the Grand Dragon, saying he could not eat with Catholics and Jews. An *Anniston Star* sketch showed the followers of Kilby, Musgrove and Hugo: the Kilby supporters were the businessmen of Alabama, successful businessmen; the Musgrove partisans were the literary men of Alabama, with their collars turned back; while Black had just a few measly supporters, but he was wearing a double-breasted suit. (Hugo thought this was funny.) But the more the publishers tried to discredit Black, the more their readers rallied to him.

None of the other candidates had caught the voters' fancy. Bankhead persisted in repeating that he was his father's son; while this was undeniably true, the difference was painfully apparent. This cold turkey "wouldn't really mingle with the people," remembered one observer. (Mayfield, whose health was not good, pitched his campaign at his fellow lawyers.) Kilby was the biggest disappointment. For stretches, while probably engaged in his business enterprises, he did not campaign or even issue any statements (and when he did campaign and held a baby, it looked as if it might cry). The Big Mules likely pressured potential backers to support Bankhead.

Black's strength, meanwhile, kept growing. "Had the primary been held the week I announced for the Senate," he later wrote, "I think it probable that I would have been the fourth man in the race. This does not mean that I did not expect to win. I thought that by an aggressive campaign I could win. . . . Several months before the date of the election I was confident that the people would give me the nomination." His opponents realized this, and their statements quoted in one of his ads implied it, but only Bankhead admitted it. "Keep your head up and claim the earth till this is over," he said to his family, "but I want to tell you that Hugo Black will be the next United States Senator from Alabama. I just want to prepare you now for what I think is coming."[6]

All the candidates angled for the church vote. Black, unlike the others, spoke to the people in church and many men's classes afterward. "He held that crowd spellbound," Charles Harrison recalled of one such talk to a Baptist congregation in Birmingham about "the dramatic life of Moses— dramatic in birth, dramatic in life and dramatic in death." Nearly all of his speeches throughout the entire campaign included a biblical quotation. He also attended the Baptist and Methodist state conventions, addressing the Baptists on religious liberty as guaranteed by the First Amendment; the Baptist state secretary backed him. The Reverend L. D. Patterson, the brother of Hugo's beloved first-grade teacher, Miss Lizzie, and now the pastor of a large Birmingham church, wrote a letter that was reprinted along with the secretary's remarks as part of Black's basic flyer. Then it was given wide circulation as a large advertisement with Hugo's picture in the *Alabama Christian Advocate*, a Methodist publication. "He is the kind of prohibitionist to go to the United States Senate now when such an onslaught is being made to nullify the Eighteenth Amendment," Patterson wrote. "Christian People of Alabama, do not be misled! Hugo Black is the man WE want in the United States Senate." Black long felt that article "undoubtedly got many votes for me."

So openly did he use the churches that two years later the *Mobile Post*, admittedly hostile to him since the rum trials, in an editorial entitled "The White Sepulchre of Hypocrisy" ridiculed him as "playing with the bones of dead and stinking hypocricies": "He got himself an old Ford and stumped the evangelic churches throughout the state. In justice to Black it should be said that if the ritualistic churches, the Catholics, Jews and Episcopalians, had been on top in Alabama, and if the dignity of their worship did not preclude politics in the pulpit, Black would have been found stumping through those churches too. He is just that sort of a bright young fella."[7]

Shortly after Black gave his "star of hope" speech in Ashland, J. Sanford Mullins withdrew from the race, unable to gain the support of Esdale and other Klan leaders. Breck Musgrove soon became an official candidate. This paladin of prohibition was friendly to labor and threatened to take votes from Black. And the national Klan officially supported him. Imperial Wizard Hiram Evans in Atlanta, wishing to express gratitude for the close primary battle Musgrove lost to Underwood six years earlier, sent an emissary to threaten the Alabama Realm that it must switch from Black to Musgrove or risk losing its charter. (In 1937 Evans said of the Black campaign: "We were jes' in favor of him, that's all." But circumstances were different by that time.) Esdale did not budge, refusing to transmit the orders to the various Provinces and Klaverns, and the national office backed down.

"Look out, money. You're gonna be spent!" warned the *Montgomery Advertiser* upon Musgrove's entrance. "Money may run like water and many have heard in this campaign of the tinkle of golden streams," Black said in Ashland, "but I have an abiding faith that the thought and vote of Alabama will run true to the highest ideals." His faith was severely tested. Several weeks before the election, recalled Grand Dragon Esdale,

> Breck Musgrove came to see me in my office in the First National Bank Building about 5:30 one day late and said he wanted that Senate seat. And I said the Klan votes were already arranged for Hugo, and he pushed a piece of paper across the table to me and it was a check for $125,000 and said, "well, these things can be changed, just by a letter from you." And I pushed it back across the table to him and said, "Breck, every man has his price. Even Jesus Christ had his price, and he died on the cross." Then Musgrove pulled one on me, he got to some of my boys and he spread around the story that I had asked him for $125,000 to change the Klan vote, when it was him who pushed the check.

An agent representing Musgrove also offered Hugo the same amount in cash as the price for withdrawal. Hugo conferred with advisers and rejected it.

Musgrove's entrance changed Black's strategy. In an effort to hold his Klan support and to secure his base in the working class, especially in Jefferson County, he attacked New York's wet, Catholic governor, Alfred E. Smith. He understood newly arrived workers' problems, Hugo said, for he also came from the country. He also reemphasized prohibition. Only half jokingly, he intimated that his opponents sought to make it effective by drinking up all the liquor themselves. While Musgrove and Black engaged in angry exchanges over who had the support of the Women's Christian Temperance Union, Hugo also stressed the danger of liquor: "Poverty and ruin follow in its wake. Crime walks with it hand in hand. . . ." "There is one little saloon every man can close," he was fond of saying, "and that is the one that is under his nose."[8]

Infighting between the national and state Klans made Alabama Klansmen work harder for Black. "Esdale would have ruined himself trying to
switch votes, " said Hugh Locke, Hugo's old friend. "He would have failed
because the Klan loved Hugo." The Klan circulated sample ballots, headed
"Official document, Vol. 4, No. 8. Issued from the office of the Grand
Dragon of Alabama," and marked with Black's name and that of Bibb Graves,
the Democratic candidate for governor and also a Klansman. This "little
brown hickory nut of a man," a wad of tobacco in his cheek belying his
aristocratic background, easily won people's affection. Downplaying his Yale
law degree and rarely mentioning that he had once saved a Negro from the
electric chair, he had been Exalted Cyclops of his Montgomery Klavern, a
paid lecturer for the Klan, a member of the legislature, and Democratic state
chairman. His ready smile and his vibrant, booming voice (his favorite
expression was "Keep on keeping on") gained him a network of loyal friends
all over the state. Esdale requested that the sample ballots be posted at every
Klavern and mentioned at every meeting. Keeping to their secrecy vows,
ranking Klan officers branded the sheets false. But at Klaverns and on the
campaign trail around the state, Graves too urged Black's election.

Black ended the campaign on a high note. His elevated newspaper
pitches now aimed to soothe. "We have fought a clean fight, and believe
victory is ours." "Hugo Black is the Winner. The moral forces of Alabama
are behind him," ran another notice. Bankhead and Kilby disagreed. "BANK-
HEAD OR BLACK?" Bankhead's daily full-page ad asked. "KILBY'S STRENGTH
MAKES BANKHEAD SEE BLACK," Kilby responded. Hugo concurred: "HUGO
BLACK IS THE WINNER. ALL AGREE HE HAS TO BE BEATEN." He had cause for
confidence. The Klan was his source of strength. Without it he would have
been a very minor candidate indeed, with negligible publicity. But the Klan
was not publicly discussed. "Whenever it was mentioned, Hugo only
laughed," Harlan Martin recalled. "But whenever he was in a large crowd,
it was obvious from his conversation that he was a Klansman. 'I know how
to talk to them,' he said. 'I know how to give them their handshake.' " His
opponents did not, and feared to antagonize the Klan in any way. "No
politician dared cuss 'em," David J. Davis said later. Bankhead publicly
called it a patriotic organization engaged in good works. Kilby did not talk
about it, perhaps because in winning the governorship in 1918 he had
condemned Catholics and Jews. Klan activity on Black's behalf was subtle.
But, as a young Kilby worker noted, an observer "could smell it."

"Backed by no political machine, aided by no paid workers," read Black's
advertisements, "my election will prove that the people of Alabama vote

their honest convictions." Klansmen were volunteers, after all. So were the hundreds of Sunday school class members who worked for their "young dynamo." He financed his campaign completely from his own pocket. The year before, he received a $10,000 fee for handling the divorce case of a prominent Birmingham woman, but did not spend it all on the primary as he had planned. His total cost, he reported, was $6,510, including a $600 depreciation allowance on his two cars.[9] The Klan supplied the rest in money and services.

Black won the primary with surprising ease. The final tally was: Black, 84,877; Bankhead, 63,865; Mayfield, 50,994; Kilby, 39,710; and Musgrove, 33,052. Nearly fifty years later, his voice still filled with pride, Crampton Harris said, "We got the royalists smacked down by a country man."

Receiving 30 percent of the first choice votes and enough second choice ones enabled Black to prevent a runoff under Alabama's complex election system. He carried forty-two of the sixty-seven counties, running best in Jefferson County and in the countryside, the areas where the Klan was strongest. His victory, the *Birmingham News* observed, was "a tremendous tribute to the effectiveness of his organization." Black "is a campaigner of great energy and shrewdness," the *Montgomery Advertiser* noted; "but above all he is the darling of the Ku Klux Klan." The Klan paid the $1.50 poll tax in many counties for white men who could not afford it and, through its control of the voting machinery, enfranchised many citizens who would not otherwise, under Alabama's restrictive and complex suffrage require-ments, have been be allowed to exercise this basic democratic right. The total number of votes cast was considerably larger than in any other Senate election in Alabama for nearly the next twenty years. "I would have had a much easier time had there been no poll tax law," Black later said.

The final tally showed that Black's total number of votes closely par-alleled the total Klan membership in the state. It was the same with Graves who won the four-man gubernatorial primary in a contest that was similar to Black's. Klansmen had been stimulated to vote. In Jefferson County an estimated 95 percent did. The county's entire legislative delegation members were Klansmen (with the possible exception of corporate lawyer James Simp-son who, Esdale claimed, had joined). Sixty-five of the sixty-seven county sheriffs statewide were on the hooded order's rolls. Esdale "openly boasted that knights of the fiery cross had gone into the fight and 'finished it.' " Every constitutional officer in the state was a Klansman. The Klan had swept

Alabama. It was now "the most completely Klan-controlled state in the union."

The month after the primary, the Klan held its annual Klorero (convention of the Realm) in Birmingham. It was a victory celebration. Thousands of masked and hooded men paraded through the streets before numerous Klan dignitaries. Black and Graves were each awarded a "grand passport" which, explained the Grand Klaliff (Esdale's assistant), was "good as long as you are good." "The day you decide to get out of the Klan," Esdale told them, "you mail these back to me." The passport read in part: "The bearer Kl. Senator Hugo L. Black is a citizen of the invisible empire and . . . he may travel unmolested throughout our beneficent domain and grant and receive the fervent fellowship of Klansmen." Accepting the gold card, Black said:

> I know that without the support of the members of this organization I would not have been called, even by my enemies, "the junior Senator from Alabama." I realize that I was elected by men who believe in the principles that I have sought to advocate and which are the principles of this organization. . . . I desire to impress upon you as representatives of the real Anglo-Saxon sentiment that must and will control the destinies of the Stars and Stripes, that I want your counsel. . . . My friends, I thank you. I thank the Grand Dragon. He has stood by me like a pillar of strength. . . . The great thing I like about this organization is not the burning of crosses, it is not attempting to regulate anybody—I don't know, some may do that—but, my friends, I see a bigger vision. I see a vision honored by the nations of the world. . . .

He was warming up.

> With my love, with my faith, with my trust, with my undying prayer that this great organization will carry on sacredly, true to the real principles of American manhood and womanhood, revering virtue of the mother of the race, loving the pride of Anglo-Saxon spirit—and I love it—true to the heaven-born principles of liberty which were written in the Constitution of this country, and in the great historical documents, straight from the heart of Anglo-Saxon patriots, with my love and my faith, and my hope and my trust, I thank you from the bottom of a heart that is yours.

Grand Dragon Esdale rarely gave interviews, preferring to work behind the scenes as kingmaker and manipulator. Partisanship and members' seeking public office, he somehow maintained, tainted the Klan's moral and patriotic mission. But shortly before the November election, which was the usual formality, he told a reporter, "I never meddle in politics."[10]

*   *   *

After the election, Black said he planned to close his law practice entirely. But he had time on his hands and practicing law was what he did for a living. That he continued to practice gave him pause in later years. To one lawyer, who asked him to testify about a case he had filed in September 1926 and sent him copies of the papers with his name on them, he wrote, "I ceased the trial of cases when I was elected to the Senate." He gave his family the idea that a senator should give up practicing because "it stunk of using pull up. I took down my shingle," he said—as if no prospective client knew where to contact the senator-elect.

The firm was now Black and Fort. Hugo had tolerated Crampton Harris's drinking and laziness because of his analytical brilliance and his friendship with Esdale. But now that he was in office he could not accept Harris's gambling and association with gambling professionals. Too many people knew, and if the stakes were sometimes high for Harris, they were much higher for Black. He would give all these as reasons why they separated: when it came to friends, he would give all sorts of excuses, and rarely the right reason. Fort agreed that Hugo would receive two thirds of their receipts and he one third, as Harris had. (They also had three associates on salary.) Their office remained the same, and so did the types of cases—largely personal injury and negligence (including medical malpractice)—as well as appellate courts' continuing to overturn Hugo's jury verdicts.

In the last case, a malicious prosecution action, one of the opposing lawyers, Frank Bainbridge, later remarked that he was "so angry" that he "was ready to arrest Black for being too good, too tough. He was strong competition. That's why we worked so hard to elect him." They might even want to reelect him, one courthouse wag suggested. "Court rooms are so much more comfortable without him on the other side of the case." He cost corporations so much money that their lawyers were glad to be rid of him, to get him out of Alabama. In 1926 Black made $28,753, almost all of it after the August primary. He earned $25,360 from his part-time practice in 1927; and, added to his $8,225 Senate salary and other investments, he was able to deposit $46,642.02 in the bank that year.[11]

....

For the first time in several years he had a relatively normal family life. With part of his ambition assuaged, Hugo relaxed some. He stayed home more than ever with Josephine and their two boys. The housekeeper, Mary Marble, spent the days with the boys—she, not Josephine, brought them up—and he put them to sleep at night. There was almost another child. During the campaign, Josephine was pregnant and Hugo, who had returned to Birmingham for a short time, took her to the hospital. He walked her down the corridor—and left her with the nurses. Later she said, "He must have been ashamed to have been there"; he admitted it. Josephine, who saw Hugo infrequently throughout the pregnancy and during the whole thirteen-month campaign period, suffered a miscarriage. By then he had already resumed glad-handing on the hustings.

He assembled a staff for his Senate office. His young Birmingham stenographer, Esther Wood, went to Washington; for months she was the only one there and had little to do. Then, as his secretary (now called administrative assistant), he hired Hugh Grant, a Birmingham newspaperman. Wood handled routine office matters, and there was also one typist. That was all the help a United States senator was thought to require in the mid-1920s. Mostly, Hugo stayed in Birmingham. To prepare for his new job he began an extensive reading program. He started reading more books on economics: the first one was Adam Smith's *The Wealth of Nations*. Many other books on political economy followed.[12]

*　　*　　*

The rituals of rural violence and race relations had long been familiar to Black. He knew Will Smelley, a well-liked white farmer who was killed in Talladega County near the Clay County line, only by reputation. On December 7, 1924, Smelley took a trip to Clay County with his brother-in-law William Farmer, his son-in-law Leland Haynes and Luke Ware, a Negro who was a tenant farmer on Haynes's land. The purpose of the trip was never truly explained, but that all four were drinking heavily was unquestioned. Police officers arrived to find Smelley dead, his body slumped over the steering wheel. Although evidence was at best spotty—Farmer and Haynes differed in their accounts—Ware was arrested the next day and charged with the crime.

Some leading Talladega businessmen believed Ware had been framed and they raised money for his defense. A respected Anniston law firm was hired to represent him. In a short trial Ware was found guilty of manslaughter. The Alabama Court of Appeals reversed the conviction. Ware would have another chance to prove the widely shared suspicion that he had been framed. To do so, his word would have to prevail over that of the two whites who opposed him. And a year later, in May 1927, another jury, after deliberating only two hours, returned a verdict of not guilty. Twelve white men had acquitted a Negro. In the Deep South of the 1920s that was the rarest of courtroom events.

A grateful and triumphant Luke Ware walked out the door of the court-house with his wife, shaking hands and accepting congratulations from about thirty people, all Negro. Word of his innocence spread quickly in this small town. George (Chum) Smelley, the affable and popular brother of Will Smelley and a farmer in Sylacauga, had asked a friend to loan him a holster in which to put the gun he was carrying. "I'm going to shoot Ware," he said. He stayed in the corner of the square by the courthouse until Ware came outside, then moved resolutely across the lawn, heading for the knot of people clustered around Ware. Several shots were fired into Ware's back and the people began frantically to run for cover. The portal of the courthouse was quickly deserted except for Luke Ware. He lay on the steps, conscious but mortally wounded, as Chum Smelley stepped over him and entered the courthouse to surrender to the sheriff.

Smelley's trial for first-degree murder opened on November 14, 1927. His counsel had let it be known that he planned to plead insanity as a defense. Soon, however, after a recess, Hugo Black suddenly entered the courtroom and took a seat between Smelley and his lawyer. In mid-afternoon, after less than three hours and having presented four witnesses who con-tributed little, the prosecution rested its case. The defense had by now dropped the insanity plea and turned instead to a plea of self-defense. This claim rested on two types of evidence. One was a penciled letter, written in a semi-literate hand by a Negro cellmate of Ware's, that Smelley alleged he had received several days before Ware's second trial. The other was Smelley's own claim, opposed by the testimony of Negro witnesses and supported only by a single white man, that Ware had lunged at him as if to attack and that, in order to protect himself, he had shot Ware from a distance of four to five feet. Ware was facing him at the time, Smelley said. Black put Smelley on the stand and went over the letter. He then recounted his actions after Ware was acquitted. On the lawn in front of the courthouse he heard someone call his name. "I turned around and the negroes around Luke began to run and Ware came towards me like he was going to grab me.

When he did I pulled my gun and shot him." "How is it then," prosecutor James Sanford asked, "that he was shot in the back?"

The key question was out, but its obvious implication was not pressed. Black and Sanford then clashed; this was a tactic Hugo often raised at crucial points during trial in an attempt to throw opposing counsel off track. The judge overruled several motions of his. Both the judge and the prosecutor called him Senator throughout. "He never raised his voice," recalled one of the prosecution witnesses, Flory Tucker. "He never got hostile with anyone. He was a diplomat. He knew how to work people to get what he wanted." Black soon introduced fifteen character witnesses who testified as to Smelley's character and reputation; and another ten testified that Ware was "violent, dangerous, turbulent, and bloodthirsty." The state began its rebuttal the next day. George Cantrell, the assistant custodian of the courthouse, said that Ware was shaking hands with him, and had his back toward Smelley, when the shooting took place. He denied categorically that Ware had made any threatening move toward Smelley. But Cantrell was a Negro. To discredit his testimony, the defense had only to introduce the word of a white man, who claimed that Cantrell was on the second floor of the courthouse at the time of the shooting and that they ran down the stairs to the scene together.

Black made his closing argument, reading from Rousseau's *Social Contract* and Sir Henry Maine's *Ancient Law*. These books were not the usual fare for Talladega juries at the time. Only recently Black had consulted Maine's classic for an address on the majesty of the law at a Civitan Club's convention. When the father had died, Maine wrote, it was the duty of the oldest son to avenge the killing of other members of the family. As Hugo pleaded with the jury not to send Smelley to jail, a tear rolled down his cheek.

In his charge to the jury the judge, Walter B. Merrill (whose brother Hugh had defended Ware at his second trial), came close to ordering an acquittal. The jury retired to deliberate. Twenty minutes later, they returned with a verdict of not guilty. Crowds around the courthouse broke into scattered murmurs of approval. Many moved forward to congratulate Smelley, now a free man. Negroes were few and far between.

....

Even though Black believed that Smelley killed Ware, he defended him. It was "inexcusable," he said, but Chum was "my friend." Smelley grew up in Talladaga County near the Clay County line, and when Hugo tagged along with his father to Talladega for supplies, they would sometimes stop at the Smelley farm and be friendly in the way of country people. They met again in the Klan. Then, because of their long acquaintance, Smelley drove Black around the state during the first part of the Senate campaign. "They really became pretty good buddies going all over," recalled Smelley's son-in-law H. L. Dozier.

It is tempting, but wrong, to say that Black defended Smelley because of pressure from the Klan or fealty to the hooded order. "An almost blind personal loyalty to friends" was one of Hugo's strongest traits. In 1915 he was asked to support his friend and sponsor Judge A. O. Lane for Birmingham city commissioner. He would have done so anyway but replied: "When the time comes when I must repudiate friendship such as existed between Judge Lane and myself and prove myself unworthy of gratitude, I am willing to resign every claim I have upon the friendship of any city or any community. So long as I believe my friend to be honest, I am for him." In Chum Smelley's case the only issue to Black was friendship. After the verdict Smelley said: "Thank God, Hugo. You got me off." Hugo replied: "Don't thank Him. Thank me. God knows you're guilty."[13]

Three days later Hugo and Josephine Black took the train to Washington.

II

THE SENATE YEARS

CHAPTER 8

THE FRESHMAN

T HE NEW CONGRESS was formed in March 1927 but did not meet until December. On December 5, accompanied by Alabama's senior senator, J. Thomas Heflin, Black strode the aisle of the United States Senate and took the oath administered by Vice President Charles G. Dawes as a member of the Seventieth Congress. Washington was a dowdy, drowsy and provincial town then. Parking spots were easier to find than political excitement. President Calvin Coolidge believed in talking in public only slightly more than he did in government; he took little part in either. Privately, he was a pretty garrulous fellow. Black liked him. "I thought he had a wonderful sense of humor, and he was honest," Hugo said many years later. He "just sat up there and let the country run, in the main. . . . I'm not sure that much needed to be done at the time."

"I expect to occupy an inconspicuous place in the Senate for some time," Black had said after his election. "A bundle of activity, physically and mentally" was all one reporter could write of him. He was assigned to minor committees—claims, interstate commerce and military affairs. "He didn't do much at first," recalled his colleague Burton Wheeler. "He hardly took part in anything. He just sat at his desk quietly, greeting everyone and looking around," observing his colleagues and the Senate's practices. The first bill he introduced was a private claim to aid an Alabama veteran. Passed without opposition, as such courtesy measures to individual senators traditionally are, it aimed at helping one constituent out of some legal difficulties. This Mobile man was a former client of Black's.

With few demands on his time, Black spent a great deal of time in the Senate library. "I have done more reading since I came to Washington than

ever before," he said the month after he was sworn in. Guided partly by a
Will Durant article entitled "One Hundred Best Books," which asserted
that if one read these books, he would become "better educated than any
new-fledged Doctor of Philosophy in the land," Black systematically went
about filling the large gaps in his education. "I'm trying to use what the
Greeks and Romans did," he told a friend. He was on familiar terms with
Herodotus, Thucydides, Plutarch, Seneca, Cicero, and, of course, Aristotle
and Plato. Hearing one of Hugo's infrequent speeches, studded with references to such worthies, a press gallery wag said he sounded like a talking
encyclopedia with a southern accent.[1]

Black's alleged Klan affiliation was frequently mentioned—in private many
liberals hissingly denounced him as "that Kluxer"—but only conservatives
tried to turn it against him. Senator William C. Bruce was a furiously wet
Maryland Democrat, imperious and Catholic, and bitingly critical of the
Deep South. For several months he hurled charges of hypocrisy at every
southern senator who espoused prohibition. He disparaged Black as "so ill
informed" and Alabama as the "Ku-Klux" state of rampant lawlessness. Hugo
couldn't take it anymore. He rose to defend "the honor of Dixie," a reporter
wrote, "with the same tense earnestness that characterizes him when he has
a point to make." The South, Black said, was "a land composed of noble
and brave and patriotic and loyal law-abiding citizens."

> I have no apology to make for being from the "Confederate States," as my
> colleague terms them. . . . There repose the ashes of my ancestors. When
> my time shall come to join the throng across the unknown shore I hope
> that I, too, shall there lie down to rest peacefully under the calm sunshine
> of Dixie. Yet these Southern States are mentioned from day to day as though
> it is a crime or a disgrace for a man to be a citizen of the South. . . .
>   Let the Senator from Maryland hurl his darts and charges thick and
> fast. Let him drop his loaded shrapnel into their midst, and still, when the
> din of the explosion is ended, the people of the South will be there, back
> in their homes on the hillsides and in the valleys, responding to the same
> old Anglo-Saxon principle of loyalty to law and decency and government
> which seems to entitle them to be particular objects of the animadversions
> of the Senator from Maryland.

The next day, Bruce continued his attack, adding, "I have heard it said
that the junior Senator from Alabama owes his seat in the Senate to the
Ku-Klux vote." Black could simply not ignore this: "That statement, like

the others [Bruce] made, is absolutely untrue," he said. "I got all the Ku-Klux votes I could get—" "Yes," interjected Bruce expectantly. "And all the Catholic votes I could get," Black continued, "and all the Jew votes I could get, and all the Baptist votes I could get, and all the others, and I have no apology, and I am here representing them." When Bruce said he "understood" that Black was "ready to resort to any expedient to get them," Hugo replied that he was "sorry"; "[I] can not state here exactly what I think about that statement, and so I suppose the best thing to do is to let it go." Bruce: "I think so. I think you show to better advantage when you keep your seat than when you rise to your feet."

Black's counterattack won plaudits, especially from fellow southerners: even those who did not agree with him had to acknowledge its effectiveness. But this was not something that a newly elected senator normally did. Freshmen were expected to remain silent until the next class arrived two years later and perform tasks such as presiding over floor debates in order to relieve their wizened seniors whose wisdom, as often dispensed in gaudy oratory, they could then imbibe all the easier.* Although he did not talk about it much, Hugo became part of the "club" that ran the Senate early in his career. Some of this was simply recognition of his ability, some his sheer agreeableness, and some his very much appreciated collegiality (such as not hoarding the spotlight and readily yielding to a colleague on the floor). He was respectful and plain friendly when he befriended a senator (or anyone else), and appeared so genuine that the person being courted wasn't even aware of it. Long a master at winning the trust of older men, he gained the confidence and admiration of Joe Robinson, the Democratic leader. The result was that Hugo was simply a younger peer, respectful of tradition and others' feelings but outspoken on issues. "As always, he maintained a certain reserve and independence; yet from the start he got good committee assignments, and many treated him with a warmth and respect usually reserved for the senior senators."[2]

He was considered a "southern liberal" in the populist tradition. "I did not know that there was any longer any line which separated the so-called

---

* After finishing a floor speech years later, one freshman found himself sitting next to Walter George of Georgia, then the dean of the Senate, who had entered four years before Black. He tried to make polite conversation and asked George what changes had taken place in the Senate during his service. "Freshmen didn't use [sic] to talk so much," George said (Donald R. Matthews, U.S. Senators and Their World [N.Y., 1960], 94).

Confederate States from the others," Black told his colleagues. "I thought that line had been washed away by the blood of patriots" in the Spanish-American War and World War One. He quickly established himself as an expert lancer of Republican policies—except when an issue hit close to home. Then he wrapped himself in the warm blanket of political survival, that bloody old shirt southerners had comfortably worn for so long. He twice voted with thirteen other southerners in a losing effort to cut off federal aid to Howard University, and he joined nine members in a losing effort to prevent the navy from flying a pennant bearing the cross of Saint George above the American flag during church services aboard ship. "Am I to understand," he asked Bruce during their debate over the Klan, "that the Senator wants the negroes to vote down there [in Alabama]? Is that what he is talking for? . . . The Senator seems gradually to be going over that way."

The specter of Anglo-Saxon racism lurked not far in the background when Black twice proposed that all immigration be suspended for five years. "The confusion of alien tongues clamoring among themselves as to their rights in our country" convinced him of this, he said in a May 1929 radio speech. "There is no place for hyphenated citizenship in this country. . . . A man is either a German or he is an American. There is honor in being either, but no man can serve two masters or two countries. We must and will determine the character of those who enter our country upon a basis of rapid and successful assimilation with our present citizenship. We have closed our doors to certain Asiatic people because of this consideration. The time is coming when we must defend this prohibition in defense of racial purity and national traditions."*

At other times racial issues were more immediate. "While I was not born at the time the Republican Party gave the negro the upper-hand in Alabama politics," Black wrote during the 1928 campaign, "I believe I am reasonably familiar with that period. . . . I expect to do my very best to see that such a control is not possible in the future, and I believe that my method at the present time will make me more useful in preventing a repetition of that catastrophe." The next year, at about the same time he told a cousin that "Negroes are human beings and need to be given the same individual

---

* "Racially speaking, there is certainly no reason why Canadians should be kept out of this country . . . from the standpoint of race amalgamation and national absorption," he told the Senate. "I think the United States has the right to select the race and nationality in the type of immigrants who come into this country" (CR 4/21/30, 7327, 7328).

rights everyone else enjoys," he informed a constituent that a marriage of a Negro and a white woman in New York was

> indeed deplorable. New York State should have a law prohibiting this sort of thing. Our Southern states have such laws, and with the large migration of negroes into the Northern and Eastern states, I would not be surprised if similar laws were passed in these states. Until very recent years they have not had much of a negro problem, but with the increasing migration of the race into these states, the intelligent Northern and Eastern people will, in all probability, come to realize the merit in our Southern legislation along this line.

On issues removed from local concerns, his thoroughgoing Jeffersonian liberalism was apparent. He invoked the sage of Monticello several times during debates and castigated Jefferson's archenemy, Alexander Hamilton, when the Senate considered a bill to reapportion Congress every ten years. Under it, the president would submit to Congress alternative sets of computations upon which the new seats would be based. Since he had not given much thought to constitutional questions, Black studied the records of the Constitutional Convention to determine the framers' intent for himself. Reapportionment, he concluded, was a matter that belonged exclusively to the legislative branch. He unsuccessfully led the fight against the bill that he believed would work against small and rural states. He remained an unremitting opponent: "any man who will study the Constitution will find that apportionment is not necessary, was never intended to be mandatory, and the framers of that document expressly declined to make it mandatory."[3]

Hugo spent the month of June 1929 recuperating from an operation to remove part of the goiter resulting from his hyperthyroid condition. The operation was unexpected (even though sometimes driving to Alabama he had to stop and eat a steak). He had gone for a checkup and the doctor had found an overactive thyroid, which meant that he always had to be doing something. "Don't touch that," Hugo said. "If it weren't for that, I'd still be plowing in Clay County." The operation was unsuccessful: too much goiter was removed and Hugo did not take the prescribed medication (desiccated sheep's thyroid) for fear it would slow him down. Never again would he go through anything like that, Hugo said. If the operation did affect his awesome energy level, however, no one noticed. (His earlier vigor had to be almost fright-

ening.) But his secretary, Esther Wood, who had already worked for him for
ten years, thought that his disposition was never quite the same afterward.
The difference was almost indiscernible, but she felt that he was just that
much more eager and in a rush to do things.

In October 1929 the Senate debated a proposed Customs Bureau regulation
aimed at controlling the importation of allegedly obscene literature as part
of the Smoot-Hawley Tariff Act. Senator Reed Smoot of Utah, an elder in
the Mormon church, piled on his desk a number of such allegedly immoral
books and invited senators to inspect them. Considerable merriment followed
as some of the dignified solons, well into middle age, showed unexpected
interest in the exhibits. Black did not look at them. He rose to address his
colleagues. Although he had not pondered freedom of speech, he did not
consult original sources. He drew instead upon his spacious reading and his
innate persuasions. "I am so firmly convinced," he said, "that this is one of
the most sacred privileges of a democracy that I can not vote for any measure
or any legislation which tends in the slightest degree to restrict its inestimable
privilege." In the twilight zone of uncertainty, he reminded Senator Smoot,
some censors might regard the tenets of Mormonism as poison. Black mentioned the burning of the library in ancient Alexandria ("because there were
some who arrogated unto themselves the high and mighty power of determining the standards of right, not only for those of the day, but for all
posterity"), the persecution of Galileo for asserting a new theory, the abuses
heaped upon John Wycliffe for translating the Bible into English and the
crucifixion of Christ for his opinions.

> All through the ages there has been this conflict between those who believe
> in freedom of human thought and those who believe in restricting and
> shackling the human intellect. [These] principles . . . grow necessarily in
> a democracy if human liberty is to be preserved. There are some funda-
> mentals which must not be overlooked or overstepped. One of them is
> freedom of speech. Going in hand with it is freedom of religion and freedom
> of assembly. We cannot separate these. . . . I am not afraid of any word
> or any expression if it comes into conflict with the fundamental necessity
> of democracy. . . . Those who fear . . . that, with education spreading all
> over this land, we shall by admitting a few small books at the port of entry
> so corrupt those minds that we shall destroy American civilization . . . ,
> have the same attitude as those who feared the corruption of the youth of
> Greece by Socrates.

So far as I am concerned, I prefer to follow the philosophy of Thomas Jefferson, who borrowed largely from the great English writer, John Locke. Only two days ago I read a treatise on government by John Locke which . . . would be barred at the port of entry because John Locke maintained, as did other great philosophers, the right of the people to use force, if necessary, to overturn a government of corruption or of tyranny. . . . I stand today and I will stand in the future, against any legislation of any kind that would interfere with the sacred right of the American citizen to think as he sees fit and to be persuaded in no way except by logic and reason.[4]

The Senate, however, passed the regulation, giving strong impetus to a huge amount of continuing litigation trying to answer the unanswerable question of what is "obscene."

•   •   •

Compromise, not logic and reason, dictated the outcome of the controversy over the Muscle Shoals dam on the Tennessee River in northern Alabama. During World War One, the federal government had built a hydroelectric and nitrogen develement plant there, and progressives, led by Nebraska senator George W. Norris, had fought for years for its government operation to provide electric power to the area. Such a program had been part of Black's campaign platform, and it became his main interest early in his Senate term. At first he believed that the project should be leased to private companies, with the power to be used for the manufacture of fertilizer for soil rehabilitation. As he and Norris reconciled their differences, their working partnership turned into close friendship.

Norris was a plain-spoken visionary, a moralist with a stern sense of duty, who clung to principle while yielding on minor points to help make that principle turn into reality. His somber attire and melancholy bearing contrasted with his progressive ideals. He spoke in a conversational tone, using everyday language, occasionally making emotional appeals. Once he wept while advocating something on the Senate floor. "He acquired great influence in the Senate," Hugo later wrote in words reeking in autobiographical image, because of his "intellectual integrity. . . . He knew what he was for and what he was against, he believed in the righteousness of his cause before he spoke, and people who listened to him believed in his complete sincerity. Senator Norris had for many years a far greater influence than other people whose sentences were more rounded and polished and whose eloquence received universal recognition." In short time Norris became Black's "hero" and, among contemporaries, always held a singular place in his heart.

Each initially distrusted the other somewhat. Black felt that a government-operated facility would benefit only the private power companies, since Alabama municipalities had already committed themselves to buy power from the Alabama Power Company. "I care nothing for the power. It is infinitesimal in importance." Nitrates were the crux of the issue. He was sympathetic to the fertilizer bid of the American Cyanamid Company, but Norris viewed this as just a cover-up for private power interests.

It took a year for them to reach an understanding. Black convinced Norris that the Southeast needed fertilizer as much as rain; and Norris gave him a sense of the potential of public power that he had not realized. "Legislation," Black said in announcing that he could vote for Norris's joint resolution, "is a matter of compromise." As he had written a constituent, "Causes have been injured more by people of rash and radical thought, who attempt to coerce every person to their exact line of thinking, than by the enemies of the causes themselves." But Coolidge's pocket veto of the carefully negotiated measure as he relinquished office to Herbert Hoover was upheld by the Supreme Court. An hour after the decision was announced, Black was on the Senate floor demanding that the Senate remain in session until it passed a bill for the operation of the Alabama project. He promptly introduced two bills for the operation of Muscle Shoals for the production of fertilizer. One provided for leasing the Shoals to the American Cyanamid Company, the other for a similar lease to the Farmers Federated Fertilizer Corporation.

Norris was resolute in his belief that private fertilizer was a cover for private power and, as chairman of the Judiciary Committee, he wanted to investigate the matter. But he was too busy and named a subcommittee, which included Black. Black had noticed unusual zeal on the part of Shoals lobbyists and suggested that their activities be examined. From January to April 1930 hearings were held sporadically. At one session Black accused an Alabama editor, J. E. Pierce of the *Huntsville Times,* of accepting a bribe to change his editorial policy to favor the American Cyanamid proposal. Black's insinuations were a "contemptible lie," Pierce said.

"I'll see you outside about that," Black replied. "Everyone knows you are by nature a coward."

"We'll go outside right now," Pierce shouted, leaping to his feet. Black

felt the matter could wait to be settled. "Then you admit you are a contemptible liar?" asked Pierce.

Chairman Thomas Walsh pounded for order. "I rise to the point of
personal privilege," Pierce yelled as he stood up. "This man Black said I
was known as a coward. I call him a contemptible cur in return." After the
tumult ended and the hearing was adjourned, Black immediately left the
committee room. "All I was trying to do was to bring out the facts and let
them speak for themselves," he said. He waited in the lobby for several
minutes but Pierce did not show up. When a quorum call summoned all
senators, he left for the Capitol with Walsh, a broad smile creasing his face.

The alleged bribe, a $1,000 check, came from J. W. Worthington,
executive secretary of the Tennessee River Improvement Association, of
which Pierce was vice president. Colonel Worthington, as he was called,
was a civil engineer who wrote speeches filled with technical information
that Black delivered. (So did Norris and Congressman Lister Hill of Montgomery, the chief House sponsor of Muscle Shoals.) "He had a shop on B
Street and had his staff going day and night," Hill's assistant Robert Frazer
recalled. "Black astounded the Senate with his erudition. His speeches
impressed people terribly. Three or four senators told me that. They said
the speeches showed profound study, that he must have spent a lifetime
studying Muscle Shoals. Then Black got mad at Worthington."

The committee subpoenaed Worthington, but he pleaded ill health and
refused to appear. He disposed of his records and fled to a Detroit hospital,
where he remained throughout the hearings. His subordinates maintained
they did not know where the files were. And even though another committee
member, Thaddeus Caraway of Arkansas, declared that Worthington had
misappropriated association funds, no supporting evidence was found. Black,
however, accused Worthington of taking money from the power company at
the same time he was working against it. Moreover, Worthington headed a
group working in cooperation with the Farm Bureau, which campaigned
extensively against members of Congress who had not supported the American Cyanamid proposal.

A disgraced Worthington dropped out of the power fight as the committee released its finding that American Cyanamid was combining its lobbying efforts with the Union Carbide Company, which provided nearly
$35,000 of the $45,000 the two companies spent jointly. Carbide had no
fertilizer objectives, but by secret agreement was to obtain a large share of
the Muscle Shoals power for non-fertilizer purposes if Cyanamid received

the lease it sought. Norris paid tribute to Black for "ripping the mask off . . . the grab" that the power companies were trying to put over. "He has been of almost invaluable assistance. . . . We cannot praise the Senator from Alabama too highly."

Black soon called on the Judiciary Committee to investigate the fertilizer interests and other groups who kept large staffs of lobbyists in Washington permanently. "Let us drive out these lobbies and do our duty to the farmers who have been long ground under the heel of the oppressors. . . . It is a crime that the fertilizer interests and the power trust continue to come to the door of this Capitol and fight legislation to carry out the people's wishes." In the strength of the lobbies he had found another issue and another enemy to be pursued. Both would be long-standing.

Norris, assisted by Black, continued to fight for Muscle Shoals legislation. In February 1931 a Senate-House conference approved a compromise bill providing for the public operation of the power facilities and public-owned transmission lines. In return the Senate conferees agreed to the private leasing of the nitrate plants, with the provision that should the president fail to find a satisfactory lessee within a year, the bill as Norris introduced it would become law. Black played a central part in ironing out the differences between the two versions. He was flexible so long as he could reach the main objective: "I would like to see the provision to construct transmission lines by the government retained, but with all other items agreed upon I would not let that provision wreck the compromise. The South wants and needs cheap fertilizer." Hoover's veto of the bill deeply disappointed Black. The White House, he said, would have to take responsibility for the veto; it was "the opening blast of 1932." Muscle Shoals legislation would have to await the arrival of a more sympathetic administration.[5]

In February 1930 Hoover nominated Charles Evans Hughes as chief justice, to replace the late William Howard Taft. As governor of New York, associate justice of the Supreme Court, Republican presidential candidate in 1916 and secretary of state under Harding, Hughes had cut a large swath on the American scene. He had over the past several years represented utilities and other major large corporations before the Supreme Court—the American Cyanamid Company among them, as Norris pointed out. Senate progressives felt that these affiliations would color his economic views. "Opposition was attributable in part to the fact that a number of senators disagreed with what they considered to be [Hughes's] basic judicial and constitutional philosophy," Black recalled. They ignored Hughes's prior record on the Court, which roughly paralleled many of these senators' own beliefs. Black took no part in the spirited floor debate and voted against the nomination. Nevertheless, Hughes was handily confirmed.

The next month, Hoover chose John J. Parker of North Carolina to succeed Justice Edward T. Sanford, who had died. Parker was a judge of the Fourth Circuit Court of Appeals; his record had been one of a faithful southern Republican. His nomination appeared assured when the American Federation of Labor announced its opposition, claiming Parker was an anti-labor judge because he had upheld (in the *Red Jacket* case) a "yellow dog" contract* as the basis for enjoining a strike for union recognition. "I feel very strongly that a senator should take into consideration the Supreme Court nominee's background, the environment in which he was raised, his growth and development, and most important of all, his philosophy," Black later said. A nominee's creed was now examined in unprecedented depth.

Senators Norris and Borah in particular were "very anxious" to defeat Parker. Black read the record in the *Red Jacket* case. The injunction, he later said, went "mighty far": it "prohibited the union from buying food for its members, caring for the sick, and burying the dead. There was no basis for this under constitutional or case law. . . . But members of that union had a contract, a kind of policy of insurance, with their union which obligated the union to pay them so much money in the case of a strike. . . . He had enjoined the union from complying with that obligation to any extent. As far as I knew, that had never been done before. Nothing in any of the Supreme Court opinions had mentioned it." That was why Black voted against Parker. He never doubted Parker's "integrity or basic qualifications, but just couldn't bring myself to vote for a man that would sign that Red Jacket injunction . . . such an inhumane order." After the nomination was narrowly defeated, Hoover quickly named Owen J. Roberts of Philadelphia who was unanimously approved. Parker continued as an appellate judge for twenty-eight more years. Ironically, his opinions thereafter gained Black's approval far more than those of Roberts on the Supreme Court. "John Parker was a better judge after the hearing than before it," Black said.

. . . .

---

* This was an agreement between employer and employee by which the latter promised not to join a union in return for the privilege of employment.

For a freshman legislator Black had been unusually outspoken and productive. He "remained for a time an obscure figure in inconspicuous garb," a reporter later wrote, "a spare, thin man who said little and that little without rhetorical flourishes. When he hit his stride, his speeches on the floor of the Senate were characterized by a business-like approach to the problem." He "soon achieved a reputation for his learning and wit"—beneficial attributes for developing and passing legislation but not of prime import for an Alabama politician. On Alabama issues he necessarily trod warily, and tightroped his way through dangerous situations.[6]

*   *   *

The leading candidate for the Democratic presidential nomination in 1928 was New York's soaking-wet Catholic governor Alfred E. Smith. "His personal views on immigration have given aid and comfort to our ancient enemy and estranged many of our friends," Black told a colleague. A poll of Protestant ministers in Alabama showed not one who would support Smith. "If the vote were to occur today," Black wrote in July, the Republicans would carry the state. Hugo could not afford to offend party regulars or drys. The Klan did not cause much concern. Its strength had waned substantially in Alabama since its glory year of 1926. Dissension divided its ranks. An informer hired by the *Birmingham Age-Herald* infiltrated it and successfully penetrated its secret meetings. And the hooded order overreached: the conviction of those responsible for the brutal flogging of an illiterate white orphan, Jeff Calloway, galvanized white Alabamians and led to the swift passage of an anti-flogging bill. Membership in the Alabama Klan dropped from 94,301 in 1926 to 5,524 in 1928 and 1,349 in 1930; James Esdale resigned the next year. The hooded order was never again a major factor in state politics. Soon Josephine found Hugo's Grand Passport in a drawer and threw it away.

It was hard to back Smith, Black later said. "He was encouraging violations of Prohibition. That may be O.K. when you're a private citizen, but not when you're in government." Because Smith had signed bills, passed by the New York legislature, repealing the state prohibition law and permitting the sale of beer and wine, Black felt he

> would not whole-heartedly seek to execute the laws of this govern-
> ment. . . . I consider him to be the most over-estimated man in America
> as to ability. I think him to be the living exponent of the predominating

sentiment of the foreign element in the City of New York, and that the ideals of that element are totally at variance with the traditions and sentiments of the people of the South. In fact, I believe him to be the selected and chosen instrument of groups all hostile to old fashioned Jeffersonian Democracy. These are some of the reasons I believe the Democratic party would be almost committing suicide to select him as the standard bearer of the followers of Jefferson and Jackson.*

Black's choice for the nomination was Senator Thomas J. Walsh of Montana—Catholic but dry and not a Tammanyite.

Senate Democrats recognized the delicacy of Black's situation. He had quickly impressed Joe Robinson who marked him as a "comer" in the party. His ambition had already impelled him to seek the post of secretary of the party caucus, similar to assistant leader. One veteran senator asked Black directly if he was a member of the Klan and warned that if Black was, he as well as other Democrats would not support Hugo's candidacy. Black replied that he had gladly accepted Klan support and in doing so was only following an "old Spanish custom" among southern Democrats then in Congress and in high state office. The response apparently sufficed: Black was named to the position (and held it throughout his Senate service). This was an extraordinary tribute to a senator who had served only a few months.[7]

---

* Black also wrote in this letter:

> You asked if in my judgment, Al Smith as President would appoint Catholics to office where possible. . . . I . . . imagine that prompted by the old rule, that *to the victor belongs the spoils,* if actuated by no other motive, there would be a large percentage of Catholics presented to office.
>
> You ask also if I think our Government would be in danger with a Catholic President, and if so what danger. The Catholic Church considers that it has been persecuted in Mexico. . . . If the Baptists had been selected as a particular object of persecution in Mexico, and a loyal Baptist should be president, he would be more than human if persecution of his fellow-churchmen played no part in his decision with reference to the nation persecuting his church. Whether Governor Smith would be able to rise above such natural human sympathies, no person can say. . . .
>
> I think that his conduct in signing bills in the State of New York which, in effect, defied the will of the people as expressed in the Constitution of the United States, which he had sworn to obey, and committed a State to the doctrine of non-cooperation with the Government in the enforcement of its Constitution, proves him to be too small to hold the exalted position of President of the United States, charged with the special duties of executing its laws. . . .
>
> Lest you do not understand exactly, I will state that I consider that a person in America has the right to belong to any church in any state he sees fit. There are times, however, when a man's alignment necessarily shows to some extent the bent of his views, and when such is true, it is not improper to consider them. [Originally emphasized.]

It was also pressure of the most direct kind to keep him regular. Being a senator, Black later said, he "had no choice but to remain in the Democratic Party." He wrote the Reverend Bob Jones, then a budding evangelist on the road to national prominence:

> My election in this state was due largely in the voters who believe in the cause of prohibition and a restricted immigration. My usefulness in standing for those principles would be practically destroyed if I should take a stand against the Democratic Party. My voice would be worth very little in the United States Senate. . . . I should probably be removed from the committees on which I am serving, and could do very little for the good friends who sent me to the Senate.

"Cautious leadership alone can preserve Democratic leadership" in Alabama, he thought. He campaigned by mail, sending long letters to political and other leaders around the state, diplomatically but realistically explaining his situation. It was not the Black usually confident of his course who wrote one publisher that he had "more or less reluctantly reached the conclusion that it is not to the best interests of the Party for me to make any speeches at the present time." He could better serve the ticket by not campaigning. Stirring up the people, thought the man who always believed in the people, would hurt and "disrupt" the party. By October he felt Alabama would undoubtedly go Democratic, although not by the usual majority.

Black did not have the courage to tell southern Baptists, whose ancestors thought of the pope as the "whore of Rome," to vote for a Catholic for president. During a golf game with his friend Hugh Locke and afterward, Hugo asked if he should lead the campaign against Smith in Alabama. He was very torn, Locke said later. Some Alabama Democratic leaders soon asked Black to serve as chairman of the anti-Smith campaign in the state. He did not reject the offer outright but considered it before refusing, and spent a full day, he said, unsuccessfully urging the dissidents not to bolt the party. Smith's positions, except on immigration, were "a clarion call to progressive democracy," Black wired the *Montgomery Advertiser* from Geneva, Wisconsin, where he was attending a Knights of Pythias convention when Smith was nominated.

But that was all. Daring to be cautious, Black made no other public comment during the whole campaign. It burned with a religious fire in many circles as election day approached. Smith carried Alabama by only 7,000 votes over Herbert Hoover out of nearly 250,000 cast, and may well have been "counted out." Black served on the special state Democratic campaign committee, appointed to run the campaign because of the hostility to Smith. But he did not attend a breakfast when his friend Josephus Daniels, formerly secretary of the navy under Woodrow Wilson, visited Birmingham to help raise money. The week before the election he campaigned to help one congressman whose seat was thought to be in danger. Vote the straight Democratic ticket, Black urged. His only public appearance in the state that fall was to urge city residents to support the Community Chest.[8]

*   *   *

Alabama's other senator, J. Thomas Heflin, was virulently anti-Catholic. Tom-Tom claimed that the cross and rosary decorated dollar bills; that the papal banner flew above the American flag on navy ships (it actually was a pennant to indicate church services); and that the "Roman hierarchy" was responsible for opposition to a cotton bill. "He [Heflin] has strangely over-looked what is probably the most striking proof of the papal invasion of the United States," the Cincinnati *Catholic Telegraph* wrote. "The telegraph pole bears the form of the cross from one end of the country to the other." In frock coat and string tie, entertaining his audiences with stories which often began, "Once there was a nigger and an old mule," Tom-Tom advanced the cause of political buffoonery. He had served in Congress since 1904 and his only achievement had been to introduce the resolution creating Mother's Day. His views repelled Black as much as the man amused him. "Personally, I liked him," Hugo said. "All I heard when I was growing up was Tom Heflin," recalled Sterling Black.

Using Heflin's congressional frank, Klan headquarters in Birmingham mailed to voters thousands of copies of his Senate speeches, all thundering about rum and Romanism. Soon he toured the country. If Smith were elected, "the Pope will sail up Mobile Bay in a submarine," Heflin said; "you'll hear the creaking of the oars when he lands on the beaches." The claptrap became too much for Democratic leader Joseph Robinson. He sharply criticized Heflin on the Senate floor in January 1928 and said he would do it in Alabama too. "Yes," Heflin replied, "and if you do, they will tar and feather you." Robinson took the dispute to the Democratic caucus, where he won a 35-to-1 vote of confidence. Black abstained.

Heflin was adamant. The chairman of the state Democratic executive committee, Edmund Pettus, warned that any person who voted against Smith in the general election might run the risk of being barred from the Dem-

ocratic primary in 1930. This threat did not faze Heflin. "So help me God,"
he soon told a cheering Montgomery throng in September 1928, "I will
vote against Al Smith if they read me out of the Democratic Party and drive
me from every Senate committee!"

They did. In December 1929 the executive committee barred as a candidate any person who "either voted a Republican Presidential ticket in
November 1928 or openly and publicly opposed the nominees of the Democratic Party, or either of them." Black believed that this action violated
state laws requiring the same qualifications to apply to voters and candidates
alike. Heflin was up for reelection in 1930 and Black advised him to take
his case to the people, to have those voters who favored his nomination
write in his name. So William Bankhead reported to his brother John who
was planning to run against Heflin. But Heflin wanted to run in the Democratic primary. On his behalf Horace Wilkinson sued to prevent Jefferson
County officials from holding the primary under the rules the committee
laid down. Wilkinson's lawyer was Crampton Harris; Forney Johnston represented the party. Heflin's hopes were dashed when the Alabama Supreme
Court ruled it could not interfere in party squabbles.[9]

Still, Heflin would not be deterred and he ran as an independent "Jeffersonian Democrat." Also running was the somewhat liberal Frederick I.
Thompson, who owned newspapers in Montgomery and Mobile; Bankhead
won handsomely. Black kept his silence throughout. He disagreed with, but
could have endured, Heflin's racism. But what he could not abide was Heflin's
lack of effectiveness in working with other senators and for Alabama's interests. He did not say this then, however. Thirty-five years later, he admitted
to an interviewer that he voted for Thompson.

Hugo Black was a yellow-dog Democrat—he would vote for a yellow
dog or any flea-bitten mongrel if it were a Democrat. "I must confess that
sometimes as I voted I felt like vomiting, but nevertheless I voted the straight
Democratic ticket," he noted at the end of his life. He campaigned more
on behalf of the party than for either Bankhead or Thompson. The Democrats, Black told a Montgomery crowd in October 1930, reflected the
philosophy of its founder Jefferson who was

> the instinctive and able champion of the struggling many; the spokesman
> of their unexpressed hopes, ambitions and desires. . . . The Republican
> party control is today of the few, for the few, and by the few. It is completely
> and wholly under the domination of a few powerful plutocrats who have
> grown bloated and powerful as the direct beneficiaries of Republican sec-
> tional greed and special privilege. . . . We cannot, we will not, we must

not destroy the party which brought the sunlight of peace, happiness and
security to the white men and women of Alabama.

Without attacking the Jeffersonian Democrats, he urged the election of a
regular party candidate as the Democratic Party was the only salvation from
the Depression. For the first time Alabama newspapers covered Black's
speeches enthusiastically. The reaction of the *Tuscaloosa Banner* was typical:
"At the close, the crowd, to a man, remained seated, captivated and en-
thralled in the silence of approval and then, like a mainspring of recovery,
they rose to their feet and burst forth with cheers."

The day after the election in which Heflin and Hugh Locke, who ran
on the same ticket for governor, lost overwhelmingly, Heflin stated he would
ask the Senate to probe the contest. Black wrote a friend that he would
defend Alabama if Heflin carried his charges of fraud too far. He wished to
avoid "any contest with my colleague," he told the Senate. "The election
was as fair as any election ever held in any state in the United States."
He requested that the Senate clerk read a resolution passed by the Alabama house of representatives condemning Heflin's "very poor sports-
manship." Black would never be a good enough sport to condone fraud,
Heflin replied.

"The two principals are as unlike . . . as one could imagine," a reporter
observed. "Heflin is robust, dynamic, long-spoken, vociferous . . . the best
showman in the Senate. He dresses the part. . . . Black is almost the opposite. Of medium height, youthful in appearance . . . , he makes only
infrequent remarks on the floor. He usually wears dark blue double-breasted
suits and likes to walk around with his hands thrust deep into his coat pockets.
His voice is strong and clear and earnest." Heflin's charge should not appear
without denial, Black stated. It would take "wholesale fraud and corruption"
in order to steal an election in fifty-seven of the sixty-seven counties that
Heflin lost. He did not object to having a Senate committee, at Heflin's
urging, investigate the matter. But, he said,

I deny the right of the Federal Government to go down into the State of
Alabama, sir, and tell the people who shall vote or who shall not vote.
["We had entirely too much of that in the days when the carpetbagger and
scalawag were running the State," he had said earlier.] I do not favor, sir,
the extension by one inch or one particle of an inch the rights of the
Federal Government to enable it to invade the sacred rights of franchise
in the Southern States of this Union or in any other States of this Union.

I am opposed body, soul, mind, and spirit, to any additional step which
gives the Federal Government the right to go into my state.

A year's investigation turned up no fraud or corruption. "Heflin didn't
have a defense in Washington," Black later said. "He was beaten in the
election." Bankhead even gained votes in the recount. After the committee
recommended by a one-vote margin that Bankhead should be seated, the
fight went to the Senate floor. Black was Bankhead's leading supporter,
"fighting like a bantam cock against that veteran raven," noted Senator
Hattie Caraway (who had succeeded her husband Thaddeus). Describing the
election irregularities as "petty, trivial, small, trifling," Black accused Republicans of "bowing at the shrine of technicality instead of trying to get
at the justice of the case."

In April 1932 the Senate voted overwhelmingly to seat Bankhead and
gave Heflin the unusual privilege of addressing his former colleagues. Pointing
to "my one-time friend . . . the junior Senator from Alabama," Tom-Tom,
his face flushed, denounced Black who, he claimed, championed Bankhead
to please the "machine" and the Alabama Power Company, an unlikely
combination.[10] Only amused spectators and Heflin's fellow clowns and dem-
agogues shed a tear at his departure. Black gained the lasting gratitude of
Bankhead, his brother Will, who was an influential congressman, and many
of their friends and supporters in Alabama. And with the state constitution
barring Governor Bibb Graves from running for reelection, Black was now
Alabama's most prominent political figure.

CHAPTER 9

"I CHANGED AFTER I GOT TO WASHINGTON"

Bʟᴀᴄᴋ ᴠɪᴇᴡᴇᴅ ᴍᴀɴʏ ɪssᴜᴇs, especially the major ones, in terms of a Jeffersonian-Hamiltonian dichotomy. This was a popular approach at the time due to the pro-Jeffersonian books of Claude Bowers. Writing dramatically, and relating an Armageddon-like battle with "the forces well defined—aristocracy against democracy," as Bowers wrote in his 1926 volume, *Jefferson and Hamilton,* he aimed to have the Democrats return to Jeffersonian democracy in its original state. His work about Reconstruction, *The Tragic Era,* was equally partisan. Both books deeply appealed to Black and he frequently referred to Bowers in Senate debates. Even more often, and on all sorts of matters, did "the scholarly senator from Alabama," as a colleague called him as he spouted quotations from Jefferson on the Senate floor, mention the sage of Monticello. "None of my books do I prize more highly," he said, than the rare first collection of Jefferson's writings, "and none have been read by me with more interest and sympathy than those which contain every word that was ever uttered by that great American." "In practically everything . . . he said, I agree with him."

The contrast between Jefferson and Hamilton was a constant theme of Black's speeches and actions. The mere sight or sound of Hamilton's name launched him on a fit of oratory. And especially now, with people hungry, Hamilton—"the darling of wealth and privilege" who "admired extravagantly the monarchy of England" and called the people "beasts"—made an even more inviting target. How happily different was Jefferson—"the instinctive and able champion of the struggling many; the spokesman of their unexpressed hopes, ambitions and desires"—who "expressly recognized that the people were sovereign and their every right must be protected." The

Democrats reflected this philosophy. "The chief issues which should, and must, bring about the liberation of the masses from economic slavery, are economic," he wrote in 1930.[1]

The Depression changed Black's concerns. Hoover insisted that prosperity was "just around the corner." But it was a very long street. Black attacked Hoover's uncertainties with fervor. The Senate should spend all its time trying to put people back to work, he insisted. "Senator Black waxed eloquent on the subject of the seven million unemployed and lectured the Senate on taking any other votes," Senator Caraway noted in her diary. In December 1931 he urged a $1 billion public works program lest the clamor for the public dole become irresistible; but the idea got nowhere. The next day, he announced his candidacy for reelection.

He meshed political necessities with plans for combatting the deepening human misery. States' rights was a theme Black trotted out when needed. In February 1932 he led the fight against a proposed bill authorizing a Federal Emergency Relief Board that would distribute $375 million. His opposition surprised and displeased many progressives, for Black himself helped circulate reports that the Depression was striking Alabama with full fury. Birmingham was especially hard hit. Unemployment had reached nearly 25 percent, and 60,000 to 75,000 of the metropolitan area's 108,000 wage and salary earners were working only part-time, the city's congressman, George Huddleston, had reported at a Senate hearing on the bill the month before. Over 12,000 applicants responded to an advertisement for 750 laborers to do "the hard, dirty work of digging" a canal at $2 for a ten-hour day. Jefferson County had ended all subsidies in rural sections. "Many . . . go into remote quarters of the community and beg from door to door where they think they are not known, trying to get a little something to eat," Huddleston said.

Edward Costigan of Colorado, co-sponsor of the measure with Robert M. La Follette, Jr., of Wisconsin, twitted Black by reading his earlier comments in behalf of direct relief. Black had then urged that $25 million be appropriated, and distributed by the Red Cross, to victims of the southern drought. The current proposal, Black charged, created a new bureau in Washington "to corrupt, to undermine, to bribe the poor and the hungry and unemployed, and take their minds off of the healthy political discontent that should result from injustice and abuse." He assailed the "Hamiltonian theory that bureaus are vested with infinite wisdom and infallibility while the people . . . can not be trusted."

His fiery Jeffersonian rhetoric was rooted in the old southern animosity toward any federal project that might upset "social habits and social customs." He "became hysterical," one reporter noted, "over the prospect of a . . . plan which might feed Negroes as well as whites, and gave an exhibition which brought a blush to the face of Tom Heflin, lurking in the rear of the chamber." "Trust the states and the people to distribute [the money] as they should," Black told the Senate.

> Personally I prefer to trust the administration of affairs touching human need and human want to the kindly and generous sentiments of those who live close by where want has made its habitation and where hunger emaciates the frame and weakens the blood. . . . The real liberal, who has come down through the ages holding aloft the torch of human liberty, has not stood for concentration of power in a centralized government or in the hands of any particular group. . . . Remember that bureaus seem to be the only thing in all history that have discovered the secret of immortality. They never die; they become more greedy with each passing year—greedy for power, greedy for money, greedy for enlarged personnel. . . . Power! Hamiltonianism! No province of Rome in the days of its greatest glory was ever made any more subject to the imperial purple in that city than the States of this Republic will be subject to bureaucratic control if this bill should become law in its present form. . . .
>
> No, Mr. President, the price of relief is too great if it must be obtained at the loss of every vestige of self-respect of the sovereign States of this Nation as they appear, hat in hand, before an inferior bureau of the United States of America. . . .*

Black joined with Senators Walsh and Robert J. Bulkley of Ohio to introduce a substitute bill, proposing $375 million in loans to those states that could demonstrate that relief funds could no longer be borrowed, with a similar amount to be allocated for public works relief. "Political trickery," La Follette called it, an unworkable replacement that would enable Democrats to tell voters they had proposed something. It, too, was defeated.[2]

---

* "Mr. Black making a rather good speech," Senator Caraway noted, "—very energetic and much stress and useful. . . . Bankhead presides while Black waves his arms and orates. I wrote to Sen. [Marcus] Coolidge [of Massachusetts], 'Will Mr. Bankhead find heaven tame in comparison to the thrill he's getting now?' And he wrote, 'He has reason to.' . . . Mr. Black has finished his speech but he doesn't know it—and I'm afraid he's fixing to make it all over again. Please sit down Mr. Black!" (Diary, 2/8/32, Caraway papers.)

....

Black was shoring up his political base in other ways. In 1931 he told a Birmingham audience: "Our country is Christian. It is not infidel. It can never be so until it departs from the foundation stone. The great [Daniel] Webster [the early-nineteenth-century senator from Massachusetts] spoke right when he said that Christianity is the common law of the United States." A principle close to heaven was Black's subject at a reunion of Confederate veterans in Montgomery: the real cause of the "War Between the States" was not slavery but states' rights. "It was to preserve her constitutional rights that the South established the Confederacy," he said. * "Eternal principles of government guided [its] course." The South should be proud of its history; its ideals must not perish. "No man can find in a true history of the South any just cause for apology."

The recent conviction of the "Scottsboro boys" heightened racial tensions in Alabama. Eight Negroes were under death sentences, and a ninth, only thirteen years old, faced life imprisonment. When four students from Vassar and Wellesley called upon Black to protest, "I asked these young ladies if they had read the evidence and had really made themselves familiar with the facts concerning the trial and conviction of these negro rapers. The young ladies admitted to me that they had not and I advised them to do so before they registered any further protest." He would be glad to discuss the case after they read the trial transcripts, he said, adding that there was much crime in northern cities to concern them. That was the closest he came at the time to this tragedy.[3]

He was not willing to talk much about prohibition, either. Although many drys in the state, recognizing the futility of enforcement, now favored modification or repeal, Black feared the reaction if he changed his position before the May 1932 primary. One of his opponents, the self-styled "dripping wet" J. Morgan Burns of Selma, accused him "with attempting a beautiful straddle on the prohibition issue. Black's delay in issuing a platform is characteristic. He is a politician and never was anything else. The only official anxiety he ever felt was to discover the tide and ride its crest. That's the way he rode the bone dry sentiment into the Senate. Now he wants to find first if the tide has switched." As a French revolutionary of 1848 said while

---

* This phrase was the result of Josephine's editing. Hugo had originally written: "It was to preserve their rights to control their own domestic institutions, as they saw fit, that the South established the Confederacy."

sitting in a café and seeing a mob pass by, "I am their leader. I must follow them." For the time being Black remained an "arid dry."

He went back to Alabama four days before the May 3, 1932, primary. He could not return earlier, he explained, "without neglecting my duty to my state." Soon he received $1,312 as his fee from a 1927 trial in a case that had finally been concluded. "No check was ever more warmly welcomed," Black wrote William Fort, who sent it, and he used it to cover the cost of distributing a résumé of his Senate activities. Constituent service had always been high among them. When storms flooded the South in the spring of 1929, he sponsored a bill providing money to rebuild Alabama's roads and bridges. The press now cheered him as a hero who had saved Alabama from the disgrace of a voided election.

Four hopefuls challenged Black in the primary. Besides Burns, they included former state attorney general Charles McCall and Henry L. Anderton, a Birmingham attorney and former judge who boasted that he was drier than talcum powder in a desert. And, once again, Thomas Kilby was Black's major opponent. (He was "glad" the popular congressman Will Bankhead did not run against him.) Since Black refused to debate on matters not touching "all-important questions affecting the economic stability of the nation," Kilby was left looking for an issue close to home. He charged that Josephine was on Hugo's Senate payroll.[4]

Hugo was infuriated. "I never saw a man get as angry as Hugo did then," her sister said. The skirts of pure white southern womanhood were not to be soiled by political mudslinging. At first "I came very near going too far. . . . It is hard to know just how a man should restrain himself under an attack like this," Hugo wrote J. J. Willett, who brought the matter to his attention. "I can frankly state that I am glad I was not in Alabama when I first read it." Josephine had worked for Hugo the previous summer when a regular secretary could not accompany him to his Alabama summer house, Hugo acknowledged. Nepotism was a common practice on Capitol Hill. (He also employed a niece for a short time and her husband for an extended period as well as his assistant's wife.) Quick to defend his action, Hugo reminded voters that Josephine had been a stenographer in the navy during the world war. "She earned her money then, and she earned every penny she received during the few months she did temporary work." Kilby "hit below the belt there," said Crampton Harris.* The accusation quickly died.

---

* Willett wrote Black: "I know of no one who profiteered more than the Kilby Car & Foundry Company did during the great war, who manufactured axles and other supplies for the

But soon Kilby and Black happened to meet in an elevator in a Birmingham office building. Kilby cowered behind the other passengers, fearing that Hugo would physically attack him.[5]

The results of the primary pleased Black. He won nearly half the votes, only 659 short of a majority—"an impressive exhibition of political strength . . . almost unheard of," opined the *Birmingham News*. But under Alabama's new election system, a lack of a majority meant that a runoff, against Kilby, who came in second place, was necessary. Prohibition was a major issue; but with people starving as the Depression tightened its grip on the country, Black no longer thought it was a matter of supreme importance. Now he announced that he favored a nationwide referendum on prohibition. He had come to believe that it was an experiment that had failed, but he could not admit that he had been wrong originally. By waiting to change his position, Black left Alabama prohibitionists "high and dry"—without a candidate to support. Kilby made "wily Hugo" his campaign theme.

"Mr. Black seems to be constitutionally opposed to taking a definite stand on any issue," Kilby charged. His "false stand" tricked thousands of strict prohibitionists. Waving a copy of the Grand Passport that the Klan presented Black in 1926 (which the *Montgomery Advertiser* now printed on its front page) and calling him "The Arch Deserter," Kilby said, "He would double cross the Ku Klux Klan too except for the fact that he is a life member of that order." Black replied in the shade of Tom Heflin that he was a Jeffersonian Democrat; the people should decide the fate of prohibition. In Kilby's hometown he pointedly said, "I have no patience with a man who will ride into office on the dry issue and proceed to try to keep the state dry by drinking up all the liquor in existence."

"Kilby is spending as usual a great deal of money," one of Kilby's former supporters told Black, "and as it is well known here he is now in financial straits, the question arises who is financing his campaign and paying for all these workers and newspapers. Can it be the Power Company which has never been able to control you?" Apparently it was not. One of the company's vice presidents, Colonel Sidney Z. Mitchell, "didn't like Kilby." He and

railroads after they were taken over by the Government. In fact he [Kilby] got rich during that time and it comes with poor grace from him to talk about any one taking advantage of the Government" (Willett to HLB, 4/15/32, Willett papers).

Clifford Durr, a lawyer in the firm that represented it and the husband of Josephine's sister Virginia, "began talking about the situation," Virginia recalled. "He would call Cliff up to his office and would get on the phone with the power company local managers and tell them all to vote for Hugo Black."

One of Kilby's main backers was Black's old courtroom antagonist, Forney Johnston. By now a rabid reactionary, he placed a full-page ad in the *Birmingham News* asking, "Why did Black Sulk in His Tent?" In Washington, Black read Johnston's broadside with mounting anger and, to blow off steam, scribbled that Johnston, "a so-called Democrat" and "traitor to his party," had just attacked every Democratic senator and congressman in office.

> He says what the Senate of the United States needs is new faces fresh from the troubles back home, ready to lash out, lion fashion. . . . To make his meaning clear he says that I am "part and parcel of a Senate that has legislated this country to the point of disaster and revolution." . . . If he were not [a political traitor], he would have said that the Republicans were in control of both Houses of Congress during the past five years, and were responsible for the added burdens. . . . If he had wanted to be candid and truthful he would have told the people that at every session of the Senate since I went there, I have vigorously protested against every added invasion of the rights of the States by the Federal Government. . . . He would have told the people that I fought the creation of the new Two Billion Dollar Federal Bureau, to take care of the railroads and big business interests whose spokesman he is. No, Mr. Johnston does not oppose bureaus like this!

Johnston's remarks backfired, and Kilby was desperate. He tried to taunt Black to debate, but Hugo refused, saying Kilby only wanted an audience for himself. While Kilby closed his appeal by sending one hundred speakers around the state, Black spoke for himself over radio. He had established that mystical bond between a candidate and the electorate. "Hugo had Alabama in the palm of his hand," as Crampton Harris said. A smile often came across his face as he circulated among crowds. Their roar and feel tapped something elemental in his nature, perhaps the longing to be accepted, but on his terms. Their cheers reassured him as to the rightness of his course when those inevitable inner doubts arose. He campaigned with adrenal zeal. On the stump he ad-libbed wonderfully. Once he nearly walked into some manure. "I almost stepped on the Republican platform," he told the crowd. And on June 14 he won renomination by a 58 to 42 percent margin.[6]

....

Back in Washington, out-of-work World War One veterans formed a Bonus Army to request early payment of a promised bonus. President Hoover refused to meet with them. When some marchers resisted leaving the shacks they had set up on the banks of the Potomac River, he ordered the army to remove them. On July 28 General Douglas MacArthur led the troops. The shacks were torched, and tear gas drove the veterans and their wives and children to flee without any of their possessions. Two veterans, two babies and two policemen died. Black was the only senator who publicly criticized Hoover's use of force. It was "wholly unnecessary and ill-timed," he said. "As one citizen I want to make my public protest against this militaristic way of handling a condition which has been brought about by wide-spread unemployment and hunger." "Babies yet unborn," he told an Alabama audience moved to tears by his depiction, "suffered from the colossal blunder of President Hoover."

At the same time Black was using his public office to protect his private holdings. He, Albert Lee Smith, William Engel and Engel's cousin David Meyer had formed the Lee Real Estate and Investment Company in 1924. One of the properties they bought, in 1929, was in downtown Birmingham; the Prudential Insurance Company held the mortgage. They defaulted on the mortgage in the summer of 1932 and Prudential moved to collect on the note. This failed, and Prudential proposed to foreclose with the expectation of obtaining a deficiency judgment against the mortgagor. This would reimburse the company for the difference between the amount it received on foreclosure and the amount of the mortgage—a total of about $30,000. Its lawyer wrote Black and associates to try to reach a mutually acceptable agreement. "My instructions have been . . . to file suit in the United States Court in the event something is not done toward getting the matter straightened out." An incensed Black drafted a reply:

> It may be possible that the Company has the right under the cold letter of the law to sue the endorsers of the note in the Federal Court, without foreclosing the mortgage. It may be possible that by this method they would succeed in extracting for themselves not only the property which was given as security for the debt, but something in addition to this. These rights may be given to them under the law now, and it may be such rights may

be permanently retained. There is nothing new in their proposal. It was made useful long before Shylock made it famous.

He sent the draft to Smith who talked it over with their lawyer, Frank Spain, and they decided not to send the letter. "Frank seems to think we could probably work the proposition better with syrup than with vinegar." Black then wrote Spain:

> The attitude of the insurance company in this case has just about convinced me fully and completely that the jurisdiction of Federal Court, in connection with diversity of citizenship, should be abandoned. In a number of other instances companies have adopted exactly this method. They take the position that it is first right to get every possible dollar from people who owe, and they want to get in a court where the cold steel of the law can be applied to the limit. They want to get far away from a court that might be at all affected by principles of human justice. The attitude of many of the companies during this depression has confirmed a belief, which I had somewhat entertained before, that the chief object of these companies is to get all they can, and take advantage of every situation possible.

Spain thereupon wrote Prudential's agent, setting forth Black's views and implying that, since the Lee company was unable to pay, a bill then pending in the Senate might pass if Prudential persisted. The Senate Judiciary Committee in April 1932 had unanimously reported to the floor a bill, introduced by its chairman, George Norris, proposing to prevent both individuals and corporations from entering suits in federal courts on the basis of diversity of citizenship. * Black was then a member of the Judiciary Committee. He did not participate in hearings about the bill in March 1932, and there was no debate when it reached the floor. After Prudential agreed not to file a suit against him and his partners, and thus accept the loss of $30,000, he withdrew his threat to press for its passage. The bill died on the Senate calendar.[7]

*   *   *

Black spent much of the fall campaigning for the Democratic ticket headed by Franklin D. Roosevelt. Both carried Alabama overwhelmingly. While FDR promised a "new deal" for the American people, Black was undergoing

---

* Diversity of citizenship grants to federal courts jurisdiction in cases between citizens of different states. Insurance companies carefully guard it because local juries, in state courts, are frequently prejudiced against them.

a political and personal transformation of his own. He had not been satisfied with his first term in the Senate, and his frustration boiled over. He was playing it safe, he told Josephine in December 1932, following too much what he thought the voters wanted, and not what he really believed; he was like a powerful angel with its wings nailed to the ground. He could continue doing this and remain in the job for as long as he wished.

But Hugo was too independent to be anyone's property, even the voters', and too determined to have an impact on his times. The devastation around him, and his ideas which could help alleviate it, aroused him to a fury. He resolved to be a true leader, to take the risks involved and (largely) to throw caution to the winds. If he weren't reelected being his own man, he said to Josephine, "we'll go back to Birmingham and I'll become the richest lawyer in the state so you can have all that money you talk about." No longer would he tack and sheer and trim expediently, riding out the storms of controversy. He would navigate by the stars, release the self-imposed restraints, and sail— on his own.

Hugo Black was a different man from the one he had been six years earlier. Being away from Alabama, in a new environment less provincial and more tolerant of diverging opinions, exposed to different ideas—all this affected him. With time for reflection, he read many books, about philosophy and law and morality. He reexamined his convictions. "I changed . . . after I got to Washington," he later said. Under the impetus of the Depression his basic humanitarianism rushed to the fore, covering almost all else. As the Republic faced its greatest internal crisis in his lifetime, Black received a letter from the recent head of the Alabama Anti-Saloon League. "The greatest problems of government relate to economic questions, and not to sumptuary legislation . . . ," he replied. "Another thing of which I have become convinced is that the churches of the nation have been greatly injured by prohibition activities. Divisions have been created in the churches on the basis of politics. . . . The idea that beer legislation or liquor legislation would remove the manifest injustices and discriminations in our economic system is to me more or less nauseating."

> Every minute of my time that is possible to use, I am devoting to a study of questions, with a view to alleviating human suffering and to an adjustment of the machinery in such way that our government can continue to be a real people's government. . . . The prohibition question, along with other questions, is used by a great many designing people on both sides of the controversy for the purpose of trying to ride into office, to perpetuate special privilege in this nation, and to increase trusts, monopolies and

injustice, with the view to having the products of all utilized largely for the benefit of a few.

I hope you will believe me when I say that my course is not now, and will not, be actuated to the slightest extent by its effect upon any future election of myself. If I can make any real contribution to the numerous millions, who are ground down under the heels of special privilege and monopoly, during my next six years, I shall be happy. For such services, I shall ask and expect no reward, except the satisfaction of my own conscience.

I have not yielded one inch of my opposition to liquor. I am opposed to it. I wish it would be made impossible ever to manufacture another drop. I realize, however, that those political philosophers are correct who say that sumptuary laws must follow public sentiment. Sentiment does not follow laws. All history shows this. . . . For the next six years, I hope to devote my time and attention to those kinds and types of legislation that I believe will make this government function for the benefit of all of its people, instead of for the benefit of a few. In this work, so far as it is humanly possible, I intend to forget that there will ever be another political election in which I might be involved.[8]

His emphatic reelection and its aftermath boosted Black's confidence and increased his political clout. He could be more outspoken and his opponents had fewer opportunities for revenge. He was now a senior majority senator who could expect to become chairman of a major committee during his new term. The incoming administration naturally generated hope—how much nobody had any way of knowing. Its leader, secure in some inner faith, brimmed with aplomb and buoyancy. His direction was liberal; his mode experimental; his technique sparkling; his manner enchanting and captivating. Franklin Roosevelt was a leader Hugo liked, respected and could follow in his own independent way.

CHAPTER 10

A NEW DEAL
FOR WORKERS

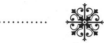

THE RELATIONSHIP between crime and the economic system had intrigued Black since his days as county prosecutor. Crime would decrease if poverty were reduced, he concluded. But whatever plans he had how to achieve this, he kept to himself; he made no proposals. Such subjects were out of fashion during the prosperity of the 1920s. Then came the Great Crash. As Hoovervilles sprouted and breadlines lengthened, all assumptions were questioned, all notions were examined. Fresh answers became imperative.

Previously, he viewed government largely as a legal mechanism, to correct wrongs; the great exception was Muscle Shoals. Now he believed it had to take the initiative, and be a positive instrument to help people. Their rights and welfare became its purpose and only justification for existence. The power of some groups over the economic destinies of other groups had to be taken away to make the system function. Black was concerned with those who ate from their lunch pail, not those who (in the phrase of historians Charles and Mary Beard) dined "at the table of acquisition and enjoyment." Laws to distribute the flow of wealth more equally would be needed. An economic democracy would have to be created in order to save democracy.

Black's reading after his Senate election widened to include many books on unemployment. Stuart Chase and other technocrats wanted to abolish the price system and to run government on the basis of scientific standards. "I probably read everything written on the subject at the time," Black recalled, as well as numerous books on the minimum wage law in England and on reduced working hours per day in England and Europe. With an increasing sense of urgency he studied social legislation that various European

154

countries had adopted. He found that England "had always been about forty years ahead of us—or fifty. And I found that it had unemployment insurance, that they had been able to fix the hours, fix the wages, and they had done numerous other things that we were just now considering."

The day "of individual initiative and rugged individuality," Black told the Senate, where "we [in] government leave it to you to stand or to fall upon your own business cunning and acumen . . . has passed. We are now . . . putting into the life blood of commerce and trade, as represented by individual business enterprises . . . the funds that come from the tax-payers of the nation." He spoke over radio for unemployment insurance ("most of the people thought I had gone wild," he recalled); for "some kind of insurance business controlled by the government that would give people medical services and medicine. And that was thought to be pretty bad"; and for wage and hour protection.[1]

The Depression traumatized Black. He agonized when broken and dispirited men and women, with sacks wrapped around their feet for shoes, stopped him on the street to beg for government jobs. In Birmingham in late 1932, he recalled, an estimated "forty per-cent of the population was on relief of some kind, some kind of relief job, or support from government." Real estate lost almost all its value. Charitable organizations were feeding one quarter of the population. Thousands of people wrote Black asking for work. Roosevelt soon referred to Birmingham as "the worst hit town in the country." The situation reached its nadir when Black announced he would be at his Birmingham office in the Federal Building the next day. He found the hall filled with people. For three full days he listened to them. "I was constantly sitting there hearing stories from some of whom were my oldest and best friends, some people who were threatening suicide if they didn't get a job.* They were all resentful and said they didn't want any charity, they wanted a job." The self-reliant lost their reliance, the independent became dependent on others, the proud went into shock. The terrible suffering hit Black as few other things could.

＊　　＊　　＊

In the autumn of 1931 he had contacted various liberal groups—farmers, American Federation of Labor (AFL) unions and the railroad brotherhoods—that were interested in recovery legislation that he was preparing.

* One friend, Albert Lee Smith's brother-in-law, did commit suicide (ALS, Jr., int.; HLB to ALS, 10/1/32).

Sidney Hillman, the head of the Amalgamated Clothing Workers Union, happened to be in Washington to testify at congressional hearings. He called upon Black to say that drastically reducing work hours, as Hugo had in mind, would spread hardship as well as work, and that a provision setting a "floor," or minimum under wages, was needed. Black explored the possibility of enacting such a minimum wage law. "At that time," he recalled, "the AFL unions were strongly opposed to a minimum wage, holding that it would tend to become a 'maximum' "; but with equal vehemence they advocated a shorter hours and work bill. Partly this was to counter unemployment caused by advancing technology. There would never be enough jobs to go around unless everybody worked less. Labor's emphasis now switched to preventing layoffs through cutting hours. Since the onset of the Depression, work hours had drastically increased (up to seventy a week in some states) and wages had dropped equally. A coal miner in Birmingham earned $1.50 a day.

Black favored legislation to provide a shorter work week "for several reasons. One was that I thought it would help more people to get jobs and that even though they worked at shorter hours it would be impossible for industry to lower their wages in anything like the proportion of the reduced number of hours. I became convinced . . . that this country can produce as much as it can possibly use under our present system with a number of working hours much lower than we have yet achieved." He wrote the bill sitting at his desk on the Senate floor and introduced it in the lame duck session in early December 1932.

Remarkably simple, the bill prohibited interstate or foreign shipment of goods produced in establishments "in which persons are employed more than five days per week or six hours a day." The idea was that available work would be shared. Six million new jobs would be created, Black predicted. "No economic proposal," wrote two Brookings Institution economists, "has ever been advanced which is more revolutionary in its economic and social implications." Later Congressman William P. Connery, of Massachusetts, chairman of the House Labor Committee, asked if he could offer a similar bill in the House. Black agreed. Although he introduced his proposal solely on his own volition, he included the thirty-hour limit to win labor support. A forty-hour-week bill was his goal "sometime in the future." Hearings were held in January. William Green, the usually cautious AFL president, predicted a "universal strike" if Congress did not pass a thirty-hour law. "Which would be class war, practically?" interrupted Black. "Whatever it would be, it would be that . . . ," Green said, adding, "that is the only language that a lot of employers ever understand—the language of force."[2]

All of this took place before the Democrats regained power, while Hoover was still in office. Black's other recent proposals also indicated a new cast of mind, a willingness to use government power to better the lives of desperate people. Hugo Black was a New Dealer before there was a New Deal.

On March 4, 1933, Franklin D. Roosevelt was inaugurated. "The only thing we have to fear is fear itself," he told an apprehensive nation. Within a week Black notified FDR that he intended to resubmit his "imperatively necessary" thirty-hour bill to the Democratic-controlled Congress. "I can see little chance of putting many people to work unless my short work bill is passed," he wrote to a niece; he always believed that his was the only conceivable response to any predicament, and if it were not adopted, despair would inevitably result.

He had a major obstacle to overcome. In 1918 the Supreme Court had ruled (in *Hammer v. Dagenhart*) that a law Congress had passed two years earlier, excluding the products of child labor from interstate commerce, was unconstitutional, as it "exerts a power as to a purely local matter to which the federal authority does not extend." For five years Black had been on the Judiciary Committee, gaining familiarity with constitutional law, and he spent the past "six months, most of the time," at the Supreme Court's library, housed in the Court's chamber in the Capitol. "I studied it and was ready on it. And argued it. I knew what I was doing on that case. But they don't all do that. They're just awful."

In his committee report sending the bill to the Senate floor, Black tried to distinguish his proposal from the old law. "Conditions today are different. . . . Laws must be interpreted to meet conditions existing when the law is interpreted." The Constitution is a living, breathing charter of government, always evolving, inviting change. It "has been interpreted from time to time to meet new situations and conditions that could not have been foreseen by the writers of that great document. . . . If change is needed to cure evils growing out of old practices, change must come." On the floor he said the "Constitution is final," noting that six new members had joined the Supreme Court since 1918. "No doctrine of stare decisis [precedent] applies to opinions on constitutional interpretation," which was, he insisted, a product of the times. The framers of the Constitution had made it possible "to adjust laws written under its terms to fit alike the oxcart and the airplane, the handloom and the swift spinning of modern factories. . . . The tendency of today is to give a new and exalted emphasis to the more sacred right of human beings to enjoy health, happiness, and security justly theirs in proportion to their industry, frugality, energy, and honesty."

The proposal reflected Black's towering view of the scope of the commerce clause of the Constitution. Roosevelt shared that belief and Black's general objective, but the rigidity of the bill appalled him—it was too cold and inhuman. It did not allow for seasonal variations or for the special hours some occupations demanded. Farmers couldn't work their hired hands only a certain number of hours. "There have to be hours adapted to the rhythm of a cow," he said. More important, merely spreading out the available work would not reach the crux of the problem. A measure creating new employment and stimulating business confidence was needed. Black's bill did neither, he felt; "he was convinced [it] was unwise," noted Raymond Moley. And because it did not consider a minimum wage, take-home pay would be slashed. FDR also believed the bill to be unconstitutional, as did every lawyer the administration consulted.

Still, Roosevelt did not want to embarrass those senators who supported it. And to Black he conveyed enthusiasm. "The first time I ever saw President Roosevelt," Hugo recalled, "he indicated that he was for a measure of that kind. He continued to urge me to have the bill passed through the Senate from time to time. He personally called up Senator Joseph Robinson and asked him to have the bill taken up for passage. Senator Robinson and I then made the bill the next order of business." At the same time, Roosevelt was doing what he could to water it down, having Secretary of Labor Frances Perkins tell the Senate Labor Committee that a minimum wage and a flexible application of the work week were needed, with the administration deciding the numbers of hours. The ballyhoo of the photographers, the klieg lights, the reporters and the radio microphones made testifying "a trying experience . . . ," she wrote. "This was a full dress affair. Senator Black apparently wanted it that way."[3]

The Senate spent a week debating the bill. Opponents read telegrams from steel manufacturers, canners of perishable goods, milk producers and other interests who protested that the measure would ruin their businesses. Farm laborers and milk industry workers were exempted from the bill's provisions; another amendment limited its effect to a two-year period. It became more of a short-term experiment than a permanent cure-all. Roosevelt asked Black to offer an amendment to raise the maximum hours from six daily and thirty weekly to eight daily and thirty-six weekly. Black refused. At the last moment Robinson submitted it; it was rejected. Under pressure from organized labor and the American Legion, the Senate on April 6 passed the bill by a vote of fifty-three to thirty.

House Speaker Henry Rainey immediately threatened to tie the bill up, saying it was not part of the president's program. FDR publicly said nothing but sent Perkins to the House Labor Committee to express administration sympathy, but not necessarily support. She largely repeated her Senate testimony, adding that minimum wages should be established through industrial boards representing management, labor and government. Was this simply a tactical stratagem? Or was it part of an evolving administration policy? No one knew. On May 10 the committee unanimously reported the bill to the House floor, but Representative Connery had insisted on adding an embargo against foreign goods not made under the conditions the proposal specified. Both Roosevelt and Black opposed this "immigration amendment," as Hugo called it, and, given the president's unenthusiastic backing for the entire measure, it died.[4]

Soon Black charged that lobbyists had filled Washington to kill the measure. He hinted at a congressional investigation. Congressmen, even some who backed labor (meaning Connery and others), tried to "amend the bill to death," he said, scoring labor leaders, including one AFL lieutenant, who had thrown cold water on the proposal. "If they had kept their hands off, we could have marched the bill through the House, with the President's helping," he told *Labor* editor Edward Keating. "The delay enabled the opposition to rally its forces. The employers brought in lobbyists from every state. There's been nothing like it in my time."

Roosevelt's hand was forced. He had played for time somewhat while Black's bill was winding its way through Congress, and his hands-in-pocket support was partly responsible for its defeat. But pressure remained great. He had to recommend another plan for industrial recovery. When passage of Black's measure seemed assured, FDR sent New Deal policy chefs scurrying to their kitchens; some were already there. They cooked up the National Industrial Recovery Act. It was based on an idea forwarded by Henry I. Harriman, head of the United States Chamber of Commerce, Black felt. He was wrong as to the provenance of the proposal; several dozen people of varying persuasions were involved in its complex preparation. But the president "wanted me to handle it," Black said, and FDR deputized Harriman to persuade him. Harriman "sent for me and got me out of the cloakroom," Hugo recalled, "and said that they were going to offer a bill that was along my line—that I'd done more than anybody to bring the country to a realization that something was needed, and that they wanted me to offer this bill."

I said, "Well, I don't know. I haven't read it. I want to see it." I took it home and read it. I found it was for more than 36 or 40 or any kind of hours. But it created committees of businessmen at various parts of the country to set up commissions and draw what I considered to be laws. And it also provided for the suspension of the anti-trust act.

I brought it back to him the next morning and he said, "What do you think about it?" I said, "I don't think I can offer it." He said, "Why, we have Section 7 in there that will give the people you're interested in, give the labor unions the right to be recognized." I said, "Well, I am interested in a lot more people than labor unions. That doesn't relieve the situation. I'm interested in the consumers, and as I understand this bill, it proposes to do away with the anti-trust act and leave the control of prices to businessmen meeting in common. I remember from Adam Smith that he said if you let a group of businessmen get together even for a dinner to talk among themselves, that the public's going to suffer. And that's the way I feel about this NRA," I said.

"Besides, Alabama now has two Senators representing the views with reference to any laws like this or any laws governing business and labor. But it won't have two representing it in these business groups. That won't do it any good. There are many things about it that I just can't be for, and I won't offer it." And I didn't. And then they went to Bob Wagner and he came to me and said, "They want me to offer this bill to the Administration, but I've told them I won't do it if you'll offer it." I said, "Well, I'm not going to offer it. I'm against it, and I'm not going to support it. There's much about it that I don't like and I don't support."

Black vigorously opposed the NRA, except for those provisions that provided for an appropriation for public works. He spurned the idea that it would achieve a single purpose of his thirty-hour bill. "This bill, if it shall pass and become law," he said, "will transfer the lawmaking power of this nation, insofar as the control of industry is concerned, from the Congress to the trade associations." And to a staunch antitruster it was a price-fixer's dream; businesses, Black felt, would simply increase prices, goods would become even more expensive, and businessmen even richer. He voted against it in various forms two out of three times. Two years later, when Black and other senators were trying to repeal it, the Supreme Court voiced the same objections he did. It unanimously declared the NRA unconstitutional in the Schecter "sick chicken" case, an action he had predicted.[5]

*   *   *

Black shifted his attention to the subsidy program for private shipping lines. Since his early days in the Senate, he had looked suspiciously at the United States Shipping Board. It sold surplus warships to private operators at cheap prices in an effort to stir up the flagging merchant marine. Black sensed something suspect. In February 1928 he sought an investigation, but the Republicans blocked him. He tried another avenue. The board paid large salaries to forty-seven lawyers who handled only 258 cases in 1927, he complained from the Senate floor. This was "rank, organized robbery." "Five reasonably good lawyers" could easily do the job. The Senate accepted an amendment he offered to an appropriations bill to limit the salaries of board officials and the number of lawyers that could be hired to ten.

During Hoover's last days in office, Joe Robinson told Black that he had heard that the Post Office Department was hurrying to sign one final mail contract, with a Philadelphia steamship company for $1 million for ten years. Robinson's informant came to speak to Black. Dangling that kind of lead before Hugo was like turning hounds loose after the fox. At Robinson's request the Senate passed a resolution creating a special committee to investigate air and ocean mail contracts. Black became chairman. "You name anybody on it you want, and just get into it," Robinson said. Black began work on May 1, 1933. His goal was to determine what the government got in return for spending $25 million yearly on overseas mail delivery. The Shipping Board supplied information and he immediately sent questionnaires to all companies holding mail contracts, asking them to detail their government relations and the terms and amounts of their contracts; to identify all executives and stockholders; and to state whether relatives of members of Congress were employees. Just as quickly, the National Committee of the Merchant Marine declared that American lines operating foreign trade would be destroyed if mail contracts were seriously curtailed. The Senate soon authorized additional funds for additional staff, and Black spent the summer poring over the data dug up.

Shipping officials frankly admitted that government mail contracts were meant as subsidies to compensate for the difference in operating costs between American and foreign carriers. One company received subsidies for delivering empty pouches and even for not delivering mail at all as its ships could not get through to certain ports. Black charged that the subsidies were spent on fat salaries, dividends and highly paid lobbyists. Shippers who claimed otherwise faced an unnerving prospect. The president of one line brought his physician with him to the witness stand to check his pulse. "It's obvious the government will never get anything back," Black commented, "but it is worth while to show how it lost all this money."

On and off for nearly six months, he continued the investigation. He attracted some attention—*Newsweek* called his a "useful Torquemada"— and won some allies but did not arouse much public indignation. He worked quietly and steadily, examining the material his small staff uncovered, sifting through the responses to questionnaires, public records, financial statements and correspondence. Black acted as his own special counsel in a probe fully as intricate as the one Ferdinand Pecora, with a corps of assistants, was undertaking into banking, stock exchange and security practices for the Senate Banking Committee.[6]

Black was plugging away when an unexpected source gave him a boost. Through the grapevine he heard that Fulton Lewis, Jr., a Hearst reporter, had collected much information on airmail contracts that his newspapers were refusing to print, perhaps, Black speculated, because of financial ties to the aviation industry. Lewis turned his files over to Black, who immediately promised startling disclosures. Roosevelt disapproved of subsidies but realized that American ships must be kept on the high seas. He favored a five-year contract with the shipping companies. When they wanted ten years, he asked Postmaster General James A. Farley to effect a compromise. Black then appeared in Farley's office to assure Farley that he had gone through all the records and all post office employees had carried out their duties properly. No compromise with the shippers was achieved and hearings began in October. The airmail probe and its consequences became front-page news for several months.

A Post Office Department clerk testified he had burned papers relating to airmail contracts on orders from Hoover administration Postmaster General Walter Brown. Brown had distributed contracts so that three holding companies, with interlocking directorates, controlled 92 percent of all airmail revenue. He did this to forge a rational, efficient airmail system and at the same time to fashion a viable commercial aviation industry; and this was simply businesslike management. But Black charged that Brown regularly awarded contracts to large aviation holding companies, ignoring small operators: "The control of American aviation has been ruthlessly taken away from the men who could fly and bestowed upon bankers, brokers, promoters and politicians sitting in their inner offices, alloting among themselves the taxpayers' money."

To garner popular support for his inquiry Black took to the airwaves. He was one of the first politicians to use radio regularly at times other than during campaigns. An immediate result was that his committee received thousands of communications; and he also gained exposure throughout the country. The government, he said on one of his several nationwide hookups, must get out of the subsidy business: it must operate airmail transport itself or completely revise the federal aid system. Black then called airline executives before his committee. Persuading them that he merely wanted to confirm for the record facts he already had, he led them into admissions of which they were often unaware. At one session he kept referring to a paper he held in his hand, giving the impression that the facts were written on it. The witness caved in and told his story. Reporters later found out the paper dealt with another subject.

Black was a "hunch player," wrote journalist Raymond Clapper, and "once in a while he hooks a fish." Ever courteous, he "sits back easily in his chair, puffs slowly on his cigar, rolls his large, open eyes quite innocently, and with a wise smile, undertakes to refresh the memory of a squirming witness." He made his daily summations just at press time so that any reply would have to wait for the next edition. Destroyed records, competitive bidding shunned, questionably large salaries and profits—the picture that emerged was depressingly familiar.

Roosevelt urged Black to press the inquiry to the limit. On the evening of February 1, 1934, William P. MacCracken, Jr., assistant secretary of commerce under Hoover and now a Washington lawyer representing airline companies, met with some of his clients. He gave files to L. H. Britten, vice president of Northwest Airlines, who promptly destroyed them, and to Gilbert Givvin, the secretary to the president of Western Air Express. The next day, Black demanded that MacCracken produce them. MacCracken claimed they were "personal" and, additionally, that the lawyer-client privilege protected them. But Givvin said they dealt with airmail contracts, as their eventual recovery confirmed.

"Senator Hugo Black and I were close friends, and our wives were great pals," MacCracken later said. At parties they danced with each other's wives, twirling them around. He came to see Black one afternoon. "I have to summon" your files, Hugo told him; MacCracken firmly maintained that the confidentiality privilege held. He saw Black again that evening. "We spent hours together while I tried to persuade him," Hugo recalled. " 'You just can't do that, Bill. . . . I'll have to prosecute you, and I don't want to do it.' " "That's exactly what's right," MacCracken replied. ". . . But I think it's my duty not to divulge those papers." Black pleaded: "I want to urge you not to do it as your friend. . . . Don't do it, Bill. I don't want to hurt you." MacCracken left with the papers in his hand.

Black introduced a resolution ordering the Senate sergeant at arms to arrest MacCracken, Britten, Givvin and Harris Hanshue, the head of Western Air, for contempt of the Senate for attempting to destroy evidence sought by a Senate committee. The resoulution was quickly adopted. Dressed in gray striped trousers and black morning coat topped by a sheriff's ten-gallon hat, and brandishing a silver-headed cane and a red carnation, sergeant at arms Chesley Jurney cut a colorful figure. He returned after several hours of a none too strenuous search to say he could not find MacCracken who was by now sitting in his office. MacCracken's lawyer, Frank Hogan, thought after speaking with Black that Hugo agreed that the courts, not the Senate, should decide the question of the applicability of the lawyer-client privilege. But Black didn't want to arrest MacCracken only to turn him over to the courts. Arrest him now, Black told Jurney, and take him into the Senate chamber. Meanwhile, Hogan hustled MacCracken out of the building. The next night, he appeared at Jurney's home (their fathers were good friends) and spent a night there so he could be arrested when the Senate was in session the next week.

In a rare procedure, MacCracken and the other defendants were brought to trial before the bar of the closed-door Senate. Black was prosecutor. He confronted them with the missing letters post office employees had pieced together from scraps of paper found while searching three hundred bags of trash taken from MacCracken's office building. At the top of some of the letters was written "MacCracken's copy." The Senate acquitted Givvin and Hanshue but found MacCracken and Britten guilty, and sentenced them to ten-day jail terms. MacCracken appealed all the way to the United States Supreme Court, which upheld the conviction, and served a ten-day jail sentence.[7]

While lunching at the White House in late January 1934, Black told Roosevelt that the president had the power to cancel or modify airmail contracts. Some legislation would probably be needed, he believed, but an executive order could correct most of the problem. "That would indicate the cancellation of contracts here and there?" a reporter asked Roosevelt afterward. "Yes," he replied. When the Post Office Department solicitor found that fraud was involved in obtaining contracts, Farley canceled contracts with the major carriers that were part of a "spoils conference" Brown had held in May 1930. Roosevelt instructed Farley to annul all existing airmail contracts and to direct the army air corps to carry the mail, starting February 19, until new bids were approved.

Brutal winter weather whipped across the country. Three pilots were killed during training. Within a week six pilots, flying in open-cockpit planes, died; six more were injured, and eight planes were wrecked. By March 10 ten had been killed. The program was temporarily halted, but as the weather improved, so did the army's performance. Public opinion ran strongly against the entire operation. For the first time the New Deal was on the defensive. Eddie Rickenbacker, flying ace of the world war, called it "legalized murder." Aviator Charles Lindbergh, perhaps the most popular American save FDR himself, sent a public telegram to Roosevelt: "Your present action does not discriminate between innocence and guilt and places no premium on honest business. [It] condemns the largest portion of our commercial aviation without just trial." The conservative press denounced the administration. After the Hearst newspapers said in a front-page editorial that Black and Farley were "blood-guilty of the death of every army navigator," postal inspectors trailed visitors to Hearst's chief editorial writer, James T. Williams, Jr. He feared Black's committee would seize his files.

Roosevelt began to back down. "General," he snapped at his air corps chief, Benjamin D. Foulois, "when are these air-mail killings going to stop?" On March 8 he proposed that airmail be returned to private carriers under conditions "barring evils of the past." The corps phased out its operations by June 1, 1934; twelve pilots died in all.

Two weeks later, Black was one of a small group invited to the White House to witness the signing of the Air Mail Act of 1934. "I cannot tell just how far we shall be able to get," he wrote as he and Kenneth D. McKellar of Tennessee were steering the bill through the Senate. "Powerful influences are at work as usual." Talking about inside department lobbyists, Black said, "Let's just put in a section which says thou shalt not steal." But he and McKellar held firm and the bill passed with practically no revisions. It stressed competitive bidding, economic regulation and airmail awards; commercial aviation was not specifically promoted, and holding companies that had participated in the spoils conferences were denied contracts. Barred from the airline business were any person who had "entered into any unlawful combination to prevent the making of any bids for carrying the mail" and any corporation that had employed as a director, an officer or an executive any such person. "Without the determined fights of these two senators aviation in America in all its phases would now be controlled by a monopoly operated out of New York," later wrote Karl Crowley, the Post Office solicitor who drafted the law. "They deserve a tablet of honor placed in the head-quarters of every independent [operator] in this country."

In June 1935 Black sent President Roosevelt the final report of his mail contracts investigation. The country, he concluded, had little to show except for a fleet of antiquated ships for the $800 million it had spent on the merchant marine since the end of the world war. His hearings and report had stimulated the nation's conscience and created demand for reform. They provided the basis for the Merchant Marine Act of 1936. The shipping industry, standing to lose greatly from any changes, hired the "superman of lobbyists" to prevent it, noted Crowley, who also drafted this bill.

A new agency, the United States Maritime Commission, replaced the old shipping board. Stipulations for government aid were completely re-worked; all ocean mail contracts made by the postmaster general were can-celed after the following June. Especially satisfying to Black was the provision that any subsidized company could not pay any employee an annual salary of more than $25,000.[8]

The conflicts over shorter working hours and mail contracts kept Hugo Black very busy. Other, personal matters were also on his mind.

CHAPTER 11

CASES AND DEPRESSIONS

W HEN BLACK CAME TO WASHINGTON, he thought the money he had saved would make his family "comfortable for life." Soon he found that his $10,000 senatorial salary was "wholly inadequate to support senators with families who had to live in two locations," he wrote later. "What I had saved as a lawyer—even insurance—was almost completely exhausted during my ten years in the Senate." The main reason was his single experience in banking.

Back in 1915, he became a director in the Merchants and Mechanics Bank in Birmingham. He did not know anything about banking, but it looked like a good way to make money. Soon the bank failed. Its officers arranged with the Birmingham Savings Bank and Trust Company to take over its assets and signed an agreement to pay its obligations. (Stockholders were then directly accountable to depositors and creditors, and had to reimburse losses.) Birmingham Savings leisurely collected on the collateral due while officers of the defunct bank delayed settlement. Finally suit was brought against them. Black was exempt from suit since the world war had begun and he was in the army. Informed of the case while he was at home on leave, he went immediately to court, asked to be heard and stated that the plea had been entered without his knowledge or consent and that, since the debt was honest and should be paid, judgment should be entered against him. He turned over the assets of his home, such as they were, and said that if he returned from the war, he would eventually pay the entire debt. The bank extended him all the time he needed, with 8 percent interest.

Several Birmingham lawyers were surprised to find their old nemesis opposing them in court after he was elected to the Senate. "Hugo saw nothing wrong with continuing his practice," Hugo, Jr., wrote, "as long as he didn't

167

represent clients who had any interest in matters pending before the Senate"—even though he rarely had that type anyway. Black had occasional trials in Birmingham, even less frequent appeals in Montgomery. These cases, largely personal injury and wrongful death claims, probably totaled no more than a dozen, but the last one was not settled until September 1935. The results did not differ much from when Black was practicing full-time: the Alabama Supreme Court reduced the jury's award in a wrongful death claim. Black had written the brief and he took the ruling almost as a personal insult. "The court has decided that $12,500 would shock the conscience of the court, and $9000 would not shock the conscience of the court," he immediately observed. The phrase had not appeared in the court's opinion, but Hugo used it several times in a motion for rehearing which was denied. It would not be the last time he would scorn the phrase.

One of Black's opponents in court in a few cases was Joseph F. Johnston, Forney Johnston's son. "They were sure losers," Johnston recalled. "I was just out of law school and Father figured I might learn something by going up against Black in a few cases. It's not something I'd want to repeat."

> I never will forget one case. We represented the railroad. One of the workers got injured on the job and the railroad obviously was going to be liable. When we got through with the arguments, the time came to take exceptions; various exceptions had already been taken. Black asked the judge to have a session at the bench. "Now Mr. Johnston objected to this here," he said. "Do you still object to that, Mr. Johnston?" "Oh, yes," I said. "Oh, well," he said, "his objection is not good but I'll agree to that. Yes. Tell the judge what you wanted to say." And he did that all through the record. To everything I said, he said, "it's all right with me." He cleaned out the whole record and there wasn't a single exception left in the whole damn thing, not a chance to do anything on appeal. He just wiped up with me. I've never come across a better trial lawyer.[1]

"I'm taking these cases because I need the money," Hugo told Johnston. His financial responsibilities were manifold. Besides supporting his own family (and supplementing the salary of his senatorial assistant Hugh Grant), Hugo had also paid "several thousands of dollars" of his brother Lee's debts to bankers and wholesalers in a vain attempt to keep Lee from bankruptcy after losing money investing in Clay County graphite mines and playing the cotton futures. Lee never worked afterward. His many children took care of expenses and Hugo put several of them through college. No one else could help. His sisters Ora and Daisy could not, and his brother Orlando had died in 1917, working himself to death as a country doctor and disregarding Hugo's suggestions to move to Birmingham.

For years he had helped subsidize his in-laws. Since Dr. Foster left the ministry, they had "lived in genteel poverty, trying to keep our best foot forward on very little money," their daughter Virginia said. Foster's latest investments in oil and real estate fizzled, wiping out much of his sizable inheritance. "He would say he was a failure and make everybody perfectly miserable," recalled Virginia. During the Depression, the banks took over what he had left. Hugo and Josephine had long been putting money under the Fosters' threadbare carpet. No words were, or could be, said; appearances were maintained.

Mrs. Foster's institutionalization added another burden. In February 1932 she was briefly hospitalized for melancholia. Josephine knew about it and began to fret over the possibility of inheriting what the doctor called a "mental disorder." So, with the help of Cliff Durr, who told his wife Virginia not to mention the matter to Josephine, Hugo kept any further news from her. The doctor informed Hugo that the "modern view" is that "heredity has its greatest influence as a suggestion. The dread of a nervous disease . . . will do a thousand times more harm than a bad heredity." Mrs. Foster and Dr. Foster went to live with the Durrs, having rented out their house for the money. Then Mrs. Foster began not eating and sleeping, and "her mind seemed confused." In November 1932 she entered Hill Crest Sanitarium in Birmingham where she would remain through January 1934. "She begged and begged to come home," Virginia said later. "She cried and cried. That was a horrible period." Since Cliff was not working, having left the blue-ribbon law firm he was with, the monthly $105 cost fell to Hugo to pay. He took on some more cases.

Several years of drafting his own speeches and press releases had greatly improved Hugo's briefs. They were written more smoothly, were better organized and made their points more clearly and succinctly. They reflected his boundless self-confidence, as the Bennett case showed. George Bennett had been crushed to death by a railroad engine while working for the railroad. After the Alabama Supreme Court upheld a Birmingham jury's judgment of $15,167, the railroad appealed to the United States Supreme Court in 1933. Forney Johnston drafted the railroad's petition for certiorari. Black wrote the brief opposing it (on the back of Senate Foreign Relations Committee stationery). In twenty-one fact-crammed pages he rebutted Johnston's contention that Bennett was in any way responsible for his own death.

"The legal principles involved are neither complicated, new nor novel," Black noted at the outset. "It is believed by the writer of this argument that citation of authorities, or quotations from them, would not aid this Court. This is because the Court is so thoroughly familiar with these often applied legal principles that the evidence in this cause and the inferences from it need but to be pointed out to demonstrate the justice of the judgment and its support by primary legal rights. . . . Legal definitions and citation of authorities are not needed to establish the railroad's liability for such conduct. The facts speak for themselves." The Supreme Court agreed. In October 1933 it refused to hear the case. ("I am more than ever convinced now that when there are no real legal questions involved, there is no reason for citing cases," Black told the lawyer who handled the trial.)[2] He received a fee of $3,129, which improved his finances.

Josephine's years in Washington had been cluttered with luncheons, teas and receptions. At her first White House function she tried to remember what to say and do. Calvin Coolidge was president, and she introduced herself as the wife of Senator Black, the junior senator from Alabama. He nodded in recognition. Mrs. Coolidge, however, could not place the senator. Josephine said that he replaced Underwood. Whereupon Mrs. Coolidge replied, "Nobody can replace Senator Underwood." Josephine was "almost devastated," a friend recalled. Every Monday, senators' wives held "at homes." "We went and left cards at everybody's house—everybody who had preceded your husband in being elected, everybody on his committee, everybody in your state delegation, and the White House, at a minimum . . . ," noted Lady Bird Johnson, whose husband, Lyndon, was elected to Congress in 1937. "So you simply went around and dropped little white cards. Occasionally the lady would be at home and say, 'Do come up.' " Small talk followed.

Hugo wanted Josephine to become friends with all the senators' wives, since "real information" in the Senate came through social life, he insisted. For the meetings of the Ladies of the Senate Luncheon Club, wrote Frances Copeland, the wife of the senator from New York, "Tuesdays are set aside during the session. Only for a very good reason does anyone miss it. We sit where we please . . . but, naturally, temperament and personal qualities result in special friendship and group formation. The ladies gather at ten o'clock and sew on Red Cross work until luncheon at one o'clock. The food is brought and served by about eight members at a time. These gatherings are a lot of fun. . . ." Josephine was groomed for them and she collected friends as quickly as she attended the events. Gradually, however, the meetings lost their appeal; she found them artificial. But she kept her feelings to herself and dutifully continued to attend. It helped Hugo and it was simply something a senator's wife was supposed to do, with no questions asked. Still, her focus was shifting. In 1930 she started taking courses at American University. Underneath she was searching. For what? Harmony with forces larger than mankind? Perhaps. She did not know. She could not know.

Publicly, she gave the impression she was thriving. A Birmingham friend invoked a muse in her appreciation: "Yesterday I passed where once you lived, my dear. The place looked quite the same, how strange! . . . And passing, I looked the other way." In Washington it was the same. With her sparkling eyes and gentle sense of humor, and with Hugo's storytelling, they were in regular demand at dinner parties; rarely did they dine at home alone.[3]

But privately Josephine was going through routine hell. On many days in these early years in Washington she sat in the living room with the curtains drawn, crying. "I belong to those whose place is at home," she said. Servants had always surrounded her and she never developed any domestic talents. One day in October 1932, when the housekeeper, Mary Marble, was sick, Josephine noted, "and I was the cook and maid and trained nurse all in one. I rather enjoyed cooking spinach for a change and washing dishes though I must admit I wouldn't like it every day, and the children would hate it. They frankly said the spinach had grit in it, and the potatoes were rather raw, but it would just take time and practice and I know I could be a good cook."

She harbored doubts as to her worth and ability. She had always been overshadowed, first by her mercurial, self-centered father who considered himself a failure, and then by her husband who was anything but mercurial or a failure. Hugo tried not to be domineering but he could not help it. Her sister observed:

> She never was independent after she married him. . . . Hugo absolutely worshipped Josephine. I never saw a man love a woman more than he did. He did everything in his power to make her happy, except give her freedom. He gave her everything he could think of. There was not a wish of her heart that he didn't satisfy, but she never had one hour's freedom from that time on. She was Mrs. Hugo Black. He expected her to subordinate herself to his life and his ambitions. It never occurred to him otherwise.

He never realized that she might occasionally want to be free to do something she wanted to do. He was kind not only to her but also to her
family. . . . But Sister was always in a state of dependence, total dependence. . . . She was beautiful and sweet and charming. Everybody adored
her, and he above all. But after she married, I don't think Sister ever was
able to have a free moment.

Josephine enjoyed distancing herself from worldly concerns in order to
read and contemplate. "I've found a place in the attic," she wrote in her
diary, "—a nice snug, cozy little hole where I can go off and be alone. . . . I
must have been an animal in some reincarnation who burrowed in a hole
all winter and luxuriated in having one little spot in the world where no
one could reach him and he could be quiet. As a little girl I used to have
a trunk in a closet where I went at times to play 'by myself.' It seems to be
a necessary part of my makeup." She read much about spirituality, nature,
existence, the universe, humanity's relationship to a higher being; meta-
physics and psychical research interested her. In her commonplace books of
these years she recorded dreamy thoughts of existence. ("Lord, what will
thou have me to do?") Occasionally juxtaposed on opposite pages were remarks easily applicable to Hugo: "The individual who is strongly based in
the concrete mind may disparage imagination as something childish because
he so lauds the faculties of logic and reason."

Her bent had always been artistic. She enjoyed writing, and some of
her articles, which were not without some style, had been published in *Junior
League* magazine under the name Josephine Foster. In the early 1930s her
thoughts turned again to writing. During the summer of 1932, which the
family spent partly at Point Clear, Alabama, off Mobile Bay, she wrote a
short story. It told about the essential uselessness of a politician's wife, how
she is not needed and has nothing to do. Revealingly, she entitled it "The
Fifth Wheel."

Many writers draw on their experiences for their best material; Josephine
was no exception. But one can only guess at her choice of subject and her
motivation. Could she in some way have been getting back at Hugo for so
controlling her life? To her delight *Harper's* magazine accepted the story for
publication. As happy as Hugo was for her, he made her write the magazine
that she could not have the story published because it might reflect, however
obliquely, on some of his supporters in south Alabama. Josephine was trying
to assert herself and boost her self-esteem, making a long-delayed stand for
independence. And Hugo shot her down. But her spirits were still high. "I

wrote a short story today," she noted in her diary in October 1932, "and was shocked at the sordidness of my sub-conscious mind in conceiving such a plot! However, the story was based on one of Hugo's law suits—tried about twelve years ago—and evidently never forgotten by me."

The spring of 1933 saw Hugo under great pressure. To relax, Josephine liked to invite Mary Knox Moore, an Alabama friend and a professional singer now living in Washington, to dinner. "She would call me and say, 'Mary Knox, it's so *dead* here. Come on over and liven things up.' When I got there, Hugo would be sitting so stiffly, with no smile, looking so serious. I'd play the piano and sing, and he joined in. Then he'd play some. It was hard to get him to loosen up. He did, very slowly, but the whole time he looked a little like he felt almost ashamed that he was. Josephine kidded him about it."[4]

Josephine's mood changed too. A stressful event, such as separation and loss, which her mother's institutionalization matched, can trigger depression in predisposed individuals; and the vulnerability to depression can be inherited in families in the same way many physical illnesses are. And the stress soon increased for Josephine, as she was expecting another child. Both she and Hugo wanted a daughter very much. For several months, she had no noticeable depressions, recalled Hugh Rozelle, Hugo's nephew who was working for him and living in the house. But as her time approached, and her mother's depressions deepened, Josephine's own depressions increased. "To a Baby Yet Unborn" she wrote:

> You who are folded there
> Underneath my heart
> Hold fast to me in my utter loneliness.

> You who but for a day
> Between this span of life and death
> Are *wholly mine*
> Take away this utter loneliness.

> You who one day soon
> Will break from my body
> And be a man
> Dispel now this utter loneliness.

Speak to me while you are mine
Tell me some deep truths.
—Are these chains in life we wear?
Or are we freer here than there?

What of life and what of death?
Have you ever lived before?
And did you choose to come?
Or were you sent by me above?—

Speak to me in language that I might understand
Tell me truths that might forever dispel this utter loneliness.

A daughter was born on October 27, 1933, and named Martha Josephine but called JoJo by all except her father who resolutely called her Josephine (or Little Josephine); and she quickly became the apple of his eye. Cigars were passed out, and a burden was lifted—temporarily.[5]

CHAPTER 12

THE INVESTIGATOR
LOBBYISTS AND PUBLIC UTILITIES

As the New Deal shifted emphasis from recovery to reform, one of Roosevelt's main goals was to abolish public utility holding companies. Pyramiding schemes meant that one company dominated others which in turn held stock in scattered operating companies. Higher utility rates across the country resulted. A holding company, said Will Rogers, "is a thing where you hand an accomplice the goods while a policeman searches you." At the heart of FDR's effort was the so-called "death sentence," which would allow the Securities and Exchange Commission to dissolve any holding company after January 1, 1940. Participants and bystanders alike called this titanic clash between the New Deal and Wall Street, with its Republican allies, in the summer of 1935 "the greatest congressional battle in history."

The Wheeler-Rayburn bill, named after its two sponsors, Senator Burton Wheeler and Congressman Sam Rayburn of Texas, had no stronger supporter than Black. "I have no more sympathy with attempting to regulate a holding company than I would have with attempting to regulate a rattlesnake," he said when one senator argued for regulation of the holding companies. They were "an inquisitorial system . . . a blood-sucking business, a vampire, taking the lifeblood of commerce and trade and extracting money from those who have earned it by honest toil and putting it in the pockets of people whose only right to it is that by chicanery, by fraud, by manipulation within and without the law, they have been able to obtain that which they did not earn."

The Senate passed the bill with the "death sentence" intact in June 1935, as the lobbying campaign conducted by the utilities was reaching its height. Industry spokesmen, resorting to an old standby, argued that widows and orphans would be hit hardest by the financial crisis that could be expected following the dissolution of the holding companies. Their agents outnumbered legislators. Missives by the ton flooded Congress; Western Union delivered about four thousand messages per hour to the Capitol. The utility mobilization, Roosevelt said just before the House voted, was "the most powerful, dangerous lobby . . . that has ever been created by any organization in this country." The campaign was successful. The House defeated the bill. Then a modified measure, without the "death sentence," was approved. FDR indirectly answered reporters' questions about these events by quoting a stanza from Robert Southey's poem "Battle of Blenheim":

> And everybody praised the Duke
> Who this great fight did win.
> But what good came of it at last?
> Quote little Peterkin
> Why that I cannot tell said he;
> But 'twas a famous victory.

There was, however, a victor at Blenheim, and Roosevelt was determined to win here.

After a Republican congressman charged the administration with coercion in return for his vote, the House agreed to investigate lobbying on bills affecting public utilities. The Senate quickly approved a resolution to appoint a special committee to investigate every effort to influence the holding company bill. Thomas G. ("Tommy the Cork") Corcoran, the chief White House operative on Capitol Hill, asked Wheeler to introduce it and to conduct the inquiry. Wheeler refused, claiming he was too busy with the bill and that the public would see him as a prosecutor and not an investigator. He went to Black, who readily agreed.

A special committee was promptly appointed, with Black as chairman, Sherman Minton of Indiana and Lewis Schwellenbach of Washington (both freshmen with whom he had quickly become friendly) as the other two Democratic members, and Lynn Frazier, a progressive from North Dakota, and Ernest Gibson of Vermont, in his first term, as the Republicans. The Black Committee, as it was called, got down to business quickly. The other members all worked hard but could not keep up with Black. As soon as he appeared at committee meetings, one reporter wrote, "all is unity. His natural leadership plus superior knowledge of subject plus diplomacy accounts for the fact that he is the predominating factor in private committee discussions."

He always asked "What do you think?" and waited while the other members talked. Then, as Minton noted, "we always followed Hugo's lead." He treated the Republicans as fairly as he did the other Democrats. At one point Gibson publicly defended the committee, saying he was sick of efforts to make it a partisan matter. Every action the committee took was unanimous.

The Black Committee "virtually set up a grand inquest on Capitol Hill," noted the *New York Times*. (Its powers had been expanded to investigate "any other matter or proposal affecting legislation [in the current] and succeeding Congresses.") With its fifteen regular staffers (others were hired as needed), Black was even-tempered, never fussy and loyal. "The most he will allow himself to say in rebuke is, 'John shouldn't have done it that way,' " noted a reporter. The White House was counting on Black to unearth evidence of corruption that would turn public opinion against the holding companies. Until then the bill would remain stalled in conference; and Vice President Garner threatened to keep Congress in continuous session until it passed the bill. The administration had regained the initiative on the holding company issue.[1]

Capitol Hill's hidden persuaders had long irritated Black. In 1929 he proposed a law requiring lobbyists to register with Congress, to name their employers, to state their objectives, and to report their salaries and expenditures. They represented "powerful interests and combinations intent upon special privilege, public pillage and public plunder," he said. When one lobbyist had implied that nine of the twelve senators (including Black) who had voted against a Coolidge administration measure to build fifteen new navy carriers had Communist ideas, Hugo told a reporter, "Men and groups who work behind a mask deserve no sympathy." (Could this choice of words have been a way of putting the Klan further behind him?) "They are enemies of true government or they would not fear public knowledge." The Senate inquiry into lobbying, he said, ought to "result in our hearing the flapping of the wings of the vultures as they fly away."

With the proliferation of government business under the New Deal, more than five thousand of these "pressure boys" had swamped Washington like bees by the mid-1930s. They plied their trade in the halls of Congress and stalked the city's leading nightspots. Their omnipresence maddened Black. He reintroduced his proposal in 1935, broadly defining lobbying as "any effort to influence the action of Congress upon any matter coming before it. . . ." The Senate passed it, and he attached a similar provision to the Public Utility Holding Company Act. The next year, provoked by William Randolph Hearst's attack on Congressman John McSwain of South Carolina, the House passed similar but weaker legislation: only representatives of organizations engaged "principally" in lobbying were required to register. It was the first time that both houses passed lobbyist registration bills. As they went to the conference committee, Black announced he would push for a measure "with some teeth in it." "Lobbying is lobbying," he said. But, pressured by lobbyists, the House overwhelmingly rejected the conference version. Not until 1946 was general lobbying legislation passed, as part of the Legislative Reorganization Act.[2]

As Black's committee convened for its first public hearing on July 12, Black shouted, "Tell the boys of the press to come in. The show is about to begin." The first witness was Philip H. Gadsden, chairman of the Committee of Public Utility Executives. Senate investigators had surprised him while he was working in his hotel office and whisked him by taxi to the Capitol. Black shot questions at him, often without waiting for answers before firing the next query. Gadsden revealed that soon after the Wheeler-Rayburn bill was introduced, public utility executives, meeting in the New York offices of the Edison Electric Institute, formed a group to defeat the measure. He was to guide the battle without revealing his affiliation with the Institute. Despite the stakes involved, and the industry's having already spent $1 million, the executives preferred not to keep minutes of its meetings. "We did it all openly and without any subterfuge," Gadsden insisted. "We always had our names to the masthead."

> I think there are two classes of what we call lobbies. One is a group that comes down here trying to get some selfish advantage out of the Government in preference to other taxpayers. I think the other group is a group like myself, that comes down here to do what they can to resist the effort of their Government to destroy their property. That is what we are up against. Gentlemen, just give me a moment. [No further question had been asked.]

Black adjourned the hearings to await return of financial questionnaires that had been sent to public utility holding and operating companies. He then received a tip from Congressman Denis J. Driscoll. Driscoll had received over eight hundred telegrams against the bill from one town, Warren, in his western Pennsylvania district. He was suspicious because nearly three fourths of the names started with letters in the first part of the alphabet; the B's alone accounted for 14 percent. Many people denied sending the telegrams; the post office returned some marked "addressee unknown." The local office of Associated Gas & Electric (AG&E) of Ithaca, New York, one of the nation's largest public utility holding companies, had directed one of its salesmen to "develop" at least one thousand telegrams to Congressman Driscoll; and he started with the letter A in the city directory.*

"Where are those original messages now?" asked Black. "They were burned in the stove in our cellar," the manager of the Warren Western Union office answered. "I do not know who definitely burned them." Even though regulations of both the Federal Communications Commission and Western Union required that the issuing office retain original telegrams for at least one year, AG&E had ordered its salesman to destroy every possibly incriminating record. The torching aided efficiency, the company claimed: all papers on the holding company bill would only "clutter up" the files. Black: "There was nothing of consequence so you were told to burn it, huh?"

AG&E used other means to gather signatures, such as paying messenger boys 3 cents for each one procured. One of these messengers, Elmer Danielson, came before the committee. He got six signatures—from his mother, a friend, a neighbor, and three others. (The telegram of the friend, fifteen years old and obviously well informed, read: "Don't let politics influence good judgment, oppose utility bill.") How, Black wondered, did nineteen-year-old Elmer, gangling and pink cheeked, win over six citizens? "What did you tell them?"

"I just asked them if they wanted to send a telegram."

"Did you tell them what they were signing?"

Beaming and wide-eyed, Elmer said he explained the Wheeler-Rayburn bill to them. After the laughter subsided, Black asked, "And where do you stand on that question today?" Elmer's eyes shifted. He opened his mouth, shut it, then smiled. "Well, I guess I'm neutral today."

Black was in high spirits afterward. His questioning of Elmer, Tom Corcoran later wrote, "really turned the tide of almost certain defeat for Roosevelt on that critical finishing blow to Roosevelt's financial enemies." "Another revelation like that," Black told a friend, "and we will compel the House to approve the 'death sentence.' " But victory was nowhere near certain.[3]

---

* Driscoll lost reelection because of utility money spent against him, but enjoyed a measure of revenge when he became co-trustee of AG&E when it went into bankruptcy in the 1940s.

....

After the House-Senate conference committee considering the bill adjourned indefinitely on July 24, AG&E vice president Frederick Burroughs appeared before the Black Committee. He discussed the company's finances. Since February he had worked against the holding company bill; AG&E had spent over $800,000. Twice Black asked about the correspondence he had generated. Burroughs: "I don't think I had any"; "We used the phone."

Gradually, a pattern emerged. The utilities organized and funded an elaborate front to fight the bill. The Edison Electric Institute, a lobbying organization hiding behind the inventor's name, pulled the strings, forming the Committee of Public Utility Executives that in turn set up another front, the American Federation of Utility Investors which sent out literature to every shareholder—all with money charged to operating expenses and passed on as costs to customers. Strange contradictions appeared. Innumerable identical messages over different signatures were sent from different areas. At least one "signer" was dead for two years—quite dead. The utilities paid for all but three of the 14,782 messages against the bill sent from New York, Pennsylvania, Texas and Florida, according to a committee staff canvass. In less than two weeks of hearings Black showed that the utilities had dispensed over $1 million. Later he estimated the total cost to be at least five times that.

He ferreted out the real purposes behind the high fees paid to various advisers. Did one utilities public relations man write a speech for a New York radio commentator? "No, Sir. . . . I supplied material for her." "Look at that, Mr. Carter," Black said. "This is my document," Carter acknowledged. "I guess it says 'draft.' I consider it a memorandum." Likewise, he found a thin line between legal services and outright lobbying, as one exchange with Philip Gadsden showed:

> BLACK: They did not have anything to do, of course, with trying to defeat the bill?
> GADSDEN: Oh, no; not a thing. Their job was to advise us.
> BLACK: They were to advise you how to defeat it.
> GADSDEN: That is right. . . .

Still, Black needed publicity and his methods turned rough. Committee agents roused a New Jersey advertising man from bed at 1 A.M. and immediately took him to Washington to testify. Edward Cramer, who worked for Edison Industries and was a member of the Utility Investors federation, had proposed back in March that utility executives, as one way to defeat the bill, instigate a "whispering campaign designed to create popular suspicion that the 'new dealers' and especially the 'New Dealer in Chief' are either incompetent or insane." With a weary and rumpled Cramer sitting in front of him, Black quoted *Time* magazine:

> For a fortnight Washington correspondents have been plagued by queries from editors and publishers back home. All queries begin alike: is the story true that ***? The stories also had one central theme: Franklin Roosevelt was on the verge of collapse, physical, mental, or both. He had, according to the tales roaring through the country in whispers, grown mentally irresponsible.

Black looked up. "That was exactly the kind of campaign that you suggested, was it not?" "Yes," Cramer answered, "that is one of the things." "Do you claim you had any basis on earth," Black demanded, "to try and circulate a report to the people of the United States that the President was insane? If so, give it now." Cramer replied, "No, none whatsoever," confessed that he was ashamed of himself and admitted that his suggestion was despicable; he was sent packing.[4]

Yet despite the many intriguing facts turned up, the investigation was a political failure. Black tried to bide time so that his findings would force the House to vote for the "death sentence" clause. But on August 1 the House defeated it again. Black took his case to the people over network radio. Americans had a constitutional right to petition the government, he said, but no "sordid or powerful group" had a right to present its views "behind a mask concealing the identity of that group. . . . The lobby has reached such a position of power that it threatens government itself. Its size, its power, its capacity for evil; its greed, trickery, deception and fraud, condemn it to the death it deserves. . . . You will destroy it."

Clearly, Black was making a powerful case. But a single identifiable villain was missing. He had announced back on July 14 that he would attempt to subpoena Howard C. Hopson, AG&E's founder, mastermind and president.* Committee investigators had been searching for him, with subpoenas

---

* Black targeted Hopson to the exclusion of other utilities executives, such as Wendell Willkie, who might have presented a cleaner image to the American public. Pinning down the articulate and appealing Willkie would have also been a difficult task.

in hand, since July 20. Black had in effect tried and found Hopson guilty in absentia, but that was not the stuff of which policy, and headlines, were made. Through a representative Hopson sent word that he was too ill to testify. Private detectives as well as dozens of government agents searched for him in New Jersey and Washington. He was switching hotels in the Washington area, and taking drives in Virginia and West Virginia to avoid process servers. After two weeks, he let himself be found. House Rules Committee chairman John O'Connor, whose panel had been assigned the House probe, announced Hopson was "under watchful eyes just outside of town," but would not say where or let Hopson out of his jurisdiction, because "the Black Committee might grab him." Hopson could expect gentle treatment from O'Connor, since O'Connor was trying to sabotage the holding company bill by focusing on "administration lobbying."*

Hopson sauntered into the packed House caucus room for a hearing the next day. So easy were the questions that one reporter likened the proceeding to a "gathering of old friends." Hopson left the room, still smiling cockily, only to be confronted by the Senate committee's process server. In the melee that ensued, Hopson's guards pushed the committee representative aside and rushed Hopson to a hotel, where he registered in his chauffeur's name. The Senate sent its sergeant at arms, Chesley Jurney, to find him. Dressed in a Prince Albert coat, polka-dot tie and straw hat, Jurney took three reporters with him in a Senate limousine; two more carloads followed. The spectacle of the machinery of government not catching up with a florid-faced, bald, roly-poly (230-pound) millionaire made colorful copy. "Eliza crossing the ice, hotly pursued by bloodhounds, had nothing on Howard C. Hopson," reporter Robert S. Allen wrote. A score of government agents drove through nearby Virginia and Maryland, and combed Washington hotels to no avail. Jurney ran into O'Connor in another hotel lobby. "We've got Hopson in custody, and we're going to keep him till we get through with him," O'Connor said.

After an inconsequential appearance before O'Connor the following morning, Hopson was served with a subpoena instanter by Jurney. Black confidently expected he would soon appear. When he did not show up by 4 P.M., Black rushed onto the Senate floor to urge that a warrant be issued

---

* "To have Mr. O'Connor head a committee to investigate the power trust lobby," pointedly observed John Rankin of Mississippi, a leading House spokesman for the "death sentence," "reminds me of the old woman who caught a mole in her garden. She was so exasperated at the little creature for eating her vegetables that she took him right to the scene of his depredations and cruelly buried him alive" (*NYT*, 7/7/35).

for the arrests of Hopson and his attorney for "contempt of the Senate." The motion was passed unanimously, without any debate, questioning or roll call. To avoid prosecution Hopson made himself available to Black, but only after O'Connor's committee defied him and turned Hopson over to the Senate.[5] Black had won his prize.

Hopson was worth the hunt. AG&E's holdings had grown so complex that he could not recall the businesses of all the companies he directed or even some of their names. Despite its annual income of over $100 million, AG&E had not paid dividends in recent years. Foes—Hopson had few friends— condemned his ethics. Utilities executives disliked him intensely, blaming his recklessness for causing much of their present trouble, and they had omitted AG&E from their lobbying operation to defeat the holding company bill. Hopson had to do his own bidding: he admitted to Black that AG&E had spent $875,531.95 up to the time of the hearings. Black immediately cross-examined him for two hours, demanding only facts and yes or no answers and stifling his determination to make speeches.

Slowly, Hopson's story came out. He gave AG&E's advertising only to those newspapers whose editorials and reporting satisfied him, warning others that "the heat would be turned on them." His telegrams to Hearst were sometimes reprinted as editorials without change. The destruction of records daily was standard procedure for interoffice memoranda, he explained. Black used file copies of Western Union telegrams to refresh his memory. The audience laughed at Hopson's comment that he would have kept the copies if he had known that Black would be able to get the originals. "You have me on the hip, Senator, as I don't know what you're reading from." He became evasive and rambling. "I want the truth," Black told him, "but I do not care to have any discussion or arguments or philosophies. We are asking for facts. If we want philosophies, we will ask for them." Piled high in front of Black at the next session were Hopson's subpoenaed interoffice telegrams from Miami to New York the previous winter. They showed how he personally approved almost every phase of the lobbying campaign. He admitted that he had devoted his entire organization to fighting the Wheeler-Rayburn bill since its introduction. "Our house was burning down and we were doing everything we could to save it," he said. The hearings had become so effective that the holding company bill itself was almost forgotten in the furor over who had spent how much in opposition.

Hopson charged that the committee was treating him roughly, "putting

words in his mouth" and "holding him to half truths." Black repeated that
Hopson was not to make any speeches. "Then you don't want the truth,"
Hopson shouted. The next day, Black interrupted Hopson to read a statement
drafted by the full committee that if there were not a more responsive attitude
from Hopson, it would bring additional contempt charges before the Senate.
As he finished reading, "Hopson's truculence melted magically," Paul Y.
Anderson of the *Saint Louis Post-Dispatch* wrote. "His fountain of speech,
which had spouted indefatigably for weeks dried up, and his manner became
strangely subdued."

The committee moved into AG&E's business operations. Hopson began
to answer questions directly and with some candor. Roosevelt had made the
company's tax records available to the committee (but not to the House
Rules Committee) by executive order. Hopson's personally owned service
companies netted profits of $3,187,064. The audience laughed as he con-
fessed that AG&E had issued a series of gold debentures due January 1,
2875.

Hopson proved Black's case. As helpless as a shackled turkey as Hugo,
with pleasure, plucked his feathers one by one, he personified almost every
crooked practice the holding company bill sought to eradicate—a caricaturist
could not have done better. He left the witness table humiliated but with
his arrogance intact, still scorning Black and the whole proceeding. Hopson
had unintentionally spotlighted the abuses of the holding company system. *
Black had proved no specific wrongdoing, but his intimations were clear
throughout. Guilt by circumstance suited his purpose well. The case against
the public utilities was tried before the people, his favorite forum. He never
more effectively employed his lusty suspicion of entrenched interest.

The House and Senate soon compromised on a bill. The bill dissolved
all holding companies more than twice removed from the operating companies, and all combines had to register with the SEC, which had the power
to eliminate companies once removed unless they met specific criteria of
efficient operation and regulation limiting them to a single, integrated system. FDR grumbled but finally accepted the bill. On August 26, 1935, he
signed it into law, hailing it as his greatest legislative triumph.[6]

* Hopson, whose personal fortune had been estimated at $47 million, went to jail in the
early 1940s on charges of defrauding stockholders of $20 million (Karl Schriftgiesser, *The
Lobbyists* [Boston, 1951], 72).

Black changed tacks in 1936. The committee now probed the affairs of pressure groups, focusing exclusively on ultra-conservative, self-styled patriotic, high-sounding anti–New Deal groups. Leading the list was the Liberty League, an organization of financial and industrial chieftains and leading corporate lawyers that issued a deluge of New Deal–despising propaganda on the principle it was teaching respect for property rights. Questionnaires concerning contributions made to the Liberty League and similar groups were sent to hundreds of business leaders in early 1936. Soon Black charged that the League was established so that corporations could circumvent laws that prohibited them from contributing directly to political causes. It was the "screen behind which certain groups could intervene in national affairs and remain within the law." He subpoenaed the heads of satellite lobbies around the League whose public images were more vulnerable (even if their incomes came from the same sources) than those of League leaders such as Al Smith and former Democratic National Committee executives John J. Rascob and Jouett Shouse, who had independent followings of their own. In this way he could attack the same opponents without focusing on the League. Much of the opposition to the New Deal, he wanted to prove, was an artificial creation of big business. In a presidential election year his findings in the machinations of the money aristocracy could supply fuel for the Democratic campaign.

He inquired into the activities of fourteen groups, such as the Farmers Independence Council of America, the Southern Committee to Defend the Constitution and the Sentinels of the Republic. All presented themselves as springing from grassroots, while withholding information about their financial support. Black called the farmers council's officers "Wall Street farmers." His committee revealed the links between these groups and the Liberty League, and how their revenue came almost exclusively from the money aristocracy—a handful of families, such as Du Pont (which alone provided one third), Morgan, Mellon and Rockefeller, and a few companies, such as Kellogg and Armour. When one source of contributors turned out to be *Poor's Manual of Directors*, even Senator Gibson, from rock-ribbed Republican Vermont, was moved to call the sources a "sucker list." Black had made another point about Roosevelt's political enemies.

Preparing for these hearings, Black used the dragnet subpoena duces tecum ("under penalty bring it with you") to gather evidence by examining telegrams. Among the many files the committee subpoenaed were all telegrams the Chicago law firm of Winston, Strawn and Shaw, which represented many large corporations, sent or received between February 1 and December

1, 1935. "When Hugo was investigating," Sherman Minton later said, "it was like the Wild West—he rounded them all up." Committee investigators undertook the enormous task of examining these messages for evidence of lobbying irregularities. The press, both moderate and anti-Roosevelt, excoriated Black for conducting an "inquisition." The *Chicago Tribune*, owned by the reactionary Colonel Robert R. McCormick, went further than any other paper. It sent a reporter to Birmingham and titled his front-page story "Klan Boasts of Sending Black to U.S. Senate"; and it published a cartoon entitled "The Night Riders: An Old Southern Custom," with Black in full Klan regalia riding over a countryside, flag ablaze, his object the "intimidation of all who oppose Roosevelt," and then it bought an entire page in the *New York Times* to reprint the cartoon.[7]

On March 2, 1936, on behalf of the law firm, Silas Strawn brought suit in the District of Columbia to prevent Western Union from handing over copies of his telegrams to Black. He argued, not without grounds, that the Senate was "conducting a general inquisitional investigation and fishing expedition into the private affairs and business of persons, firms and corporations." A judge immediately granted a temporary restraining order prohibiting Western Union from releasing any more telegrams.

Three times over the next two weeks, Black defended his committee's actions on the Senate floor. The lobby investigation was consuming almost all his time. When he was not conducting a hearing or was not on the floor, he was reading court cases or books and articles dealing with Congress's power to investigate. They reaffirmed his belief that, as he said upon hearing of the court's action, "The Senate can protect its interests when the time comes." If the court order were made permanent, he would seek Senate action to compel production of the telegrams. He defied any court to interfere with the Senate's ability to gather information.

> If I ever had any idea that any judge would issue an injunction against this body's getting certain evidence, I would have long ago introduced a bill to take away that jurisdiction which enabled the court to do that. Either this body has a right to summon witnesses or it has not. . . . If the time ever comes, when each time the Senate has an investigation different courts can issue injunctions to each separate witness to prevent the production of papers, then, of course, the power of the Senate to investigate will be lost.

He defended his methods as necessary to disclose "secret activities of privileged groups who sit behind the scenes and attempt to direct the economic

and political destinies of 120,000,000 free born citizens." "A loud clamor
has been made about private telegrams," Black said over a radio hookup.

> Be not deceived. Their noise comes because it was thought that all evidence
> had been burned and it is the telegrams that relate to public affairs that
> now frighten the spokesmen of privilege and the highly-paid mouthpieces
> of greed and grab. . . . The real opposition to this Committee's action,
> just as in all others, comes from a desire of those who want to work in
> darkness, who avoid the light, and who dread the condemnation of the
> honest, patriotic people of this nation for their pernicious practices and
> their secret and conniving efforts to conceal their sinister activities behind
> lofty names and sonorous phrases. Men quote the Holy Scripture for their
> own unholy purposes, and, if this is true of the Scriptures, may not men
> also quote the Constitution for the same unholy purposes?

He dismissed the complaints of "unreasonable" searches and seizures and
unlawful intrusion of privacy* during the holding company investigation as
"all this noise. . . . The destroyers of papers are not interested in privacy,"
he told senators, "but in continuing to conceal from the people of this nation
the devious and subterranean methods used to defeat legislation—to the
advantage of a few plutocrats in this country and to the disadvantage of the
great masses of the people. . . . Look behind the smokescreens to the citadel
of the great in the sanctum sanctorum of powers, of position, of privilege
whose instructions go out as to exactly must be written for the press. It is
then they begin to talk about constitutional rights. . . . They see they are
about to get caught. They thought the evidence had all been burned. . . .
The greatest enemy of a free press in America is the man who is willing to
subordinate it and to invade the sacred rights of the privacy of American
citizens whenever he can do so to put filthy dollars in his pocket."

Meanwhile, Chief Justice Alfred A. Wheat of the District of Columbia
Supreme Court heard Strawn's case. After Strawn's lawyer had been speaking
for two hours, Wheat suddenly said, "I do not believe I want to hear any
more," and granted the injunction. "This subpoena goes way beyond the

---

* The relevant constitutional provisions are the Fourth and Fifth amendments. The Fourth
  Amendment states:

  > The right of the people to be secure in their persons, houses, papers, and effects,
  > against unreasonable searches and seizures, shall not be violated, and no Warrants
  > shall issue, but upon probable cause, supported by Oath or affirmation, and partic-
  > ularly describing the place to be searched, and the persons or things to be seized.

  The Fifth Amendment provides that "No person shall . . . be deprived of life, liberty, or
  property, without due process of law. . . ."

legitimate use of the subpoena duces tecum." Western Union did not have to release the telegrams, since the committee had violated the Fourth Amendment's protection against unreasonable searches and seizures. It was one of the few times in American history that a court had restrained a congressional investigating committee. Black vehemently protested the ruling. Calling it "deliberate" and "malicious," he retaliated by threatening to introduce a bill to forbid courts from interfering with *any* legislative inquiry.[8]

At the same time Hearst seized the opportunity Strawn's case presented and sought to enjoin Western Union from delivering one specific telegram that Black subpoenaed. Black had given a copy of it, dated April 5, 1935, to Congressman John McSwain, chairman of the House Military Affairs Committee. In it Hearst had written: "Why not make several editorials calling for impeachment of Mr. Swain [sic]. He is the enemy within the gates of Congress, the Nation's citadel. He is a Communist in spirit and a traitor in fact. He would leave United States naked to its foreign and domestic enemies. Please make these editorials for morning papers." After McSwain read the telegram on the House floor (to the laughter of members who cheered when he denounced Hearst), Black withdrew the subpoena in the hope of deterring the suit. Hearst was insistent. The following day he broadened his request to protect all other subpoenaed telegrams.

"We are having quite a little controversy with Mr. Hearst," Black told an Alabama political friend. He was in his element, trying to uproot special privilege. "Those engaged in the fight will have all kinds of invectives hurled at them by those who fear that they will lose some of their unjust privileges," he wrote a sympathetic lawyer. "It is really quite an honor in this country to be abused by newspapers such as those operated by Mr. Hearst and the Chicago Tribune." To another correspondent he gave his explanation of the stakes involved: Hearst's suit challenged Congress's right to "make any investigation of any type of the press of the nation. If successful in this suit, investigations by Senate and House Committees for the purpose of passing legislation would hereafter be subordinated to the courts and would include a subordination to the District Courts of the nation. If this country is to continue to have a system of government by three coordinate branches, it is necessary that this suit be defended."

Hearst's novel request for an injunction against the Senate was denied. Courts do not have the authority to enjoin Congress's use of even illegally

seized documents, Chief Justice Wheat held. Hearst appealed. Defending
the committee after Richard Rives turned down an offer was Black's old law
partner Crampton Harris. In his brief he presented a straightforward position—that the separation of powers mandated that courts had no power to
prevent a coordinate branch of government from performing its duties in
the way it saw fit—and won an unanimous decision. (Whether the allegations
of Hearst's complaint were true was not in issue.) Hearst did not appeal to
the U.S. Supreme Court. Black had won by default.

Savoring it all was Franklin Roosevelt. In early May 1936 his old brain
truster Raymond Moley paid a visit. They discussed Black's investigation,
Moley recorded in his journal, and FDR "went into a long discourse of how
Black's invasion of privacy had ample precedent in Walsh and Seabury.* . . . The inference was that the end justified the means." It would
be better, Moley commented, to let people "go free than to establish the
principle of dragnet investigations. I said that sooner or later there would
be great public indignation at such methods, and he reverted once more to
the moral indignation theme," that people were angry and fed up with the
sins of others.[9]

·   ·   ·

Then and later, Black's investigating methods were bitterly criticized. His
use of the subpoena duces tecum was especially condemned. "He didn't have
to use it," said New Dealer Benjamin V. Cohen. "He went too far." Black
was more prosecutor of immovable foes than impartial investigator. "There
is no power on earth," he wrote, "that can tear away the veil behind which
powerful and audacious and unscrupulous groups operate save the sovereign
legislative power armed with the right of subpoena and search."† After an
investigator "has tried every technique, politeness, kindness, blandish-
ment, . . . he is sometimes driven in the presence of a witness who is
deliberately concealing the facts to attempt to shake it out of him with a
more drastic attack." If a witness refused to answer questions, Black con-

* Roosevelt was referring to Senator Thomas Walsh, whose investigation broke open the
Teapot Dome scandal, and to Samuel Seabury, the New York judge whose investigation of
corruption in New York City led to the removal of Mayor Jimmy Walker and several
convictions.

† "The power of the probe," he continued, "is one of the most powerful weapons in the hands
of people to refrain the activities of powerful groups who can defy every other power. That
is because special privilege thrives in secrecy and darkness and is destroyed by the rays of
pitiless publicity."

tinued, "In each instance with which I am familiar, the House and Senate have steadfastly adhered to their right to compel reply, and the witnesses either answered or have been imprisoned."

He wrote this in an article *Harper's* magazine commissioned and ran in March 1936. It was, he recalled, "pretty well received until Walter Lippmann gave it a very vigorous criticism." The legislative inquiry was "by way of becoming an engine of tyranny in which men are denied the elementary legal protection that a confirmed criminal caught red-handed in the act can still count on," Lippmann wrote in calling for an investigation of legislative investigations. Coming from the public paradigm of rationality, this had the sweet aura of truthfulness.

"I was completely surprised at his interpretation of the article," Black recounted. "Unfortunately, however, in reviewing it in the light of Mr. Lippmann's criticism, I was compelled to admit to myself that his interpretation was wholly reasonable." And thirty years later, he privately admitted that the exposure of individual wrongdoing was not a necessary investigative function of Congress. Otherwise, Black adamantly defended his actions. But he exhibited a touchiness that he did about few other subjects. The Klan he could always attempt to rationalize; anyway, that was politics. This dealt with his official duties, and with people's rights. When a representative of the American Civil Liberties Union questioned him about invading individual liberties, he took the offensive: "It is to be regretted that a group that claims to stand for the liberties of the people should unite with a group that recognizes no right of liberty except for themselves."

> If the views which you have been asked to support had been adopted a long time ago there would have been no Teapot Dome exposure of crookedness; the credit moblier grafters would have escaped without the public's knowing the wrongs they had committed, and every other Congressional and Senatorial investigation would have been unable to accomplish the purposes intended. It just seems a little strange to me that an organization which has led the public to believe that it wants to protect the masses of the people from loss of their economic liberty should suddenly discover that it is called upon to join the so-called Liberty League and utility lobbyists and others in protesting against the practice which has been accepted as constitutional for more than a hundred and fifty years.

This criticism, moreover, involved something that was at least as important to Black: "I do not believe that any witness who appeared before us can truthfully say that I did not treat him with courtesy, even some witnesses whose own deportment was at the opposite extreme from courtesy." He emphatically denied that he ever "browbeat" or "bullied" witnesses. "If even at this late date [1959] I knew that I had ever browbeat a witness, I would apologize to him if I found him living." One of those, of course, was Howard Hopson. "Strange as it may seem," Black wrote, "I developed far more admiration for Hopson—who was bold and frank about what he did—than I did for other witnesses who thought it was better at least to evade than to answer all inquiries truthfully."[10]

Black's success as an investigator was based on several factors—his diligent preparation, his ability to put his finger on the important issues, his persistence, and his firmness as presiding officer. He sat at the center of the committee table, calm, ever courteous, a smile wrapping his face as he gazed at the witness facing him. He would launch a cordial conversation. The witness relaxed and gained confidence. "Suddenly the unlit cigar* would be shifted to the corner of his mouth as his lips drew into a tight line. It was the tip-off. Black would let loose a machine-gun fire of questions, his eyes blazing, his hands working in quick nervous gestures. And the hapless victim was nailed to the cross of his own indiscretions."†

He demanded information on the spot. A witness suffering from a sudden attack of amnesia was quickly cured. He tolerated no nonsense. Utilities agents who appeared before him were "so frightened that they instinctively address him as 'your Honor,' " journalist Raymond Clapper noted. Black investigated, said James Landis, then chairman of the Securities and Exchange Commission, "with bare fists." His purpose was to advertise what he had already learned. Hugo put aside other activities to study files, read correspondence, draft questionnaires, analyze the returns; and he stayed up all night if necessary. "He comes to the committee room about fifteen minutes before the hearing opens," one newsman wrote, "calls for files on the witness, and re-reads or scans them for the second time. This is all the preparation he makes for hearings. It's amazing to an outsider. At hearings he seems to know more about the witness's business than the witness." "So far as Mr. Gadsden and Mr. Hopson were concerned," Black felt, "if I 'bested' them

---

* He chewed an old black stub. A doctor told him in 1932 to quit smoking; this was his "compromise" (WS, 8/13/37).

† Wallace Werble, who covered the hearings for *Newsweek*, wrote: "He starts out seemingly along some inane line, sets about twenty traps for the witness and keeps up along a straight line, going easy all the time, until the witness falls into one trap" (*Newsweek* files).

it was due in no small part to the fact that I had made extensive study of their past activities in preparation for asking them the questions I did."

His elephantine memory was Black's greatest asset. When AG&E vice president Fred Burroughs finished testifying, he asked for the witness fee of $3 a day and expenses. Black pointed out that Burroughs said he made $60,000 a year. "I was forced to take up my time to come here," Burroughs said, "and I want my fees." Black flipped right to a page of Burroughs's testimony: "Forced? Why this transcript shows you testified: 'I want everybody to know I came here of my own volition and I've been trying to come before this committee for a week.' " Burroughs didn't get the fees.

Black was tough—very tough—but impersonal. He stuck solely to the grounds of the inquiry. His job was to get the facts and he was merciless in that. But he did not question motives or slander reputations or impugn patriotism as later investigators did. Black wanted to know what people did, not their opinions; their actions, not their thoughts. "Sarcastic at moments, he can remain friendly enough to shake hands with his witnesses when they leave the stand." After heatedly interrogating one witness, he smilingly bid him "good day" and went over to discuss calmly how newspaper photographers mistreated both of them.

Equally indispensable was Black's ability to work effectively with the press. He had a knack for knowing what reporters needed. They appreciated that he arranged sessions, sometimes long and dull, to provide a bit of scandal in the morning for the afternoon papers and another newsworthy item in the afternoon for the morning dailies. "Chairman Black's Three-Ring Circus," they dubbed the hearings. He made wonderful copy—eminently quotable, with good leads, and full of revelations. They appreciated that, unlike most investigators, he relied upon finesse and shrewdness; and they did not mind that he personalized congressional investigations more than other legislators. Veteran newsmen considered him "the best investigator the Senate ever had."[11]*

His delight was obvious. He was exulting in a new role, playing it with the greatest of éclat. The job was made for him—or perhaps he made it in his own image. Black was where he always wanted to be, fighting for the

---

* Frequently seen leaning over Black's shoulder was reporter Paul Anderson, a brilliant but troubled man who spent his whole career digging up scandals. Also behind him virtually as an assistant sat Ruth Finney of the Scripps-Howard chain (the only major news service backing FDR on the issue). Both not only worked actively with Black in developing the investigation but passed him notes and questions (some from other reporters) and spoke with him during hearings.

people against the "interests," exposing corporate chicanery, rooting out entrenched privilege. "His eyes sparkle," a reporter wrote, "and the more difficult a witness becomes the more Black seems to enjoy it. If a witness continually answered 'I don't remember,' Black pounded away. 'Who did you say was in the dinner party?' the scenario would go. 'What did you talk about?' 'Well, what did "A" say to "B"?' 'Now this dinner was only 24 hours ago. Can't you remember what happened?' 'Let me see, what did you say your salary is?' " Back came the answers, sounding frailer and more tired and defensive all the time. Black exploited all the possibilities in his dual role as judge and prosecutor—setting the tone of the proceeding with his manner of questioning, admitting or rejecting evidence and replies, examining and cross-examining, acting on his trained intuition for inconsistencies and evasions, engaging in asides, refusing to share documents—and he did it with an unmistakable glee.

It was politics as theater. His natural showman's instinct came to the fore. Black thrived in the white glare of publicity. The trial lawyer, with his shrewd flair for melodrama, was acting on a larger stage. At times Black was guilty of excess zeal, and he was driven, as all successful investigators must be, by a conviction of righteousness, that his cause was morally above reproach. It was a job suited for a trial lawyer. The facts have to be dug up, presented in an understandable way; the courtroom skill of asking short, incisive questions is essential; and, as *Newsweek* observed, "the Senator from Alabama seems to know the answers before they're given." By making the iniquitous image of Howard Hopson stick as the embodiment of the entire public utility holding company system, Black greatly eased the bill's enactment. "Hugo was invaluable," said Burton Wheeler. "It couldn't have passed without him."

———

Black's hatred of business interests caused him to trample over witness's rights protected by the Fourth Amendment. He used to the fullest the investigatory powers of Congress—few have used, or can use, them more so—but directed them only toward hard-core conservatives. If they had been aimed at the other end of the political spectrum, he would have been the first to howl at the infringement of constitutional rights.

He always realized the intensity of the interests' hostility to anyone who challenged them, and the lengths to which they would go to destroy anyone who proposed change that harmed them. Such rancor only hardened his determination, and made him more aware of the dangers he faced. The utilities secretly tried to "get something" on him, to dig up some hidden facts. Black found out about this clumsy effort and it failed on its own—as had a similar attempt by the *Chicago Tribune*, which sent reporters to Alabama during his 1932 reelection campaign. That was when the paper had learned about his Klan connection, which it used in the cartoon about him. The Alabama Power Company barely reduced its rates after buying electricity at very low cost from the TVA's Muscle Shoals dam. Its head at the time was Thomas Martin. "And he really hated Hugo Black," recalled Virginia Durr. "I don't think I've ever seen a man hate another man with such passion as he did Hugo Black. He really despised him."[12] In his feelings Martin did not stand alone.

CHAPTER 13

PORTRAIT OF A NEW DEALER

T HE STERILE CONSERVATISM of Alabama's ruling hierarchy practically invited dissent. And Hugo Black was in constant intellectual rebellion, questioning fundamental assumptions most people cheerfully swallowed, his sense of outrage perpetually rekindled. On the surface he was an unlikely rebel. His dress, speech and manner were utterly conventional, and he often said that one could not win people over by offending them or making them feel uncomfortable and that it is easier to gain support on major issues if one is as orthodox as possible on unimportant matters. But sometimes he did things differently just to be different. He often sang "I Am a Good Old Rebel," a bitter piece written by Major Innes Randolph, who served with J. E. B. Stuart: "I'm just a dirty rebel, and that is what I am. For this fair land of freedom, I just don't give a damn. . . ."

Within Black was a touch of the jacquerie. He saw the world in terms of a battle between the dispossessed and the comfortable. But he was too sincere and sober to be a demagogue. In a time of despair he raised people's hopes and offered optimism, the chance of a better life. His rhetoric dealt more with proposals than with personalities. It quickened people's emotions—and then he'd stop, as if he had a sixth sense that told him a crowd shouldn't be *overly* provoked. His awareness of the excesses of power, reinforced by his extensive reading, tempered his actions. "Study people as well as books," he liked to say.

He studied majority leader Joe Robinson and Huey Long. Black hit it off well with Robinson from the beginning. Conservative to the core but more loyal to the Democratic Party than to any other earthly institution, the temperamental Robinson struck some as autocratic: he had the final say on the appointment of Democrats to committees and in deciding which bills would come to the floor, and in what order, for debate and vote. But he so greatly admired Black that he modified his style. Once Robinson did not appear at a meeting of a joint House-Senate committee that he chaired. The waiting senators were irked and restive. When he finally showed up, Robinson said, "Senator Black was speaking and when he talks, I never want to miss a word."

"Huey Long has one of the very best minds I've ever met," Black said. They shared broadly similar backgrounds, thought almost alike and were the Senate's best debaters. On one occasion the issue was, as Long phrased it, "whether or not, in the case of a corporation owned by farmers, the stockholders ought to be made individually liable and the other corporations allowed to shield their members and stockholders from individual liability." If he had had Long's assistance the last time the matter came up, Black said, "I believe I would have won."

"No," roared Long. "I gave the Senator votes by being against him and he does not realize it."

"That is likely true," said Black to the laughter of colleagues.[1]*

Joe Robinson hated Long and turned to his best weapon. By June 1935 Black had grown tired of Long's obstructing legitimate Senate business. So he happily agreed to Robinson's request to stop Huey's latest filibuster. He organized a group of freshmen to stay on the floor to force Huey to talk until he dried up. Huey started to talk shortly after noon. At four o'clock Alben Barkley of Kentucky suggested that Long sing instead of talk. At five Huey asked for a recess. Black objected successfully, as he also did at nine o'clock and eleven. Long continued to speak, discussing his favorite recipes and the place of Frederick the Great in history. At 2:52 A.M. five freshmen objected in unison to his call for a recess. One hour later, at nearly 4 A.M., hoarse and "as groggy as a punch-drunk boxer," Long yielded the floor and, in response to nature's demands, rushed to the men's room.

Black was "as proud of this effort as he was of much of what he did on the Court," his son Sterling recalled. It was no coincidence that the next month both Schwellenbach and Minton were named to his lobbying investigation committee. Huey knew who was behind the freshmen. The next

---

* "I was born forty years too soon," Long said another time. "I'm not being appreciated." Hugo rose. "Will the senator yield?" Huey did. "Mr. President," Black said. "I just wish to concur with the sentiments of the distinguished senator from Louisiana that he"—and Hugo stopped. Huey scratched his leg as if to say, "That's pretty good, old Hugo," recalled one observer, Hugh Rozelle (int.).

day he and Black met in the Senate restaurant. "What'd you want to do me
that way for?" Long asked. Hugo explained that Huey had simply filibustered
him into missing supper once too often. The Kingfish's response is not
recorded but in the three months that remained before he was assassinated
he tried only one more filibuster. After a few hours the Young Turks, Hugo's
"Out of the Senate by Supper Bloc," again foiled it.[2]

Whether he was leading senators, speaking or debating, Hugo could be as
passionate as a great artist or as hard as a great general. He had about him
that indefinable aura of control. His voice spread both a sense of authority
and of calm. His eyes could seem cold. His temper was always under control.
He conveyed intensity. * "He was serious-minded and didn't have much sense
of humor," Burton Wheeler noted. In the cloakroom "he didn't swap yarns
too much," observed Claude Pepper, who served briefly with him. A man
of primary colors, Hugo could also mix the pastels on his palette to the
appropriate shade. Wheeler: "Hugo was an emotional sort of fellow, one
who could be swept off his feet on some issues, and sweep you off them too
if you didn't look out. He planned to be emotionally effective."

  He approached his job with gusto and almost all his work was exclusively
his own. He rarely tired even though he worked like a Trojan. "We are doing
the best we can to keep Senator Black from working too hard," an assistant
wrote, "but are not very successful except for short intervals at a time." His
entire personal retinue consisted of four secretaries and an administrative
assistant who kept the office going. To his staff Hugo was never stodgy or
nasty and rarely critical. He had a contagious laugh and his bright shoe-
button eyes snapped all around. He usually wore a rumpled dark gray or blue
suit and a beat-up felt hat in the winter, and was always rushing. But barring
urgent Senate matters, he made himself constantly available to Alabamians
visiting Washington. Periodically, he wouldn't be in the office for several
days, but would call in a dozen times daily. Then he would whiz back in
and pull papers out of a file or his pocket. Since he didn't carry a briefcase,
he often lost letters. "We have to get a new filing system," he would say
before going on to something else. No one who worked in his office recalled
him as mean or impolite. Situations, not individuals, got him angry. Some-

* "I saw Black as successful, aloof, somewhat cold, not an easy man, terse, curt, not quick
  either to friendship or informality, a get-business-over-with-dispatch type," noted David
  Ginsburg (int.), who worked for the public utilities division of the SEC and reported to
  him on various matters.

times people who hadn't previously met him came to the office looking antagonistic; almost always they left smiling. "He was one of a kind, a breed apart," one staffer said.[3]

The press corps regarded Black highly. He was honest, straightforward, an original with dash and verve. "He read, he thought for himself and he honestly told you what he thought," said Joseph Alsop. "He made you feel he trusted you. All that is rare among senators, even then. You couldn't pigeonhole him. He was just different, an original and I simply liked him." Many reporters concurred. They appreciated that he was "always willing to talk or give a reporter a helping hand," as one observed. "He's not a publicity hound, but makes himself into good news by instinctively making big stories. He also has a faculty for creating mystery [which] gives political reporters a big chance to speculate. He is modest, unassuming, etc., but fancies himself as pretty smart though. He says he doesn't care for favorable stories as long as the facts are told." Since he sometimes lisped slightly, his remark that "This will fwottle the fweedom of the pwess" was often mimicked in the press gallery. To pass time when things got dull, remembered Turner Catledge of the New York Times, some reporters polled each other about the senators. Park Trammell of Florida was considered the most "useless." Black was voted the most persuasive.

While newsmen respected and largely agreed with him on issues, he vehemently opposed their publishers. Most were "merchandisers of the First Amendment" who used their freedom to escape their responsibility, Black believed. He had a good word for few newspapers. When a Birmingham friend, William Hendrix, joined the pro–New Deal New York Daily News, Black wrote, "it has seemed to me that this paper really wants to help all of the people, and it does not permit itself to be a propagandist for the small privileged group of racketeers in America."[4]

*   *   *

For a spell Josephine's depressions had lessened. Helping to run the house and to bring up three children kept her busy, and in 1935 the Senate wives elected her president of the Senate Ladies Luncheon Club. But in early 1937 the depressions returned, if with less frequency. Feeling mournful for herself and not knowing what to do, she occasionally asked Hugo to leave politics. But it was his life and his career, and she catered to him and to it. In her gentle way and with her intuitive understanding Josephine frequently corrected him with humor about the feelings of persons he dealt with, and helped smooth out his rough spots. He accepted her advice, as he accepted no one else's. She made him realize anew, as he continually needed re-minding, that he could not bulldoze his way through situations and that holding firm, martyrlike, would not necessarily prove anything, that his dry humor left a sting.

Although they were not regulars on the social circuit, Hugo and Jose-phine went to many dinners and parties. But mostly they preferred to en-tertain at home. Cliff and Virginia Durr "were continually in and out of the house"; and Lister Hill, then the congressman from Montgomery, as well as Senators Robert La Follette of Wisconsin, Shay Minton and Lew Schwel-lenbach and their wives often visited. Even though Josephine (really the housekeeper, now Annie Campbell) set a splendid, informal table, Hugo sometimes wrapped a large apron around himself and cooked dinner, usually a steak. A doctor long ago had told him to eat steak every day to protect his health; he faithfully followed this advice. Hugo regaled friends with Clay County stories or campaign and courtroom tales, or he played on the piano or harmonica songs that all joined in singing, while Josephine's instinctive friendliness and sympathy, delightful sense of humor and ability to puncture pretense painlessly kept the fun going.[5]

He was the undisputed master of his house. To his sons he was a tough father and a strict disciplinarian—but not to Jo-Jo, with whom as a reporter noted, he carried on "a love affair" in a (barely updated) southern version of the double standard. His notions about child rearing could have come right out of Dickens, a century earlier. Perhaps he hoped that the continual discouragement he gave his sons—he did not reward them when they did well, only punished them when they did wrong, while pitting them against each other—would somehow stimulate them. He demanded perfection. If Hugo, Jr., didn't receive all A's in school, he yelled, "Why do you have to swoop after you soar?" Convinced that comics in the newspaper caused this lapse from perfection, he banned his sons from reading them. But Sterling's report card was perfect, and Sterling didn't think the edict should apply to him.

So, early the next morning Sterling called a friend and they just started to walk. But by night they had become tired and the friend called his father to pick them up. When Sterling came home, neither Hugo nor Josephine said anything or asked why he had run away. Hugo immediately locked Sterling in the attic for several days of solitary confinement, and warned the rest of the family not to see him. He did, however, bring Sterling two meals daily. (Josephine, without telling anyone, brought him water and food when-ever she was home.) "He was hardest on those he loved the most and rarely said a harsh word about anybody else," noted Sterling. "He was such a strong personality that you couldn't resist him. He just beat you down."

Children should be brought up Spartanlike, Black believed. Thinking his sons lacked discipline, he sent them to the Florida Military Academy in St. Petersburg, Florida for two years in the mid-1930s. That regime would keep them from becoming conceited. It was important to be a "plain fellow." That meant being frugal: he often had his one pair of shoes resoled. After dinner, even at friends' houses, Hugo helped wash the dishes. Josephine feared he might do this at a formal dinner or White House affair. Live simply and within your means, he urged, otherwise you'll be tempted to sell out your ideas and principles. Once, after Hugo, Jr., had ordered the most expensive item on the menu, he forced him, to the point of tears, to finish eating it. Even nonworking time should be spent productively. One Sunday afternoon, hearing his sons laughing, he came in and said, "I'm going to read something that fits you boys," and proceeded to read from Oliver Goldsmith's *The Deserted Village:* "The loud laugh that spoke the vacant mind." Birthdays, holidays and sports he viewed as unnecessary. Yet on occasion he allowed himself to enjoy life enormously and relished times with the family together—barbecues, music, dancing (usually at the Army and Navy Club with Josephine), playing golf with her or pitching softballs to the boys, allowing them to teach him Monopoly and, especially, picnics in the country.[6]

Hugo's reflective and scholarly side complemented his activist temperament and gave a solid foothold to the bold solutions he proposed. Many of the recollections of Black as a senator revolved around his reading. An offhand listing he made in 1948 of books read largely during these years came to several hundred volumes. Predominating were history, "innumerable biographies," the works of the Founding Fathers and Enlightenment *philosophes,* political theory, poetry, English and American literature ("Shakespeare's works—some many times"; "Dickens—all"; "many of Mark Twain's books"), and, of course, ancient classics. Although he omitted economics and noted, "I could give you many more by reflection," it is an astounding list for a public officeholder and one that would keep any full-time university faculty member busy.

His desk in his office, and later in a little, bare hideaway on the first floor of the Senate Office Building, to which he escaped in order to read and write speeches and (especially on Saturdays) dictate letters, was piled so high that one caller, David Lilienthal, said Black could hardly be seen when leaning back in his chair behind them, "chewing a cigar and up to the elbows in papers." He often had a load of books under his arm as he pranced through the Capitol with an easy gait that to one reporter vaguely suggested a Tennessee walking horse. During debates, his desk on the Senate floor was stacked with legal cases and economic treatises, with place marks stuck in them, giving him ready ammunition to make a point or to pounce on an errant colleague. From slouching in his seat—he didn't sit in a chair; he restlessly bivouacked in it—Black would suddenly jump up and interrupt, "Will the Senator yield?" and gladly joust with his adversary.

The largest purpose of his reading was for specific information that he could apply to solve the economic problems of the day. "He was always quoting various economists," said his colleague Wheeler. "He had studied them." But he had his other favorite authors. There was Jefferson of course. Charles and Mary Beard's *Rise of American Civilization* appealed strongly to Black. But he never mentioned Beard in any of his Senate remarks, partly because the historian's outspoken liberalism would not go down well at home. In a selective use of history he referred to Walter L. Fleming's *Civil War and Reconstruction* to make a point during debate on the 1932 relief bill, even though he did not find Fleming's marked southern bias appealing. The intellectual currents such as regionalism and agrarianism that whipped across the South in the 1930s did not affect Black. Returning to the land was impossible and impracticable in a machine age, he believed. The South, part of the Union, had to adapt to modern conditions. The system had to remain in kilter. "If you don't like the idea," noted one reporter, "the chances are that Mr. Black can quote Aristotle to you to prove it is a sound one."

His reading also had an exhortative purpose. Thus it was Plato's caveman fable in *The Republic* that Hugo took as his typically extemporaneous text upon receiving an honorary doctorate from Auburn University in 1935. "This subject was chosen," he wrote in 1966, "because Auburn had already begun to teach that to be free, people must struggle out of the lower world of shadows and echoes and seek knowledge in the upper world of reason."[7]

*   *   *

Books were a necessary avocation; politics was his profession. Senator Black kept a vigilant eye on his home base. In 1935 an antilynching bill was reintroduced. It called for federal prosecution of any public official if a mob, defined as three or more persons acting in concert, tried to injure or kill any person in its custody. In lengthy remarks on the Senate floor, Black said he wholeheartedly favored the bill's objective—"I yield to no man in my hostility and my antagonism to the crime of lynching"—but he could not support the measure. For, remembering the 1908 Birmingham coal strike, he viewed it as an antilabor bill: "In the name of antilynching, to crucify the hopes and aspirations of the millions of workers of the country is beyond my conception." If three union members (a "mob") gathered, and one were charged with injuring a strike breaker, and the prosecutor decided that the striker was not guilty, Black hypothesized, would the prosecutor then "dare not to tell the jury so? He would not . . . because he would know that his Government . . . had passed a law which subjected the prosecuting attorney to five years' imprisonment, and [he would] have the stigma of felony put upon his brow, if he neglected to do everything he could to convict that man." All sheriffs and police officers, Black warned, would become strike breakers for fear of being prosecuted for failing to protect company property.

Black had read in Thomas Macaulay's *History of England* that when native Englishmen killed Normans after the Norman conquest, the idea of trying someone other than the person who committed the crime had been judged a failure. Officials here would be forced to prosecute strikers if any deaths occurred during a strike, Black predicted: a proper title would be "A bill to prevent strikers from meeting together and injuring the property of their employers, or, as a consequence of their meeting together, injuring or killing strike breakers or other individuals." The senator from Alabama came to the heart of the situation. The proposed law would also separate the races. "Is it fair to use at this time," he asked, "when we are working in peace and harmony the one with the other, to do something which will bring about again the spread of the flame of race antagonism, and instill prejudices which, thank God!, have been stifled in the hearts of the people of Alabama and the other States of the South?"

He meticulously analyzed the bill in an example of somewhat specious, if sophisticated, reasoning. Unspoken was his contention that states should handle these matters themselves. But his discussion brought legal doubts to the fore. Whatever his substantive feelings, Roosevelt did not want to endanger his legislative program by offending southerners who held strategic positions in Congress. "I've got to get legislation passed by Congress to save America," he told Walter White, the secretary of the National Association for the Advancement of Colored People. Other liberals were also unsure about the measure's constitutionality. Norris and William Borah of Idaho (whom many, especially Borah himself, considered a great constitutional lawyer) joined in speaking against the bill, effectively killing it for the session.

A majority of Black's voting constituents certainly agreed with his opposition. Antilynching legislation symbolized the attack on the Jim Crow system of segregation. That system "reached its perfection in the 1930s." It "prevailed . . . in all aspects of life," as two laws passed by Birmingham in 1930 showed. One ordinance required separate taxicabs; the other, getting down to specifics, made it "unlawful for a Negro and a white person to play together or in company with each other" at dominoes or checkers. To be against the bill was not to be a devotee of the rope and fagot. "We can proceed most successfully against this crime without the enactment of this bill," Black wrote a friend in 1937. "I am not persuaded that you can prevent lynching in any particular county by providing for a penalty against the taxpayers of the county, with the right to levy execution on county property. . . . It is very necessary to consider the local reaction to a Federal bill, which reaction might arouse much resentment, that instead of deterring the practice, it might actually aggravate it." Unlike other southern senators, Black did not camouflage his opposition in a torrent of high-sounding but empty rhetoric. But if he had favored the proposal, he would have lost much of his influence toward assuring that Alabama would send a pro-Roosevelt delegation to the 1936 Democratic convention.[8]

By the mid-1930s Black had become "fast political friends" with Alabama's other senator, John Bankhead.* Lacking the light touch, almost self-consciously serious, with an occasionally searing temper, he never forgot that in large measure he owed his seat to Black's maneuverings. (Socially they did not see each other much.) Bankhead's primary interest, agriculture, did not clash with Black's main concerns; and, he always remembered, Hugo was the senior senator and senior partner in the alliance. Their relationship, he wrote Bankhead, "has created a friendship that I would greatly regret for any disagreement to threaten."

An informal but binding arrangement required both senators to approve all federal patronage and appointments in Alabama. Even before the death of Birmingham federal judge William I. Grubb in October 1935, many lawyers had mounted vigorous campaigns for the post. The judgeship held special importance, since by statute it had jurisdiction over all TVA action.

* Bankhead's brother Will, the House majority leader, liked Hugo too. Usually he "kept pretty quiet on other people," recalled Will's chief assistant Carter Monasco (int.). "But he talked about Black and said Black simply got more done than any other senator."

David J. Davis had long wanted the post, and since coming to the Senate Black never had any other candidate in mind, as Bankhead knew. That they had been roommates, partners, and "particularly close" friends was immaterial to Hugo. Bankhead wanted a man "widely known as an outstanding lawyer of high convictions." Davis, although a former president of the Birmingham Bar Association, had a wide-ranging general practice but few corporate clients, which attorneys like Bankhead considered essential to being an "outstanding lawyer." Only after several exchanges of letters with Black, and assurance that Davis had voted for him in 1930, and, even then, he told Hugo, "more on your account than all of the others combined," did Bankhead support Davis's nomination.

In the midst of his exchanges with Bankhead, Black explained his views on judicial appointments. "In almost all instances," he explained, "judges in the federal court have been men, who whether by instinct or by environment, have not been sympathetic enough with the plain people, and have been too sympathetic with wealth and privilege. It is my intention to do everything within my power to see that this greedy group has nothing whatever that it can expect from the judge of the Northern District of Alabama, except *even handed justice*" and that "no man sits [there] who is not in sympathy with the progressive ideas absolutely essential to bring about economic justice in America."[9]

CHAPTER 14

COURT-PACKING
AND WORKING HOURS

BLACK'S INVESTIGATIONS had won him Roosevelt's favor. The two shared the same bitter enemies, whom they relished routing in the forthcoming presidential election. The campaign would be a vehicle for educating the public, its theme a war against entrenched privilege. "We have only just begun to fight," FDR said at its climax. In June 1936 Black attended his first Democratic convention. As a member of the Alabama delegation he served on the platform committee, where he and Michigan governor Frank Murphy helped draft the labor plank. For the first time a political party pledged to do something about "minimum wages, maximum hours, child labor and working conditions."

As one of the Democrats' most effective speakers, Black enjoyed heaping invective on Republicans, pounding away on their demand for the return of the "good old days" (a favorite phrase) "when the Constitution was safe for Republicans." Perhaps only FDR himself was better at turning on the faithful. One occasion was the Missouri Jackson Day banquet in early 1936. Black "proved to be a man of not more than medium size," a reporter noted, "with a tired, serious face, thinning hair, a very high-bridged nose, an unusual small, thin mouth, and an intermittent frown, with eyes which are unusually bright and penetrating, brown, shrewd and quizzical. Great animation lights his face, which is unusually expressive. There is an oddish combination of humor, appreciation of the situation, and iron." He continually moved around the speaker's platform. "When Roosevelt came into office," Black said, "the only successful business operating was the bankruptcy courts." Now "these gentlemen" (administration critics) "are seeking to crush the people of the cities into industrial serfdom, the people of the farms into agricultural peonage." In all, the reporter concluded, Black

> held them spellbound for an hour and a half with dramatic oratory com-
> paring Franklin Roosevelt and Andrew Jackson, ridiculing "the sage of Palo
> Alto" [Herbert Hoover], damning the "pillagers and plunderers" of pre-
> Roosevelt days, and blasting New Deal critics with burning sarcasms. "Pour
> it on them," yelled the happy crowd. "Lead on! Where you lead, America
> will follow!" the speaker cried in a dramatic peroration to "the peerless
> leader of American democracy," that "man of flaming courage and unsur-
> passed daring." And the crowd went crazy applauding.

In June Black told the national committee that he would "be glad to speak at any time, in any place and before any audience, where it is believed that my services will be helpful to our Cause."

Alabama was not a place where he would be needed. The Democrats had the election there won before the votes were cast. But Black spent much of the summer touring the state, stumping sixty-one of its sixty-seven coun-
ties. He called on probate judges and newspaper publishers, spoke at Rotary Clubs, went to barbecues (only men attended). He stopped people on the street to get their ideas on legislation and to ask if they had any problems he could help them with. If they did, noted Lee Rhoads who chauffeured him around, "he'd invite them to come see him in the office set aside for him in the county building or the post office. A person would tell him the problem. He would say, 'Fine, I'll do something about it,' and tell the person to wait outside. He'd call me in and dictate a letter. I'd type it. Then he would call the person back in and sign it in his presence." He was securing himself with the voters, but he was also trying to educate Alabamians to political realities of the world: that they are part of one nation whose government cares, that it can and should help all people when they cannot help themselves.

Black was doing all he could to advance the cause of liberalism in Alabama. He was trying to reshape the state's political context, to move the various forces and factions closer toward his idea of the political good. Black continually encouraged Alabamians to involve themselves in public affairs. Those who ignored the dead, comforting hand of the past to confront the problems of the day received his special attention. And three progressive candidates were elected to the House in 1936.

He had a staunch supporter in *Montgomery Advertiser* editor Grover Hall.

Passion and tolerance enveloped Hall's witty stiletto of a pen. "A heavy rain was falling," he wrote of the 1920s. "Instead of buying a poncho, which soldiers wear in wet weather, [Black] bought a hood and a knight-shirt." His editorials denouncing the Ku Klux Klan won him a Pulitzer Prize in 1928. Because of the Klan he and Black were very wary of each other at first. But by the mid-1930s "Grover really warmed to Black," recalled his assistant Gould Beech. "That fellow is truly charming," he said after one of the typically freewheeling conversations they had whenever Hugo went to Montgomery. "Grover came to feel that the Klan was long past and was such a technical matter." "You are grade A company," he told Black after spending much time with him at the convention to which Hall was also an Alabama delegate.[1] Of few people he met in public life was Hugo more fond than he was of Grover Hall.

Roosevelt appreciated Black's value to the party and to liberalism. When Robert La Follette told the president that he was organizing a group of liberals such as Norris, New York mayor Fiorello La Guardia, former brain truster Adolf Berle and United Mine Workers chief John L. Lewis into the Progressive National Committee to advocate the president's reelection, FDR urged La Follette to include Black at a conference the group would hold in September. La Follette invited Black, passing along FDR's comment, and he attended. He then spent six weeks in the North and Midwest speaking on behalf of Roosevelt and other Democratic candidates in twelve "battleground" states. Traveling alone by train, he made over forty speeches, sometimes two daily. On October 10 he left Iowa to join congressional leaders meeting at Roosevelt's Hyde Park home to plan a whirlwind finish to the campaign. The next day Black departed for Illinois. "No longer is the Republican party of the common people," he said. "Why, can you imagine Lincoln walking side by aside with Andy Mellon and the Liberty League?"

War clouds were on the horizon. That month Hitler and Mussolini established a Berlin-Rome axis, and Hitler had militarized the Rhineland, without retaliatory action from France. "Do you want an administration influenced by friends, such as the Du Ponts, whose sole business is war and the production of implements of war?" Black asked one crowd. From Indianapolis he wrote Roosevelt, "The fear of our possible embroilment in another European War is more widespread than I dreamed before on this campaign tour." He urged the president to "leave with the people in your last speech, preferably near the close, your firm determination to keep our people at peace." FDR felt no need to do so; but Black worked this theme into his speeches.

On election eve Black predicted that Roosevelt would carry all states except Vermont and Maine. Except for Jim Farley, few other politicos were so bold. But Black had traveled widely and had felt the enthusiasm of the masses. And he was right—as Farley memorably said, "As Maine goes, so goes Vermont." A week later Black told a reporter, "if the President had entered these states, he would have won them too." Black's political stock received a big boost. He was becoming a force in the country, as he was in the Senate. "Already there's talk about him in connection with the national ticket for 1940, based in part on the conspicuous service he rendered in the recent campaign," wrote the *Birmingham News, Age-Herald,* now combined into one newspaper. "Not since the days of Senator Underwood has an Alabamian loomed so large upon the national stage as Senator Black now bids to do."

In the Senate he was a power. One reason was that he plied his authority quietly, without fanfare and not talking about it much. He just went ahead, got what he wanted (largely) done and avoided unnecessary antagonisms. As the chairman of the Labor Committee, he held a blank check within his bailiwick. Committees accomplished only what chairmen considered important; a committee could do nothing without his approval. Black placed on his committee, sight unseen, Claude Pepper, fourteen years younger than he, who grew up down the road from Ashland and had been elected to the Senate from Florida in 1936 with the help of Roosevelt's long coattails. "Hugo took me under his arm and helped me," Pepper said.* He would serve in Congress for most of the next half century, the last New Dealer. Also elected in 1936 was William Smathers of New Jersey. Tall, handsome and wavy-haired, he and Hugo, and their wives, hit it off immediately. In later years they spent many happy hours playing tennis.

The Democratic landslide buoyed the party. Roosevelt was turning slightly but noticeably leftward. Soon he would be where Black had been all along. He dominated the national awareness as no American had ever done

---

* Hugo later joked about Pepper. When Pepper was a student at the University of Alabama, he supposedly went to Washington to see Black, mentioned his political ambitions and asked for advice, at which Hugo, eyeing a future competitor, replied, "Move to Florida." It always got a laugh (which was its purpose), but it was not true: Hugo was practicing in Birmingham when Pepper was graduated from Alabama in 1921 and from Harvard Law School in 1924; and Pepper didn't move to Florida until the next year, one year before Hugo was elected to the Senate.

in peacetime. But neither Roosevelt nor anybody else knew what he would do with his mandate. (Thirty years later, Black, Thomas Corcoran and fellow New Dealer Benjamin Cohen, reminiscing after dinner, speculated whether Roosevelt could have established a dictatorship then if he wished. "He was powerful enough," they agreed.) The New Deal was riding at high tide, but one flagrant current was threatening to negate many of its achievements.[2]

* * *

The Supreme Court had invalidated six major New Deal laws over the previous two years. Its decision finding the Agricultural Adjustment Act unconstitutional led Justice Harlan F. Stone to remark in dissent, "Courts are not the only agency of government that must be assumed to have capacity to govern." The ruling, Black contended, meant that "five men now rule 120,000,000 people." They "have left themselves free to decide all legislation in any manner they see fit. They have thrown away the charts." The lower federal courts, moreover, were also dominated by Republican judges who regularly issued injunctions suspending the application of New Deal statutes. One injunction, in Birmingham in early 1935 by Judge Grubb, prevented the Tennessee Valley Authority from selling electricity to municipalities in Alabama. Black, angered, responded by introducing a bill that would have allowed for direct appeal to the Supreme Court from federal courts when injunctions prohibiting the enforcement of federal statutes were issued. Chief Justice Charles Evans Hughes and Justices Louis D. Brandeis and Willis Van Devanter appeared before the Judiciary Committee to oppose the proposal successfully on the ground that the Court's authority to grant review before an appellate court heard such a case was adequate.

Speedy justice—quick court action that did not encumber the New Deal—was Black's goal. It was also Roosevelt's. Pending before the Supreme Court was the validity of such legislation as the Social Security Act and the Wagner Labor Relations Act. Six of the nine justices were in their seventies or eighties, and came to maturity during the heyday of the Robber Barons. The two most senior ones led well-defined alliances of "the Nine Old Men." Roosevelt's whole program for economic recovery and reform was in danger of being washed away in an elderly black-robed sea.* By the end of January

---

* Brandeis was the oldest, eighty-one, and most progressive justice. (Aligned with him most of the time were Stone, sixty-five, and Benjamin N. Cardozo, sixty-seven, relative young-sters.) The next oldest, Van Devanter, seventy-eight, was the guiding intellectual force of the Court's reactionary Four Horsemen, the others being James C. McReynolds, seventy-five, George Sutherland, seventy-five, and Pierce Butler, seventy-one. This tight bloc of

1937, after the State of the Union address, the Senate sensed something was up. "Strange things are being said in Congress," a columnist noted. But nobody knew what Roosevelt would propose to make the Court more sympathetic to New Deal measures.

Black prepared to deal with whatever came his way. Starting after the 1936 congressional recess, he studied the history of the Supreme Court and the Constitution "with more diligence and closeness" than he had ever done. He reread the debates in the Constitutional Convention and in the state ratifying conventions, and studied the Court's decisions. Then he read the debates of 1802, in which, as he noted, "the Federalists made more serious charges against President Jefferson than have yet been made against President Roosevelt. They charged him with attempting to concentrate all power in his own hands; with destroying the independent judiciary; and with absolutely subverting the Constitution." Indeed, "this Court question has been studied by me as much as anything I have ever investigated since I have been in the Senate."

One result of this reading was that he started to focus on the wording of the Constitution and the background of its provision at issue. No longer did he emphasize the evolution of the document to meet changing needs as he had when pushing his thirty-hour bill. That was now only one part of his thinking as he began to talk about the "writers of the Constitution," the background of the charter and of the judges themselves, and of the limits on judges. "I regret to say that a real study of impartial history has changed a great many of my preconceived ideas about the aloofness of the Supreme Court on political issues. In my judgment, it has simply not been 'aloof.' On deciding these political interpretations they have always followed the economic predilections of the individual members." "Nothing is clearer than this. . . ."

Slowly, almost without even realizing it, Black was developing a theory of the Supreme Court's role. "Trained in the traditions of law and influenced by the Federalistic propaganda through the years as to the infallibility of judges, I might not have supported [the Court-packing plan] before this study." He now had the rudiments of a mature philosophy. His reading and natural inclinations led him to accept the necessity of judicial review of legislation in certain types of cases. He often stressed "human rights above property rights," and courts had to uphold them: "It is my belief that the

---

Tories usually picked up a fifth vote, from Hughes, seventy-five, or Owen Roberts, a mere stripling of sixty-two, to form a majority.

part of the Bill of Rights which protects free speech, free religion, and a free press constitutes the real bulwark of liberty and that a suppression of these rights would destroy our Nation as a Democracy."

Restricting the scope of judges, imperfect men with a mortal desire to expand their province, is an eternal problem of governance. "Judges after all," Black concluded, "will always determine whether or not policies adopted are contrary to the Constitution. The next and logical step is, of course, to confuse constitutional prohibitions with personal prejudices or predilections." The Constitution is the law until the people change it. "I do not believe that the judges have the right to make this Constitution say what it clearly does not say as written by the framers." They "left upon Congress the imperative duty of preventing judicial encroachment upon the rights of the people, the states and the national government."[3]*

Roosevelt shocked the country on February 5, 1937, with his Reorganization of the Judiciary proposal: for every Supreme Court justice who did not retire after the age of seventy, the president would be empowered to appoint a new justice, up to a total of six. While FDR later called this "the answer to a maiden's prayer," angry opponents howled Court-packing. And for once he was too clever, his motive too transparent. The Court was a sacred symbol in the American covenant. A direct assault was the political equivalent of sacrilege. Roosevelt had equated age with incompetence, or at least hostility to the New Deal, forgetting (or ignoring) that ideology, as Brandeis observed, is the product of genes rather than of years.

"I favor the plan," Black immediately declared. "For many years more Federal judges have been needed to adequately transact the business of the courts. The message of the President represents this necessity with unanswerable statistics and logic." The Court was "jeopardizing the Constitution," he told a friend. Roosevelt's proposal would "preserve our theory of government." But privately, he was not as optimistic. "I asked him his assessment of the Court Plan's chances," Corcoran later wrote, "and got an ambivalent answer: 'Something's got to happen to the Court and I'm with anyone who wants to modernize it reasonably. But I don't think you'll make it with this proposal.' " These feelings notwithstanding, Black fought for it wholeheartedly, and more.

The Court-packing battle was one of the most bitter in American po-

---

* In 1936 Black wrote a former congressman: "I have always believed that it would have been better not to have had the Supreme Court judges *appointed* for life with the vast powers which they are capable of utilizing under the constitution" (to B. F. Welty, 1/12/36; originally emphasized).

litical history. Senate Republicans, outnumbered seventy-six to sixteen (plus four "others"), quickly decided to "lay low" in order to let dissident Democrats, working in conjunction with the American Bar Association, lead the resistance. Although he was a progressive Democrat, Burton Wheeler spearheaded the opposition. "Hugo was very mad at me," Wheeler recalled. "He didn't talk to me for a while. I told him we should talk even if we disagreed, and we finally did." Black attacked the Court's interpretations but not the justices individually. An income tax, he pointed out, was constitutional only when the Supreme Court said it was. During the eighteen years starting in 1895 that the Court held it was not,

> The Constitution itself had not changed. The writing was the same. The same charter was in the Library of Congress, and it was perfectly constitutional to have an income tax. Then along came five judges who decided it was unconstitutional, and for 25 years, though the Constitution was still the same in the Library of Congress, it was a violation of the Constitution to collect an income tax. It is clear the Constitution changes as the judges change. . . . Truly, the Constitution was not what its framers wrote, but what the judges from time to time said the framers meant.[4]

Black took the same tack in a radio address. The Court's dominant philosophy was "the exact philosophy of the political group that could obtain only eight electoral votes in the last Presidential election. . . . When our great charter is changed, the people should do it—not the courts." A "bare majority" of the Court had been "sitting as a continuous constitutional convention . . . ," he charged in a New York speech. "Assuming the right on their part to determine the reasonableness of State and Federal laws," these justices had "usurped and taken over the rights of the people. . . ."

Two constitutional provisions were at issue: the commerce clause—"The Congress shall have power . . . To regulate commerce . . . among the several States . . ."; and the due process clause of the Fourteenth Amendment—"nor shall any State deprive any person of life, liberty, or property, without due process of law. . . ." Black strongly supported the viewpoint, first expressed by Chief Justice John Marshall over a century earlier in the landmark case of *Gibbons v. Ogden* (1824), that Congress can regulate "those internal concerns which affect the States generally." It was a broad, virtually all-encompassing grant of power, but one within given limits. "When our country was young," Black explained early in the struggle, there was very little commerce among the states. In fact, the roads were so bad interstate commerce on a large scale was impossible, but now some statisticians contend 90 per cent of our commerce is interstate. Anybody can see that much of our trade is carried on nationally without regard for state lines, so why should we not state the thing in so many words and proceed to have Congress regulate it? All we have to do is face the fact.

The due process clause was another matter. It was "totally incapable of definition," Black told the Senate. "No one has ever defined it" or "marked its boundaries. It is as elastic as rubber" and "means one thing to one citizen and another thing to another citizen." It gave courts a means to deny "the rights of human beings as human beings the first importance" they deserve. "I supported the President on the Court bill because of due process," he said late in life. "My goal was to get judges who were objective. Four men, four justices, were unreasonable then." The fray was really over matters such as minimum wages, maximum hours, child labor and farm relief, not the president's right to enlarge the Court's membership, Black said at a Town Hall meeting in Washington. That was the nub of the problem. From Town Hall to Carnegie Hall in New York to Yale University to delivering several radio addresses to writing letters to newspapers, Black defended the Court-packing plan. The administration had no more zealous or active champion.

From the outset the plan was in trouble. Roosevelt had prepared it in great secrecy, consulting only with Attorney General Homer Cummings and, secondarily, Solicitor General Stanley Reed. No one on Capitol Hill or Roosevelt's usual advisers, such as Corcoran and Cohen, knew. It also did not help that, when the Senate Judiciary Committee hearings began, Black was no longer in his spot as ranking majority member able to help with his resourceful parliamentary skills; he transferred to the finance committee, because judiciary "never did anything." Nevertheless, he acted as one of Joe Robinson's most trustworthy lieutenants, feeling out individual senators, talking compromise (adding only two new justices) as the plan foundered, and reporting to Robinson, who held the legislative reins firmly in his hands. Opponents were unusually united and determined, Black warned the president at lunch at the White House on April 1, 1937, and would delay in every way possible. "We'll smoke 'em out," Roosevelt the stubborn Dutchman breezily replied. "If delay helps them, we must press for an early vote." Three days before, the Court had upheld a Washington minimum wage law similar to a New York statute it invalidated only the previous year; and two weeks later, it found the National Labor Relations

Act constitutional. Both rulings were by a 5–4 vote, as Justice Owen Roberts changed his position. It was, Joseph Alsop quipped, "a switch in time that saved nine."

On May 18 Justice Van Devanter announced his retirement. Roosevelt had the vacancy he wanted, and he had long promised to appoint Robinson, loyal but conservative. Senators, pumping Robinson's hand, called him "Mr. Justice" in anticipation of the honor to be bestowed. Within a week, the Court in two more 5–4 decisions sustained the unemployment insurance provision of the Social Security Act, and ruled by a 7–2 vote that old-age pensions were constitutional. Not only was the Court abreast of its work, as Chief Justice Hughes showed in a devastating letter to Senator Wheeler, but now there seemed to be little need for Court reform. Later, Roosevelt claimed he had lost the battle but won the war. It was a costly victory. A "constitutional revolution" had been achieved at the expense of an angry and divided Democratic Party.[5]

*   *   *

The Court's approval of a state minimum wage law cleared the way for the introduction of a federal bill. Black had reintroduced one in 1935 and the Senate had defeated it. During the 1936 campaign, Roosevelt promised to find some way to restore government wage-hour regulation. "What happened to that nice unconstitutional bill you had tucked away?" he asked labor secretary Frances Perkins after reelection. She produced it. He gave it to Cohen and Corcoran to redraft, with the thought of submitting it early in 1937. In late January Roosevelt discussed the situation with Black. Hugo had clung tenaciously to his theory that the basic cause of the Depression was a lack of purchasing power; profits were not distributed as higher wages but were concentrated in the hands of a relatively small number of individuals. "Our economic system exists to sell," he wrote in a 1936 article. A shorter work week would stimulate production by spreading the ability to buy, and also create a scarcity of labor, which would be "a wholesome economic tonic for America." Nevertheless, in meeting with Roosevelt, Black agreed to abandon his pet thirty-hour measure. Democratic appointments to the Court, Roosevelt believed, were also needed if an effective bill were to pass judicial scrutiny.[6]

Over the next few months, in spare moments taken from the Court fight and as an epidemic of sit-down strikes swept the nation, Cohen and Corcoran worked on a comprehensive fair labor standards bill, with Cohen as the chief draftsman. * Black did not like the draft. It included a board with unlimited authority to set the minimum wage at whatever it deemed appropriate and also to set different standards on the work week. He knew this broad discretion would draw strong antagonism from southern Democrats and most Republicans. Corcoran and Cohen came to discuss it several times in May. "The four of us sat around the table," recalled Lee Rhoads, one of Black's assistants. "I was the markup man, taking notes. They would play Harvard lawyer, using legalese. Black told them he thought these things could be said in simpler language. Neither got his full way on the bill. The Senator said he couldn't get through everything they wanted. They'd question him on that, and he'd look at them with a smirk, as if to say 'you guys don't know what you're talking about here.' They didn't see eye to eye on everything and discussed things pretty strongly sometimes."

In late May, as the administration's prospects for a victory on Court-packing dimmed, the proposal was ready. Roosevelt hoped it would reunite the party. Black introduced it in the Senate, and William Connery in the House. The Supreme Court had changed its heart and the bill relied on the newly reinvigorated commerce clause. Besides empowering Congress to set minimum wages and maximum hours, the draft called for an independent five-member Fair Labor Standards Board, to be appointed by the president, which would have the authority, if collective bargaining failed, to increase minimum standards; and it prohibited child labor under sixteen. An estimated three million persons would enjoy higher labor standards. "We have promised it," Roosevelt said in an accompanying message to Congress. "We cannot stand still."[7]

Black spent June chairing joint Senate and House hearings, a tactic FDR suggested in order to speed action on the bill. Hugo continued his habit of getting his own views into the record. At the end of each witness's testimony, he made a long statement summarizing it, then turned and asked if it were correct. One novice reporter wondered, "Which is the witness?" ("Chairman

---

* One problem was whether there should be a national minimum wage, 25 or 35 cents an hour, or whether the rate should be flexible and allow for differences among occupations. Pecan pickers in Texas would be put out of work if the minimum were fixed, since they were not being paid nearly that much. Corcoran, Cohen and Reed debated for a while at the White House before Roosevelt, his cigar sticking out of his mouth. Finally he said, "Let's have a flat minimum," and it was included in the proposal (Louchheim, *Making,* 86).

Black," replied a former NRA official who was now covering the proceedings.) Testimony was mixed. Business and industrial groups spoke against
the bill. Individual businessmen broke along sectional lines, northerners
supporting it as a means of countering low-wage competition from the South,
and southerners opposing it; farm and agricultural processing groups requested exemptions.* Organized labor was even more divided. Both the
American Federation of Labor (AFL) and the Congress of Industrial Organizations (CIO) favored it, but with major reservations. William Green
of the AFL feared, as he had in 1933, that regulation of wages and hours
might interfere with collective bargaining. For his part, John L. Lewis of
the CIO, although indifferent to the bill, thought its minimum wage scale
was fixed far too low to benefit his members.[8]

Senatorial reaction was as vigorous as Black foresaw. Many southern
senators "actually froth at the mouth when the subject is mentioned," Homer
Cummings observed. They wanted to maintain the southern "differential"
of lower wages and viewed the bill as another step toward federal despotism.
Josiah Bailey of North Carolina thought about "issuing a statement declaring
for minimum wages and maximum hours and the millennium. I think we
ought to add the millennium to the program otherwise it would not be
complete." Only one other southern senator "actually wanted to support
it," Black recalled (forgetting Claude Pepper who wrote in his diary, "The
South which I love must grow"). That was Theodore Bilbo of Mississippi,
later to gain notoriety for his fanatical racism.

From its inception wages-hours was intertwined with Court-packing. As
early as March 9, in a Fireside Chat the night before Senate hearings on
the Court bill were to open, Roosevelt said, "We need a wage and hour law,
and we need it *now*," hitting the word. Court-packing absorbed his time
and emotional energy, and depleted his political capital with Congress. And
Corcoran, for one, felt that Roosevelt's heart, for whatever complex of
reasons, was not truly in the wages and hours measure. "I don't want the
bill," Roosevelt told him. "I want the issue."[9] The bill, then, belonged to
Black.

He took his argument to the people, over radio, in speeches in and out
of Washington, and in letters to editors. One speech, delivered over NBC

* One witness testified to the effect that northern workers were more efficient than southern
workers and gave several reasons for his belief. It might be true now that southerners were
not as efficient, energetic and alert as their northern neighbors, Pennsylvania congressman
Matthew Dunn replied, but from what he had heard about Robert E. Lee's expedition into
Pennsylvania, he felt that could not be said about Lee.

on June 7, showed Court-packing's connection. Michigan Senator Arthur Vandenberg had said that the effect of the wages and hours bill would be "the essence of fascism" because of the discretion the proposed board would have. In response Corcoran wrote a draft for Black, stressing the difference from the NIRA. Hugo gave it "a quick, speedy overhauling," he told Corcoran. "Language may not be the best. Think we should not antagonize anti-Court group. Some of them will be with us."

He elaborated on his reasoning behind the measure in a letter to Birmingham journalist John Temple Graves II, which he knew Graves would use in his column, syndicated throughout the South. Black still objected to government setting of wages "above an amount necessary for decent American living." His standard was that a minimum wage "construed as a wage adequate in amount to buy life's necessities is certainly the right of every citizen who is ready, able and willing to work. . . . The workers of this nation have not been able to obtain a fair wage based upon the idea of competition for a long time," certainly not since 1929, and had "little prospect" of doing so in the immediate future. That justified legislation that would "provide a mere subsistence for the millions of workers whose wages are kept down because of a surplus of workers, and who have no chance to bargain for themselves. . . . At the present time we are faced with a reality. In the face of stern realities, theories frequently fail to fit conditions."[10]

Following the hearings, Black moved quickly. He had to mediate carefully, balancing political considerations with the concerns of many factions. He "knows when to wear a twinkle in his eye and when to lash out like a vicious prosecutor," a reporter wrote. "He personally was never more effervescent and his tenacity never more apparent" than now. Black was working at a feverish pitch: "for the past few weeks, I have been so busily engaged in committee work and Senate work that I have hardly had a chance to see my office. I have not had a chance to talk with my secretary for three days." Lost in his task, he "seldom stopped to eat at meal time, but constantly whipped away." (He agreed to pose for a photographer, but continued working. "Your hair—," the photographer began, proferring a comb. "Oh yes," said the nearly bald Hugo. "My wife's been telling me to get a haircut for a week." The picture quickly taken, he returned to work.)

Many groups were pressuring Congress to exempt their field from the bill's scope. Corcoran and Cohen conferred continually with Black about it. "Ben and I worked with it day and night, and day and night," Corcoran recalled, "and that's why I got my great and tremendous admiration for Hugo." Black was willing to make concessions to keep as much support for the heart of the bill as possible. Different fields were exempted. To the dismay of northern liberals, farming and dairying, fishing and forestry, one by one, then railroad employees, cannery workers and those persons engaged in local retailing were all excluded. But the votes of halfhearted backers were now secure, and the formerly lukewarm were mollified. In early July the committee, including the one Republican present, unanimously approved a sharply revised bill. The powers of the proposed board were drastically curbed. It could not set wages at over 40 cents per hour or a standard work week at less than forty hours. Minimum wages and maximum hours were left to the board, however, not to Congress. And child labor standards were lowered, to permit children under sixteen to work in jobs that would not injure their health or interfere with their education.[11]

As the bill's sponsor, Black opened floor debate. He admitted that it "would be wholly and completely . . . impossible to bring about overnight a complete leveling of the wage scale" nationwide. But "wherever a man may live, . . . when he is compelled to work in order to obtain food and clothing for himself and his family, he is entitled to receive a minimum wage sufficient to prevent him from dying from the slow undernourishment and slow starvation." Black was speaking directly to the bitter resistance of southerners who wanted to continue paying lower wages than other sections. They were trying to preserve the basis of a way of life that South Carolina's "Cotton Ed" Smith called "the splendid gifts of God to the South." Black replied dramatically. He waved mill vouchers, showing payment of $2.68 for four days' work and $4.48 for four and a half days' work. "That figures up to about eight cents an hour. I subscribe to the gospel that a man who is born in Alabama and who can do as much work as a man born in any state in New England is entitled to the same pay if he does the same work."* When Mississippi's Pat Harrison sarcastically noted that the bill had "a lot of lovely poetry in it," Hugo turned lyrical:

> I should thank God if it had. I cannot forget that the great poets of the world have never failed, down through the ages, to raise their voices in

---

* "It is my own belief that the South will be a great beneficiary of fair and decent wages for our working people. I do not understand why anyone would believe that a native worker of Alabama is worth less when he is employed by some company that employs people in the North and in the South than he would be if the same company employed a boy born in some part of the North" (HLB to William E. W. Yerby, 7/3/37).

behalf of the helpless and the weak. . . . Somehow I have always thought that the poetic phrase, "Come unto me, all ye that labor and are heavy laden," was perhaps more than anything else responsible for the unpopularity of the One who spoke it. I do not forget that "man's inhumanity to man makes countless thousands mourn." I do not forget the Song of the Shirt, the lilting melody of which, with all its beauty and all its purity, did so much to awake the people of its generation to a realization of abuses that must be stopped. . . .

My friends, thank God for the poetry in this bill if it but reaches but a single heart, if it but reaches the standards of American citizens, if it but cuts off unnecessarily long hours that people are toiling, while others live on the dole. . . . I come from the South, and I am proud of it. I believe I speak the language of its people. My ancestors have been buried under the soil of the South since before the Revolutionary War.

"I speak for the little men and women of Alabama and of the Nation," he concluded.

The bill, narrowed further, passed the Senate 56–28 on July 31. Leading the administration forces was the new majority leader, Alben Barkley of Kentucky.[12] Joe Robinson had died two weeks earlier, drained by the Court-packing struggle. He was found dead in his apartment, the *Congressional Record* at his side. Roosevelt had to find a new appointee to the Supreme Court.

"AN ABSOLUTE
ANOMALY"

B**LACK'S SPONSORSHIP** of the wages-hours bill involved grave political risks. By putting more money in the pockets of working people, it threatened to dent the rigid class structure the Big Mules, other industrialists and their Black Belt allies held so dear. Many Alabama businessmen did not accept Black's continual assurances that he was simply carrying out the Democratic platform and that the bill would not harm the South. One manufacturer said it would be more ruinous to the South than the War Between the States. (The loss to slave owners then was $4 billion, he figured, but this bill would cost the South $10 billion. To this way of thinking human values apparently played no role in the Civil War.)

Diehard anti–New Dealers had always loathed Black and in the spring of 1937 they comprised virtually his only opposition to renomination the next year. Little could they suspect that for a spell that February he considered not running because of financial restraints. He was unable to afford the mortgage on the Birmingham property he owned with Albert Lee Smith and feared that the bank would call in payment at the time of the May 1938 primary election to embarrass him. He put the whole matter to Barney Whatley. "You have been more than a brother to me and you will not find me ungrateful now or any time," Barney replied. He did not want to buy the property, as Hugo proposed, but offered to assume Hugo's immediate burden yet still let him reap any future benefits. "I do not hesitate to go the limit with you. . . . Rest assured that no one is going to bring about your downfall for the want of a few dollars—not while I have these few." Barney, who had struck it rich in mining, paid the mortgage and eventually forgave it as well as other loans he made to Hugo over the years.

The progress of the wages-hours bill led to a firestorm of protest against Hugo starting in June 1937. A report that he would replace Attorney General Homer Cummings received considerable publicity in Alabama, encouraged by the Bourbons in hopes of weakening his candidacy. Hugo minimized it by stating, as a reporter likely using his language wrote, that even though he had been broached about it "several times," he "did not want the place in that all he wants is what he now has." Farmers joined with business in criticizing him, but softened their attitude because of his efforts to stop the fall of cotton prices in the South. Roosevelt signed his bill allocating $3 million for road construction and improvement in Alabama, enabling farmers to get their goods to market more easily.

Despite the fact that the amended wages-hours proposal specifically excluded forestry, Alabama lumbermen headed the opposition to Black. This activity influenced the press. Wondering whether Black was "failing in his usual political sagacity," a Birmingham reporter claimed that "he has, in fact, become an extremist in a government of extremists." But to deny him renomination, as the Bourbons wanted, would be a tough job. They were a distinct minority of the electorate, far outnumbered by the masses for whom Black fought every day. Nevertheless, names of potential opposing candidates floated about, congressmen Lister Hill, Sam Hobbs, Henry Steagall and Frank Boykin being the most prominent. They all faced an uphill fight. "Hugo would've won," said Cooper Green, postmaster of Birmingham on his recommendation. "The people were still supporting him." Montgomery lawyer Richard T. Rives, a power behind the scenes, partly dissented: "Black probably faced a real battle in '38. He didn't continue his contacts as much as before. But then they weren't as necessary." "In Alabama," a reporter noted, "it is easier to talk aout the Civil War and local issues than it is to demand the 30-hour week for the men who make steel in the furnaces of Birmingham. But this fellow Black has a way about him."

The most serious challenger would be Hill. Personable and articulate, the son of the first American doctor to perform a closed heart operation (who was also the largest landowner in Montgomery County), Hill had been serving in Congress since 1923. As with many southern politicians, a deceptively casual bonhomie overlaid both his intensity and his well-developed ambitions. "I wanted a Senate seat then, very much so indeed," he acknowledged. But Hill was a very cautious politician. In 1930 he wrote out a proposed announcement for a primary race against Bankhead or Heflin before deciding not to run. He did not challenge Hugo in 1932 because "he and I represent too much the same people and agree too well. I really do not know an issue I could raise with him." Friends thought Black treated Hill, who was eight years younger, "as a sort of protégé" and that "Lister didn't mind" (at the time; "I've always been my own man," he later seethed. "Everybody knows that"). He brought out a playfulness in Hugo as only Barney Whatley otherwise could. "They just cracked each other up," said Hugo, Jr. And their wives were dearest friends.

Through the grapevine Black heard that Hill was seriously thinking of running. One night Hugo called him. "I've been hearing these reports from all over that you're going to run against me, but you haven't said anything about it to me. You have a popgun but where's your pop? Let me know if you're going to use it because I want to get my people ready. I look forward to it and we'll see who'll win. But still, I want to tell you, Lister, you're my friend."

"Oh well, Hugo," said Hill, "if you want to put it that way . . ."

In retrospect, Hill claimed he "would not have run against Hugo because he was my friend." Then came the complete truth: "Anyway, he had the state won in '38, no question about it."[1]

Black's opponents did not know this. Nor would it have stopped them if they did. A new acerbity appeared in editorials berating him from small town and weekly rural newspapers across the middle and southern part of the state especially. The *Wiregrass Farmer* was the most savage: this "zealot" and "firebrand" who serves "only" that "lawless element called Labor" should be removed from public life and installed as "General Counsel of the Affiliated Labor Unions of the United States, with headquarters, perhaps, in Moscow." Black replied in what one experienced observer, Atticus Mullin of the *Montgomery Advertiser*, called "the worst castigation we have read in years from a public official regarding a newspaper editor." Concerning one part of the editorial—that he was "particularly good at opening other people's mail to see what secrets could be found"—Black wrote, "I could not properly refer to it without violating the postal laws." He accused the editor of "deception." But "the reason for the big noise" being made against him was "that I do represent all Alabamians, and I decline to permit myself to be the representative of a small group who carry out the secret orders of their holding company masters who issue their directions for action from a distance many miles removed from the State of Alabama." Perhaps, as Mullin suggested, Black believed he could end the mounting criticism with one devastating blow. If so, he was correct. By early August no challenger had come forward. The Bourbons had shot their load.

"I have been somewhat surprised that this pre-primary campaign has not accomplished more than it has," Black wrote a supporter. "I am really looking forward with a great deal of pleasure to a fight to the finish." He would carry Roosevelt's "great Democratic platform directly to the people of Alabama." In conversation with friends his usual confidence was apparent. "Hugo didn't show any worries about re-election," remembered Claude Hamilton, Jr., an Alabamian who got his job as Reconstruction Finance Corporation assistant counsel through Black and became a good friend. "He thought it would take some work but that he had it without any real problems." He expected to win by his biggest majority ever. Behind his opponents' determination to defeat him, he contended, was "Muscle Shoals, and the question of who shall develop the remaining streams of the nation, and for whose benefit. I shall continue to fight to have them developed for the benefit of the American people, instead of exclusively for the benefit of Mr. J. P. Morgan, the Electric Bond and Share Company and their associates."[2]

He was developing campaign themes. In Mobile he planned to talk about the *Mobile Press Register*, that its management "was launched through the activities of the Alabama Power Company and their representatives (as instigated by the holding company). . . ." The groups that "now hire Washington lobbyists and spend large sums of money to defeat President Roosevelt's program, did not do this in 1932," Black wrote the head of the Montgomery County farm bureau. "They were not able. They were too busy at that time attempting to steer clear of the open doors of the Bankruptcy Court to hold big meetings at big hotels." He was collecting material about these groups. The Alabama Power Company, he noted, gave more advertising to newspapers that already started to campaign against him. And "I have direct information that paid workers have been sent into Alabama within the last ten days to stir up opposition among farmers and others. These facts will all be brought out at a later date."

But even before the ruckus over the wages-hours act, Black was not taking any chances. In early 1937 John L. Lewis invited him to a small dinner at the Cosmos Club in Washington. Pending before the Senate, having passed the House, was a bill that, although it guaranteed collective bargaining for miners, created a national commission that would set prices and allocate and control production; its effect would be to make coal a public utility subject to federal regulation. Even though many miners lived in Alabama, Black opposed the proposal. Why? "Really for antitrust reasons," said James Landis who was there that night. "He had a feeling that it gave too much power to management. . . . His opposition was completely genuine, but it was . . . an opposition that springs from a Sherman Act approach. The old populist concept"—unfettered competition among small businesses. ". . . But the purpose of this meeting was to induce Black to change his position."

"It was argued out for some time. After people were getting on the philosophical argument, Lewis turned to Black and said, 'Senator, I understand that your term's expiring next year.' Black admitted that." Lewis continued, "Senator, of course you'll have a primary fight on your hands, and as I recall it, the last vote in your primary was"—and he rolled off the figures. "You know there are a lot of coal miners in Birmingham, Alabama. There are a lot of other people who are allies of theirs, and they have aunts and uncles and nieces and what not, and if you didn't have their support, as I believe you had it last time, you might have difficulties in this primary."[3]

Black voted for this bill—without saying anything during debate.

*   *   *

A decade in Washington, the Depression, reading and reflection had changed Black's views. He had thought his way "beyond state boundaries" to deal with broad economic problems. "All that is wrong here in Alabama can never be righted if we try to right it in Alabama alone," he told a Birmingham reporter. "Great wrongs in the nation must be corrected in the nation as a whole and not in Alabama alone." Problems of education and public works were too big to be handled only by states and counties, he pointed out to Alabama's county commissioners. "It is the purpose of all governments that all the people move forward in unison." He wrote a friend: "I can understand and appreciate the note of sadness running through your realistic discussion of a changing governmental philosophy, brought about by a changed economic order. National business control, as distinguished from local business control, has made it necessary that many of us reshape and maybe remold traditional concepts that we really love."

His activities during this torrid political season showed how far he had come. Like a one-man think tank, Black dropped new proposals into the legislative hopper. He urged that the Civilian Conservation Corps, which had already employed two million youths in two years, be made a permanent agency. Federal aid to education had long been on Black's mind. In 1937 he joined Senator Pat Harrison in introducing a bill calling for an initial $100 million in direct aid to the states, with an additional $200 million over the next four years. No people could be ignorant and still be free, Black stressed in a radio speech urging support. Hearings were held shortly before the Education and Labor Committee, and "no one appeared in opposition to Federal assistance." Since the proposal "vitally affected the Negro people of the South . . . they appeared in great numbers," William Borah of Idaho said the next year.

> The most difficult problem was to work out absolute protection for the colored children in the enjoyment of the fund proposed to be set up. I must say that I never knew a person more meticulous, more determined, more vigilant to protect the colored students in the employment of that fund than was . . . Black. I was impressed with the fact that there was a determination upon his part to teach the Negro at the point in his life where he could best serve him not only with reference to general citizenship but as to the reduction of crime.

Walter White and Charles Houston of the NAACP discussed the measure with Black. They had prepared an amendment that all aid should be granted without discrimination in states where segregated schools existed. Black opposed it because it would alienate southern votes needed for passage. "Education is the answer to the race question," he said. "When white Southerners are educated and given economic security there will be less prejudice against the Negro—fewer lynchings, more jobs, greater justice for the Negro." Having been disappointed by Black's stand on the antilynching law, White "learned" that he "was not only capable of intellectual growth but was one of the ablest men in the Senate. The dead hand of tradition was anathema to him. . . ."[4]

He was also ahead of his time in another field. In 1934, just as Roosevelt charged the Cabinet-level Committee on Economic Security with formulating a social insurance program, Black, trying to persuade the group, said:

> I am firmly convinced that the health of the nation should be of national concern. . . . Whether the betterment of national health can be worked out better by a system of national hospitals, or by a system of state or national health and accident insurance, nobody knows, but humanity and social justice demand that it must be studied—it should also be studied from a viewpoint of national defense.

Early the next year, he introduced a bill designed to provide a health insurance system under which the great majority of people earning less than $3,000 a year (which meant most people) would receive essential medical services and partial compensation for loss of income from illness. This plan became part of the unemployment insurance provision of the Social Security Act, which Congress passed that June. A more general system of health insurance had been omitted from the act because of pressure from the American Medical Association (AMA). Roosevelt still favored such a system, however, and quickly established an interdepartmental commission to coordinate health and welfare activities.

Black submitted a resolution in January 1937 calling for an investigation to determine "the best and most effective kind of federal legislation to provide a system of health insurance throughout the entire United States." The Education and Labor Committee, of which he was now chairman, "indefinitely postponed" this proposal. The AMA, up in arms, contacted Hugo's physician to urge him to dissuade him from fostering "socialized medicine." "Well, I tried," the physician reported, "but the trouble is that he is sincere." Black submitted a slightly reworded resolution in June 1937. This time, he noted, the AMA "is ready to cooperate with the government in making such a study." Black planned to draft a bill incorporating its findings, providing comprehensive medical coverage.[5]

———————

In the summer of 1937 Hugo Black was one of the most intriguing figures in American public life. An "absolute anomaly—an intellectual leftist liberal from below the Mason and Dixon line" and "probably the most radical man in the Senate," Joseph Alsop and Turner Catledge wrote. He strove for what he called a "regulated capitalism," with government as "policeman." "You can't get far with revolution," he said. "The best system must always be worked out by evolutionary processes." He felt that nearly all New Deal measures pointed in the right direction. By distributing wealth more equitably, they helped break up the combination of money and power that impeded the full promise of democracy. He expressed his own credo best in 1934 when the Senate was debating the nomination of Roosevelt brain truster Rexford Tugwell to be undersecretary of agriculture. Black supported Tugwell because:

> In everything he has spoken, in every word he has uttered, we find him striking a sledge-hammer against inordinate profits, against long hours,

against children in factories. . . . I am not for Mr. Tugwell solely because the President has appointed him. I am for him because I think he represents a school of political thought of which the country has long been sorely in need . . . which will not deify money and property to the extent of adding to the destitution and human misery of the men, women and children of the United States who produce the wealth which the people themselves are entitled to have.

(Virginia senator Harry Byrd asked Black if he really professed to understand Tugwell's abstruse theories. "Yes, I do," Black said. Whereupon Byrd read one of Tugwell's observations: " 'Chance has substituted itself for the anthropomorphic interpretation of history as a causal sequence.' Does the senator understand *that?*" "I thoroughly understand," Black replied, "but I would not undertake to explain it to the Senator from Virginia.")[6]

He was caustic when other senators made the welkin ring with their bombast. In offering to make a document available for a colleague to read, he said, "I presume he can write and I presume he can read." Once, sunk back in his chair with his chin cupped in his palm, he listened to a colleague deliver a three-hour speech. Black rose to compliment him: "There is just one thing I'd like to know. Is the senator for or against the bill?" Yet Hugo carried his likes and dislikes rather casually, and didn't let them interfere with his work or his life too much. He was self-sufficient, with a woodpecker's industry and a penchant for colorful action, and had a shrewd and realistic expediency that enabled him to cooperate with almost anyone.

If his intellectual interests set him apart from most senators, he was otherwise a southerner—genial, social, an amiable companion who fit the situation and looked little different from the numerous southern legislators who also escaped from the black-hat tradition. Except for his accent, said James Landis, "I don't think you'd take him for a Southerner . . . No, he gets down to business pretty quickly." Briskness was one of his outstanding characteristics. A bundle of energy—raw but harnessed driving power—he moved, thought and acted quickly. "When he has addressed the Senate," a reporter noted, "he has appeared more like a business man in a hurry to get a pointed message over to a director's meeting than like a professional statesman." He employed the theatrics of the art of public speaking, pausing dramatically, varying his voice, holding his lapels, cocking his head. And he waved his arms, sometimes in a wide arc, or he chopped at the air. His remarks were delivered for maximum effectiveness. Problems were something to be solved, not merely to be talked about.

A bill before Congress in 1936 provided that only large creditors could put a corporation into bankruptcy, and it had a retroactive clause that benefited only one company—Howard Hopson's Associated Gas & Electric. William O. Douglas, a new member of the Securities and Exchange Commission, was concerned: the Senate had just passed the bill. He raced to the Senate cloakroom and asked to see Black. "Senator," he said after introducing himself, "you have just done Associated Gas & Electric the greatest favor." "Never in my life," Black flared. Douglas pointed out that the bill, for which Hugo had voted, would enable AG&E to evade bankruptcy. "Wait right here," Black said. Forty years later, Douglas remembered how Hugo "literally trotted onto the floor." In a few minutes he returned to thank Douglas and to say that the Senate would recall the bill. (Until this, Black and Douglas had never met. They would meet again . . .)

With Roosevelt, Hugo had an easy, open relationship. The supreme political performer enjoyed the good show Black always gave. "He talked about that a few times and you could see his face brighten up," recalled his son James Roosevelt. "It was more than that Black was scoring points. He liked the way Black went about it." Hugo's crusty independence, as essential to his functioning as his vitals, also appealed to the president. FDR understood the compromises that any southern liberal had to make and admired the manner in which Black jealously guarded his political turf. But above all, Roosevelt appreciated his loyalty and efficiency. He told James, " 'If you want something done in the Senate, give it to Black. He'll do it.' Father felt that Black was indispensable to the New Deal's success," James continued. "He appreciated Black's willingness to go as far as he did, even if he did not always agree with Black. Several times Father said that the New Deal would not have been the same without Black."[7]

·   ·   ·

"What manner of man is he?" asked Grover Hall in the *Montgomery Advertiser.*

> There are few anecdotes about him. He is not funny, nor is he a highly gregarious animal. Rather does he seem to be a wary, cagey fox, nervous, alert, trim and ready. While he is warm enough, I doubt if he has ever been freely intimate with many people. He is liked because he is not personally angular and unpleasant. He is surprisingly urban for one with a purely rural background. But he is no back-slapper. He is plainly the scholar and thinker, as well as the suspicious prosecutor. As an inquisitor and a prosecutor he is terrible in action. . . .
>
> I doubt if Black trusts as many people as deserve to be trusted, but he

is no icicle intellectually or personally. Primarily he is a humanitarian who has . . . the gift to make a purely intellectual approach to every question. As a Senator he has never said a cheap or shabby thing. He has thought of himself as a philosopher. He knows something of literature and is rarely seen without a good book. The last time I saw him was in a Montgomery hotel room, when he tried to make me read Aristotle when he shaved for dinner. I have forgiven him some of his earlier political aberrations, but it will be a long time before I overlook that.

Black is a radical of the Norris, LaFollette, Holmes, Brandeis school— perhaps the first genuine philosophical radical that the deep South has sent to the Senate. . . . He always surprises people who know him best . . . , but his friends long since learned not to take this man lightly. Even his enemies no longer do that.

Spare, inconspicuously dressed, usually in a double-breasted suit, with an unlined face, a neutral complexion and sandy-colored, receding hair, Black could have easily passed for younger than his fifty-one years. In the heat of battle his eyes took on a cold, steely look that could wither distant trees; but when he relaxed, they twinkled with the appearance of a man thoroughly enjoying himself. "The physiognomist's delight," Duncan Aikman of the *New York Times* called him, "because the play of expression on his features reveals both emotional aspects"—of being prosecutor and philosophical student.

The harsh, relentless prosecutor's look energizes his whole face when he tells of combats with the forces he opposes or of specific grievances against his enemies. But a moment later, though he still may be speaking of the same enemies, his features light up with responsive intellectual curiosity and humorous philosophy, as he explains how they got the way they are and charitably, often gayly, analyzes their motives.

For that matter, the very design of the face suggests the dual quality in the Black temperament. The upper part around quick, intelligent eyes has, without being in any sense gross or sensual, the well-rounded curves of a lover of good living and genial society. Tout the jaw below, slightly receding without a trace of weakness, narrows to a point suggesting ruthless, almost ascetic, determination.

He fused opposites naturally. A writer later inquired of Black about his colleague Claude Swanson of Virginia, who often came up with terse, humorous epigrams. The three that Hugo recalled are revealing: "First, 'There comes a time in the life of every man when he must rise above principle'; Second, 'For the first four years after his election each senator can be a statesman, for the last two he is bound to be a politician'; Three, when answering a charge that he had originally been a prohibitionist but later changed, the Senator replied that 'The people of Virginia cannot change their minds a damn bit quicker than Claude Swanson can.' "

"Hugo was always optimistic and jovial in an easy quiet way," said Claude Hamilton, Jr. "His personality didn't change much under stress." He adapted to the circumstances. "He had a decided view of things, with no extra verbiage. He let others carry the conversation. But when he had to do something he didn't like, he'd simply clam up and you just couldn't get a word out of him." His skin hardened over the years but his sensibility and caring deepened—a colleague called him "an evangelic progressive."[8] He liked nothing better than a good, hard-fought political scrap; and he had complete faith as to who would win. Destiny, Hugo Black had confided to a diary he kept shortly after entering the Senate, had great things in store for him.

III

TO THE
SUPREME COURT

CHAPTER 16

CHOOSING
A JUSTICE

F ROM THE BEGINNING of his presidency Roosevelt had given great consideration as to whom he would nominate for the Court. But much as he may have wanted, he could not get around his promise to appoint his Senate wheelhorse Joe Robinson. Robinson's death meant that Roosevelt had to choose carefully. The sharply divided Senate "had relapsed into a mood of seething irritability from which another great rebellion could easily flare up." The sweltering weather contributed. Dire physical consequences were predicted if the session lasted much longer. One newsman noted "the rage-quavers of the voices" of legislators as they "snap at each other in floor debates" and bite the heads off secretaries, prompting him to report "a new high in headless . . . secretaries."

At the end of July Roosevelt said that he was exploring the possibility of making the appointment after the Senate had adjourned. But that changed once some senators murmured threats. At Roosevelt's request Attorney General Cummings and Solicitor General Reed searched "the whole judiciary" and bar for possible appointees, Reed recalled. "They were all canvassed and discussed." (Cummings could have had the appointment if he wished, but told Roosevelt he did not want it.) A list of fifty-four names was assembled quickly. Included were federal judges, eminent law professors, leading liberals and loyal Democrats.

Almost daily in early August Cummings quietly called on Roosevelt at the White House. They first laid down their specifications for the ideal appointee: a thumping New Dealer, easily confirmable and reasonably young, and from the South or the West since neither section was well represented on the Court. Each day they cut more names. Within a week seven names remained: federal appellate judges Samuel H. Sibley of Georgia, Joseph C. Hutcheson, Jr., of Texas and Sam G. Bratton of New Mexico (a former senator); North Carolina chief justice Walter F. Stacy; Reed (from Kentucky); Senator Sherman Minton; and Black. Various party powers pressed the claims of the different candidates. But Roosevelt was genuinely undecided. Tom Corcoran went to Massachusetts, presumably at FDR's direction, to consult Harvard law school professor Felix Frankfurter, an old friend of the president's and the most prominent liberal legal academic in the country. Frankfurter preferred Reed because he would be "thoroughly at home in the procedural problems that come before the Court" while Black would "have to muster an immense amount of rather technical jurisdictional learning."[1]

By the first weekend in August, Roosevelt concluded that the four judges were not liberal enough. The Senate's impatience was growing. Some senators, fearing the appointment of a New Deal "brain truster," "were gathering their forces to resist confirmation to any appointment you may make," William Smathers of New Jersey soon told Roosevelt. He had to move fast. The next Supreme Court justice would be Reed, Minton or Black. Minton, however, did not want to join the Court whose justices he had attacked so personally and unsparingly. It would embarrass him and might make them more inclined to rebuke the president. He was strongly urging Black's claims to Cummings at dinner on August 8 when Cummings suddenly asked him to find out Hugo's feelings.

This was not the first time Black was mentioned for the Court. In January 1937 George Norris, Robert La Follette and Minton had urged Roosevelt to appoint him. That spring various Alabama friends wished to recommend him. "I have told all of them that I shall not be an applicant under any circumstances," Black wrote one inquirer. He preferred to remain in the Senate. "A term of twelve years has given me a familiarity with the various legislative problems, which leads me to believe that I can probably be of more value here than I could anywhere else." Yet he never said he wanted his name removed from consideration.[2]

August 9: Minton visited Black in the morning. "Someone of importance" had asked how Hugo would feel about accepting the Court appointment, Minton said. He could not state who would get it but pointed out that since information was desired, this "must mean something." Hugo responded frankly. He did not wish to leave the Senate. He preferred being in the center of policy making to the secluded eminence of the Court, and was confident he would win the primary in Alabama in 1938. But Josephine, he continued, had for some time been after him to return to his Birmingham law practice. "She's in Alabama and called yesterday about our son Sterling's hearing. I must talk with her." "Okay," Minton said, "but let me know."

Only recently had Hugo and Josephine discovered that Sterling was partly deaf. They found out only because Josephine's sister Virginia had noticed it and told them. "They were so involved in what they were doing that they didn't know," Sterling later said. Black was now taking him to the Johns Hopkins Hospital in Baltimore. "For a while we thought Sterling might lose his hearing completely." (He did not.) Black immediately called Josephine, who was spending the summer in Point Lookout, Alabama, with the children and her family. "I told her to come up to Washington. She said she'd come on the day coach, but not on the Pullman, because 'we're hard up.' I said, 'we're not completely broke and this is very important so come on the Pullman,' and she did." Since the lease on their house had expired, Hugo was staying at the Army War College, where their friend General John L. DeWitt was commandant. "They talked most of the night and did not come downstairs until after lunch the next day," recalled Sterling. "Their meals were brought to them."

They had much to talk about. "At first," Josephine said later, "Hugo didn't want to go on the Court." For he wanted to be president. He thought he could succeed Alben Barkley as majority leader, despite the problems he knew it would create with his constituency, and then he hoped to run for the presidency. ("You shouldn't be elected to the Senate unless you want to be President," he often said.) This culmination was his goal long before he entered politics, since he was just a boy in Clay County. So Hugo was reluctant to leave the Senate. A friend had once told him, as they were walking in front of the Supreme Court, that he hoped Hugo would be appointed. "Life would be dull," Hugo replied. "But Josephine thought the Court would be good for him," Frances Arnold said. "She built up his confidence." She saw it as the refuge from political life for which she longed. The next day, then, Black told Minton that while he would not ask for the appointment, "I would take it" if it were offered. Josephine's influence was decisive. As Sterling said, "My mother wanted him to do it."[3]*

August 10: Southerners were gloating at a motion to be introduced the next day by Robert Wagner to consider an antilynching bill. They declared their

---

* "Hugo thought he'd be able to get to the presidency easier from the Court," Lister Hill observed. Being outside the normal political picture, "he wouldn't have as many people to go around" (Robert Frazer int.).

intention to debate it until Christmas. Black was preparing to lead the
opponents. Democrats held a "harmony dinner" for Barkley. Cheek by jowl
sat staunch New Dealers and rebellious southerners. A "dove of peace"
fluttered above the senators; even the ice cream was dove shaped. The
brooding nighthawk that perched on a Capitol column outside the Senate
chamber would have been a better symbol of their mood.[4]

August 11: Cummings told Roosevelt of Minton's report of his talk with
Black. The attorney general once again pressed Reed's credentials. The
president was still pondering his choice as Cummings left. "FDR admired
Black no end for his steadfast helping," said Tom Corcoran. He thought
Hugo was "a fighter for principle and liked his aggressive leadership of the
liberal bloc." And "to give the rebels' part of the country so important an
appointment," wrote Joseph Alsop and Turner Catledge, "yet give it to one
of the two or three left-wingers in the Senate was a neat and cruel irony to
the rather vengeful President." Roosevelt was nothing if not vengeful at this
time. Lunching with him a few days earlier, former NRA official Donald
Richberg felt the president was "a bitter man . . . He did not joke about
opponents as he used to do, although Roosevelt kept everything on a bright
light level and tried not to show his feelings." These were as apparent to
those around him as his tilted cigarette. "Father was very angry at the Senate,
hopping mad almost," said James Roosevelt, then a presidential assistant.
"He really wanted to get back at them, stick it to them if he could." Black
was the perfect vehicle for retaliation.

In the afternoon Roosevelt reached his decision. He had one of his
secretaries call Black to ask if he could come to the White House that
evening. The invitation was put blankly, for Roosevelt had kept his own
counsel. Nervously, Black said he'd be delighted. Roosevelt received Black
in his upstairs study. Hugo remembered his talk with Minton, but the president could have wanted to discuss the wages-hours bill. After some small
talk, Roosevelt reached into a drawer for a piece of paper. It was a commission
that must be completed when a presidential nomination goes to the Senate.
The president had already written on it "Associate Justice of the Supreme
Court of the United States." He smilingly pointed to the empty space and
casually asked if he could fill in Hugo's name. Black said, "Mr. President,
are you sure that I'll be more useful to you on the Court than in the Senate?"
"Hugo," the president replied, "I wish you were twins because Barkley says
he needs you in the Senate" (even though FDR had not spoken to Barkley),
"but I think you'll be more useful on the Court." The president wrote in

Black's name, signed the commission and told him not to mention it before the next noon.[5]

August 12: Cummings went again to see Roosevelt, carrying with him a memo that listed the pros and cons of Black and Reed. The president was lying down in his bedroom ("providing a very formal and dignified background for affairs of state," as one frequent caller noted). "Did you make up your mind?" Cummings asked. Smiling widely, Roosevelt shook his head positively and told Cummings what had happened the night before. He showed Cummings the sealed envelope with the commission inside. Then they laughed at the joke they were playing on all the politicians and pundits in Washington.

Roosevelt met with Will Alexander, a progressive southern educator. He asked Alexander to guess whose name he had submitted for the Court— "someone from our part of the country," FDR said, becoming the southerner by adoption that he sometimes did because of the Little White House in Georgia. Alexander mentioned an Atlanta judge, but when Roosevelt told him it was Black, his first thought was that Black had probably been a member of the Ku Klux Klan. He started to mention this, then changed his mind. Otherwise, only Roosevelt, Cummings and the Blacks knew what was to come. In the course of a long talk that morning with James Farley, who was also Democratic national chairman, FDR did not once mention Black.

Shortly before noon, presidential press secretary Steve Early indicated to reporters that Roosevelt was still considering a list of "sixty or seventy names" and that no appointment might be forthcoming for a couple of weeks, perhaps not until the congressional session was over. Suddenly the bell from the president's office rang for him. After excusing himself for a moment, he returned to the reporters. "Jesus Christ!" he exclaimed. A Court appointment had been sent up. "You'll have to get the rest of it from the Senate." It was now noon. A White House messenger, commission in hand, was standing at the Senate door. FDR was grinning.

The messenger entered the chamber. Vice President John N. Garner rapped for attention and shouted: "A Message from the President of the United States." Black sat slumped in his seat, nervously twisting a piece of paper. Josephine, wearing a big black linen hat, looked down from the front row of the senators' family gallery. A clerk gave the envelope to Garner. "I nominate Hugo L. Black . . ." A gasp went through the chamber; Black half flinched. For a moment only hushed silence could be heard. Then senators began stirring around; irritation slowly replaced incredulity for most. Black stayed quietly at his desk, his face not showing any unusual excitement, until some colleagues, mainly liberals, came over to congratulate him.

Henry Ashurst, chairman of the Judiciary Committee, rose to move that the nomination be taken up in executive session immediately under "an immemorial rule" that the Senate confirms a member "without reference to a committee. . . . No amount of investigation or consideration by a committee could disclose any new light on the character or attainments and ability of the nominee, because if we do not know him after long service with him, no one will ever know him." He extolled Black as a "lawyer of transcendent ability, great, industrious, courageous in debate, young, vigorous, of splendid character and attainments . . . I cannot conceive how the President could have made a wiser selection." Even Hugo could not have agreed more.[6]

Hiram Johnson of California and Edward Burke of Nebraska objected. Black turned white-faced. "I think the nomination should pursue the regular course," Johnson said. Within an hour Ashurst named a subcommittee to consider the appointment; it consisted mainly of Democrats who had supported the Court-packing plan. For the first time since 1888 a committee would consider a colleague's confirmation. Burke had suggested that a formal opinion from Attorney General Cummings should be sought. Since Black had voted for the Supreme Court retirement bill, providing full pay for retired justices, Burke contended that the constitutional bar forbidding appointment of legislators to posts for which emoluments have been increased during their term of office prevented the appointment.* This had not been raised, even privately, when Joe Robinson was virtually justice-designate in May. Nor did it concern most senators now. But after Cummings and Reed hurriedly conferred at the Justice Department, Roosevelt held a press conference to say that Cummings had informed him that Black's nomination was perfectly constitutional.

Majority leader Barkley felt it would be "unwise and futile to go into executive session at this time." Black sat at his desk, his chin cupped in his hand, as the Senate resumed discussion of the antilynching bill. He quickly left the Senate floor so photographers could take the obligatory shots. Then he went for lunch with his wife, Sterling and a Birmingham reporter.

* Article 1, Section 6 of the Constitution states: "No Senator or Representative shall, during the Time for which he was elected, be appointed to any civil Office under the Authority of the United States, which shall have been created, or the Emoluments whereof shall have been increased during such time. . . ."

The nomination dropped like salt into already raw political wounds. While liberals erupted in paeans of joy, "conservatives were very skeptical," said Burt Wheeler. "I wasn't surprised at the appointment—I knew what Roosevelt was up to—but many senators really were. They felt Hugo went a little too far in support of Roosevelt and that on the Court he would vote the New Deal line." Most conservatives, stunned and horrified, went into spasms of teeth gnashing. "If he had picked the devil himself, he would not have aroused nearly so much resentment in the reactionary camp," labor leader Edward Keating happily noted. "This was a kick in the face and the President used our own foot to kick us," one anti–New Deal senator said. When asked for a comment, Virginia's Carter Glass replied, "Don't start me off again." All this appealed to Roosevelt's sadistic instinct and he loved every minute of it. "Just now I have a thoroughly discombobulated Congress, running around in circles . . . ," he wrote.[7] Only those who knew Black well were not alarmed.

August 13: Roosevelt was exulting in the open frustration and confusion of his senatorial enemies. He knew that the Senate's sense of collegiality would prevail. "They'll have to take him," he told James Farley. The Judiciary Committee subcommittee swiftly approved the nomination 5 to 1. Warren Austin of Vermont, claiming that the emoluments matter made Black ineligible and demanding open hearings, cast the only "no" vote.

From the moment the nomination was announced, Black's connection with the Ku Klux Klan was a major topic of conversation in the Senate cloakroom. No senator had the audacity to discuss it in public. "No comment," Black replied when a·reporter put the question to him directly. The *Washington News,* a Scripps-Howard paper sympathetic to the New Deal, and the *Chicago Tribune* quickly noted in editorials that the Klan had supported him in 1926. "It is difficult to find a sketch of Senator Black which does not contain some reference to the Ku Klux Klan . . . ," *Washington Post* columnist Franklyn Waltman wrote. "Where there is so much smoke, there must be some fire." Some anti–New Dealers tried to start a blaze. Alabama newspapers of the 1920s and other political records were carefully examined. One northern publisher inquired about Black's role in the Father Coyle murder case in 1921. The Republican National Committee researched his senatorial comments. If "anything of a documentary nature" were found, one senator said, it would be submitted to the Judiciary Committee.[8] But no proof of Klan involvement was found, only strong but unsubstantiated rumors of the hooded order's support.

August 16: Walter White of the NAACP called on Black. "I told him that while I personally had confidence that he would take an enlightened point of view, there was much apprehension" among Negroes, White wrote later. Black was willing to receive but would not answer the telegram White was sending him, as he had declined to answer other questions while the matter was before the Judiciary Committee. He promised to make a statement if hearings were held or another appropriate opportunity presented itself. "Very frankly," he said he hoped to measure up to what White and his other friends expected of him.

Roosevelt told chairman Ashurst it was "time for the Democrats to get hard-boiled and push the Black matter through the [Judiciary] Committee." In a tempestuous session Senator Borah raised the question of Black's eligibility for the Court; Senator Burke wanted Black to appear before the committee. Their efforts were in vain. When William Dietrich, an Illinois Democrat, then charged that unnamed committee members tried to "besmirch" Black in the press, Burke had to be physically restrained from attacking him. Calm quickly returned, however. The nomination was easily approved and sent to the floor.

The efforts to expose Black's reputed Klan connections continued. The *New York Sun* quoted from a 1926 newspaper report that Black had been elected "with Alabama's most powerful political organization [the Klan] backing him. . . . The Alabama Klan has a loyal and devoted friend." This was admittedly small fruit. But rumblings continued that he would be accused of being a Klan member. Only such a startling disclosure could stay quick confirmation, all Senate leaders agreed. Two powerful influences were working in Black's favor: senatorial courtesy, perhaps the body's most sacred tradition, and the stampede for Congress to adjourn by the end of the week.[9]

August 17: The nomination came before the full Senate. Crammed galleries heard a handful of foes pound away all afternoon against the appointment. Some, such as Borah, still insisted that no legal vacancy existed. To others the Klan issue was paramount. Royal Copeland immediately raised it, merely repeating rumors about Black's connection. "Oh! Mr. President," he declared in quavering tones, his voice reaching a dramatic crescendo, "I beg of you to withdraw this name and send us another, that of a New Dealer, if you must, but one free from the taint of religious and racial prejudice." Not only did he and Black share a mutual antipathy, but Copeland was running as the Tammany candidate in the Democratic primary for mayor of New York City. He had announced his strong opposition to Black the day before (calling the nomination "an insult to the nation"), and his remarks were calculated to garner votes from the city's polyglot population. His colleagues listened in "stony silence," one reporter wrote.

Senator Burke stated that two men (unnamed) living in Washington were ready to testify they witnessed Black's Klan initiation. He claimed to have known this since Saturday (it was now Wednesday), "but the Judiciary Committee never asked for any evidence." "Who is this unnamed person from whom the Senator gets his information?" Sherman Minton asked. "Could it be Elisha Hanson, a Hearst lawyer? I ask because I happen to know that some of the information used in a speech yesterday by the Senator from Maine [Republican Wallace White] was supplied by Hanson."

Black's supporters took up their cudgels while several friendly colleagues asked him to make a statement on the Klan matter. Borah, representing the Judiciary Committee and a Republican, spoke for them; he was abrupt but sympathetic. Black weighed his response, uncharacteristically hesitating before answering. He would make no statement, he replied; all he would say, even to them, was that he was not now a Klansman. "I did tell Senator Borah, a member of the Senate Judiciary Committee, that I had had no affiliations of any kind with the Klan since I had come to the Senate," he later wrote. But he added that if any of his friends were concerned that he might have been a member in the past, he would ask that man to vote against confirmation. Without actually saying so, he let his callers understand that he had been a Klansman.[10]

The Judiciary Committee, quickly canvassing the situation, decided that Black had no prejudices and that the best thing to do was to "forgive and forget."* Borah took it upon himself to speak for the committee. As the body's senior senator he exercised great moral weight, and the Lion of Idaho roared: "There has never been at any time one iota of evidence that Senator Black was a member of the Klan. [He] has said in private conversation, not since this matter came up but at other times, that he was not a member of

---

* "Several years ago, when the Klan question was being discussed," Borah wrote the next month, "it was generally stated around Washington that Black had been a member of the Klan. He had stated to his friends, so I was informed, he was not a member. . . . Rumors had all been to the effect that Black was not any longer a member. When the matter was brought up in committee, no one had any facts further than this general rumor which had long prevailed" (Borah to R. W. Owens, Jr., 9/18/37, Borah papers).

the Klan, and there is no evidence to the effect that he is. What is there to examine?"

Black waited with Josephine in the office of Edwin Halsey, secretary of the Senate, during the six-hour debate. Opponents forwarded technical objections and called for further inquiry, a sure sign they had run out of arguments. Tom Connally of Texas stated: "Hearings are for the information of the committee, not for the purpose of public amusement; not to have a legislative rodeo." To those who ridiculed Black's only judicial experience being a police court judge, he pointed out that "all but two [current Supreme Court justices] never sat on a bench, except perhaps a park bench, until they took office."

The roll was called. Fellow southerners (except for Glass and Harry Byrd of Virginia) supported Black mainly due to regional fealty (and also because the Deep South had been complaining for years that not a single justice had represented it). Most Catholic senators as well as many who opposed the Court-packing plan refused to be recorded on the merits of a colleague. Black was confirmed 63 to 16, with 17 senators not voting. After the vote he walked into the chamber, smiling broadly. Senators crowded around to congratulate him. He returned to Halsey's office. Barkley, Claude Pepper, Pat Harrison and Key Pittman of Nevada were there. They discussed whether Black "should make an adieu to the Senate. Agreed he might—short," Pepper wrote in his diary. Leaving the Senate, with its clubby atmosphere and his friends, and the setting of many satisfying accomplishments over a decade, was not easy for Black; he later confessed to suffering from a "depression of spirit."* He "said he would like to go back to Clay County, Alabama, birthplace, where mother and father [are] buried to take the oath, almost a tear in his eye," Pepper noted. "Harrison and I urged him to do it whether it looked spectacular or not." He decided against it.

"So Hugo Black becomes a member of the Supreme Court while the economic royalists fume and squirm and the President rolls his tongue around in his cheek," chortled Harold Ickes.[11]

*   *   *

---

* John Bankhead was almost emotional: "Shake partner shake," he wired Hugo upon hearing of the nomination. "I am tickled to death on your account." Then he wrote: "I have a feeling of dejection and lowered spirits because of our separation in public service and our personal relations. I know that I shall miss you tremendously and I never hope to have a colleague who will provide the same degree of friendliness and cooperation as you have consistently done" (8/12,13/37).

"But what a sensation the appointment caused in your beloved Alabama!" wrote a delighted Grover Hall ("I am as proud of you personally as if you were my brother"). "The apple cart was completely turned over." Black tried to keep the wagon rolling in the same direction. Before the Judiciary Committee met, he called Lister Hill's confidant, Richard Rives, in Montgomery. His confirmation "almost a certainty," Black wanted to contact Hill, who was touring Europe as part of a delegation dedicating war monuments, and asked Rives to reach him. "The Boss [FDR] and I discussed who should be my successor," Black told Rives. "We both think Lister is an outstanding House member. I want my work carried on and we think Lister will do it. If there's any weakening in our position, some forces could turn against him. Tell him to get on the first boat, and have him make an announcement that he will be a candidate. This is strictly confidential, but I feel so strongly for the wages-hours bill."

Rives reached Hill who quickly sailed home; and, together with Montgomery postmaster Roy Nolen, Rives drafted a purposely equivocal announcement on the wages-hours bill. The power to appoint an interim senator belonged to Governor Bibb Graves. As soon as Black's nomination was announced, several candidates geared up to run; a possible party bloodbath was in the offing. After conferring with Roosevelt, Black called Graves: they agreed he would name his politically active wife, Dixie Bibb Graves, to serve until a special election to be held the next January, when both he and Roosevelt would support Hill. (After one of her several radio broadcasts to her new constituents on her first day in office, Graves remarked, "Who said I didn't appoint a good senator?")[12]

August 19: Black lunched at the White House with Roosevelt. Thirty years later, after reading an article about his appointment, he dictated a statement to "correct for posterity any idea about President Roosevelt's having been fooled about my membership in the Klan":

> President Roosevelt, when I went up to lunch with him, told me that there was no reason for my worrying about having been a member of the Ku Klux Klan. He said that some of the best friends and supporters he had in the State of Georgia were strong members of that organization. He never in any way, by word or attitude, indicated any doubt about my having been in the Klan nor did he indicate any criticism of me for having been a member of that organization. The rumors and statements to the contrary are wrong. On the other hand, Senator Copeland, who opened the attack on me in the Senate about the Klan, had a dinner party for the Klan

lobbyists shortly after I came to Washington. He invited my wife and me to the dinner and we went. The dinner was held at the Wardman Park Hotel. I had been told in Birmingham by members of the Klan that Senator Copeland was a member of that organization himself. His association with the Klan lobbyists led me to believe that these statements about his Klan membership were true.

This statement deserves comment. Other than this assertion, no evidence has ever come to light that Roosevelt then knew about Black's Klan membership. Most likely, he was simply trying to make light of the reports to put Black at ease. He gave no indication to anyone around him that he recalled the 1926 series of articles in the *New York World* by Charles Michelson, who was now publicity director of the Democratic National Committee, when in fact, recalled James Roosevelt, "he sometimes talked about them when something from the South came up." Almost everybody in political Washington knew that Black was regarded at least as a beneficiary of the Klan. In any event Roosevelt's remark about his Georgia Klan supporters was "true," said James Roosevelt. "I could well picture Father telling Black that. It was the type of thing he would laugh about as he would be talking about it."

Black never chuckled about Copeland. Not until several years after the doctor-senator's death in 1938, however, did he start claiming that Copeland was a member of the Klan. He needed a rationalization for those who opposed his confirmation—it was part of his guilt about joining the hooded order—and imputing Klan affiliation to a dead, disliked former colleague made a good one. But it cannot explain why the Klan in western New York wanted to replace Copeland; why he received an award from the National Conference of Christians and Jews; or why he was long a close ally of William Randolph Hearst, who, whatever else may be said about him, was notably free of prejudice and whose publications were outspokenly anti-Klan.

Black left the White House with his Supreme Court commission rolled under his arm and "smiling like a schoolboy on commencement day." The rest of the afternoon he spent closeted with Governor Graves, who had come to Washington with his wife. Many years later Black remembered "the anxious moments" the governor spent pacing his office "because of his desire that I resign my seat in the Senate at the earliest possible moment for his wife to be named my successor." "I told [them] that I was going to take the [Supreme Court oath] a half-hour after I resigned. I told them I wouldn't want time to get an injunction against taking my seat. They said, of course, there wouldn't be anything like that, and I told them they didn't know that crowd—that I knew them better than they did." A quirky former federal judge and Justice Department official, Albert Levitt, had just filed suit to require Black to prove his eligibility; many other individuals angered by Black's activities would need no prompting to join.[13]

Once most senators had left the Capitol for the day, Black wrote out his resignation at his desk on the floor and gave it to the page. It was now six o'clock. The courts had already closed. He called the trusted Senate secretary, Halsey, to make arrangements for the oath; he wanted no other witnesses. Charles F. Pace, the Senate's financial clerk, acted as notary. In Halsey's office off the Senate chamber, Black took a simple constitutional oath, the same declaration required of all federal officers.*

Barney Whatley had gone to Washington shortly after the nomination "to see that everything is done in true Clay County style." In his pocket was a large amount of cash. He knew Hugo had long yearned to visit Europe. (The cost of the 1932 reelection campaign prevented a trip then.) Now he plunked the money down on Hugo's desk and told him to take Josephine and go. Not until Hugo was confirmed and travel arrangements were hastily made, did Barney return to Colorado. The following week, Hugo and Josephine joined him for a few days. Black had the Supreme Court ship volumes of cases so he could reread as many as possible when they were not playing golf.[14]

Back home, he closed out his Senate office and secured jobs in the federal government for members of his staff. He needed a secretary at the Court. Since rumors about some Klan affiliation were still circulating, he had to make a clean break with his past, and to Black this meant hiring a Catholic. Esther Wood had worked for him for nearly twenty years, since just after the world war. Because she was Protestant, however, he came up with one of his most preposterous stories: he told her she could not go to the Court with him because the Alabama Democratic Executive Committee had passed a resolution that it had to approve his choice. Then he asked one of his young secretaries if she would serve at the Court. She was Catholic. But she wanted to return to Mobile to get married, and declined. So he asked another assistant—she too was Catholic. She readily agreed. Thousands of letters had poured in and, with the help of his staff and friends, he began to answer them.

---

* The usual Supreme Court custom at the time was for a new justice to take a general oath, administered by the chief justice, in the Court's robing room on the first day he assumed his duties. This is the oath that Black took in Halsey's office. A second oath was taken in the courtroom, just before the new justice ascended the bench.

One dispatch carried the once familiar letterhead of the General Robert
E. Lee Klan No. 1, Realm of Alabama ("The Oldest Functioning Klan in
the Invisible Empire"). Black read: "A man representing the Birmingham
News came and asked what connection you had with the Klan in your first
race for the Senate. . . ." This did not surprise him: he knew "that crowd."
Even in one as self-contained as Hugo Black this had to trigger a momentary
alarm; certainly here were the seeds of a potential crisis. But he was already
sworn in as a justice, and he would not let this interfere with his plans.

The furor waned as Congress adjourned and congressmen went home.
Black's name faded from the newspapers; the controversy seemed to be over.
On August 26 he and Josephine sailed for Europe, scheduled to return on
October 1. In Washington, however, wags were still quipping, "Hugo won't
have to buy a new robe; he can have his white one dyed black."[15]

CHAPTER 17

HIDING THE ROBES

To Black high in "that crowd" were industrialists, financiers and publishers. The press had largely condemned the appointment. Most newspapers frowned, some grimaced, others pouted, and columnists also split on ideological lines. Mere mention of the Ku Klux Klan, however, brought memories and raw emotions to the fore.

The weekend of the nomination, Herbert Bayard Swope, editor of the *New York World* during its crusading heyday in the 1920s, was vacationing with banker Robert Lehman at Saratoga, New York. He proudly recalled the fight the *World* under his leadership had waged against the Klan in the early 1920s. Black was the Klan's candidate in 1926, Swope noted; somebody should get a reporter to look into it. Lehman told this to his friend Paul Block, New York–based publisher of the *Pittsburgh Post-Gazette* and other papers. Like Swope and Lehman, Block was Jewish. "Father just wanted to go after Black because of the Klan—he just abhorred it," said Paul Block, Jr. He was also a staunch Republican and an acid critic of the New Deal. Block hurried to call Pittsburgh. City editor Joe Shuman suggested assigning Ray Sprigle to the Black story.

It was an appropriate choice. "Sprigle could smell a story," recalled Shuman. "He enjoyed going out and getting things for himself." With his corncob pipe, which he smoked incessantly, and his huge sombrero, he was as colorful as his flamboyant, dramatic prose. He liked to "pick up the paper by the corner of the page—and watch the blood drip out" of his stories, he said. Since it was Sunday, Shuman passed the hat for money so Sprigle could fly to Birmingham immediately. Block had already swung into action. In Birmingham Sprigle made a beeline for the office of Black's old enemy Forney

247

Johnston, who took him to Charles R. Robinson, a member of the state Republican committee and a law partner of George Frey, a onetime high Klan official. Robinson's office became Sprigle's base. Sprigle was well bankrolled and money flowed easily. "Sprigle offered me a very lucrative fee," Robinson told Frey. Ten former Klansmen rounded up by Frey were paid to give affidavits stating that they sat at meetings with Black and saw him receive a lifetime membership.

For a few days Sprigle followed up leads, but got nowhere fast. While everyone was certain Black had been a Klansman, Sprigle wanted proof. He went to the one-room office of James Esdale. Reporters from all over the country were trying to pin down the former Grand Dragon who was cynically fencing with them. Sprigle left. That evening he took a cab to Esdale's farm. They quickly found a subject of common interest—chickens. Esdale was setting up his son with a flock of leghorns. Sprigle, who raised white wyandottes on his farm, persuaded Esdale not to stock them as he had planned. Then they got to comparing different types of tobaccos. "Sprigle would put up his feet and talk away while drinking, a real regular guy," a colleague recalled. Esdale took to him. "All right to drop in on you tomorrow?" Sprigle asked upon leaving at midnight. "Surely, any time" came the reply.[1]

Sprigle spent the next day checking out Esdale. After leaving the Klan in 1931, he returned to practicing law. In 1935 the corporate lawyers who ran the city and state bar associations charged him with illegally soliciting legal business. The state bar disbarred him and in April 1937 the Alabama Supreme Court upheld the action. That night, after a long telephone conversation, Esdale asked Sprigle to come to his office in the morning. Sprigle did. He had telexed Pittsburgh, "send six 5 Brothers chewing tobacco," and he gave it to Esdale. Then Esdale swung around and opened a safe. He shoved an armful of documents across the desk—Black's application for Klan membership; his service card, with a record of his initiation and dues (Hugo never paid one cent) and a listing of every office he ever held and every committee he had served on; his scrawled resignation on the Grand Dragon's letterhead; and the stenographic record of the great Klorero in Birmingham to celebrate the Klan's power in the 1926 elections. Chronicled was Black's life in the Invisible Empire.

"That what you wanted?" Sprigle gulped. Esdale wanted to go over it with him and to know how he would handle it. "But the general idea is that you get it," Esdale said, continuing to pull material out of the safe.

Sprigle urged they quickly get it out of Alabama, where much of the federal legal machinery was indebted to Black. Esdale planned to leave with his family for a two-week vacation in Florida on Monday, August 20, three days hence. Sprigle offered, instead, an all-expenses-paid holiday in New York, with a car and driver at the Esdales' command and box seats at the theater and baseball games. Esdale readily agreed. He left the next day with two suitcases of Klan documents safely buried under the family luggage. Sprigle met him at the Hotel McAlpin in New York on Monday.

Why did Esdale turn over the records to Sprigle? At the time he was in difficult straits. Sprigle told Paul Block, Jr., that he paid for the documents. More important, Black's behavior in office had annoyed Esdale. Hugo never associated himself with the Klan, although he never publicly denied his membership. Esdale had expected him to "play ball"—at least to give jobs and patronage to Klansmen. This Hugo did not do, favoring unaffiliated "laymen" instead. And when Hugo's friends denied he ever had any association with the Klan, Esdale was vexed. This came after Esdale's disbarment. He had sought Black's intervention then (through Crampton Harris). "There was no doubt that it would have been extremely helpful," Esdale told Sprigle. "It was not forthcoming." Years later, to an interviewer who specifically asked why he turned over the documents, Esdale gave "a vague answer connoting revenge."[2]

*   *   *

Hugo and Josephine arrived in Paris on September 1, 1937. Soon he received a letter a Birmingham court reporter sent his Senate assistant: "a mug by the name of Sprigle," stating that his mission was "to look into Senator Black's affiliation with the Klan," had asked the reporter to certify the transcript of a 1926 Klan meeting; Sprigle would be willing to pay. (The reporter refused the request.) Hugo put the letter away. He and Josephine enjoyed Paris. The purpose of the trip was simply "to give us both some rest," as she said. Their pleasure was lessened on Friday, September 10, when the *Pittsburgh Post-Gazette* announced that a series of articles on Hugo's relation with the Klan would begin on Monday. Reporters called his hotel. "A Hearst man in order to spy on us got a room commanding our rooms," Black said later. "He might have seen us disrobing. I wanted to punch him but that wouldn't do."

They went to England on the thirteenth as planned. The series started, running in leading papers across the country. Written in Sprigle's flowery style, touching the right emotional chords, the articles made engrossing reading, as the lead for the first one showed: "Hugo Lafayette Black, associate justice of the United States Supreme Court, is a member of the hooded brotherhood that for 10 long blood-drenched years ruled the Southland with lash and noose and torch, the Invisible Empire Knights of the Ku Klux Klan. He holds his membership in the masked and oath-bound legion as he holds his high office in the Nation's Supreme Tribunal—for life." Black's connection with the Klan was now conclusive and undeniable. Most significant, Sprigle was claiming that Black was *still* a member of the Klan.

The resulting uproar could be heard in London. Some senators and congressmen demanded that Black resign, others talked of an investigation or impeachment, and Catholic groups were especially insistent that some action be taken. ("How could they impeach me?" Black said later. "I hadn't done anything.") "The Klan was a shocking thing even though I wasn't surprised by it," said Claude Pepper, expressing a widespread opinion on Capitol Hill. "Most senators regardless of party, and most of the southerners, liked Hugo personally and knew that he was not a Ku Kluxer in behavior or sentiment. They knew his liberal record and thought the Klan was just politics. I wasn't sure he'd get through it. The thing just sizzled. The Senate was embarrassed but didn't know what to do." There was nothing it could do.[3]

Friends rallied to Black's defense. Attorney General Cummings stated that his "record of public service . . . made his suitability beyond question." To Senator Bankhead the whole issue was "a rattling of old bones that have long been dead and dry." Liberals gave Black continuing support. He is "the people's lawyer," said Senator Norris. "That's the reason for all this furor. If he had been a corporation lawyer, all of these issues would not have been raised." But they were being raised, savagely and unrelentingly. Even some newspapers that strongly supported the New Deal joined the many urging Black's resignation. A chorus of condemnation drowned out the few editorials and columnists who, even though they were startled, hurt and genuinely outraged, counseled patience to hear Black's side of the story. It was a ready-made situation for cartoonists, and they outdid themselves portraying a white-hooded figure in divers settings.

Roosevelt was in a quandary. Piqued at Black for getting him into this predicament, FDR was paying the price for his own secretiveness. (He readily understood Hugo's action; indeed, had he been in Hugo's shoes, he would have not informed the president either.) "The Klan thing hit me like a clap of thunder," he told Lister Hill. "It knocked me out of the damn chair." He didn't know what to do, his loyal secretary Missy LeHand said. Opinion was divided within his own circle. Molly Dewson, an old political friend now on the Democratic National Committee, went to see him. "The disturbed look on Roosevelt's lined and tired face is unforgettable," she later wrote. "He said without preface, 'Molly, I did not know Black belonged to the Ku Klux Klan. This is very serious.' "*

The day after the *Pittsburgh Post-Gazette* series started, FDR told the press that until Black returned from Europe, "there is no further comment to be made." He was stalling to see what developed, with Black, himself and public opinion. Soon he announced that he would leave on a two-week tour, ostensibly a vacation and inspection trip, which would take him to the Northwest. From the administration came only silence.[4] Rumors and fulminations from its enemies filled the void.

In London, Paul Ward phoned the Blacks' hotel. Their close friend Richard Hogue, whom Hugo had met as part of the public power movement and who was helping handle matters at home for him, had alerted Ward, a Washington reporter now heading the *Baltimore Sun*'s London bureau, that Hugo would be coming and asked that he meet the "right people." Hugo and Josephine spent much time with the Wards. After one of their several dinners together, as they were returning to their room, a reporter sprang out from a corner, said he was with the *New York Times* and the Associated Press, and demanded a statement. Hugo, comforting a frightened Josephine, said he would comment if and when he desired. He was "shocked that the Associated Press was using such tactics to get a scoop," Josephine wrote in her diary. "The man got very angry and started most of the ugly stories of our isolation and chagrin in a London hotel about our stay in London." (The reporter was young James "Scotty" Reston.)† Under the door were "all kinds of notes." Hugo told Josephine he would put a sign over their bed at

---

* But Roosevelt, ever the practical politician who knew the uses of humor, still found something to laugh about in the situation. Joseph P. Kennedy, then chairman of the Maritime Commission, told FDR of a conversation he had with reporter Arthur Krock. Krock had expressed shock that Black had not informed FDR of his Klan membership. Kennedy's reply (cleaned up for publication) was "If Marlene Dietrich asked you to make love to her, would you tell her you weren't much good at making love?" (Joe McCarthy, *The Remarkable Kennedys* [New York, 1960], 68–69).

† At a dinner years later at which Reston was also a guest, Black said he asked what paper the reporter was with. When the reporter said, "the *New York Times*," Black replied, "I don't believe it. You have got to be from the *Chicago Tribune*." Black was being kind and Reston, who was stringing for the *Times* in 1937, didn't say anything. Reston's memory of the incident was that he went to Black's room and introduced himself, "I'm from the *New York Times*," upon which Black said, "That's enough for me," and closed the door (ESB, *Rebel*; ESB, Reston ints.).

home, saying, "This too will pass." He knew what the press commotion was about.

Reporters descended on the hotel the next morning at breakfast like a horde of locusts. "They seemed determined to destroy us like the locusts in 'The Good Earth' did the wheat fields," Josephine noted, "but we were determined not to be destroyed." English libel laws made it difficult to determine just what was behind the glaring headlines. Black was afraid the Klan transcript might be altered. "What's new about this?" he asked Ward. "The Chicago Tribune sent men down during my reelection in '32." If it really were the right version of the Klan's 1926 Klorero, he was happy: he had mentioned Protestants, Catholics and Jews. "I have nothing to apologize for." Ward cabled home for clarification. A summary sent to London "deep-ened Black's suspicions. He was taken by surprise," Ward recalled. "He said that there was a conspiracy to get him, but that he couldn't do much about it because then it would be conduct unbecoming a Justice, and he didn't want to give further impetus to any movement against him."

If not quite the typical tourists, Hugo and Josephine took in Hyde Park, Westminster Abbey, Parliament and the Tower of London, as well as the old haunts of Ben Jonson; undiscoverable in the city's crowds, they went to the theater almost every night. In bookstalls Hugo found books he wanted— a volume of Grote's *Aristotle* and Thucydides' *History of the Greek Wars*; he sought out Toynbee Hall. Ward arranged luncheons for Black with Fleet Street journalists and with Harold J. Laski, the prominent English liberal intellectual. While he was eating in the *London News Chronicle* board room, both the British and the American press were writing that he was barricaded in his hotel room and that he was leaving London. Raymond Gram Swing, the American correspondent for the British Broadcasting Corporation, was saying ominous things on radio. Black gave the hotel instructions that he was "permanently out." "You simply want to ask me questions so you can write: 'Black refused to answer,' " he told one reporter. To another he said, "I don't see you. I don't know you. And I don't answer you." Ward, serving as Black's unofficial press agent, reluctantly told colleagues his whereabouts and that he was planning to visit his ancestors' home in Ireland and sail home from there.

Soon all this got too much for Black. Tom Corcoran called from Wash-ington on his own initiative to urge Hugo to stand fast and not to answer the charges until he returned home, when he could do so in a radio broadcast. Beleaguered and harassed, Black called Ward and asked to talk off the record. "He didn't want to tie his hands," Ward recalled.

He talked about the Klan. He starting telling me the good things he had done before the Senate, that as prosecutor he cleaned up crap shooters. He told me how he brought a pauper's case to the Supreme Court. He talked about that with a lot of pride. He said that in a way all this controversy was to the good, that regardless of the fact that he was involved members of the Supreme Court shouldn't be considered above criticism. He talked to me almost as if it were a confessional. He was trying to show that he wasn't a bad guy, that the Klan story meant nothing.

Black decided to cut short his trip and go home. Josephine canceled their reservations on the liner *Manhattan*, to sail on the small ship *City of Norfolk*. Hugo attempted to mislead the press by sending his luggage in the early morning to Ward's house. But a limousine he hired to take him and Josephine to the port failed to appear. He called the booking agency. "You want to get rid of these fellows?" the clerk asked. "What fellows?" Black asked. "The newspapermen," replied the clerk. The English reporters were around the corner from the agency, peeping out. The limousine (an Austin cab) came and took a back route to the port. "The reporters took turns driving alongside us, waving," Ward remembered.

It was like a Mack Sennett chase through the London suburbs. The reporters would wave and we would duck, then we would sit up and the reporters would duck. Up and down, up and down. It was crazy. We went a round-about way. Then I saw no reporters behind, and I told the driver to take off. We had lunch at a countryside hostel. At the port, a guy from the ship line jumped out and said, "We'll keep it quiet." They held the ship for him. A reporter said, "I didn't think you were coming," and left. We went up the gangplank to the captain's cabin. I told friends I knew from when I had crossed on the boat not to say anything. And Black went home.*

"Klandestinely," a newspaper noted.[5]

While the Senate was debating Black's nomination, Senator Henry Ashurst declared that "no scenario writer this year will produce a more delightful film or one more opulent with gentle irony than the scene we have here." High among the ironies was that the Roman Catholic Church came to Black's

---

* "The whole experience from the beginning made me uneasy," Ward added. "I had the old-time respect for the Supreme Court and I was a reporter. That was my job. But Black was also my friend. He was a good guy and on the right side of issues. And he needed help."

defense. The Protestant Roosevelt had cultivated Catholic political leaders throughout his career. And with none of any faith did he hit it off better than with Chicago's Cardinal George Mundelein. Despite strong criticism of Black's appointment in the Catholic press, the hierarchy did not protest. On September 17 James Roosevelt called Bishop Francis Spellman of Boston, on his way to being FDR's "favorite bishop." Black's "only answer," Spellman said, "was to admit he joined the Klan, that he resigned, did not believe in it and repudiated it." Monsignor John A. Ryan ("Right Reverend New Dealer," his biographer called him), a friend of Black's since before Roosevelt took office, echoed these thoughts. "He has been a great advocate of social legislation," Ryan said in an interview that received wide publicity. In their relations, he added, he had found Black notably tolerant.

Ray Sprigle returned to Birmingham, where Forney Johnston handed him $500, saying "You're doing a good job. Keep it up." Former governor Kilby, private detective Fred Bodecker, and Horace Wilkinson, prominent Klansman and lawyer, furnished more information. Twenty other former members, including two ministers who had attended the Klorero, gave Sprigle affidavits describing the ceremonies. The *Birmingham Age-Herald* later assigned a reporter to expose the background of the whole matter, showing the role Esdale and Johnston played; but his editor killed the series he prepared.[6]

*   *   *

The eight-day voyage gave Black time to ponder his course of action. His enemies were saying that the ship wasn't going fast enough, that he jumped off and swam. Later, he claimed that he had word indirectly from Roosevelt to handle the situation as he thought best, and that the idea of speaking over radio came to him in Europe "in order to tell the complete story directly without fear of newspaper slanting." But whether or not he was referring to Corcoran, while Black was sailing FDR told Harold Ickes that Black should say to reporters upon his return: "I have been in Europe and all that I have seen have been headlines. I want to pause just long enough to read what charges have been made and at the end of two days I will have a statement to make." The only question was when the speech should be delivered. En route Black and Thomas M. Woodward, a friend and member of the Maritime Commission, exchanged several telegrams. Black initially wanted to talk from Norfolk upon landing. "Immediate action probably outweighs disadvantages," he thought, and the press could not misquote him. Delay twenty-four hours to consider all angles, advise with friends, and get a larger radio audience, Woodward replid. "Opposition evidently playing something [at] Norfolk," Black responded. "Maybe with stacked crowd. Agree [with] you no rush."

September 29: A throng of seventy-five reporters and photographers greeted Black when the boat docked in Norfolk at dawn. "Just show them your teeth," he told Josephine before she went to chat with friends in the press. Smiling and seemingly in high spirits, he was affable to everyone. Many reporters still called him Senator; he greeted several by name, but did not recognize Sprigle whom he had never met but was smoking his pipe and readily identifiable in his ten-gallon hat. "This is a great reception," Black said several times, "really delightful." The irony in his description was not lost. He would go by car to Washington ("it's a splendid road"), to his office at the Supreme Court. "If you want to come along, I'll be glad to have you," he added in that combination of bluntness and sarcasm that the Washington press was accustomed to from him. "When I have any statement you can accept it as definite and final that I will make it in a way that cannot be misquoted and so the nation can hear it." Did that mean he was going to speak over radio? Black, grinning: "What do you think?"

Only when the questioning touched the Klan did Black betray any emotions. He shut his lips tightly and twitched his lips when he spoke. "That and the smile which twisted his mouth," wrote William M. Mylander of the *Pittsburgh Post-Gazette.* "His eyes divorced themselves from the expression. It was the same smile which has fooled many an unsuspecting witness. . . ." "Mr. Justice," Mylander said, "here are copies of the newspapers carrying the six articles in which we all are interested. Would you care to look them over?"

"Who are you?" Black demanded.

"Mylander of the Paul Block newspapers."

Black hesitated, replied "Suppose you take them back to Mr. Block," and quickly closed the door to his cabin.

Cliff Durr drove him to the Durrs' house in Alexandria. Having leased their own home, Hugo and Josephine accepted the Durrs' invitation to stay there until they found a place of their own. They turned down General and Mrs. DeWitt's invitation to lodge at the Army War College; one could easily imagine the headline: BLACK SEEKS PROTECTION OF THE U.S. ARMY.[7]

....

One of the first things Black had done upon arriving in Norfolk was to cable Crampton Harris in Birmingham: "Meet me in Washington tomorrow." Black knew that Esdale had given the Klan documents to Sprigle—no one else could have. And Harris knew why Hugo wanted him: he was perhaps Esdale's closest friend, and only he could possibly keep the former Grand Dragon from damaging Hugo further. When Harris got there, Black said, "I go on radio tomorrow night. I want you to help me with my speech." Where they would write it presented a problem. Working at the Supreme Court was not seemly. They went to the office of a vacationing colleague of Durr's, at the Reconstruction Finance Corporation. Durr and Claude Hamilton, also an RFC assistant counsel, served in effect as Black's bodyguards, Durr keeping the press at bay, and both reading some of the many drafts that Durr's secretary typed.

At first Black thought of disclosing his childhood membership in the Coming Men of America (a secret society, with a secret handshake and password, which he read in a magazine he could join), as well as his later affiliations in the Knights of Pythias, Masons and similar groups. But he quickly changed his mind: he had to confront his Klan membership while saving as much face as possible and not appearing too suppliant. He read the *Post-Gazette* series and analyzed the controversy. By dinner he knew "pretty well" what he would say and had completed a "very rough draft."

"I do not ask the American people to dismiss these charges lightly," he wrote in the draft. Nor did he ask them "to endorse every act and deed which I have done in the last fifty years." Yes, "I did join the Klan in September, 1923, persuading myself that an organization which had made so powerful an appeal to Southern loyalties might be a force for good and not evil. I soon discovered my mistake": its "out-door meetings were so devised as to work up the frenzied passions of intrinsically decent and law-abiding citizens" that he "resigned without reservation or qualification in July, 1925. . . . I owe no allegiance to the Klan." The draft concluded on an upnote. "I want to see tolerance and fair play not only on the Supreme Court but in all walks of life." In the Senate he tried "to act with fairness and good-will towards all. As God is my witness, so long as I sit upon the Supreme Court I shall administer equal justice towards all."

Corcoran came on his own to see Black in the evening, telling of the pressures on Roosevelt to get Hugo to resign. Hugo was sure FDR would not do so, but Corcoran urged him to explain why he joined the Klan. He read the draft and thought it was "terrible." He showed Black excerpts he and Ben Cohen had drafted for Black's possible use, calling for abject repentance on Hugo's part and a plea for forgiveness, along with an indictment of Klansmen, past and present. Black looked at them, then said, "I know everyone in the South is waiting for the broadcast and what they are saying is let's see if old Hugo will chicken out. Well, old Hugo is not going to chicken out."

Corcoran left. Black and Durr worked late. The next morning Hugo told Harris the draft "doesn't express exactly how I feel." He didn't want it known that Harris was there, which Harris understood and accepted; Durr never saw him, even though he was only a few doors down the hall. Durr told the press in his office that he didn't know where Black was. Joseph Alsop was the only exception among reporters: Black took him into his confidence and showed him a draft. "It still needed some work," Alsop remembered. Black and Harris revised it several times, finishing shortly before Hugo went on the air.[8]

In the middle of the day Josephine Black called to say that photographers were already in the trees outside the Durrs' house, preparing to set up long-distance and telescopic lenses. The radio networks feared sabotage of their lines. Black refused to speak from a network studio; he did not want to face crowds. So Claude Hamilton offered his house in northwest Washington, at the edge of Chevy Chase. The press did not suspect this. Black spoke from there.

He arrived early. One photographer from *Life,* however, was there, and his picture of Black in the alley, with his hat half pulled over his eyes and two packs of cigarettes in his hand, made him look like a well-dressed fugitive. Hugo entered by a rear cellar door and calmly rehearsed the speech. After the women came, in evening dress (leading Virginia Durr to call it "just a good old Southern gathering"), Black threw a letter in the fire. "Wish I could read a little more of my mail and get rid of it," he said. Throughout, said Hamilton, "Hugo was the calmest one of us all. If he showed any nervousness I didn't notice it."

The scene was unprecedented in the history of radio. Black sat in the middle of Hamilton's living room, a pencil sticking through his lapel, his family (except for his secretary and the Hamiltons) off to the side, microphones, wires and his script before him. All three networks and some independent stations, 318 in all, carried the speech. At 9:30, when the broadcast began, almost nothing else was on the air in the United States. The nation gathered to listen to Black. His audience of an estimated forty million was the largest ever except for that which heard King Edward VIII abdicate the throne the year before.

"The Constitution is the supreme law of our country," Black opened. "The Bill of Rights is the heart of the Constitution." Religious freedom was "one of the most sacred of human rights." The "planned and concerted campaign" against him was "calculated to spread racial and religious hatreds." To help avert a catastrophe that might bring the "political religionist" back into a position of governmental influence made it necessary for him to break with precedent and speak, Black said. He pointed to his record in the Senate, claiming it "refutes every implication of racial or religious intolerance." He admitted his early Klan membership—"I did join the Klan. I later resigned. I never re-joined"—and he denied any present or recent connection with it. He did not explain his motives for joining and then leaving: to do so might well have confused rather than clarified the issue; an elaborate apology would have only added to the controversy. Nor did he denounce the Klan by name, its members, past or present, or those who believed in its ideals.

He talked more about matters of conscience, "the un-American power to interfere in the slightest degree with complete religious freedom." Race and religion played no role in his support of political candidates and endorsement of government applicants, he stated. Not only did he "number among my friends many members of the colored race," but "some of my best and most intimate friends are Catholics and Jews"; this remark did not strike some Jews the way he intended. Then he recounted his friendship with Herman Beck.

It was time to finish. "When this statement is ended my discussion of the question is closed. I believe that the character and conduct of every public servant, great and small, should be subject to the constant scrutiny of the people. This must be true if a democracy is to serve its purpose. It is in this spirit that I now bid those who have been listening good night."

He spoke for only eleven minutes, in plain language and more slowly than normally, as if measuring every word, with an occasional sentence or phrase emphasized. The speech was dramatic only in its sobriety and its careful abstinence from drama. It was deliberately anticlimactic. He did not deny any of the major points in Sprigle's articles, especially his speech at the Klorero after accepting the "unsolicited" membership card; or say whether his resignation from the Klan was made in good faith or for political reasons; or explain why he had joined the Klan.[9]

....

Ray Sprigle heard the speech in Birmingham with a small group of former Klan leaders. When Black finished, one of them said with a grin, "That ain't the way we heard it the night he almost kissed our feet in gratitude for making him senator, is it?" The others agreed. Some of them had been prepared to furnish material concerning his role defending Edwin Stephenson in the 1921 Father Coyle murder if he denied his Klan connections. But Black had confessed membership and Sprigle saw no need to write anything more.

The clamor following the speech nearly matched the uproar preceding it. The press still engaged in an orgy of vituperation. It was almost completely united in continuing to denounce Black—except for southern publications, which largely supported him. Calls for his resignation continued. Even those who admired him and favored the New Deal were not completely satisfied. *
"Hugo Black's address to the nation was the work of a brilliant prosecutor suddenly turned to the defense," editorialized the Scripps-Howard newspapers. "It was an eloquent plea for tolerance. It was clever. But like too many of the recent happenings in the region of the Supreme Court, 'too damn clever.' " Better that Black had advanced the "simple, tho not so clever, plea that to err is human but to forgive divine, or had adopted the still more picturesque excuse of Falstaff who, upbraided by the Prince, replied: 'Hal? Thou knowest in the state of innocency Adam fell; and what should poor Jack Falstaff do in days of villainy?' "

Reactions of politicians were likewise mixed. "I think he satisfied the people generally," Burton Wheeler said, expressing the consensus. Black thought so and, years later, pointed to the Gallup poll as vindication. Before the speech, 59 percent of those questioned said he should resign from the Court if he had been a Klan member; afterward 56 percent said he should remain. Roosevelt did not hear the speech. The White House said that he was riding in an open car without a radio as he was inspecting Fort Lewis, near Tacoma, Washington. Soon he read the transcript. "It was a grand job," he told Jim Farley when he returned east. "It did the trick; you just wait and see."

* H. L. Mencken, who initially distrusted Black because of his investigations, now wrote that the speech "made a powerful impression on me. It was unquestionably the most noble public utterance heard in this country since the Gettysburg address," he told Theodore Roosevelt, Jr. "I am having 200,000 copies struck off to send to all the schoolchildren of Baltimore. I was particularly affected by his opening strophes in celebration of the Bill of Rights. How beautifully he proved his faith in the case of Silas Strawn and Hearst!" (Mencken to Theodore Roosevelt, Jr., 10/6/37, Roosevelt papers, LC.)

Black had dug Roosevelt (and himself) out of a political crater. While some Alabama editors called the furor "a tempest in a teapot," Tom Williams of the *Talladega Daily Home* cracked, "a gale under a bedsheet would be more appropriate." And those former Klan leaders most intimately involved with Black in the hooded order knew he was not being candid. Only much later, however, did they mention it to trusted friends. "Jim Esdale said that what Black said was not completely true. He was very peeved," recalled Leigh Clark. "Hugo's speech was a damn lie," Walter Brower, by then embittered, later told Whit Windham. "He was interested in politics and wanted to use the Klan. It was a political necessity. That's all there was to it."[10]

From the beginning Black was confident of the outcome. It was "nothing but a plain political fight" by "the same old crowd," he said—he was in his métier. The press "really did a most magnificent propaganda job," he admitted. It "had no difficulty in making the public believe that they had broken a startling piece of news." The attacks, he claimed, did not surprise or even disturb him, for he realized their motive. They would "continue as long as some people can bring about the slightest interest. As a matter of fact, if it had not been this, it would have been something else."

Black liked to portray himself as a sitting duck for Roosevelt's many enemies, a convenient victim because of his economic views, while the people knew what was going on. He never really grasped, or could admit, the genuine outrage that the Klan caused, and not only among Catholics, Jews, and Negroes. Even Grover Hall wrote, "The hostility to the new Justice was honest hostility in the main"—both for his beliefs and for the Klan. His adoring niece Hazel wrote to ask if Roosevelt would have appointed him if he knew of the Klan. Two weeks after the speech, he replied: "With all of their deliberate falsehood, of every conceivable kind, [the press] have convinced the public of their utter insincerity and unreliability. The country—in spite of their false clamor—knows what the noise is about."

There was nothing new in the articles written in the *Pittsburgh Post-Gazette*, except the venom and the false implications. All of the statements have been thrashed out in Alabama political campaigns. Governor Kilby supplied the "gold card" memorandum from his campaign files. It was widely published in Alabama in 1932, and all the leading papers throughout the nation as well as the magazines have repeatedly published the fact that I was formerly a member of the Klan. Of course, these papers knew it and were aware that everybody else knew it who had kept up with politics in the country.

> . . . I never missed a single minute's sleep, and have never had a single fear as to what would occur. Not having applied for the position, and accepting it with some hesitation, it was wholly immaterial to me as to what might be declared to be the legal status. The newspapers, however, in the zeal to destroy, have given me a national prominence and following which I have not sought and do not really desire. Their conspiracy to ruin me has not worked. . . . My enemies have not caused me to suffer. I have followed my course and my conscience approved it. This armor has protected me and will continue to guard me from their poison shafts.

Black did not answer the question directly. No publication had previously claimed that he was actually a Klan member. And toward those newspapers that attacked him he retained at least a trace of bitterness.[11]

The animus with the *New York Times* ran both ways. While its news coverage of Black was fair enough, the editorial page reflected the sensitivity to the Klan of publisher Arthur Hays Sulzberger. "We might pass a bill retiring all justices under the age of 60," stated one editorial typical of many. "This would fit the case very nicely, as . . . the youngest of the other eight justices, Roberts, is 62." As Black was about to take his seat, a friend told him that Sulzberger had said that he would "get" Black if it were the last thing he ever did, and that he had sworn to print an anti-Black editorial every day he served on the Court. "I'm 51 years old," Black replied, "and I think my health is good. Before I get ready to quit, the paper would be bankrupt." He sent word to Sulzberger that the publisher would lose all his readers if he tried to do so because they would tire of reading about it. The conduit for these messages was New York lawyer Edward S. Greenbaum, Sulzberger's lifelong friend and the Sulzberger family lawyer for more than forty years. He also represented the defendant, Robert S. Allen, in the only lawsuit occasioned by a Supreme Court nomination.

In September the *Nation* published an article by Allen, "Who Exposed Black?" The "real author" of the *Post-Gazette* series, Allen asserted, was Frank Prince, a former Hearst reporter and now operator of a New York City detective agency, who "dug up the material on which the Black-Klan articles were based." Sprigle had written the articles at his desk in open sight; Prince had nothing to do with them. Paul Block's lawyer, Max Steuer, demanded that the *Nation* withdraw the charge. When it continued to defend the article, Block sued for libel.

The whole matter was handled very quietly. Greenbaum delved into the

"Klan business" somewhat with Black, but at much greater length with Cliff Durr, to whom Black had in effect delegated the matter. But Hugo had told Cliff very little about the Klan, and Cliff was innocent of such things. In Birmingham Cooper Green usefully summarized Sprigle's activities as he understood them. And while Crampton Harris said he would do whatever was possible ("of course we are leaning on him heavily," Greenbaum told Durr), he also had his livelihood and friendships to consider. So his usefulness was limited. Much more helpful was Gould Beech. He had left the assistant editorship of the *Montgomery Advertiser* to accept a fellowship at the University of North Carolina. One of his friends there was Michael Clark, the son of *Nation* publisher Freda Kirchwey. Clark asked Beech to help in connection with Block's suit. "Greenbaum wanted to know how Ray Sprigle was provided the material," Beech recalled.

> I went to Birmingham and Black's friends, especially Cooper Green, said to see Congressman Luther Patrick, and he gave me a lead to see Fred Bodecker. So I went to the Bodecker detective agency. He had a trunk of information there. He told me, "Yeah, information was made available to Sprigle. I did work for these other fellows." From that I assumed the detective agency was working for Sprigle. "But it wouldn't be right for me to tell you everything. See my brother." So I saw his brother and his brother said, "I know everything but it'll cost you $1000." I said thank you and went on my way. I made a report for Greenbaum on what I did and knew, and didn't hear anymore from him.

Greenbaum's response to the suit reflected Black's beliefs as relayed through Durr; Black reviewed it and kept a copy. Its gravamen was that "administration-hating interests"—Hearst, Forney Johnston and Block together with Prince, Alabama Republicans and local Klan officials—combined forces, virtually conspired, to reveal Black's Klan membership. Hearst's financial and business relationship with Block was discussed at length: not all the contentions were correct.

By the 1930s Hearst and Block had become "quite intimate," according to their sons, collaborating in varying ways to serve their individual interests.[*] In 1937 Hearst, deeply in debt, was sitting on a tottering throne. His company's survival was on the line and he was forced to sell some of his

---

[*] They also shared an admiration—for Marion Davis. When Block's relationship with her progressed to the point that she began to suggest marriage, he introduced her to Hearst, with whom she lived for the rest of his life (John M. Harrison, *The Blade of Toledo* [Toledo, Ohio, 1985], 209–10).

assets, including profitable newspapers. "Father was trying to save his life's work," said William Randolph Hearst, Jr. "He wasn't interested in a court appointment." A fortnight before Black's nomination, Block bought the *Post-Gazette* from Hearst. The transaction remains in dispute. "Paul Block was a front man for my father," said Hearst, Jr. "He put up the money for Block to begin with and let Block buy the *Post-Gazette* when he was divesting himself of papers." Block's sons, William and Paul, Jr., with firsthand knowledge that Hearst's son could not have, adamantly denied this. Their father, they claimed, used his by then considerable money.

After Greenbaum filed his papers in April 1938, Block's resolve to win his suit against the *Nation* lessened. "When it came time for depositions," recalled Gould Beech, "he didn't want to answer questions about his financial relationship with the Hearst papers." On discovery the defendant could have demanded such information. "That is why Block softened." He balked when Steuer advised him to drop the suit. "Father wanted to keep the door open for the Pulitzer Prize," noted Paul Block, Jr. "It never came to court because, as I understand it, Max Steuer got $25,000 for bringing it," said Greenbaum. "It had served its purpose. It had started the action, and victory was achieved when Sprigle got the Pulitzer. The lawsuit became unimportant thereafter."

When the *Nation* in July 1939 published an apology, the case was over. Winning the Pulitzer raised some journalists' eyebrows. For despite Sprigle's superb sleuthing and dramatic presentation, Black's Klan "grand passport," which figured so prominently in his stories, had been reproduced in the *Montgomery Advertiser* back in 1926. To Alabamians it was all old hat, so much so that a joke went around Birmingham: "Poor old Sprigle! He only got $1000 for the Pulitzer prize, and he paid out $1200 for information that he could have had for free because everybody knew it already."[12]

IV

THE COURT YEARS,
1937–1949

CHAPTER 18

JUNIOR JUSTICE

THE PRESS WAS HOWLING as Hugo Black drove to the Supreme Court early on October 4, 1937. Hundreds of demonstrators wearing black armbands marched in front of the building in the steady rain. He purposely drove into the basement entrance to avoid marchers at the rear, then went to his chambers, in a choice corner facing northeast. There he met his law clerk. The job came about in an unusual fashion. Before Black left for Europe, Harvard Law School professor Felix Frankfurter (likely after conferring with Tom Corcoran) recommended Bernard Monaghan, a Birmingham native who had just received a Harvard law degree and was going to Oxford on a Rhodes Scholarship. He received a cablegram from Frankfurter that Black offered to appoint him as his clerk while sailing to England in September 1937. Monaghan, who was Catholic, remembered that in 1921 Baptist Hospital would not admit his father because of his religion. Then, just after Black returned to the United States, the *London Times* ran a notice that he had just picked a Catholic secretary and was assigned an elderly Negro messenger (who was also Catholic). This "just smelled too much"; Monaghan cabled Frankfurter to reject the offer.

The day after Black gave his speech, with Court opening in two days, he called his old friend Judge David J. Davis. He accepted Davis's suggestion to take his clerk, Jerome A. (Buddy) Cooper, also a recent Harvard graduate. A Supreme Court statement noted, "He is of the Jewish faith." Black met Cooper early and noted that he had known Cooper's father from a Masonic Lodge in Alabama. After a while, he had to go to the bench. He popped out of the chair, barged up to the door and suddenly stopped, and said, "I am very proud and grateful for this moment. I wish one person were alive to be here—my mother." Then he bustled off.

In the robing room he met most of his colleagues for the first time. Black knew two of the justices. Benjamin N. Cardozo had visited him at the Army War College after the appointment and had gone to see him again just the day before. "He was the only one," Black recalled. And he had long admired Louis D. Brandeis. Upon arriving in Washington, Black went to considerable effort to meet him; it took over a year. But starting in 1929, he saw Brandeis regularly and never once missed calling on the justice before his family went to Cape Cod for the summer. Brandeis told a friend when the Klan revelations appeared that from long personal acquaintance he considered Black thoroughly well qualified.[1]

"Oyez! Oyez! Oyez!" the crier chanted to a packed courtroom. "All persons having business before the Honorable, the Supreme Court of the United States, are admonished to draw near and give their attention, for the Court is now sitting. God save the United States and this Honorable Court! The Chief Justice"—the center curtain portal was drawn for Charles Evans Hughes and James McReynolds and Brandeis, the senior justices—"and the Justices of the Supreme Court of the United States." The two portals on either side flushed a covey of black-robed figures. Black, the last one to file in, went to his seat on Hughes's extreme left. He cast a swift glance to his right and, as the other justices pulled back their chairs, sat down. Another justice's wife thought he looked very nervous. Josephine was smiling at him. His face set, as it was throughout except for one brief smile, he looked until he found her in the rows reserved for justices' family and friends. Then he took his hands off the bench and half closed his eyes.

Hughes announced, "Hugo L. Black, of Alabama, a former member of the Senate of the United States," had been confirmed by that body, presented his commission and "taken his oath in the form prescribed by law." After twenty-three minutes, during which the Court accepted, only to dismiss the following Monday, two motions that Black was illegally seated, Hughes declared the court in recess. The justices rose. Black looked unsure what to do. Justice Owen J. Roberts, seated next to him, motioned to leave through the same portal he had entered. He returned to his chambers to lunch with friends and later had tea with Justice Harlan F. Stone and his wife at their home.

Hughes soon called on Black. With his erect carriage and well-trimmed beard and long, flowing gray-white mustache partly hiding his fine features, Hughes looked and acted like God. (Every person in the room stood up when he and his wife entered the dining room at the French Pavilion at the New York World's Fair in 1939.) Black was apprehensive about how Hughes would greet him: he had, after all, voted against Hughes's confirmation as chief justice in 1930. But "when I viewed his Jovian countenance and heard the warmth of his greeting, I was overwhelmed," Hugo recalled. "In no way did he ever reveal anything but friendship." ("Of course, what would one expect?" Hughes said about the spirit of that first meeting. "I was the Chief Justice.") Hughes escorted Black through the Court building and helped him feel at home.[2]

Black appreciated the kindness. Photographers at the time were climbing trees near the Durrs' house to take pictures through upstairs windows, and "death threats were coming in all the time," Virginia Durr recalled, as they had since Black first arrived there. Since he was completely unprotected, Hugo and Josephine stayed at the Army War College for a while. Reporters were continually calling the Court, asking to see him. He refused to talk to them (the one exception being William Hendrix, an early Birmingham acquaintance and now a New York journalist, who wrote an article at his urging and with his substantial assistance). "Time is on my side," Black confidently said. He started answering most of the thousands of letters he received, but his staff—his secretary and his law clerk—did not know how to address him. Should it be Justice Black, Mr. Justice Black, or Mr. Justice? And his secretary was still calling him Senator. They asked him. He thought for a couple of seconds and said, " 'Judge,' just call me 'judge.' " And so to a legion of law clerks and to his secretaries over two generations he became simply Judge. Josephine, who called him Hugo, found a house to lease on Seminary Hill near the Durrs. "The Judge" settled down to his "very heavy but interesting" work.

"The New York Times is now heading the fight on me," Black told labor editor Edward Keating, repeating what Edward Greenbaum had said. Its publisher, Arthur Sulzberger, was "trying to induce litigants to challenge my right to sit in various cases." He "fears Roosevelt, thinks he's headed for Communism! Hitting the President through me." Black wanted to see Roosevelt but thought he should wait until after an opinion he was writing, in which the government was a party, came down. One of the Court's customs allows a new justice to choose his first opinion. *Federal Trade Commission v. Standard Education Society* was argued the third week Black sat and was decided unanimously three weeks later, in mid-November. An encyclopedia publisher had told prospective buyers that their prominence led to their being chosen to receive free sets of encyclopedias if they also ordered a loose-leaf extension service at a reduced price. Actually, the price charged was the same as the regular price for both the books and the service. Black held for the Court that FTC findings of unfair trade practices are conclusive if supported by evidence.

> There is no duty resting upon a citizen to suspect the honesty of those with whom he transacts business. Laws are made to protect the trusting as well as the suspicious. The best element of business has long since decided that honesty should govern competitive enterprises, and that the rule of *caveat emptor* [let the buyer beware] should not be relied upon to reward fraud and deception. . . . The courts do not have a right to ignore the plain mandate of the statute.[3]

The consumer had a friend in court.

Politics could not get out of Black's blood, and despite being *"really busy"* he always had time for it. On November 1 he again sent for Ed Keating. He showed a letter from an Alabama friend predicting that Tom Heflin would defeat Lister Hill in the Democratic senatorial primary in January unless Roosevelt supported Hill and "labor got busy." Heflin was running with the support of corporations and denouncing the wages and hours bill. "The big plantation owners in the Black Belt are against it because they fear it will force them to raise the wages of their negroes," Black said. "As a matter of fact, the negroes should get more, but of course you can't convince the plantation owners of that. Heflin also has all the utilities back of him." "I was Hugo's candidate," Hill later said, and not long after Black saw Roosevelt, "FDR called me to come to Key West so pictures could be taken together. He was there dedicating a naval installation." As Hill rode the presidential train back to Washington, the pictures adorned campaign posters all over Alabama. He won the primary handily.

"I am entirely too busy to know much about the noise that has been raised," Black protested to Birmingham congressman Luther Patrick. But when a Montgomery friend, Marion Rushton, came in, he laughed as he said, "Catholic boys had the Knights of Pythias, Jewish boys had the B'Nai B'Rith and we Protestant boys had the Ku Klux Klan."* Black could not

* Black told David Lilienthal in January 1938: "I rather enjoyed the fight they made. I knew there would be a howl; in fact, I would have been rather suspicious of myself if there had

have chuckled much when Patrick read a poem at a National Democratic
Club dinner:

> A fellow never knows when he takes his hat in hand
> An' starts into politics exactly where he'll land.
> In the State of Alabama away down yan
> Two politicians joined the Ku Klux Klan.
>
> They each wanted office and the members knew it too
> But they let 'em with a kluck-a-doodle-doo,
> The lads of the order knew the habits of man
> So they passed down word through the Ku Klux Klan.
>
> In that day and time it looked pretty good
> An' they sang a little song to the wearin' o' the hood
> An' one is now governor and the other is a judge
> Appointed by the President and he ain' a-goin' to budge.
>
> A lot o' folks think it's a mighty bad sign
> If a man ever marched in bed sheet line
> I've never been a member, so I can't tell
> But these two brethren have done pretty well.
>
> So fill 'er up boys, a sody pop'll do
> An' drink a little toast to the kluck-a-doodle-doo
> We'll pass a little grin and wink sort o'sly—
> It may have been tricky, but the boys got by.

At the annual Gridiron Club dinner in December Black did not laugh
at all. The entire government, press, industry, and labor hierarchy was present
to hear the satires. In one skit hooded figures sang to the tune of "There Is
a Tavern in the Town":

---

been unanimity about my appointment. Guess I would have gone out and joined something
else. . . . The fight . . . had one very good effect. It showed that the Court and the members
are human and that they can be attacked, just as a Senator or anyone else. The thing that
amused me most was the notion some of them had by some kind of way they would get me
to resign. I laughed a lot over that" (Lilienthal, *Journals*, 69).

There is a klavern in the town,
In the town.
And there some Baptist let me down,
Let me down.
And on my breast he pinned a little note:
"Explain when you get off the boat!"
Fare thee well . . .

The curtain fell while the Klan Klorus sang:

K-K-K-Klansman,
Beautiful Klansman,
You're the same old K-K-K-Klux I knew before,
When the m-m-m-moon shines,
Over the White House,
We'll be watching at the K-K-K-Kourthouse door!

Hugo stalked out in a rage, and didn't attend another Gridiron dinner for fifteen years. (After the Christmas holidays, Josephine talked about how the family had come over. "Quite a gathering of the clan," she said to a moment of frozen silence, which she broke with a laugh and a frenzy of conversation.)[4]

Every new justice regardless of background or prior occupation goes through a season of adjustment. Black was no exception. The circumstances surrounding his appointment notwithstanding, his period of acclimation to the Court seems to have been shorter than most. He avidly embarked on his new task, even before the motions as to his eligibility were dismissed. With his sort of wound-up nervousness, he would spring out of the chair. He was on the spot, steamed up with determination and bent on vindicating himself because of the Klan revelation as he studied the records and briefs in each case.

He liked his brethren. George Sutherland, one of the conservative Four Horsemen, he found "an entertaining, charming man. He and those other fellows really believed that the country was following them," Black felt. James McReynolds of Tennessee was another one of them, and he also had a well-deserved reputation as rude, mean and bigoted. No justice had ever gotten along with him. Black was the first southerner to serve with McReynolds and he would be different. He instructed clerk Cooper to time

McReynolds's daily arrival at the Court precisely. One morning by seeming happenstance, as McReynolds got off the elevator, who should be passing but Hugo, smiling widely and saying in the broadest of accents, "Good *mawnin'*, Mr. Justice *MacReynolds.*" The crude old grouch was almost forced to smile: it was just one southern gentleman greeting another. With all the other justices Black quickly developed smooth working relationships, and with Owen Roberts he formed a warm friendship. They sat next to each other on the bench, where Roberts liked to chat. Roberts's flexible convictions were irrelevant; he was outgoing and simply delightful company. Until January they were the two youngest justices. Then Sutherland, whose fluent pen had often spoken for the Old Court, retired and he was replaced by Solicitor General Stanley Reed, solid, hardworking, straightforward and somewhat plodding. Black was no longer the justices' baby brother.

The neophyte's early opinions, largely in relatively simple cases of minor importance that Hughes assigned,* read like those of a novice. They lacked the penetrating self-assurance of his Senate addresses. Their mediocrity drew the criticism of Justice Harlan F. Stone. Black admired Stone and felt a general judicial rapport with him. It was Stone who had written a memorable dissent in the 1936 Agricultural Adjustment Act (AAA) case: "Courts are not the only agency of government that must be assumed to have the capacity to govern." Nevertheless, the former Columbia Law School dean complained about the "poor quality" of Black's early draft opinions. "They're not even acceptable by law school standards," Stone said.[5]

By December, however, Black had become eager to strike a blow for his beliefs. Hughes wrote a *per curiam* (unsigned "by the court") opinion, returning to the lower court a utilities rate case begun seven years earlier just because the methods used in determining costs were obsolete. Here was an old enemy, and Black prepared an unprecedented dissent to such an opinion. He criticized the "reproduction cost" theory of rate-making valuation (which applied the current, higher cost of replacing the total investment). In the "confusion of language—too frequently invented for the purpose of confusing—" it was the consumer who paid for the impotency of the regulatory system.

"I am a good deal troubled . . . ," Stone wrote Hughes. "I see in Justice Black's dissent the handiwork of someone other than the nominal au-

---

* The chief justice, when in the majority, assigns the Court's opinion to himself or another member of the majority. When he is not in the majority, the senior justice in the majority makes the assignment.

thor. . . ." Whom Stone had in mind is unknown, but soon rumors started popping up in Washington that Ben Cohen and Tom Corcoran were writing Black's opinions, that "Ben was law clerk number one and I clerk number two," as Corcoran later joked. Anyone who knew Black even slightly would have guffawed at the suggestion.

In late January 1938 Black dissented alone twice more. One of the cases involved a California tax on a corporation's privilege to do business within the state. For the Court, Stone held that the tax was void under the due process clause of the Fourteenth Amendment. Black believed that the tax was valid, even if the due process clause protected the corporation. But, he argued, the Fourteenth Amendment the Court was applying was not the same one adopted in 1868: "I do not believe the word 'person' in the Fourteenth Amendment includes corporations." The idea had been in his mind for several years. He first came across it while reading Charles and Mary Beard's *Rise of American Civilization,* which Josephine bought for him as a Christmas present in 1932. Three years later, while debating the antilynching bill in the Senate, he asked, "Did any Member . . . hear me read the word 'corporation' as I read the Fourteenth Amendment? He did not. The word 'corporation' does not appear in the Fourteenth Amendment."

Many of the cases Black cited to support his conclusions harked from over a half century earlier. Due process had then been limited to *procedural* safeguards. In 1886, however, the Court held, without discussion, that corporations were "persons" within the meaning of the Fourteenth Amendment. This led to an expansion of due process to include the *substantive* determination of social policy. Exalting the right of property ignored the fact that, as Black wrote, "the history of the amendment proves that the people were told that its purpose was to protect weak and helpless human beings and were not told that it was intended to remove corporations in any fashion from the control of state governments." For "corporations have neither race nor color." The amendment "was intended to protect the life, liberty and property of *human* beings."

Prior constitutional interpretations should not be binding, Black had told Cliff Durr while driving to work a few months earlier. In following their oath to uphold the constitution, justices were obliged to try to determine for themselves what it meant rather than follow blindly what a court said it meant fifty or one hundred years ago. The Court often changed its reading of the Constitution. "A constitutional interpretation that is wrong should not stand," Black wrote.[6]

Black's dissents "really startled" Stone. Occasionally he went to see

Black. Seating himself in a chair by Hugo's desk, Stone took the opinion out to show Hugo where he went wrong and how he should correct his errors. He did this with very little humor and seemed unaware that Hugo felt a certain intellectual rapport with him. As he would leave, Black, courtesy written all over him, would tell Stone what a pleasure it was to see him. Technical matters especially concerned Stone. "Black has a good mind," Stone said, "but it needs training." Someone had to teach him. "Do you know Black well?" Stone wrote Felix Frankfurter.

> If you do I think you might be able to render him great assistance. He needs guidance from someone who is more familiar with the workings of the judicial process than he is. With guidance, and a disposition to follow it until he is a little surer of himself, he might do great things. I am fearful though that he will not avoid the danger of frittering away his opportunity for judicial effectiveness by lack of good technique, and by the desire to express ideas which, however valuable they may be in themselves, are irrelevant or untimely. There are enough present day battles of importance to be won without wasting our effort to remake the Constitution *ab initio*, or using the judicial opinion as a political tract.

"A dissent represents a disagreement," Black told a friend, "and a failure to dissent where there is not agreement would be strange for one who has opinions." Activity was Hugo's nature and crusading was in his bones. He would not let a different post keep him from doing what he perceived to be his calling. In dissent his creative urge found an outlet. He would continue to go his independent way.

Nearly every weeknight Black dined with his clerk, Cooper, at the Methodist Building near the Court (with his secretary usually joining) or, less frequently, at home. The meal was brief, as they had to get back to work—invariably until at least eleven o'clock. "Most people say they've arrived when they reach the Court," Black told Claude Hamilton at dinner in January 1938. "This is my second night since September that I'm not at the books." He read only for cases now, except for a pile of grammar books Josephine brought home one day early in the term. "I think these might help you, dear," she said. That was all he needed and he "devoured" them. He was learning very rapidly. From the first his opinions had been as clear as a mountain stream, but the writing improved as he wrote more. ("The most difficult thing about coming on the Court was learning to write," he later said.) He recited the facts, sharply defined the issue, stated his argument and marched straight to its goal. "The arguments seem obvious—once Black has made them," observed one commentator. Black used italics for emphasis; he relegated citations, sources, and lengthy quotations to the footnotes, leaving the quick staccato of the text intact. "Black is certainly popular with newspaper men," Heywood Broun noted in the middle of the term, "because he recently wrote a dissent in English as plain and simple and clear as a good running story on the first page. And, naturally, reporters take to those who speak their own language. And it is a finer tongue than that invented by Mr. Blackstone."[7]

On April 28, 1938, the Court handed down a decision heralding as great a change as that of the constitutional revolution of the previous year. The case was *U.S. v. Carolene Products*. Through a footnote ("Footnote Four") in this otherwise unimportant case, which upheld the Federal Filled Milk Act, Justice Stone fashioned a charter for the protection of individual rights.* He rejected a constitutional challenge to the act and summarized the modesty of the Court's recent decisions: hereafter federal legislation would generally be upheld if there was a "rational basis" for the legislative judgment. This was a self-effacing test; but Black went to the Court believing that the power of judicial review of legislation should be sharply circumscribed.

Stone's draft, he felt, "approves the submission to proof to a jury or a court under certain circumstances to determine whether the legislature was justified in the policy it adopted. This is contrary to my conception of the extent of judicial power of review. . . . In matters concerning policy I believe the right of final determination is with the Congress." He agreed with the

---

* Footnote Four reads:

There may be narrower scope for operation of the presumption of constitutionality when legislation appears on its face to be within a specific prohibition of the Constitution, such as those of the first ten amendments, which are deemed equally specific when held to be embraced within the Fourteenth.

It is unnecessary to consider now whether legislation which restricts those political processes which can ordinarily be expected to bring about repeal of undesirable legislation, is to be subjected to more exacting judicial scrutiny under the general prohibitions of the Fourteenth Amendment than are most other types of legislation.

Nor need we enquire whether similar considerations enter into the review of statutes directed at particular religious, or national, or racial minorities; whether prejudice against discrete and insular minorities may be a special condition, which tends seriously to curtail the operation of those political processes ordinarily to be relied upon to protect minorities, and which may call for a correspondingly more searching judicial inquiry.

opinion except for the part in which the footnote appeared. Stone's clerk, Louis Lusky, immediately spoke to Black's clerk, Cooper, to ask Black to reconsider. "Stone isn't advocating substantive due process. He's not pushing anything Black isn't for." This was on a Friday. Cooper mentioned it to Black, but Black had to attend a funeral over the weekend and was not doing any work. He said he'd get to it the next week. But the opinion came down Monday as planned.

The *Carolene Products* rationality test indicated that the Court would hold unconstitutional only those laws that no one would reasonably have enacted. Combined with *Erie Railroad Company v. Tompkins*, another case that came down that day, this meant that the Court's new role would be significant only in regulating federal-state relationships, interpreting federal statutes and developing areas of law, such as patent and admiralty, that the Constitution left to the states. The *Carolene* footnote, however, opened up a new area and caught Black in a dilemma: he preferred human rights over property rights; he was philosophically and emotionally committed to a broad reading of the Bill of Rights—all without the judiciary's playing a central role in guaranteeing them. The Court's dismantling of major portions of the New Deal had horrified him. He believed the capacity of courts should be limited. "Would you ever hold any statute unconstitutional on grounds of substantive due process?" Stone asked him. "If not, then of course you could not agree with the third [section] in the opinion in the *Carolene* case." As Black later said, substantive due process was "why I came on the Court. I was against using due process to force the views of judges on the country."[8] To remain true to his convictions Black would have to solve this predicament.

For several months Stone had been taking morning walks with reporter Marquis Childs of the *Saint Louis Post-Dispatch*. Stone—a man who, as William O. Douglas put it, was "a little gossipy, who relished saying something a little snide about someone . . . a fine, fine man but he just talked too much"—talked about how each justice must keep up with the Court's heavy workload and know how to write opinions lest delay result. That was Black's problem. Stone also feared that new appointees would not be lawyer-like and would express their prejudices and predilections as the Old Court had. Childs set out these views without attributing them to Stone in a *Post-Dispatch* article. "This must have a national reading too," a pleased Stone said. When an expanded version appeared in *Harper's* in May 1938, it set off a storm of protest. Black's "lack of legal knowledge and experience" and "deficiencies in background and training" led him "into blunders which have shocked his colleagues," Childs wrote. He was "unable to carry his share" of the work. "Several opinions he has written have been rephrased by other members of the Court and . . . subsequently released with something less than satisfaction."

"I did a terrible thing to Black," Childs later said. "It was the worst thing I ever did in my career. I've been sorry about it ever since. Stone had no malicious intent at all" and naturally he denied any hand in the article. He was letting off some steam while also trying to signal Roosevelt not to appoint any more similar justices. Stone felt genuinely friendly toward Black and looked at the new justice as sharing similar judicial views. He feared Black would waste his energies attempting to accomplish the impossible instead of concentrating on efforts that might be surely and swiftly gained. The object of Stone's comments took them calmly. "I can assure you that I am not disturbed in the slightest . . . ," Black told Irving Brant, a friend both of Stone and of many New Dealers. He well knew just what Stone was up to. But in Childs's article and the press response he saw "a newspaper plot" against him.

Stone went to see Black. "He swore to me that what Childs wrote wasn't what he told him," Black recalled. "He told me that Childs distorted it." Years later, Childs admitted to Black that he printed just what Stone told him. "I think," Douglas said, "that Black got the impression that Stone . . . was out to whittle him down in public, to make fun of him, and so I think that froze Black somewhat. Not in terms of amenities, because he was always very gracious, but I don't think that he had the respect for Stone that he had at the time when he first came on. And I think that his real feelings about Stone were of a man that he didn't greatly admire."

Very different was Chief Justice Hughes's attitude. He already held Black in increasing regard. Even though he said he did not agree with all the criticism of Hugo for his dissents, Hughes encouraged him to dissent when he felt he should. "The Court will be a great institution only so long as bold men have the courage to state their separate views," Hughes said. Dissents are "our lifeblood."[9]

Black's nine sole dissents during the term troubled Justice Brandeis. When Brandeis was asked in the spring how the new justice was getting along, he replied, very well, indeed, that he was carrying his share of the work. The inquirer said he meant the next to newest member. Brandeis shook his head and waved the question aside. "Oh, that's different." His concern was not a matter of ideology, for Brandeis likely agreed with the substance of Black's opinions. After the rate-making valuation case, in which Black stated the position Brandeis had been arguing for many years, he came to extend his compliments and to encourage Black to keep to it. But institutional considerations weighed heavily with Brandeis: "The great difficulty of all group action . . . ," he once said, "is when and what concession to make. Can't always dissent." Just before the term ended in May 1938, he expressed his apprehension to Felix Frankfurter, who was in Washington.

Frankfurter now met Black for the first time. He had earlier congratulated Black on his appointment, characteristically enclosing articles he had written on Justice Oliver Wendell Holmes and on Brandeis, and later he sent a copy of his latest book. They now had tea and dined together with their wives. Frankfurter spoke "in passing," he wrote Brandeis, "about the importance of choosing one's ground for dissenting. . . . Black has such admiration and veneration for you that I am sure you could do great things with him if you could spare the energy to treat him on the basis of cordiality and confidence, instead of allowing barriers to grow up between you and him through formality and the insulation of non-intercourse."

Hugo and Josephine spent much of the summer away. While they were at Barney Whatley's ranch in Colorado during July, and then in Birmingham, the legal world continued buzzing about Hugo. Commentators agreed that Black was something new on the Supreme Court, but nobody was quite sure what. His independence was disquieting. Between sets of tennis in Birmingham, columnist John Temple Graves II asked what he deemed his mission to be. Human advancement within the limits of constitutional interpretation, Hugo said. He was trying to expand those boundaries, to force the Court and the legal profession to reexamine accepted constitutional postulates. "He regards sacred cows as ordinary heifers," wrote an admiring Walton Hamilton in the *New Republic*. A functional, practical realism, not the barren slogans and labels of an arid formalism, should rule. Given his evangelistic passion for democracy, Black was impatient; even his nominal concurrences were in effect dissents. Law served the public interest; people should not be sacrificed to its ceremonies. Black was bringing "a breath of fresh air into a rather musty courtroom."[10] Would the windows remain open?

CHAPTER 19

FINDING
HIS NICHE

Roosevelt's appointments ventilated the Court. The nomination of Felix Frankfurter in January 1939 to succeed the late Benjamin Cardozo delighted Black. They were already on a first-name basis. Frankfurter "has entered into the work with his usual energy and understanding," Black soon told Harold Laski, "and I am looking forward to the pleasure of many years of service with him." Their relationship would span much of the range of human emotions and have long-lasting intellectual repercussions. In March, to replace the retired Brandeis, Roosevelt named William O. Douglas, the forty-one-year-old chairman of the Securities and Exchange Commission. His brilliance fully matched Black's and Frankfurter's, and he quickly became Hugo's most dependable ally and closest friend on the Court. The next year Frank Murphy, FDR's attorney general, at once mystical and practical, took Pierce Butler's seat.

At conference Black battled Hughes and Frankfurter to hear economic and workmen's compensation cases. He was "still fighting mad" upon returning to his chambers and talked about these clashes, Buddy Cooper recalled. "When describing things, he would gesticulate and, especially, grimace and also parody someone's voice. And he'd make these faces when talking about Frankfurter. He said, 'Felix'—he always called him Felix— 'Felix said, "Hugo, the trains have to run," and I said, "Yes, Felix, but they don't have to run over people's legs." ' " "The changing complexion of the Court meant that Black was writing more majority opinions, in a wider variety of cases; although he continued dissenting alone on occasion, his concurrences lessened. Legislatures have exceedingly wide scope to legislate, he believed. They "determine the necessity for regulatory laws, considering

both the evil and the benefits that may result. Unless prohibited by constitutional limitations, their decisions as to policy are final," he wrote in a
1938 case.

Hughes dominated this Court in transition. Indeed, with his marvelous
powers of concentration (he would inhale a page), his incisive intellect, his
imposing presence and an impish wit that erupted unexpectedly (when an
elderly lady recognized him at a New York City hotel and said "Oh, I thought
you were dead!" Hughes smiled, bowed slightly and replied, "Sorry to disappoint you, madam!"; and at first he referred to "Professor Frankfurter"),
Hughes could dominate any gathering. Firmness, mastery of the issues, and
intellectual dexterity made him "the perfect presiding officer," Black said
in 1968. "We haven't had another like him since." When he stated the
case, "you could be sure it was correctly stated." He might lay out four or
five possible lines of decision, then assert, "I think we should follow the first
line. It will keep us away from the troublesome problems opened up by the
others."

He made the strongest impression on the youngest justices. One day at
Christmas time in 1938, Hughes left the Court early to put gifts under the
Blacks' tree. Hugo, working at the Court, knew nothing about it. Hughes
was down on his hands and knees under the tree when Josephine came home.
All she could see at first was a man's rear end, so she asked, "Who's there?"
"It's just me," Hughes said. He got up and his face fell: he had been caught.
As he left, Josephine said, "You know, Mr. Chief Justice, I think you're just
great." That night Hughes sent her an autographed picture.[1]

Chambers v. Florida reached the Court in fall 1939. Within a day after an
elderly white man was robbed and murdered in Pompano, Florida, near Fort
Lauderdale, twenty-five to forty Negroes were arrested without warrants and
confined to the county jail. Officials sharply questioned and cross-questioned
them while threatening, abusing and not allowing them to see counsel or
confer with any other person. This continued for six days, during which
suspects were released until only four remained—"ignorant young colored
tenant farmers." Just after daybreak the next morning, after fifteen straight
hours of relentless interrogation, the suspects confessed. Their convictions
and sentences of death were affirmed. Although Black voted not to hear the
case, fearing it would be wrongly decided, the Supreme Court accepted it
as a pauper's petition. The confessions were reversed with little opposition.

"I think Chief Justice Hughes assigned *Chambers* to me because I was a

Southerner," Black said. "And there were these Negroes here who were so mistreated. He forced me to write the case. At first I didn't want to. He said, 'Don't worry, I'll get the Court for you.' So I saved all my views and wrote them since I knew I had the whole Court with me." The Fourteenth Amendment was at the heart of the case. But Black did not want to be drawn into a necessarily controversial discussion of its sweep, as he noted in a discarded early draft. He focused instead on its due process clause, which "has led few to doubt" it was intended to guarantee procedural standards to protect persons suspected of or charged with crime. The opinion reflected his long-standing hatred of coerced confessions. It brimmed with emotionally charged language: "The circumstances were calculated to break the strongest nerves and the stoutest resistance" and "to fill petitioners with terror and frightful misgivings"; "the haunting fear of mob violence was around them in an atmosphere charged with excitement and public indignation . . . To permit human lives to be forfeited upon confessions thus obtained would make of the constitutional requirement of due process of law a meaningless symbol." Then Black worked to a crescendo of a conclusion:

> Today, as in ages past, we are not without tragic proof that the exalted power of some governments to punish manufactured crime dictatorially is the handmaid of tyranny. Under our constitutional system, courts stand against any winds that blow as havens of refuge for those who might otherwise suffer because they are helpless, weak, outnumbered, or because they are nonconforming victims of prejudice and public excitement. Due process of law, preserved for all by our Constitution, commands that no such practice as that disclosed by this record shall send any accused to his death. No higher duty, no more solemn responsibility, rests upon this Court than that of translating into living law and maintaining this constitutional shield deliberately planned and inscribed for the benefit of every human being subject to our Constitution—of whatever race, creed or persuasion.

"There's been no case which I put more work in," Black said. "He knew what it meant to him," Cooper recalled, and he had "a real feeling of satisfaction writing it. But it was also a real struggle for him." He had to reverse a jury verdict. And that was hard indeed. He had made his living persuading southern juries; the former trial lawyer would be reversing himself. But slowly Black came to realize that judicial review in this area was needed if the Founders' intentions were to have effect.

Black circulated his opinion within two weeks after the case was heard on January 4, 1940. McReynolds and Reed decided not to dissent, making the Court unanimous. The case was scheduled to come down on February

5, but Hughes decided to hold it over until the next session, February 12. On Lincoln's Birthday the former senator from Alabama delivered the opinion—"one of the enduring utterances in the history of the Supreme Court -and in the annals of human freedom," as Frankfurter wrote Josephine.

Any doubts about Black's commitment to the Constitution and civil liberties were quickly stilled. Commentators heaped praise on him; to his supporters it was vindication. *Catholic World* ran a laudatory article. "Far and away the most direct, sweeping and brilliantly written application of the Fourteenth Amendment to human rights that has come from our highest Court," opined the *New York Times*. It "will ring with power as long as liberty and justice are cherished in our country," wrote Charles Beard. A reporter asked Roosevelt if he would care to supplement the praise. "If I were," the president replied, "I would put in a general dig that some of the press should not give a little praise but also a modicum of apology for things they have said in the last two years. Is that fair enough?"[2]*

First Amendment cases were initially few. Jehovah's Witnesses were responsible for most of them. The Witnesses' sense of divine mission led them to aggressive and intrusive proselytizing and to resisting laws that intruded upon their beliefs. (They brought so many cases that Justice Stone suggested that these "pests" deserved an endowment for their contributions to civil liberties.) In 1939 the Court found unconstitutional the regulations of several localities restricting the distribution of leaflets on public streets. Black rewrote much of Roberts's draft opinion for the Court but did not circulate his changes. It is the best indication of his First Amendment views at this time. Freedom of speech and press was "made secure against all invasion by express prohibitory language of our supreme law—the Constitution," Black wrote. It is "an indispensable prerequisite" to the Constitution's "existence and perpetuity." Courts must "scrutinize legislation with zealous eyes whenever it is challenged as an infringement of the rights constitutionally declared to be inviolable." The burden of maintaining the streets

> is inspired by the constitutional solicitude for free interchange of ideas. The Constitution has declared this right of free men to be so sacred that

* *Chambers* made Black recall the grand jury report he prepared on third-degree confessions at Bessemer in 1915. He reread the newspaper reports and mentioned their specific dates to journalist John Temple Graves (HLB to Graves, 2/14/40). In his column Graves wrote that Black "was turning no corners in his philosophy. . . . He had said the same things . . . a whole quarter of a century before" (BAH, 3/2/40).

it must not be abridged whatever the monetary cost of its preservation and protection. And the spirit of the bill of rights is such, that its authors and supporters would doubtless say, that the cost of cleaning streets is too small to attempt to balance against the priceless privilege of free expression of ideas. Besides, the fact that cities may not prohibit dissemination of ideas by prohibiting distribution of literature, does not deprive the city of all power to prohibit street littering.

The First Flag Salute case offered an opportunity to apply these views. *Minersville School Board v. Gobitis* presented the question whether a pupil could be expelled from school for refusing to salute the flag, as required by a school board regulation. It was argued April 25, 1940, two weeks after the Nazi army had quickly subdued Denmark and Norway; in May, Holland and Belgium were invaded. "I come up to this case like a skittish horse to a brass band," Hughes said in introducing the case at conference. ". . . I simply cannot believe that the state has not the power to inculcate this social objective." Frankfurter spoke passionately about patriotism and the role of public schools in instilling love of country; Black long recalled his emotion. Stone and Black passed when the justices voted; but the others sided with Hughes who, feeling, as he told Douglas, that "an immigrant could really speak of the flag as a patriotic symbol," assigned the opinion to Frankfurter. The opinion held that it was constitutional to expel children from public schools if they refused to salute the flag. "Personal freedom is best maintained . . . when it is ingrained in a person's habits and not enforced against popular policy by the coercion of adjudicated law." The battle of France began two days later, on June 5, 1940, and soon the ruling was being called "Felix's Fall-of-France Opinion."

Stone circulated a powerful dissent on the day before the conference at which Frankfurter's opinion was approved. Black did not know about Stone's plans. A majority of the Court, he later said, might have bolted from Frankfurter's opinion after reading Stone's dissent—the rush of work at the term's close prevented the justices' looking at the dissent until after the opinion came down—but Black, Douglas and Murphy found Frankfurter's argument so moving they had assured him they would support him and were loath to break their word. Immediately, "we knew we were wrong," Black told an obituary writer in 1967, "but we didn't have time to change our opinions. We met around the swimming pool at Murphy's hotel and decided to do so as soon as we could." At once they notified Stone that they would stand with him at the first opportunity.

Over a half century later, Black's excuse still sounds lame. He never needed anyone to join him to take a stand he believed in. From the beginning he had reservations about Frankfurter's opinion and persuaded him to make minor changes. Black would have decided the case on due process grounds: compelling the children to salute the flag was a repugnant act that denied the free exercise of religion protected against state action by the due process clause of the Fourteenth Amendment. Unmentioned in all his (and Douglas's) rationalizations are the forcefulness of Hughes's statement at conference and that no justice wished to change his position to vote against Hughes.[3]

More so than any other chief justice since "the great chief justice" John Marshall in the early 1800s, Hughes ran the Supreme Court. The same image recurred: "The Chief Justice sits there like a god," Justice Murphy wrote during one conference. "Magnificent Olympian roaring out his wisdom." Hughes stated his positions with boldness and assurance. In conference each justice, speaking without interruption in order of seniority, stated why he agreed or disagreed with Hughes's views. The Chief reviewed the discussion, pointing out his concurrence or dissent. Then, with his positions freshest in their minds, the justices voted. Hughes treated them all as equals, except that he was first among them, as they all knew.

Friendships developed as factions disappeared. For several years Hugo and his family spent many weekends at Roberts's Pennsylvania farm, especially in the spring, and they also visited each summer. Each time they thoroughly enjoyed themselves; when they were with the Robertses, politics dropped several ranks in importance. After Roosevelt won a third term in 1940, Roberts wrote to Hugo of "the returns of the late lamented election. I am still an economic royalist or in F.D.'s latest phrase economic imperialist!" To Hugo that was (largely) insignificant. More important, as Roberts noted while inviting the Blacks to stay a week two summers later, was the "good dishes of talk" he assured Hugo they would have.

This affability paled beside Hugo's harmony with Bill Douglas. They shared the same patron, many of the same friends and enemies, and an extraordinary ideological affinity. Before Douglas joined the Court, they knew each other only slightly. As a member and then chairman of the SEC, Douglas was a calculating crusader who never stopped fighting Wall Street for running the stock exchange like a private club. Black was always senior in their relationship. Routinely Douglas went to him; rarely did Black go to Douglas. Douglas held "in awe anyone who had been elected to office," noted his longtime friend journalist Eliot Janeway. "He said that Hughes had made it into the club on his own, that no one appointed him. And because Hugo was also a member of the club, Douglas felt comfortable playing a subordinate role to him."

Like Douglas, Frank Murphy came to the Court believing that Frankfurter would be his intellectual and spiritual knight. But Frankfurter's professorial habits and his disdain for Murphy's intelligence led Murphy to shift allegiance to Black. "I must say," Murphy told Roosevelt in May 1941, "that Black in the event he lives a decade or two will be numbered among a small company of great Supreme Court justices. Black has a primitive, powerful intellect, great capacity for work and the heart of a lion." He would trust Black as he would few others to defend "liberty of conscience." This comment came shortly after Black's dissent in a picketing case in which the Court held that states could ban peaceful picketing "enmeshed" with admittedly illegal conduct. "Banned from public discussion" were "matters of public concern," Black noted.

> I view the guaranties of the First Amendment as the foundation upon which our governmental scheme rests and without which it could not continue to endure as conceived and planned. Freedom to speak and write about public questions is as important to the life of our government as is the heart to the human body. In fact, this privilege is the heart of our government. If that heart be weakened, the result is debilitation; if it be stilled, the result is death.[4]

Four terms had given Black a ready grasp of the Court's processes. He now dealt easily with intricate matters. His initial doubts about the legitimacy of judicial review had almost completely evaporated. Even in his first year, he spoke "a good deal about the crucial importance of the Court. This is where the 'pattern' is going to be cut," David Lilienthal recorded in his diary after talking with Black early in 1938. He "drew an analogy with the Platonic conception of government; those things which were right and wrong depended upon whether that coincided with the philosophy of Plato." "You and I," Hugo wrote Douglas, "know that the Court has the last word on questions of law which are determinative of questions of public policy upon which the course of our Republic depends." Outmoded doctrines, bulwarks of business civilization, were being overruled and discarded. So fast was the rate of change that before Harvard law professor Thomas Reed Powell made any statement to his class on Monday mornings when the Court sat, "I always take out my watch to see what time it is in order to know whether I am safe in making the remark," he said.

In June 1941 Hughes, now seventy-nine years old, stunned his brethren by announcing that he was resigning for health reasons. "During my four years' service on the Court," Black wrote him, "you and I have differed on many questions. But these four years have given me far more than an impersonal and detached admiration for your extraordinary intellectual gifts and your loyal devotion to the public service. And I would be untrue to my own impulses if I should fail to tell you that as a result of our association I entertain a genuine personal affection." Hugo never lost it. He respected and admired Hughes as he did few others: "He was a wonderful lawyer, a patriotic citizen and a genuinely fine man to work with," Black wrote in 1962. "I now rank him close to the top of the eminent men who have served as Chief Justices." Hughes lived until 1948 and although Hugo saw him little, "when he died I felt that I lost one of my best friends ever."[5]*

To fill Hughes's seat Roosevelt appointed Justice Stone, and to take Stone's he named Attorney General Robert H. Jackson. Since McReynolds had also retired, the president nominated Hugo's former Senate colleague James F. Byrnes, of South Carolina. Only Stone and Roberts remained from the Old Court. The New Deal Court had been formed.

FELIX

They were very different men with equally different tastes in other men and women. What kept them together was their love of country, their devotion to its institutions, the quality of their minds and their lust for learning, and their ultimate goals. Their means to achieving these ends clashed dramatically but never broke their tie. They blended as they battled, combining rare charm and rare intellect, their arguments reaching greater pitch because of their similarities and greater depth due to their contrasts. The Supreme Court without Felix Frankfurter would have been a very different place— as different as it would have been without Hugo Black. If eventually in many, and among the most important, ways the Court was Black's lengthened shadow, his conflicts with Frankfurter played a significant part. Frankfurter did not stop trying to teach just because he left the classroom. His ceaseless importuning and questioning maddened all within hearing distance, but

* "The day [Hughes] retired, when walking from the Court House to his home, as was his custom, with a newspaperman who was a friend of mine, he discussed in that conversation, confidentially, some of the members of the Court and he said that in his judgment Justice Black will go down in history as one of the greatest Justices of the Supreme Court" (James Farley to VH, 7/18/69, VH papers).

they helped lead Black (without admitting it) to clarify his premises, to hone his rationales and to sharpen his analysis. The conflict was pivotal to the Court's final product, central to the body's functioning. But it never really threatened their friendship, for too great was their mutual respect and regard. Both the friendship and the conflict were present from the beginning.

During their first term together, Frankfurter told Black he was a Benthamite, a follower of the Enlightenment English law reformer Jeremy Bentham. Black did not know much about Bentham. So he ordered two of his many works, *Fragment on Government* and *Introduction to the Principles of Morals and Legislation,* and marked them up extensively. To Bentham legislatures devised all law; he deemed judges' attempts to usurp that power "judicial legislation." Statutes were the grist of the court's business. Black looked at them from the perspective of the legislators who enacted them. Their words have a fixed and definite meaning, and courts must apply it to the facts of the case, he thought. Significance cannot be read into silence.

Discussing such matters in the context of a case provided the kind of "intellectual ping-pong" Frankfurter thrived upon. He was a hyperkinetic, effervescent busybody, a man of passion who, a colleague said, had "more fizz than Coca-Cola."* In Black he had an adversary who, upon provocation, gave as well as he took. Frankfurter inscribed *Law and Politics,* a newly published collection of his occasional writings: "For Hugo Black, whose fault it won't be if my mental veins harden." Black made sure of that. Their friendship was warm in 1939, recalled Archibald MacLeish, then Librarian of Congress who occasionally drove Black to the Court. Frankfurter was talking about Black to old friends. Increasingly, he told Harold Laski, he felt "the greatest possible respect for [Black's] character. . . . Our friendship is being steadily forged through free and untrammeled exchange of minor differences and differences in experience in reaching common ends." And when Hugo was sick in early 1941, Felix wrote: "But there is something much more important than [this] or all other opinions, ad that is that you should get wholly fit and therefore let nothing whatever interfere with the

---

* English legal scholar Arthur Goodhart later told the story, in Frankfurter's presence, of how a group, including Felix, went to the races and sent the economist among them to lay 20 pounds on a horse in a pooled bet on a 10-to-1 horse. The horse won; the economist went back and collected 200 pounds. They promptly told the economist that he had made a mistake—that their original bet money should have been returned, for a total of 220 pounds. The economist firmly refused to go back to argue with the man, so they finally sent Felix. He went over, and after twenty minutes of intensive argument the bet-taker said: "The hell with it. It's not worth 20 pounds to have to argue with you any more" (ESB to girls 9/7/60, in ESB, *Rebel*).

recuperative powers of nature. I feel very strongly about it but I shall say no more because both Josephine and you know my deep feeling on the subject. Affectionately yours."[6]

The matter of excess profits came to the Court in 1942. At issue in *United States v. Bethlehem Steel* was the amount a shipbuilder claimed under World War One contracts. Bethlehem had earned 22 percent (plus more from selling itself the necessary steel), and the government moved to recover the portion that was beyond "just and reasonable." "As much as I abhor the [contract] system," Black said in conference, ruling in Bethlehem's favor "is the best way to stop it.",These profits, "seen in their commercial environment, cannot be considered exceptional," he wrote for the Court. They "may justly arouse moral indignation. But indignation based on the notions of morality of this or any other court cannot be judicially transmuted into a principle of law of greater force than the will of Congress." He told Jackson, who as a former attorney general did not participate in the case, that although the contract was "outrageous," he would vote to uphold the contract, hoping "to knock out the contract system and have the government build its own ships." The opinion was a letter to Congress to take action, and the Renegotiation Act was quickly passed. The Court was stepping into the policy-making domain, Frankfurter contended in a lone dissent. If he meant urging Congress to draft or modify a statute, he was later guilty of the same offense he accused Black of committing.[7]

Bridges v. California opened eyes in other ways. Originally argued during the 1940 term, it pitted freedom of the press against a defendant's right to a fair trial in a classic constitutional clash. A California judge had ruled in a bitter dispute between warring labor factions against the union of which Harry Bridges was an officer. While a new trial was pending, Bridges sent Secretary of Labor Frances Perkins a telegram calling the decision "outrageous" and threatening to tie up the port of Los Angeles and perhaps the entire West Coast if it were enforced. At the same time the *Los Angeles Times*, in an editorial entitled "Probation of Guerrillas?" warned the judge he would be making a "serious mistake" if he granted a pending application for the probation of two of the defendants, who had been convicted of assault. "This community needs the example of their assignment to the jute mill." The judge held Bridges and the Times-Mirror Company in contempt.

As usual Hughes set the tone of discussion at conference. "The facts here transcended the limits of reasonable discussion and I think [the lower court] should be affirmed," he stated. Black voted to reverse while Frankfurter leaned toward Hughes. The Court followed Hughes's lead, with McReynolds, Stone, Roberts, Frankfurter and Murphy joining the Chief, and Black, Reed and Douglas wanting to reverse. Hughes assigned the opinion to Frankfurter. He based his comprehensive opinion on the state's power under the due process clause to punish publication as contempt of court, a power "deeply rooted in history"—Anglo-American history. "The civil liberties here invoked depend upon an untrammeled judiciary whose passions are not even unconsciously aroused." ("Who can prevent it?" Black asked.)

Black worked from entirely different assumptions. "First in the catalogue of human liberties essential to the life and growth of a government of, for and by its people," began his draft dissent,

> are those liberties written into the First Amendment to our Constitution. They are the pillars upon which popular government rests and without which a government of free men cannot long survive. History persuades me that the moving forces which brought about the creation of the safeguards contained in the other sections of our Bill of Rights sprang from a resolute determination to place the liberties defined in the First Amendment in an area wholly safe and secure against any invasion—even by government.

The Court's "basic fallacy" was the belief that First Amendment liberties "can be restricted in whole or in part by reference to English judicial practices current, recent or remote. . . . Perhaps no single purpose emerges more clearly from the history of our Constitution and Bill of Rights than that of assuring Americans a freedom of religion, conscience, expression and press, which it was generally known had been denied to people of Great Britain." "It may be true that there are no such things as absolute liberties," Black wrote in his fourth draft, which he circulated as his dissenting opinion. *
He was seemingly basing his opinion on "absolutes" and, in doing so, downplayed the importance of English precedent. The former was the object of Frankfurter's deepest scorn his entire professional life, as the latter was the

---

* "Narrow abridgments have a way of broadening themselves," Black also noted, starting in his second draft, "and in this field as elsewhere the lines marking these narrow limitations are not only somewhat unclearly marked but are susceptible of being pushed out beyond their original confines."

object of equally intense veneration. "Freedom of public expression," Frankfurter now wrote, ". . . is not an absolute and is not predetermined." Black's "doctrinaire overstatement of its scope" gave it "an illusory absolute appearance."

By the time the opinions were completed in June 1941, McReynolds had retired and Murphy had changed his mind. This left only three votes to affirm the convictions and four to reverse them. The case was put down for reargument the next term. During the summer, Black picked up a scratch pad and listed his differences with Frankfurter's opinion in question and answer form. He disagreed with each point in Frankfurter's reasoning. The "construction and enforcement of Amendment 1," not the due process "concept of ordered liberty," would be his yardstick. Courts and the First Amendment must not be placed on a "parity": "Amendment ranks higher— [Frankfurter] says opposite." Black would not "construe an exception to right to free press to exist as to public discussion of matters involved in cases pending before judges." Nor could contempt citations be justified simply because courts had historically done so.

When the Court reconvened in October 1941, the two new justices divided on *Bridges*, Byrnes choosing affirmance and Jackson casting a secure fifth vote for reversal. Black had gained a majority. He revised and moderated his opinion, necessarily working within the Court's prevailing First Amendment standard, the "clear and present danger" test first enunciated by Justice Holmes in 1919. "The question in every case," Holmes had written in *Schenck v. U.S.*, "is whether the words used are used in such circumstances and are of such a nature as to create a clear and present danger that they will bring about the substantive evils that Congress has a right to prevent. It is a question of proximity and degree." Given this vagueness, the pummeling the test received over the years was not surprising. Nevertheless the test remained sturdy enough for Black to expand its orbit:

> What finally emerges from the "clear and present danger" cases is a working principle that the substantive evil must be extremely serious and the degree of imminence extremely high before utterances can be punished. These cases do not purport to mark the furthermost constitutional boundaries of protected expression, nor do we here. They do no more than recognize a minimum compulsion of the Bill of Rights. For the First Amendment does not speak equivocally. It prohibits any law "abridging the freedom of speech, or of the press." It must be taken as a command of the broadest scope that explicit language, read in the context of a liberty-loving society, will allow.

"It is a prized American privilege to speak one's mind, although not always with perfect good taste, on all public institutions," Black noted. And no construction of the "clear and present danger" test suffices to justify restricting his right to free expression.

The effect of this "sudden break" with the past, Frankfurter charged in dissent, was to permit "trial by newspapers," and that was to misconceive the idea of freedom of speech. But his differences cut deeper: "Free speech is not so absolute or irrational a conception as to imply paralysis of the means for effective protection of all the freedoms secured by the Bill of Rights." Issues were joined.[8]

The styles of Black's and Frankfurter's opinions in *Bridges* contrasted as much as their views, and in their blending of history, facts and analysis were the forerunners of many disagreements to come. Frankfurter's lengthy opinions often seemed to be learned essays masquerading as opinions, the impressive scholarship not directly related to the issue; the verbiage sometimes made it difficult to discern the holding. Black's more varied background led him to believe that other people besides lawyers might want to read Supreme Court opinions. He wrote so that "my uncle down on the farm plowing the fields can read them" (except that he had no such relative when he said this). As he finished simplifying an opinion, Black would say, "Now they'll be able to understand that." "They" were the people, the general public. He wrote American—plain, direct and forceful; one felt his personality as a presence, not as an obstacle performing intellectual acrobatics. Black decided cases in language all readers, lawyer and nonlawyer alike, could understand. His words were unadorned for the greatest possible impact. He tried to show that law as an institution exists for the benefit of human beings.

He chose to interpret the *American* constitution. For the first time he read extensively about the drafting of the First Amendment. Black saw something distinctly American in it and, in forthrightly basing his *Bridges* opinion on what he learned, freed the First Amendment from English law. He used English history "to determine the full breadth" of the First Amendment's scope "by a consideration of the evils at which they were aimed," as he wrote in a draft; but he would not be bound by it. English judges, he noted, had inflicted penalties such as boring and clipping men's tongues and cutting their hands off. For Frankfurter such remarks denigrated one of the great glories of civilization.

Black's decision "went far to dissipate the legend that there is a divinity that doth hedge a judge," Judge Jerome Frank said. Soon Black appeared on the bench without his judicial robes. He scurried behind the purple curtain and returned appropriately attired. Although the dignity of the Court may have been preserved, Black would have preferred wearing his usual double-breasted suit.[9]*

Divine judgment seemed to be the goal to which Frankfurter strived in ascertaining the meaning of the due process clause. Its interpretation has been a constant source of contention since its adoption in 1868. After holding in 1897 that the Fifth Amendment guarantee against taking private property without just compensation was included in the Fourteenth Amendment, the Court rejected periodic attempts to "incorporate" other portions of the Bill of Rights into that amendment's privilege and immunities and the due process clauses. Then in 1925 it announced that it "assumed" that the First Amendment's protection of free speech was applicable to the states via the Fourteenth. Ironically the one amendment in the Bill of Rights specifically addressed to Congress became the first one "incorporated" into the Fourteenth Amendment.

Early during Black's first term, Justice Cardozo in a major opinion, *Palko v. Connecticut,* rejected the claim that the Fourteenth incorporated the right against double jeopardy and other guarantees of the Bill of Rights. The amendment "absorbed" within its meaning those rights "of the very essence of a scheme of ordered liberty," Cardozo wrote. The opinion was suffused with the kind of "natural law" rhetoric Black had scorned in the Senate ("so acute and shocking"; "those 'fundamental principles of liberty and justice . . .' ")—yet he voted with the majority. Why? "I loved Cardozo," Black said, recalling Cardozo's visits after his appointment. "He was deathly ill when we decided *Palko.* I believed that I should vote for someone who had done so much work. It would be a pity not to do so. I hadn't then concluded that *Palko* was wrong." Black joined the opinion "with some difficulty," his clerk recalled, while praising Cardozo personally.

Two years later, Black began promoting the very incorporation thesis

---

* Black believed that judges should be unfrocked, to the extent of robes at least; but nary a judge other than Frank agreed. "For this reason," he wrote Frank (10/17/45), "I shall be compelled in the very near future to purchase a new garment at an outlay of about $100— a sum which could buy many other things I would prefer to have. At any rate, I am with you in your sacrilege."

that *Palko* rejected. Early in the consideration of *Chambers v. Florida,* he referred to "the 'Fourteenth Amendment' as an entirety." Frankfurter wrote to ask what criteria he would use to select which amendments would apply. Black did not reply. He started to draft but finally eliminated any substantive discussion of the matter, simply alluding to the controversy in a footnote. He decided the case on the prevailing flexible, fair trial approach demanding fundamental standards of procedure. He noted, however, a "current of opinion—which this Court has declined to adopt in many previous cases—that the Fourteenth Amendment was intended to make secure against state invasion all the rights, privileges and immunities protected from federal violation by the Bill of Rights (Amendments I to VIII)."[10]

Smith Betts was a Maryland farmhand. Indicted on a charge of robbery while he was unemployed, he told the judge he was too poor to hire a lawyer and asked that counsel be appointed to defend him. His request was denied. He served as his own lawyer, and was found guilty and sentenced to prison. "I believe he is entitled to a lawyer from the history of the 14th Amendment," Black said at the Court's conference in April 1942. "It was intended to [be] made applicable to the states [by] the Bill of Rights. The court has rested on due process. Due process under the prevailing doctrine" means that "if you can find in history a practice [which] violates [judges'] instincts, then they hold that is [a] violation of due process." This turns judges into "law makers, and if I am to pass on what is fair and right I will say it makes me vomit to think men go to prison for a long time. No man should be tried against the constabulary of the government without a lawyer."* "The 14th Amendment did not incorporate the first ten," Frankfurter countered. "If it did, you would uproot all the statutes of the states. . . . We ought not to make due process something to shrink from. It has an ancient lineage. It is for the protection of individuals. . . ."

Black aimed his dissent of less than four pages at Roberts's holding for the Court that the Sixth Amendment applies only to the federal government and that "every court" could appoint counsel if deemed to be in "the interest of fairness." "I believe the Fourteenth Amendment made the Sixth applicable to the states," Black wrote, joined by Douglas and Murphy. "Discussion of the Fourteenth Amendment by its sponsors in the Senate and House shows their purpose to make secure against invasion by the states the fundamental

---

* "How many times in your practice," Black asked, "do you think that any man could plan his defense, summon witnesses and otherwise conduct [a] trial in [the] face of organized opposition?" This was a loaded question, since few justices had actual experience in the practice of criminal law.

liberties and safeguards set out in the Bill of Rights." The Court had already labeled the right to counsel as "fundamental," and in his first term Black wrote for a unanimous Court that in a federal prosecution counsel must be appointed to represent a defendant who cannot afford to hire an attorney. He now condemned a practice that "subjects innocent men to increased dangers of conviction merely because of their poverty." Most state constitutions, statutes or "established practice judicially approved" assured counsel to the indigent. "Any other practice seems to me to defeat the promise of our democratic society to provide equal justice under the law."

The debate continued on a low simmer off the pages of the United States Reports. An occasional remark by Black could entice Frankfurter, adopting a pose of innocence, to ask what materials led Black to his conclusion about incorporation.[11] But another case would be required to ignite the matter.

The battle line had shifted to civil liberties. All justices had expressed agreement with, or at least no public opposition to, the concept that human rights are to be preferred over property rights—"preferred freedoms," as they came to be called. "The power of the states to regulate property," Black wrote in a draft for a 1940 right to counsel case, "must be distinguished from constitutional procedural rights protecting human life and liberty." When the Court in 1942 extended the principles of the First Flag Salute case to uphold laws requiring licensing fees to sell books, Black, Douglas and Murphy appended a one-paragraph statement (written by Black) in dissent—"we now believe that it also was wrongly decided." Democracy "has a high responsibility to accommodate itself to the religious views of minorities, however unpopular and unorthodox those views may be."

Wiley Rutledge's replacement in early 1943 of Justice Byrnes meant that the dissenters had gained a majority. Warm-hearted, unassuming and a devout civil libertarian, Rutledge was a delightful colleague. The Court reversed itself in one of the first cases he heard (*West Virginia Board of Education v. Barnette*). The preferred freedoms doctrine reached its apex in Jackson's eloquent opinion overruling the First Flag Salute case and was implicit in Black and Douglas's short concurrence (drafted by Black). The "ceremonial" flag salute, they noted, "when enforced against conscientious objectors, more likely to defeat than to serve its high purpose, is a handy implement for disguised religious persecution."

Frankfurter rejected the preferred freedoms doctrine in a long, anguished dissent, one of the most personal opinions in Supreme Court annals. "One who belongs to the most vilified and persecuted minority in history . . . ," he began. At length Frankfurter laid out his cramped view of the judiciary's role. Its power "does not vary according to the particular provision of the Bill of Rights which is invoked. . . . In no instance is this Court the primary protector of the particular liberty. . . ." He had come to profess that the Court's function in protecting civil liberties was the same as in protecting property rights; there was no hierarchy of values to safeguard. That was not the position he ascribed to Holmes and adopted for himself when discussing Holmes's philosophy in 1938. Nor was it what he told Stone during First Flag Salute: "I agree with that distinction; I regard it as basic."

Another Jehovah's Witnesses case, in 1943, pitted free speech against privacy in the context of a city ordinance that prohibited the door-to-door distribution of handbills. "People in [the] bona fide exercise of religion are not peddling," Black said the year before, when the Court discussed over-ruling the First Flag Salute case. He would have approved a narrowly drawn law against house-to-house solicitation. *Martin v. Struthers* now gave him that opportunity.

"Can a community be barred by the First Amendment from passing this kind of a law?" he asked when the Court considered *Struthers* at conference in March 1943. "The line is not distinct but there are means which appeal to me. If you can't protect a church from interruption, how can you do so with a home?" Otherwise, "I am fearful that the next case will be Jehovah's Witnesses' invading a Catholic Church." The Court voted 5 to 4 to support Black, with Roberts, Reed, Frankfurter and Jackson joining; and Roberts assigned Black the opinion. His first draft closely tracked a memorandum his clerk John Frank had prepared. A law could regulate conduct "which to some extent limits the dissemination of knowledge" if it advanced legitimate community interests, Black wrote. These included maintaining the quiet of the home and preventing house-to-house canvassing for fraudulent purposes. Stone then circulated his dissent. Its notes persuaded Black that he was wrong and he changed his mind (a rare occurrence). Stone graciously assigned him the new majority opinion, in which he incorporated them. "Door to door distribution of circulars is essential to the poorly financed causes of little people," Black now wrote. "Freedom to distribute information to every citizen wherever he desires to receive it is so clearly vital to the preservation of a free society that . . . it must be fully preserved."[12]

*   *   *

Felix Frankfurter came to the Court expecting to be the dominant figure, at least among the Roosevelt appointees. He quickly found out very differently. What happened? What went wrong?

The Flag Salute cases have traditionally been used to show the embrace and rejection of Frankfurter's "leadership" on the Court. That leadership was more symbolic than real. These were only two cases, despite their importance, and other factors were at work (such as Hughes's being Chief for half that period). Well before the Second Flag Salute case, Douglas recalled, reflecting what Black felt but would never say,

> we had become pretty well separated from Frankfurter. This is nothing that happened overnight. It was an evolutionary thing. Frankfurter had lost the respect of Black and myself and Murphy, just generally speaking. We learned that he was utterly dishonest intellectually, that he was very, very devious. None of us had known him very well, but he spent his time going up and down the halls putting poison in everybody's spring, setting, trying to set one justice against another, going to my office and telling me what a terrible person Reed was or Black, going to Reed's office telling Reed what a stupid person somebody else was, and so on. So we got a full measure of the intrigue of the man and of the manner of his operations. *

Frankfurter's modest view of the Bill of Rights "was beginning to unfold in our minds," Douglas continued, "and we began to realize that here was a man who instead of being a friend and a champion of civil liberties was using his position on the court to line up allies for a constitutional doctrine that we didn't, we couldn't go with. . . . So the explosions in the conferences had become more and more frequent, particularly between him and Black, and between him and me, and we had become more and more suspicious of the good faith of the man, his intellectual honesty." And in those conferences Black's comments, much more than Frankfurter's, structured discussion. [13]

At heart Frankfurter remained a law professor, an emotional intellectual gadfly who preferred to question endlessly rather than to answer. His ploys toward his ends—flattery and ridicule, cajoling, twitting and teasing colleagues, being a master of the vertical pronoun in a collegial institution and

---

* "In an institution this small, personalities play an important role," Justice William J. Brennan, Jr., has said. "It's inevitable when you have just nine people. How those people get along, how they relate, what ideas they have, how flexible or intractable they are, are all of enormous significance" (Jeffrey T. Leeds, "A Life on the Court," NYT Mag. 10/5/86).

reminding his colleagues of his expertise—were self-defeating. Once he said to Black's clerks, with Hugo in earshot, "If I could just be Justice Black's law clerk for one year, how the law would be greatly improved."* Frankfurter had always personalized differences of opinion, and had transformed disagreements about tactics into controversies about the intellectual morality of himself and his opponents. Now he invented and wrote down supposed conversations—with Douglas about Black and the First Flag Salute case, claiming that Hugo changed his mind because he had been "reading the newspapers"; with Brandeis about Black and the *Bridges* case, claiming that Brandeis had said "Black & Co. are going mad on free speech"; and in his files he attributed other, similar remarks to Black and Douglas.

The last of these comments was recorded in June 1942. By then Frankfurter had become massively frustrated. His expectation of dominating the Court had failed. "It was a bad time between him and Black," said Maxwell Isenberg, Black's clerk and Frankfurter's former student. "FF would tell something to his clerk Phil Elman who would tell me," and Isenberg would pass it on to Black. Hugo hated such a way of operating, whether by design or happenstance. For the first six months of 1943, during an exceedingly charged term ideologically, Frankfurter kept a diary. Very little he wrote about the Court is, if true, verifiable; much is outright false. ("The most reliable diaries," he later said, "are those that come from the dullest men." If nothing else, Felix Frankfurter was never dull.) What emerges most clearly is his extraordinary capacity for projecting his own personal traits onto other people.

Frankfurter's initial nod of deference toward the legislative and executive branches had hardened into an ideological commitment. He had reacted to challenges to his beliefs and to what he assumed should be his intellectual domination as if he were under siege, boxing himself into a jurisprudential corner. There he would spend his career on the bench, occasionally extricating himself while deciding cases on the basis of a philosophy he had formulated long ago to deal with different problems. To his acute distress he was fighting from the rear guard. Hugo Black, he knew better than anyone, was occupying the foreground.[14]

---

* In 1943 Justice Murphy wrote:

> Harvard had a little lamb
> its fleece was white as crimson
> and when it had its own sweet way
> its manner was most winsome
> But came der Tag when . . . [FM papers.]

CHAPTER 20

ONE JUDGE,
TWO COURTS

THE COURT and Hugo Black's home were the twin centers of his life. On one he served; over the other he presided. Josephine began looking for a house shortly after he joined the Court. They wanted to stay in Alexandria, preferably in the Seminary Hill area, where they were renting and where her sister was also living, but it was too expensive. In the Old Town section, just before the land slopes down to the Potomac, Josephine saw a run-down Federalist-style home, built about 1790.

The Snowden House, at 619 South Lee Street, had a checkered history. At various times it had been a brothel and a residence for sea captains, and unreconstructed slave quarters were still on the property. The house itself was in very bad repair. All this, as well as the remnant of the widow's walks that an earlier owner had built, made Hugo dubious, but Josephine had grasped the potential immediately and persisted. In early 1939 they bought the house and went about fixing it up. They also bought, and Hugo personally knocked down, an old dwelling next door. He was getting very enthusiastic and wanted to buy more adjoining small plots so he would own the entire southern part of the block, but Josephine put her foot down. They had borrowed enough money from the Glidden Paint Company in Birmingham in which he still owned a share, she said. The centerpiece of the property, extending through to the next street, was the half-acre garden—with its rhododendrons (which, along with his turnip greens, Hugo faithfully watered every night), scuppernong grapes (from Clay County), several varieties of trees, and vegetables and berries which Hugo also planted. A wall around the property afforded much outdoor privacy. It was a place unto itself, not just a home on the street. To those who knew Black outside the Court, the man and the home were interrelated.

Josephine planned the house with Hugo's happiness uppermost in mind, as a self-contained sanctuary befitting his station in life. It was not the epitome of modern luxury (the water did not run too well at times) but an eighteenth-century haven in the twentieth-century world. The family could frolic there and guests could relax, with wonderful meals served inside and refreshments outside amidst much good conversation. Guests left remembering "the feeling of the pleasantness of the company and the charm of the place," as Jonathan Daniels, one of Roosevelt's assistants, wrote long years later.

A large, comfortable upstairs study became the center of Hugo's intellectual life. Like him, it was formally informal, with an innate dignity. Many of his waking hours were spent at his desk in this only slightly updated version of an Enlightenment drawing room. Two of the walls were lined with bookcases filled with his burgeoning collection of books. He bought most of them second hand—his most treasured volumes were purchased from the catalogs of used-book dealers he occasionally scanned—and many were gifts. He continued reading and rereading Greek and Roman writings in translation as well as books about those civilizations. A book about ethical, knowledgeable advocates appearing before "jurymen of good sense" in ancient Rome showed "there is very little new in the world at all," he wrote an Alabama friend. Black regularly analogized from literature. "Like FDR" and "like Pearl Harbor," he marked in Livy's *History of Rome*. After reading *War and Peace* in the summer of 1942, he said, "there's a character in Washington to match each character in the book and a scene in Washington to match each scene."

The South remained close to his heart; he consumed almost as many volumes on it as he did on American history in general.* After reading Hudson Strode's uplifting *Finland Forever*, he wrote Strode, "I can only regret that every thinking person in our country—particularly in the South— has not read the story." In 1938, upon receiving an award from the Southern Conference for Human Welfare, he half froze a Birmingham audience by

---

* In another way, too: He was "a pushover for southern dishes—pecan pie, black-eyed peas and onion soup," a reporter noted after seeing him lunch at the Court (Harlan Miller, "Cloakroom Closeups," *Minneapolis Journal*, 10/23/38).

giving an address that reeked with radical ideas. Nearly all his words came from Jefferson.[1]

Going on the Court changed the nature and focus of Black's reading in different ways. Works about law became more important. For the first time he read Holmes's pathbreaking *The Common Law* and Cardozo's contemplative *The Nature of the Judicial Process*. Studies of the Constitution and its history, of the Court and the justices—Black devoured tomes. He devoted each summer to a different subject; he tried to read a book daily. In the summer of 1943 he focused on legal philosophy. Max Lerner's *Mind and Faith of Justice Holmes* caused Black "to make a number of forays into outside reading. . . . I found your comments to be far more objectively detached than many of the discussions about Justice Holmes which manifest an exaggerated adulation," Black told Lerner (for whom he had "great respect. He has an excellent mind on constitutional questions"). ". . . You brought out rather clearly, I think, that Holmes' economic ideas (so far as he had them) were not of the kind which many of his devoted followers would have us believe."

The discovery of Vernon Parrington's *Main Currents in American Thought* was a happy moment for Black. It gave him "a much clearer understanding of the basic philosophical conflicts which have throughout the ages divided thinking people into groups some of whom favor the exploitation of the many by the few and others who took exactly the opposite position." Parrington conceived of belles lettres as the battleground between conservatism and democracy. "No book that I have read in recent years has given me more food for thought"; Black continually recommended it to friends. Equally attractive was Parrington's style, "something which many people shoot at but which few achieve—simple, clear and most impressive." Hugo increasingly noted phrases that emphasized easily understood language. Next to Montaigne's "Some there are so foolish that will go a quarter of a mile out of the way to hunt after a quaint new word," Black noted in the margin: "Writing—substance is words." "Simplicity, clarity, force led to effectiveness," he scribbled in a biography of Cardozo, and underlined "How I envy you, I sweat blood over every page" of an opinion.[2]

Black and books, books and Black—they went together like Black and tennis. At home, when he was not reading, he could often be found on the tennis court. As the house was being renovated, Hugo announced he had decided to build a court. He had not played much since he came to Washington. The Senate doctor had told him that no man in his forties should play singles, he liked to say, so he waited until he was fifty. He picked up tennis again in the spring of 1938, playing with Cliff Durr on Seminary Hill. Now he studied surfaces, consulted experts and supervised the construction of a clay court. More than once over the next thirty years this court seemed to Black personally to rival in importance the marbled one across from the Capitol.

Stories about Hugo and tennis became legion. Every day the weather permitted he played, far into the fall. (During the winter he sometimes used a makeshift court in the Supreme Court's attic, with balls that the Court's marshall had dyed orange in a futile effort to improve the visibility.) Hugo recruited neighbors to play with, or he'd hit basketfuls of serves, knock balls against the backboard he built on the wall around his property, or use the machine he bought to improve his baseline game. Over time he became a good player, steady but without much range or pace, and better in returning shots than in hitting winners. A stranger once came to the door to ask whether the court was for public use. Josephine said it was not, but invited him to play with Hugo. He did, but no one ever found out who he was. Noon was Hugo's favorite time because he believed one played best when the sun was at its strongest. He often played with Henry Wallace, vice president during Roosevelt's third term, who brought along V-8 juice. Or his opponents were law clerks, his or those of other justices. After a set, the clerk might be panting, but Black simply asked, "Why don't we play just one more set? I believe I could beat you." One clerk called his bad days on the tennis court "tennis the menace" days.

Hugo was as competitive in tennis as in anything else. "I lived down the street from Black and knew him mainly from playing tennis when I was with the Solicitor General's office from 1938 to 1942," said Richard Salant who later became president of CBS News. "My most vivid impression was his intensity. You could hit an overhead on to the fence and he'd climb the fence to get it." Frequently he played seven or eight sets of singles at a stretch. "The last games we had together indicated that you were about to get too good for me," he wrote Hugo, Jr., in early 1943. "This makes it necessary that I do some practice before you arrive." The next year, Sterling "frightened" him by almost winning, and he prepared to "keep [him] in a proper subordinate position." Once he had switched from a western to an eastern grip, he told his sons, he felt "sure that neither of you need get your hopes up, because I can beat either one of you yet." "I see no reason at all why you should be embarrassed at telling anyone that I beat you . . . ," he told Hugo, Jr. And he couldn't resist bragging of a match with Sterling: "We played three sets, nineteen games. He won a game."[3]

At small dinners or outside near the tennis court, Hugo and Josephine entertained friends. The Durrs, Lister and Henrietta Hill, Tom and Peggy Corcoran, Claude and Mildred Pepper, Bill and Mildred Douglas, Thurman and Frances Arnold, Drew and Luvie Pearson, Bill and Mary Jim Smathers, Alexandria friends Marion and Ferris White—all were household familiars. In such settings Josephine shone, with her penetrating, irrepressible eye for the ridiculous. She sometimes teasingly addressed Hugo as "Mr. Justice," which always sounded like "Mr. Jestice." "Dinner with Black was wonderful," said Creekmore Fath, a White House aide, who had "a few dozen" with him over several years. "The Durrs and Bill Douglas and Walton Hamilton and their wives would be there. The conversation just kept on moving. One subject would make Black think of another, and before you were through you'd have covered twenty subjects."

The Blacks, Hills, Peppers, and Corcorans often dined or spent relaxing evenings together, sometimes going to the Olney Theatre. "We'd talk about everything and just have a lot of fun," Pepper recalled. Of all the couples, the Blacks and the Hills were the closest. "It was, 'we'll go with my friends this weekend and yours next weekend,' that type of thing," said Henrietta Hill Hubbard. "Daddy always called Hugo his best friend." (For a while in the summer of 1942 Hill lived with the Blacks.) Theirs was a friendship rare in political Washington, rife with its rivalries. At times Josephine and Henrietta were seemingly inseparable, going to lunches and teas together, and shopping at secondhand stores (if someone recognized them, they would say they were buying for the servants). "It was really something between them," recalled Mary Jim Smathers who had attended finishing school with Henrietta. "One would start talking and the other could finish the sentence." Outside the family, only Henrietta and Mary Jim knew the true extent of Josephine's depressions.

Finding and furnishing the house, taking more courses at American University and writing stories that were rejected—all had kept Josephine busy since Hugo's appointment. But moments of gloom were never far from the surface. "I detected an ominous note which has grown increasingly louder," Josephine wrote in her diary on her anniversary in February 1939 when doctors told her she could not have another child. The next week: "I still feel like I am walking on the edge of a razor blade, but maybe I can work up out of the hole." Further tests revealed she would soon need a hysterectomy; the only consolation was that the tumor was not cancerous.

In November 1940 Josephine underwent the operation. She made out her will and told Hugo, as she did many times, he wrote his beloved niece Hazel Davis, the daughter of his brother Lee, that "if anything occurred to her she wanted me to move heaven and earth to get [Hazel's husband Joseph] the position he would like in Washington so you could take care of our daughter." Hazel had "always loved and adored, admired and followed" her uncle Hugo, and he returned the devotion, penning hundreds of letters to her and confiding in her as he did in hardly anyone else outside his wives and children.

A long period of convalescence followed the operation. Josephine never truly recovered. Although she adored Roosevelt, she did not attend his inauguration the following January because, Hugo wrote Barney Whatley, "she did not want to be mixed up in the excitement." A psychiatrist, Solomon Katznelbogen, whom she consulted at the suggestion of her physician Paul Dickens, suggested that she get away as much as possible. Hugo enjoyed Dickens's company and, atypically when it came to the medical profession, trusted him; and Josephine felt close to Katznelbogen and Hugo also liked him. She traveled throughout the South for a month with a friend in the spring. They stopped at hotels and tourist camps, and stayed on the beach in Florida. What she coveted was calm and quiet. Back in Washington her condition worsened. She started crying when another woman just looked at her in a store. For a while she just largely stayed at home. Dr. Katznelbogen recommended that Josephine receive further treatment. She had at least one stay (in the Fall of 1941) at Washington's Saint Elizabeth's hospital where she underwent shock therapy. Preoccupied, Hugo had his clerk draft many opinions.

Josephine spent increasing amounts of time away, altogether close to one quarter of the 1940s. For weeks on end, several months yearly starting in the late 1930s and continuing into the mid-1940s, Josephine stayed with Mary Jim in Atlantic City. "She worried about JoJo because she felt that she couldn't really be a mother to her," recalled Mary Jim. "She liked talking to children better than to adults. She said they weren't phony and pretentious like adults. And then she'd go back to Washington and start crying. She just couldn't take it there. She was so fragile and so gentle. She wouldn't complain about Hugo, just say how much she had to get away, that there was too much pressure in Washington for her."

To others, however, Josephine would complain. At a small dinner she cornered Irene Hamilton, the young wife of Yale law professor Walton Hamilton, and "talked about how hard it was to live with Hugo. I hardly knew her but she went on about the strain she felt she was always under and made Hugo out almost to be an ogre. She poured out her heart to me so that I felt sorry for her." Josephine even told Sterling: "Your father doesn't understand. He doesn't know how much I have to struggle to do anything."[4]

*   *   *

If the Supreme Court was one of Hugo's courts and the tennis court the other, politics was his third arena. In April 1938 he sent Claude Hamilton advice intended for transmission to Roosevelt. The House had just defeated the president's government reorganization proposal, calling it an attempt to centralize power into the executive's hands. Black urged him to drop the matter and to focus on issues that appealed to the country: "wages and hours, protecting rights of workers, better income for farmers, a job for every man who wants to work supplied by government if not by business, cheap power, *taxing* those most able to pay instead of putting burden on those least able to pay, *peace.* These were the paramount issues in 1936, and they *are yet with the people.*" And late in 1938 he spoke at length to Allan Knight Chalmers, a New York minister who was spearheading a movement to have Alabama governor Bibb Graves pardon the Scottsboro Boys, and wrote and (likely) spoke to Graves.

"After his appointment," said Lister Hill, "Hugo and I talked politics continually. He kept up an active interest in Alabama politics. He advised me on my re-election campaigns in 1944 and 1950. He had friends down here, probate judges and county commissioners, and spoke to them on my behalf." Hill also consulted with Black about the appointment of federal judges, and Black quietly but actively influenced appointments to the Court of Appeals for the Fifth Circuit. "Since 1937," he later said, "I have helped keep off the bench people whose racial antagonism and prejudice I thought made [them] unfit to judge others." Similarly, in letters and private meetings, he encouraged moderate southern politicians. He thought the future of his region lay in their hands.[5]

Politics and government were also on the agenda during his many evenings of conversation with George Reynolds, a neighbor and Agriculture Department official during the war. "Roosevelt was very much on Hugo's mind," recalled Reynolds. "He never criticized Roosevelt directly" (although he once noted, "We need a President who reads more than detective stories"). "And he was never highly critical in an hysterical way about anybody

or said something like, 'That was a dope.' But he made it clear that someone
made a mistake. He would say, 'If I were running the show, I would do
this . . .' And he would make his points so succinctly and give his reasons
for each, in order, one, two, three, and with such logic. It was just wonderful
to watch. He always gave the impression that 'I wish I could get in the fight.'
He'd say, 'If I were running, this is what I would say to the people at this
time.' "

He never lost his desire to be president. Roosevelt knew this. Indeed,
"we all did," said James Roosevelt. "Tommy Corcoran sometimes talked about
Black as a vice-presidential candidate, or even a presidential candidate but
that, of course, would be only if Father were dead or not running." And in
the spring of 1939 nobody knew whether Roosevelt would run for a third
term in 1940 or not. Black predicted that he would, but that was only a
guess. At dinner in late June, Senator Josh Lee of Oklahoma told of having
recently seen Roosevelt. "Mr. President," he said, "I am getting all enthused
over this third term talk." The president's answer, Josephine wrote in her
diary, "was to remember what happened when they warmed up a big league
pitcher too soon, and he also said that a Democrat might rescue a drowning
man before long and the whole country would have to take notice! Lee said
the President . . . never would answer him seriously about a third term."

On July 14, 1939, Roosevelt invited Black to lunch at the White House.
Hugo came home and told Josephine, who recorded:

> He said he seemed in fine spirits and definitely toying with the third term
> idea. He said the President went over the potential candidates at great
> length and eliminated them one by one. Harry Hopkins he discussed as
> too frail. Jim Farley he wouldn't even consider. Frank Murphy couldn't get
> the nomination. Stanley Reed [!] didn't have enough personality. Bob
> Jackson would be ideal but wasn't well enough known. Bill Douglas he
> seemed to think had vast potentialities as vice presidential timber and
> possibly later presidential material but couldn't be developed by 1940. He
> seems to be more or less sitting on Paul McNutt to see how he hatches—
> flesh, fish or fowl.
> Hugo got the impression at this time he does not feel there is anybody
> emerging over the horizon—and he might have to run himself.
> Hugo stayed with him for three hours and he said they had a fine time.

The next month, a trial balloon promoting Black as a vice presidential
possibility went nowhere. (Joseph Alsop raised it in the *New York Herald-
Tribune* at Corcoran's suggestion.) By the spring of 1940 Roosevelt still had
not made his intentions known. Black felt Roosevelt would run. But he also

told Douglas he was seriously considering running in the upcoming Florida primary, even against Roosevelt if the president ran: "I may have to run against the President."

Roosevelt was undoubtedly aware of this activity, at least some of it. Others were more directly so. "Black spoke to people about the vice-presidency," said Carter Monasco, assistant to House Speaker William Bankhead and his successor. "He was quiet about it but word got around." During the 1940 convention, Douglas recalled, Corcoran "and others associated with him" tried to get Roosevelt to select Douglas, without Douglas's authorization or interest, instead of Henry Wallace for the vice presidential nomination. "And one of the persons that they had approached was Hugo Black. . . . They were trying to get my Brother Black to call. But Black didn't want to call F. D. R. because Black was anxious to get into the campaign himself and be F. D. R.'s running mate."

Roosevelt, however, was giving no consideration to Black. When he was choosing a successor to the retiring Chief Justice Hughes in June 1941, Justice Murphy mentioned Black for the post. Roosevelt replied that selecting Black would revive the Klan issue. It would be infinitely more true during a presidential campaign. Black knew this as well as anybody. From Alabama in July 1940, he wrote Roosevelt:

> With knowledge of your preference for retirement at the end of your term, I was among those who urged you to accept another nomination. I am happy that you concluded to do so and congratulate you on your magnificent acceptance address.
>
> The 1940 campaign will, I fear, be even more bitter than those of '32 and '36. And I hope that the strength of the forces that seek your defeat will not be underestimated.
>
> The election of Mr. [Wendell] Willkie would, in my judgment, threaten our country's peace and security at home and abroad. As an Associate Justice I am barred, however, from taking an active part in this crucial contest you have patriotically entered. Nevertheless, I stand ready to resign my position and enter the fight, should you conclude you need my services.

"I was touched by your expression of such real friendship and loyalty," Roosevelt answered. "I do appreciate it, and I want to see you when you do come back." They did not see each other during the campaign. But when in mid-October journalist Robert Allen wrote Black that "the situation in the mid-west is extremely serious and requires the President's personal attention," Black (as he noted on the letter) "called this to attention of

President."[6] Administration troops fanned out through the heartland, in accordance with quickly evolving plans, and helped Roosevelt win a comfortable victory.

World War Two changed everything for Josephine as for everyone else. Hugo, Jr., and Sterling both served in the army but medical problems—Hugo, Jr.'s, asthma and Sterling's hearing—kept them from the battlefront. Josephine stayed up many nights, crying because of her fear that Sterling's defective hearing might lead to his death. During the day, she contributed to the war effort in her quiet, personal way. She volunteered at an Alexandria child care program, served as a Gray Lady of the Red Cross and attended soldiers at Fort Belvoir Hospital. All sorts of people came to her at home to pour out their souls when they were upset. (A family saying went that Hugo represented Justice and Josephine represented Mercy.) They left with an inspired sense of self-worth and their feelings soothed. Among these people was Mamie Eisenhower, who cried because she found out Ike was having an affair with Kay Summersby in Europe.

None of Josephine's callers knew of her depressions. To almost everyone she seemed the same gentle, sweet, caring soul she had always been, "a genius with people who could put anyone at ease," as one young friend (journalist Eliot Janeway) said. But the effort she exerted from not revealing her condition to others and her preoccupation with soldiers dying combined with the effects of menopause to deplete further her low reserve of strength. Virginia Durr brought their mother to live with her on Seminary Hill. Mrs. Foster, whose malady had always been more serious than Josephine's, "wept and wept all the time," and her physical condition also deteriorated. Josephine faced the prospect of her mother's death when she herself was suffering terribly: twelve depressions yearly in 1942, 1943 and 1944, each one lasting for three weeks each month. Her hopelessness increased, and she slept little. "You have this feeling of simply cluttering up the earth's surface," she wrote in the diary she now kept only occasionally. "You are contributing nothing and you have lost the will to take hold anywhere."[7]

This was mid-1944. Roosevelt left the choice of a running mate in the forthcoming presidential election to party politicians, who chose Harry Truman to replace Henry Wallace. But before this, Tom Corcoran had been working on both Douglas's and Black's behalf: he was more interested in being the king-maker than in who the king was. He had established a lucrative law practice since leaving the government, one of the first examples of those who, as he later said, went to Washington "to do good and stayed to do well." Even after Roosevelt had retreated from his promise to name Corcoran solicitor general (fearing it would reopen the Court-packing fight), Corcoran retained contact with FDR, doing occasional, unpublicized political chores.

Since 1940 Black had cemented his standing as one of the leading progressives in the country besides Roosevelt himself. The Klan issue was that much further in the past. More than any other political figure, except for Lister Hill, Corcoran knew how badly Black wanted to run for national office.* As "family" to Hugo, he would not have misled his close friend. Nor would Corcoran have undertaken such a task on his own if he thought Roosevelt would disapprove. And few knew better Roosevelt's high opinion of Hugo.

"We've got labor and the liberals lined up for you, and the money is there," he told Black, urging him to come to the convention in Chicago. "The nomination is yours if you want it."

And Hugo said no. He would do nothing. "My mother's health was the reason," Sterling Black said. Josephine was in the midst of one of her worst spells of depression; Hugo frequently gave her testosterone shots. So he lost out directly on the steppingstone to the political prize he wanted above all others.[8]

*   *   *

Josephine's health suddenly improved in the fall of 1944. She took a college course and played golf almost daily, Hugo told his sons that November. "Your mother is better than she has been in ten years." Then she suffered another long spell of depression. Perhaps it was a delayed reaction to her mother's death in September. A murky cloud descended on her mind. "Complete aimlessness," Josephine wrote, "no direction, just marking time for something to happen outside yourself. The power within you has escaped, oozed out a little at a time and life has lost all meaning or purpose."

Carl and Jane Allen, friends from Alexandria who had moved to California, told her about an endocrinologist there who also dabbled as a faith

---

* "Black was like the old ads for bad breath: his best friends wouldn't tell him certain things," said Eliot Janeway (int.). "There was no way you could tell him he wasn't going to be president. He just had it in his head." Lister Hill sometimes wondered whether Hugo would run for president, saying, "I wouldn't put anything past him" (Clarence Allgood int.).

healer and practitioner of "Far Eastern religion." Josephine spent the summer of 1945 living with the Allens and their young children near Los Angeles. Hugo wrote her daily. He assured and reassured her of his and their children's love for her. He tried to lift her spirits: "It has always been my insistence that you depreciated your *physical* disabilities and wanted to attribute every ill to nervous or mental disturbances. . . . You do not have an *incurable* trouble." He told her of his trip to Miami to see Sterling: "I fear I must do the cooking. Maybe this *is* a rather lonely job for an Associate Justice, but such is the state of the world and my appetite that I shall perform the duty without shame—for a T bone steak." Back home, with JoJo away at camp and the boys in the army, this man who cherished times with his family above all was terribly lonely. He read constantly, played tennis nearly as much and ate dinner out almost nightly, and wrote Josephine about his activities and household matters, all sprinkled with observations on current affairs. At successive White House and French embassy dinners Hugo sat next to Charles De Gaulle. He found the general

> as unscintillating as his pictures indicate. Never once did I see a simple flash of humor on his countenance. If, as many think, gaiety of spirits is a typical French attribute, De Gaulle is not true to type. He looks as solemn as that monkey which visited us again yesterday, without any of its alertness or sprightly movements. If there is a single tinge of imagination in his makeup, it must be too deeply buried to find an outlet. Compared with him I should be constrained to label Coolidge as an iridescent luminary.

Hugo's mood brightened when Hugo, Jr., had a short medical leave and JoJo came back from camp. "In celebration of the occasion," he wrote Josephine, "I have bought her some chewing gum (which was a monumental concession) and a milky way." "We are all homesick for you." She returned at the end of September, her condition little improved. Testosterone shots had caused hair to grow on her shoulders and down her back, making her "look almost like a gorilla," according to one friend.* Still, she continued trying to help others. In a prospective (but never published) article, "The Psychological Menopause," she wrote: "Everything began to cave in. There

---

* Hugo was dubious about this treatment from the beginning: "I am so solicitous about the good or informed faith of people who claim such extraordinary results from such a strange diagnosis and such a shower of pills and capsules." "In spite of all my doubts, however, and they are many, the lady's treatment may work. Stranger things have happened in this age" (HLB to JFB, 8/19,20/45).

was no perspective anymore to anything. The slightest little decision seemed to loom into a gigantic peak which I was powerless to scale. . . . I write this article now after five years have elapsed since the operation. They have been five years on the torture wrack—no words can describe the agony of mind and body that I have experienced."

Those five years had coincided with World War Two. Of all the letters Hugo had written Josephine that long summer, probably the most welcome was that of August 15:

> There is a strange quietness today following the bedlam that broke loose last evening immediately after Truman announced the Japanese surrender. Staid old Alexandria broke loose then. You heard the radio report of what happened elsewhere and it was the same here. As for me, I rode through streets with racing, blowing cars, went to the Hot Shop, had a very commonplace and unenticing dinner, and then returned and read until 11. How long the noise kept up I do not know, but it awakened me several times.[9]

World War Two was over, taking with it one source of Josephine's suffering. But its root would never leave her.

CHAPTER 21

"HARDSHIPS ARE
PART OF WAR"

T HIS MAN HITLER means every word he's written," Black said after reading *Mein Kampf* upon English publication in 1939. "He wants to take over the world and we must do everything to stop him." War was inevitable. Black spoke with Roosevelt about the preparedness program three times the next Spring. The government, he said, should nationalize the armament and munitions industries, and hire some businessmen as dollar-a-year men to run them and not, in effect, have to prepare the corporations through the Defense Plant Corporation. He feared big business would try to monopolize competition or exploit the government for lavish profits by overproducing or underproducing and then charging exorbitant rates, and that a kind of domestic fascism might result as a backlash. Roosevelt listened patiently. "Hugo, we got the sons of bitches during the war," he said, referring to World War One. "We'll get them again."

Late in 1940 Claude Pepper showed Black a draft of the Lend Lease bill that the Senate was preparing to help England. "We talked about it in his library," Pepper recalled. "He gave me some very helpful comments that were incorporated in the final version." Lend Lease made Black's apprehensions all the greater when FDR named businessman William S. Knudsen and Edward Stettinius as two of the directors of a hydra-headed Office of Production Management early in 1941. They would think only of profits and ways to help their companies, Black said. The general situation in the production field continued to worry Black. He spoke about it often to Harold Ickes, the interior secretary, with whom he was becoming ever closer friends. On December 7, 1941, he and Josephine were lunching at Ickes's Maryland farm. Senator Tom Connally was amusing the several guests with funny

312

stories. "Naturally, we talked of the possibility of war," Ickes recorded in his diary, "but we had been on the edge of it so long that it didn't seem real, after all." Over the car radio on the way home came news of the Japanese attack on Pearl Harbor.

"We have gone back to work," Hugo the next day wrote Josephine, who had gone to New Jersey to visit Mary Jim Smathers, "but it seems difficult to concentrate on individual disputes between Americans at a time when the entire country is participating in a world dispute. The atmosphere at the joint session [of Congress which Roosevelt had addressed] was grim and determined. Japan has done something Roosevelt could not—it has brought about a greater spirit of unity than ever before existed when this country went to war. And since the war has seemed inevitable for quite a time our loss of lives brought about by the surprise attack can be considered as the contribution of some to their country's welfare—a tragic price to pay, but perhaps a necessary one."[1]

World War Two had no more zealous prosecutor on the Supreme Court than Hugo Black. In its early days he was fearful as ill-prepared armed forces geared up for worldwide conflict. The nation is "in such desperate danger," he said in April 1942. That June at Roosevelt's direction Black went to Birmingham as an undercover presidential emissary to investigate production slowdowns in mines, steel plants and shipyards caused by racial friction. FDR asked him to look into wildcat strikes, because whites refused to work alongside Negroes, and into reports that workers of both races in Mobile shipyards and other plants were going to work armed. These situations continued as Roosevelt took little action: production was more important than a frontal attack on discrimination in private enterprises. The next month, at Roosevelt's urging, Black addressed a Southern Win-the-War Rally.

Panic had followed the attack on Pearl Harbor. Anti-Japanese hysteria swept California. Three Japanese submarines sank American tankers. Some civilian and military leaders, fearing that the West Coast stood in danger of invasion, agitated for action against both alien Japanese and American citizens of Japanese descent (Nisei). "A Jap's a Jap," General John L. DeWitt, area commander, soon told a congressional committee. "It makes no difference whether he's an American citizen or not. There is no way to determine their loyalty."

In February 1942 Roosevelt signed an executive order authorizing the War Department to remove all Japanese from the military zone that covered most of the West Coast. "The President is authorized in acting under his general war powers without further legislation," Attorney General Francis Biddle assured him. The next month Congress gave these provisions the force of statute. The army required all persons of Japanese ancestry to report to designated centers for transportation to and imprisonment in "resettlement camps." Roosevelt himself later more aptly dubbed them "concentration camps." Concentration camps American style.[2]

Soon this program was challenged in the courts. Gordon Hirabayashi was convicted for disobeying both the order to report for evacuation and the curfew requirement that the military had imposed. In 1943 the Supreme Court upheld the conviction. A majority of justices agreed with Chief Justice Stone's suggestion at conference to rule only on the validity of the curfew; Black warned against dealing with the evacuation issue. Applying the lowest level of judicial scrutiny, Stone wrote, "It is not for any court to sit in review" of the wisdom of the military's choices.

Black told Frankfurter that if he were commanding general, he would refuse to allow the Nisei to return to the West Coast even if the Court established their loyalty. In this instance the commander was an old friend. Josephine renewed her Birmingham friendship with DeWitt's wife Martha in Hugo's first term in the Senate. The two couples saw each other socially on occasion. And not only had Hugo stayed at the Army War College, headed by DeWitt, before and after his nomination to the Court, but Hugo's messenger, Spencer Campbell, was now working with the DeWitts in California. Black's faith in DeWitt added to his belief that the commander in the field had the right and the power to make the decision who should remain in an area. Although Stone's opinion sufficiently satisfied Black, he drafted but never used a statement summarizing his own views:

> When an enemy Army imminently threatens a particular area of our country with invasion, the immediate responsibility for defense must necessarily rest on those who direct our armed forces. Inability to make quick and final decisions in order to meet actual or suspected dangers might bring about disastrous consequences. Purely military orders, limited to the comings and goings of occupants of an area which may at any minute become an active war zone, call for the exercise of a military, not a judicial judgment. A curfew regulation in a zone of imminent danger is such a regulation. The regulation here under consideration was made by the Commanding General, and the Congress conferred jurisdiction upon the Federal courts to punish those who violated it. Final authority to say what persons in the area were to be subjected to the curfew regulation was, I think, not in the courts but in the military department charged with

protecting the country against pressing danger. Therefore, I find it unnecessary to appraise possible reasons which might have prompted the order to be issued in the form it was. It is enough for me that both Congress and the Commander-in-Chief of the Army made a decision that the regulation as made was necessary to provide for the common defense in an area in which no man could say whether or when armed invaders would appear.[3]*

Over 120,000 persons of Japanese descent, 70,000 of them American citizens, remained in the concentration camps to which they had been herded like cattle—solely because of their ancestry. There they lived under crowded, extremely spartan conditions, with dust and sand blowing across the fields and seeping through the cracks of their barracks. The army permitted each detainee to bring a single duffel bag and two suitcases containing only bedding, clothing and cooking utensils. Anything else was forbidden or confiscated. "We don't propose to have the Japs back in California during this war if there is any lawful means of preventing it," California governor Earl Warren told his fellow governors in 1943. Fred Korematsu, unwilling to leave his Caucasian girlfriend, was one of the few who did not report for evacuation. He had recently undergone facial surgery in an attempt to conceal his racial ancestry; he was picked up in a dragnet search and eventually convicted.

At oral argument before the Supreme Court the government claimed, as Douglas wrote in an opinion thirty years later, "that if the Japanese landed troops on our West Coast nothing could stop them west of the Rockies. . . . Enclaves of Americans of Japanese ancestry should be moved inland, lest the invaders by donning civilian clothes would wreak even more serious havoc on our Western ports." This claim impressed the justices. In conference Stone pressed for a narrow construction of the case: he was anxious to separate the exclusion order, which allowed detention in an assembly center, from detention in a relocation center. The Court voted 5–4 to uphold Korematsu's conviction. Rutledge, the junior justice, reluctantly followed *Hira-*

*. Privately, however, very privately, Black harbored doubts. "He wasn't sure," recalled George Reynolds (int.), "moving the Japanese was the right thing to do to people who had lived in the country quite a long time, but he supported it on the ground that you couldn't take any chances of domestic bombing in wartime. He told me that we shouldn't second-guess the President. Second-guess was the word he used. He indicated that during a war the Court shouldn't exercise independent judgment in the way it should otherwise. He also led me to believe that he wouldn't have done that to the Japanese if he were President. He never criticized Roosevelt, you have to remember. In his usual indirect way he said, 'If I were President, I'm not sure I would have done that. These people are American citizens and have lived here for a long time.' "

bayashi and came down on Stone's side, joining Black, Reed and Frankfurter. Roberts, Douglas, Murphy and Jackson went the other way. Murphy had initially dissented in *Hirabayashi* and Douglas's grudging concurrence there almost assured that he too would vote to reverse Korematsu's conviction.

Also before the Court was *Ex parte Endo*, a challenge by a Nisei to her continued detention in a camp after she was no longer suspected of disloyalty. Black thought the same judge should write both decisions. That was the usual practice when cases dealt with aspects of the same situation. But Stone assigned *Korematsu* to Black and *Endo* to Douglas, and Hugo "was hopping mad about it," noted Murphy's clerk. "He says he hates to write against civil liberties." "This was the most upset he ever was toward Stone," observed John Frank, who had clerked for Black two terms earlier. To a later clerk Black indicated that *Korematsu* was the only assignment he ever received that he had reservations about writing. Douglas wrote Stone to change one of the assignments, but it was to no avail.

Korematsu was "very much discussed, very much considered, very much debated up and down the halls of the corridor of the Court," recalled Douglas. "Black was very eloquent in defense of the power of the military to do what they did. And he had no doubts [or] reservations." Black wanted to immunize the military completely from judicial review during wartime. He looked at the case as one of administrative finality. General DeWitt's decision, he told his clerk, was the same as if it were made by a court or a regulatory agency. In his mind no question existed about the legality of the exclusion order Korematsu had violated. It was virtually a case of first impression; only *Hirabayashi* was even somewhat analogous. And like Stone there, Black purposely ignored the possible application of the *Ex parte Milligan* (1866) doctrine that "military necessity . . . is not a self-justifying plea" in the absence of martial law. He strove to confine his opinion as a response to the specific situation and to limit its value as a precedent.

"Exclusion and detention under guard are separate situations," Black wrote, contradicting his admission earlier in this first draft that the exclusion order led directly to detention. "Racial prejudice" was not involved, and he denied that "all danger of Japanese invasion of the West Coast had disappeared, and that there was no longer any military necessity for taking precaution against espionage and sabotage in case of attack."

The dissenters all quickly circulated opinions. Jackson's was the most personal. Military power "wholly removed from judicial examination," he noted, might well lead to an absolutism that "would approximate Lenin's definition of a dictatorship." Black's opinion suggested that "we may as well say that any military order will be constitutional and have done with it." Frank Murphy was much more impassioned: the Court's "legalization of racism" ignored that "guilt is personal and not inheritable," a maxim fundamental to Western law. "Exclusion goes over 'the very brink of constitutional power,' " he justifiably asserted, repeating a phrase he used in his *Hirabayashi* concurrence, "and falls into the ugly abyss of racism."[4]

Douglas's dissent, based on statutory rather than constitutional grounds, was surprisingly mild. He had already written the opinion for a unanimous court in *Endo*, having reluctantly agreed to restrict it to holding that Congress had not authorized detention of any citizen whom the government conceded to be loyal, and was waiting for it to come down. Stone, however, was in contact with the administration (as on a daily basis was Frankfurter) and held it until December 18, 1944, a day after the army announced the total exclusion of Japanese-Americans from the West Coast would end on January 2, 1945. Despite his "complete satisfaction," Black was also delaying *Endo's* release, hoping to find some way to persuade Douglas to change his mind on *Korematsu*. In early December they met in Black's chambers to go over his draft. Black made many changes to satisfy Douglas. Most were inconsequential, concerning tone; he did not retreat at all from his position of "military necessity." With "some reluctance, some hesitation" (and to his later regret), Douglas withdrew his dissent. The court soon approved Black's amended opinion.

In an early draft Black insisted that "a factual foundation of record" existed to support the evacuation. "Compelling urgencies of national defense" compelled it.* "All laws directed primarily at racial or ethnic groups are immediately suspect. But that is not to say that they are all unconstitutional." This was an obvious allusion to Stone's Footnote Four, but Black provided no citation. He revised the paragraph: "All legal restrictions which curtail the civil rights of a single racial group are immediately suspect. . . . Courts must subject them to the most rigid scrutiny." Then he carved out

---

* The FBI had investigated claims in the Army's *Final Report: Japanese Evacuation from the West Coast, 1942*, prepared at DeWitt's direction, about a possible connection between the sinking of American ships by Japanese submarines and alleged Japanese espionage activity on the West Coast. The report had inferred, as one government lawyer noted, that "frequent signaling by unlawful radio transmitters from Japanese-Americans on shore to submarines at sea" was "among the most important factors making evacuation necessary." But the FBI and the Federal Communications Commission had found no such activity. To conclude that DeWitt "in all probability" knew that his justifications for evacuation and detention were "incorrect" was not only a violation of legal ethics but would harm the government's case. The government's brief was purposely ambiguous on the point (Peter Irons, *Justice at War* [New York, 1983], 285–92).

a wartime exception: "Pressing public necessity may sometimes justify the existence of such restrictions; racial antagonism never can."

Black rested his opinion on the *Hirabayashi* case: "we could not reject the finding of the military authorities that it was impossible to bring about an immediate segregation of the disloyal from the loyal."

> We are not unmindful of the hardships imposed by [the exclusion order] upon a large group of American citizens. But hardships are part of war, and war is an aggregate of hardships. All citizens alike, both in and out of uniform, feel the impact of war in greater or lesser measure. . . . When under conditions of modern warfare, our shores are threatened by hostile forces, the power to protect them must be commensurate with the threatened danger.
>
> . . . We are dealing specifically with nothing but an exclusion order. To cast this case into outlines of racial prejudice . . . merely confuses the issue. Korematsu was not excluded from the Military Area because of hostility to him or his race. He *was* excluded because we are at war with the Japanese Empire, because the properly constituted military authorities feared an invasion of our West Coast and felt constrained to take proper security measures, because they decided that the military urgency of the situation demanded that all citizens of Japanese ancestry be segregated from the West Coast temporarily, and finally, because Congress, reposing its confidence in this time of war in our military leaders—as inevitably it must—determined that they should have the power to do just this.[5]

Korematsu troubled Black for the rest of his life. He did not like to talk about it to his clerks, and when he did, he was usually defensive. The West Coast was going to be invaded, General DeWitt had made a determination and that was that, went his standard reply. "Slight differences in circumstances," Black wrote to a law student in 1956, "can be so important in times of threatened danger to the country that it might be difficult to conceive of a situation precisely like that the Court had before it in the *Korematsu* case." In 1967 he told an interviewer:

> I would do precisely the same thing today, in any part of the country. I would probably issue the same order were I President. We had a situation where we were at war. People were rightly fearful of the Japanese in Los Angeles, many loyal to the United States, many undoubtedly not, having dual citizenship—lots of them. They all look alike to a person not a Jap. Had they [the Japanese] attacked our shores you'd have a large number fighting with the Japanese troops. And a lot of innocent Japanese Americans would have been shot in the panic. Under these circumstances I saw nothing wrong in moving them away from the danger area.

He stood by the opinion until his death. "I had a long talk with Black the month before he died," recalled Sidney Davis, his clerk during the term of *Korematsu*. "He said, 'Under those circumstances we did the right things. Under those precise circumstances we couldn't have done anything else. I still think I did the right thing.' " He still couldn't admit he was wrong about *Korematsu*.[6]*

---

* Historical happenstance a decade later brought Earl Warren and Tom Clark together with Black on the Court. The contrast in their attitude toward these matters is instructive. "I have since deeply regretted the removal order and my own testimony advocating it," Warren wrote in his *Memoirs* (149). "It was wrong to react so impulsively without positive evidence of disloyalty." And he cried during an interview as he talked about the faces of children being separated from their parents (EW int., 6/22/72, ROHO, UC). Clark, who in the early years of the war coordinated the evacuation program, in 1966 likewise admitted it was a "mistake": "We should not let [wartime hysteria] influence us. The reason I say that I think it was bad is because, well, even way back a citizen always had a preferred position. In the Bible it says, 'I am a Roman citizen . . . and am entitled to this and that . . .' It's the same with an American citizen in my book. We picked up these people and . . . put them in concentration camps. That's the truth of the matter" (Weaver, *Warren*, 113).

CHAPTER 22

FEUDS AND ALLIES

T HE ASCENSION of Harlan Stone to the chief justiceship changed the atmosphere of the Court. He had chafed during the taut conferences Hughes conducted and determined to change them. Stone was ill equipped for the task—a weak and indecisive leader, Black thought, who lacked the sense of group discipline needed to preside successfully. He presented the cases in detail, then joined the debate, interrupting colleagues as they spoke and making little effort to moderate the crossfire of arguments. What had been a four-hour Saturday conference under Hughes dragged out into the evening, and once until midnight, only to be resumed and continuing until midweek. The meetings were openly abrasive—"raw and personal," Murphy said. Black's concise remarks generally shaped the discussion—"a *fierce* advocate," both Stone and Frankfurter called him. And while Douglas said that in conference Black "never once spoke an unkind word, never, never spoke a mean word or a malicious word," the power and intensity of his advocacy could sting as it influenced the others.

A kaleidoscopic collection of personalities sat around the table. There were the survivors of the Old Court: Stone—garrulous and open-minded, a creative judge versed in equity and the common law tradition; Roberts—bluff and hearty, who sometimes knew his own mind. There were the New Deal judges: Frankfurter—an outsized personality in a small package, brimming with learning and ready to let the world know it; Reed—a southern gentleman's gentleman, never known to play one person or point against another; Douglas—with whom Black had a truly brotherly relationship (if one hiccuped, the other would practically say "excuse me"); Murphy—self-absorbed, an unblushing libertarian evangelist of whom a kind critic said that he "thinks with his heart, not with his head"; Rutledge—an unpretentious teddy bear of a man who stood out as a hard worker even in this crowd. (Byrnes made a negligible mark in his restless, unhappy one-year-plus on the Court, spending most of his time at the White House as "assistant president.")

Then there was Robert Jackson. Roosevelt had often told Jackson that, when Hughes retired, he wanted to see him as chief justice; he knew Jackson coveted the position. But with the threat of war looming, the need for national unity, combined with Hughes's advice to Roosevelt that prior experience on the Court was "invaluable" to a chief justice, led FDR to name Stone, a Republican. Jackson went on the Court believing he would succeed Stone. Roosevelt had virtually said that (prompting Jackson to remark, "I will be happy to serve at the end of his term"), and Jackson believed the president who promised with the promiscuity of a hooker. Roosevelt did tell his son James that Jackson " 'needs more seasoning. He's a little too young.' Father liked Bob but thought he was the type of guy that if you said something nice about him, he'd remember it forever and forget all the not so nice things you or anyone else said about him." Jackson's ambition was presently stifled, but it would not go away.[1]

A gifted stylist whose freshness and pungency broke through the page, Jackson had charm and surface glitter. (He also struggled with a sharp temper: more than once he blew up at a lawyer on the bench.) At first he and Black were "friendly but not intimate," Jackson later wrote. But Jackson's praise of Black's courage and ability quickly turned into disdain. His stance in economic cases led Black to suspect his motives, to look upon him as sympathetic to big business and established institutions, and to regard him as somewhat duplicitous and devious, since he liked to mouth progressive sentiments while denying their claims; his adherence to the New Deal had been only temporary, Black said. The antagonism started during Jackson's first term when they had some flareups in conference. "It was very evident in almost all our conferences," Douglas said, "that Bob Jackson thoroughly disliked Hugo Black and was out to destroy him . . . in the sense of discrediting him, and his words were very vivid, very derogatory."

In an opinion for the Court in a March 1943 tax case, Jackson went out of his way to discuss at length Black's Senate remarks and to make them a central part of the bill's legislative history. They came "after he had already begun the antagonism he later indicated . . . ," Hugo noted in 1961. Letting off steam after a difficult term in the summer of 1943, Black told Sterling, "I may have to resign. I can take attacks on what I believe but not on me personally like Jackson is doing." And several times over the next two years both the trend of decisions on the Court and Josephine's health led him to discuss the possibility of resigning.

Behind Jackson's provocations, as behind most intrigue on the Court, was Frankfurter. By 1943–44 he had run out of justices to convert. His manner had deeply repulsed Douglas and Murphy, much more than their substantive disagreements. Rutledge, the newest justice, was already meeting with them and Black to plot strategy. Stone and Reed went their own ways, the former always trying to persuade someone on the merits, the latter always available, smiling and annoying no one. Only Jackson and Roberts were left, and Frankfurter never passed up an opportunity to tell them the worst about Black. No one else on the Court went out of his way to make trouble with colleagues (not yet anyway). But Frankfurter always had been a divisive force. No group that he joined would be happy, Judge Learned Hand once told Douglas. (When an interviewer said how good Felix was at making friends, Hand replied, "Yes, and enemies.")[2]

Nine scorpions trapped in a bottle, Holmes once called the justices, and on January 3, 1944, they splintered, issuing twenty-nine opinions in fourteen cases. The day before, columnist Drew Pearson in his weekly radio broadcast stated that the Court was divided "four to four, with the ninth justice trying to make up his mind by today." This was incorrect: Douglas's opinion in a rate-making case was for a 5-to-3 majority, with Roberts not participating. Nevertheless, Roberts demanded that Stone call a conference to deal with the furor raised by Pearson's comments. Stone acceded. At the conference Roberts pulled out the newspaper story with Pearson's remarks. He insisted that a justice had leaked this information to Pearson. "And Frankfurter made it very plain in the conference that he had so advised Roberts," Douglas recalled. He directed "the finger of suspicion" at Douglas and Murphy. They both said they didn't know where the leak came from, that it was "just the old guessing game." The other justices agreed—but not Frankfurter and, especially, Roberts, who wanted to "explore the matter further." Roberts was "very, very, very worked up"—even though he was not sitting in the case. Over his protestations, the case came down.

Roberts went to see Black. Hugo said he was "positive" that neither Douglas nor Murphy had ever said anything to the press, and that since they said so, he had "implicit confidence" in them. Roberts thereafter became very embittered. Never again did he come into the justices' robing room for the traditional handshake before going on to the bench. He waited outside in the hall, then silently stepped into line. He arrived late at conferences, speaking only to Frankfurter and Jackson, believing every other justice "sort of a conspirator against him."*

Hugo lost a valued friend with whom substantive disagreement took second place to rapport. He enjoyed the witty remarks Roberts wrote on Hugo's own draft opinions. "I stand, naked and exposed, but unashamed!" Roberts noted in one case. And in another: "I agree. As the old lady said, 'It is short, sweet and to the point.' " Gone, too, were the weekends together at Roberts's farm and relaxing evenings at Hugo's house discussing life and ethics (and law). "I do know," Douglas said in 1961, "that Hugo Black to this day would put down Roberts as, not the man he admired most, by any means, but the man whose company he enjoyed the most of almost anyone that he had met."[3]

The month was not over before the justices were quarreling again. Roberts, dissenting on a white primary case, bitingly wrote of the majority opinion overruling a past decision that it brought the Court's cases "into the same class as a restricted railroad ticket, good for this day and train only." Ever partisan, Black thought that Roberts "sounded off" to furnish the Republicans with "some campaign literature" for the 1944 elections. "Variation of differences is evidently thought to be desirable by those who wish to attack the present Administration during this political year," he wrote Sterling. Roberts did not shake hands with Black and Douglas at the next conference.

Black tried to downplay the conflict. "The so-called rift in the Supreme Court," he told Hugo, Jr., "is nothing more than a difference in views, and not an indication of personal animosities, which, of course, should have no influence upon judicial opinions." But personalities naturally played a role. It could hardly be otherwise in a small institution. Hugo talked about it with trusted friends who knew the justices, such as interior secretary Harold Ickes (a good friend of Roberts's) and Thurman Arnold, formerly a trust-

---

* "Owen Roberts was a fine man," Douglas later wrote Fred Rodell. "But Frankfurter got Roberts to believe that new judges were scheming behind his back, giving stories to the press, and playing politics. While he was doing this to Roberts, he was saying behind Roberts' back, 'I would hate to be Roberts. I couldn't sleep nights if I were. I would think his conscience would keep him awake—the way he votes.' He once said that to me" (5/9/49, Rodell papers).

busting assistant attorney general and now a judge on the federal appellate court in Washington. "People who are familiar with Supreme Court history," Hugo informed Sterling, "know that there has never been a time since it was first instituted where there were not sharp differences of opinion among the Justices. As you suggest, it would be bad for any institution of this kind to have men who constantly profess to be of one mind on all issues. It would indicate either that they have no minds at all, or that they subserviently yield to their own views. The Court's activities in the past have indicated that its membership has not been limited to men who do not think for themselves."[4]

Tension was palpable when the brethren heard the *South-Eastern Underwriters Association* case, one week after Roberts had blown up. The government had brought an antitrust action against the association and its membership of nearly two hundred fire insurance companies, charging conspiracy to fix rates and to monopolize the insurance market. Bound by an 1869 Supreme Court decision holding that states could regulate insurance because it was not commerce, the lower court held the statute inapplicable. At issue now was whether insurance constituted interstate commerce under the commerce clause.

Black, Douglas, Murphy, Jackson and Rutledge voted to affirm the proposition and to reverse the lower court. Assigning the case to himself, Black prepared an opinion granting to Congress "the power to regulate insurance transactions stretching across state lines." On March 12 Drew Pearson predicted the outcome over radio. Once again, Roberts did not participate but charged that Douglas was the source;* once again, Douglas denied it. Pearson refused Stone's call for his transcript. Attention turned to the law clerks. After each judge questioned his clerk, word came that Stone wanted to meet with all clerks; then he called off the meeting. Roberts was so adamant that in mid-March 1944 the Court decided to continue working on the case but not to release it for a spell, "merely to avoid giving credence to Pearson's prediction." It did not come down until June.

---

* Why Roberts disqualified himself here and in *Federal Power Commission v. Hope Natural Gas Co.*, decided earlier in 1944, remains unanswered. Perhaps the man whose action occasioned the quip about "the switch in time that saved nine" back in 1937 was especially sensitive to guises. He found appearances of impropriety where few others did—once complaining that the name of one of Murphy's clerks, Eugene Gressman (int.), who had previously worked at the SEC, appeared on a brief in a case that Murphy wrote for the Court—yet Roberts long sat in many cases in which his former firm appeared.

The business of insurance was commerce, and subject to regulation under the Sherman Act, Black held for a majority of four. (Reed also disqualified himself, and Jackson switched his vote.) Insurance was national in scope. Quoting liberally from the Federalist Papers, Black wrote that Congress had "the power to legislate concerning transactions which, reaching across state boundaries, affect the people of more states than one." The Sherman Act aimed to abolish "trusts" and "monopolies," which were "the terror of the period." Stone, Frankfurter and Jackson dissented on various grounds, their main point being that while Congress could regulate insurance, it had not done so under the Sherman Act. "Of course that part of the bar that dislikes regulation of business will holler its head off," Jerome Frank wrote Black, "but intelligent honest lawyers who read your opinion are bound to be convinced by its amazing clarity."[5]

Black could take deep and complicated concepts and clothe them in easy, graceful, direct, almost simple language that was concise, clear and crafted perfectly to his purpose. His sharp and simple assertions cut through soft tissue, crushing myths. One law clerk recognized Black's bent when he inscribed a book of his own "To the Judge, who taught me that the language of the countryman can rival the measured discourses of Oxford." Black wanted litigants, people in barber shops, "your momma," he once told a clerk, to understand his opinions. "Writing in language that people cannot understand is one of the judicial sins of our times," he said. Once he had time to read only the last paragraph of a colleague's dissent, which noted that Black's opinion for the Court was " 'unintelligible.' What's the matter?" Black asked. "Are our words too big or something?"*

His general procedure was to dictate or write a first draft in pencil on a yellow legal pad. He usually did this at home. "He sits at his desk," his wife wrote in 1959, "completely oblivious to anything except working on his dissent. . . . He is a little island, completely surrounded by mountains of books, yellow pages—some of which have been crumbled up—large pieces of eraser crumbs, and many written sheets lying in more or less organized heaps. There is a little buffer or pocket of concentration that hangs over the desk like an aura—an impenetrable light of thought rays going out in every

---

* When a former clerk told Black that one of his opinions appeared long, Black replied, "I think I better go back and look at it with a view to truncating it. (You see, I do know at least one rarely-used word)" (HLB to Vernon Patrick, 1/11/58).

direction." The draft would then be revised and given to his clerk. "See what you can do with this," he would say. Sometimes he added, go find the case that Bill Douglas, for example, wrote concerning, say, peanuts and that came up from the state courts in about, and he would give the approximate year, state and holding. Especially about cases he didn't write, he often remembered everything except the name.

Since the opinion peaked for complexity after the clerk's revisions, they reviewed it together, word for word, taking out commas and every unnecessary word. Often, and especially in early years, Black read it aloud: his inflection made it difficult for any listener to disagree with him. Black breathed life into a clerk's prosaic changes. He wanted this draft, which he considered the second, to be half the length of the first. Then it will be twice as good, he said. But in going over it he often reached a point that excited him, and it was as if he were making a stump speech. The clerk just wrote down Black's words as fast as he could. Black's momentary passion was more than he felt on reflection, and his excesses had to be removed; this partly accounted for, especially in later years, the gloomy language he invoked when he was on the losing side. Sometimes several additional drafts went by before Black felt he had an opinion he wanted to circulate, but not before going over the opinion again to eliminate any syllable not needed. ("Too long," Black replied when asked about a concurring opinion of seventy-five pages. "It'll hurt in the future. You can't tell which part is important.")[6]

The indispensable centrality of clerks in this process made their selection one of the most important decisions any justice made each year. (Each justice had only one clerk, and the chief justice two, until 1946, when Congress authorized adding one more for each judge.) Black's first three clerks were former Frankfurter students, chosen by Felix or his present clerk. After the 1941 term, Hugo determined to change this. He did not have another clerk from Harvard until 1955 (with the exception of Lister Hill's nephew, whose father took Sterling under his wing during World War Two). His first two clerks in 1942 (both southerners)* were called into the service; a third stayed all year. Walton Hamilton of Yale suggested all three, and over the next dozen years a large majority of Black's clerks came from Yale. Black chose his clerks largely on recommendations from friendly law professors and federal judges, and some were the sons of friends.

---

* "What's your name, son?" he asked the second clerk, obviously knowing it full well. "Christian Dixie" came the reply. "Great name to run for office in the South with," Black said (Dixie int.).

His ideal clerk was a liberal, tennis-playing Alabamian or, failing that, someone from the South who led his class at Yale Law School and wanted to go home and do something for the cause. "At first I wanted someone from the South," Black told a clerk in 1959. "Then I wanted the best." "He was vague why he changed," recalled John McNulty, to whom he said this, "but indicated Frankfurter was part of it." All his clerks became virtual members of his family. They were over at the house regularly for work and meals, and he lunched with them in the Court's cafeteria. Better than anyone else they felt the steely crackle of his mind. He viewed the clerk's role as being a student at a graduate law school, with himself the major professor. In a different way but almost as much as his sons, the clerks represented his personal investment in the future. Clerking "is bound to make a man more willing to challenge platitudes generally accepted as infallible truths," Black wrote. He selected the person who "gives the greatest promise of being the most outstanding contributor to the public welfare." This did not mean limiting himself to persons who "want to hold public office." A clerk "should have greater aspirations than that of becoming the most successful lawyer, meaning by that the most highly paid lawyer."[7]*

*   *   *

Life at the Court is like a turtle—it moves slowly and quietly. At least to the New Dealers among the "nine young men," being a Supreme Court justice left them with extra time. Looking for other things to do with their excess energy, some threw themselves into extrajudicial activities of all sorts, from politics to shadow journalism to becoming virtual appendages of the executive branch. Some justices never really acclimate themselves to the Court's pace. Bill Douglas never did. He was a study in contrasts—a man of public strength and of private weakness. His outspoken positions were temperately phrased and he spoke quietly, often with a literary and almost a feline quality; with friends he could burst into a guffaw on little provocation. His manner ranged from introverted and frosty (especially with underlings) to witty and winsome. His humor could be wicked: once Douglas got up

---

* "What is a lawyer, why be one?—394," Black wrote in the back of Tacitus' *Works*, where it was written: "Can we possibly be employed to better purpose, than in the exercise of an art which enables man, upon all occasions, to support the interest of his friend, to protect the rights of the stranger, to defend the cause of the injured, to strike with terror and dismay his open and secret adversaries, himself secure the while, and guarded, as it were, by an imperishable potency?" In the margin he substituted "integrity" for potency" ("A Dialogue Concerning Oratory" in *The Works of Tacitus* [New York, 1869, Oxford trans.], II, 394; HLB Books).

when Frankfurter came into the conference room, gave him a stiff Nazi salute and said, "Heil, Führer!"

Douglas brought to the Court an unmatched financial expertise ("That guy can look at a corporate statement," one justice said, "and tell you in a minute if there's any fornicating going on in the back room"), a gut instinct for civil liberties and a fluid pen. He was a quick study for whom work always came first. Initially "I found the court a very unhappy existence . . . ," he recalled. "It took about two or three years to get caught up in the enthusiasm of the broad group of ideas that the court dealt with." After that, "I was quite happy there."

Black was a big part of the reason. "They just clicked. It was a real friendship from the beginning," said Black's first clerk, Buddy Cooper, who observed it. Like Roosevelt and Joseph P. Kennedy, who sponsored Douglas with FDR, Hugo had that unshakable self-assurance that Douglas lacked. He found Hugo's emotional stability and equanimity about himself comforting and reassuring. And Hugo's candor and unpretentiousness; his fairness and respect for differing views; his ability to work long, hard, and quickly; his loyalty to his beliefs, his friends, and to the institution—all quickly captured Douglas's mind and heart in a way no other justice (or public figure except possibly Roosevelt) had or ever would have. Hugo always took the lead, and Douglas listened as Black talked about how to view Congress from the Court and how to craft opinions with congressional nuances and vibrations in mind when necessary. Before committing himself, Douglas liked to know what Hugo felt and would often go to see him. Occasionally Hugo's subtlety irritated Douglas, and upon returning to his office he would briefly imitate Hugo, mimicking his accent, manner and walk; but these moments quickly passed. When Roosevelt wanted Douglas to leave the Court both before and during the war for a "more active job" involving the national defense, Douglas turned first to Black, who strongly counseled against it. And when Roosevelt nominated Stone for chief justice, Douglas wrote Hugo, "I am sorry that it did not go to you. I thought you *deserved it*. And I know it would strengthen the Court greatly if you were the Chief."[8]*

Douglas had hardly taken his seat before pundits started touting him as a running mate of or successor to Roosevelt. Then and later he adamantly

---

* "It is a burden but at the same time an opportunity for whoever holds the position—I mean an opportunity for service, not merely for the individual," HLB wrote Douglas about the chief justiceship (6/11/41, WOD papers).

maintained that he never wanted to be a candidate. "I had no idea of getting into politics," he told an interviewer in 1962, and "never had any discussion with Roosevelt about me running for any office." He even went as far—in 1944, when there was talk he might join Roosevelt on the ticket—as to draft a statement for possible newspaper use, "In case the unlikely or improbable happened and the [vice-presidential] nomination were offered to me, I would refuse it—I definitely would not accept it." Yet, at the same time, never did he discourage or in any way try to stop the stories—he enjoyed the publicity too much.

Black deeply resented this, the more so since Douglas agreed, when they talked about it with Corcoran and Eliot Janeway of *Time* (who were the prime pushers of Douglas's supposed availability), that if any justice were to leave the Court to run for office, Hugo was the one. And Douglas had also told him, "I want nothing but the opportunity to slug away alongside you for the next 30 years." That Douglas then would even think of leaving the Court to run for office upset Black. "No justice should do that," Hugo said. "Once someone is appointed to this court, he should stay here"—noble thoughts that never stilled Hugo's own political ambitions.[9]*

*   *   *

Black was essentially a political being. Part of his duty, as he saw it, in every position he held was to improve the civic culture, to expand the polity, to facilitate the democratic process. The Court in 1947 upheld the Hatch Act, which prohibited federal employees from engaging in certain political activities, as a way to protect the integrity of the civil service. These workers should not be "political eunuchs," Black said in conference; their "full participation in political affairs" was essential in a democracy. "Legislation which muzzles several million citizens threatens popular government . . . ," he wrote in dissent.

Similarly, courts step into the political process when necessary to guarantee the equality of voting. Gerrymandering electoral districts was an old American tradition. Illinois had not redistricted the state since 1901 and had the most malapportioned congressional districts in the country. One of

* Reports that James Byrnes might run with Roosevelt in 1944 especially annoyed Black. He felt he deserved the nod over Byrnes and liked to recall Wyoming senator Joseph O'Mahoney's jibe about Byrnes as "just a fixer." Black was certainly aware of Byrnes's feeling, if not specifically his remark to Jackson, that in the Senate Black had been "a lone wolf" who "oftentimes could not get anyone to go along with him but that in the Supreme Court he had three votes nearly all the time" (Janeway, "Douglas"; Blum, *Wallace,* 250).

the appellants in *Colegrove v. Green* lived in a district of over 900,000 people; other districts had as few as 112,000 people. Was this a matter for courts to consider?

Chief Justice Stone thought not: the only question to him was how to affirm the lower court that had denied Colegrove's claim. Similarly, Black insisted that relief be denied. "I find it difficult to make of this a controversy," he said in conference. "I assume the court below acted on the basis that there is no cause of action. I don't want to get involved in control of elections in states and nation. I didn't think courts had power to make them [states] act. If courts had power," the plaintiffs "have made a clear case." Several justices expressed the view that, as Reed put it, "this is something that is left to Congress." With Jackson not participating and Murphy passing, the Court initially voted 6–1 to deny Colegrove's petition for relief. Only Douglas would have granted it: this is "not a political question. It is equitable," he said. Stone assigned the opinion to Black. Immediately, "the clerks for the liberal justices—Black, Douglas and Murphy—ganged up and put pressure on him," Black's clerk David Haber recalled. "It made him feel uncomfortable." Black spoke to Douglas and changed his vote. Four days later, Stone reassigned the case to Frankfurter. "Courts ought not to enter this political thicket," Frankfurter wrote for a plurality. "The remedy for unfairness in districting is to secure state legislatures that will apportion properly, or to invoke the ample powers of Congress." How the people could obtain a remedy from the body that perpetuated the abuse was never explained: it is to admit there is no remedy. *

Black's belief that he was now right increased as he worked on his opinion. What came through in his discussion was his egalitarianism—his belief that the Court was devaluing a basic element of democracy, the equality of each person's franchise—and his populist background. Malapportionment in Alabama, he long remembered, had given a "small bloc of Whig planters" disproportionate influence in government. "They thought I was crazy," he later said of his colleagues when he circulated his opinion. Douglas and Murphy did not. They joined his dissent, which argued that the matter was indeed justiciable: the petitioners were asserting rights granted by Article

---

* Frankfurter had a majority because of the vote of the other "liberal" justice, Rutledge. Rutledge's preference was largely tactical: he concurred because the short time to the 1946 election would have hurt more than helped the petitioners (and have rendered the case moot); and he was unwilling to have an undermanned Court decide an issue of such importance, fearing that a full, reconstituted bench would reverse it, which he thought would be a disastrous blow to the Court's prestige. (Rutledge told this to Irving Brant; see Brant's "Introduction" to Harper, *Rutledge,* xv; and Brant to Harper, 11/7/61, Brant papers.)

I, Section 2, of the Constitution which provides that congressmen "shall be chosen . . . by the People of the several States" and, more fundamentally, by the equal protection clause. Federal courts have an obligation to exercise their equity powers in order to give "all the people an equally effective voice in electing their representatives as is essential under a free government." The Illinois law at issue resulted "in a wholly indefensible discrimination against petitioners and all other voters in heavily populated areas in heavily populated districts." The equal protection clause "does not permit the States to pick out certain qualified citizens or groups of citizens and deny them the right to vote at all."

Certainly Black had taken a novel position, yet it was one whose import could hardly be overestimated. Each common coin of democracy deserves to be counted equally.[10]

One of the many lessons World War Two taught was that democracy requires unimpeded discourse to survive. Company towns traditionally try to control what residents can know. Black had seen many such towns in Alabama, going back to the miners' strike in 1908. *Marsh v. Alabama* involved a company town, Chicakasaw, Alabama, similar in all respects to an ordinary municipality but wholly owned by a private corporation. Company regulations prohibited any solicitation on town streets. Nevertheless, a member of Jehovah's Witnesses distributed religious literature in the business section and was convicted under a state criminal trespass law. "It makes no difference to me" who owns the town, Black said in conference. "A person has a right to be there and has a right to speak his thoughts. I call this a political subdivision."

Citizens in the town were entitled to the same First Amendment rights against the town's owners that they would have against the government of a municipality, Black held for the Court in early 1946 in overturning the conviction, the first time property rights were held not to be all-controlling in a company town. "The public in either case has an identical interest in the functioning of the community in such manner that the channels of communication remain free." These people must, like all other citizens, "make decisions which affect the welfare of community and nation. To act as good citizens they must be informed . . . their information must be uncensored."

Black's clerk had added in the draft, "The [First Amendment] liberties include both the right of inhabitants of company towns to keep outsiders from invading their dwellings as well as the right to receive them." Then Black dropped the idea without explanation. The concept that *recipients* as well as purveyors of information have rights—a fresh notion—was already implicit in his opinion and explicit in his thought.

"It would be strange indeed . . . ," he wrote in a 1945 case, "if the grave concern for freedom of the press which prompted adoption of the First Amendment should be read as a command that the government was without power to protect that freedom." This came in *Associated Press v. United States*. The government had sued on antitrust grounds, claiming that the AP's bylaws prevented nonmembers from using its services. For the Court, Black held that "arrangements or combinations designed to stifle competition cannot be immunized by adopting a membership device accomplishing that purpose." The First Amendment "rests on the assumption that the widest possible dissemination of information from diverse and antagonistic sources is essential to the welfare of the public, that a free press is a condition of a free society. . . . Freedom to publish is guaranteed by the Constitution, but freedom to combine to keep others from publishing is not."[*]

Slowly Black—"Mr. Jefferson," Frankfurter once called him, likely in connection with the AP case—was developing a theory of the First Amendment consistent with his view of what democracy means and demands.[11]

---

[*] At the time, Black was reading Polybius' history of Rome, and he likened attempts to suppress liberty in the United States to Roman history. He liked to talk about the period of Tribunes (of Martinis) (Haber int.).

CHAPTER 23

BOMBSHELL FROM NUREMBERG

CHIEF JUSTICE STONE was losing his grip by 1945. His energies and mental sharpness were noticeably lessening, and he was rapidly becoming more conservative. The bent of his legal thinking had initially attracted Jackson, but now Jackson was irritated with and curt toward Stone. "Any fool would know that this should be reversed," Jackson would say. Since Black's ideas were now dominating the conference, to Jackson that "fool" was Black.

If the bitterness in conference had taken on a tone of personal venom, a dinner in March 1945 honoring Black increased it. The Southern Conference for Human Welfare once again presented him its Thomas Jefferson award. Senate Majority Leader Alben Barkley presided, reading a letter from President Roosevelt. Administration and liberal luminaries spoke. Mrs. Roosevelt attended, along with much of political and official Washington, nine hundred persons in all. In retrospect it was the last hurrah of the New Deal. All the justices were invited. Reed, Douglas, Murphy and Rutledge came (with Douglas and Murphy listed among the patrons); Stone, who did not believe in such tributes, Roberts, Frankfurter and Jackson did not. (Another sharply divided "decision.") Jackson felt the dinner was "grossly improper." If this had happened in the "old days" and a "big business association" had hailed a conservative justice, he said, "every liberal in the country would have screamed his head off over it."[1]

One week later came the *Jewell Ridge* case. The same question of what constituted working time in underground mines had been before the Court the previous year. In *Tennessee Coal Company v. Muscoda Local* the miners claimed they should be paid on a portal-to-portal basis—from the time they entered the mines until they left them—which would entitle them to substantial overtime pay without violating War Labor Board guidelines. The Court agreed, with Justice Murphy holding that underground travel in iron ore mines constituted work and thus was included within the meaning of a "compensable work week" in the Fair Labor Standards Act. That bill, of course, was Black's baby: he had conceived it, sponsored it and helped draft its final version, which the Senate was considering when he was appointed to the Court.

In *Jewell Ridge* "Black was very, very strong and vocal" on behalf of the miners at conference, recalled Douglas. He thought the act covered the amount of travel time the miners spent while Jackson was "very vociferous in thinking that it [did] not. . . . There was pounding of tables," not unusual in itself. But this "seemed, for some reason or other, to stir Jackson very, very, very deeply. Both of them poured it out with great vehemence and emphasis and at great length. . . . " A 5–4 majority agreed with Stone that the basic wage paid to coal miners took travel time into account. He assigned the opinion to Jackson but when Reed quickly changed his mind, Black, the senior justice in the majority, gave Murphy the assignment. "The sole issue," Murphy wrote, "is whether any different result must be reached as regards underground travel in bituminous coal mines." So phrased and with *Tennessee Coal* as precedent, the result was obvious.

Murphy circulated his opinion on April 5, 1945. The next day he sent a note to Jackson, who was writing a dissent (after having concurred separately in *Tennessee Coal*): "Some of the brethren . . . spoke of offering a motion tomorrow to hand down on Monday the judgment in portal-to-portal. I don't want you rushed . . . take all the time you want. But I thought you would want to know how some feel about delaying this case." To Jackson this meant Black and Douglas. "What is the rush?" he wondered. "Maybe they have changed their minds since negotiations ended," Murphy replied. "I rushed my opinion to accommodate others." Negotiations between the government and the United Mine Workers collapsed April 6, one day after Murphy circulated his draft opinion, but resumed the next day. On April 10 the government seized the mines, and the following day a new agreement was signed, providing full pay for underground travel, subject to the approval of the War Labor Board, which was waiting for the Court's decision. Rushing opinions for policy reasons was not uncommon. Frankfurter had recently done so, and the Court would soon do it again; the losers always resented the pressure.

That the decision did not come down at this time was only because it could no longer help the miners, Jackson privately charged. He believed that Black was trying to mastermind a shocking and sinister judicial impropriety, manipulating the judiciary to drive it toward his economic views, a form of "collectivism" mistaken for liberalism, "far to the left of anything that I had associated with the New Deal," Jackson later wrote. And, he contended, Black was using the justices who went along with him as his pawns, controlling their votes from his hip pocket.

Jackson's cutting dissent pitted Justice Black against Senator Black. As proof that Congress had not intended the Fair Labor Standards Act to interfere with collective bargaining agreements, Jackson cited both the report on the bill of the Senate Education and Labor Committee, which Black chaired, and his remarks on the Senate floor. (Jackson never mentioned his own role as a draftsman of the act who testified on its behalf before the joint congressional hearings chaired by Black.) Stone, who joined Jackson's dissent, thought this legislative history was not very relevant. Murphy warned Jackson that he was quoting Black out of context. His quotations, Black told the Court, related to an "entirely different" version of the bill than the one finally enacted. Jackson's inference was "wholly unjustified," and if the dissent were unchanged, "it will not be a fair representation of the facts." Jackson did not change his opinion. He was, he later admitted, "seething."[2]*

In late May the coal company filed a petition for rehearing, claiming that Black should not have sat, because his former partner Crampton Harris had argued for the union. Jackson insisted that Black disqualify himself. This had not been discussed at the original conference—indeed no one had mentioned it. "I think the thing would have been dismissed as ludicrous," Douglas said, "as silly, as something not worthy even of considering, but for Bob Jackson, who for some reason or other was steamed up. How he thought

* Jackson had earlier aimed pointed remarks toward Black. In January 1945, he held for the Court that the Fair Labor Standards Act did not cover Western Union messenger boys, since Congress had refrained from banning child labor "employed directly in interstate commerce"—"purposely," he wrote in *Western Union v. Lenroot*. To call telegrams "goods" and their transmission a "shipment" was "a ridiculous job of construction," he said in conference (Fine, *Murphy*, 316). In his opinion he quoted extensively, and by name, from Black's Senate hearings. "Everything Jackson wrote can be taken apart," Hugo said, asking Murphy to write a dissent (Gressman int.). Murphy did, charging Jackson with "fastidious adherence to linguistic purism" and overlooking Western Union's procedures; Black, Douglas and Rutledge joined Murphy. "Perfect!" Black wrote Murphy. "Particularly do I like to see a man's own weapon turned against him" (Howard, *Murphy*, 387).

anything would be accomplished by getting Hugo Black out of the case is difficult [to understand]. Because if Hugo had not sat, the case would have been a firm four to four. The result would have been the same": the lower court decision would have been affirmed. But Jackson did not want the Court to be put in a position of seemingly approving Black's sitting in a case in which he felt Black should not.

Jackson had raised a singularly touchy matter. Every justice has tradi- tionally been the keeper of his own conscience when a potential conflict of interest arises. Black had disqualified himself in all cases in which the Federal Communications Commission was involved, however remotely, because Clif- ford Durr, his wife's brother-in-law, was a member. Otherwise, with ex- ceedingly rare exceptions, he sat, as was his duty, ruling both for and against counsel and parties he knew. To deal with the rehearing petition, Stone suggested a compromise per curiam opinion stating that the Court lacks authority to pass upon its members' participation in cases. "If this goes down," Black told Stone, "please put the names of the justices who agree to it, and leave mine out." He wanted silence. The others in the *Jewell Ridge* majority agreed.

The next week, in mid-June, a donnybrook of classic proportions ensued. "That was quite a stormy conference," Douglas recalled. Jackson was "highly personal . . . highly emotional, and it was a feud. Not a feud in the sense that Black was feuding against Jackson or retaliating, because he was always perfectly proper in his relationships. He never was personally vindictive. I've never seen him do a vindictive thing in his life. But Jackson was quite the opposite." A "very bright, able, strong fellow with his head on backwards," Black described him, "a great argufier," naturally combative, who "just loved to fight. He went around picking fights. He beat up on people, pummeled poor Murphy." Several other justices felt Jackson was unstable, a walking time bomb in a way, overheated. Rutledge said that he could foresee the position any justice would take except for Jackson. "Bob's just too mercurial. You never know what he's going to do."

After Stone canvassed the Court about the rehearing petition, he said, "We'll deny. It has no substance." Frankfurter spoke up: "This is a little peculiar. The motion is basically a motion for disqualification. It's not prop- erly addressed to the court. The court has no authority to consider it. I want to write a short paragraph pointing out that it should have been addressed to the justice involved." This was aimed directly at Black. Hugo kept his outward calm. "At this level of discussion Black was always the perfect Southern gentleman," noted Douglas. "He never, never got personal.

Top and bottom: Two homes: Hugo Black's birthplace, near Ashland in Clay County, Alabama; and the Federalist-style house in the Old Town section of Alexandria, Virginia, that he bought in 1939. (Life *magazine and the Library of Congress*) *Center:* Hugo at about age six with his parents, William LaFayette (Faet) and Martha Ardella (Della) Toland Black, and his oldest sister, Leora,on their porch in Ashland. (*Associated Press*)

OFFICE OF
GRAND

REALM OF ALABAMA
1801 FIRST NATIONAL BANK BUILDING
BIRMINGHAM

July 9 — 1925.

Mr. Jas Hamilton, Klizrd.

Birmingham Ala.

Dear Sir & Klansman,

Beg to tender you herewith
my resignation as a member of the
Knights of the Ku Klux Klan, effectiv
from this date on—

Yours I.T.S.U.B.

Hugo L. Black

Top: Resignation letter from the
Ku Klux Klan, which Black
had joined in September 1923.
(*Pittsburgh Post-Gazette*)

Bottom: Hugo Black as a young man.
(*Josephine Black Pesaresi*)

Top: "Now when did you say that dinner was?": the investigating senator in 1935. His close friend Sherman Minton is at right. (*Collection of the Supreme Court of the United States*) *Bottom left:* As jurors, opposing lawyers, and judges saw him in court in the early 1920s. (*Josephine Black Pesaresi*) *Bottom right:* Josephine Foster Black in the early 1930s. (*Bachrach /Josephine Black Pesaresi*)

Top left: Black explaining his membership in the Klan over radio in October 1937, three days before he first sat on the Supreme Court. (*AP/Wide World Photos*)
Top right: The nomination which Franklin D. Roosevelt casually asked Black if he could fill in. FDR didn't date it. (*University of Alabama Law School*)
Bottom: Cartoonists had a field day when Black's former Klan membership was revealed to the nation. This cartoon by the *Washington Post*'s Elderman was titled "Reform of the Judiciary."
(*The Washington Post*)

The White House.
19

To the
Senate of the United States.

I nominate Hugo L. Black
of Alabama to be an Associate Justice
of the Supreme Court of the United States.

Franklin D. Roosevelt

Reform Of The Judiciary.

Top: The New Deal Court, 1943: (front row) Stanley Reed, Owen J. Roberts, Chief Justice Harlan F. Stone, Hugo Black, Felix Frankfurter; (back row) Robert H. Jackson, William O. Douglas, Frank Murphy, Wiley Rutledge. (*Harris & Ewing/Collection of the Supreme Court of the United States*) *Bottom left:* William O. Douglas, the friend and ally whom Black called "a genius in his own right." (*Peter Ehrenhaft/Collection of the Supreme Court of the United States*) *Bottom right:* Felix Frankfurter, the intellectual adversary who said Black had "the best mind on the Court." (*Peter Ehrenhaft/Collection of the Supreme Court of the United States*)

Top left: With his children, Sterling, Josephine (JoJo) and Hugo, Jr., and Elizabeth in 1966.
Top right: Hugo and Elizabeth on their wedding day in September 1957. *Bottom:* On his other court, in 1971, three months before his death. He was always ready for the ball on either court.
(*All from Josephine Black Pesaresi*)

Top: The Supreme Court in 1965 and 1966: (front row) Tom Clark, Hugo Black, Chief Justice Earl Warren, William O. Douglas, John M. Harlan; (back row) Byron R. White, William J. Brennan, Jr., Potter Stewart, Abe Fortas. (*Josephine Black Pesaresi*) *Bottom:* With Lyndon Johnson at the White House, 1965. (*Collection of the Lyndon Baines Johnson Library*)

Top: Swearing in Thurgood Marshall as Solicitor General, 1965. Unidentified person, Thurgood, Jr., Cecelia Marshall, Lyndon Johnson, unidentified person, Marshall, Black, Elizabeth Black. A bust of John F. Kennedy is in the background. (*Collection of the Lyndon Baines Johnson Library*)
Bottom: The justices after Black's death and the retirement, one week earlier, of John Harlan. (*Atlanta Constitution*)

. . . Where Do We Go from Here?'

He always kept it at the purely professional level," impersonally strenuous in his assaults in pursuit of his principles. "Personal attacks do not make a favorable impression," he believed. "They do not win any *new* votes." ("From long experience," he told Hugo, Jr., "I can tell you that there is no benefit at all to be derived from getting angry with someone.")* "Felix," he now said, "you have no basis for saying that and for wanting to write an opinion." It seemed to be just another chapter in their ongoing battles.

Jackson had not yet spoken. He found Black's comments outrageous and felt Frankfurter was just being a stickler for proprieties, he later admitted. But now he said, "If Felix doesn't write a concurrence, I'll write it." He made it clear that he was in no way willing to imply approval of Black's role in sitting. Black reacted "with fiery scorn to what he regarded as an open and gratuitous insult, a slur upon his personal and judicial honor," journalist Doris Fleeson later wrote. "Nor did he bother to conceal his contempt." According to Jackson, Black said that "any opinion which discussed the subject at all would mean a 'declaration of war.' " Jackson replied that he would "not stand for any more of his bullying" and would have to write a separate opinion "to keep self-respect in the face of his threats." There were no smiles when the conference ended.

The Court denied the rehearing. Jackson issued a statement, revised by Frankfurter, who joined him, noting that he knew of "no authority" by which "a majority of the Court" could "under any circumstances . . . exclude one of its duly commissioned Justices from sitting or voting in any case" and therefore indicating that Black should not have sat. Since none of that majority was willing to reconsider his vote, "no good" could come of reargument. The denial was issued June 18, 1945. That day Jackson left for Europe as chief Allied prosecutor for the Nuremberg war crimes trials. The new president, Harry S Truman, made the appointment.[3]

" 'President Roosevelt is dead.' When these words sounded in my ears, I repeated them—I could say no more." So Black wrote in the *Washington Star* three days after Roosevelt's death on April 12, 1945. Like most Amer-

---

* "There was no fierceness directed to his opposition—only to their ideas," Douglas wrote. "I never heard him say an unkind word about any Justice, no matter how deeply opposed the two were. He never indulged in any personal aspersions, no matter how heated the arguments" (*Go East*, 450). "When he is convinced," John Frank observed in 1949, "he is cool steel hard . . . he is absolutely impervious to any blows that may fall upon him . . . His temper is usually in close control, but he fights, and his words may occasionally have a terrible edge. He can be a rough man in an argument" (*Black*, 134–35).

icans, he found it hard to believe: it had been so long since there had been another president. The Court was part of the procession in Washington, and Black went to the funeral at Hyde Park. "The faces of the people along the way," he wrote a friend afterward, "reminded me of Claude Bowers' pen picture of the days following the assassination of President Lincoln."*

The night after Roosevelt died, Black dined with Claude Pepper, Thurman Arnold, Tom Corcoran, Lister Hill, and their wives, and Ben Cohen. They were all thinking about how it affected the country and them politically (although not necessarily in that order). All knew Harry Truman well enough, but none had an inkling how he would perform in office. Hugo told Cliff Durr that he was not "a big enough man for the job." Within a fortnight Truman offered Jackson the Nuremberg post. Jackson hesitated but briefly before accepting: it presented a splendid opportunity to escape the continuing dissension enveloping the Court. He took an unprecedented official leave of absence, giving little thought to the fact that he would be executing an explicitly executive function in apparent violation of the separation of powers. He was led to believe it would be a short affair, that he would prosecute Nazis during the summer and receive the verdict in time to return for the Court's next term, in October 1945.

That term would begin without Justice Owen Roberts. Since early 1944 he had retreated into himself, coming out of his shell to oppose anything Black, Douglas, Murphy and Rutledge favored. His feeling toward Hugo came through in a letter he wrote Frankfurter in September that year about a recently decided case: "And when I guess that maybe . . . those rich and crooked s.o.b.'s of the glass industry . . . think they are honest men, I just turn Black in the face." In July 1945 Roberts retired—without ever receiving even a lukewarm version of the traditional letter of appreciation for his service from his colleagues.

He had told Roosevelt of his plan to retire. After consulting only with Attorney General Francis Biddle, FDR decided to name Herbert F. Goodrich, a respected, liberal federal appellate judge and a longtime friend of Biddle's from Philadelphia. The nomination was on Roosevelt's desk, ready to be sent to the Senate, when he died. History changed when it fell to Truman to make.

In mid-September, Sherman Minton asked Black to speak to Truman

---

* Black never deviated from what he said on television in 1968 about Roosevelt: "I thought what most of the people did. I liked him. I thought he was magnificent. . . . He was our greatest man."

on his behalf. "What can be done is anybody's guess, but my fear is very little," Hugo wrote Josephine. "Anyhow, I could not refuse Shay's request." By the time Hugo saw Truman the next morning, he had already nominated Senator Harold H. Burton of Ohio, his former colleague on the Truman Committee, "*the* Committee," as Truman called it in inscribing a copy of his *Memoirs* to Burton, whose wife he called Skipper. Nevertheless Truman "insisted that I give him my views which I did," Hugo told Josephine. "He thinks Burton is a genuine liberal all the way, which I doubt, although he is less hidebound than most Republicans. He said he would be greatly pleased if my apprehensions about Burton proved to be wrong, and I told him that I would be too. He expressed himself as believing that I was the only man on the Court whose views he could wholly depend on, and asked that I talk to him from time to time, which I agreed to do. Notwithstanding all this I am disappointed that he did not appoint Shay."[4]

Black had known Truman since 1934, when he stumped for him in Missouri as part of his general strategy of campaigning for aspiring senators, but it took time for their political rapport to cross the line to personal friendship. As Hugo basked in the spotlight during the public utilities investigation in July 1935, Truman, writing his wife, included Black among "several so-called people's friends in the Senate," which "would be in a hell of a fix if there were not some good old work horses here who really cause the Senate to function. . . . There isn't a so-called progressive who does anything but talk."

Truman quickly changed his view, however. "You don't know how much I appreciated [it]," he wrote after Black called to congratulate him on reelection in 1940. "Hope to see you before very long." And the next year they conferred about Truman's investigation of defense waste and confusion. First they talked briefly at Justice Brandeis's home. Truman then came to Black's house for several lengthy discussions. He accepted Hugo's advice about how to run the investigation and Hugo had "only praise" for Truman's "excellent work." By 1945 they had developed a mutually high opinion of each other. "I think the country is to be congratulated on the fact that we have a man like Justice Black on the Supreme Court," Truman wrote early that April while still vice president. Later that year, as president, he said he regarded Black as "the best man on the Court."

Black admired how skillfully Truman handled the presidential succession. After attending a White House dinner in August 1945, he wrote Josephine that Truman's "conduct was as natural as it would have been in Independence, Missouri. His handshake with each person was hearty and behind it a smile which bespoke genuine pleasure that the guest had found it possible to come. The country boy was at home. If he can keep this attitude, his success is certain." But still Truman was no Roosevelt: Black always spoke warmly of Truman but it was nothing more than plain warmth. When he talked about Roosevelt, his eyes glittered. FDR to him was in a special class.[5]

With Jackson in Nuremberg the Court limped along with eight judges. His absence annoyed his colleagues and increased their burden. Black wrote more opinions both overall and for a majority that term than in any other. He, Stone and Douglas thought Jackson should have resigned before taking on what Stone called a "high-grade lynching party." They (and likely the rest of the justices as well) believed the trial was illegal by American standards. Black always thought the defendants were being tried for ex post facto crimes and that no one should be tried for acts that were not punishable when committed. "What a mistake those trials were," he later said. "If you want to punish people like that, take them out and shoot them." "One of the most evil effects of the affair was, I think, that it diluted the general meaning of 'judicial proceeding,' " he wrote in the margin of Charles E. Wyzanski, Jr.'s, 1965 book, *Whereas*. Was this a case of "disguising vengeance under the facade of legality"? Black: "I think we did." Were the proceedings "a model of forensic fairness"? "I think not." And as to Wyzanski's conclusion that the world "has every reason to be profoundly grateful to" the lawyers who "persisted until they demonstrated the justice of the *ad hoc* method adopted at Nuremberg," Black wrote, "I wholly disagree."

"There will be much public interest for a short time when Jackson's Court (?) sentences some of the Nazis to death," Hugo told Josephine in late August 1945. But logistics and preparations alone took months, lives were put on hold, wives and children left behind. A miasma surrounded the trials. "Almost everybody there acted in a shocking way," observed Warner Gardner, who had served under Jackson as solicitor general. "People lost their balance, their rationality. They became preoccupied with their task. It was the only thing in their lives." Jackson was the prime example. He grew increasingly irascible, feeling isolated, and feared for his safety. His cross-examination of Goering, central to his case, flopped tragically; the master advocate was not a skilled trial lawyer. The inevitable bickering and argument within his large, talented staff over how to present the case took its toll. By the spring, as the trials dragged on, his impatience was noticeable.

One judge felt he was "unhappy and beaten"; another said his nerves were "frayed." "I thought Bob was very nervous and agitated, not the same he had been at home," said Claude Pepper, who went to Nuremberg as his guest. "He was cordial but very much on edge, not as relaxed."[6] Jackson had lost his balance wheel.

On April 22, 1946, while preparing to deliver an opinion in open court, Chief Justice Stone suffered a stroke; he died a few hours later. "I expect a lot of casting of lots to divide the clothes of Christ," said Tom Corcoran. "There might be some hesitancy to attend funerals." But "Washington adores a funeral—especially if it ushers in a vacancy," as Jackson, the prime contender for the spot, later wrote. Truman wasted little time trying to fill it. He immediately consulted with party leaders and with former Chief Justice Hughes, who recommended both Jackson and a Republican, New York University Law School dean and New Jersey lawyer Arthur T. Vanderbilt, soon to be that state's chief justice. Truman thought very highly of Jackson— "one good man" doing "an outstanding job" at Nuremberg—whose experience and talents, he said at the time, made him think that he should promote Jackson to be his successor if he did not run in 1948. Now Truman was strongly considering nominating him for chief justice.

Two events soon gave Truman pause. He called Black to ask whether Jackson would make a good chief justice. "Douglas would make a much better one," Hugo replied. And Lister Hill called Truman to make an appointment. He made it on his own. "I'd do anything on earth for Hugo," he once said. "That sounds just like Lister," noted Claude Pepper. "He and Hugo were so close." They "were eating together, associating together all the time," recalled Hugh Rozelle, Black's nephew, who was then working for Hill. "But Hugo would've never told Lister to go get the Chief Justiceship for him. If Lister said he was going to do it, Hugo would have never responded. He might have smiled."*

"I have urged Hugo's appointment as strongly as I could," Hill wrote a constituent after meeting with Truman. "I shall do everything further that I possibly can for Hugo." Senator John Bankhead could not attend the meeting, but noted that Hill "made as strong a statement as he could, for

* "Like he did," Rozelle continued, "when we were sitting on the front porch in Ashland before the war, talking about his being president. My parents, sister, Josephine and I were talking, and Hugo was smiling very broadly."

both of us, in support of Justice Black. He did not, however, receive any positive encouragement." Hugo did not mind. "The administrative work of the Chief Justice is a very heavy burden," he wrote Sherman Minton, "and while I could perform it if I were compelled to do so, it is not the kind of task which adds glamour to the position." He felt he was too militant a New Dealer and too publicly associated with it to be appointed, and told friends he was not a candidate. But "it is important that the right type of man be named for the place. . . . The appointment made, however, might have considerable effect upon my future course."[7]

Knowing this, Hill also told Truman that if certain contingencies Black had seen mentioned in the newspapers occurred, meaning the appointment of Jackson, the Supreme Court would no longer be a place where he could usefully serve. "Two members" of the Court might resign—it was not necessary to identify them—Drew Pearson had written in his column before Stone was buried. His likely source was Corcoran. Corcoran, Hill and Thurman Arnold knew Black's feelings about the Court better than anyone else off it (as Corcoran and Arnold knew Douglas's). "I think either one of them would resign and quit if the other man went in," Corcoran said.

Was Black really serious? Would he forsake the Court—the institution to which he had devoted himself for almost a decade and which upheld those ideas he increasingly cherished—just because he disliked somone so much? Granted, he had talked with Corcoran the year before about retiring early, and now he did not look forward to working with a person as chief justice who, when he later compared him to Frankfurter, he thought was malicious in a way Felix wasn't; and who was personally motivated (he claimed that Jackson voted a certain way because others did), while Frankfurter was just misguided. He attributed most of his problems with Jackson to what Jackson had done. There was something of a bully in Jackson, he felt, and this aroused Black's pugnaciousness. Yet—especially because he was working together with Douglas—could it all have been a bluff, part of a strategy to force Truman not to appoint Jackson? In combat politicians use many techniques to reach their goal. Survival is most important, and Black always protected himself.

Tommy the Cork swung into action, talking with senators, political operatives and journalists. He was in continual touch with Hill and told Justices Douglas and Reed what he found out. He did not call Black from his office: Truman intensely disliked Corcoran and was wiretapping his phone for political surveillance. Instead, Corcoran's law partner James Rowe, formerly one of Roosevelt's chief assistants, contacted the highest levels of the administration directly. Labor made its voice heard for Black. But few people of influence pressed Jackson's claims. He will not be appointed, Robert Hannegan, postmaster general and chairman of the Democratic National Committee, assured a visitor in early May. A Jackson nomination was quickly sidetracked.

Other than not wanting Jackson, Black had no particular preference for the center chair. His first choice was Douglas (who did not want it), then Reed (who did so very much); either "would have been perfectly satisfactory," he said, and Lloyd K. Garrison, former law school dean and National Labor Relations Board chairman, would have been acceptable. But Black thought it "unfortunate" that a justice should be "a candidate for chief justice. The court in my judgment is not helped by any member's candidacy for office." None of these candidates was a likely appointee, especially after Truman called in Owen Roberts, who told him for the first time of the rift within the Court. Who, then, would it be? On May 3 Truman told the press he was "in no hurry" to make the appointment."[8]

Matters took a new turn with the publication of Doris Fleeson's syndicated column on May 16. Entitled "Supreme Court Feud: Inside Story of Jackson-Black Battle Laid Before a Harassed President," the article breached the confidentiality of the Court's conference by describing the deliberations in *Jewell Ridge*. Fleeson described Black's angry reaction to Jackson's statement on the Court's denial of the rehearing petition, which she quoted at length. "This inside story of the clash of strong wills has been laid before President Truman . . . a southerner himself," who "was quick to perceive the affront which Mr. Black feels he suffered. He [Truman] has confided to a Senator: 'Black says he will resign if I make Jackson Chief Justice and tell the reasons why. Jackson says the same about Black.' "

Who told Fleeson this? "Somebody who was present at that conference table," Jackson later said. That could well have been Black. Fleeson was a good friend of his and Josephine's, and often came over to the house for dinners and parties. Whoever it was, the reaction was immediate. Douglas spoke with Truman by telephone the next day, perhaps reinforcing the strong implication he and Black might resign. This and Truman's earlier call to Black are the only recorded contacts any justice had with Truman during this period. And it is likely this is what Black was referring to when he told a former law clerk that "another Justice," whom he did not name, had played the "role" of "having opposed and possibly prevented Jackson's appointment

as Chief Justice." Soon the president again saw Owen Roberts, who recommended former federal judge Robert P. Patterson and Fred Vinson, secretary of the treasury and Truman's close friend. He spoke with Vinson,
James Byrnes, now secretary of state, and Attorney General Tom C. Clark,
who also called former Roosevelt adviser Samuel I. Rosenman.

In Nuremberg, absorbed in trying an arduous and exhausting case, Jackson knew little of these political machinations. On May 17, however, his
Washington lawyer friend Francis M. Shea wrote him: "I understand that
for a few hours it seemed a sure thing for you. Then, Black got word to the
President that there would be a row if you were appointed. At this he began
to make wide inquiries and to appreciate, perhaps exaggerate, the rifts in
the Court." Despite Jackson's apparent belief that he should be offered the
post because Roosevelt had seemingly promised it, nobody was spearheading
his longing for it. In late May, a lawyer on his Washington staff sent him a
copy of the Fleeson article. Jackson then drafted a four-page memorandum
for Truman setting out his view of the "case." He did not send it.[9]

Truman nominated Vinson on June 6 almost by a process of elimination.
"We had some growing pains with Fred . . . ," recalled Tom Clark. "Some
sources seemed to think Vinson was more political than he was judicial."
But that did not bother Truman or Clark: "We had to figure out just who
would be the best peacemaker," and there were few better in government
than Vinson. After a decade of close friendship, he enjoyed Truman's unlimited confidence and was now the president's "favorite poker companion."
If his jowls and his heavily hooded and pouched eyes made him look like a
"hungover sheep," they concealed a shrewd competence. Nobody had spoken
to him about going on the Court, Vinson told Corcoran in early May, and
he wasn't "too interested." During a reception at the White House in early
June, Truman asked him to step outside on the balcony with him. "Fred,
how would you like to be Chief Justice?" "That's just about the greatest
honor a man could aspire to," Vinson replied. "Well, you *may* be." At that,
Vinson recounted, he knew he was going to be or Truman would not have
mentioned it at all. Then Truman told Vinson he wanted him to serve as
chief justice. Vinson did not have much time to decline even if he wanted
to, for an hour later Truman sent his name to the Senate. Vinson accepted
as much out of loyalty to his friend as for anything else. "Once the President
heard about the problems in the Court, I rather doubt he seriously considered
anyone else," said Clark Clifford, his closest assistant.[10]

When news of the appointment reached Nuremberg, Jackson redrafted his unsent statement to Truman. His frustration, hopes and ambition had boiled over, and he could not control himself. Malice ran through the cable, even watered down. After congratulating Truman on his nomination of Vinson, Jackson pointed to the rumors of Black's threats to resign if he were named: "I would be loath to believe that you would concede to any man a veto over court appointments. . . . The alternative impression sought to be created is that something sinister has been revealed to you which made me unfit for Chief Justice. If that were true, I am also unfit for Associate Justice." He recounted at length his side of the *Jewell Ridge* story and closed by noting that unless Truman suggested otherwise, he would be "compelled" to ask the president to release the statement.

"I am afraid you have been grossly misinformed," Truman cabled Jackson immediately. "I have not discussed the question of the appointment of a new Chief Justice with any member of the Court. I received no information from anyone that even insinuated that you were unfit for promotion. There may have been some newspaper comment regarding differences existing within the Court, but I took no notice of them nor did they enter my decision in any way. I did not see the [Fleeson] article . . . nor had I ever heard of it before. Justice Black has given me no information either orally or in writing on this subject. The reputation and the position of the Court are of paramount interest to me and no purpose can be served by making this controversy public."

Jackson did not think so. Consulting only with his son, two years out of law school, and with his close friend Gordon Dean, both of whom were on his staff and neither of whom tried to dissuade him, he released the statement, now addressed to the chairmen of the Senate and House judiciary committees. He did not notify Truman. Deleting the more personal references to Black, Jackson further breached the confidence of the conference room to focus on *Jewell Ridge*. (He justified these revelations on the ground that Fleeson had already done so and that he had to set the record straight.) Black, he wrote, had threatened a "declaration of war" and had now "apparently made good his threat." Jackson wanted the practice of having former law partners arguing cases "stopped. If it is ever repeated while I am on the bench, I will make my Jewell Ridge opinion look like a letter of recommendation by comparison." Before leaving for a vacation in Denmark, he told the press: "I prefer to have my escutcheon clean."

The cable jolted political Washington and commentators nationwide. It was, and remains, unprecedented. Black was dumbfounded, nearly disbelieving when he heard about it. "Bob shot from the hip," he told a relative. His colleagues' remarks were in character. "Too bad, but it's just like Bob," Rutledge said. "I'm not surprised." He was "thoroughly disgusted with Jackson," wrote one law clerk after talking with him several times. Murphy sent an understanding message to Black. Reed thought that the statement "will have some unfortunate results. Open sores are hard to heal," as he wrote Frankfurter. "[Bob] and Hugo will be enemies while both serve. If Bob resigns, as I fear he will to avoid this unpleasantness, we lose greatly. There is no third alternative to me." Frankfurter said, so another clerk reported, that Jackson "had done the right thing, that he wished he had had the courage to do it himself, and that if the time came, he'd take his stand publicly in support of Jackson."

Why did Jackson send the cable and take what he admitted was "this audacious and desperate step"? "I admired Bob and was devoted to him, but something happened to him at Nürenberg," wrote Francis Biddle, one of the tribunal's judges. "This showed . . . in his outburst about Black—an exhibition which shocked all of us, particularly the two British judges who found it indefensible." Under enormous strain for an extended period away from home and out of his element in a political battle, Jackson helplessly witnessed the latest in a series of disappointments. And now he snapped. When he later recorded his reminiscences he mused, half humorously, that perhaps he had been overwrought. Some commentators had forwarded a stress theory, he said, "that I was under the enormous strain of the Nuremberg trial, which resulted in an irresponsible act for which there is no rational explanation." He paused, then added, "Well, I may have been mentally irresponsible. That, someone else will have to judge." (Upon editing the taped transcript, he crossed out "mentally irresponsible.")

Jackson "has surely gone haywie," Truman wrote his wife. " . . . He was so dead sure he would be Chief that he had to take it out on somebody." Truman was certain Jackson would have to resign. He called Black to tell him not to answer Jackson: "Hugo, let him sink in his own piss mire." Black had already decided not to dignify the charges with a response. To a law clerk he said he "will never say anything or do anything" about the whole matter. Resignation was "the last thing" on his mind. He claimed he had not even read Jackson's statement and did not know whether he would—a remote prospect indeed.[11]

Drew Pearson phoned Black, wanting to know if he could help in any way. Over the next week he wrote several columns defending Black. Hugo was leaking like a sieve. He also spoke with columnist Robert Allen, Pearson's former partner, who likewise offered his assistance. Allen similarly pictured Black as the "blameless victim" of his colleagues. One of them was "a scheming, power-hungry manipulator" while the other was "a jealous and disappointed job seeker." It was not hard to figure out Allen meant Frankfurter and Jackson.

Other friends came to Black's defense. "Why the hullabaloo?" a "damn angry" Sherman Minton wrote, giving the horse sense of the matter. "Did Owen J. Roberts get off the bench when Goerge Wharton Pepper came in to argue the *Butler* case when everyone whose brains were as thick as buttermilk knew he was employed to bring Roberts in! He brought him with his voice filled with sobs and tears and Roberts wrote the opinion and Stone made him look like a justice of the peace and made himself immortal by his great dissent! Did Pierce Butler come down as his railroad pals argued? Hell no! He wrote the opinion. . . . " Black's reply showed his ability to take shafts philosophically:

> The recent statement made by my colleague has undoubtedly done great injury to the Court as an institution. You can rest assured, however, that I am not at all disturbed or bothered as to its ultimate effect on me personally. This is due, I suppose, to the fact that I have an abiding faith, naive, maybe, that the long-range judgment of people is usually sound.
>
> A slight familiarity with the history of individuals who from time to time have dared to assert that the status quo may not be perfect, led me to realize long ago that one who expressed such views would be subjected to many and repeated attacks. Any time an attack is made upon such an individual will be found a propitious one, insofar as the enlistment of sympathizers is concerned. Long ago I became convinced that the only way a public man could escape smears was either to actively espouse or acquiesce in conditions and practices abhorrent to his sense of justice. Since I could not follow this course with any inward satisfaction, I concluded that the only thing to do was to accept criticism as an incident of my work.

Black did not let the strange events disturb his tennis. Nevertheless, since Jackson had now publicly raised the matter of disqualification of judges, "someone in Black's corner had to defend him. So I did," said John Frank. In an article in the *Yale Law Journal* Frank concluded that in hearing an ex-partner twenty years after the association ended, Black "seems to have done pretty much what all judges do. . . . Had Black disqualified, he would have departed from the [Supreme Court] traditions of 150 years."

Harry Truman threw a "grand ceremony . . . with all the trimming" for Vinson's swearing in at the White House on June 24, 1946. The Court, ambassadors, the Cabinet, Congress and the "Common People" were there, accompanied by a band. "If that doesn't recreate some respect for the Court, I know of nothing else to do." When Vinson took his oath, Truman said it was "a lucky day for the United States and a lucky day for Mr. Vinson." He paused and tentatively added, "At least I hope it is."

Black did not talk much about the Nuremberg bombshell or the events surrounding Vinson's nomination. Only two years later he called them "a very small event in my life." "Oh, that was nothing," he told a secretary with a wave of the arm. He always tried to brush aside past unpleasant incidents so he could concentrate on winning the next round. "Well, I can understand what happened at Nuremberg," he said in 1949, almost completely diffusing Jackson's pique insofar as it affected him.

But a week after the blast he wrote a former law clerk: "Today the publisher of the *Macon* [Georgia] *Telegraph* sent me an issue of last week. On the editorial page appeared an editorial . . . entitled, 'Jackson is an Unmitigated Ass.' On the same page appeared an article written by John Temple Graves on the same subject. I have nothing but sympathy for John Temple."[12]

CHAPTER 24

"THE GREAT DESIGN
OF A WRITTEN
CONSTITUTION"

JUSTICE BLACK'S CONSTITUTIONAL TREE had many branches. At the top, overlooking the other limbs, was the protection of individual rights. Giving government and the economy room to operate occupied a bough just slightly lower. At the root was limiting the discretion of judges. History provided the tree's nourishment, allowing it to flower. Yet the tree needed continual tending, by sympathetic caretakers, lest it be abused or ravished. High among those potential assailants, according to Black, were those who advocated the flexible conception of due process. The struggle against this approach formed the core of his constitutional outlook and consumed much of his career.

He wanted to eliminate substantive due process completely. The idea that some forms of liberty are so fundamental that government may not abridge them in any way seems eminently reasonable at first blush. But it was simply a grab bag out of which judges could pull their version of what was "just," "fair" or "reasonable," a blank sheet of paper on which they could rewrite the Constitution and the Bill of Rights, Black maintained. The Court had arrogated its prerogative with its accordionlike method of expanding or deflating due process, including or excluding rights, with each case. Black sought to establish the constitutional text, read through the guiding lens of history, as his source of authority.

Soon after he got on the Court, "I began a great, intensive study of the Fourteenth Amendment since the Court took on too much power itself," Black said. He was looking for the end that the Fourteenth Amendment incorporated the Bill of Rights and applied them against the states. "There has been [such] a current of opinion," he wrote in a 1940 opinion. And that, he wrote in the 1942 *Betts v. Brady* right to counsel case, was the purpose of the amendment's congressional sponsors when it was adopted in 1868. He also hinted obliquely there that he might eventually elucidate his reasons. But in 1943 he lost both an article asserting that view as well as his copious notes. So he started over. Frankfurter's comments spurred him on. Time and again he would return from conference scoffing, "Felix invented this. It's natural law," that undefinable scourge which resided only in each judge's mind. Black spent summers and spare moments during the terms searching through the Congressional Globe and other records of the ratification of the Fourteenth Amendment, and had his clerks do the same. [1]

In early 1945, while the Court was considering a coerced confessions case, Black wrote the other justices about Frankfurter's circulated concurrence claiming that the prosecution's action failed to meet "civilized standards": "In the past, this broad judicial power has been used, as I see it, to preserve the economic status quo and to block legislative efforts to cure its existing evils. At the same time, the Court has only grudgingly read into "civilized standards" the safeguards to individual liberty set out in the Bill of Rights. . . . When the matter does hereafter arise in a proper case, I shall discuss it. . . ."

Willie Francis's case seemed appropriate. On May 3, 1946, the fifteen-year-old Negro, having been convicted for murder in rural southwest Louisiana, was strapped into a portable electric chair, and a hood placed over his head. The prosecution had presented only his two written, semiliterate confessions and witnesses who testified that the confessions were made voluntarily; nobody saw the murder and the murder weapon was "lost in transportation" after having been sent to the FBI in Washington. Counsel for the defense rose and "announced to the court that it had no evidence to offer on behalf of the accused," the sheriff recalled, and then sat down. The attendant threw the switch to kill him, saying in a harsh voice "Goodbye, Willie." But the portable generator did not produce enough voltage to kill Willie. He merely sizzled. The attendant threw the switch back and forth frantically to no avail. Straining at the straps, Willie gasped, "Let me breathe." The sheriff ordered him to be returned to his cell.

Could Louisiana now have a second chance to kill Willie? Chief Justice Vinson and Justices Black, Reed, Frankfurter, Douglas and Jackson voted to affirm the state court which had rejected his double jeopardy argument; Justices Murphy, Rutledge and Burton would have reversed. Vinson assigned the opinion to Reed. His early drafts relied on the due process clause, but Black disagreed with his definition. Then Douglas switched to the dissent: Reed had to hold Black's vote. So his next draft explicitly assumed that the Fifth Amendment's double jeopardy clause and the Eighth Amendment ("cruel and unusual punishment") were applicable to the states. Only partially placated, Black decided to note that he concurred in the result. But the next day he circulated a concurring opinion. Even though he reached the same result as Reed, he differed with Reed's reasoning. *

There was "ample" historical support for incorporation, Black noted. The flexible approach to due process—he was directing his comments largely to Frankfurter, who had concluded that the execution was not "repugnant to the conscience of mankind" without saying how he reached that conclusion—ultimately left judges without guidance, requiring that they "measure the validity of every state and federal criminal law by our conception of national 'standards of decency' without the guidance of constitutional language. . . . Conduct believed 'decent' by millions of people may be believed 'indecent' by millions of others. Adoption of one or the other conflicting views as to what is 'decent,' what is right, and what is best for the people, is generally recognized as a legislative function. Our courts move in forbidden territory when they prescribe their 'standards of decency' as the supreme rule of the people."[2]

But Black never published the opinion. Douglas, Murphy and Rutledge, his likely allies in an incorporation campaign, dissented, joining Burton's opinion.† Another case, *Adamson v. California,* to be argued two days after

* Jackson also drafted a concurring opinion, which opened:

> If I am at liberty, in the name of due process to vote my personal sense of "decency," I not only would refuse to send Willie Francis back to the electric chair, but I would not have sent him there in the first place. If my will were law, it would never permit execution of any death sentence. . . . I have doubts of the moral right of society to extinguish a human life, and even greater doubts about the wisdom of doing so. . . . A completely civilized society will abandon killing as a treatment for crime.

> To which Justice Rutledge replied: "I consider it to be more than absurd for the prosecutor at Nuremberg to say that he doesn't approve of capital punishment. If he didn't approve, he should never have taken the job" (RHJ draft, 12/46; WR memorandum, [no date], both Rutledge papers).

† Reed's opinion upheld the Louisiana court and sent Willie Francis back to the electric chair. His lawyer wanted to pursue the matter and had grounds to do so, but Willie said, "No, don't go back. I'm ready to die. I'm ready to go." This time the switch worked (Arthur S. Miller and Jeffrey H. Bowman, " 'Slow Dance on the Killing Ground': The *Willie Francis* Case Revisited," 38 *DePaul Law Rev.* 1 [1983]).

Francis came down, seemed like a more promising vehicle. Black had spent the previous summer preparing for it.

Admiral Dewey Adamson, not a naval officer but a poor, ignorant Negro, had been tried for murder in Los Angeles. He did not take the stand as a witness in his own defense since the prosecutor could have impeached his testimony with questions about his prior record (he had twice served time in prison). Because he did not deny the evidence offered against him, the prosecutor argued, as California law permitted, that the jury could infer guilt. Adamson was convicted and sentenced to death, and he appealed to the Supreme Court. Black asked more questions than usual at argument. He tried to force counsel for both sides to concede that the Court could rule on the basis of either the traditional due process standard of undefined fairness or the Fifth Amendment's right against self-incrimination, incorporated through the Fourteenth. In conference he did not vote. He passed, saying he was uncertain whether allowing comment on a defendant's failure to testify infringed the Fifth Amendment.

The Court voted 5–3 to affirm the conviction, with Douglas, Murphy and Rutledge in dissent. It is "settled law," Reed wrote for the majority, that the self-incrimination clause "is not made effective by the Fourteenth Amendment as a protection against state action on the ground that freedom from testimonial compulsion is a right of national citizenship, or because it is a personal privilege or immunity secured by the Federal Constitution as one of the rights of man that are listed in the Bill of Rights." Nor was it a fundamental principle inherent in due process under the "concept of ordered liberty" test of *Palko v. Connecticut,* decided in Black's first term.

Black swallowed his doubts soon after conference and started drafting a dissent. He ranked it as his most important opinion. "I think it really is, no question about it," he told this author. "There I laid it all out." It culminated years of research and reflection. "I write when I'm ready," he continued. "I waited because I feared that my opinion on the Fourteenth Amendment might be too firmly fixed at too early a date. It takes a while to make up your mind on something so important. I didn't write until I came to the complete conclusion that I was reasonably sure of myself and my research. It was my work from beginning to end. I went through all of that myself."

"That" was the history of the Fourteenth Amendment in the 39th Congress, which passed it. He concluded that its framers meant to apply the Bill of Rights to the states. "If I didn't find that this was their view, my career on the Court would have been entirely different," he said in 1967. "I would not have gone with due process and I'd be considered the most reactionary judge on the Court." History as he read it was his means of limiting judicial discretion and maximizing individual freedom under the Constitution. Black worked long hours with his clerk, culling from the huge collection of notes, phrases and jottings he had compiled, organizing and writing anew. "The 'natural law' formula which the Court uses to reach its conclusion in this case should be abandoned as an incongruous excrescence on our Constitution," he wrote.

> My study of the historical events that culminated in the Fourteenth Amendment, and the expressions of those who sponsored and favored, as well as those who opposed its submission and passage, persuades me that one of the chief objects that the provisions of the Amendment's first section, separately, and as a whole, were intended to accomplish was to make the Bill of Rights, applicable to the states. . . . In my judgment the people of no nation can lose their liberty so long as a Bill of Rights like ours survives and its basic purposes are conscientiously interpreted, enforced and respected so as to afford continuous protection against old, as well as new, devices and practices which might thwart those purposes. I fear to see the consequences of the Court's practice of substituting its own concepts of decency and fundamental justice for the language of the Bill of Rights as its point of departure in interpreting and enforcing that Bill of Rights.
>
> If the choice must be between the selective process of [Palko v. Connecticut] applying some of the Bill of Rights to the States, or the Twining [v. New Jersey] rule applying none of them, I would choose the Palko selective process. But rather than accept either of these choices, I would follow what I believe was the original purpose of the Fourteenth Amendment—to extend to all of the people of the nation the complete protection of the Bill of Rights. To hold that this Court can determine what, if any, provisions, of the Bill of Rights will be enforced, and if so to what degree, is to frustrate the great design of a written Constitution.

The Fourteenth Amendment's "historical purpose has never received full consideration or exposition in any opinion of this Court," Black wrote in Adamson. "For this reason, I am attaching to this dissent an appendix which contains a resume, by no means complete, of the Amendment's history." He essayed an almost exclusively legislative history. This befitted his background, but it did not tell anywhere near the whole story. A constitutional amendment, not a statute, was being enacted. But Black neglected the ratification process in the states, and when legislators vote on a proposal, they cannot escape the enveloping atmosphere. Black also ignored that, as well as the Amendment's historical antecedents, especially the rich lode of abolitionist thought. He had to overcome a major obstacle: the 1873 *Slaughter House Cases,* only five years after the Amendment's passage, had gutted the privileges and immunities clause of any meaning. Thus Black spoke of "the provisions of the Amendment's first section, separately, and as a whole." It was on the "whole" that the amendment was largely considered. But while the sponsors, Jacob Howard in the Senate and John Bingham in the House, were explicit in their intention to incorporate the Bill of Rights (while some of Bingham's remarks were often confusing), a hazy ambience surrounded its passage in Congress.

Black's was an advocate's history: he proved too much and ignored or swept away all doubtful evidence. But Black had always been an advocate down to his bones. Try as he did, he could not get advocacy out of him—just as no one, despite every best attempt in the world, can remove one's past. "There is no charge," he told the Senate shortly before his appointment to the Court, "against the integrity of any prospective judge that with reference to economic predilections after he goes on the bench he will still be the same man that he was before he went there."[3]

The initial criticism of Black's history and its implications came from Frank-furter, as Black knew it would. He had his clerk, Louis Oberdorfer, deliver the first draft to Frankfurter by hand instead of having his messenger, Spencer Campbell, take it over. Oberdorfer stood while Frankfurter read it. When he finished, he flung it across the desk and said, "At Yale they call this scholarship?" The recent Yale Law School graduate collected the pages, now strewn on the floor, and excused himself. "Hugo is trying to change the world and misreading history in the attempt, just making things up out of whole cloth," Frankfurter told his clerk. He expanded his earlier, brief concurrence just to counter Black's opinion. The due process clause required of judges a determination whether a particular case offended "those canons of decency and fairness which express the notions of justice of English-speaking peoples even toward those charged with the most heinous crimes," Frankfurter wrote. Although these standards are "not authoritatively for-mulated anywhere as though they were prescriptions in a pharmacopoeia," they must be divined to make a judgment. But Frankfurter never said *how.* *

---

* He misread Black, claiming Hugo "merely" meant to incorporate "some but not all of the

Black's history was open to valid criticism, but Frankfurter did not make it. This was surprising. "For nearly twenty years I was at work on what was to be as comprehensive and as scholarly a book on the Fourteenth Amendment as I could make it," he had told Black in 1943. "That book was aborted when I came down here, and now there is nothing to show for those twenty years except the poor things in my head and a mass of largely illegible notes." It is unlikely he ever delved directly into the passage of the amendment: he relied upon secondary works. So when Black had called Congressman John Bingham, the House sponsor of the Fourteenth Amendment, "the Madison of [its] first section," and quoted extensively from his speeches, Frankfurter remarked, "What was submitted was his proposal, not his speech." That was undeniable, but it was a lame response from a judge justly praised for his historical acuity.[4]

Extensive criticism came from Stanford law professor Charles Fairman in the *Stanford Law Review*. At first glance, Black wrote John Frank, "I must confess a very great disappointment at Fairman's article. I had supposed he was more of a detached historian."

> One of the reasons I had for putting in *some* of the evidence indicating that the purpose of the 14th Amendment was to adopt the Bill of Rights, was that a national discussion of the subject would be brought about. After reading Fairman's article . . . , I was reminded of my old senatorial colleague, Senator Heflin. Many times I have heard him make speeches until his clothes were wringing with perspiration. Almost invariably he would close . . . by saying, "Now, senators, the subject having been fully debated, let us vote."
>
> I would thoroughly enjoy engaging in this debate with Mr. Fairman and his associates were I free to do so. I must say that Mr. Fairman's article reminds me of those advocates who come into court with the belief that

provisions of the first eight Amendments, selected on an undefined basis," when that was Black's fallback position. That, as a practical matter, under his theory the Seventh Amendment requirement that civil suits involving less than $20 be tried by a jury would have to be scrapped, did not faze Black. "A constitutional amendment will be easy enough" was his standard response. "Hugo would overrule state laws to give every man jury trial and require grand jury indictment," Earl Warren told Drew Pearson. "Many states don't require jury trial for civil cases over $20 and prevent indictments on bills of information. To change this would make states topsy-turvy. [I told him,] 'Hugo, the only reason you're taking this position is because you don't have other [votes]. If you did, you'd be the first to reverse yourself.' Hugo didn't like this at all" (*Adamson*, 332 U.S. at 65, 67 [FF]; JPF, "Black and Declaration," 614 [easy enough]; diary, 8/5/[66], Pearson papers [EW]).

strained inferences conclusively settle a matter. Even if Bingham were as corrupt in his lifetime as this article implies, and if Howard were the muddleheaded individual that Mr. Fairman seems to think he was, I should still think that there might be an opportunity for rebuttal. This is true in spite of the fact that by my agreeing with the conclusions of Flack in his nearly 300 page argument,* it appears that I have committed an unpardonable sin. What governors did not say about the 14th Amendment appears to have much more weight with Mr. Fairman than what the sponsors of the Amendment said themselves. And he seems to think there is no weight to be given any statement of the *general* purposes of the Amendment. Only those who enumerated in detail its specific purposes said anything that would influence Mr. Fairman and he of course is not influenced by them because he thinks they were either crooked or stupid.

Naturally I am not interested in his charges that I misquoted Flack. Anyone who reads Flack will know that is not true. Besides I would suppose that a *historian* trying to find out what actually occurred would not be interested in whether one person writing about a historical event may have misinterpreted the full effect of what another historian said. At any rate, I now think of Mr. Fairman as an advocate, not a historian, and I would not rank him at the top of the advocates of the world.†

Black never changed his mind about Fairman. He believed Frankfurter "got" Fairman to write the article and that Fairman did it "to get a job at

---

* Horace Flack wrote *The Adoption of the Fourteenth Amendment* (1908), which Black cited several times.

† Fairman had hoped the article would not be considered an "attack on Justice Black." Frank told this to Black, who replied:

It is entirely possible that Professor Fairman had no intention whatever of making a personal attack in his article. Advocates for the cause frequently fail to appreciate the full significance of what they say. Books on history are replete with instances which show deviation from historical detachment. Historians like other writers have their heroes and their villains although it would doubtless be hard to persuade them that they do. After rereading what Flack said, what I said, and what Fairman said, I am still inclined to think that Mr. Fairman momentarily slipped from his historical pedestal. In fact, I may add that the lack of persuasiveness in Mr. Fairman's article tended to confirm my former opinion concerning the historical purposes of the 14th Amendment. In my judgment there could have been far better arguments on Mr. Fairman's side than he presented, arguments that more acute students would have found. He lacks a familiarity with the operation of forces that bring about legislative and constitutional changes. He is apparently unable to dissect the integral part of broad general arguments. Approaching present and past problems on the same level he used in his article, he would find nothing for instance in any states' rights argument except a broad abstract belief either for or against states' rights. Fully to appreciate such broad general arguments, one must of course try to find out what particular existing privilege is sought to be protected.

(JPF to HLB, written on JPF to Fairman, 2/28/50 [first quote]; HLB to JPF, 3/2/50.)

Harvard." "Neither [Fairman's] arguments nor his vigorous reflections upon my accuracy," Black later wrote Boston lawyer Charles Curtis, "shook my own belief in the interpretation of the Fourteenth Amendment I expressed in *Adamson*. I do not deny that there are better, more detached and even less biased historians than I am, but that does not mean that I think Professor Fairman is one of them." His writings do not "necessarily mark him as the most detached and unemotional historian who writes today. It is my hope that sometime the history of the Fourteenth Amendment will be explored and discussed by some person who has your detachment and who is experienced in how legislative bodies and legislative committees work." Black talked with Louis Oberdorfer about Oberdorfer's publishing a rebuttal to Fairman but decided against it. He wanted his opinion to stand by itself, to have people talk about it and not to have it diluted by further commentaries.[5]

Adamson's radiations rested uneasily for several years. Within the Court, Black did not want to press a view for which he lacked enough votes. But in 1952 there was an eruption. Los Angeles police, suspecting that one Rochin was selling narcotics, entered his house and forced open the bedroom door. There they spied two capsules. Rochin seized them and put them in his mouth. After officers "jumped upon him" in an unsuccessful effort to extract the pills, they handcuffed him and took him to a hospital, where he was strapped to a table, his mouth forced open, and his stomach pumped.

Two capsules containing morphine were found. They led to Rochin's conviction. The Court agreed to reverse it. Black forecast that anyone writing the majority opinion would face difficulties. But pumping a suspect's stomach made Frankfurter "puke," he said in conference, and he thirsted to write for the Court—to show "what kind of instrument the Due Process Clause is against the States, thereby restating the conception of [it] which this Court has enforced ever since the Fourteenth Amendment was adopted, and rejecting the notion that that clause is a handbag for the eight original Amendments," he told Chief Justice Vinson. The police methods here, he wrote, were "too close to the rack and the screw to permit of constitutional differentiation." As Black read Frankfurter's draft opinion, he marked these passages: "We may not draw on our merely personal and private notions and disregard the limits that bind judges. . . . Considerations deeply rooted in reason and in the compelling traditions of the legal profession" are guiding. " 'Due process of law' requires an evaluation based on a disinterested inquiry pursued in the spirit of science, on a balanced order of facts exactly and

fairly stated [and] on the detached consideration of conflicting claims. . . . *
Prosecutions cannot be brought about by methods that offend 'a sense of
justice.' . . . Conduct that shocks the conscience" demanded that Rochin's
conviction be reversed.

This language predictably angered Black.† His response had nothing to
do with his feelings for Frankfurter personally. "Felix is one of the nicest
guys anywhere," he said. "If I had to find someone in the world to tell me
what's right or wrong for society, I'd pick him. There's no other man I would
rather leave that choice to." Black's reaction had everything to do with their
constitutional approaches. Due process was not to him, as he believed it was
to Frankfurter, a vessel into which a judge could pour any content he chose,
or none at all. "You can't put Felix into a bottle and see what comes out
for due process purposes, just drop his stomach there and see what color the
litmus paper turns, whether it's blue or red. There have to be some fundamental rules."

Black gave some consideration to not dealing with the due process
argument. He had his clerk go through the entire transcript of this "gangster
trial" to see on how many pages the tax law was discussed. This did not
suffice on which to base an opinion, so he confronted the majority on its
grounds. Even before Frankfurter circulated his draft opinion, Black composed some thoughts for his planned concurrence. "The rounded periods of
the majority opinion express many lofty governmental ideas that are the
ultimate goal of every good society," he wrote. " . . . But no express constitutional language grants judicial power to invalidate all kinds of state laws
deemed 'unreasonable' or contrary to the Court's notion of civilized
decisions."

He wanted his opinion to be slightly sarcastic. Why, Black wondered,
should the notions of only the English-speaking peoples be considered to
determine what are immutable and fundamental principles of justice? No
express constitutional language grants courts power to invalidate "*every* state
law of *every* kind deemed 'unreasonable' or contrary to the Court's notion
of civilized standards," yet these "evanescent standards" had been used to
"suppress evil economic practices." But "of even graver concern" to Black

---

* "You may understand what [this sentence] means," Black said in 1968; "I do not, and yet
I believe that the *Rochin* defense of the philosophy of due process which I oppose is the
best one ever written to justify that philosophy" (*Faith*, 30).

† Nearly twenty years later, Frankfurter's language still angered Black. "Imagine 'shocks the
conscience' as a constitutional basis," he said at lunch with this writer. "Could you imagine
that? How does your conscience shock? Mine can get shocked pretty easily."

was using that doctrine "to nullify the Bill of Rights. I long ago concluded that the accordion-like qualities of this philosophy must inevitably imperil all the individual liberty safeguards specifically enumerated in the Bill of Rights."[6]

Three times in less than three pages Black referred to *Adamson,* but not its historical argument. He talked about it now only to his clerks. "I read the original proceedings. That convinced me. The Court had never had that kind of original research before," he proudly said. Or he wrote about it on the pages of books he read. When Paul Freund contended in 1961 that *Adamson* represented for Black "the maximum protection of civil liberties with a modicum of protection for interests of property," Black scrawled "Not true" in the margin. ("Right," he declared next to "the compulsion of the constitutional words.") And when Alexander Bickel claimed that Fairman had "conclusively disproved Justice Black's contention; at least, such is the weight of opinion among disinterested observers," Black noted (in 1966): "He did not"; "That is his [Bickel's] view and the 'weight of opinion' for him is his own view."

Like the snake that kept rising up, Fairman's article was always on Black's mind. He had no doubt he was right historically. In 1968 he used the article as a stalking horse. The Court in *Duncan v. Louisiana* applied the Sixth Amendment's right to trial by jury to the states. Black expanded his one-paragraph concurrence to ten pages to answer Harlan's lengthy dissent. His *Adamson* opinion was "the product of years of study and research," Black wrote.

> My appraisal of the legislative history followed 10 years of legislative experience as a Senator of the United States, not a bad way, I suspect, to learn the value of what is said in legislative debates, committee discussions, committee reports, and various other steps taken in the course of passage of bills, resolutions, and proposed constitutional amendments. . . . I have read and studied [Fairman's] article extensively, including the historical references, but am compelled to add that in my view it has completely failed to refute the inferences and arguments that I suggested in my *Adamson* dissent. Professor Fairman's "history" relies very heavily on what was *not* said in the state legislatures that passed on the Fourteenth Amendment. Instead of relying on this kind of negative pregnant, my legislative experience has convinced me that it is far wiser to rely on what *was* said, and most importantly, said by the men who actually sponsored the Amendment in the Congress. I know from my years in the United States Senate that it is to men like Congressman Bingham, who steered the Amendment

through the House, and Senator Howard, who introduced it in the Senate, that members of Congress look when they seek the real meaning of what is being offered.* And they vote for or against a bill based on what the sponsors of that bill and those who oppose it tell them it means.

Black believed that the Constitution should be interpreted to agree with its framers' intentions. He searched for the "original understanding" of a constitutional clause and with rare exceptions felt it bound him. History becomes, then, essentially a command to future generations living under that charter. This marked him as a practitioner of "intent history." It contrasts with "ongoing history," of which Frankfurter was an avid proponent, which emphasizes the currents and lessons of experience as one tries to capture patterns, to elucidate themes, to raise dilemmas. The Constitution to Black was a constitutive act of the people assembled, dealing with timeless problems. As he wrote in *Adamson:* "I cannot consider the Bill of Rights to be an outworn 18th Century 'straight jacket' as the *Twining* opinion did. Its provisions may be thought outdated abstractions by some. And it is true that they were designed to meet ancient evils. But they are the same kind of human evils that have emerged from century to century wherever excessive power is sought by the few at the expense of the many."

The American Constitution resulted from thousands of years of history. Forged out of strife and turmoil, it erupted in a new country like a crescendo of thought, aiming to preserve hard-won freedom. To understand it one must know not only what brought it into being but how its ideas were refined. But Black did not believe in blind adherence to dead letters, lest they fetter us. He strove to find what animated them and their framers. This meant going to the original sources, without the intervention of interpreters, the historians. "History is one-sided, such as Livy's *History of Rome,* or biased and selective," he said. "It has its shade-offs. Livy is great reading but he was a reactionary historian. The history of the U.S. government tracks the history of Rome. Hannibal or Carthage—one thing is destroyed and another takes its place. Nothing is ever final with reference to human knowledge."[7]

---

* "Anyone acquainted with the realities of the United States Senate," Black wrote in a 1969 dissent, "knows that the remarks of the floor manager are taken by other Senators as reflecting the views of the Committee itself" *(Zuber v. Allen).*

CHAPTER 25

STRUGGLES

Religious freedom is the first freedom listed in the Bill of Rights: "Congress shall make no law respecting an establishment of religion. . . . " History generated the content of the Founders's quest to make America a haven for the integrity of the individual conscience. Yet not until 1947, in *Everson v. Board of Education,* did the Supreme Court interpret the provision. The occasion was a New Jersey statute that authorized local school boards to reimburse parents for the cost of public transportation of students to both public and private schools. An economy-in-government group challenged the repayment for travel to church-related schools. Before the case reached the Supreme Court, it took on overtones of a Protestant-Catholic clash.

Discussion at conference was spirited. Vinson, Black and Reed believed the statute should be upheld. Frankfurter thought "otherwise, but with difficulty." He talked vehemently of "the absolute separation of church and state the framers had in mind. Freedom of speech is spurious about this. These are contributions to parochial schools and it makes no difference to me that it is Catholic or Jewish schools. This leaves out the profit-making schools. . . . If joint buses why not joint gyms and joint lavatories, all bit by bit the whole equal support of parochial schools under the guise of promoting the general welfare of our citizenry. . . . I do think due process protects me against blending of ecclesiastical and state affairs." Rutledge strongly agreed: "We ought to stop this thing right at the threshold of the public school." Approving busing for parochial school children would lead to state aid for other religious purposes and there was "no telling where the end [would] be." "All that Wiley said is true but his conclusion," Jackson retorted. "If the state decided to support private schools, it could do so. I

361

don't see how you can read it in." By the Fourteenth Amendment, Frankfurter said. Black spoke up again. A line could be drawn between different
types of state aid to religions, he thought. "I do not affirm on a ground that
went as far as protection [of] church. Logic would not compel me to support
schools and church. But this is not enough here."

The Court voted to affirm the statute, with only Frankfurter and Rutledge dissenting, and Murphy, the Court's sole Catholic, passing and saying
nothing, and wondering whether it might be best if he abstained altogether.
Black was assigned the opinion. Then Burton and Jackson, who had thought
that "the argument that [it] is for children and not schools refuted everything," switched to dissent. But Murphy, his conscience torn, went with
Black, giving him a majority. The first of his six drafts conceded that the
busing law gave the Catholic Church "an indirect benefit" and therefore
that it approached "the verge of state support to a religious sect." A later
draft portrayed the law as a welfare measure aimed to benefit all schoolchildren regardless of their religious beliefs. Parochial schools derived an
"indirect benefit" from the law, Black admitted; but this was not "support."
(Under this "child benefit" theory the child in a sectarian school, not the
school, gets the benefit of incidental aid; in conference Jackson called the
theory "phony.")

Rutledge's powerful dissent went through eight drafts, and he hit hard
at Black's assertion that the state had not entered into any kind of partnership
with the church. Black's next draft omitted all such references—just as he
eventually did not admit, although he did not deny, that parochial schools
gain indirectly. So it went. Rutledge pecked away at Black's arguments; Black
tightened them up, revised them, or dropped them completely. His discussion
of the background of the First Amendment's establishment clause, but not
its legislative history in Congress, came only in response to Rutledge's lengthy
discussion.

The clause, now applicable to the states through the Fourteenth Amendment, Black wrote, "means at least this":

> Neither a state nor the Federal Government can set up a state church.
> Neither can pass laws which aid one religion, or prefer one religion over
> another. * Neither can force or influence a person to go to or remain away

---

* To say that government may not "pass laws [to] aid" religion is a sweeping statement that,
  if applied literally, would forbid tax exemptions and many other collateral benefits to religious
  organizations.

from church against his will or force him to profess a belief or disbelief in any religion. No person can be punished for entertaining or professing religious beliefs or disbeliefs, for church attendance or nonattendance. No tax in any amount, large or small, can be levied to support any religious activities or institutions, whatever they may be called, or whatever form they may adopt to teach or practice religion. Neither a state nor the Federal Government can, openly or secretly, participate in the affairs of any religious organizations or groups and vice versa. In the words of Jefferson, the clause against establishment of religion by laws was intended to erect "a wall of separation between Church and State."

These stirring words—adopted from Charles Beard's 1943 volume, *The Republic*, which Black called "a great book" whose "title might almost have been 'The Origin and Aim of the American Constitution' "—were certain to warm the heart of the stoutest civil libertarian. But then Black swiftly pirouetted: "The First Amendment has erected a wall between church and state. That wall must be kept high and impregnable. We could not approve the slightest breach. New Jersey has not breached it here."[1]

"When I started to read the Everson case," Rutledge's friend and Madison biographer Irving Brant wrote him, "I flipped the leaves and missed the break in it, therefore thought it was a unanimous decision. As I read along through Hugo's opinion, I got a real lift; it showed such a complete understanding of the principles which governed the writing of the First Amendment. At one point, I got out the manuscript of one of the chapters of the unpublished volume on Madison and read parallel sections to [Mrs. Brant], to show how even the wording was almost duplicated. Then, by gosh, on a point negatived by his own prior reasoning, he jumped over and affirmed the decision." Black had hurdled the wall, negating his own evidence and reasoning to uphold the program on the grounds that the state aid was a public safety measure designed to protect students and in no way could be construed as aid to church-related schools. This was a harsh letdown, as Jackson noted in dissent. The "most fitting precedent," he thought, was "Julia who, according to Byron's reports, 'whispering "I will ne'er consent,"—consented.' "

The opinion drew criticism from all quarters. Black's rhetoric and dicta contrasted too sharply with his conclusion and holding to satisfy anyone. If he had not written it as he did, he said later, "Bob Jackson would have. I made it as tight and gave them as little room to maneuver as I could." He regarded it as going to the verge. His goal, he remarked at the time, was to make it a pyrrhic victory and he quoted King Pyrrhus, "One more victory and I am undone." His friends could not understand how he could consider this a victory of any sort. "One of the strange things about it, however," Black wrote Max Lerner in 1949, "is that the most severe and consistent criticisms of the opinion have come from leading Catholics. In fact their criticism . . . began at the very time when others were criticizing the opinion on the ground that it accorded the members of the Catholic church something which they were not constitutionally entitled to receive. No week passes and few days pass that I do not have criticisms either by way of letters or magazine article written by members of the Catholic church."[2]

The related question of the use of public school buildings for released-time religious instruction came before the Court the next year, 1948, in *McCollum v. Board of Education*. With Black's dicta in *Everson* as the crucial issue, all justices except Reed thought a Champaign, Illinois, plan was unconstitutional. Once again Black was assigned the opinion. Resting solely on *Everson* for support, he wrote that the religious instruction program "is beyond all question a utilization of the tax-established and tax-supported public school system to aid religious groups to spread their faith." He rejected the argument that government need only treat all religions equally. "In this delicate field it would seem wise to have a Court opinion," he told Justice Burton, but injection of "the parochial school issue" might prevent that. And the *Everson* dissenters were reluctant to accept it as binding precedent. Meeting at Frankfurter's invitation, they decided he would draft a concurring opinion expressing their continuing opposition.

Burton tried to play peacemaker by reconciling Black's and Frankfurter's opinions when Jackson circulated a concurrence that closed, "We are likely to make the legal 'wall of separation between church and state' as winding as the famous serpentine wall designed by Mr. Jefferson for the University [of Virginia] he founded." This sentence caught Frankfurter's eye. "I am prepared to delete all references to *Everson*," he told the brethren, even though he was convinced it was "wrong and mischief breeding." An angry Black replied:

> I have just been handed a memorandum from Justice Frankfurter. . . . I will not agree to any opinion in the *McCollum* case which does not make reference to the *Everson* case. Time has confirmed my conviction that the

decision in the *Everson* case was right, and since I attach great importance to the constitutional question involved, I desire to supplement the record made by Justice Frankfurter by stating this fact. Of course, there is nothing unusual about one who entertains the belief that the views opposite to his are "mischief breeding."

He was willing, Black told Rutledge and Burton, to "agree to any opinion which decides this case on the basis of [*Everson's*] principles," but he would not "repudiate them expressly or by failure to refer to them in a Court opinion."

"These tempers flash too fast," Rutledge advised Burton. "But often they cool after the flash." Burton persisted in his efforts at mediation. "He seems to look upon the world with an idealistic generosity concerning other people's motives," a reporter had written of Burton in the Senate. This gentle man needed every bit of his considerable sincerity and frankness to persuade two strong-willed colleagues. He suggested changes in their opinions and shuttled between offices to discuss them. Finally, Frankfurter removed explicit criticism of *Everson* and Black deleted some references (as well as the observation that the released-time plan was "union" of church and state).[3] And six justices subscribed to Black's opinion for the Court.

The loud, intense and swift criticism from Catholic spokesmen convinced Black that it was "impossible to write so as to satisfy all persons on questions which so vitally touch the lives of people and which may so greatly influence the course of the nation," he told Lerner. Catholic writers "claim that the *McCollum* opinion was the natural result of what was said in the *Everson* case, and of course that was what we said in the *McCollum* opinion." But *McCollum* turned out differently: Black's rhetoric became the basis for his holding. After *Everson* was decided, he received a letter suggesting he read *Annals of Congress*, the proceedings of the First Congress. "Get volume 1 and let's see what was said," Black scribbled on the letter. He discovered the framers' indisputably broad view of the establishment clause—no government aid to any religion under any guise, even without preference to any church. As historian Leonard Levy stated after examining the evidence exhaustively, "Nowhere in the making of the Bill of Rights was the original intent and meaning clearer than in the case of religious freedom." At the time that Americans were being guaranteed such broad religious liberty, Black's forebears came to the United States in search of freedom. "All of my religious decisions are influenced by what happened to our Toland ancestors in Ireland," he once told a nephew.[4]

....

The one justice absent from the maneuverings in these as well as in most other cases was Chief Justice Vinson. Beyond presiding at conference and assigning cases, he hardly seemed present. He tried to bring the justices closer together early in his first term by inviting them to his apartment. There he had them sing around the piano. The effort fell flat. At conference he presided amiably and the discussion proceeded orderly enough, but he stated the cases tentatively and summarily, and did little to sharpen issues. Vinson underwhelmed with his lawyerly qualities. Some who dealt with him earlier thought he was "quite fuzzy-minded." On the Court, dealing with issues he did not fully grasp, he never gave any reason to dispel that conclusion. Vinson's best "writing" took place when he left the room; his papers show that he never contributed more than a sentence to any opinion, and in no more than a dozen instances did his pen touch the paper of a draft. This devoted public servant, who never wanted to be on the Court, was simply far out of his depth.

Vinson's fumbling ineffectiveness left a vacuum at the center. If he ended some of the tensions that existed under Stone simply because he was not Stone, others continued and new ones started. Black did not let this affect him. "The new Chief Justice is getting along well," he wrote John Frank. "He is courteous, companionable, and according to my experience, as easy to reach as my messenger. Our conferences are short, snappy, and so far as I am concerned, adequate. . . . So far as I know, everything goes well." His analysis continued to dominate the conference, but by no means the opinions. Frankfurter's nature prevented that; and Jackson, the other possibility, was still absorbed with Nuremburg and found it hard to focus on the Court's work. When he and Black saw each other in the hall for the first time after Jackson's return, they pleasantly exchanged greetings ("Hi, Bob," "How are you, Hugo?" "Oh, just fine") as if nothing had happened and they were good pals. But there was a real strain, Black later indicated. It was touch and go for a while; the forms were observed, the Nuremberg blast not mentioned. At the first conference they shook hands and "joined in a brief discussion—all in the best of quiet manners," Burton recorded in his diary. But emotions were still running high and soon Jackson "took Black on almost as if he were a subversive person," according to Douglas.[5]

Keeping working relationships amiable was rarely more important. Privately, Frankfurter "referred to Black in very personal terms," recalled television reporter Martin Agronsky, who saw both periodically after World

War Two. "Black's Klan connection was always in the back of his mind. He didn't trust Black." Stanley Reed made a similar point in his kind way. "Black will put something in this opinion that he plans to pull out and use five opinions down the road," he told a clerk, "so you better be very careful about the future implications of what you see in things that he circulates." Much the same thing came from Bill Douglas. "Hugo understands everything," he said to his clerk. "You have to watch Hugo. He's tricky." But Douglas would never intimate this to Black. By the late 1940s, theirs had long been an unbreakable tie. They shared so much—ideas, friends and opponents, a sense of alienation from the self-satisfied. Douglas reserved for Black a warmth and respect he gave no one else. If he treated his own law clerks like hired help and worse ("the lowest form of animal life," he called them), he viewed Black's as junior associates working together in a common cause, and some he later counted as among his closest friends.

It was, as it had to be, slightly different with Frank Murphy and Wiley Rutledge. As the years went on, Black regarded them with brotherly warmth. "I don't think Murphy was ever upset with Black," said Murphy's longtime clerk Eugene Gressman. "He was grateful to Black because he assigned him good opinions." Black was deeply fond of Rutledge but thought the former professor, like many academics, lingered unnecessarily over every point. Sometimes he complained, "Why does Wiley feel he has to answer that?" Black worried that Rutledge, who regularly labored until after midnight, would work himself to death; and he could never persuade Rutledge to slow up. With Douglas, Murphy and Rutledge, Black had an attachment that went far beyond words or mere expressions of agreement.

He did not talk much about other justices, even though he liked them all, Robert Jackson being in a separate category. Black hardly mentioned Fred Vinson. Reed, he would tell one and all, was a delightful colleague. An article by Drew Pearson claiming that Harold Burton was not carrying his share of the Court's load upset Black, for he highly admired Burton as a human being and knew how hard he had to work. Toward Frankfurter, Black showed, rather than expressed, much disappointment, feeling that he backtracked from his professorial days. They visited socially and were always personally cordial, sometimes a little artificially so. The Court was operating under bright lights, its every raised eyebrow scrutinized by the press and the academy. In January 1947, Arthur Schlesinger, Jr., published an article on the Court in *Fortune*. While preparing it, he spoke at length to recent Frankfurter clerk Philip Kurland and Harvard law professor Thomas Reed Powell, an acerbic critic of the Court who was convinced of Black's "intellectual crookedness and meanness." Black still came off well: "courteous and friendly in person, cold and tough were issues are concerned . . . his emotions center around ideas, not personalities . . . his clear, driving intelligence . . . an honorable person."

Soon Black talked about the article with Judge Jerome Frank, who, with Black's permission, gave Schlesinger his views. Black liked Schlesinger and admired his recent book, *The Age of Jackson,* Frank told Schlesinger. He continued, "You would, he [Black] thought, by your writings, contribute much to the desirable development of this country. Your point of view . . . on the Court was 'naive,' and probably ascribable to your inexperience in this field, with a consequent inability to appraise accurately misinformation coming to you from prejudiced sources." Black, Frank said, had become so accustomed to adverse, unfair criticism that he ceased to resent it, being content to let his record speak for itself. But, typically Hugo, "He did, however, regret your unfair criticism of Douglas."[6]

Personal aspersions had no place in the Court's opinions, Black believed.* When Douglas asked about the wisdom of filing a memorandum noting who voted to hear a case ("It puts Bob in an untenable position"), Black replied: "I am not so sure. Probably the response evoked might be so bitter that we would be surprised, even though we are accustomed to biting criticisms from this source I rather lean to the view that for this reason it might be best to drop the matter here. His bitterness would be attributed to us by the press regardless of the merits of the controversy." Douglas did not publish the memorandum. Jackson had returned from Nuremberg changed by his exposure to the horrors of totalitarianism. He now voted more often than not to uphold restrictions on free speech. In several cases his vote made the difference between an advance and a setback.

One of these cases came in 1949 when the Court upheld a law prohibiting the operation of sound trucks that emitted "loud or raucous noises." It was an old problem in a modern setting, and Black, dissenting, claimed this repudiated a decision the year before, striking down an ordinance requiring permission of the police chief before a sound truck could be used within

---

* In an early draft of Black's opinion in *Rogers v. U.S.* (1951), his clerks added the name of the mean-spirited prosecutor. Black took it out, saying "When you're on top, you've got to be careful how you use your power. You can't be ad hominem" (George Treister int.).

town limits. He outlined his First Amendment views: The "basic premise" is that

> all present [and future] instruments of communication . . . shall be free from governmental censorship or prohibition. Laws which hamper the free use of some instruments of communication thereby favor competing channels. Thus, unless constitutionally prohibited, laws like this Trenton [New Jersey] ordinance can give an overpowering influence to views of owners of legally favored instruments of communication. This favoritism, it seems to me, is the inevitable result of today's decision. . . .
>
> There are many people who have ideas that they wish to disseminate but who do not have enough money to own or control publishing plants, newspapers, radios, moving picture studios, or chains of show places. Yet everybody knows the vast reaches of these powerful channels of communication which from the very nature of our economic system must be under the control and guidance of comparatively few people. On the other hand, public speaking is done by many men of divergent minds with no centralized control over the ideas they entertain so as to limit the causes they espouse.

Black's first Senate campaign—when he was dependent on street corner gatherings and meetinghouse speeches, and when large newspapers refused to cover him or slanted their reporting—remained vivid in his mind. Small papers, he believed, could get news out as well as big ones. So could sound trucks convey ideas in a world in which wealth and the profit incentive increasingly controlled mass communication.

This opinion typified Black at the time. He viewed a case not only in terms of its result on the parties but also in terms of its future consequences on constitutional vitals. He searched for the governing principle with the meaning and objective of the broad constitutional design in mind. He interpreted the Bill of Rights generously but gave government latitude to enact reasonable restrictions.

The reasonableness had been present, if overlooked, in his philosophy from the beginning. In the early 1940s he wrote and joined in opinions that upheld the state's power to regulate certain types of conduct and speech, noting, however, that such statutes must be narrowly drawn. This belief came to the fore in 1949. At issue was an injunction issued by a Missouri court against labor picketers who attempted to pressure an ice supplier not to deal with nonunion peddlers. This was not different from forbidding a newspaper to publish something that might violate a law, Black said in conference, contending again that restraints on picketing must be narrowly drawn. But

picketing was "more than speech," observed Frankfurter. "All speech" was
"designed to influence [or] coerce," Douglas rebutted. The court voted 5–
4 to reverse on the ground that the injunction was too broad, and Black,
the senior member of the majority (along with Reed, Douglas, Murphy and
Rutledge), assigned the opinion to himself.

The more he worked on it, the more he became convinced it wouldn't
come out the way he wanted. He changed his mind, he told the justices,
and they all agreed with his new position. But he still searched for a rationale.
With the help of his former clerk John Frank, who reviewed most of the six
drafts, Black tried to define picketing. It is not publicizing, he wrote in the
fourth draft, and he started focusing on the placards the picketers used. The
main purpose of the picketing was to induce a violation of state law forbidding
agreements in restraint of trade, Black concluded. The First Amendment
does not protect speech that is an inseparable part of conduct and whose
"sole, unlawful immediate objective" is the infringement of a valid law or
public policy. Picketing undertaken for an illegal purpose could be regulated.

"I entirely agree," Frankfurter said. "You have written an opinion that
is hard to get around," noted Rutledge (who tried but could not). Enshrined
was a doctrine that picketing could be prohibited if its objective were contrary
to "public policy." Left unexplored was how picketing was more than speech,
and this gave the Court, and Black, a strong tool to use under certain
circumstances.[7]

*   *   *

The aftermath of World War Two saw the emergence of a loyalty mania
unequaled in American history. In March 1947 the Court refused to hear
a case arising from the dismissal of a federal employee as a result of a Civil
Service Commission finding that there was "reasonable doubt as to his
loyalty." Four days later, President Truman issued an executive order establishing the federal employee loyalty program. Over two million workers were
immediately subject to a cruelly inhumane regime that blithely ignored
traditional standards of due process and fair hearing. The frenzy raged across
the country, emulated by state and local governments. To politicians the
order worked: the officeholder who resisted it was soon looking for a new
job. That it trampled on American freedoms was given little thought.

The loudest protest against these practices if the Court had weighed
their merits at this time would have come from Black. He would have applied
the Fifth Amendment's "flat prohibition" against self-incrimination, which
aimed at "using a man's compelled testimony against him," as he wrote in

a 1944 dissent. But Black barely peeped when invasions against Fourth Amendment rights were charged;* even his remarks in conference were unusually short. Much of the reason derives from his experience working closely with police officers while he was prosecutor in Birmingham. He developed respect for their integrity and courage. "Soldiers in the cause of the law," he called them in his memoirs. Black always had a hardnose streak in him, a prosecutor mentality. "The method of getting [the suspect] is not the supreme thing; what happens to him after that is supreme," he once said. Punishment of dissenters for their heretical views concerned him more than "ordinary criminals." His whole career involved civic governance—it was the locus of his being. The following statement in an opinion, then, does not startle as much: "it is not surprising that the men behind the First Amendment also insisted upon the Fifth, Sixth, and Eighth Amendment. . . . " Black did not mention the Fourth Amendment.

That amendment's enforcement is the exclusionary rule—evidence obtained illegally cannot be used against a person at trial. Black dealt with it in two 1949 cases. Although the principle behind it goes back hundreds of years, he called it in the first case "an extraordinary sanction, judicially imposed." In *Wolf v. Colorado* he went further. A physician had been convicted for conspiring to perform abortions; the conviction was based partly on information (the names of patients listed in day books, who subsequently testified against him) that police had seized in his office without a search warrant as an incident to a warrantless arrest. In conference Black passed before voting to reverse the conviction. Eventually he decided to write a concurrence to Frankfurter's opinion for the Court.

Since his service as assistant United States attorney forty years earlier under Henry L. Stimson, that walking embodiment of old-fashioned rectitude ("Gentlemen do not read other people's mail"), Frankfurter had been passionate about the Fourth Amendment. "I am nuts about it," he told the brethren two years earlier, "because there is no provision of the Constitution more important to be nuts about." But his opinion in *Wolf* was so abstract it did not even mention the facts of the case. He extended the Fourth Amendment's "core" to the states, but not its enforcement feature, the exclusionary rule itself. (To do so by judicial command would have gone

---

* The Fourth Amendment reads:

> The right of the people to be secure in their persons, houses, papers, and effects, against unreasonable searches and seizures, shall not be violated, and no Warrants shall issue, but upon probable cause, supported by Oath or affirmation, and particularly describing the place to be searched, and the persons or things to be seized.

against Frankfurter's principles of federalism.) And he hinted that the rule was one of evidence and subject to annulment by Congress.

Black's opinion jelled finally after Frankfurter circulated his own, and he tracked part of Frankfurter's analysis in his two-paragraph concurrence. "A plain implication" of the Court's opinion, he wrote, was that the exclusionary rule was "not a command of the Fourth Amendment but . . . a judicially created rule of evidence which Congress might negate." ("I do not here question the wisdom of the rule . . . ," he wrote in a draft but deleted from his published opinion.) Black's position, John Frank observed shortly after the case came down—and no one supported him more overall— "may well be the most restrictive interpretation of the Fourth Amendment by any Justice in the Court's history."[8]

Black's philosophy involved Supreme Court intercession in some areas to secure the intent of the Constitution or of legislation, and a hands-off attitude in others. To ensure a fair trial in accordance with constitutional safeguards was one of his major legal goals. No stronger proponent of jury trial has ever sat on the Supreme Court than this old trial lawyer. "The jury is like rock music," one law professor wrote. "Classical theory frowns; the masses applaud. And in a democracy the felt need of the masses have [sic] a claim upon the law." When a jury decides against someone, Black liked to say, the losing litigant knows he has gotten a fair shot, whereas if the judge decides against someone, the litigant often thinks that the system is rotten. The right to jury trial was almost as much a star to him as was Thomas Jefferson himself. The Supreme Court has a responsibility to review actions brought under laws protecting injured workers. For a judge to disregard, to order a jury to enter, a particular verdict was to Black nothing less than judicial sin.

Nor may courts interfere with the operation of the economy, with rare exceptions. Congress had the sweeping power to regulate whatever affected commerce, Black believed. In the absence of this direction, states could regulate. (Of the commerce clause's "outside boundary," he wondered "if there is any.") In 1945 the Court struck down, as a restriction on state power, an Arizona law limiting the length of trains. To Black this smacked of the Old Court's knocking down legislation it did not like. That the earlier decisions "rested on the Due Process Clause while today's decision rests on the Commerce Clause" was beside the point: elected representatives rather than appointed judges "can best determine the policies which govern the people." These provisions, he later noted, "have been used like Siamese twins in a never-ending stream of challenges to government regulation. The reach of one twin may appear to be longer than that of the other, but either can easily be turned to remedy this apparent handicap."

Under the due process clause, courts could not consider the appropriateness of legislation. This doctrine had been "deliberately discarded," Black wrote for the Court in 1949. The states had power to legislate "so long as their laws do not run afoul of some specific federal constitutional provision, or of some valid federal law." It is difficult to overstate the centrality of this tenet of his creed, and as long as Black remained on the Court, no state economic regulation was invalidated on grounds of denial of substantive due process. Reappearance under any form or any name alarmed him, and he remained ever vigilant.

So strong was this belief that even when a state law required racial segregation in public transportation, Black would not intervene. He wrote a concurrence, sustaining it under the commerce clause. In doing so, he was being deliberately inconsistent. He believed the law's policy was both abhorrent and unconstitutional. In conference he suggested it could be held to violate the equal protection clause. Whereupon Frankfurter replied it was unnecessary to decide the constitutionality of state-mandated segregation now: "We should wait for that case."[9] . . .

*   *   *

Lyndon Johnson's case could not wait. In September 1948 the young Texas congressman ran against Governor Coke Stevenson in a brutally fought primary for the Democratic nomination for senator. Johnson was a New Dealer at heart but painted himself more conservative to appeal to the statewide electorate; Stevenson was so reactionary that the twentieth century was foreign to him. Each side tried to count the other out. Votes were manufactured but the Johnson camp produced more—203 were "found" in ballot box 13 in the town of Alice in Jim Wells County in south Texas. The final tally gave Johnson an 87-vote victory, and the party certified "Landslide Lyndon," as he called himself, as its candidate. Then, on September 15, Stevenson's lawyers obtained from a federal judge a temporary restraining order forbidding the party to place Johnson's name on the November ballot as its nominee. The judge, suspecting fraud, appointed two special masters to investigate charges of vote stealing; if they found it, he would invalidate the primary results. And Stevenson would become senator.

Time was urgent: the Fifth Circuit Court of Appeals judges who would hear the case would not sit together until mid-October, a month off, after absentee ballots had been printed. (A single appellate judge acting alone could not grant a stay of the order.) The Supreme Court justice assigned to the circuit could, however, hear cases individually under emergency circumstances. After the Fifth Circuit denied the stay, as expected, Johnson's lawyers appealed to Black.

Leading this group of what one member (Paul Porter) called "the greatest collegium of legal talent that Washington could supply" was Abe Fortas. * His generation produced no better lawyer, and Fortas framed the issues precisely. Since federal courts had no jurisdiction over state primaries, he had little doubt that Johnson would win on appeal. The motion was presented to the Court on September 25. Its main point was simply that federal courts are supposed to stay out of state elections; it is a matter for state courts only. On the twenty-sixth Black's clerk told Thurman Arnold, also Fortas's partner, that Black would hear the case on the twenty-eighth if Stevenson's counsel was present; former Texas governor Dan Moody, a talented advocate, agreed to fly up.

The hearing brought together strands of Black's past and present. He had known about crooked elections long before Johnson and many of those now helping him (including Fortas) were born. And for a dozen years now he had a friendly acquaintance with Johnson, as well as scores of mutual friends, and Virginia Durr was a dear friend of Lady Bird Johnson and had raised money for Lyndon. Accompanying Fortas to Black's chambers were Arnold and Porter, Hugh Cox, Alvin Wirtz (Johnson's Texas lawyer, friend and mentor) and former Texas governor James Allred. Moody represented Stevenson alone. They sat in a semicircle around Black's desk. While he rocked in his swivel chair, they presented their arguments. [10]

Jurisdiction was the issue, Fortas claimed, and time was critical. Unless the order was overturned by October 3, state law dictated that no Democratic candidate would appear at all on the Texas ballot, which would be "perfectly appalling." Fraud was the issue, Moody argued, and Black lacked power to rule on the injunction, which was justified under a post–Civil War statute designed to give federal protection to voting rights of Negroes. Black asked "sharp, relevant" questions, recalled Porter. He "knew more of these Re-

---

* This group included former attorney general Francis Biddle, Ben Cohen, Tom Corcoran and his partner James Rowe (also one of Roosevelt's former assistants), Hugh Cox, and Joseph Rauh, as well as Fortas's partners, Thurman Arnold and former FCC chairman Porter. "Tommy was the leading personage and Abe was the leading lawyer," said Rauh (Kalman, *Fortas*, 202).

construction cases than any of us had had an opportunity to research." The previous day he had looked for precedents with his clerk and Hugo, Jr., who was in his last year of law school and happened to be in town, but they could not find any. When Black indicated that he wanted counsel to address the Court's power to interfere with the electoral process, Moody felt that Black was suggesting what Fortas should assert and that he "had no chance to win after that." But Black, privately having little doubt that Johnson stole the election, was trying to give Moody a lifeline, however flimsy. He did not take it while Fortas subtly shifted his argument. The federal judge had overstepped his domain, Fortas concluded. Texas laws gave Johnson an "irrevocably and incontestably vested" right to be on the ballot. The whole case was "a political controversy, neither more or less."

Black recessed the hearing for lunch while he drafted a statement (a shining example of gastronomical jurisprudence). His clerk summoned the lawyers to return to chambers, where Black announced his decision. The Constitution gave him the power to act, and this controversy was "a matter of supreme importance, not only to Texas but beyond the borders of Texas," he said. Stevenson had recourse to other than the federal courts: "The Senate is the judge of the qualification of its own members, finally." Black could find no statute that empowered a federal judge to intervene in a state election. And to permit that to happen "would be a drastic break with the past." Black granted a stay "until the full Supreme Court has an opportunity to consider it." The chance the Court would overturn it was small, and it was upheld October 5, two days after ballots were printed. Johnson was easily elected the next month.

Later, as Johnson's prominence grew and Landslide Lyndon's larceny took on a life of its own, stories spread that someone had spoken to Black on his behalf. Joseph Rauh thought Tom Corcoran did, as if that might convince Black. Sam Rayburn's name was mentioned (Black denied it). Johnson's balanced biographer Robert Dallek raised Attorney General Tom Clark as a possibility; since "Clark was indebted to Lyndon for helping him" get his job, "something of the kind might have occurred," hardly a weighty claim. On a higher level is James Reston, Jr.'s, undocumented declaration that President Harry Truman "would call Black from his campaign train outside San Marcos, and urge Black to enter the case and decide for Johnson." But the Truman Library has no record of any such call, nor does any survivor of the train ride recall one. Indeed, no evidence has ever been produced to support these assertions. Any such contention, moreover, makes little sense. No one had to tell Black about the importance of the election or the need, as he saw it, for progressives in the Senate or the viciousness of ideological politics in the South: more than any messenger, he had already been there.

To Black it was simply another case ("Texas case," not "Johnson" or "Stevenson," he wrote on the letter reporters sent asking to be present), although highly unusual and of obvious importance. The legal principle involved was not complicated: federal courts are supposed to stay out of state elections. It ensured the making of a senator and Lyndon Johnson never forgot who, by granting the stay, saved his political life. In 1966, to celebrate Black's eightieth birthday, he threw a small party in the family quarters at the White House. Some of the same people who were involved in the 1948 episode were there. Johnson referred to it in vivid detail in his toast. "If it weren't for Mr. Justice Black at one time, we might well be having this party," he said. "But one thing I know for sure, we wouldn't be having it here."[11]*

---

* "Lyndon didn't talk about the case much," said Lady Bird Johnson (int.). "It was the kind of thing that you just take a deep breath and say, 'I'm glad it's over.' He was so relieved and somewhat surprised. I think he was too grateful to Justice Black to talk about it much."

CHAPTER 26

IN THE FAMILY

THE SUPREME COURT was the focal point of Hugo Black's life. Its work came ahead of anything else. He could play, but there really wasn't much play in him and he felt guilty about being frivolous. He did not take his own advice to Lister Hill: "I have an idea that a man can probably accomplish more, and be happier, who has a long life of intermittent work rather than a man who tries to pack constant work in the narrow limits of a short life." Politics, play (tennis), family and reading also kept Hugo perpetually busy.

Perhaps it was symbolic that he lived in Alexandria, where the statue in the middle of town is of a Confederate soldier and faces south. For he often looked southward, to Alabama. The itinerary of many Alabamians visiting Washington included a visit to their former senator in his chambers. Hugo was always eager to hear how things were going back home, to swap old tales, to find out how mutual friends were. He never asked anyone to leave; the visitor would determine when that time came. He had the politician's sense of easiness with people without giving away any secrets. When he went on the Court, he said, an "old and very wise friend" told him the only subject he would discuss with the press was Chinese art. "Mr. Justice," asked a newsman, "what do you know about Chinese art?" "Not a thing" was the reply. He did know about politics. Through his continued subscriptions to Alabama newspapers and his discussions with Lister Hill—"just about whenever we got together," Hill recalled, which was very often— Black kept abreast of Alabama politics. Occasionally he lunched with the state congressional delegation in the speaker's dining room on Thursdays. In 1946, even more than usual, the talk was political.

Into a state whose political leaders focused exclusively on local concerns,

377

strolled James E. (Big Jim) Folsom, running for governor of Alabama with a hillbilly string band called the Strawberry Pickers, a cornshuck mop and a wooden suds bucket, which he passed around for contributions. He espoused progressive reforms in education and pensions, urged repeal of the poll tax and called for the fair apportionment of the state legislature. It was a conscious replay of Black's first Senate campaign. ("Hugo Black was the greatest man Alabama ever produced," Folsom later said.) His opponents, joined by their press and business supporters, ridiculed him. But the sneering quickly stopped once Folsom won the June primary. In August he went to Washington. After meeting Truman and other Democratic leaders, he drove to New York with Black and Hill. The ostensible reason for the trip was for Hugo and Lister to take a vacation in New England. But its real purpose was to tutor Folsom, who had no plans and was making none, on how to be governor. In thanking Folsom for sending his inaugural address, with its "simple but wholesome ideas" that held out hope that Alabamians might become "a happier people," Black laid out his own precepts:

> You may not find the road towards it either smooth or well lighted. To march along it will require not some but all of your energy and devotion. You will find ambuscades along the route. There will be flowers, good to look at but poisonous to the touch. False friends will invite you to go the wrong way. If flattery fails to swerve you from your course, and if caution enables you to escape traps and pitfalls, your courage will be tested by intimidation, abuse, and fusilades of hostile criticism. Much of this will come from good people who have been misled. All of these things you can overcome if you get wisdom and understanding. They teach a man to put the public good above personal glory.
>
> Along with your other friends, I hope for you that you may be able to walk the highroad with safety. Always remember that you live in a goldfish bowl.[1]

In the waning days of World War Two, Black started to speak publicly about foreign policy. He felt frustrated at being out of the political arena. "One of the deprivations of holding some positions is that it is sometimes necessary to withhold publication of views which one would like to express," he told *Nation* publisher Freda Kirchwey after turning down for the second time an opportunity to support its beliefs publicly. Especially after Roosevelt's death and Truman's elevation, Black often spoke about wanting to be a news commentator like Drew Pearson. So he unleashed himself, within limits.

Addressing a Russian war relief program in Los Angeles in June 1945, he denounced talk about another war before the present one was over. The United States and the Soviet Union shared a joint interest in peace. "Certainly this country, dedicated to democracy and to freedom of expression, has nothing to fear from Russian ideology. Our safety rests in the good sense and loyalty of our people." He was "convinced that the Russian people would like to look forward to our help and our friendship in their task of great reconstruction." Ben Cohen gave him much information and wrote "quite a lot" of the speech, qualifying many of the conditions for American support to Russia; but Black insisted on eliminating them. He attended the closing session of the initial United Nations conference in San Francisco, and left with hope: "Everything now points to a world organization which offers some promise that future generations will not have to give up a part or all of their life in order to engage in war."

Black did not want to "get tough" with the Russians. At a dinner at Joseph Alsop's house in January 1946 he "made the point that we had no more business messing in Rumania and Bulgaria than Russia had messing in Mexico and Cuba," Henry Wallace, then secretary of commerce, wrote in his diary. "He said that we would no more tolerate an unfriendly government in Mexico than Russia would tolerate an unfriendly government in Rumania." By September 1946 Black felt "we were headed straight for war" with Russia. "The only thing that troubles me at the present time," he wrote his old Senate colleague Homer Bone, "is the effort of many people, allowedly backed by most of the press, to plunge this country into a new war with Russia. Such a thing is especially frightful to contemplate. . . . There seems to be a widespread opinion that what this country should do is to attack Russia at once, destroy her cities with atomic bombs, and thus win an easy victory. Even if this could be done, the prospect of our engaging in such wholesale slaughter as we did at Hiroshima is not inviting to a man of peaceful instincts." (He thought that dropping the atomic bomb on Hiroshima, however, was "a regrettable necessity to save further lives.")

Wallace's call on Russia to meet the United States "halfway" in the quest for peace had gotten him fired from the Truman administration in September 1946. "Of course" Wallace's criticisms of Russia were "well founded," Black told him, "but you couldn't confuse the people by presenting both sides of the case." (Black later called Wallace "a good man although a very, very poor politician.") The "only thing" to remember was that "the Army and the State Department were carrying us into war with Russia just as fast as they could." Black struck a familiar theme: the people did not realize this because they could not get the "facts." "When you touch the emotions of people they don't reason things out." Russia has no "aggressive designs" against the United States. Black's fear of war overshadowed most other competing foreign policy considerations. The Republicans, he said, were waiting for the Democrats to get the country into war so they could win the 1948 election using the slogan "The Democrats got us into war."*

What, Wallace asked, was Black's impression of Truman in the Senate? He "always voted right," Hugo replied. "He was with us on practically every progressive issue. His heart is in the right place; he is not dishonest. Those who claim that because he was part of the Pendergast machine he was therefore dishonest are altogether wrong." The trouble was that Truman had "no background or understanding . . . no fundamental philosophy and very little knowledge of history." He "could not realize how nations react once a certain channel for events has been created." It was "a tragedy that Truman should be President." Alben Barkley, the Senate majority leader, "would have been much better." Roosevelt's sickness caused "the whole trouble."[2] Black's frustration was showing.

These differences did not affect Black's feelings toward Truman. They shared many things. Hugo simply liked Harry and always quickly came to his defense. "My own belief is that he is thoroughly honest; that he has exceptional common sense; and that this country could be in far worse hands," he wrote Hugo, Jr. "I rank Truman pretty high," he said in 1968. " . . . He does know some history." And history "is the basic thing a man ought to know to have good ideas about government. How's it been done before? What was the weakness of this government here? What was done to relieve the weakness? And to give it strength." The president, Black told a friend just after delivering a stinging rebuke (in the Steel Seizure case) in 1952, is "a man of very high principles, honest, and not only loyal to his friends but loyal to the best traditions of the country. . . . High motives" have prompted his "every action. . . . Any disagreements I have had, however, have never led me to doubt for one moment his complete integrity of character."

On no domestic issue did Black disagree with Truman more whole-

---

* Black blamed this partly on the media. When the radio and the press "constantly beat the tom-toms, the result is not difficult to predict," he wrote a former clerk. The public would not complacently accept the inevitability of war if the accompanying civilian death and destruction were given equal emphasis. "The idea that no country but the United States can make use of such discoveries is probably a vain illusion" (HLB to Charles Luce 4/8/48).

heartedly than on the loyalty oath. Black believed that it and the attorney general's list of subversive organizations, which Truman also revived, were patently unconstitutional, utterly immoral and thoroughly counterproductive; and he hated their every word. So did Clifford Durr. To Durr, Hugo Black was special. "We were like brothers," Durr noted. In 1966 Black put into print what he had long felt:

> Cliff is one of the best men I have ever known. All of his life he has been the personification of gentleness, kindness and tolerance. His course in life has been marked by courage, not by expediency. He has never been afraid to advocate what he believed to be right and to oppose what he believed to be wrong. He has never compromised with what he believed to be evil and against the best interest of his country. As a public servant he fought valiantly for the public interest and not for what he thought was the best interest of Cliff Durr . . . a man without greed and without guile. . . .

As a member of the Federal Communications Commission since 1941, Durr had outspokenly advocated a democratic radio and public television system. Truman's "mindlessly cruel" loyalty program shocked and sickened him. He refused to cooperate in its implementation within the FCC and attacked it publicly whenever he could. And he decided not to accept reappointment when his term expired in June 1948, even if it were offered. Two people disagreed: Harry Truman and Hugo Black.

Truman offered Durr reappointment through Black when Hugo came to the White House on March 29. Durr's opposition to the loyalty program— he was its leading critic in government—made no difference, Truman said. Whatever Durr's views, Truman knew him "as a man of sturdy honesty and courage, and for that reason alone" he wanted him to continue serving. Not only would he reappoint Cliff, but he would fight to the end for Senate confirmation. Durr sent back his thanks and "regrets" without specifying his reasons for declining, Black told Truman when the president called the next week. Durr then saw Truman. The loyalty program would "tear this country to pieces with fear and suspicion unless it was arrested," he pointed out. Truman professed agreement: he was only trying "to take the ball away" from Parnell Thomas, the new chairman of the House Un-American Activities Committee, to keep something worse from happening, he said, and he was "not at all happy" about it.* His purpose was to protect government

---

* The loyalty issue "was a political problem," according to Truman's counsel Clark Clifford. He "was going to run in '48, and that was it. . . . I felt the whole thing was being

employees from the unjust accusations Thomas was making. If the program did not accomplish this goal, or resulted in any hardship or unfairness, he assured Durr, he would amend it or even repeal it if necessary. But Durr was convinced it would be wrong to accept reappointment and then fight the loyalty program policies. He left government.[3]

Truman's behavior "was an exhibition of his greatness of character concerning fundamentals," Black told Durr after writing about the incident in a letter to the *Nation* in 1966. Hugo "came out of this experience with the belief that there was something strikingly alike in the character of these two men—that both profoundly believed in plain, simple, homey honesty, and that neither could be swerved from doing that which he thought would best serve the public interest." It also made Black put into words how and when a public figure should choose his spots for maximum impact, something he did (seemingly naturally) rather than talked about. Cliff "frequently makes fights that are not completely necessary and thereby impairs his influence in matters of more importance," he wrote a clerk in 1961. Shortly before his death, he talked with Durr's daughter, Tilla, about how ideals could get in the way of effectiveness. "Cliff chose to be a martyr and lost his effectiveness. That was a tragedy since he is a most talented man." Black admitted to "the necessity for taking stands and living by one's ideals. Yet one should not lose his capacity to effect change." That is what he felt Cliff Durr had done.[4]

*   *   *

Issues such as the loyalty oath led some liberals to seek an alternative to Truman. They first turned to William O. Douglas, who lost interest in the Court's work after the war. Discussion about Douglas and politics irked Black; Hugo sloughed over clerks' comments that Douglas wanted to run for president. They were more intellectual and judicial companions than bosom friends now. The fondness was there as always, but the personal closeness of former years had lessened. But Bill continued to look upon Hugo as a stabilizing influence, someone who could counsel him on different types of matters. He needed it now. His behavior had become increasingly erratic. He started showing up late for various functions; little things like that always bothered Hugo. And Douglas's marriage to his wife of twenty-five years had turned on-again, off-again. Hugo and Josephine (who was one of

---

manufactured" (Carl Bernstein, *Loyalties* (New York, 1989), 195, 197; see Clifford, *Counsel* 182).

Mildred Douglas's closest friends) arranged a dinner to try to keep them together and also invited the Corcorans and the Arnolds. Douglas was sullen and frigid the entire evening. He wanted to stay on the Court (for the security it offered as much as for anything else), and orchestrated a charade, indicating interest in the vice-presidency to politicians and pundits while writing letters denying it, then rejecting Truman's offer of the vice-presidential nomination. He remained on the bench, speaking out publicly on any and every issue that engaged his constantly active, trenchant intellect.

Black never commented on Douglas's odd political ways. "The Supreme Court is unto itself," he said. "It is unbecoming for justices to toss their hat back into the political ring." He believed this deeply—but he found it easier for the rule to apply to others than to himself: the presidential fire still burned within. In 1947 he and Josephine dined with their friends Mamie and Dwight Eisenhower. Crowds cheered Ike as they walked down the street from the restaurant. He flashed that grin and waved back. "I knew then that he wanted to be President," Black later claimed. Hugo probably wanted to have dinner to gauge Ike's interest. In early 1948 he went to Birmingham to determine if he could garner backing for a possible presidential run. The odds were small, but Black's dream was too strong not to try. He spoke quietly with his old friends Hugh Locke, who made discreet inquiries, and Ben Ray, still powerful in the state party; and with Montgomery postmaster Roy Nolen, Lister Hill's closest political operative. The responses were uniformly negative.

Revolt was brewing in the Alabama Democratic Party. The threat of mass Negro voter registration had catalyzed conservatives already chafing at national Democratic spending and racial policies. The year before, Lister Hill had resigned as Senate whip (and presumably the next majority leader) because he saw an inescapable clash between the party's southern and national wings, and wanted to protect his seat. He knew how badly Black wanted to be president (even if Hugo didn't show it much). Lister "often talked about Black and the presidency," recalled his friend Clarence Allgood, later a federal judge. "We'd go fishing a few times a year and he'd always talk about it. Lister thought Black would be a great President and said there was nothing he couldn't do if he put his mind to it. To Lister the question was more how Black would find a way to run while on the Court. He said Black would never step down." Hill would try to move mountains for Hugo; and his political partners would strive mightily. But they did not command the party machinery. The party's executive committee was headed by a blustery, reactionary Mobile lawyer, Gessner McCorvey, and controlled by

Black Belt interests and big business representatives, who supplied its funds. For Black to try to budge these forces would be fruitless. Only political lightning—in the form of a presidential nomination—would change his mind. That was highly unlikely.

Harry Truman knew nothing of Black's activities and dreams. What would have happened if he did? "President Truman lacked confidence in himself as president for a long time and decided to run in 1948 much later than anyone realized," said Clark Clifford, the person in the White House closest to him. "If he knew Black wanted to run, I believe one of two things would have happened. He would have redoubled his efforts to have Eisenhower accept the nomination, which of course would have failed. Or, considering his respect for Black stemming from the Senate and Black's standing in the party and among liberals and labor, the President would have stepped aside."[5] And Hugo Black might have been president.

Unsurprisingly, then, a mid-May 1948 dinner with Hill, Corcoran, Claude Pepper and their wives was a glum occasion: "All of us against Truman," Pepper recorded in his diary. But Truman's fighting speech at the Democratic convention in July excited Black. He told Truman that if he said that all over the country he would win the election. Truman was already thinking that himself; and his whistlestop ("Give 'em hell, Harry") campaign proved it to the pundits. Black had discovered Truman's campaigning ability in Missouri in 1934. "I have also heard him talk at every Gridiron meeting since he became President," Hugo told Sherman Minton. "There has been no instance in which he came off second best upon any of those occasions. He leaves his audiences with the impression that he is exactly what I think he is—a man of simple integrity and honest purpose."

Black discussed the race several times with Truman and listened to the results at Lister Hill's house. "How happy they all were!" recalled Truman Hobbs, Black's clerk and the son of an Alabama congressman, who was there. "I told Harry that if he went to the people, he couldn't lose," Hugo said several times. "That was a grand victory and it was *your* victory," he wrote Truman. "You have proven again that the people cannot be fooled when they are told the truth. I had no doubt that what you had done as a candidate for senator you could do on a nationwide scale. The people recognize integrity. My best wishes. Take care of yourself, the people need you." In thanking Black, Truman added by hand: "Want to see you one of these days when I get back. We've lots of things to talk about—'shoes & ships & sealing wax.' "

"What happened the other day did not send me to bed from shock or disappointment" or "with illness brought on by disappointment," Hugo told friends. And he happily wrote Hugo, Jr.: "I understand that a lot of weak-kneed Democrats in Washington who anticipated that the 'little man' would be overwhelmingly rejected by the people are now trying to release the houses which they had given up in view of the approaching calamity. At the same time I understand that a lot of formerly cocksure Republicans who had leased houses in Washington are struggling to get out from under. Too bad!"[6]

Black tried to separate his fondness for Truman from the monstrous cruelty the president unleashed in the name of "loyalty." He talked about the human and legal tragedies the policy produced but not about its originator. Starting in 1949, he saw and spoke to Truman less. And Black never felt quite the same toward him after the United States entered the Korean War the next year. "It was a mistake to go into Korea because among other reasons I did not believe it would be possible to fight any large armies successfully so far away from home," Black told a former clerk. "Maybe our officials have done all they could to prevent such a catastrophe" as a third world war with Russia, "but people who abhor war are always prone to wonder that more could not be done." That was late 1950. Soon he wrote, "I still have some hope, though faint, that there may be sufficient statesmanship somewhere to prevent World War III." Truman's relieving General Douglas MacArthur from his command was appropriate, Black believed. His feelings about MacArthur came through in early 1948 while having a drink after playing tennis at *New Republic* publisher Michael Straight's home with Robert W. Barnett of the State Department and Jiro Kato, a member in good standing in the Japanese establishment. Barnett recalled: "Justice Black spent the whole time, in effect saying what a son of a bitch Douglas MacArthur was. Why? Because he was a military man, who was all right as a military man, but trying to shape up a presidential boom, and Black felt that for constitutional and policy reasons this was an outrage."[7]

*   *   *

Josephine's depressions continued. Hugo felt frustrated because he could not help her. He took books on depression out of the Library of Congress and pored over them at home by the hour, trying to fathom a subject that could not have been further removed from his inclinations. But will cannot overcome depression. He searched his memory for reasons for her depression, and wondered if he had done anything to cause it in any way. Her assurances that he had not did not lessen his sense of guilt. He asked Cliff Durr for advice. "I've done everything I could think of," he said. "I don't know what else to do." Occasionally he cried because he could do nothing. "I am helpless," he admitted. *

He agreed with whatever her psychiatrist said. She went away at times, and when she came back she felt much better. Hugo felt that was her cure. "See how good she's feeling now. That doctor is good." He never understood that her getting away from him and from Washington for a while partly explained the improvement. Then the doctor suggested that she paint. It was marvelous therapy, satisfying her yearning to accomplish in her own right. Some of her self-worth returned, and she appeared more serene and at ease with herself and the world. She took courses and worked in a studio in an old shed she fixed up in her backyard, where she was joined daily by Dorothy Goldberg, whose husband Arthur was then a leading labor lawyer. Eventually, Josephine won several contests, and her paintings were displayed at exhibitions in Washington and New York.

Her moods still fluctuated sharply and they affected her health. These were the days before medication could control depressions. Her presence remained striking but she suffered from regular depressions as well as a variety of minor physical ailments that baffled doctors. "Constant headaches—constant pains in shoulder, legs—numbness of legs and arms—sleeplessness weeks on end and constant cramping of heart and palpitation—complete exhaustion—almost prostration—constant fight to keep from destroying myself," she wrote in 1948 in a record of her health during the decade. More than ever, she turned to nature as a refuge from the turbulence around her. "I seem always to have been conscious of tremendous forces operating on all the planes of manifestation—physical, emotional and spiritual," she once

---

* In the 1960s Black wrote to a former assistant whose wife was suffering from depression: "The fact that she is able to be up and around and engage in most normal activities should be encouraging—and, of course, it takes a lot of courage on the part of all concerned to meet a situation like this. I am confident that you have developed a philosophy of your own which will enable you to come out of it all with an even better philosophy than you have had before. It takes an extraordinary amount of kindness, generousness, courage and love. It is bad for little children not to have the full benefits that come from a mother with an abundance of health and energy to help them along through their hard days. That makes a daddy's problem all the more. Please give [her] my love."

wrote Hugo, Jr. "Life was never a simple thing for me even as a tiny little girl." In Miami she once sat with her daughter, just looking out the hotel window at the rolling waves and currents of the ocean. Hugo had asked JoJo to stay with her in their room. "She might jump," she said.

In the summer of 1950 Josephine's physician advised her not to have anyone else stay at her house. For that reason her father, whose own health was failing, could not come live with her and went to a nursing home in North Carolina. Dr. Foster had long been a pain to Hugo. Vigorous and optimistic as he supported himself on various small government sinecures, he both amused and irritated his son-in-law. "If I do anything, I'll outlive him," Hugo said. Foster's occasional visits to Washington always produced a crisis as he poured out his continual business disappointments to Josephine. But he was always entertaining and lively, stimulating and intellectually curious, even after his health started to decline. He died in 1952, after Hugo had helped to pay his expenses in a nursing home for two years.

Money troubles shadowed Hugo. Occasionally, they made him talk of leaving the Court. After a decade on the bench, despite a $20,000 salary, double his senatorial earnings, he still had not erased the debt he had incurred while in the Senate. Josephine's medical expenses and his support of Dr. Foster forced Hugo to borrow money from Barney Whatley. Albert Lee Smith's restructuring of the lease on the Birmingham property he and Hugo owned helped, but what really pulled Hugo out of the hole was selling his share of the partnership in 1954.[8]

Yet such matters did not prevent him from enjoying life. It is "a pretty gay experience, after all," he wrote Sterling, "in spite of the fact that a great many people are greedy, selfish, thoughtless, and even incapable of appreciating the blessings that surround them every day of their lives if they would just look around." He practiced what he told Hugo, Jr.: "In your associations with people, as everywhere else, it is a question of balance, and the Greeks just about hit on the best doctrine when they adopted as the slogan of life, 'Never Too Much.' "

Hugo and Josephine regularly got together with the Arnolds, who lived nearby, the Hills, the Corcorans and the Durrs (often on the spur of the moment). Some of the parties at their or the Arnoldses' house were uproarious, such as the time Thurman smoked the candlesticks. Occasionally, Hugo even took a drink. And Bill Douglas got drunk as often as not. Or

Hugo got a few people together to sing, only somewhat on key. "A few nights ago," he wrote Sterling, "I heard [Kentucky senator, later baseball commissioner] Happy Chandler sing to an accordion accompaniment played by Tom Corcoran. Both of them have agreed to come out to my house and play some evening, and I suggested that I hoped it would be when you and Hugo were here. They also promised to bring with them the new musical Senator from Idaho, Cowboy [Glen] Taylor, whom I have not yet heard. We could have a great time on such an occasion."

In the late 1940s he and Josephine went to New York. Let Hugo tell the story of dinner:

> They've got lots of good restaurants in New York, don't they. Expensive though. I remember about twenty years ago a doctor friend took my wife and me to the 23 Club—or was it the 21??—anyway, it was *some* place. Must have cost him a fortune. He had 50 single dollar bills in his pocket when we walked in, and not one left when we walked out. And that didn't include the bill!
>
> Well, he just kept giving those dollar bills away. Even the butter boy got one! And the salad boy, and I'm sure the headwaiter got ten, at least. Well, he was a very successful doctor, did ear operations. But even so, when he tried to give a dollar to the hat-check girl, to retrieve my hat, I had to stop him. "I resent that," I told him. "My wife's been trying to get me to throw out that old fedora for 15 years now, and nobody's going to pay to get it back. Give the dollar to me."

Another meal started off differently. In March of 1948 Hugo was the guest of honor at a party in Saint Petersburg, Florida, given by local newspaper publisher Nelson Poynter. He was standing in the receiving line when another guest walked in, wearing a pillow case with holes cut for eyes and nose and a pair of dime-store white gloves. Black's face turned crimson when he looked at New Orleans newspaper editor George W. Healy, Jr., in what strongly resembled Klan regalia. Healy exposed his face and explained that he meant no offense but that he had a severe case of sunburn and a doctor told him not to expose himself to the sun. Black was incredulous, then enjoyed the embarrassment and insisted that Healy need not apologize. Soon he was laughing aloud, and asked Healy to put his protective gear on so they could be photographed together.

He did not laugh, even if others did, when reading a story about himself. Protocol required that he attend the funeral of a colleague he had cordially long detested. "How far has the service gone?" asked a colleague who walked in late. "They just opened the defense," Black whispered back.

And, of course, there was tennis. It continued as unsurpassed therapy for him. He jokingly insisted that he preferred the Supreme Court to the Senate because it gave him "more time for tennis." How much tennis is "too much"? he asked. "I have not yet been able to find out." Tennis in summer is "the best tonic I can take." When he developed tennis elbow, the right-handed Black played lefty. "I find very few here who have enough endurance to keep me occupied when [the Supreme] Court is not in session," he noted in 1952. The only book he ever asked his daughter to return was *Tennis Made Easy* by Lloyd Budge, who gave him lessons in Miami. (Through Budge, Black got to know his champion brother Donald.) Hugo was always telling his sons that his game was improving. "At 64 I am still going strong on tennis," Black wrote them in 1950. "In fact, unless you two have improved considerably, I think your ambition to 'clean up the old man' is not yet in prospect of immediate fulfillment." That goal would take them several more years to achieve.[9]

After the war, Hugo, Jr., and Sterling returned to college, Hugo at the University of Alabama, Sterling (who had gone to Dartmouth for a semester before the war) at the University of Arizona, near where he had been stationed. Then (without receiving his degree) Sterling went to Columbia Law School, which pleased Justice Black. An Ivy League school had originally been Hugo, Jr.'s, first choice for college. His father felt differently. "Although he always tried to convince me and himself that he let me make my own decisions," Hugo, Jr., wrote, "he worked on me" to attend Alabama. He had a political career in mind for his son and there Hugo, Jr., would make friends from all over the state who could be helpful later. And Alabama it was, "because I knew he wanted me to." But Hugo, Jr., enjoyed writing courses at college and thought of becoming an English professor or writer. This did not suit Justice Black. At first he encouraged Hugo, Jr., but once he saw his son was serious, he subtly changed emphasis. The thought of a Professor Black did not meet with the approval of Justice Black, a public figure for over thirty years now.

Black believed in taking vigorous action. If he had been a physician, he would have been a surgeon. He sometimes mentioned an Alabamian he knew who had won a Rhodes Scholarship and gone to Oxford. He mimicked his friend, saying "oxe" with a pinched mouth and emphasizing "furd." "This fellow got a Rhodes Scholarship and you know what he landed up doing? He ran a girls' boarding school." People should go out and *do* something. The leisure of the theory class is often not realistic. "One of the troubles of so-called intellectuals," he wrote Hugo, Jr., "is that they frequently attempt to live in an isolated world. They somehow feel that those who have attained not their own intellectual level are inferior beings. This is wrong. . . . " And while admitting that teaching is an "inviting career," with "charm and opportunities," Black was "compelled to admit that professors and scholars too frequently live wholly in the world of theory. As a result, they from their ivory towers too often attempt to chart courses for a good society without a proper appreciation of the common-place motives which make the average man tick." *

Hugo, Jr., decided to go to law school and he was accepted at Yale. "I do not believe there is any better training going on at the present time than one can get in the Yale Law School," Black felt. Most faculty members, almost all liberal Democrats, were his friends. "They welcome ideas at that institution, both conventional and unconventional. . . . Most graduates at the Yale Law School have learned how to think for themselves." But first came a summer of intense preparation. Black gave his son a reading list of works on legal theory and history, and on philosophy, culminating in Aristotle. After each book, he questioned him, contradicting each answer with a counterproposition, and drilled him on syllogisms and drawing inferences. The purpose was that books are not only sources of information but usable tools for argument. It was in the tradition of John Stuart Mill's being trained by his father. But when a tired Hugo, Jr., took a nap, he woke up to see his father standing over him shaking his head and saying, "Go to the ant, thou sluggard, and consider his ways." The training helped. Hugo, Jr., made the *Yale Law Journal,* and the justice advised him with his assignment and counseled him for his moot court appearance.

For years Hugo, Jr., suffered from a form of asthma. As a child, he wrote, "I had a way of escaping things by getting sick. The night of scout meeting I was always ill with one thing or another—a cold, an asthma attack or hay fever." The condition kept him from combat service in World War Two but otherwise not from a very active life, including much tennis. The symptoms slowly lessened as his father's grip on him loosened. Even in his last year of law school, Black wrote, Hugo, Jr., suffered from "a tendency

---

* "Theoretical contemplation is a highly valuable means of moving toward improved techniques in many fields, but it cannot wholly displace the knowledge that comes from the hard facts of everyday life," Black wrote in a 1964 opinion (*Jackson v. Denno*).

toward asthma under certain circumstances." But it was definitely, if slowly, lifting. Being out of his father's house, away from his domineering presence, his attitude that he knew what was best for his sons—all served to abate Hugo, Jr.'s, asthma sharply, and he gained self-confidence as he embarked on his career.

Hugo Black insisted that his sons exercise regularly ("It means you will do more work and better work"), and urged they adopt those traits that "anyone who aspires to be a leader in any way"—which he assumed they would be—"needs to learn."* All the while he gave them the benefit of his vast experience. And he demanded self-discipline, never realizing that a scant handful of people at any time could possess it in the way he did. ("The next time you have an inclination to brood over something," he told Hugo, Jr., "read Parrington, or read that part of the Bible which says in substance that he that controls his temper is better than he that ruleth the city.") If one did not control oneself financially, he warned, that person might become "a slave to his immediate desires" and then to "special interests," a "tragic representative of a large group of people" who, despite their "brilliant minds, finally become the paid employees of men with stodgy minds, fat stomachs and long cigars." It was all part of his special type of tough love for his sons, admittedly and sometimes brutally frank and continually constructively critical—for their self-improvement.

And it continued in the trying early years of professional life (and marriage: Hugo, Jr., married in 1947, and Sterling early in 1949). Black commented on their cases and other legal work, and he regularly suggested and sent them books to read. Tacitus' and Cicero's writings on oratory he recommended as "useful to a man whose career depends to a very large extent on his capacity to persuade. . . . I do not think that any real eloquence is ever achieved except when it comes from a good person." And, "I am still optimistic enough about people to believe that there are many who would not use Cicero's general's subterfuge in order to violate an obligation. Even so, there are too many of this kind of people. There are probably many more than you think who try to live with the Golden Rule

---

* He wrote Hugo, Jr., in law school, 11/27/46: "Given good health which is preserved by careful living; and indomitable resolution to go ahead; and ability to keep up courage and self-confidence in the face of temporary difficulty and disappointments; and a fair amount of interest, no person need fear that he cannot achieve what are considered to be great accomplishments. . . . Sleep enough, eat enough, exercise enough, and work enough. Do no one of these things too much, and worry not at all. Such a budgeting of your time and control of your habits will bring you fabulous returns."

although many of them perhaps would be ashamed to admit it in public. I am also naive enough to believe that it pays in the long run, at least in self respect and self contentment."*

Hugo, Jr., accepted much of this counsel and advice as his father meant it. Sterling did not. He wanted to go as far west as possible to escape his father's heavy-handed, if (usually) benevolent, paternalism; and landed in Los Alamos, New Mexico, where he worked as a lawyer for the Atomic Energy Commission. Their relationship became as much contentious and adversarial as loving. Father would write how he thought Sterling should do something. Sterling would reply, taking issue point by point why he did it his way and that he did not want to be ordered what to do. Behind Black's behavior was his fear that Sterling's defective hearing would prevent him from earning a living as a practicing lawyer, and his belief that, as a result, Sterling should be a backroom government lawyer.[10]

To the satisfaction of his parents, Hugo, Jr., went into practice in Birmingham. He joined the firm of his father's first clerk, Buddy Cooper, and soon Cooper, Mitch and Black was the city's leading labor law firm. But the justice urged him not to concentrate too much on labor law, lest he "adopt highly specialized or narrow views." That he differed with the dominant thinking in Alabama on both racial and economic issues did not make his task easier. But the additional tutoring Black gave him before he moved— reading and discussing more classics, then concentrating on writing and speaking as simply, naturally and precisely as possible—helped in persuading clients, juries and audiences. Black also counseled Hugo, Jr., how to deport himself in his profession: A lawyer should not attack an adversary personally; one can always represent the client faithfully and loyally "without saying things that may leave lasting scars. . . . Always remember that the best lawyer is a perfect master of himself." And he advised how Hugo, Jr., could improve his next speech: "Strip it of all language which might engender personal bitterness on account of personal charges or implication; appeal to high and lofty motives; be calm; in references to [an opponent] be certain

---

* Black "particularly liked" Tacitus' "Dialogue Concerning Oratory" because it "urges the necessity for a person who wants to speak to fill his mind with knowledge. . . . Tacitus also agrees with all the other worthy writers on this subject that one who wants to appeal to exalted ideals of his hearers must himself possess internal wisdom and goodness" (HLB to HLB, Jr. 11/29/49).

not to overstate his delinquencies. Above all, do not get mad. In this way you will lay the ground for . . . public esteem. . . ."

Hugo Black wanted few things more than to have his namesake follow in his political footsteps. And personable young Hugo was politically involved from the moment he arrived in Birmingham. He had hardly unpacked before he started helping Lister Hill in his reelection campaign. Soon Hill said it would be an "excellent idea" for him to run for state Democratic committeeman from Jefferson County. He would be "practically certain" to be elected, and it would give him good standing with the party. "There will be some hot discussion, however," Black warned, "before the state Democratic party finally settles back in the national Democratic fold." After the 1950 primaries, Hill told Black that Hugo, Jr., should prepare himself to run for Congress in 1952. (Indeed, as far back as 1943 he said Hugo, Jr., should be a candidate after the war.) He wanted more congressmen who would vote with him on economic issues and thought Hugo, Jr., would win.

Hugo, Jr.'s, "plan" was to win the congressional seat and wait for Hill or John Sparkman, the other senator, to retire or die (while Hill and Black would try to persuade Sparkman to step down), and then run for the vacant seat. "From there who knows?" he wrote. His friends—the justice's old ones and their children—and labor would be his political base. And Hill's potent organization would stand at the ready. Black was already unobtrusively cultivating prominent Alabamians who visited Washington. The decision, he said, should be Hugo, Jr.'s, and his wife's, alone to make. He had only one suggestion: "Your best preparation for making decisions in my judgment is to take time enough to read the ideas of the great ethical, moral and spiritual teachers to enable you to put first things first."[11]

With JoJo it was very different. Josephine's indispositions meant that Hugo was virtually a single parent. He drove JoJo to school in the carpool as other parents did, making a game of it along the way and never once complaining that it might be keeping him from doing something else. Then he went to the Court or came home to work or play tennis; on weekends he took her to friends or to school functions. "You must be popular and behave yourself or your mother won't feel good," he told her when she was twelve in 1945. Thereafter, she headed every group and won every award in school. For college he wanted her to go to Sweet Briar. "That's where Southern women are supposed to go," he said, because Josephine went there for one year. ("I never met a graduate of Sweet Briar that I didn't like," he noted six months before he died.) But when JoJo insisted on coed, intellectually more stimulating Swarthmore, and stood her ground, he gave in. He always found it very hard to say no to her.

Hugo decided to throw her an unusual high school graduation party. He had her invite her classmates over to the house while he had all his colleagues and President Truman for a stag dinner. After the meal, he called for her to bring the girls down. "President Truman wants to play the piano for them." JoJo replied, deadpan: "You can't fool us." Truman sat down at the piano and said, "Call your numbers, anything at all." He played the first one, a current tune, and many more. The justices grinned and joined in the singing, as delighted as the astonished girls.

Black came to maturity at the high tide of the idea of progress. It was an Enlightenment concept. Civilization was moving in a definite and desired direction, all things were possible, and tomorrow was going to be better than today. World War One shattered this belief, but Black retained the conviction tightly and acted upon it. "While human progress is slow, it is nevertheless sure . . . ," he wrote Sterling.

> This country has during my lifetime moved in the direction of a better distribution of justice, in the large sense of the word, to the advantage of the people of the nation. No one can doubt but that individual human beings have many weaknesses, both physical and mental. It cannot be expected that societies composed of such individual units will somehow achieve perfection over night. Realization of this fact should now, however, *not ?* impel a person to conclude to become a member of the Edgar Allan Poe Melancholia Club. . . . From long experience in many governmental affairs, I have long since decided that it [our government] works about as well as anybody could expect, despite the petty political mistakes which crop up in the activities of those engaged in public service. Furthermore, I think we have a much better government than we had in 1789, and will have a still better one in 1989.[12]

He had faith, optimism and high hopes for his country. His idealism remained intact. He would need it all in the years ahead.

V

THE COURT YEARS, 1949–1962

CHAPTER 27

THE DARKLING
PLAIN

If a special size street riot puts you flat on your back,
Be philosophical with Douglas, Murphy, Rutledge, Reed and Black;
As you lie there bashed and bleeding, with your muscles badly hurt'n,
Say a little prayer for Vinson, Jackson, Frankfurter and Burton.

Robert Jackson's doggerel after one closely divided First Amendment case in the spring of 1949 caught the essence of the Court's uneven course in most civil liberties cases. The trend of decisions led Wiley Rutledge fleetingly to consider resigning, to accept an offer of a law school deanship. The results sapped his strength somewhat but not his determination to change them. Frank Murphy's health, however had not been good for several years, and in July 1949 he died. He was fifty-nine. Forty thousand people turned out in Detroit to honor a man of whom Black said, "If he ever did the wrong thing, it was for the right reason."

President Truman appointed Attorney General Tom Clark. Easygoing on the surface, accommodating and agreeable, the fifty-year-old Texan both put the government in the legal battle against segregation for the first time and stalwartly endorsed all internal security programs (he ordered one admitted Communist "picked up because he had been making speeches round the country that were derogatory to our way of life"). Douglas suspected what Clark's nomination portended for future cases. The matter "has been gnawing away at me," he wrote Black. "It is really a dreadful thing. I have thought that perhaps the best thing that could happen would be for you and me to resign. I have been seriously considering it."[1]

The fourth member of the civil liberties quartet, Wiley Rutledge, took

Murphy's death the hardest of any justice. They had been so close they often joked that one would not want to remain on the Court without the other. Then on September 10 Rutledge died. He was fifty-five. At the Rutledge funeral Black "looked old and worn," noted Drew Pearson. Hugo told Murphy's brother George that he would retire "in a year or two." Then, one day before the Court's new term was scheduled to open, Douglas fell off a horse in Washington State's Cascade Mountains and broke twenty-three of his twenty-four ribs. "He just lived because he wanted to live," said Elon Gilbert, who was riding with him. It would obviously be months before he would be able to return to the Court. In many cases, and especially in the most important ones, Black was down from four almost certain votes to one.

A gloomy Hugo Black sat at the Court's first session listening to Chief Justice Vinson conclude his memorial remarks: "We turn to the work before us." Quickly, the country knew that this work consisted largely of rejecting Murphy's and Rutledge's civil liberties views. Without them to vote to hear these cases, the Court reduced its docket over the next few terms to the smallest in perhaps a century. And when the Court did agree to hear a case, the result (in upward of twenty cases in the 1949 term alone) would likely have been different had Murphy and Rutledge been there.[2]

Black hoped to gain an adherent with the appointment of his old Senate friend Sherman Minton to replace Rutledge. To him it was, despite Minton's uncertain health, almost the only bright spot in an otherwise dismal picture. Minton had recently expressed agreement with his position on the Fourteenth Amendment, and Hugo hoped that this would carry over to other areas. He applauded one of Minton's early efforts: "It manifests a keen form of analysis to hit the jugular as you have in this case. This is good writing that follows the classic rule Aristotle laid down in his *Rhetoric*. Start—continue—finish. After all this, I agree." But Minton would continually reject challenges asserting violations of individual liberties in both national security and criminal cases. Serving on the Court of Appeals had made him become "a bit more hidebound on precedent and procedure than I would have liked," Black said in a typical understatement when it came to another person's (especially a friend's) views. This "grand fellow" greatly disappointed him.

But if the Court did not sanction many liberties, relations were essentially civil. Clark's industry pleased Black. "Information which I consider reliable," he wrote John Frank in a way he rarely spoke about a colleague, "is to the effect that [Clark] cannot only write opinions but can write with fluency—even a first draft. . . . Experience on the court thus far and diligent and unremitting work have combined to enable him to write opinions with much more rapidity and with much less meticulous detail than that he formerly practiced. I consider him to be open-minded, fair, and earnestly devoted to his job. He can discuss cases with considerable clarity due I think to the fact that he studies and understands the points raised." And Minton's presence helped improve relations. His plain affability appealed to all ("Shay could talk about anything, just anything," Black said), as did his unpretentious earthiness. In 1953 the Court heard a challenge to baseball's exemption under the antitrust rules. Holmes had written the opinion in a similar case thirty years earlier, and Frankfurter told his colleagues in conference that Holmes would know when to change his mind but this was not such an occasion. Suddenly Minton said loudly, "Bullshit, Felix. Baseball is a sport. It's the all-American sport, our national pastime, like motherhood and apple pie. So I say to you, bullshit, Felix." The brethren laughed long and noisily.[3]

Hugo missed Bill Douglas terribly. It was more than the comfort they gave each other in cases. Hugo provided a sympathetic ear for Douglas to pour out his antipathy for Frankfurter, and Bill would listen as Hugo talked about Alabama or made a sly wisecrack; and they talked cases and politics regularly. They could kid each other, and although Douglas was often a great practical joker with friends, he was never one with Hugo. Here, Hugo did most of the kidding. By spring 1950 speculation had already begun as to who would succeed Truman. Douglas was always among the names prominently mentioned. One day, having arranged to lunch together, Black got his meal in the Court's public cafeteria and took it on a tray into the justices' private dining room. There he saw Douglas being served by a messenger. "Where," Black said, "is that so called man of the people?"*

From the moment he heard of Douglas's injury Hugo had been solicitous. "Your letters are a great joy to me," Douglas replied. "Write whenever you can." In November 1949 he was flown from Washington State to a ranch near Tucson, Arizona, to continue his convalescence. Soon he urgently invited Hugo to visit. But Hugo could not afford it. Then Barney Whatley arranged for him to address the Roosevelt Memorial Committee of Colorado (and paid for the entire trip). From Denver Hugo went to Tucson, where

---

* There was no teasing, only tautness, in early 1950 when both turned up for dinner, each thinking the other would be honored, having been told so by an ambitious, young Lebanese diplomat in Washington, Clovis McSoud, who later (as Maksoud) became head of the Arab League (Warren Christopher int.).

he played tennis on each of the several days he otherwise spent just loafing with Douglas.

Black had hardly returned to Washington when Senator Joseph McCarthy of Wisconsin announced, "I have here in my hand a list"—of Communists in the State Department who were "known to the Secretary of State" and "still working and making policy." Whether McCarthy mentioned a number and what it was (57 or 81 or 205 or merely "a lot") was unimportant and irrelevant. And whether the speech was a ploy by a psychopath or a shrewd move by a politician unsure about reelection and needing an issue, it came a fortnight after Alger Hiss, a former State Department official who had been denounced as a Communist spy, had been convicted for perjury. All most Americans heard was the word "Communist." A shiver went up the country's collective spine. The "red hunt" became the nation's fixation.

The Cold War was at high tide. Fear spawned more fear; anxieties of all sorts were intensified, suspicion stimulated, timidity encouraged. In Madison, Wisconsin, generally considered a progressive community, only one of 112 persons a reporter approached would sign a "petition" composed exclusively of excerpts from the Declaration of Independence; the reporter was accused of having Communist sympathies. In California a three-year-old girl was hired as a model at a public college. Her mother was told that the girl could not be paid unless she signed a loyalty oath. Since the girl could not write, she was never paid. "From sea to shining sea" morale was undermined, initiative stifled, courage throttled—all in the land of the free and the home of the brave.

In this spirit the Court in March 1950 upheld the contempt conviction of Eugene Dennis, the general secretary of the Communist Party, for refusing to testify before the House Un-American Activities Committee. Seven members of the jury were government employees. They "have good reason to fear," Black wrote in dissent, "that an honest vote to acquit a Communist or anyone else accused of 'subversive' beliefs, however flimsy the prosecutor's evidence, might be considered a 'disloyal' act which could easily cost them their job." The case frustrated him greatly. The government expended large resources in prosecuting Dennis, and Black could not understand why, if it felt its case was strong enough, a majority of government employees was needed on the jury. When delivering the opinion, Black turned to Solicitor General Philip Perlman, not one of his favorites, looked at him coldly, lowered his voice and said scornfully, "Nor should the government *want* such an unfair advantage." Perlman turned several shades of red.[4]

Even after Douglas returned to the Court late that month, Black was discouraged at being so irretrievably in dissent. Occasionally he wondered what he was doing on the Court: he just couldn't make colleagues see what to him were simple truths. He never talked of leaving the Court. But to a man who was always convinced he was right—at home he sometimes walked around saying, "I'm always right"—it was highly frustrating. And it only got worse. In June the Court upheld the non-Communist affidavit provision required of labor union officers under the Taft-Hartley Act. Black passionately protested the power of Congress to proscribe beliefs and political affiliations, and he was the sole dissenter. (Douglas did not participate.) Test oaths had been effectively inflicted on "obnoxious minorities" throughout European as well as both English and American history, he noted. "And wherever the test oath was in vogue, spies and informers found rewards far more tempting than truth."

> These experiences underline the wisdom of the basic constitutional precept that penalties should be imposed only for a person's own conduct. . . . Like anyone else, individual Communists who commit overt acts in violation of valid laws can and should be punished. But the postulate of the First Amendment is that our free institutions can be maintained without proscribing or penalizing political belief, speech, press, assembly, or party affiliation. . . . It is the heart of the system on which our freedom depends.
>
> Fears of alien ideologies have frequently agitated the nation and inspired legislation aimed at suppressing advocacy of those ideologies. At such times the fog of public excitement obscures the ancient landmarks set up in our Bill of Rights. Yet then, of all times, should this Court adhere most closely to the course they mark.

"Most of us know that constitutional liberties have a pretty hard time when people get too frightened," Black wrote in February 1951. He was not scared: he viewed only war with alarm. "I confess to one obsession," he told a Tennessee audience—"those provisions written in the Bill of Rights, which are intended to preserve the individual liberty of the citizen, free from unwarranted invasions by any person anywhere, however high his position may be in Government." Lawyers were even ducking this "chief responsibility." But being "decidedly in the minority," Black soon said, "is not likely to stifle all my views."

He was distinctly in the minority on the Supreme Court. The affirmance of a conviction of a street corner speaker after police told him to stop for fear violence might break out when a listener threatened to "get" him, "was a long step toward totalitarian authority," Black wrote in dissent. ("Ingenuity of the policeman on the beat will be sufficient to stop a meeting when the police do not like it," he said from the bench.) He continued to adhere to the "preferred position" philosophy granting favored status to First Amendment liberties. But the Court disagreed. As he wrote in another dissent, "A new First Amendment philosophy," disregarding precedents established over most of the previous two decades, had triumphed.[5]

*   *   *

The unfortunate apogee of this philosophy came in *Dennis v. United States.* Few cases have caught the public interest as much. The arrogant and provocative courtroom behavior of publicity-seeking federal judge Harold Medina in New York overshadowed the conviction of Dennis and cohorts for conspiring to teach or advocate the overthrow of the government by force or violence. The prosecution did not offer any proof that Communist theory was about to be translated into revolutionary action: it did not have any. Medina sparred with the defense lawyers from the opening curtain, refusing to let them introduce crucial evidence as they derided the proceedings and then citing them for contempt and summarily sentencing them to prison. The Second Circuit Court of Appeals upheld the verdict in an opinion by Judge Learned Hand. Before the Supreme Court the issue became the reach of the clear and present danger test.

"The amazing thing about the conference in this important case," Douglas wrote in his conference notes, "was the brief nature of the discussion. Those wanting to affirm had minds closed to argument or persuasion. The conference discussion was largely pro forma. It was more amazing because of the drastic revision of the clear and present danger test which affirmance requires." The discussion came out in the opinions. Speaking for the Court in June 1951, Chief Justice Vinson explicitly adopted Hand's reformulation of the clear and present danger standard: "In each case," courts "must ask whether the gravity of the 'evil,' discounted by its probability, justifies such invasion of free speech as is necessary to avoid the danger." If the "evil" is serious enough, any speech can be suppressed unless it is totally harmless. It was an ambiguous yardstick to apply, especially to a situation where no overt acts were charged or implicated. The petitioners were simply charged with agreeing to assemble and to advocate and publish certain ideas later— just teaching and advocating. Their affiliation blinded the Court, and the nation, to basic values.

Black lashed out on Vinson's drafts in vicious marginal comments. The new clear and present danger standard "permits courts to sustain anything," he scrawled. It was "as much an element of the crime as death is in a murder charge." "In other words courts can approve suppression of free speech at will and despite 1st Amendment," which is "words but not therefore a 'semantic straightjacket.' " "Now puts 'speech' and 'armed internal attack' in same category." "How could anyone have suspected five years ago that membership in a party could be held a crime? John W. Davis, Charles E. Hughes, Jr., and Tom Clark thought not." "How can one explain without fear that he will be charged with advocating?" Vinson's attempt to distinguish the decision by emphasizing the increased threat of worldwide Communism made Black write, "The goblin'll get you." "Emergency, crisis, always the plea of those who would give dictatorial power to rulers." Next to Vinson's remark that "government . . . must wait until the putsch is about to be executed," Black scribbled, "Good semantic emotionalism and ghost conjuring!" "These people [were] not convicted for 'acts,' " but whether this was an issue for a judge to decide was "the old dodge of judges who want to be jurors too." "In other words since [petitioners] are guilty of violating the vague statute, it must be held good as to them. Strange American doctrine! They are guilty of something, therefore they cannot attack the statute." "Bad men! To jail with them!"

And on Jackson's draft concurrence Black scrawled: "World War II revolutionary techniques were not new." "Strategy of stealth" is "what hostile groups always say about each other. Russia today accuses our people of this." "But does the Constitution prevent agreement to teach by words to be classified as illegal 'conspiracies' "? It was Black's last comment that summed up his view: "1st Amendment presumes that free speech will preserve, not destroy, the nation."[6]

Hugo Black would have none of this judicial subjectivity where First Amendment freedoms were concerned. His courage in *Dennis* never flinched. Authorities could control violence at Communist meetings "if they tried hard enough," he said. That they did not was no reason to keep these people from talking. Upholding that right was his job and his duty. But as the spring of 1951 stretched along and Douglas did not submit an opinion, it seemed Black's might be the only dissent. The thought of impeachment attempts was not that fanciful if he dissented alone. Black also feared Douglas might forsake his convictions to keep alive what he believed Douglas really felt were his presidential possibilities, a concern that Douglas's eloquent dissent only partially allayed. "Free speech—the glory of our system of government—," Douglas observed, "should not be sacrificed to anything less than plain and objective proof of danger that the evil advocated is imminent."

Black went further. Even before the Court heard the case, he knew he would lose. He went back and forth several times whether to write a long or a short dissent. Finally he decided his disagreement with the majority was so fundamental that expressing it at length was useless. "A reasonable legal opinion," he said, referring to the typical Frankfurter or Jackson opinion, "is not a persuasive document. That's why I put rhetoric in my opinions. The most effective dissents are short ones"—especially when so hopelessley outvoted. In a dissent of little more than two pages he stated the essence of his view of the First Amendment. He asked Douglas to join it, but Douglas refused. * "What does the Constitution say?" Black often asked his clerks. He would be standing up, sometimes walking around the office as he said it, "as if to talk it into himself, to convince himself," recalled Luther Hill, one of his clerks. And he answered himself: "It says 'no law.' That means no law. It doesn't make for any exceptions." He took that position in his *Dennis* dissent: "At least . . . in the realm of public matters,"

> laws suppressing freedom of speech and press cannot be sustained on the basis of Congress' or our own notions of mere "reasonableness." Such a doctrine amounts to little more than an admonition to Congress.
>
> Public opinion being what it now is, few will protest the conviction of these Communist petitioners. There is hope, however, when present pressures, passions, and fears subside, this or some later Court will restore the First Amendment liberties to the high preferred place where they belong in a free society.

Black was no longer marching to the clear and present danger theme or playing with its semantics. He had always paid it homage, as he had to do, but it was always a difficult melody to play, requiring the balancing of imponderables, and current strains added discordant notes to the chorus.†

---

* This year Black and Douglas thought on parallel lines rather than being friendly. They were sort of estranged. They signed each other's dissents, but did not work together much on them. Black did not know what Douglas's *Dennis* dissent would be until he saw it (George Treister int.). Neither joined the other's opinion; Douglas was still committed to the clear and present danger test.

† "The problem with my brethren," Black said early in 1951, "is that they have no philosophy or otherwise no rational explanation for their views. In deciding cases, you can't hop from one side to the other in a rational way" (Luther Hill int.).

"Prejudices, hate and fear are constantly invoked to justify irresponsible smears and persecution of persons even faintly suspected of entertaining unpopular views," he wrote in another opinion. At times like this, when freedom needed to be protected most, courts protected it least.[7] The preferred position doctrine was also implicitly a balancing process. It did have the great advantage of heavily favoring First Amendment freedoms, but it could not always ensure that result. Black was moving toward complete protection of political speech ("public matters"), a position unprecedented in Supreme Court annals.

*   *   *

Repercussions of the Court's decision were not long in coming. The legal community consulted its dictionaries for variations on that elusive phrase, clear and present danger. Lost in the details of many of the semantic analyses was the fundamental importance of the Bill of Rights in a free society. "I know what those fellows meant," Black had been saying about the Constitution's framers for several years. "I know what they were thinking." He had digested their debates and could practically regurgitate them whole. Their faith in human reason warred against finding reasons to prevent people from exercising their constitutional rights. Jefferson best embodied the framers' dreams. He was "for rigid adherence to constitutional language," Black marked in a biography of Jefferson.* Books were much on Black's mind. "I am very happy that court has adjourned for the summer," he wrote Hugo, Jr. "During the next few months I expect to do a lot of reading and tennis playing." Soon he started on George Bancroft's mammoth *History of the United States.*[8]

From Black's viewpoint, the cases on the Court's calendar in the 1951 term were no more promising than those in the previous session. He would have to decide them, moreover, without the lively presence of his daughter JoJo, who was now away at college. Even where he would write much of the

---

* HLB wrote this on the inside rear cover of Dumas Malone's just-published *Jefferson and the Rights of Man*, which he read that summer. Malone's words are just as applicable to Black as to Jefferson: "His doctrine of strict construction cannot be detached from the larger setting of his general attitude toward public law. He himself was not unwilling to construe Acts of Congress liberally, upon occasion . . . and as a practicing statesman he could not have been expected to be wholly consistent. Even with respect to statute law, however, he tended to be a literalist, and he was characteristically scrupulous about fundamental law as embodied in constitutions. . . . To him laws in general, and constitutions in particular, were shields against tyranny; and he coupled a positive faith in human beings with a predominantly negative attitude toward political agencies and institutions"(341–42; HLB Books).

opinions was not certain. He and Josephine recurringly thought of selling the house, which had always been expensive to maintain but was now, they claimed, too big for just the two of them. They did not act on the idea, however, and remained in their familiar surroundings. There Josephine continued her painting as therapy. "I have never felt such peace in all my life," she told Hugo, Jr., that summer. But her daughter's absence and her father's gradually deteriorating health contributed to her suffering another spell of depression. On her occasional sunny days she could see an escape from her agony, from the sense of hopelessness that often leads to total despair.

Those days were few in November 1951. At the end of the month Hugo accepted an offer to judge the moot court competition at Columbia Law School in mid-December. Josephine planned to go with him; they would go to the theater and spend a couple of days in New York. Perhaps that would lift her spirits. Before that, Sterling came to Washington on business. He spent several days at the house; she seemed happy, no different than whenever she was not depressed. Because of a cold, she could not see him off and instead left a note that she wanted to come to New Mexico to see her grandson the coming spring. Then she went to his old room to sleep.

The next morning, December 7, 1951, ten years to the day after Pearl Harbor and the beginning of the war that changed her life so, Josephine Black was found dead. She was fifty-two.

The children quickly returned. Black's first words to Hugo, Jr., were: "I waited and waited because I didn't want to marry a woman who would die before me." Someone asked, what should we tell the press? Although Josephine had a rheumatic heart (as once did Hugo, Jr.; they occasionally joked who would die first), Black said, "That she died of natural causes." Which was what the press printed, noting she had been ill for several days. No autopsy was performed, contrary to Virginia law. She was buried at Arlington National Cemetery, overlooking the Jefferson Memorial, on a cold, rainy day. Tears unabashedly flowed from the eyes of many in attendance, men and women, on and off the Court.

Her death almost devastated Hugo. He wanted to be alone. But the children thought somebody should live with him. One of his clerks, Sam Daniels, stayed with him until JoJo transferred to George Washington University for the spring semester. Black was an ascetic. He presented a jovial exterior most, if not all of the time, no matter what bothered him. Repression was his method for survival. Now he repressed everything and joked a lot. "The Judge was a real cut-up," Daniels said.

All his clerks gathered round. The first one, Hugo, Jr.'s, partner Buddy Cooper, spent a night with him. "We were standing in the kitchen," Cooper recalled. "The judge had just cooked some steaks and he was talking about Josephine. He said, 'Maybe I should have stayed in Birmingham and made all that money for her so she would have been happy.' Then, when we were eating at the table, he'd go back into the kitchen from time to time and start crying. He'd come out and say, 'Maybe I should have resigned and gone back to Birmingham.' He had no idea that wasn't her problem." He did not know what was—or could not admit it. She had wanted a television set and air-conditioning. But he adamantly refused, saying they weren't needed and, besides, cost money he did not have. Now he bought a TV and an air-conditioner for the study and, on a visit to Florida during the Court's Christmas recess, aluminum chairs to replace the waterlogged ones she had had. Could he have been assuaging part of his guilt? Or was there more? "I think Hugo Black went to his death not knowing two things," observed Aline Berman, who knew him well for fifteen years. "How to respond to being a member of the Klan and how Josephine died."

He answered by hand each of the several hundred messages of heartfelt sympathy he received. "Never before had I dreamed how much comfort could come from the sympathy of friends," Black wrote Max Lerner. "It was a long, hard job," he told Dr. Foster, "but I felt that each person was entitled to an individual, handwritten response." Part of his letter to his niece Hazel Davis was typical: "I cannot write of her without tears. This I know should not be since I keep telling myself how fortunate I was to have had her for thirty years."* He contemplated selling the house. An apartment would

---

* In Black's papers is a typed sonnet, the author unknown, entitled "To Josephine":

> You came that day like some lovely thing,
> Like some frightened bird with a broken wing,
> And your cry not heard by the ears of man
> Gripped my heart, like a bird's cry can,
> I knew that the road you traveled was long,
> That weary, you'd almost forgotten your Song,
> And the only thing that I knew to do
> Was to ask of God to help you through;
> I watched you—a flower in a garden space
> Seeking the sun with a lifted face
> Saw you turn with the bravest bloom
> And open the door of your in-most room.
>   . . .
> I think as I walked along with you
> That the Angel of Light walked with us too.

"probably be better," he thought. But he and the children realized he needed the tennis court. It was his therapy, a virtual lifesaver. His mental health could be gauged by whether he would play.

By the spring, however, discouraged by the Court's decisions, he was talking of leaving. "It will be four more years before I am old enough to retire and go to Coral Gables to play tennis," he lamented to Austin Rice.[9] But Hugo Black was never a quitter and he did the only thing he knew—continue working as hard as he could for what he believed.

CHAPTER 28

THE WORST
OF DAYS

T HE NEXT TWO YEARS WERE the bleakest time of Hugo Black's life. At home he often seemed in a trance, doing things by rote. He needed all his steely, gritty determination to work, but work he did. He did not have any self-pity and simply refused to submit to depression. He continued to come in to the Court at nine o'clock, whistling "Dixie" or another lively tune, in an obvious attempt to get his spirits up. Often he left early to play tennis. Happy stories cheered him up; time and again now he repeated the same ones and laughed. Gradually he talked less about Josephine and the children as he returned to his usual twelve-plus-hour working day, and his conversation mainly concerned it.

The cases were getting only worse. American freedom was under perpetual seizure, being assaulted on all fronts. The Court was ignoring the procedural safeguards enumerated in the Constitution. Especially where Communists were involved, the majority saw red. The Court was proceeding in the undemocratic spirit of the 1950 Internal Security Act, passed by Congress over Truman's veto. This new Statute of UnLiberty contrasted with that majestic first sight of America to many aliens seeking refuge, the Statue of Liberty. Under this law the Court upheld the Immigration Service's arrest of longtime resident aliens, on the basis of secret charges by secret informers, and holding them in jail without a hearing and *without bail*, pending a determination whether they were deportable as Communists. "Maybe the literal language of the framers lends itself to this weird, devitalizing interpretation when scrutinized with a hostile eye," Black protested in dissent. "But at least until recently, it has been the judicial practice to give a broad, liberal interpretation to those provisions of the Bill of Rights obviously designed to protect the individual from governmental oppression."

The Bill of Rights was being weakened almost every time the Court sat. The Court even sanctioned the deportation of an Italian who had been a Communist as a young man more than twenty years earlier, and more than ten years before such membership was made a deportable offense. Such a case was harsh, but none approached the cruelness of Ignatz Mezei's. He had lived in the United States for twenty-five years before being stopped at Ellis Island on his return from seeing his dying mother in his native Romania in 1948. For two years he was held, without charges or a hearing, on the "basis of information of a confidential nature." Then he was put on a boat and he went to Europe and back; so intimidating were unidentified American fears that no other country would accept him. Finally he sought habeas corpus, to be released on bail. * But the government objected: even telling the judge any of its reasons would jeopardize the national security; nevertheless bail was granted.

The Supreme Court reversed. The reason: stating the causes for the exclusion "would be prejudicial to the public interest." It was the vaguest of conceivable explanations. Mezei was ordered, as Black wrote in dissent, to "go back to his island prison to stay indefinitely, maybe for life. . . . No society is free where government makes one person's liberty depend upon the arbitrary will of another. Dictatorships have done this since time immemorial. They do now. . . . Our Bill of Rights was written to prevent such oppressive practices." After drafting the opinion, Black read it to his clerk, Melford (Buddy) Cleveland. "Then he gave it to me," Cleveland recalled, "put me on the other side of the room and said, 'make it ring.' " But Black already had.† When he delivered it, noted Douglas's clerk Charles Ares,

---

* Habeas corpus is the right of any prisoner convicted in a state court to have the constitutionality of his conviction, or his sentence, reviewed in a federal court.

† "The Founders abhorred arbitrary one-man imprisonments," Black wrote.

> Their belief was—our constitutional principles are—that no person of any faith, rich or poor, high or low, native or foreigner, white or colored, can have his life, liberty or property taken "without due process of law." This means to me that neither the federal police nor federal prosecutors nor any other governmental official, whatever his title, can put or keep people in prison without accountability to courts of justice. It means that individual liberty is too highly prized in this country to allow executive officials to imprison and hold people on the basis of information kept secret from courts. It means that Mezei should not be deprived of his liberty indefinitely except as the result of a fair open court hearing in which evidence is appraised by the court, not by the prosecutor.

"suddenly you could hear the Senator speaking. It was an oration. He went from a whisper to thunder. The courtroom was transfixed."[1]

*   *   *

"This country is in the most desperate trouble on the First Amendment than it has ever been in, much worse than during the Palmer Raids," Black told the Court's clerks at lunch in late 1952. "The present period of fear is even more ominously dangerous to speech and press than was that of the [1798] Alien and Sedition Laws," which prohibited criticism of government or its officials. With "a creeping censorship loose in the land," more was needed than the evanescent, will-o'-the-wisp standards the Court was applying to protect First Amendment freedoms. Freedom of speech, after all, inheres in the concept of self-government. If the people are to rule, they must be able to discuss all relevant subjects openly and freely. Otherwise, the compact between the rulers (the people) and the ruled (the government) is broken. At the heart of this argument, forwarded by philosopher Alexander Meiklejohn in 1948, was a distinction, easier to state than to maintain, between public and private speech: public speech related to governance and was therefore constitutionally protected; private speech could be subject to regulation. Black read Meiklejohn's contention immediately upon its publication. It was the philosophical counterpart of the structure he was developing in opinions.

A new word began to appear in those opinions. When the Court in March 1952 upheld a New York law requiring dismissal of teachers for knowing membership in an organization advocating the violent overthrow of the government, Black dissented. "Quite a different governmental policy rests on the belief that government should leave the mind and spirit of man *absolutely* free." The next week he wrote, again in dissent, "My belief is that we must have freedom of speech, press and religion for all or we may eventually have it for none. I further believe that the First Amendment grants an *absolute* right to believe in any governmental system, discuss all governmental affairs, and argue for desired changes in the existing order."*

---

* "This freedom is too dangerous for bad, tyrannical governments to permit," Black continued.

But those who wrote and adopted our First Amendment weighed those dangers against the dangers of censorship and deliberately chose the First Amendment's unequivocal command that freedom of assembly, petition, speech and press shall not be abridged. I happen to believe this was a wise choice and that our free way of life enlists such respect and love that our Nation cannot be imperiled by mere talk. This belief of

At issue in *Beauharnais v. Illinois*, decided in April 1952, was a conviction under the state's "group libel" law for circulating a pamphlet attacking Negroes and asking action to halt their spread into white neighborhoods. In conference the Court voted 5–4 to uphold it; Black, Reed, Douglas and Burton would have overturned it. Then Burton switched to join Frankfurter, who wrote the majority opinion, while Jackson shifted to the dissent. Frankfurter treated the statute as "a form of criminal libel law." Adopting the extremely deferential "rational basis" test toward legislation, he devoted only three sentences to the First Amendment almost as a throwaway at the end of the opinion and did not mention it once. He stopped short of sanctioning governmental control over expression that defamed the government—but only barely. To this repression of free speech Black vigorously dissented:

> No legislature is charged with the duty or vested with the power to decide what public issues Americans can discuss. In a free country that is the individual's choice, not the state's. State experimentation in curbing freedom of expression is startling and frightening doctrine in a country dedicated to self-government by its people.
>   . . . This Act sets up a system of state censorship which is at war with the kind of free government envisioned by those who forced adoption of our Bill of Rights. The motives behind the state law may have been to do good. But the same can be said about most laws making opinions publishable as crimes. History indicates urges to do good have led to the burning of books and even to the burning of "witches."

The Amendment, Black concluded, " '*absolutely*' forbids such laws without any 'ifs' or 'buts' or 'whereases.' " And any minority groups which hailed this decision should consider the ancient remark: "Another such victory and I am undone."*

He was powerless, a voice crying in the wilderness, lashing out plaintively in dissent. But from the beginning Black's First Amendment opinions had

---

mine may and I suppose does influence me to protest whenever I think I see even slight encroachments on First Amendment liberties. But the encroachment here is not small. True it is mainly those alleged to be present or past "Communists" who are now being jailed for their beliefs and expressions. But we cannot be sure more victims will not be offered up later if the First Amendment means no more than its enemies or even some of its friends believe it does.

* Plutarch's report of these words of King Pyrrhus after defeating the Romans in the battle of Asculum in 279 A.D. had long been a favorite of Black's. Now he quoted them to Frankfurter about another case (in a 1/31/52 letter as he was preparing his *Beauharnais* dissent).

pointed toward the idea of the heart of it as an "absolute." In the summer of 1952 he explained what he meant. "The Bill of Rights means what it says and there are absolutes in it," he told his clerks. "Now I know that some people say there are no absolutes. Some people would say that this table top"—and he pointed to his secretary's shiny desk—"is not completely smooth, that if you put it under a magnifying glass you'd find some rough spots. But for practical purposes it's smooth. And in the same way there are absolutes in the Bill of Rights." This explanation might not satisfy a philosopher, but Black reached it from his extensive readings on the speech-conduct distinction. Protection for "speech" under the Constitution was "absolute."

An idea entering Black's mind often seized it. Soon, the concept of First Amendment absolutes became the centerpiece of his thought. Boston lawyer Charles Curtis wrote an article noting the necessity of keeping "open the area in which we are free to act as we choose, . . ." as Black wrote him. "This is reminiscent of the 'Thou shalt nots' of our Constitution which appear to be stated as precisely as was thought possible by those who drew them," Black felt. Not even the Court's overturning an Oklahoma loyalty oath (really a "test oath" as he pointed out in his concurrence) for all state employees later in 1952 fully gratified him:

> Governments need and have ample power to punish treasonable acts. But it does not follow that they must have a further power to punish thought and speech as distinguished from acts. Our own free society should never forget that laws which stigmatize have a way of reaching, ensnaring and silencing many more people than at first intended. We must have freedom of speech for all or we will in the long run have it for none but the cringing and the craven. And I cannot too often repeat my belief that the right to speak on matters of public concern must be wholly free or eventually be wholly lost.[2]

Half a loaf was not better than none.

*   *   *

Black had much time to develop his new First Amendment theory. Leading a sheltered life, rarely going out, he spent much time wondering about Josephine's death, asking himself, could I have done it? what have I done? At the Court he was particularly friendly now with Shay Minton and Tom Clark ("the only man I know who wears a ten gallon hat who makes sense"). But Minton was the only colleague Hugo had over for dinner; they reminisced

about the Senate. But that was rare now, no more than twice yearly. And
it was the same over the next two years with the Arnolds and Tom Corcoran. Even Lister and Henrietta Hill came over irregularly. For vacation
Hugo went, usually with JoJo, to see the boys in Birmingham and Albuquerque or to Miami, even in the summer, to play tennis with his friend
Austin Rice. In July 1952 he camped in Maine with Douglas and Fred Rodell.
It was the farthest north he had ever been. "I've never been so cold in my
life," he said when he came back. "I almost froze to death." Hugo's closest
companions were his law clerks. "My family says I need someone to stay
with me," he told his new clerk Cleveland in 1952. "That was his invitation
to move into his house." The next term both his clerks lived with him. "Just
pay me the same rent you'd pay someone else." All three became like sons.
"We did everything together—cooked breakfast, washed dishes. Everything," said Charles Reich, who was with him that year. "There was no
pretension with that man. He was so warm and human." At breakfast Black
commented on any article of general interest in the newspaper; he wasn't
too interested in international affairs, his main fear being that a small country
with an egotistical head would get the world embroiled in war. "You can't
believe anything you read in the newspaper except the advertising and comics," he said.

They drove to work (the clerks took turns) and stopped to shop on the
way back; Black picked out the best steaks, grilling them on Sundays. Before
dinner he poured himself a drink, claiming liquor couldn't hurt a man his
age, while telling the clerks not to drink or smoke. Then he read from the
classifieds, including ads for convertible tops. (It was hard not to notice the
rain dripping through the tattered roof of Reich's car.) From early morning
until bedtime they talked about the Constitution, the Bill of Rights, due
process. These were "philosophical conversations, but not philosophy as
distinct from life or daily business," Reich noted. "Black is . . . a romantic
fundamentalist." But not even such lofty thoughts could fill a void: Black
was lonely and expressed it. "This is my wedding anniversary," he said one
night in February 1953, "and the worst one I've ever spent." Years later,
Reich, by then a best-selling author, penned a memorable portrait of living
with "an authentically great man."

> In a city that lived by display, power, gossip, and publicity, his way of life
> was simple and old-fashioned and wholly without artificial trap-
> pings. . . . In a world that was "realistic" about power, Justice Black was

passionate about justice for each individual, no matter how inconsequential the person might seem to the world. He was utterly uncorrupted and incorruptible. He was powerful because he possessed the power of love— love of the Constitution, of justice, of democracy, of the people, of his family and friends, of his country. . . . I never stopped marveling that here I was, sitting at dinner with Justice Black and talking about freedom of speech while the Justice divided a steak three ways, and we passed the corn sticks and greens. . . .

We sat in the kitchen, eating the eggs the Justice had cooked, while he read aloud from the *Washington Post* or talked about the Constitution. The sun streamed in through the windows of the small, low-ceilinged, old-fashioned room that looked out on a garden. There sat the grand old man, in pajamas and bathrobe, his face serious and majestic, talking about the framers of the Constitution and the deep and terrible experience out of which had been born the protections of the Bill of Rights. He foresaw that we would become "a nation of clerks" if we could not remember what it meant to be a free people. And I knew this was my unique and magical moment to sit with the Prophet, the old man of the American Testament, and absorb his stern passion, his belief in truth, and carry it forward when I could.[3]

Teaching gave Black great joy and he conducted an informal academy for his clerks daily. Technical legal training was only part of it. "You always took time to find me one more book, discuss one more point, or outline one more area of philosophy for me to study," Buddy Cleveland told him. He would just as soon have them read good books and talk about them as read Court papers. In 1952, to celebrate his fifteen years on the bench his clerks presented him with a "Free Speech Library," several dozen volumes on loyalty, security and the First Amendment. "I love the library," Black said. One of the books he especially enjoyed was John C. Miller's *A Crisis in Freedom,* "one of the best discussions of the alien and sedition period that I have seen," he wrote. "One cannot help being impressed perhaps by the fact that extreme prosecutions continued under those old laws until Thomas Jefferson was elected president on a platform of bitter hostility to such suppressions of speech and press. I think of no leaders in governmental affairs today who have Jefferson's views and his opportunity to put those views into effect." Having been defeated by Dwight Eisenhower in the 1952 presidential election, Adlai Stevenson did not have the opportunity, but Black believed his "public utterances manifested a steadfast loyalty to the noblest legal traditions of human freedom."

The election filled Black with trepidation. Shortly afterward, he dined with Drew Pearson. "He sees increasing encroachments on freedom of the press," Pearson noted in his diary. "He is fearful that the new administration will bring on fascism and war." Sterling's job with the Atomic Energy Commission, Black observed, "might be in jeopardy," since he was "the son of a Democratic justice. . . . I must say that I would prefer that he lose his job and be something else rather than enlist under the Republican banner"—a remote possibility in any event. Black despaired for his country. "The present trend is away from the American way and the Constitution and bodes ill for the future," he told Claude Pepper in Miami in early 1953.* He was losing almost every case, yet upon returning from conference he would say, "Well, we'll go back tomorrow and try again."[4]

·   ·   ·

In one sense the Steel Seizure case came as a relief to Black: it took him away from dissenting in cases involving individual rights. At issue was the very structure of government under the Constitution, a matter of different but no lesser import. Fearing that a nationwide strike would shut down the steel industry and stop the flow of military matériel to the troops in Korea, President Truman directed the secretary of commerce to seize and operate the steel mills. He emphasized his "distaste" for this and announced the intervention as temporary. As he admitted, he lacked specific statutory authority. But the inherent power of his office, stemming from his capacity as commander in chief, granted him the power, he claimed. Because of the case's importance, the federal courts handled it on an accelerated basis; in the Supreme Court only one month lapsed from its filing to its decision in June 1952.

Arguing on behalf of the steel companies was the country's preeminent appellate advocate, John W. Davis, whom Black considered, depending upon his mood of the moment, either equal to or just below Robert Jackson as the best lawyer to appear before the Court. Truman's action, Davis told the justices, was not only a "usurpation" of power, not only a deed "without parallel in American history," but "a reassertion of the kingly prerogative,

---

* "I have read your opinion holding that this petitioner was entitled to bail and fully agree with your action," Black wrote Douglas about *Yanish v. Barber*, which the Court refused to hear. "The steps taken by the Attorney General to supervise the daily life of this person on the basis that no court can review that supervision shows how far some people think we are on the way toward the kind of government they appear to have in Russia, Spain, Argentina, and a number of other places in the world. Freedom is being whittled away in the name of freedom. I regret to think so, but I am very fearful that our Court will back the Attorney General" (HLB to WOD 5/17/53).

the struggle against which illumines all the pages of Anglo-Saxon history."
By contrast Solicitor General Perlman, on behalf of the administration,
could not complete a subject, so often did the Court interrupt him to ask
questions or make comments. "Let me finish," he implored.

At conference all the justices spoke at length. They voted 6–3 to hold
Truman's action unconstitutional. Black assigned himself the majority opinion. As Frankfurter said from the bench, prefacing his own opinion, "Justice
Black's opinion is the least common denominator on which five of us can
agree." It was necessarily an unadorned exposition of the doctrine of separation of powers, and it remained the same through three drafts. Black
avoided the basic questions created by emergencies, and he did not cite a
single case on the central constitutional issue. No emergency, not even one
created by war, could alter the fact the Constitution vested the lawmaking
power exclusively in Congress. He could not faithfully hold that the president
has "the ultimate power as such to take possession of private property in
order to keep labor disputes from stopping production. . . . The Founders
of this Nation entrusted the lawmaking power to Congress alone in both
good and bad times."

His opinion was "consistent with my philosophy of law and government,"
Black wrote a former clerk. "No one familiar with that philosophy should
have been surprised at anything I wrote." That was true enough—just as it
is difficult to disagree with a basic textbook treatment of a complicated
subject: the reader leaves it just wanting more. In his way Black obliquely
admitted this. Majority opinions could not be eloquent, he once told economic historian Joseph Dorfman, who believed that this opinion fit in that
category. "I wonder, however," Black replied, "if you are not a little too
generous in its appraisal."

Vinson's long, passionate dissent pressed the same advice he had privately given Truman in early April: that the president had the legal power
to seize the steel mills as a wartime emergency measure. A furious Truman
composed a letter to Douglas about "that crazy decision that has tied up the
country," but he did not send it. Black knew how angry Truman was. Three
days after the decision, he called the president to invite him to dinner with
the Court the following Monday. Hugo held it outside; steaks were served.
"Truman was gracious though a bit testy at the beginning of the evening,"
Douglas recalled. Then "everybody was mixing it up pretty well and here
was Truman, who was just given a body blow by the Court, saying, 'Well,
Hugo, your decisions stink but your bourbon's pretty good.' "[5]

....

In April 1952 the Court upheld New York's released-time program allowing public school students to receive religious instruction during school hours. Justice Douglas's majority opinion explicitly reaffirmed Black's 1948 released-time case while distinguishing it: New York did not permit the instruction on public school grounds. Hugo felt hurt whenever Douglas did not go along with him, but this left him astonished and virtually speechless. It was not only the result but Douglas's statement "We are a religious people whose institutions presuppose a Supreme Being." That was undistilled Douglas: he had a strong, nonobservant religious, almost mystical, streak. But to Black, dissenting, Douglas was approving nothing less than the "combination of Church and State." Douglas's opinion, Jackson wrote in dissent, "will be more interesting to students of psychology and of the judicial processes than to students of constitutional law."

Jackson well knew what he was saying. Douglas's behavior had turned more erratic recently. Mercedes Davidson, who helped research his books, moved in to live with him in 1951; this annoyed Black greatly. And at the time Douglas was playing his usual game of ego massage about his supposed availability for the Democratic presidential nomination. It was sadly familiar. (The Democrats' nomination of Alabama senator John Sparkman for vice president upset Black. If anyone from Alabama got it, he thought he should. Lister Hill, Hugo said, also deserved it before Sparkman, whom both considered a high-level mediocrity at best. Black rationalized about Sparkman's fortune. But his real reason for his displeasure, noted one former clerk, was that he could not bear the thought of another Alabama senator being one heartbeat away from the presidency.)

Outside of conference Black and Douglas did not speak to each other much that year. Douglas was not at the Court much anyway. This changed some the next year, but Black's unhappiness at Douglas's domestic situation did not. Still, he could persuade Douglas when no one else could. Five seamen had drowned when the boat they were on collided with a pier and overturned. This was the type of case that brought out all of Hugo's humanitarian instincts, and when he heard that Douglas was giving strong consideration to denying the claims of the estates of the deceased he wrote Douglas at unusual length. "Surely, it is not for us—at least for me and you—to bring up conceptualistic ideas to make that law [an 1851 federal liability act] mean more than it has to mean by its plain language. . . . I have expressed myself fully and frankly to you because it is the only way I know for us to deal with one another. The position you have taken here seems to me to be unsupportable in the law except on the part of people who, unlike you, are usually willing to construe laws to the advantage of groups who need that construction least." When the case was decided the next year, Douglas joined Black in dissent.[6]

Well before these cases, Chief Justice Vinson's lack of intellectual acuity had proved a source of unspoken embarrassment at the Court. * The tone any presiding officer sets becomes all the more important when the institution is fractured intellectually. Knowledge of precedents is obviously helpful but a feel for the legal and policy implications of the case to be decided is even more so. In this Vinson was sorely missing. He spent more time with Truman (who made few important decisions without some input from him) and his friends in Congress and the administration than on Court matters. Vinson assigned few opinions to himself—"just plain lazy," Jackson called him— and was slow to make assignments to others. His ineffectiveness led Black to state that "there should be no chief justice. The job should be rotated among the justices as some state courts do." Several justices said this in Vinson's presence and "made no bones about regarding him . . . as their intellectual inferior." Black never uttered one derogatory word about Vinson. (The closest he came was when he told a nephew, "Truman's appointments were mediocre at best. We didn't get the best people.")[7] Black understood Vinson as a congressional type unable to make the leap to the judiciary. Despite their conflicts on issues, they never lost respect for each other personally.

*   *   *

Hugo and Robert Jackson were now friends. His ambitions behind him, Jackson had calmed down and was once again the true gentleman he was above almost anything else. "Hugo has class and polish," Jackson had been saying for several years now. "He may have been wrong, but he believes in what he says." From the time he returned from Nuremberg, Jackson told an

---

* Eugene Nickerson, a former Stone clerk and later a federal judge, argued a 1950 deportation case, during which he cited *Mahler v. Eby*, a 1925 Court decision. Vinson said, "Counsel, government also relies on that case." "Well, yes," Nickerson replied, "but I take considerable comfort in it and if you'd look at it, you'd see what I mean." "Vinson got absolutely red," Nickerson recalled (int.). "Black, Frankfurter and Jackson put their hands over their mouths to keep from laughing. Only Minton didn't laugh. I saw Jackson call for one of the bailiffs. I thought I'd be given a hearing before being disbarred or even be cited for contempt of court. Then the bailiff gave me a note from Jackson in which he said, 'However the case comes out, I'm going to vote to affirm the last two paragraphs on the page where you cite *Mahler*.' "

interviewer in 1952, "Justice Black has treated me with respect as one gentleman to another. We've never had a word." They were even agreeing in cases they likely would have not done so earlier.

By the early 1950s they were each other's most frequent visitor. "Bob Jackson and I shook hands in his office in 1953 about what happened about the Chief Justiceship," Black recalled. "We had a drink and laughed about it. We agreed that it was just one of those things." It was not that, of course, but both felt they should (try to) put it behind them. Yet the past could not be forgotten completely. In 1952 at the private memorial ceremony for Charles E. Cropley, the Court's longtime clerk, each justice spoke. Black said that when he first met the austere Cropley, he didn't know if he would like him. "It took a while but I changed my mind as I warmed to him and grew to like him very much." Jackson got up. "I'm also happy to be here for two reasons. I joined everyone in paying tribute to Cropley's memory. And I'm glad to hear Justice Black confess error."

Jackson's unpredictability remained, but if an opponent was a gentleman, Hugo could forgive almost anything—even his views. "Some people as judges are different from what they are as personalities," Black once said about Jackson without naming him. He felt Jackson tried to be too cute and didn't stand for something, as he believed Frankfurter did. Jackson's opinions no longer reflected the "preferred position" he had embraced for freedom of speech before joining the Court and continued to hold until after Nuremberg. Jackson took pains in his always refreshing opinions to justify his restrictions on free speech. And his switch of votes in several cases changed the result in favor of state power over assertions of individual rights.

"If Bob and I could just get together, back to back, we could break down what is happening to the country," Black was telling his clerks. "But Bob can't go with me because of what he said at Nuremberg." Hugo was more sorry than angry.[8]

In February 1953 Hugo went to Miami for a few weeks. He stayed with Sam Daniels, his clerk the previous year. Daniels was then suffering from shingles, and not long after Black returned home, Hugo caught it. It struck from his left hip down; his foot became lame. The pain was intense. The doctor told him, he said, "to go home, get as comfortable as I could in bed and make a mint julep every so often." For over three months Hugo could not wear a shoe. He did almost nothing besides going to the Court, for conferences, and to sit on the bench, and writing short opinions, usually dissents. Douglas came out to his house three times to review cases. Yet despite the agony, in his pajamas at night Hugo would search his library for a certain passage in a book to show to his clerk to teach him, or discuss one more point or outline one more area of philosophy for him to study.

A ten-day hospital stay in May helped. Soon Hugo could sleep without sedatives. Doctors' fears that the condition would be permanent proved to be unfounded. "My foot still bothers me a great deal," Hugo reported in late June, "although I was able to put on a shoe and come to town this morning for the first time in several months." By July he was on the way to recovery: he played some light tennis. Later Hugo felt he lost a great deal because of shingles; if so, no one else knew. He spent much time tending his garden over the summer.[9] Usually he did this with the help of Spencer Campbell, officially his messenger but really his assistant of all trades. But Spencer had suffered a breakdown and was in an institution. JoJo was home when not at college, and his clerks were with him. Hugo and Douglas, despite his quirks, always gave each other by their mere presence a sense of reassurance. And there were some steadfast friends. But Hugo Black felt very much alone.

•   •   •

The Court had already considered the Rosenberg case when it returned in full force in May 1953. Julius and Ethel Rosenberg had been convicted in 1951 for violating the 1917 Espionage Act in what some people even before trial called "the crime of the century"—passing the secrets of the atomic bomb to the Soviet Union. New York federal judge Irving Kaufman, no model of judicial detachment, sentenced them to death. After the sentences were upheld on appeal, they came to the Supreme Court.[10]

The Court voted on the Rosenberg matter in different guises nine times in all. By the time the justices closed the term on June 15, 1953, they had already refused to hear the case twice, vacated one stay, and denied another; each time Black voted to bring it before the Court. The next day, two new lawyers, intervening on the couple's behalf, went to Black's house with a fresh claim: that the Rosenbergs should have been tried under the Atomic Energy Act of 1946 rather than the earlier statute, and that a stay should be granted to consider this. But Black was in the hospital, preparing to undergo a hernia operation. He had even left word with his secretary that he would consider no petitions and mentioned the Rosenberg case by name. The lawyers went to Jackson, who oversaw the judicial circuit from which the case came. He passed the matter on to Douglas.

In his chambers Douglas listened to the Rosenbergs' counsel. Of the five times the case had thus far been before the Court, he had not once voted to hear it. Now, since his law clerk had already left to take the bar examination, he called Black, who loaned one of his clerks. They worked intensively until 11 P.M., when Douglas went to see Chief Justice Vinson at home to say that he would issue a stay the next morning. Earlier that evening Vinson had another meeting—with Attorney General Herbert Brownell. "Vinson was hot under the collar," Brownell recalled. "He was mad and said that what Douglas was doing was wrong, that he should not have even considered a stay. I asked Vinson to convene a special session of the Court." Vinson said he would call the full Court into session to vacate the stay, FBI documents reveal.

Not knowing any of this, Douglas granted the stay on June 17. The lower courts could then consider this new matter in an expedited fashion, with the expectation it could come before the Supreme Court in the fall. Black left the hospital without having his operation, postponing it until the next month, as the Court held feverish conferences. He vigorously objected to the special session, denouncing it to his colleagues. "The Chief Justice has no power to summon the Court." He was not like the manager of a baseball or a football team, Black continued. It was "terrible to come in and consider this issue as though we had it before us." The Court could convene in special session only by a majority vote of its members, as Chief Justice Stone took in the case of the Nazi saboteurs in 1942.

Black was right, Douglas said. But Douglas decided "to waive the point," as he later put it, to "defend the right of the Chief Justice to summon the Court to take a vote on whether or not a Court should be convened . . . I would cast my vote to convene the Court." Hugo must have winced as he heard this; his heart had to sink as he heard Douglas deserting him. Thereupon he withdrew his opposition.

The justices went into the courtroom on June 18 to hear argument under conditions unparalleled in the Court's annals. The FBI had been monitoring the activities of Black and Douglas for a while, apparently because of their First Amendment views. Now it posted agents in the courtroom who, in Hoover's words, "kept abreast of the actions of the Supreme Court, the individual judges, and defense attorneys," and did so with the assistance of Court employees. Two days later, Hoover thanked the Court's marshal (and the clerk and police chief the next month) for cooperating in the surveillance of the justices. Brownell was aware of this. "I didn't authorize surveillance of the Court and never told Hoover to do it, and don't believe he did.

Certainly he would not have gone to Ike on something like this without my approval," Brownell later said. "Vinson likely requested it. No one else could have." (Vinson might have spoken with his old friend Ike about approving informing on his own colleagues.) And Hugo Black knew about it.

After the argument, the justices went back into conference to vacate the stay and to remove all other avenues remaining in the way of the execution. "It is terrible to take this matter up without more information," Black said.

> None of us knows enough about it. Even if we did, I would oppose any action today. This is a race for death. I know of no case that has been so handled. This will be a black day for the Court. I plead that it not be decided today. My inclination is to hold that the statute applies that provides for the lesser penalty. Anything I say is wholly useless. I never could vote on a picked up session like this to vote to over[ride] a Justice during vacation time. [This is about a] conspiracy to do something over a number of years, 1944–50. Where there is a conspiracy that continues before and after the enactment of a statute, then we must apply the lighter punishment. We should not pass on the merits at this time, but should have argument and not be swayed by the winds of the time.

To the majority, however, the legal questions were frivolous and insubstantial. Douglas sided with Black only on the question of the stay; and Frankfurter had agreed with him ever since the original refusal to hear the case the past November, even if nearly all the time he did not dissent but only filed a memorandum or a statement expressing his views. "Our general direction in re civil liberties is very much the same," Black wrote John Frank then, "although I continue to think (as I tell him [Frankfurter]) that he tries to go by the wrong route and stops so short that he defeats his own purpose." The fact remains: of all the justices, *only* Black voted to hear the Rosenbergs' case *every* time it came before the court.[11]

June 19: The justices filed their hastily written opinions. Black, Frankfurter and Douglas each dissented. "In view of what you said, " Black told Douglas a day or two earlier, "I think it best for me simply to note a dissent because I agree with your opinion and disposition of the case." Douglas replied, "I think something should be filed—opinions explaining the point—at least my opinion on the stay"; and Black thought it best to write an opinion. In strong language he summarized all his complaints on this deviation from procedural regularity. Above all, he objected to the unseemly rush in a capital case: "More informed arguments" and "more deliberation . . . would be more nearly in harmony with the best judicial traditions." As he later said, "I believe [the Rosenbergs] to have been guilty but the prosecution wasn't conducted under the right law."

At a mass demonstration in Lafayette Park, across from the White House, protesters, mostly well dressed and middle class, held signs that the Rosenbergs should burn and shouted intensely anti-Semitic remarks. It was "perhaps the ugliest scene I ever witnessed in Washington," journalist Marquis Childs wrote after forty years there. Vinson, who, as Douglas noted, "was filled with passion to such an extent that he could hardly utter a calm word," received a note from the Acting Solicitor General that the attorney general advised from the White House that the president was entertaining a clemency petition: the executive branch was informing the judicial branch about the executive's own business. In the early evening Eisenhower denied it.

After the Court's session, Black left for home in a windowless laundry van. He did not want the FBI to locate him. One of the Rosenbergs' lawyers nevertheless went to his house, hoping for another stay. Black was playing tennis with JoJo when Lizzie Mae said someone was at the door. JoJo answered it. When she came back to tell him, he was standing on the tennis court, in his shorts, racket in hand, facing her, crying. "I can't do it," he said before she could say anything. "Josephine, tell them I can't do it."

The Rosenbergs were executed that night.[12]*

A dispirited Supreme Court finally rose for the summer. All the justices were glad simply to get away. The FBI's spying on the Court, initiated by Vinson, was much on Black's mind. So was its wiretapping of his home telephone for several years at Hoover's instigation. When the FBI found out nothing, it ended the tap. "Black had only the greatest of contempt for Hoover and talked a great deal about what a menace he was," recalled Martin Agronsky. He well knew Hoover's ability to ruin people's reputations and

* Vinson attended the American Bar Association meeting in Boston in late August, and when he heard that Douglas's brother happened to be staying at the same hotel, called him in "and went into the whole Rosenberg case," Douglas recalled. "The mob had tasted its blood and Fred Vinson was a sad man. He was sorry at what had happened. He had looked at this with sorrow and misgivings, regret. And he told my brother that I had been right. And he wanted to do everything he could in the rest of his life to try to clear my name of any wrongdoing and to make up for this great injustice that had been done. It was rather sad" (WODM, 318–28).

was not going to let it happen to himself. Mutual friends contacted New York lawyer Morris Ernst, who, although a prominent liberal and outspoken champion of freedom of speech, served as an FBI informant. Ernst put in a good word for Black to Hoover. That only got rid of an obnoxious immediate problem. In late August, leaving his office to go home, Black said, "They will soon be back deciding all those cases wrong again."[13]

CHAPTER 29

BROWN v. BOARD
OF EDUCATION

F RED VINSON'S SUDDEN DEATH on September 8, 1953, shocked the Supreme
Court. Black, as senior justice, served as acting chief justice until a successor
was named. Late in the month, the Court made its customary ceremonial
visit to the president. Limousines and a police escort, along with sirens and
flashing lights, were provided for the trip down Pennsylvania Avenue. Black
murmured he would drive his own car. So, leading the procession was his
1948 green Plymouth. He drove slowly, in contrast to his usual practice,
and stopped at every red light. As he pulled up at the White House gates,
the limousines went through them and the justices alighted. Black looked
for a parking spot. He found one in the Ellipse a block away; when he
returned, he had gotten a parking ticket.

In early October, President Eisenhower nominated California governor
Earl Warren for chief justice. Then in his third term, Warren had had an
extraordinarily successful political career. In 1946 he ran as the candidate
of both the Democratic and Republican parties. Two years later, when he
ran for vice president with Thomas Dewey, Truman said, "He's a Democrat
but doesn't know it." ("Yes," Warren replied, "but with a small 'd.' ") And
in 1950 he embarrassingly defeated the bearer of the most famous name in
American politics, James Roosevelt. Warren was a progressive moderate who
would take two steps backward if necessary to take one leap forward. He
courted all factions with a suave inconsistency, uniting groups and creating
consensus. In the process "he practically took over the Democratic Party in
the state," noted John P. McEnery, vice chairman of the party in California.
A man of robust good will, ever glad-handing, with a contagious smile and
a hearty greeting for all who had not crossed him, deliberate and methodical

in a low-keyed but determined way, an emotional fellow who usually kept his passions in check—Warren was a masterful *political* leader. No one ever noticed any intellectual depth or subtlety on his part.

His first move, after visiting his new office upon arriving in Washington, was to head straight for Black's. Hugo's warmth and political background immediately put Warren at ease. Hundreds of new cases, including "some of the gravest importance," were awaiting consideration, Black explained. Warren knew nothing about them or the Court's procedures. He asked if Black would preside at conferences until he could familiarize himself with the procedures. Black agreed, took Warren to meet the other justices and gave him the public oath, and the Court went right into conference. Within three hours the atmosphere had already changed. Earl Warren, fresh and energetic, was not the tired, worn-out Fred Vinson. And if he was conveying a new spirit to the Court, he was bringing dawn to Hugo Black.

Toward the end of the week Warren unexpectedly went to Black to ask with some urgency, "Could you recommend some book I might read on the subject of opinion writing?" Black leaned back in his dark leather chair. "There's one book which is by far better than anything published before or after." Warren leaned forward. "Aristotle on Rhetoric," Black announced. As midnight approached, Warren was still reading it in chambers. "The new Chief Justice is a very attractive, fine man," Black wrote his sons in the middle of the month. "Just a short acquaintance with him explains why it was possible for him to get votes in both parties in California. He is a novice here, of course, but a man with his intelligence should be able to give good service. I am by no means sure that an intelligent man, with practical, hard common sense and integrity like he has, is not as good a type to select as could be found in the country." In other words, Black was completely sure.[1] He never lost that feeling.

Those "gravest" cases were the school desegregation cases. The Court would have "some significance in pegging out new frontiers for groups whose rights were abused and in aiding them to move forward in their attempts to win their constitutional rights," Black told Ralph Bunche in 1940 (on the day after *Chambers v. Florida*), but he cautioned that it "cannot change political opinion in the South." Negro political rights there "cannot be widely won through court actions until the white community is at least no longer violently hostile to their exercise by Negroes. No legislation can bring about overnight changes in the people's mores, nor can any decisions of the Supreme Court do so; history shows that such changes should come only gradually," through "time, education and the evolution of ideas." The "real core of the problem is economic," Black claimed, "and that must be worked out before anything significant along other lines can be hoped for."

But his thinking began to change. At least as early as 1946, when the Court considered segregation in interstate commerce, Black realized such cases would continually arise and the Court would not be able to duck them. "There is no way I could vote for segregation," he said, but if the courts ordered school integration in the South, "there'll be blood in the streets." He feared virtual revolution, almost anarchy, noting that segregation was such a central part of southerners' way of life. Only time, education and the evolution of ideas could change political opinion in the South, he stated. But he could not condone segregation at all—that he knew as well as he knew anything.

The NAACP had been engaged since the early 1930s in a carefully devised strategy to overthrow the "separate but equal" doctrine the Court laid down in *Plessy v. Ferguson* in 1896. Only one justice, John Marshall Harlan, had protested upholding a Louisiana train segregation law. He dissented in words that have since reverberated around the world: "Our Constitution is color-blind." In the field of education the NAACP decided to attack first at the graduate and professional level, and work its way down to elementary schools. Its guiding spirit for a score of years now was Thurgood Marshall. His cheer and his astute advice, his indefatigability and banter masking his relentlessly insistent professionalism were indispensable in trying to make democracy simply live up to its claims. "There can be no separate equality," he told the Court in 1938. His movement gained momentum after World War Two.

Black knew the resistance Marshall's ultimate goal would meet, both in the Court and in the country. "The Judge didn't want to make an all out frontal assault on segregation in school cases as a matter of tactics and politics," said Truman Hobbs, his clerk in 1948. "He feared what would happen in a city like Birmingham. He knew the most sensitive area of all was the schools. He felt that if you give the blacks the vote, all other things would fall in their lap." That year the Court unanimously held that judicial enforcement of racially restrictive covenants violated the equal protection clause. The Court could not easily step out of the fray now. Marshall was cautiously emboldened: in two 1950 cases he asked only that they be decided in his favor within the confines of *Plessy*. In one case (*McLaurin v. Board of Regents*) admission to a University of Oklahoma doctoral program was on a "segregated basis," and the Negro student was then forced to sit in an alcove while attending the same classes as the white students; and in the other (*Sweatt v. Painter*) a Negro, denied admission to the University of Texas Law School solely because of his race, was offered admission, which he refused, to a newly created state law school for Negroes that lacked the established school's facilities and reputation.[2]

Black viewed the problem in terms of equal rights. "I don't think the record shows equal in either case," he said when the Court considered the cases in conference in April 1950. "I would make the burden as heavy on the state as we do in discrimination on juries." The state "can't set up a new school that is equal—common sense tells us" that. Segregation was "Hitler's creed—he preached what the South believed." The South "may never accept that until the races amalgamate as they do when they live side by side." "This system was designed to set up a caste system" that was both "contrary to the Fourteenth Amendment" and "a hangover from the Civil War. It is a badge of inferiority. If we reach this question, then I shall meet it regardless of the cases of this Court." But extending the holding to elementary schools, Black continued, concerned him because of a "deep seated antagonism to commingling in the South," which would close its schools "rather than mix races at grade and high school levels." He "would prefer separate and equal but cannot have [that] here." The Court had two choices: it could rule that there was no equality in either case and "handle the cases one by one and not cause trouble," or it could hold that segregation in graduate education was "unreasonable." Black voted to reverse in both cases.

Most of the Court also looked at the question of discrimination from the vantage point of equal rights, and while Vinson, Reed and Jackson did not, all (except perhaps Vinson in *Sweatt*) concluded that equality was lacking in both cases here. As the senior justice in the majority, Black assigned both cases to himself. But five days later, at the Court's next conference, he relinquished the assignment. At the same time Vinson announced he had changed his mind in *Sweatt* and would prepare the opinions. Segregation was held unconstitutional in each case under separate-but-equal, without the Court's reaching the broader issue. Black told Vinson he would not write separately in *Sweatt* unless another justice did, and (apparently) said he would join *McLaurin* if all others did. The Court's unanimity made both actions unnecessary. Even the most careful parsing of the Court's language could leave no doubt what it meant. Significant inequalities in education are constitutionally impermissible.[3]

....

Reaction came quickly. Responding only in part to the refusal of governor James Folsom and state Attorney General Albert A. Carmichael (a Clay County native) to join other southern and border states filing an amicus brief supporting Texas in upholding segregation, the Alabama legislature proclaimed it would not permit integrated education in the state's public schools. Reports reached Black that tomatoes would be thrown at him when he planned to talk to Birmingham lawyers in July 1950. He was also scheduled to be the main speaker at the Alabama Bar Association meeting when he heard that some lawyers planned to introduce resolutions putting the bar on record as criticizing the Court's decisions. He canceled both appearances. "High emotions over the segregation cases," he wrote Hugo, Jr., "would probably be aggravated by my presence."

Even before Hugo, Jr., went to Birmingham, his father was of two minds about his practicing there. Racial matters reaching the Court's plate would make it rough for his son. Not so much practicing law but politically: Lister Hill's political lieutenants pointed their stilettos in his direction to keep him out of party matters. "I am sure it is the Senator's affection for you and me" that made them do this, Hugo, Jr., told his father. The justice's report that a new round of segregation cases would be coming before the Court changed his son's plans to run for Congress, with Hill's blessing, in 1952. "I am by no means sure myself that it would be wise for you to be in it"; but while Hugo, Jr., might get elected now, "next time they will get you unless, of course, you are willing to abuse the Supreme Court. . . . You wouldn't have to get after me—just the Court." That was not appealing to Hugo, Jr., even if to his father it was simply a legitimate, if distasteful, political tactic. He told Alabama politicians he was not ready. Puzzled, they rightly suspected he knew something they did not.

Sweatt rang like a clarion. Whether *Plessy* still retained vitality was now seriously open to question. Those with the ultimate say on the matter, the Supreme Court justices, privately believed it had been implicitly overruled. They would be unlikely to maintain the line between higher and elementary education. Sensing their problem with the distinction, Thurgood Marshall decided to bring several suits challenging segregation in public school education. It would take the better part of two years for any of the cases to reach the Supreme Court, and perhaps by then the justices would be ready to tackle the issue directly. At this point, Tom Clark said later, *all* of us thought the climate was not just ripe for change. . . . The cases were not really clear cut. The records were cloudy. They came from the South. We wanted to get a national coverage, rather than a sectional one. . . . We delayed, awaiting the filing of additional cases; we hoped to have one based on the Fifth Amendment along with those predicated upon the Fourteenth. . . . It was deliberate on the part of each of us. . . . There was no shuffling of feet, no holding back on the legal question. It was simply a question of (1) getting a broad area of coverage; (2) thereby securing the opinion of the various Attorneys General of the states; and (3) getting more light for ourselves.

The Court unanimously refused to hear an appeal from Texas, even though the evidence showed that the Negro school was better than the white one. Black made a point to tell his clerk, "I'm doing it as a matter of discretion, but if I can get enough votes, I'll make law."[4]

*   *   *

In June 1952 the justices agreed to hear *Brown v. Board of Education* (from Kansas) and a South Carolina case, and in the fall added three other cases from the North that the NAACP had brought. The four state cases were designated *Brown*, and the fifth case, from the District of Columbia, was styled *Bolling v. Sharpe*. Argument was held in December 1952, one month after the presidential election. Black prepared for the case with his usual thoroughness, but with no great intensity. After argument, he intimated he would not hold that then present practices were constitutional; at dinner a few nights later he said, "I'm not going to hold that segregation is constitutional." In talking to his colleagues now, he was explicit:

At first blush I would have said it was up to Congress, but if we can declare confiscation or other laws unconstitutional then we can segregation. I'm compelled for myself to believe the idea of segregation is because the Negro is inferior. Nor can I escape that the [Thirteenth, Fourteenth and Fifteenth] Amendments had as their basic purpose the abolition of such castes. That is what is behind opposition now. If I have to meet it, the purpose of the law is to discriminate on account of color . . . the Amendments were designed to stop it. . . . I have to vote that way.

He did "not need books" or any of the sociological evidence the plaintiffs were offering to say this. South Carolina would go through the "forms" of abolishing public education, and other states "would probably take evasive measures while purporting to obey." There would be "some violence." Resistance to a desegregation decision might place the courts on the "battle front," leading to "law by injunction." Black was "driven to" his conclusion despite the "knowledge" that this "means trouble." At conference Black, Douglas, Burton and Minton were the only certain votes to overturn segregation.

Frankfurter, despite convictions no less deep than those of Black and Douglas, positioned himself in the middle as he often did. That way he could try to gain the most leverage over the other justices (and thus have history show that he guided the Court). How a decision-enforcing decree would be framed was much on his mind. While he would vote right now to desegregate District of Columbia schools, those in states presented different problems because of the Fourteenth Amendment's history. He wanted to postpone voting so that the incoming Eisenhower administration could participate and more consideration could be given to the decree. Vinson was deeply troubled by how to make the rights in these cases "personal" (as they had been in several prior segregation cases) when they would apply to millions of children. "Boldness is essential but wisdom indispensable," he said; these were two qualities not ordinarily associated with him. Jackson would assent to abolishing school segregation, but only if the Court could find a judicial, not a political, ground for its decision. Clark wanted to delay. With him and Vinson the matter came down not to racial intolerance but a disinclination to use judicial power in this fashion. Jackson, however, was always acutely ambivalent about the question of race and never sympathetic to the drive toward equal rights.[5]

"Don't take any vote now," Jackson urged. They didn't. If they had, the only unquestioned dissent would have been by Reed. "Must start with the idea that a large opinion [holds] that separation of races is for benefit of both," he said. Otherwise, all the justices, even Jackson, wanted to overrule *Plessy* formally if they could find a way to do so. But no one was willing to rush to judgment. A substantive void resulted. The chief justice often tries to step into it. But as spring came and the 1952 term neared its end, Fred Vinson seemed (even aside from the pressures brought about by the Rosenberg case) increasingly, and unnaturally, cranky and tense. The Court's inability to find unity around a strong position distressed him. "Vinson kept his views to himself but felt fear and trepidation about the segregation cases," one of his clerks recalled. "He knew trouble was coming." But he did not know how to head it off or even try. Of the other senior justices, Jackson was likewise uncertain, Reed was out in right field, Douglas was temperamentally incapable of leadership—and shingles prevented Black from making any attempt. It was a ready-made situation for Felix Frankfurter. He made the most of it.

In late May, Frankfurter circulated a draft of five questions to be submitted to the parties on reargument in the fall. These dealt with (1 & 2) the legislative history of the Fourteenth Amendment, (3) the power of the judiciary to decide the issue raised, and (4 & 5) the possible forms of relief (the decree). "I am willing," Black wrote, "to have 4 & 5 submitted to the parties but believe 1, 2 and 3 should not be. There are too many reasons for my objections to set them out. In the main, however, I think asking 1, 2 & 3 would bring floods of historical contentions on the specific points we asked about which would dilute the arguments along broader lines. I doubt if it would be possible to isolate framers' views about segregation in the primary schools. Although willing to acquiesce as to questions 4 & 5, I still rather doubt the wisdom of submitting any questions." Then he crossed this out. His ailment kept him from attending the conference where the Court took it up. Douglas noted for him: "A majority agreed May 29, 1953, to put all the questions." Because of that "I go along," Black wrote Frankfurter after Felix made minor changes.

The Court soon restored the segregation cases to the docket and also invited the attorney general to take part in oral argument and to file an additional brief if he so chose. After shingles forced him to miss the conference at which the invitation was approved, Black sent a memorandum to his colleagues stating that the invitation should be withdrawn "in view of the political uses that are being made of [it]. I do not think that this Court should permit itself to become involved in current political controversies, and I know of no way to prevent it in respect to the subject except to change our order."[6] If the Court discussed this at its next and last conference of the term two days later, when the Rosenberg case overshadowed just about everything else, Black's contentions were easily quelled. What was likely behind the memorandum was his ancient distrust of Republicans. This blinded him to the fact that Attorney General Herbert Brownell, the solicitor general and their staffs were stalwart supporters of desegregation, as much so as any justice.

Argument lasted more than ten hours during three days in early December 1953. (Black gave one of his allotted seats in the audience to his old friend, NAACP secretary Walter White.) On December 12 the Court deliberated.

Chief Justice Warren had been presiding at conference for well over a month now. The Court, he began, should merely discuss the cases informally for as long as needed and not vote on them now. He wanted to prevent views from forming too quickly and hardening. For Warren the case was easy: the principle of equality was one of his guiding creeds. He specifically rejected *Plessy*'s "basic premise that the Negro race is inferior." By saying this, he was putting the matter on a moral footing; implied was that any justice who wished to perpetuate segregation had to candidly acknowledge this.

Douglas, Burton and Minton expressed similar beliefs. (Black was absent due to his sister-in-law's illness, but he sent in his vote.) Frankfurter's lengthy, roundabout comments established that he would also vote against segregation; and Clark was willing to go along with the majority if a flexible decree could be drawn. That meant more than enough votes to overturn separate-but-equal. But Jackson found no legal basis for this "congenial political conclusion" and he wanted to deal with both the remedy and the merits. And Reed felt that segregation was constitutional because it "was not done on inferiority but on racial differences."

By the end of the conference several justices thought Warren should write the opinion. Perhaps he could increase his rock-hard majority, Douglas recalled, "but getting nine at that time seemed to be rather remote." Who would write the opinion was not uppermost in Warren's mind: consensus was. He desperately wanted it. Daily, virtually wherever the justices met privately, they talked about the cases; Warren put them on every conference agenda. In late February 1954 he asked the brethren if they were ready to vote. They said yes. On March 1 the Senate confirmed Warren as chief justice by voice vote without dissent. (Eisenhower had named him in an interim appointment since the Senate was not then in session.) The Court in early March voted unanimously against the separate-but-equal doctrine. Warren assigned the opinion to himself. This he "originally had not intended," Tom Clark said twenty years later. "I think Justice Black was responsible for [that]. I doubt that the Chief Justice realized the added impact of an opinion authored by that office. No doubt he also felt that Black or even myself, being from the South, might be more acceptable." Warren prepared a memorandum, which a clerk essentially followed in drafting the opinion.

By now secrecy and fear of leaks had become obsessions. No justice was more mute than Black. He went to talk to students at Princeton. One student asked about the cases. Black looked around with a blank stare. "School cases?" he replied. "What are they? I'll have to look them up when I get back to Washington." This only reinforced his not wanting to go anywhere. "I think you are correct in believing that this might not be the most pleasant time for me to visit Birmingham," he wrote Hugo, Jr., in April 1954. "It would probably be wholly impossible for people to refrain from attempting to discuss court matters with me, even though some would know that such a discussion would be improper. The issue involved is too sensitive a one." His clerks were living with him but "he never said anything about [Brown] to us," recalled David Vann. His co-clerk Charles Reich concurred: "Usually we could look at anything in the Judge's files if it at all related to what we were working on. Nothing was sacrosanct. But it was different in Brown. He said, 'I don't think you boys have to know about that,' and specifically told us not to look at that file. He locked it up and kept the key."[7]

Bolling v. Sharpe challenged segregation on the basis of the due process clause of the Fifth Amendment. Warren's original draft treated it as an education case ("the very subject now before us"), and for support he cited four cases from the 1920s. These epitomized the "fundamental liberty" approach that Black had castigated as "natural law" and had campaigned so strenuously to vanquish. The second draft transformed the case into a race case: "In view of our decision that the Constitution prohibits the states from maintaining racially segregated public schools, it would be unthinkable that the same Constitution would impose a lesser duty on the federal Government." Born was the equal protection component of the Fifth Amendment. What caused the change?*

"I think that Black said something to Warren about those [citations]," Justice Douglas recalled. Black and Warren were saying a lot more to each other. They felt an instant attraction for each other, these contemporaries, former prosecutors with long careers in electoral politics. Along the way

---

* Black's support of Bolling seemingly violated his own principles: the Fifth Amendment does not contain, nor can it be read to incorporate, the Fourteenth Amendment's equal protection clause. When a clerk later asked how Black could justify this, he replied: "A wise judge chooses, among plausible constitutional philosophies, one that will generally allow him to reach results he can believe in—a judge who does not to some extent tailor his judicial philosophy to his beliefs inevitably becomes badly frustrated and angry. . . . A judge who does not decide some cases, from time to time, differently from the way he would wish, because the philosophy he has adopted requires it, is not a judge. But a judge who refuses ever to stray from his judicial philosophy, and be subject to criticism for doing so, no matter how important the issue involved, is a fool" (Guido Calabresi, "Foreword: Antidiscrimination and Constitutional Accountability (What the Bork-Brennan Debate Ignores)," 105 Harv. Law Rev. 80, 132 [1991]).

both had made their share of necessary compromises, but they looked at most questions of policy from largely the same angle. Hugo's first thought was to make Warren feel comfortable in his new surroundings. He would wait for Warren to take the initiative, confident that their backgrounds would bring them together. Soon they spent much time talking about the cases. When Black soon heard that he and Douglas had influenced Warren's "new liberalism," he protested: "Why, Warren came to the Court with the same ideas I had. He got them in California—I in Alabama."

The ink on Warren's commission had scarcely dried when Frankfurter was wearing out Warren's carpet courting him. Warren was lonely and "perfectly miserable" at first—his wife returned to California after he took his oath—and felt he was "practically a prisoner" both at the Court and in his hotel room, he recalled. Visiting Black at home was one of the few ways he lifted his spirits during this period. There he had a good steak (Black chose "the best part" for him), a good scotch and good conversation recounting political and courtroom war stories. "The Judge would masterfully steer the conversation to whatever Warren was interested in," recalled Charles Reich, who often observed it. For Warren it was a welcome relief from the pressures of the marble palace. His wife did not return until Thanksgiving, when Black hosted dinner for the whole Warren family. On these occasions law was not discussed much. (When the family was there, it was not mentioned at all.) A friendship was being formed.

It was also a hard time for Hugo. His sister-in-law Hattie, Robert Lee's wife, was dying, and he thought his brother might not outlive her. Hugo had been devoted to her since he lived in her house after his mother died in 1905. Her daughter Hazel, visiting him, wrote: "I have seen loneliness in one who tried not to let others see loneliness in him. He smiled when others smiled; he tried to laugh when funny little things happened. . . . Although he was brave, his smile looked as if pain might have had to step in and help it stretch out a bit to make a smile. . . . Silence became a noticeable part of this lonely man." He went to Birmingham to see Hattie for a sad last visit before going to Miami for the first of three extended visits. "I do not like cold weather," he told Sterling. "As a matter of fact, [it] just about knocks me out. It is for that reason I go to Florida every chance I get during the winter." He could also play tennis there daily, which helped to clear up the lingering aftereffects of shingles.[8]

He did not have many opinions to write. "My work is very light but I do find a dissent now and then that gives me some interest," he told John Frank. He stretched out drafting his opinions; the longest one this term was only twelve pages. On occasion he even had each clerk write a draft. So would he. Then he would say, "Let's pick the best one to work with." And he would always pick his. It was all part of filling up his time. This gave him leisure to read: Lloyd Stryker's *The Art of Advocacy,* A. E. Taylor's life of Socrates, and soon he was "thoroughly enjoying the speeches of Charles James Fox, the great English liberal statesman who was a thorn in the flesh of the king's ministers during the time of Revolutionary War and immediately before and after the Colonies won their liberty. Fox's speeches before 1776 contain many of the ideas that Jefferson wrote into the Declaration of Independence."[9] The first of the "truths" that he held to be "self-evident" was that "all men are created equal." That, after all, was only what the Supreme Court was trying to hold in the school segregation cases.

*   *   *

By March 1954 nobody knew when *Brown* would come down. The Eisenhower administration was becoming edgy over the case.[*] While Warren was drafting the opinion, the Secret Service came over to Black's house. "They peeked around the kitchen but I wouldn't tell them anything," Hugo said.

   Warren personally showed each of the justices his draft opinion. One of his clerks took it to Black, who was playing tennis at home. A small slice disturbed him. To support the statement that "modern authority" found that separate educational facilities are "inherently unequal," Warren appended a footnote listing seven works by social scientists, starting with an article by psychologist Kenneth Clark and ending with leftward-leaning Swedish economist Gunnar Myrdal's pathbreaking social study, *An American Dilemma.* Black told Warren "it would go badly in the South." But despite misgivings (such material never appealed to Black), he did not strongly protest the footnote's inclusion; if he had, Warren likely would have struck it. "It was only a note, after all," as Warren said later. Black also disagreed over another aspect. He believed the decision should be effective immediately. Warren felt that separating its principle from its enforcement was essential; the delay would give needed time for southern wrath to cool. Once again, Black swallowed his doubts.

[*] Even though Herbert Brownell had passed along Warren's comment that the Justice Department brief was "outstanding," Ike soon sat Warren next to John W. Davis, the lawyer who had argued the segregationist side, at a White House stag dinner where he openly praised Davis and his position before Warren (Robert F. Burk, *The Eisenhower Administration and Black Civil Rights* [Knoxville, Tenn., 1984], 140 [outstanding], 142; Warren, *Memoirs,* 291).

"My decision," he wrote Edmond Cahn in 1960 in one of his few written comments on the case, "was not the result of brushing aside history nor on the theory that time had made something unconstitutional that had been so since the Fourteenth Amendment was adopted. Some articles that have been written indicating that we did go against history in that case are not in accord with my own views." Black pronounced himself satisfied with the opinion. All the other justices likewise found it acceptable—even Robert Jackson ("*Plessy* doesn't make sense today," he told his son) and, most surprisingly, Stanley Reed ("there was an inevitability about it all," he admitted a few years later). * In a triumph of personal diplomacy Earl Warren had won a unanimous Court. The next day, after looking at a newly published article about Warren, Black predicted, "It's only the first of many. Everyone will be talking and writing about him soon."[10]

On May 17, 1954, Black gave no indication that *Brown* was coming down. But just before lunch he told his clerks, "You might want to come to Court today." They came and saw Justice Jackson on the bench, having returned from the hospital. That could mean only one thing. In a firm, unemotional voice Chief Justice Warren read the *Brown* opinion. "We conclude"—and here he departed from the printed text to insert the word "unanimously"— "that in the field of public education the doctrine of 'separate but equal' has no place. Separate educational facilities are inherently unequal." (He added "unanimously" because "I thought it was getting kind of tense in there and just wanted to liven things up a bit," Warren said to one of Black's clerks later in the day.) In Black's chambers Spencer Campbell, his loyal messenger, observed, "I have to go back to Alabama and I know what it will be like. You could always go to California. One hundred thousand people move there every month."

That was the reality of the decision. Jim Crow may have been legally dead but its spirit animated the South. Strife and turmoil would now ensue. At a dinner at *New Republic* publisher Michael Straight's house a few nights later, praise was heaped on the Court; some guests said they foresaw a truly color-blind society. "No," Black soberly warned, "that's going to take a very long time if ever. It won't be easy. There's going to be trouble and people

* It was in this sense that Justice William J. Brennan, Jr., quietly said in 1986, "That's right," when Black's clerk during the term of *Brown* noted that the decision did not come as a surprise to careful Court followers, who knew the institutional imperatives and the importance of precedent (Vann, UA remarks; the author was sitting next to Justice Brennan).

are going to die." Soon he said that "before the tree of liberalism could be renewed in the South a few candidates must water it with their blood." (When he hired Vann, an Alabama native, as his clerk, he asked, "Are you sure you want to work for me if you want to practice law in Alabama?") Equally realistic was Thurgood Marshall. "There is only but so much lawyers can do," he told a friend. "After we get the law clear, the hard job begins." That would start when the Court issued its implementing decree.

From the first Black, although he wanted to order an immediate remedy, had been leery of too forceful an implementation. "Leave it to the district courts," he said when the Court discussed it in January 1954. "Let them work it out." He did not see how they could be given any framework. Flexible enforcement was a necessity. A decree should not resolve everything at once. "If necessary, let us have 700 suits. Vagueness is not going to hurt. Let it simmer. . . . Let it take time." In the Deep South "any man who would come in [to support desegregation] would be dead politically forever." Enforcement, he warned, would give rise to a "storm over this Court."

The Court planned to hear argument in late 1954, after the November elections. But in October, shortly before the term was to begin, Robert Jackson died of a heart attack. Argument was now postponed until Jackson's successor was confirmed. Eisenhower quickly nominated John Marshall Harlan, a judge on the federal court of appeals in New York, a former outstanding trial lawyer and the grandson of the justice who had proclaimed "our Constitution is color-blind." As a lawyer he had spent much of his time representing large corporate interests in court. He was confirmed in March 1955, and *Brown II* was extensively argued the next month. These were class actions, Warren said in conference, and therefore affected more than those parties in whose name the suits were brought.* The decree would have to be more than "bare-bones." District courts should consider "physical facts" but not "psychological attitudes," which would defeat the decree.[11]

"Write a decree and quit," Black urged. ". . . The less we say, the better off we are." He recalled being raised in an atmosphere distinctly hostile to federal officials; this was only beginning to change. He did not think any federal judge in the South would enforce a "vigorous decree." He knew all those judges and, so far as he could tell, none favored the *Brown* decision. Limit the decree to "these seven children," the named plaintiffs, and enjoin the local school boards "not to refuse," so its members could "avoid con-

---

* A class action is a lawsuit brought by representative member(s) of a large group of persons on behalf of all its members.

tempt" charges. "Nothing is more important than that this Court should not issue what it cannot enforce." Only Douglas agreed. Five other justices said these were class actions and should apply to all those persons in the group. But the whole Court was united on one point: as Black put it, "If humanely possibly, I will do everything possible to achieve a unanimous result." Warren wrote a brief opinion enshrining the theme of gradualism. The Court remanded the cases to the lower courts "to take such proceedings and enter such orders and decrees consistent with this opinion as are necessary and proper to admit to public schools on a racially nondiscriminatory basis with all deliberate speed the parties to these cases."

The phrase "with all deliberate speed" immediately entered the language. Black wished it had never come in. "I wasn't happy with it," he said later, "but Justice Frankfurter wanted it. I said, 'What's "deliberate speed"?' But Justice Frankfurter said, 'We have to do it because of Justice Holmes,' " who had used it in a 1918 opinion. Black regretted its use from the first and talked about it much over the next few years. The Court, he felt, made a mistake in not deciding *Brown* on the basis of what the Constitution means, like every other case. He disliked the idea of applying law prospectively, even more so when the guiding decision was premised on a phrase whose meaning was anything but clear. Black got up on his soapbox and said, "One of the worst things I've done was to go along with Felix on that. I just don't know what got into me. How could I have ever let myself get talked into that. I should have known that if Felix proposed anything like that, it was no good." This was in 1957. "Several times later at conference," recalled Justice Brennan, "he said sadly, 'Felix persuaded me. We made a mistake.' " He went along with "all deliberate speed" just so the Court would be unanimous.[12]

*   *   *

Black's old constituents reviled him for doing what the Constitution demanded and his conscience dictated. By the hundreds they wrote their former senator. These letters hurt more than he could admit. He was called a betrayer and a scalawag, Judas Iscariot, a "renegade" who lacked the courage "to stand up for the things he learned at his mother's knee," the "Benedict Arnold of Alabama" whose "name is Black in Washington, but [is] a damn sight blacker in Alabama." Public appearances there were out of the question for the foreseeable future. Even trips to see Hugo, Jr., and his family grew infrequent. He did not want to lower the dignity of the Court by exposing himself to personal attack. When he did go to Birmingham and walked down

Twentieth Street, to see friends at the few law firms where he was still welcome, he often wore a chest protector provided by the Secret Service.

Old friends shunned him. Crampton Harris turned his inscribed picture of Hugo to the wall and "kept it there for quite a while," his granddaughter recalled. In 1955 Black played tennis at the Birmingham Country Club, then entered the dining room for lunch; he was booed, and several people walked out. The club soon passed a bylaw that members could not bring guests on the tennis courts. Black's law school class did not invite him to its fiftieth reunion in 1956, deeply saddening him. Some relatives sent him blistering criticism. Politicians blasted him. One (losing) candidate for governor in 1954 remarked, "Justice Black is not fit to try a chicken thief." The Alabama secretary of state, Betty Fink, opined, "I hope he dies and burns in hell." Jim Folsom, whose second term as governor, starting in 1955, was wrecked on the shoals of race, was being only realistic when he said, "The only man I could beat in Alabama today is Hugo Black. . . ."

Hugo, Jr., suffered more directly. Six months after *Brown*, he began to think of moving from Alabama. A country club had blackballed him the year before when a member refused to "associate with any labor lawyers," and now the noose was slowly tightening. "It is easy to understand the considerations that you mentioned," Black wrote him in December 1954. ". . . I could have come to see you most any time during this autumn, but I have doubted the advisability of making a trip to Alabama at this juncture. You understand the reasons for my doubts and I understood that you agreed with those reasons. Should I come down there at any time it will be necessary for me to get around and see some of my friends. While I know and love the people of Alabama, I also understand that they have deep feelings on certain questions—feelings that make some of them rather emotional at times. Emotional statements would not disturb me particularly, but I am not so sure about you, that is, I do not see why you should be subject to any unpleasantness that is not necessary."

Justice Black tried to put up a good front. (He retained his wry sense of humor. A lawyer arguing an Alabama case told the Court, in answer to a question from Black, that "the Alabama courts have not been reconciled to the Supreme Court in this field." "That," Black remarked, "is not unusual.") He knew the people of Alabama, had fought for them in court, had represented them in the Senate. And now this. "When Justice Black said he couldn't come back to Alabama," remembered his old friend Judge Richard T. Rives, "tears almost came to his eyes. He was very emotional about it."[13]

....

Brown was finally enforced through the efforts of four judges on the Fifth Circuit Court of Appeals. One was Rives; the others—Elbert P. Tuttle, John Minor Wisdom and John R. Brown—were Eisenhower-appointed Republicans, always a most improbable source to Black. Were it not for them, as Burke Marshall, later assistant attorney general in charge of the civil rights division, said, "*Brown* would have failed in the end." Black got to admire and like them, especially John Brown. But to him Dick Rives was special. Their fondness began when they fought together in Alabama political wars. While he was arguing a case before the Supreme Court in 1951, Rives received a note that President Truman had nominated him for a judgeship. He went to see Black when the argument was over. "I wasn't sure whether to take the appointment," Rives recalled. "I told him, 'I'm happy in my law practice. I haven't looked at a lawbook in 30 years. I'd like your advice.' He told me, 'I'll be glad to give it to you, Dick. When you get on that court, the cases are so close that,' and he paused, 'you can't do any real harm.' "

Black revered Rives as he did few other people, especially after Rives's opinion in June 1956 striking down Alabama's bus segregation law and ending the Montgomery bus boycott. A "cross" of "a lion and a lamb" was how Black described Rives to Warren when the Court upheld the opinion that November. Over the next decade Rives and federal judge Frank M. Johnson, Jr., also of Montgomery and another Eisenhower-appointed Republican,* outlawed segregation and discrimination in every facet of Alabama life. One of the reasons Black wanted the segregation cases over was that he felt they were keeping otherwise qualified white southerners out of the national mainstream. "Nobody is better qualified to be president," Black said of Georgia senator Richard Russell, "but he can't be. He's the ablest southerner. That's why he's leader of the southern bloc." Soon Fifth Circuit judges in other states followed Rives's lead, and the South was never the same again. "There comes a time when people get tired of being trampled over by the iron feet of oppression," a new minister in Montgomery said.

---

* A further Eisenhower-appointed Republican, Simon E. Sobeloff, of the Fourth Circuit Court of Appeals, was the federal judge of whom Black was perhaps most fond. "How very much I have regretted the fact that we have not been colleagues on this Court," he told Sobeloff in 1964 (3/2/64). They almost were: "I have every reason to believe that Simon Sobeloff was promised an appointment to the Supreme Court but rendered too many decisions for integration," Earl Warren later said (diary, 2/5/66, Pearson papers).

Suddenly electrified, the congregation stomped and thundered, the noise rolling on and on. The radiations of Martin Luther King, Jr.'s, oratory spread over the land. And America was never the same again.[14]

Most of the judges in the Fifth Circuit held Black responsible for *Brown* and the changes it wrought. "There was considerable opposition to him," Rives noted. "Sometimes it was pretty personal. They said he was a traitor to his section and country." At circuit conferences they kept their distance. "Some didn't want to be photographed with him," observed John Brown. A siege mentality was beginning to take hold across much of the South. The Alabama legislature nearly unanimously passed a nonbinding resolution declaring *Brown* "null, void, and of no effect" in the state; the state senate did pass one, asking Congress to distribute the Negro population of the South evenly among all forty-eight states. The next year, when a rumor got around that Black might retire, a state representative introduced a bill to provide funds to defray any expense Black might incur in locating somewhere other than Alabama. In 1959 the Alabama senate passed a resolution that it was the sense of that distinguished body that when Black died, his remains should not be mingled with the fine Alabama soil. For several succeeding years the legislature passed resolutions condemning Black.[15]

The fallout from *Brown* also affected Lister Hill. He and Black felt the same way about racial matters. This was something Hill admitted only to his immediate family and less than a handful of close friends. Hugo and Lister had seen each other less since Josephine's death, but the warmth between them had not changed. When *Brown* came down, Hill issued conventional expressions of "shock" and "dismay"; soon he would have to start gearing up for reelection in 1956. Black said, "Lister, you have got to stop being with me. You can't be seen with me. It's going to hurt you." Hill protested, "No, it won't. People already know and I don't care, you're my friend." Black was insistent. Time and again he said, "It will hurt you, Lister. You must stop." So finally, against his own desires, Hill stopped seeing Black. He removed Hugo's portrait from its prominent place in his home. For years they would have hardly any contact. Tragic circumstance forced these two dearest of friends to discontinue a relationship that had been an integral part of their lives.

Black became mainly defensive of Hill and John Sparkman when they signed the Southern Manifesto in 1956, declaring as its purpose to use "all lawful means" to reverse *Brown*. "They have to do that to stay in office," he said. It was justified; the alternatives to them were so much worse. Black gave the impression that if he had remained in the Senate, he would have rolled with the punches as Hill did. "Politicians do what they think is right," Black said at the time, "but their motives are often very complex."[16]

Postscript: "I didn't call Hugo after *Brown*," Hill told this writer after Black died. "That was a terrible opinion, the worst ever. We never discussed it. Hugo realized there wasn't much he could do for me after 1954. I severed the cord with Hugo." The former politician was remembering what he wanted to remember. It was not Lister Hill the man talking. "Are you sorry you did?" I asked. Hill's arms flailed and his voice rose. "If anybody ever saw me with him, I'd be dead.* Nobody would ever vote for me." I repeated the question. Hill leaned forward even more, put his head down between his legs, kept it there for more than thirty seconds, sighed, and said very slowly and quietly, "I'm sorry. I'm very sorry." He paused again. "In restrospect, I wish I could have seen him more in recent years."

---

* It must be assumed that Hill meant that politically, although given the temper in Alabama then, he could have meant it literally.

CHAPTER 30

"BOOKS ARE MY FRIENDS"

Pᴇᴏᴘʟᴇ ᴏɴ ᴛʜᴇ ᴘᴀɢᴇs of his books were his friends, Black liked to say. They had different personalities but just did not happen to have live bodies. Reading his books, he came to know these people as well as he did his living friends. The ancient world spoke to him as if it were breathing. Books from and about ancient Greece and Rome were Black's favorites. In them he found limitless comfort, instruction and relevance. These cultures were as familiar to him as the society in which he lived. He could never read enough about either civilization to satisfy himself fully.

Of all Black's books, Edith Hamilton's *The Greek Way* was *the* special one. "Read that," he told law clerks when he hired them. "It's the best preparation for the job I could think of." He seemingly memorized the book and regarded Hamilton as "one of our truly great thinkers." Of her many reaffirmations of his own thoughts perhaps this passage in the chapter on Thucydides is the most telling: "He reasoned that since the nature of the human mind does not change any more than the nature of the human body, circumstances swayed by human nature are bound to repeat themselves, and in the same situation men are bound to act in the same way unless it is shown to them that such a course in other days ended disastrously." The Greeks, Black noted, "would brush aside all obscuring, entangling superfluity, and see clearly, plainly, unadorned, what they wished to express. . . . Clarity and simplicity of statement" were their "watchwords." Black underlined all these passages.

Exulting in the quest was one part of the Greek world. Tragedy and suffering were another. Black had seen Josephine suffer while he was powerless to help. In the years following her death he read the classics with a new urgency. He marked instance after instance where Greek authors as well as Edith Hamilton dealt with tragedy and suffering. Could he have been searching for answers, looking for solace, for words that spoke to his anguish?

The ancients were Black's primary reference point. Aristotle he called "my favorite author." He liked to "lean back in the chair," recalled Eugene Gressman, Justice Murphy's longtime clerk, "and make some comment tying something he had just read in Aristotle into the conversation. It was just remarkable." What Aristotle gave Black essentially was a perspective, an infinitely practical wisdom. His espousal of "paideia," the educational ideal, and his insistent emphasis on individuality, so valuable lest litigants simply be considered integers on a judicial assembly line, made him an unfailing source of insight and stimulation.

Other classical writers offered different virtues. "Cicero's discussion of the *Nature of the Gods* presents most of the arguments that can now be thought about for and against religious beliefs," Black thought. Livy was "the Mark Sullivan of his period, writing always in the interest of the patrician classes. On the other hand Tacitus seemed to have a leaning the other way." Sometimes, when working on a case, he came into the clerks' room with his copy of Livy, pointed to a parallel situation in a passage, and said, "There it is. It was going on then." And "if one gets nothing else from Xenophon, his writings show a great similarity between the people of different centuries, their practices, ambitions, vices and virtues."[1]

Black treasured the calmness, purity and tranquillity of the classical world; and the order, logic, stability and reason it represented. The wisdom of Greece spoke so directly to him that he wanted to learn Greek because he did not trust the authority of the translations; but he did not, because he felt it was too late in life to do so. (He was in his mid-sixties at the time.) He viewed ancient writings as universally applicable. The citizens of Greece and Rome had much to teach us in many areas: anonymous informers,* resistance to tyranny, inexcusable punishment and human relations among them. Black habitually invoked the authority of these civilizations to establish and buttress his position. "Conquest by the United States, unlike con-

---

* Several times Black repeated a Roman emperor's instructions to one of his officials about prosecuting Christians: "Anonymous informations ought not to be received in any sort of prosecution. It is introducing a very dangerous precedent, and is quite foreign to the spirit of our age" (*Carlson v. Landon* [1952]) commencement address, Swarthmore College, 6/6/55; *Faith,* 3. And in Tacitus' *Annals* he underlined, "the guilty acts of informers, and their wages, were alike detestable. . . ." (*The Works of Tacitus: The Annals* [Oxford, Eng., 1871], II, 3, in HLB Books.

quest by many other nations, does not mean tyranny," he wrote in a 1950 dissent when the Court refused habeas corpus to an enemy alien confined overseas by American officials. "For our people 'choose to maintain their greatness by justice rather than violence.' " In a footnote he observed: "This goal for government is not new. According to Tacitus, it was achieved by another people almost 2,000 years ago." Recurring themes in human nature were a motif of his thought. He was fond of saying that "ancient ways have a way of repeating themselves." "Those people who think that this country is beset by many new problems and who think these problems insurpassable, would be greatly benefitted by studying," he observed after reading H. J. Haskell's *This Was Cicero.* In talking about freedom of speech in an address dedicated to the memory of Albert Einstein, Black instinctively linked the times of the Roman emperor Augustus, James Madison and Hitler.[2]

He grounded his convictions on the ancient premise that the purpose of history was to discover those grand moral laws that man should know and obey. This idea of history as philosophy teaching by example was an Enlightenment concept, and Black would have been at home in an eighteenth-century salon, drinking from the goblets of history and philosophy, calmly exploring differences and agreeing that disagreement is only to be expected (while saying to himself that those who disagree with him "just don't get it"). Symmetry and grace and order (amidst contemporary chaos) epitomized thought then. The Constitution was the prize product of the age. It more than furnished a structure to government: it was designed to outlaw the beast in humanity while allowing the individual personality, the creative spirit in all spheres, to flower. To a judge who must apply it, it provides an unparalleled vision and a source of perpetual optimism.

Immersion in the past made yesterday and today seem like one to Black. To venture forth to improve tomorrow without contemplation would be foolhardy. He underscored this remark by Pericles: "Instead of looking on discussion as a stumbling-block in the way of action, we think it an indispensable preliminary to any wise action at all." Next to John Adams's comment "It seems to me that man is made to act rather than to know," Black marked, "Why not both?" A creed was an incentive to action more than a refuge of reason. "The truths of the spirit are proved not by reasoning about them, but only by acting upon them," Edith Hamilton wrote. "Their life is dependent upon what we do about them." Black had a passion for finding out, for getting to the bottom of things. Intellectually he had a kitten's curiosity. He was hellbent on truth and intent on understanding. Only then could the practical idealist move to reform most efficiently.[3]

Philosophers helped in the pursuit. Certain types of technical philosophy gave Black problems. "Hegel's and Kant's works have always been a little difficult reading for me," he confessed. But public-spirited philosophers were different. Black acknowledged the influence of John Dewey's functional approach: "My daughter has frequently told people that if they want to find out what I think they should go to Dewey's works." In a different way Bertrand Russell also influenced Black. When he went in for a hernia operation in September 1956, he was on a Russell reading binge. He took several Russell books to the hospital and was talking about Russell to the doctors and nurses as they wheeled him into the operating room. By the time he left a week later he had the hospital staff reading and discussing Russell.

Black read more in the years after Josephine's death than at any other time. He was a man of regular habits—the same meals each day (light breakfasts and lunches, but a normal-size dinner), the same routine each evening, watering his garden before steak for dinner, then working on an opinion afterward—and he set aside a certain amount of time for reading daily. He kept a pile of books by his bed, and the reading lamp over it burned a hole in the mattress. To him it was part of his job. He continued his regular summer reading program focusing on specific topics. One summer it was all of Dickens and Scott. In the summer of 1950 he read all of Macaulay. The next year he told a clerk to go to a certain part of one of Macaulay's books, where he would find something on bills of attainder; Black put it in the opinion. He was necessarily selective in his reading: he enjoyed novels but read fewer over the years, as he felt he could more fruitfully spend his thinking time on books from which he could gain knowledge, perspective or understanding.[4]

No modern figure supplied any more of those qualities than Thomas Jefferson. He was Black's "number one, number two and number three" historical hero, noted Hugo, Jr.—and had been since law school. "There are few things that have been writen about Jefferson that are not interesting," Black said. He practically downed Jefferson whole. And although Jefferson's cup of libertarianism was chronically overflowing, Black did not even ask him before replenishing his supply. To Black, Jefferson epitomized the mellow respect and tolerance that are the heart of democracy, as Black's underlinings in Dumas Malone's biography of Jefferson reveal: "He hated to hurt anybody's feelings and liked to tell people what they liked to hear." "The boldness of his mind was sheathed in a scabbard of politeness, and he was conciliatory in minor matters," Malone wrote. And Jefferson continued "personal friendship, despite differences about political doctrines and public questions."* (Black also thought he shared more with Jefferson: on occasion late in life he even thought he looked like him. Pictures showed "similar noses and hair," Black said, even though he was almost bald.) The passage about Jefferson's youthful friendship with Dabney Carr, later his brother-in-law, at the beginning of Tom Watson's *Life and Times of Thomas Jefferson,* he found especially moving. It was "one of those pieces," as Daniel Meador, the chronicler of Black's reading, observed, "from which he liked to read aloud occasionally" to his clerks—just as he used to talk to juries, "with mock solemnity and pompousness, tinged with mirth and punctuated with laughter."

Black naturally invoked Jefferson most frequently on First Amendment issues. His favorite Jefferson quotation, the one he quoted most often, dozens of times in all, came from Jefferson's First Inaugural Address: "If there are any among us who would wish to dissolve this Union or to change its republican form, let them stand undisturbed as monuments of the safety with which error of opinion may be tolerated where reason is left free to combat it." But his most specific reliance on Jefferson came in 1957 when the Court reversed the convictions of fourteen second-string Communist leaders for conspiring to advocate and teach the overthrow of the government by force and violence in violation of the Smith Act. This simply "was a political trial—what the First Amendment was supposed to prevent," Black said in conference. In a concurring-dissenting opinion joined by Justice Douglas he wrote:

> I believe the First Amendment forbids Congress to punish people for talking about public affairs, whether or not such discussion incites to action, legal

---

* In 1962 HLB wrote Joseph Martin, former House of Representatives speaker and a Republican, appreciations and congratulations upon fifty years of public service:

> . . . So far as congratulations are concerned, however, I congratulate the public which has been the beneficiary of your service. I say this because I believe that your public service, while duly regardful of loyalty to party, has always placed loyalty to country first. While my admiration for public service is great, that is not the end of it. Without yielding one particle of your loyalty to your own party, you have been able, because of your warm personality, to make friends among those who disagree with you. This, to my way of thinking, is one of the marks of a man who renders distinguished public service. It is in this category that I salute you! [8/27/62]

or illegal. As the Virginia Assembly said in 1785, in its "Statute for Religious Liberty," written by Thomas Jefferson, "it is time enough for the
rightful purposes of civil government, for its officers to interfere when
principles break out into overt acts against peace and good order. . . ."[5]

Black's daughter JoJo was always looking for books or ideas that could be
helpful to him. In one of her college courses, she read selections from the
Levellers, a small band of mid-seventeenth-century English army radicals
whose proposed "Agreement of the People" read like early drafts of the
Constitution and the Bill of Rights. A constitutional convention would draft
a written constitution, which would set limits to governmental authority
and abolish arbitrary power. There would be freedom of religion, of speech
and of the press; conscientious objectors would not be drafted into the army;
and public worship would be voluntarily supported. The right against self-
incrimination would be inviolate. Only by jury trial could life, liberty or
property be taken away. There would be universal manhood suffrage (except
for paupers and servants), and the legislature would be apportioned on the
basis of population.

This sounded just like what Black continually talked about, and when
JoJo recommended the excerpts to him in the fall of 1953, he devoured
them. Thereafter he considered the Levellers "the first real constitutionalists"
and pored over their writings and books about them. He read Joseph Frank's
1955 book, *The Levellers*, upon publication; it became one of the most
marked-up volumes in his library. Black had several conversations with
Harvey Poe, who had just returned from Oxford, where he had written a
dissertation about them. "I was amazed that Black had read their early,
obscure pamphlets," he recalled. "Not even many people in England had
done that then."

Soon, when he got started talking about the Levellers and especially
their leader, John Lilburne, which was frequently every two weeks or more,
"it was hard to stop him," a clerk noted. Their "general ideas about rights
foreshadowed most of the rights sought to be protected in our Constitution
and Bill of Rights," Black noted. The Levellers strove to remove Parliament's
power "to enact all laws it desired without limitation." The people's "Agreement" had eliminated that prerogative, and now only they could change
what their representatives had determined was the supreme "law of the land."
This creed gave Black fresh theoretical footing and historical ammunition
for his insistent contention about the importance of a written constitution,

and first appeared in a speech he gave in early 1960. By the end of that decade it suffused his thinking.[6]

To go from Jefferson to the Levellers is like going from a vintage wine to uneffervescent ginger ale. But the impact of the Levellers on Black was profound. They completed the trinity of his primary intellectual influences. He clothed the approach of Aristotle, the structural essentials of the Levellers and Jefferson's spirit of humanity with his own hard-headed, ever sympathetic realism.

The contemporary authors Black felt most comfortable with personally were the celebrated popularizers. Their smooth narrative syntheses spoke to him as the latest, most fashionable academic scholarship could not. These carried the authentic voice of plain-spoken eloquence and erudition. Not just Edith Hamilton, but Claude Bowers and Charles Beard, and Eric Hoffer, the longshoreman-philosopher, Will Durant and Carl Sandburg. In Miami in the winter of 1952 Black met Durant. The man whose guide to reading had impressed him so much in 1929 was living there while working on a book on the Renaissance, the fifth volume of his *The Story of Civilization*. To Black their wide-ranging discussions remained memorable. Montaigne was a conspicuous figure in Durant's book. Soon Black bought Montaigne's *Essays* from one of the used-book dealers whose catalogs he periodically scoured and talked about Montaigne frequently to JoJo. Black and Sandburg thought on the same wavelength. After Sandburg sent a copy of *Remembrance Rock*, Black wrote that "the book faithfully portrays the American tradition as I conceive it. It contains warnings and inspirations that the country needs and will continue to need. Like your other writings it is filled with spiritual nourishment. Its appeal should grow as the years go on. For stumbling blocks to truth are less dangerous when people know how to identify them."

One of the literary friendships that gave Black the most pleasure was with publisher Alfred Knopf. Walton Hamilton's *New Republic* article about Black's first term on the Court made Knopf want to meet the justice. In December 1938 they talked about a book of his opinions. Even though Black was noncommittal, "he impressed me mightily," Knopf wrote in a memoir. "Indeed I gradually became one of [his] 'best friends.' " The next spring Charles Curtis's *Atlantic Monthly* article about Black encouraged Knopf to approach him again. At the same time H. L. Mencken asked Knopf, "Have you ever thought of doing a book on the dissenting opinions of Hugo Black? They are sometimes almost insane, but they are often written with considerable skill." Fortified in his belief, Knopf returned to Washington. Black said he would not mind if Max Lerner edited a book of his opinions. Knopf quickly signed Lerner up. Other projects prevented Lerner from proceeding, and when Black's former clerk John Frank approached Knopf with a similar proposal, especially after Black enthusiastically endorsed Frank, Knopf fairly jumped at the opportunity. Its publication in 1949 deepened Knopf's admiration for Black. They savored each other's company on the several occasions they saw each other yearly. Knopf usually took Black to dinner. (Hugo was never one to pass up a free meal.) He called the always colorfully dressed Knopf, with his bristling mustache, "strange but fine."[7]

Knopf sent many books to Black he would never have read otherwise. "All of his ideas are interesting," Black wrote about Albert Camus's posthumous collection of political essays, Resistance, Rebellion and Death: "most of them seem good to me and many of them are beautifully expressed. I finished reading the book with a feeling of sadness that the life of a man like this should have been cut off so prematurely." But mostly the volumes were on history, politics or the South. James McBride Dabbs's The Southern Heritage hit home to Black as few other books could. "As a southerner he has done a magnificent job in explaining the southern attitude on the current and historical questions, and I only wish the book could be read, or would be read, I should say, by all southerners."[8]

American history ranked with the classics and seventeenth-century English constitutional history as one of Black's favorite subjects. The formative period of the Constitution and the Founding Fathers naturally received much attention. "Among my most cherished possessions," Black noted, was Saul Padover's To Secure These Blessings, a topically arranged account of the debates in the Constitutional Convention of 1787. Shortly before his death, he gave it to his grandson for a high school graduation present, noting that he could have much more easily given him a substantial amount of money than his "treasured," marked-up copy. He did not own but likely read most of Irving Brant's monumental six-volume biography of James Madison. In 1961 Black sent Brant a telegram that almost moved Brant to tears: "Congratulations on completion and publication of your last volume on Madison which marks another great achievement of a man who has devoted his whole productive life to service of the high ideals he has always cherished."

The major political figures on the Union side of "The Second American Revolution," as Charles Beard called the Civil War, appealed to Black. He read several books about Lincoln. Autobiographical overtones were evident when he wrote Hugo, Jr., that Benjamin Thomas's biography taught him much "about the struggles of a young lawyer to acquire practice and the growth of a man from a kind of country logrolling politician into a statesman guided by high ideals and lofty patriotism." But although he wrote "Gettysburg" in the margin next to "words cannot magnify the deeds they have done" in Zimmern's *The Greek Commonwealth,* Black was no Lincolnphile. Lincoln's successor, however, was one of Black's heroes. "I have to admit that I think Andew Johnson was a great man," he told a clerk. He read, he said, "about all I could find" about Johnson and even visited his grave. Once at a dinner Tom Corcoran gave in the late 1950s, Black took Arthur Schlesinger, Jr., aside and, after saying how much he liked Schlesinger's *The Age of Jackson* "started talking about how historians do not pay enough attention to Andrew Johnson. He talked about Johnson's life, his battles against the planters," recalled Schlesinger. "The way he recounted it I felt he was telling me his own life."[9]

Among American historians, Beard stood in a class by himself for Black. His economic interpretation of events; his sense of history as endless adventure and high drama and of the American experience as a continual experiment; his expansive, sometimes overblown rhetoric and occasional flair for self-dramatization; his hard-boiled realism; his faith in history as "an instrument of civilization"; his insatiable curiosity; his self-assertion and independence; his impassioned defense of intellectual freedom—all these struck similar chords in Black. Black gained much from one whose opinions so nearly matched his own. "Watch that man: he will go far," Beard told his wife and collaborator after meeting Black for the first time at a Washington dinner in 1934 and having an "intellectual adventure" with him, discussing land tenure in ancient Rome among other subjects. So strong was Black's esteem for Beard that he did not let what has been called the historian's "impassioned vendetta" that Roosevelt purposely drew the country into World War Two keep him from writing an introduction to a posthumous collection of essays honoring Beard.[10]

Legal subjects were an obvious staple of Black's reading diet. He read law reviews published by law schools almost exclusively for the information they imparted, nothing else—for the pedantry and scholasticism of the academic treadmill appalled him, and intellectual affectations and pretentiousness grated on him. Black appreciated Charles Curtis's writings for their fairness and civil libertarian spirit, and Curtis himself for "the richness of his un-usually mature and penetrating intellect. He was one of my favorite people and I have often wished that I could have lived in the same community with him. . . ." Nearly anything Black came across about individual freedom he marked up. He admired Lloyd Stryker's biography of Lord Erskine, who resolutely defended the rights of Englishmen against the Crown at the end of the eighteenth century. The history and functioning of the Supreme Court naturally appealed to Black. He admired Alpheus Mason's writings and found his biography of Chief Justice William Howard Taft "fascinating. He would stop now and then and read passages to me," Elizabeth Black wrote. "He said Taft stood for everything he was opposed to, though he respected him for being honest in his views."[11]

He particularly relished almost anything John Frank and Edmond Cahn wrote. Black took great pride in Frank's prolific pen and looked upon him almost paternally. Both while he was teaching at Yale Law School and later in Arizona with a busy and distinguished practice, he churned out books and articles. Black enjoyed them all. One of his books, *Lincoln as a Lawyer,* Black found "as interesting as a novel and as informative as history should be." Indeed, "everything you have written has been interesting."[12] Jerome Frank sent Black a copy of Edmond Cahn's *The Sense of Injustice* after reviewing it in 1949. "Here is the most compelling discussion since Aristotle of the subject of justice," the oft-iconoclastic Frank had written. Post haste, Black advertised its wide circulation. To Cahn, a New York University legal philosopher, justice meant (and Black underlined) "the *active process* of remedying or preventing what would arouse the sense of injustice." The thrust of the book—that the function of law is to serve individuals, that law must be sculptured to meet their needs or it has no purpose in existing—was the goal to which Black's entire career was directed.

Begun was one of the most important intellectual friendships of Black's life, which continued unabated until Cahn's death in 1964. Every few months and more, starting after Black got over the immediate shock of Josephine's death, they had long conversations. At first these were sometimes in New York, on trips arranged by Black's former clerk Sidney Davis. Davis intro-duced Black to entertainer Danny Kaye, Davis's childhood friend, and to Kaye's wife, Sylvia Fine. Black was immediately attracted to them, and esteemed Kaye for his humanitariansim. For several years he occasionally went to New York for a day or two, just to see Kaye and Fine, his old friend Irving Engel, and Cahn, Davis and Jerome Frank. He discussed legal theory with Frank and Cahn but "just wasn't in their league as a philosopher," said

Davis. "He would sit there but wouldn't say that much. He couldn't keep up with them." (Also at work was a continuing defensiveness, stemming from not having gone to college.)[*]

Cahn was Black's greatest correspondent, exchanging more letters with him than even John Frank, who knew him more than twice as long. He would write the justice at the drop of an idea or an opinion and wax lyrically about Black's greatness, ("*Another* letter from Edmond Cahn saying what a great job I did," he once half complained. "I really think he loves me.") In conversation he gently prodded Black about parts of his opinions. Hardly anyone else had enough gumption to point out where he felt the justice went astray. Such was Black's respect for Cahn that he appreciated this more than he could admit. He was freer in his talks with and letters to Cahn ("a great friend with whom I spent many profitable hours") than with almost anyone, except for his family and a bare handful of friends and law clerks.

"We didn't agree on everything," Black recalled, adding, "but then no two men do." Most basically they agreed on the Bill of Rights. Both inescapably returned to the First Amendment for the bedrock values upon which all else rests in a democratic society. Without freedom to discuss issues, democracy loses its meaning. In Black's hands, Cahn wrote in 1956, the Bill of Rights "is directed toward the values that lie beyond. He reads it as a kind of people's charter of edification. . . ." The title of Cahn's article caught well the primacy of Black's belief: "The Firstness of the First Amendment." "He understands what I'm trying to do," Black said. Cahn sent Black (or otherwise Black read) virtually everything he wrote. In Cahn's work Black found, so he noted in a memorial tribute, "the same kind of inspiring arguments for equal justice for all people that is found in those enduring books which contain the maxims and precepts of the great religions and philosophies of the world." He ranked Cahn as a legal philospher "at the top of the list in his generation."

Few contemporaries ever really influenced Black intellectually in the most basic senses; George Norris, Alexander Meiklejohn and Bill Douglas did. If Cahn did not, he made Black reexamine his intermediate premises, reevaluate his evidence, even query certain assumptions, as no one else could or even would try. It was for Charles Beard and Cahn, once for each of them (Cahn posthumously), that Black wrote a foreward to a book, and only for Cahn, twice, that he gave blurbs for a book.

---

[*] Black resembled Antaeus in the Greek myth, who was invincible as long as hs feet touched his mother, Earth, but who was easily strangled by Hercules once he was lifted from the strength-giving ground.

············

Many forces, of course, helped to shape Black's philosophy. He brought to his reading his experiences in law practice and politics. There can be no doubt that part of his reading was purposive. Certainly it reinforced his preconceptions. He never stopped trying, though, to consider the opposite side of an isue. He saw little value in psychiatry, for example, yet when his daughter gave him some books on the subject late in his life, he made a true attempt to understand its benefits. After reading partially through the books, however, he gave up and clung to his original belief.[13]

Any philosophy is only a set of propositions. Standing alone, it carries little weight. Black's reading and theoretical investigations and speculations were prelimninary to action here and now. His philosophy was more than the sum of its sources. By adding to the cream of the humanistic tradition, he assured that the product would live as long as individual dignity remains important.

CHAPTER 31

THE JUSTICE
TAKES A BRIDE

To an observer in the mid-1950s Black looked like he was declining. He appeared so frail that *The New York Times* updated his obituary. His secretary's admonition to guard his health brought no response, just a blank look. He toyed with the notion of retiring. In February 1956 he would reach the age of seventy, "an event that I prefer to lament rather than celebrate." It "rather tempts me to retire," he told Hazel Davis, "but I am not quite sure that I shall do so. Perhaps when the time comes I shall prefer to remain on the Court." Whether he stayed on the bench or not, he would receive full pay for life. "Things go along all right with me," he wrote a former clerk. "I am simply grinding away with the knowledge that under the law I can quit when I please, a knowledge which is comforting." He postponed choosing his next year's clerks. "I don't want to choose them too early because I don't want to leave them stranded without a job," he said. Usually he picked them about January; in 1956 he waited until March. "I have reached the point where I do not love work nearly so much as I once did," he told Alfred Knopf. But his job was deciding cases, and he was not about to stop doing so.

For his birthday, tributes poured in. The *Yale Law Journal* devoted an entire issue to his achievements; Justice Douglas wrote a short introduction. Black's clerks threw a party at which they gave him the twenty-two-volume *Dictionary of American Biography*. He appreciated this fully as much as the tributes. "There were many times when he would have been happy to desert public service to enjoy his farm, his family, and his books": Richard Hofstadter's comment on Jefferson caught Black's eye and captured his spirit when he read it now.[1]

On his birthday Black also interviewed Elizabeth DeMeritte of Birmingham to be his new secretary.

In 1954, for the first time in thirty years, Black had financial security. He sold his half interest in the Glidden Paint Store in Birmingham, which he had bought long ago. "The result is that I have more money than I need—particularly in view of the fact that my salary is for life, whether I continue to serve on the Court or not." He gave each of his children $3,000, warning them not to spend it unnecessarily. Some of the money he used to send JoJo on an around-the-world trip with Justice Douglas as a present upon graduation from Swarthmore in 1955. They traveled to the Philippines, India and Iran (where Robert Kennedy joined them). In each country they met and dined with the head of state as Douglas conducted his own personal diplomacy. But Douglas left her stranded in Teheran when he would not let her continue to Russia as planned. She was forced to moved up her itinerary of Israel and Europe. Seething at Douglas's characteristic thoughtlessness, Black needed all of his self-control to restrain himself when Douglas returned.

JoJo came home and worked for the Alexandria welfare department for two years. During this time, they grew even closer. Her presence always lifted his spirits. She recalled the side of Hugo Black that his family and close friends knew: "He was so sentimental and kindhearted that he had to fight it all the time. He wouldn't go to the movies after we saw *Friendly Persuasion* because he cried then and that shamed him. He did not talk much about other people. Those who did he called babblers. At home, when he was not working or reading, which was not often, he usually talked about what he was reading." In 1956 she moved to New York and entered a graduate program in psychiatric social work at Columbia. "This is her plan, not mine," Black wrote, "but as fathers usually do, I accept it." She felt that by helping others she would be completing her mother's "unfinished business."

Vacations he spent in Miami, at Hugo, Jr.'s, in Birmingham or, sometimes once yearly, at Sterling's in Los Alamos. Grandchildren were coming along now, and Black took typical pride in them. (By 1947 Hugo, Jr., had three, and Sterling five children, and after Hugo, Jr., called to announce the birth of a "very beautiful" baby, Black said: "I doubt that I shall file a dissenting opinion regarding his characterization of the baby's personal pulchritude.") He often drove to Miami during the Court's winter breaks. On the way he deliberately tried to put "all you can drink for a dime" orange juice stands out of business, telling his clerk and Spencer, who usually went with him, to drink as much as they could. "It's a real good deal." His driving was not up to the standard of his opinions. When he started talking, he usually forgot how fast he was going—or where. Once a traffic cop in Washington stopped him for driving in the wrong direction in Rock Creek Park, where a two-way road becomes one-way at four-thirty for the evening rush hour. "Say, don't you know the law?" the cop bellowed. Black: "You can get an argument on that." "I have much more confidence in your taste in literature than in your automobile driving," Grover Hall, Jr., told him after one experience with Black behind the wheel.[2]

Otherwise he stayed home, reading, playing tennis and dining with a few friends. Hugo, Jr., brought his family up for a few weeks each summer. "I shall miss them when they leave," Black wrote during one visit. "It is about time for Hugo to go, however, because I have practiced him up to the point that his tennis game is getting exceedingly dangerous to me. As a matter of fact in another week he might beat me far more than I beat him!" Black was maniacal about tennis now—seven sets at midday in Birmingham in August and during summers "every day when the sun was shining, frequently playing both morning and afternoon." He felt his game was better than ever, and, when he was with those who played, it was a main topic of his conversation. *

Black's whole outlook had improved in the years since Josephine's death, but he was still in the doldrums. Even his interest in politics was no longer nearly as consuming. He was fond of Tennessee senator Estes Kefauver, a southerner with similar origins and populist outlook, and happy that he ran for vice president on the Democratic ticket with Stevenson:

> I am rather of the opinion that the Democrats nominated the best ticket they could have selected. Kefauver has impressed many people with the idea of his integrity and respect for the masses. Even his investigations [into organized crime]—which I agree can be subjected to some criticism—endeared him to many people. I am so far removed from the common run of what people are saying that I have few ideas that would be helpful to you in political activities. I am convinced, however, that most people, with complete justification, believe in President Eisenhower's good intentions.

* "Has this chap ever met you?" Black's Miami tennis-playing buddy Austin Rice wrote him after reading John Frank's statement "He . . . does not talk the game away from the court," in Frank's seventieth-birthday tribute to Black, which Frank sent Rice (Austin Rice to HLB, 5/8/56). "I am about to reach the conclusion," Black replied, "that by the time I die it will be a shame to waste my great tennis skill" (HLB to Rice, 5/14/56).

I am also convinced that nobody can make any headway against him by
accusing him of wanting too small an army. I doubt if anybody has ever
been defeated for President of the United States on the basis of fears that
he might not push the country into war quickly enough.

Black felt Ike was what came to be called a middle-American, as he
was, with a basic love of country, a true patriotism. He thought this since
they met through General John DeWitt in 1930, when Eisenhower became
affiliated with the Army War College in Washington, of which DeWitt was
a superintendent. They saw some more of each other in the early New Deal
when Ike, now Douglas MacArthur's chief aide, lobbied in Congress for the
army's budget. Black knew that although Eisenhower was never a New Dealer,
he was, as his son John said, "charitable toward much of what Roosevelt
was trying to do." And Josephine and Mamie Eisenhower had been friends
throughout; the two couples dined together occasionally. "You can't help
but like him personally," Black told an interviewer in 1968. "He's got a
winning smile, and he has it when he's out with the public. And he's not
exceedingly serious. He doesn't know much. I don't think he ever has been
a great student of history. But he's a good man. I think he did fairly well.
I wouldn't put him up with a man like the grim determination of Truman
or Roosevelt." But now, in the 1950s, more often Black simply dismissed
Eisenhower as a Republican or treated him with silence, saying that he was
"a nice man of limited ability."[3]

*   *   *

Hugo Black was a southern gentleman of his generation.* Ever paternal, he
shielded women from controversy and strife as much as he could. He underlined Thucydides' remark, "He led her with moderation and fenced her with
security." Women had their role and place. In trying to decide which part
of a steak to eat, he might say, "Give it to a woman, just give it to her and
she'll tell you." When it appeared that a niece of whom he was very fond
might not get a college degree, he wrote:

If she does not, I am one of those who believe that it will not necessarily
destroy her life. She seems to be rather learned in the science that most
women prefer above all others, though she is not willing to wash and iron

* He was also a very gentle man. Once, in the Court's basement, he got lost going to his
car. The janitor was shining the floors and yelled, "Get the hell out of here." Black said,
"The next time the marshall might be here and that might be trouble" (Calabresi, UA
remarks).

shirts even in that field. This, I think, shows a necessary independence which I hope she will be able to keep up during the rest of her life. Probably the best diploma [she] can get would come from a local court house somewhere in the way of a marriage license.

"After my wife died I sort of lived a life in the dark . . . ," Black later admitted to a cousin who had also lost his wife. It was one of his rare remarks about the subject. What he wrote but did not send also expressed his thoughts: "You undoubtedly feel now that there can never be another woman in your life." Occasionally he went to parties, usually taking JoJo with him when she was home. Old widows served tea and "I could almost hear him say 'Oh, no,' " she recalled. "He practically hid behind my skirt," showing little interest when they tried to introduce him to eligible women. One person offered to arrange for him to meet the widow of Robert E. Lee IV. He politely said no.

In early 1956 his secretary, Gladys Coates, told him she was retiring to stay home with her children. He immediately offered the job to his law clerk's sister, sight unseen. But she had just graduated from college and turned it down. Black then asked Hugo, Jr., to find a suitable replacement— an Alabamian with grace, charm and an easy friendliness that would make people feel comfortable, he said. Hugo, Jr., first approached Mary Tortorici, the chief deputy clerk of the federal court in Birmingham, but she was a widow with a son in dental school and did not want to uproot herself. He spoke with Nancy Huddleston, the daughter of former Birmingham congressman George Huddleston, who also worked in the court; she said no. At the same time Tortorici asked Elizabeth DeMeritte, one of her assistants and her best friend, "Would you be interested?" Elizabeth grabbed at the possibility. "From all I can gather she will make as good a secretary as you can get down here," Hugo, Jr., wrote Black. "Everyone has only good things to say about her. I hope that she will be so good that you will think from the interview that I have given you an extra birthday present."

One possible problem gave the justice pause: Elizabeth was separating from her husband. "I don't want a woman with middle-age problems on my hands." "But Daddy, she's so good-looking," Hugo, Jr., replied. "Send her up," Black said.

Black knew her father, Birmingham physician James Seay, and other kin who had supported him in various political races, he told her. He had no doubt she could do the job well, but he wanted her to discuss her situation with her husband. If she wanted to return to him at any point after starting work, Black wanted her to feel free to do so. "He was like a gray ghost," she recalled. "He said he was just waiting for the cemetery." At the end of the interview he followed her to the door. "This non-pompous easy-to-know man, a legend in Alabama for some thirty years or more, had been so kind and understanding to me that I felt a surge of emotion," Elizabeth later wrote. "Tears came to my eyes as he extended his hand. I took it in mine and impulsively put it to my cheek, then turned around and quickly left."

Her husband, who was running for mayor of Fairfield, a small city outside Birmingham, reaffirmed their agreement to postpone the divorce until after the November election, and asked that she keep it secret. Elizabeth quickly told this to Hugo, Jr., who passed it along, and Gladys Coates told her to report April 1. Then Black asked if she could come up on March 12. She did. "Soon the Judge will invite you to dinner," Coates advised, for he always had his secretary and clerks out several times yearly. "He'll take a great interest in you, but if I were you I wouldn't tell him anything about your personal affairs. He gets very involved in people. He'll take over and try to change your life, your personality, and everything about you. . . . He starts working patiently on [his law clerks], trying to get this one to work harder, that one to play more, and softening down another's personality. So it goes— on and on."

"You could slowly see a lift in him when Elizabeth arrived," recalled his clerk Vernon Patrick. His colleague Harold Ward agreed: "It was obvious that there was a new interest in the office." Elizabeth's liveliness kept everybody in a good mood. Before leaving, Gladys Coates said, "You just wait and watch, they're going to get married."[4]

"Josephine wants me to invite you to dinner either tonight or tomorrow night, tonight preferably," Black told Elizabeth as he trotted in the first day she was in the office on her own. "I'll come and get you," he said. "I never let the ladies in my family go out alone at night." He almost ran up the sidewalk when he came to pick her up; as he drove he talked about his children. At dinner she had "a feeling of peace and serenity, of rightness." As JoJo showed Elizabeth the house, Elizabeth said she hoped she was smart enough for the job. "Oh, Daddy hates smart women!" JoJo answered. "Really don't be nervous about your work. Daddy is a real softie. You'll have fun being around him." They all spent several hours talking in the study. On the way home Hugo questioned Elizabeth so sympathetically she found herself telling him the story of her life.

She grew up on Birmingham's fashionable South Side. Her father's medical practice was thriving when he died suddenly at forty-one. Four years later, her brother introduced her to his fellow medical student, Fred DeMeritte, twelve years her senior. DeMeritte soon dropped out of medical school and moved to Miami, hoping to strike it rich in the Florida real estate boom of the 1920s. At the same time Elizabeth's mother, Attie Seay, also moved to Miami, because of its better climate and Fred's calls and letters to Elizabeth. He wooed her, they got married, and ten months later she had a son. She was not yet seventeen. After moving back to Birmingham, she worked for a law firm, the New Deal's Reconstruction Finance Corporation and in the federal court clerks' office. Her colleagues always found her to be a live wire who kept everybody happy. "Things always happened where she was," said Mary Tortorici.

Elizabeth's marriage had been rocky for years. Her husband realized he couldn't run for office if he were separated from his wife. So they agreed that they would remain together (she had often threatened to leave him after their son was grown and she was supporting herself), and regardless of the outcome of the election, they would divorce afterward.

The next morning at eight o'clock Elizabeth's phone rang. "Last night I thought a lot about your situation. What you need is to develop a philosophy of life for yourself. You need to go on a reading program." Black gave her books to read: John Dewey, Bertrand Russell and, of course, the Greeks and Romans. Every day he asked about her progress with them and how she was. Soon he had her type copies of a quotation. "It is Virgil's Song* and it expresses my feelings so exactly that I want it read at my funeral." A look of distress came over her face—"should that remote and unlikely event ever occur," he added in mock seriousness. She began to see her boss more and more after work. JoJo frequently invited her for dinner, or Hugo took both of them out for steaks.

After Elizabeth's husband won the primary, Black told her how he thought Fred DeMeritte could get elected. "Tell him to announce that his wife has gone career-mad and has gone up to Washington to work for that

---

* The song reads: ". . . me let the sweet muses lead to their soft retreats, their living fountains, and melodious groves where I may dwell remote from care, master of myself, and under no necessity of doing every day what my heart condemns. Let me no more be seen in the wrangling forum, a pale and anxious candidate for precarious fame; and let neither the tumult of visitors crowding to my levee, nor the eager haste of officious freedmen disturb my morning rest. Let me live free from solicitude, a stranger to the art of promising legacies, in order to buy the friendship of the great. And when Nature shall give the signal to retire, may I possess no more than I may bequeath to whom I will. At my funeral let no token of sorrow be seen, no pompous mockery of woe. Crown me with chaplets, strew flowers on my grave, and let my friends erect no vain memorial to tell where my remains are lodged."

After reading it aloud, Black's eyes were moist.

reprobate Hugo Black. He will pick up a lot of sympathy votes." It might have helped: DeMeritte narrowly lost in the November general election to a Republican. Regardless, she was granted a divorce that month. Now she and Hugo were playing bridge regularly. His game was based on a recently and imperfectly mastered study of Charles Goren's manual; their partners usually were Chief Justice Warren's secretary Maggie Bryan and George Freeman, one of Black's present clerks. These sessions often lasted until 1 or 2 A.M. One night Freeman showed Hugo and Elizabeth how to dance the "Birmingham Hop," and said he would teach it to them. "I was not surprised to find that the Judge, who had a good sense of rhythm, could dance beautifully," Elizabeth wrote. "He was also without any inhibitions about tossing his partner around, swinging her under his arm, or kicking up his heels in general. As we ended our version of the Birmingham hop, the Judge swung me to him, gave me a little squeeze, and we both dissolved in laughter."[5]

Black spent late 1956 in and out of the hospital with a urinary tract infection and lost all interest in Elizabeth personally; he was worried about himself. "Daddy dramatizes himself when he is sick," Hugo, Jr., told her on a visit. "Either he is completely optimistic or he has a 'farewell to the world' attitude. I think he's going to be all right." He was, and his possessiveness toward women reasserted itself. He did not want Elizabeth to attend a friend's New Year's party in New Jersey. Finally he said, "You have made your plans now, so go ahead." As far as she was concerned, the winter frost was over. He resumed calling her on the phone the first thing in the morning and the last thing at night.

    "You hired me exactly a year ago today," Elizabeth said on his birthday in 1957. "I hope you have no regrets." "The only thing I regret is that I am not twenty years younger," he replied. As spring turned into summer, they spent many hours talking philosophically about life and about their lives before they met. He gave her more books to read. She had done remarkably well in adjusting from Birmingham to Washington, he said. "In fact you could walk with princes." Elizabeth's mother had reluctantly moved to Washington after Elizabeth did, and Hugo firmly stated that he did not think it wise for parents to live with their children and that at his age he could not accept it. He meant her mother. When Elizabeth heard this, she later wrote, she suddenly realized Hugo was "moving slowly toward marriage and that he wanted to approach it analytically."

He went to visit Sterling in August. First he stopped off to see John Frank in Phoenix. For several days he played six sets of tennis on a hard court at noon. When John took him to the airport, Hugo was singing and laughing. He had called Elizabeth that morning. "I never saw him happier," recalled John's wife, Lorraine. He arrived in Los Alamos. "In the middle of dinner," Sterling said, "he excused himself, saying he had to go to the bathroom. I got up and saw the door to my bedroom was slightly open. There he was, sitting on the bed like a teenager who was getting away with something." He had called Elizabeth. "Is there anything wrong?" she asked. "Yes, I am too far away from you. I have a song to sing"—and he started singing "I've Grown Accustomed to Your Face." He finished it and added, "And I have."

Back in Washington, he wrote Hugo, Jr.: "I have found it necessary to see her many nights since I am endeavoring to improve her bridge game and am finding it very difficult. Sometimes I think I may even have to increase the times I see her or else give up this particular task." He ended by saying if Hugo, Jr., moved west to be with Sterling, "there is always the possibility that I might decide to retire and take my secretary with me to the West to help me write a book." It was, as Elizabeth noted, "a lilting summer."[6]

"Why don't you and Elizabeth get married?" JoJo suddenly said to her father one night at dinner in September. "You're in love with her and she's in love with you." He was waiting for her approval. She never raised any objections as the relationship deepened; if she had, he might have ended it. In fact she had shamelessly instigated and encouraged it. He went over to Elizabeth's house to talk about an unusual subject—love and the Supreme Court. "I have had a prior love affair for almost twenty years now with an institution. . . . In my personal life I have to be like Caesar's wife: above reproach." He was seventy-one; she was forty-nine. "In another five or ten years you may not find me as attractive as you do now. If that were to happen and you wanted a divorce, I would give you one. But I think it would finish me and hurt the prestige of the Court." He held her in his arms. "You'd be wonderful for a man in his twilight years. With you, I could sail into the sunset—with glory!" he said, and left abruptly. When he got home, he called. "I forgot something. I forgot to tell you I love you, darling—and good night!"

Hugo came to work before Elizabeth the next morning. He buzzed for her to come in. She took her notebook and pencil in with her, even though she hardly thought she would need them. Hugo started listing all the reasons why she should not marry him. "As I have pointed out a number of times, I am too old for you. I have my habits of living and my eccentricities, and it would be awfully hard for a woman to get used to them. I am not in as vigorous health as I once was, and something might hit me at any time. Then you would be stuck with an invalid on your hands." He paused; his eyes looked like liquid pools. "But, darling, *will* you marry me?" She gave the expected answer.

He wanted to get married that day but the District of Columbia had a three-day marriage waiting period. Virginia had none, so they decided to wait until the next day. He asked his former clerk Buddy Cleveland to arrange for a marriage license; that was quietly done within a few hours. Hugo called Hugo, Jr., in Birmingham. Almost belligerently he broke the news; he looked surprised that his son seemed so happy. Hugo, Jr., came right up; but the only flight from Albuquerque would arrive too late, and Sterling did not come. Hugo felt gratified and pleased that his children were not only willing, but actually eager, for him to get married. On the morning of the wedding day, September 11, 1957, father and son went to see Chief Justice Warren to tell him. Warren said he felt relieved. "Seeing the serious look on your face, Hugo, made me think for a moment you had come to tell me you were going to retire, and that was the last thing on earth I wanted to hear."

"No, Mr. Chief Justice," Hugo, Jr., said. "An old man retires and Daddy is too young for that. He's going to take on a young man's duty."

Since Elizabeth wanted a minister to officiate, Hugo called Dr. A. Powell Davies, the eminent pastor of Washington's All Souls Unitarian Church and his old friend from Seminary Hill days. Davies came over to the house. In the parlor, with a portrait of Josephine hanging over the mantel, Hugo and Elizabeth took their vows. She long remembered how he was "shaking a little." That night, they had dinner at his favorite steak restaurant. The next morning they played tennis.

News of the wedding had leaked out, so they held a reception for the press. Only good-natured questions were asked. "She says she can cook but that hasn't been established yet." Elizabeth: "Justice Black has the most wonderful cook. I'll rest on her laurels." As they strolled through the garden, Hugo sang a little tune: "As our feet go tap, tap, tap, Hear our fingers go gaily snap." Shakespeare? "No, that's a jingle from my school days in Clay County." Who would be boss in the household? "Well, she's been running the office anyways, and I thought she might as well run the house." Hugo turned to Elizabeth: "Smile, like you do when I give an order in the office."[7]

....

"I've never been so cold and so hungry in my life," Elizabeth soon began complaining. "Hugo doesn't like too much food in the refrigerator and he likes to keep the heat down." She was learning that he didn't believe in anyone's being an ounce over what he considered the correct weight ("Fat people have flabby will powers," he thought); and even if he was warm-blooded, as he claimed, he was certainly very conscious of the cost of heating a big, old house. "A person can think better in a cool room," he said. "It is better for everybody's health."

"In other words," Elizabeth countered, "what's good for Hugo Black is good for America?"

"No," he replied. "What's good for Hugo Black is good for Elizabeth."

He was happier than he had been for longer than he could remember. So much that he had repressed was now coming out spontaneously. His playfulness at home returned. When John Frank wired, "Your grins in picture here would span Grand Canyon," Black shot back, "The inferences you drew from the pictures you saw are fully justified." John Harlan told Elizabeth he "noticed a decided change in Hugo from a silent man into a radiant scin-tillating one." On a sideboard in their home sat a silver tray, a wedding gift inscribed by the justices. It stated: "Mr. Justice Black took no part in the consideration of this case."

Elizabeth soon discovered more of his "eccentricities." He liked to talk in the middle of the night. Often he turned on the light or nudged her, and said, "Are you asleep?" If she had been, she wasn't now. And he would talk about his past, the Klan, Josephine, his children, or a case he was working on: "My brethren are about to destroy the country," he might say and go on to explain the case in simple terms. "Don't you think I'm right?" Her reply never disappointed him and he'd quickly go back to sleep. Or he told her how happy she was making his life. And, of course, tennis played a role. He said that since she sometimes got up at night to go to the bathroom, she should keep a racket on the dresser in the hallway so she could take a couple of swings on the way. "You could improve your backhand that way," he said.

Growing accustomed to her new role was not easy for Elizabeth. She kept on calling Hugo "Judge" even after they were married a while. "I was visiting them during Christmas 1957, sitting in their living room," recalled Mary Tortorici, "and Elizabeth said, 'yes, Judge,' 'that's right, Judge,' 'of course, Judge.' Finally Hugo became annoyed and said, 'Now Elizabeth, I want you to call me Hugo. Do you understand me?' She meekly said yes and started calling him Hugo." But old habits die hard and for many months she wrote letters calling him "Judge."[8]*

He educated her about Washington social ways. "There is an aristocracy of the intellectual. The achievements of individuals count more than family prestige"—in contrast to Birmingham. "Most people like to talk and they like to hear what they themselves have to say. I make it a practice to talk as little as possible and to try to learn from the conversations of others. My advice is—at least right at first—to keep your knees together and your mouth shut." Thurman and Frances Arnold gave one of the earliest parties in their honor. Drew and Luvie Pearson were also there, and Abe Fortas, Arnold's partner, with his wife, Carol Agger, who practiced law under her maiden name. Black had no more devoted friend than Thurman. He was marvelous company, if also the despair of Washington hostesses, even of his wife at times, since he was a careless and sloppy eater. (At one dinner the Blacks gave, he looked at the person he was talking to as he mixed dessert—on the tablecloth. Another time he emphatically made a point with a tomato on his fork: the tomato flew across the room.) His cigar ashes typically trailed over the tablecloth, and his cigar occasionally burned a hole in it.

Frances Arnold, elegant and sharp-tongued, was one of Washington's last grande dames. She initially took a dim view of Hugo's marriage, not only because, she later said, it was a second one but also because Elizabeth had been his secretary. Starting that night, Elizabeth worked hard at earning Frances's friendship. She left the dinner feeling graciously and warmly received. This grew into open-hearted acceptance, and Frances Arnold and Luvie Pearson became two of Elizabeth's closest friends. Word of her charm spread quickly among Hugo's friends. They had seen him a walking shadow of himself since Josephine's death—lonely, unsmiling, taut. With great relief they saw him now aglow and rosy with happiness. All his long-standing

---

* The habits also died hard with his friends. There could be a forbidding formality about Black. It took Edmond Cahn nearly ten years of increasingly close friendship, and Fred Rodell twenty-four, to address him as Hugo. They were of course a generation younger. But his contemporary Alfred Knopf, at age sixty-seven, needed three attempts to break through the last-name barrier. "Dear Hugo:—I am going to make so bold after all these years and I hope you won't mind," began his first letter. Black's clerk pointed out that Knopf had called him Hugo. "Yes," Black said. Then he smiled and dictated, "Dear Mr. Knopf." "Dear Mr. Justice," Knopf replied: "—how can I address you otherwise if you persist in 'Mr-ing' me?" Again, "Dear Mr. Justice," crossing that out and writing "Hugo." Now finally—"Dear Alfred" (Knopf to HLB, 6/17, 23/59, and 7/17/59; HLB to Knopf, 6/18/59, 7/23/59).

friendships remained fully intact—with one exception: Lister and Henrietta Hill. Lister understood, even if he did not at first fully appreciate it, that Hugo stopped seeing him for his sake politically, and his affection for Hugo never ceased. But things just could not be the same without Josephine. So, for years the Hills and the Blacks saw each other very rarely.

Remarriage changed some of Black's patterns. He worked more at home now, simply to be with Elizabeth, not going to the Court daily, as he always had. Hugo liked her jabbering away, her mere presence. He even (slightly) refurbished the house for her, bringing it into the (early) twentieth century. And he painstakingly taught her to play tennis. "I had hardly ever played before," she said. "At first I was exhausted. But I persevered. Hugo wouldn't let me do otherwise. He said, 'It's just good for you.' " Hugo thought that testosterone shots were good for him. He started giving them to himself, claiming they were partly a substitute for the thyroid shots he had taken for many years. Whether it was his main purpose or not, a side effect was to increase his sex drive, as he well knew from the beginning. "I feel almost as much a man as I've ever been," he told Hugo, Jr.[9]

CHAPTER 32

THE PEOPLE'S TEACHER

For several years the school segregation cases stood at the center of the Supreme Court's life. They were of such overriding magnitude that the justices purposely refrained from hearing many other significant issues. Only after the 1955 decree in *Brown* did the emotional exhaustion wear off and did the justices feel comfortable adding more fodder to their platter. Black had never enjoyed treading water. He wanted the Court to hear and decide cases asserting infringements of constitutional rights. He might not be able to muster enough votes for a majority, but he could file a dissent that might prick the consciences of his brethren, and, more important, serve as a building block to win in the future.

Earl Warren found Black's easy and forthright manner much more appealing than Frankfurter's intense intellectualism. They were carrying very different messages about the proper role of the Court, but whereas Hugo could separate himself from his message, Felix could not. While offering his own views colloquially, in homey terms and with a velvety resolution, Hugo gave Warren room to find his own. Nevertheless, Warren tended to vote with Frankfurter. This lasted two terms. But he was growing more confident. He had spent most of his life deciding and acting, not brooding and pondering. Results mattered most to him. Frankfurter's spell wore off. The courier had overdone it. His pedagogic approach to human relations piqued Warren. If the Chief had been asked what had happened, he might have said, "Felix irritates, Hugo soothes."

Warren now approached cases from Black's perspective. Frankfurter had lost a pivotal battle and, in keeping with his character, his relationship with

470

Warren soured. Black capitalized on this emerging antagonism. He and Warren visited regularly; Warren more often came to Black. They were simpatico, raised each other's spirits, had a wonderful camaraderie. "The Chief talked with the Judge about cases, the Court's calendar, Eisenhower, politics, anything at all," said Harold Ward, one of Black's clerks in 1955. The year before, Warren started the practice of deciding with Black, when they were in the majority, which justice should be assigned to write Court opinions. After stopping at his office after conference, he would go to Black. Hugo would tell him which cases he wanted, Warren would agree, and then they would decide who would write the others. It was common knowledge at the Court. "There's not too much around here that's secret," said Justice William J. Brennan, Jr. "If anyone complained, I didn't hear about it. It was just accepted as a fact of life here." It continued for as long as Warren and Black served together and remains unparalleled. It helped make their rapport, as Elizabeth wrote, "a lasting thing, and both had an affection and respect for the other."

Hugo Black had quietly played a formidable part in Warren's education. He had won Warren's heart and mind, with portentous consequences for the future. And Warren had so impressed him that, after Eisenhower's heart attack in September 1955 led to speculation that if Ike stepped down the next year Warren might run for president, Hugo observed that in view of Warren's "unusual qualifications" perhaps he should reconsider his attitude about any justice's being available for any other office. (Black ignored his own past desire to run for president or vice president.) "I cannot think at this time that you will have to change your views about Chief Justice Warren," Black wrote John Frank the next term. "My own belief is that he will stand out as a great head of this Court."[1*]

Black was always certain what he had to do. His mind was notable not only for its swiftness and incisiveness but also for its ability to pigeonhole any issue instantly. If someone questioned him, he could argue the problem on its own terms, penetrating to its heart in a flash, disregarding the wider consequences for the purpose of debate and overwhelming his interrogator

---

* "The smartest thing these reactionaries ever did from their point of view," Black later said, "was to shunt the Chief off onto this Court. Not that he has not been great here. But the Chief could have gone all the way. He's one of the greatest vote-getters ever. What a President he would have made. They could never have gotten him out—anti–third term statute and all—until he was ready to go" (Pollack, *Warren*, 11).

with an avalanche of plainspoken eloquence. He looked at things distinctively, which might mean that new categories and structures were set up. A detailed analytical framework, so comforting and supporting to many people, was not required. "Some minds, whether legal or scientific, are more comfortable with formal simplicities, resolving underlying complexities intuitively," wrote Harvard law professor Paul Freund. "Such minds are often the minds of the masters." The consensus of Black's colleagues and all law clerks at the Court during his tenure was, as Charles Luce, one of his clerks, said: "He had at one and the same time the keenest mind on the Court and the greatest insight how society and government function. He had the quickest and best mind in combination that I've ever known."

He looked at everything from his point of view. When he was in the minority during these years, he said with as much conviction he could muster under the circumstances that "What matters is not how a case comes out but how the position is put." "Strike for the jugular," he exhorted time and again (pronouncing it *juge*-ular). Seize upon the most important issue and hit it hard. He liked to come into his law clerks' office, stand before their desks, and debate—argue really—a case. To one clerk "his mind was so nimble it was scary." If a clerk conceived an appealing proposition, Black probed it by continually asking his favorite question: Why? "Not the sight of truth," he underlined in Edmond Cahn's *The Sense of Injustice*, "but a profound skepticism makes men free."

Occasionally he was deliberately wrong, to test his own ideas and those of his clerks. The case would be thrashed out. "It looks like we're reconcilable here," Black might say, never wanting to hurt anybody's feelings; or, the next morning, "I thought a lot about this last night and for reasons *wholly* different I agree," but not before rewording the clerk's analysis just to make him think they really concurred all along. Often he jumped to that conclusion after hearing one word or phrase, such as "jury" or "First Amendment." Then his eyes lit up and the words just poured out. To Black, American civilization under the Constitution was at stake. As an idea grew in his mind, he expanded it until it took on a life of its own. Black was a believer. He convinced himself of the truthfulness of any proposition he uttered, at least as of that moment. He tried to be as rigorously logical as possible. But, he said, "It all depends where you start."[2]

Black started with people. "The first thing he saw in a case," Charles Reich wrote, "was the human being involved—the human factors, a particular man or woman's hopes and suffering; this became the focus of all his compassion."[*] Black never hid his predilections. Piercing legal clichés to help injured workers, seamen and longshoremen secure their rights under federal statutes gave him much joy. In these cases he wrote in a distinctly satirical vein. A satirist is always a stripper. He shaves the veneer to show the grain and peels the garments to show the body. Black was dedicated to stripping away the philosophical formalism encased in boilerplate rhetoric and to laying bare the operative realities of the legal system, however unappealing they might seem to corporate legal eyes. This gave his writing in this field an unusual combination of ironic detachment and impassioned caring, which only a satirist achieves (perhaps fitting for one who was often understated and sarcastic).

He was the moving force behind the Court's hearing injured workers' claims: he voted to support them every one of the nearly two hundred times they came up for decision. When Black wrote an opinion, he presented the facts appealingly, choosing indisputable evidence that tugged at the heartstrings. Shorter sentences built up tension. He castigated the idea of judges' preventing a jury from reaching a verdict (and did so without naming the judges who did this). The city's "voice must be clothed with the impartial authority, not of a class or a caste, but of the people," he underlined in Zimmern's *The Greek Commonwealth*. Next to this he wrote "classless juries." Dismissing the voice of the people was contempt for a vital democratic organ.

Brennan's appointment modified the balance of the Court. Of liberal instinct, affable and open-minded, hardworking and technically proficient, with a sharp, quick, retentive mind, he was a delightful colleague. He had been on the Court only a few weeks when Black wrote, "I like the new justice very much. Maybe he has been a labor lawyer for business but so far his approach to cases does not indicate that such lawyers do not have just as much desire to do justice as lawyers that represent the labor unions themselves. . . . He has a very nice personality, has understood the cases argued, and has expressed himself with references to those cases in a fine wholesome manner." The changed results in personal injury cases led Frankfurter to switch his argument from maintaining that the Court should not spend its time dealing with such mundane matters to claiming that they disproportionally contributed to the Court's being overworked. When a

[*] "In deciding cases Black is frequently a sentimentalist about people. A vivid and dramatic imagination fills in details that may or may not exist." At times his "sympathies are so completely and automatically enlisted for the unfortunate that he is very nearly as much of a pleader as a judge" (Frank, *Black*, 134).

Harvard professor, Henry Hart, wrote an article echoing Frankfurter's assertions, Black said Hart "just doesn't know what he's talking about" and "didn't take into account the time I spend reading certiorari petitions in the toilet."[3]

* * *

A crisis faced the justices upon their return to Washington in September 1958. The Little Rock, Arkansas, school board had adopted a modest plan for gradual desegregation. This went too far for Governor Orville Faubus. He called out the National Guard to keep Negro students from entering Central High School. A federal court injunction got rid of the guardsmen, but unruly crowds, encouraged by the governor's intemperate opposition, continued to frustrate implementation of the plan until President Eisenhower sent in the army, solely, he emphasized, to enforce the court order, not to integrate the school. The school board appealed the injunction to the Supreme Court. Black's admiration of Eisenhower had lessened, because of Ike's diffidence in enforcing *Brown v. Board of Education*. Eisenhower believed in the principle of desegregation but also that courts and the federal government should not be involved in erasing it. Hardly anyone in public life had been more condemned personally because of *Brown* than Black. To see a president grudgingly enforce it gained only Black's indignation. Ike, he now said, was a nice fellow and would have made a good probate judge back in Alabama.

On September 11, 1958, the Court convened in special session to hear *Cooper v. Aaron*. After the school board pleaded to be permitted to "revert" to segregation until public sentiment settled, the justices quickly and unanimously agreed to issue a per curiam opinion that would, as Warren put it, "reaffirm the duty of state officials to obey the law as laid down by the Supreme Court." One month earlier he had told Brennan, "'It would be helpful if we had some kind of memo about the case.' I worked one up and it was used as the basis of the opinion," Brennan recalled. "We needed something—it was almost the start of the school year. The guts of the opinion was in the memo." Brennan circulated a draft within a week. While recognizing the difficulties facing the school board, he concluded that delay was not warranted. His colleagues were not satisfied, and in the conference room they rewrote portions of what he admitted was a "pretty dry" draft. The part of the opinion dealing with the supremacy of national law over state law needed "more punch and vigor," Black told the justices. He wrote a new opening paragraph:

As this case reaches us it involves questions of the highest importance to the maintenance of our federal system of government. It squarely presents a claim that there is no duty on state officials to obey federal court orders resting on this Court's deliberate and consistent intepretation of the United States Constitution. Specifically, it involves actions by the Governor, Legislature and other agencies of Arkansas . . . that they are not bound by our holding in *Brown* . . . that the Fourteenth Amendment forbids states to use their governmental powers to bar children from attending schools which are helped to run by public management, funds or other public property. We are urged to permit continued suspension of the Little Rock School Board's plan to do away with segregated public schools until state laws and efforts to upset [*Brown*] have been further challenged and tested in the courts. We have concluded that these contentions call for clear answers here and now.

This gave the opinion the needed tone of dramatic urgency, and the Court adopted it almost verbatim. The message could not be clearer that all state officials were bound to obey the law of the land, including the orders of the Supreme Court.

The opinion was announced on September 29. Frankfurter had early suggested that the justices individually sign their names to it to point out, emphatically, the Court's unanimity, and although Douglas and Brennan opposed this, all went along. In open court Warren pointedly said that each justice was joint author. Meanwhile, without telling anyone, Frankfurter was drafting a separate concurrence. He told the justices when they met before going on to the bench. This undercut mentioning all their names and they held their collective breaths until they saw what he wrote. It left suggestions and innuendos, they all agreed after reading it on Friday, October 3. At an emergency conference Frankfurter said that the South's failure to comply with *Brown* led him to write. He claimed he was addressing former students and other acquaintances practicing in the South: this totaled no more than a relative handful of people, as if their combined influence could end the rabble-rousing and demagoguery the situation had produced. Warren and Black said the opinion would do damage. "It was none of the Court's business" what he wrote, Frankfurter replied.

"Felix was all gung ho do for his opinion," Brennan said. "There was havoc around here, just hell to pay. The Chief, Black and I were furious." Frankfurter had added nothing of substance. "We almost cut his throat," Brennan recalled. "It's a mistake," Black told one of Brennan's clerks. Another conference was held October 6, the first day of the new term, when Frankfurter's opinion would be issued (but not announced from the bench).

The justices tried again to talk him out of it. He remained adamant. Black and Brennan proposed writing a short opinion that Frankfurter's remarks "must not be accepted as any dilution or interpretation of the views expressed in the Court's joint opinion." The other justices could not dissuade them until Harlan passed around the table a satirical opinion which defused the tension. Black and Brennan withdrew their proposed statement.[4]

* * *

Hugo Black resisted learning to play chess because he felt that those who played babbled too much. In the same way he was vexed with those who were intelligent enough to know better, but didn't act that way. Life to him was a gift, and he felt a person should make the most of it. This feeling accounted for his gradual disillusionment with Bill Douglas.

A man so enormously gifted should have accomplished more in his job, Black said. "What a waste. The guy has the best mind on the Court. He could have been the greatest justice ever." He'd shake his head. "It's a shame Bill is so lazy." If he "worked harder," Black said in 1957, "we'd be in better shape." And to his clerk the next year: "I worked on a dissent with Bill. It was good enough for him, but not for us. We owe more to the bar." Of greater importance to Black, he found Douglas's conduct and lack of human qualities and of empathy with people appalling. "Try and ease things for others," Black liked to say. Douglas did not do this. More than once, Black put his head in his hands when talking about Douglas, then quickly tried to justify him. But even if Douglas troubled and frustrated him and he sometimes didn't know how to react or to treat him, they continued to share a genuine warmth. At its base was the nearly common results they reached in cases and the fact that Black was a rock in Douglas's life. Once he came to Hugo "all heated up by something Frankfurter said. He paced up and down," recalled Black's clerk Daniel Meador. "Black calmed him down, almost like a baby." Composed, Douglas returned to his office. But these occasions were now infrequent. Black and Douglas didn't see each other much at the Court (except for conference) starting in the 1950s. One of Black's clerks in 1960 asked him to talk to Douglas just so Douglas wouldn't think Black was avoiding him. Black replied, "Have you ever tried to talk to Bill Douglas?"

Nor did they socialize much outside the Court anymore. Douglas's turbulent personal life, with his incessant womanizing, embarrassed Black. ("We all had the feeling that nobody's wife was safe around Bill," said David Ginsburg, one of his closest friends.) Nevertheless, while Hugo distanced himself somewhat from Douglas, the deep mutual attachment remained. His feelings showed when he wrote Douglas in early 1955 shortly after Douglas's remarriage: "You know, of course, that Josephine and I were very fond of Mildred, and regretted that you and she were separated. But however that may be, you know, I am sure, that you have my affectionate good wishes in your new companionship. May both of you be very happy is the hope of your friend, Hugo." Douglas long knew how upset Hugo was at the way he treated his first wife, virtually destroying her. To make Hugo feel better toward him, he offered to take JoJo on his trip to the Philippines, India and Iran that coming summer. Practically Hugo's first words to her when she returned in August were "We're going next month to Venezuela," whose government had invited him to speak. "I always had the feeling Daddy told me that just to show that Douglas wasn't the only justice traveling," she later said. It was part of the competition between them that surfaced when Black let it. For it was Douglas who in effect continued to report to his senior.

Douglas found it hard to put his emotions about Black into words. Black meant too much. "I have thought a lot about you this summer on my long and rather weary journey around the world . . . ," he wrote Hugo in August 1954. "It is one that you should have been on instead of me." Two years later, as he told Fred Rodell, "I easily agreed to do a foreword on Hugo Black for the [seventieth-birthday] issue of the Yale Law Journal. When I came down to writing it, it was the hardest thing I had ever undertaken. I actually spent eight days on it, with at least thirty-two drafts. I was just too close to undertake it. . . ."* And Douglas inscribed his 1958 book, *The Right of the People*, "For Hugo L. Black, to whom this book should have been dedicated."[5]

One of the strongest of the many links between Black and Douglas was Yale Law School. In 1954 its almost entirely liberal faculty utterly inexplicably denied John Frank tenure because of doubts about his writing. Black was deeply disheartened. Yale's action was "rather ominous," he thought. "It [Yale] has been looked upon with much hope by people who want lawyers to learn how to think rather than to be the subservient automatons of stereotyped conventionalities. It looks now like thinking may be at a premium around old Eli. . . . I very much fear that Yale Law School is about to cease

---

* Douglas understated the amount of time: it was more than two weeks.

being an institution for thinking and begin to emphasize the memorizing of formulas—conventional ones at that. . . . It is hard for me to believe that you could enjoy yourself at Yale under the new regime."

Yale was headed by a new dean, Harry Shulman, "FF's candidate—nice, conservative, no guts, timid," Douglas told Black. The Yale Corporation denied tenure to Vern Countryman, Douglas's former clerk, despite the unanimous approval of the law faculty (except for Shulman) and Douglas's attempted personal intervention with university president A. Whitney Griswold.* Shulman died the next year. His successor, Eugene Rostow, went to Washington to call on Justices Black and Douglas. "I had to repair relations," Rostow recalled. "Douglas brusquely gave me a piece of his mind about the Countryman affair. Black said. 'I think you were very wrong and made mistakes you'll regret, but let's get all this behind us.'† He was just wonderful, so gracious." They started talking about the Bible, and Black said he would judge Yale "as it develops according to the precepts of the Book of James."

Rostow tried to soothe Black's feelings further by inviting him to be the guest of honor at a law journal banquet in April 1956. Black's remarks showed where his heart lay: "This has been a great law school. It still was a great law school when my son went here. I hope it will be a school I would want to send my grandson to." Soon Black resumed taking Yale graduates as his clerks, as he had largely done for a decade, starting in the early 1940s, but had stopped during 1954 and 1955. For those years he basically sang "All hail to Harvard." One reason was his deep respect for Harvard Law School dean Erwin N. Griswold.

After the Republicans won the White House in 1952, Black hoped Griswold would be named attorney general ("unless I am mistaken Griswold would have stood like a stone wall against encroachment on the great individual liberties our founders dreamed about") or solicitor general (he "would fill this place with great credit to himself and great benefit to the

---

* Griswold "promised to fire" Countryman because of his views, which were the same as Black's and Douglas's. He refused to meet Douglas, who had come to New Haven unannounced solely to urge Countryman's promotion. Douglas showed up, wearing a cowboy hat, at Griswold's secretary's desk, introduced himself and asked to see Griswold. She went back to tell Griswold, "There's a man here who says he's Justice Douglas," and returned to say Griswold was not available (WOD to Rodell, 3/2/55, Rodell papers; Countryman int.).

† Rostow always felt "we did the right thing. Countryman never deserved to be at Yale and I still don't think Frank writes well" (int.). Rostow remained in a minuscule minority. Frank and Countryman fared the crisis well: Frank moved to Phoenix, where he became one of the country's most distinguished lawyers; and Countryman taught for many years at Harvard Law School, becoming one of the leading bankruptcy scholars in the United States.

Government"). In early 1954 Griswold gave a series of typically forthright speeches, defending the virtues of the Fifth Amendment. "It is hard for me to tell you how good I feel that there is a voice like yours to speak up for constitutional safeguards that seem to me to be absolutely essential to the continuation of a free government," Black wrote him and suggested that he ask Massachusetts senator Leverett Saltonstall to place the speeches in the *Congressional Record* for wider circulation.[6]

But Black was not quite ready to paper his chambers in crimson. He enjoyed teasing his clerks about 'Hahvard' professors.* This reflected not only his belief that many academics didn't know all the answers but also that they made issues more complicated than they really were; and that Harvard professors, especially, resembled medieval scholastics in overemphasizing "technicalities" without giving students a broad background for law in the everyday world. "Lawyer—a sort of wary and acute legalist, a repeater of forms, a catcher at syllables," Black wrote to himself in 1959. "Your law practice will undoubtedly make you a better teacher," he told one former clerk. "I sometimes wish that many law professors in influential places had more knowledge about the way law works in practice." He expanded his target to the nature of legal education. "I think that the case system, with its extreme emphasis on precedents and the method of law school teaching in general, does need searching inquiry on the part of people who are detached enough to be skeptical about existing teaching practices," Black observed in 1960. "I am by no means sure that the law schools of today are turning out graduates who are able to consider law as it may affect litigants as distinguished from interpretations thought to be compelled by judicial or professorial formulas." He urged those of his clerks who wanted to teach to practice first, and one of the reasons he wanted his clerks to go into teaching was to counter Frankfurter.

Harvard exalted the reigning orthodoxy in American law. Holmes had devised it, Cardozo (a Columbia graduate who was revered at Harvard) had given it lasting expression, and Frankfurter was its leading current exponent. But Black felt little kinship with it. "While I greatly admired and respected Justice Cardozo, I never fully agreed with his discussion of 'The Nature of the Judicial Process.' It always seemed to me that he exalted judge-made

---

* "The Judge always talked how lucky I was I didn't go to Harvard and suffer under its influence," said John Harmon (int.), who clerked for Black in 1970. "It was as if because I didn't that I could make my own way in the world. One of the clerks he chose for the next term came from Harvard. The Judge said, 'That's my missionary project.' He was going to save him from Harvard."

laws a little too much to fit into our constitutional pattern of law-making."
Indeed, "I do not agree with nearly all he says about the way judges decide
or should decide cases." Once again, Black looked further back.

Establishing a legal standard by written law was for the Greeks an
educational act. "That most excellent leading-string of the law," said the
Athenian in Plato's *Laws;* and Aristotle suggested that "education by the
laws" might serve as a bridge between ethics and politics. Law is one of
democracy's most noble teachers, guiding, training and supporting citizens
to administer their common social business as well as their private affairs.
It liberates and sets limits. The most prominent contemporary advocate of
this view was Edmond Cahn; Black read all his writings. To most traditional
legal thinkers this creed was an infidel in the temple. Black made no apol-
ogies. The Constitution required it, he believed.[7]

*   *   *

By the early 1950s Black had come to read the phrase "all criminal prosecutions" in the Sixth Amendment to mean *all,* including those for criminal
contempt. What distressed him during McCarthyism as much as the substantive results was the shortcutting of the legal system—not giving defendants their rights by not letting their lawyers defend them to the fullest.
So when Justice Harlan in 1958 reaffirmed for the Court the traditional view
that the Constitution does not require jury trial in contempt of court cases,
Black vigorously dissented. He would have had to eliminate both his twenty-
five years of practice before trial judges and his belief that a trial lawyer
should be threatened with being cited for contempt to think otherwise. Few
doctrines were more odious to him than the power of one judge in a single
breath to cite, make a judgment, and punish a person for conduct both in
and out of court, without a jury trial, by applying a seat-of-the-pants "reasonableness" test—"that irrepressible, vague and delusive standard which at
times threatens to engulf the entire law, including the Constitution itself,
in a sea of judicial discretion."*

Black recognized the human frailties of judges. But courts, and especially
the Supreme Court, should correct past errors. They "were established and
are maintained to provide impartial tribunals of strictly disinterested arbiters

---

* Compare the "reasonableness" test to the one used by Harry Cohn of Columbia Pictures
in the era of movie industry censorship to determine whether a film was suitable for viewing
by the public: "If my fanny wiggles, it can't be shown." To which his leading writer, Herman
Manckiewicz, replied: "Imagine the whole world wired to Harry Cohn's ass" (Bob Thomas,
King Cohn [New York, 1967], 142).

to resolve charges of wrongdoing," not to serve as organs of criminal prosecution. "Trial by a jury of laymen and no less was regarded as the birthright of freemen." Only through this "democratic element" could punishment be meted out. Law in the American scheme empowers the citizens and not their supposed governors. The Constitution assures this. By having absorbed the social contract, it changed the rules. The imperial attitude had viewed the prerogatives of the citizens as secondary to the needs of the state. But now the individual reigned supreme.

Alfonse Bartkus had been acquitted in a federal court on bank robbery charges. Thereupon, federal authorities assisted Illinois to try him again, in a state court, for the same offense—despite the Fifth Amendment's assertion that no person "shall . . . be subject for the same offence to be twice put in jeopardy of life or limb." Bartkus was found guilty and he appealed to the Supreme Court. At conference, after reargument in October 1958, Black stated that the Court could apply the Fifth Amendment to the states. "It doesn't say twice put in jeopardy by the same government, but for the same offense." Therefore, "When the 'feds' do what was done here, we have a direct violation of the Fifth Amendment or it is so shocking to the conscience that we can't take it under the Fourteenth."

This unlikely phrasing was a direct appeal to Justice Charles Whittaker: Frankfurter had tried but failed the year before (Whittaker's first on the Court) to induce him to affirm. What the federal government had done, Whittaker said then, " 'shocks (my) conscience' and, in my view, constitutes a denial of due process." But he had since changed his mind, leaving the Court again evenly divided; this time, however, instead of a justice's (Brennan) not participating, a justice, Potter Stewart, who was serving his first month, said he couldn't make up his mind. In a few days he decided to join Frankfurter, who led the conference argument the other way. The double jeopardy defense, Frankfurter wrote for the Court, does not apply when a defendant is charged with having violated the laws of two or more different "sovereigns."

One of the ways to get Frankfurter's vote at this stage in his career, Black said, was simply to ring the federalism bell. This case chimed it. Frankfurter eagerly answered the call. Black found such prosecutions, even more than Felix's response, "so contrary to the spirit of our free country that they violate even the prevailing view of the Fourteenth Amendment."

The Court apparently takes the position that a second trial for the same act is somehow less offensive if conducted by the Federal Government and the other by a State. Looked at from the standpoint of the individual who is being prosecuted, this notion is too subtle for me to grasp. If double punishment is what is feared, it hurts no less for two "Sovereigns" to inflict it than for one. If danger to the innocent is emphasized, that danger is surely no less when the power of State and Federal Governments is brought to bear on one man in two trials, than when one of these "Sovereigns" proceeds alone. In each case, inescapably, a man is forced to face danger twice for the same conduct.

Black wanted to make Frankfurter angry by listing the first example of a situation where double jeopardy seemed to be allowed. This was, after all, the most ancient procedural guarantee in the Bill of Rights. His clerk located the initial one. That didn't satisfy Black. "Now go find the original." Back to the library the clerk went. There it was—its heading had been missing. Black was showing that the legal protection of rights was a continual flow. When Frankfurter, in delivering the opinion, said, "This isn't St. Augustine, this is the United States," Hugo smiled. The case only confirmed his belief that "highly technical justice," with complicated rules of procedure, is "class justice," tending to favor those who can afford to hire skillful (usually urban) lawyers, Black said.

In November 1958, while opinions in *Bartkus* were being prepared, Frankfurter suffered a heart attack. He became much more rigid afterward. "Felix is obviously a sick man," Black observed. "Maybe that's why he is so hard to get along with in conference." More than ever, Frankfurter tried to browbeat his colleagues. But his most consistent target of verbal pummeling was Whittaker, for the simple reason that Whittaker held the decisive fifth vote in the most important cases. Formerly an able trial lawyer in Kansas City, Whittaker had a hankering for procedural fairness. He regretted accepting appointment to the Court from the day he arrived. Quickly, he was under medical care. "I sold myself down the river for a bowl of porridge," he said. He would agree to what anybody told him and could be easily persuaded after an analytical conversation in which he did most of the listening. That, of course, was Frankfurter's reason for being. "Felix really went after Whittaker in *Bartkus*," recalled Black's clerk Guido Calabresi, telling him he *had* to agree. Hugo similarly tried, his purpose just as transparent but his manner much more gentle. He saw Whittaker's agony of decision. Finally, he said, "I cannot destroy a man."

Stewart's initial indecision did not bother Black, for he liked and respected Stewart from the first. He saw Stewart as conscientious if conservative, and appreciated his quiet and often pungent wit. (One lawyer appearing before the Court, convinced the justices were divided four to four in his case, joked he should move the lectern down to Stewart's end and argue the case directly to him. If he had, Stewart said later, "he would have ended up losing the case by a vote of 8 to 1.") One day soon Black said he was "feeling old, which he did as a running thing. It didn't amount to anything," recounted Calabresi. "I asked, 'What would happen to the Court?' He said, 'Bill [Brennan] will be just fine, and Potter will grow. Bill is as smart as anyone on the Court. Everything is fresh to him. But when Felix and I decide a case now it's just the last chapter of a book we've been writing.' "[8]

It was a thick volume. To no small degree they helped to define each other and the history of the Court during the time they served together. Real feelings of affection from earlier conflicts remained even if the two justices were now amiable rather than truly friendly. Hugo genuinely believed Felix was his only worthy rival on the Court. In one case he pointed to his draft opinion for the Court as an example of how a position has to be built. All the other justices signed on without comment except for Frankfurter who, picking up Black's hidden meaning, wrote him: "I agree with every word, especially your essay on *Brown v. Board of Education.*" "There," Black said, "that's why I say Felix is the brightest man on the Court."

And Frankfurter was Black's greatest intellectual admirer. "I heard him say repeatedly that God Almighty gave Black the best brain in our Court," wrote his first law clerk, Edward Prichard, Jr., and he told the same thing to Judge Learned Hand and Paul Freund. And to Chief Justice Warren he admitted, "Nobody on the Court or off it has a better appreciation, I think, than I have of the intellectual powers of Hugo." Yet it is hard to picture Frankfurter writing Black as Hugo wrote Felix when some hypothetical remark was made regarding contingencies of service in the Court during conference on March 1, 1957: "I strongly hope nothing will happen that causes you to leave the Court—not on account of this case—but simply I hope you stay. Hugo."

They quarreled like two boys in a schoolyard who then make up and walk home together, continually wary of the other's tactics and vowing silently to defeat the other tomorrow. Frankfurter got angry quickly and got over it just as quickly; but part of his anger festered, never to leave him, and he acted on it. He continued to spread all sorts of calumny about Black as a man and judge. Hugo disregarded this as much as any person could.

Felix's behavior often simply bewildered him, and he refused to dwell upon it. Focusing on principles, not personalities, had been a consistent trait throughout Hugo's career. He and Felix never stopped trying to convince each other of the wrongheadedness of the other's approach.

Black wanted, above all, principles of individual rights hard and clear so that other persons in power, especially judges, couldn't squirm out of them. Frankfurter found great value in ways to keep from reaching judgment. "Rules, rules, rules—that's all Felix cared about," Black said. "As far as I'm concerned, the only rules should be about the books in which our opinions are published." Judges could make wise decisions, Frankfurter believed; they had the power and the duty to draw lines on the basis of "reasonableness" where the people's rights are concerned, even in a country whose fundamental law is embodied in a written constitution.* Frankfurter had a traditional outlook, rearranging the furniture of the mind only within a particular room. Black impatiently rummaged through the whole house and beyond, looking for articles, accessories, props, anything he could find, and added them to the foundation to develop a new structure. His concern was the individual and the political landscape. It was a battle between a carpenter, a superior craftsman at his trade, and an architect who also designed the interior of the building and oversaw its construction. A painting by Ben Shahn, *Frankfurter and Black,* has Felix sitting at a desk in front of a window, head buried in a thick book. Hugo is standing beside the desk, a small smile on his face, looking out the window at the broad, sun-drenched field.[9]

Their ideological conflicts reached a peak as the 1950s ended. At oral argument they clashed constantly. Whereas Frankfurter typically harassed counsel, Black would help him out. Hugo might ask a softly couched but pointed question. Felix would immediately harshly phrase it from the opposite viewpoint. The hapless lawyer would be caught in the middle, forced to answer queries really meant for the other justice. They put on the best show in town when they announced conflicting opinions from the bench.†

---

* Haim Cohn, Israel's founding attorney general, came to the United States to study its constitutional experience. "Mr. Justice Black," he recalled, "began our discussion by saying, 'The first thing you should do, young man, is write a constitution.' " Cohn went next door to see Frankfurter: "The first thing you should not do, young man, is to write a constitution. Good and courageous judges" could best protect civil liberties (*NYT* 10/13/75).

† "It's wonderful what Hugo can do with a bum legal position by high sounding phrases and the right tone of voice!" Harlan once wrote Frankfurter; no date, FFLC.

In announcing the *Bartkus* opinion, Frankfurter made a passing reference to "the so-called Bill of Rights." Black's voice rang with passion as he delivered his dissent: "This case concerns the Bill of Rights, not the so-called Bill of Rights."

Black did not usually talk much about the Court's conferences, in which Frankfurter had become even more exasperating, except to refer to his differences with Felix. He often anticipated Frankfurter's comments and took the initiative in responding so that Felix was put on the defensive. Back in the office, he sometimes animatedly related some of Felix's antics during conference while disparaging him. "My, how that man can go on," Hugo would marvel, and add, "but the code works"—occasionally. "Felix screamed at me so today, I thought he was going to hit me," he once told Elizabeth. He paused. "Why I could beat that little thing up with one hand tied behind my back." At one conference Frankfurter's words got too much for Black, and he started to go after Felix physically. Tom Clark, who sat next to Frankfurter, intervened to break up any possible altercation. Black walked out of at least three Court conferences because of Frankfurter, early each year in 1954, 1958 and 1961. "Felix kept on talking and talking," Hugo said to his startled secretary one Friday in March 1958 as he picked up his hat. "So I told them that if he kept on, I'm just going to leave. It's still light outside and I'm going to play tennis. See you on Monday."

Occasionally Black attributed a Svengali-like influence to Frankfurter. At times it seemed almost that his thesis was that Frankfurter was trying to undo the Republic. He would not say that Felix was leading a conspiracy against him—he was too much a politician to do that—but he felt it. He saw Frankfurter working indefatigably to defeat him and malign his beliefs. He knew that almost whenever he did anything controversial, a whole host of law professors would attack him. Many of these were Harvard trained and Frankfurter's former students or otherwise befriended by him. The fierce "Harvard-Yale" dispute over the Court's role resulted. Frankfurter instigated and perpetuated it. "You've got all those fellows out there in the law schools trying to tell the bar that I'm trying to force my views on the American people," Hugo told him. Felix, of course, vehemently denied it even as he tried to coax and entice the professoriate into believing that when Black was not acting lawlessly he was purposely misreading and mangling history for his own ends. In Aristotle's *Rhetoric* Black marked as *"sophistry"*: "But *when logic is prostituted to the support of false propositions* by the bad principles of its professors, *it is* branded with the name of *sophistry . . . that species of sophistry* by which our enlightened reason reconciles us to the gratification of our worst passions."[10]

Hugo Black believed intensely in the power of language and the power of history. He dictated the first drafts of many and certainly of his most effective opinions. These captured the spoken word's simplicity, eloquence and rhythm in a manner similar to that of the Bible and Shakespeare, with an occasional flurry reminiscent of Tom Watson's *Napoleon* (which he owned). He used the leaping and lingering of a good storyteller. He would tarry on a point with an anecdote and a moral, and then startle in a way that commanded attention. It was a continuation of the oral tradition of the South, with all the embellishment and the use of the superlative it entailed. His best opinions read as if he's talking to you; the reader becomes the listener. Black caught the traits of the spoken word in written form.

His opinions reflect a long-held view of man and life. It ran counter to the idea, represented by Frankfurter, that the Supreme Court's constitutional interpretations should build on each other, all kept attuned to the changing times. Life is an inclined road. "New occasions teach new duties and time makes ancient good untruth," wrote James Russell Lowell. As the hymn goes, "They must ever up and onward who would keep abreast of truth." But since the old-fashioned words in the Constitution can easily impede any attempt for progress, judges must approach the document in the spirit of the framers: if they were here today, they would understand our situation and view it as we do. This is an estimable notion but an unprovable assertion. But it is, by and large, the prevailing legal and political approach: pragmatic, cocky, optimistic: things will always get better, we're always going to have growth; rah rah, go go, we can fix it—all so classically American. And it is as far away from Black's thinking as the twentieth century is from the eighteenth.

Black asserted that man's life is a straight line. It doesn't necessarily go up or down. People and government are the same today, with the same problems, as five thousand years ago. That is what the Greeks and the Romans taught him. He drank ancient learning out of Enlightenment bottles and poured it into contemporary cups. He grew up imbibing the strongly individualistic character of Protestantism and its traditional pessimistic view of human nature: man is sinful and, in Lord Acton's famous words, "Power tends to corrupt and absolute power corrupts absolutely." This led Black to reject the thesis that judicial review should be limited in Bill of Rights cases as Judge Learned Hand had explicitly urged recently and Frankfurter had strongly implied at times, calling this "good as an original proposition, but it's not the constitutional system." It also led Black to envision the Constitution as a brilliant scheme that had been devised to limit power.[11]

The role of the Court was, as John Marshall had intended, to blow the whistle when necessary on the executive and legislative branches. Where Black and Frankfurter deviated was on what standards judges should follow. Black could not say that judges could do whatever their consciences told them to. The implications would have destroyed the Court. That eliminated Frankfurter's "shock the conscience" or any similar test as too subjective; judges could not be free agents. Black retreated to the Constitution, to the literal words as much as possible. It was a revolutionary step.

These beliefs reached their strongest level as Black gave the deepest thought of his life to the history and meaning of the First Amendment.

CHAPTER 33

"THERE *ARE* 'ABSOLUTES' IN OUR BILL OF RIGHTS"

B<small>Y THE LATE</small> 1950s Black had long been regarded as the dean of American judicial libertarianism. Various individuals and institutions had been urging him for years to deliver lectures on his constitutional philosophy. He felt "in somewhat of a dilemma" since Edmond Cahn and his former clerk Sidney Davis discussed how to induce him to make a formal statement of his creed at New York University, while William C. Warren, dean of Columbia Law School, had been urging him to deliver the Carpentier Lectures there. "Should I conclude to deliver lectures anywhere," he told Cahn, "it will be over the protest of certain inner voices that keep telling me that the best thing I can do is tend to my knittin' here at home."

In September 1959 Black consented to deliver the first in a lecture series that NYU was establishing in honor of James Madison. Several factors influenced his decision. He knew that any speech he gave would further fan the already flaming fires of controversy. But he also wanted an additional forum for his views. His dissents were rebuttals. He had not been able to present, without opposition, his conception of the towering purpose of the Bill of Rights. Here was a splendid opportunity. There was also the simple matter of Black's fondness for Cahn. Yet it took all of Cahn's considerable relentless persistence and determination to overcome Black's objections. "By using every persuasive device I could conceive of, I obtained Justice Black's virtual acceptance," he noted. "Edmond just wouldn't take no for an answer," Elizabeth Black said later. "And Hugo could never really say no to friends." The lecture was scheduled for mid-February 1960.

Black was always prone to procrastinate on any off-Court activities (except tennis). The speech had not assumed even a tentative written form by mid-December 1959. Cahn wanted Black to elaborate on the First Amendment. That would "require that I change my subject from 'The Bill of Rights' to 'the First Amendment,' " Black immediately responded. It "is but one part, although in my judgment, the very heart of the Bill of Rights as a whole. There is therefore at least a logical inconsistency in limiting the first of a series of Bill of Rights lectures to a discussion of the First Amendment. . . . The result of my thinking up to now is, that, unless the lecture is to be called off entirely, it might be best to postpone it to a later date." Black suspended work until Cahn and Davis came to Washington at the end of the month to speak with him. His doubts quickly dispelled, he soon started drafting the speech. Cahn's suggestion to view it as a permanent statement of his manifesto reinforced Black's desire from the beginning to say that the Bill of Rights contains "absolutes."[1]

First Amendment freedoms are "absolutely indispensable for the preservation of a free society . . . ," Black wrote, concurring in a 1958 case (*Speiser v. Randall*). "Loyalty must arise spontaneously from the hearts of people who love their country and respect their government." The House Un-American Activities Committee, in its sincere but misguided attempt to purge the nation of "Communists," put a barrier between many patriotic citizens and their government. Lloyd Barenblatt, a college teacher, had been cited for contempt of Congress after refusing to answer its questions whether he was or ever had been a member of the Communist Party and, more specifically, whether he had been a member of the Communist Club while a graduate student a few years earlier. He explicitly based his refusal on First Amendment grounds.

Justice Harlan, with scale in hand, wrote the opinion in *Barenblatt v. U.S.* for a sharply divided Court in early 1959. The First Amendment narrows the scope of legislative investigations, but the test whether those limits have been violated "always involves a balancing . . . of the competing private and public interests at stake in the particular circumstances." Here "the balance between the individual and the governmental interests . . . must be struck in favor of the latter." Despite a recent opinion suggesting that the committee had no constitutional power to question citizens about their political beliefs and associations, Harlan held that the First Amendment was not "offended" here.

Black had long yearned to put the nefarious Un-American Activities Committee out of business. It abridged freedom of speech "through exposure,

obloquy and public scorn," he noted in his dissent. His first draft was as full
of rhetoric as analysis. His clerk Guido Calabresi expanded it to include a
direct-indirect test. Some laws "directly," while others "indirectly," affect
speech; when in the latter cases the speech and conduct were intertwined,
a balancing test determined "the effect on speech . . . in relation to the
need for control of the conduct." Black instantly adopted this analysis intact.
But this was not an occasion for its application.

For even under the majority's assumption that balancing was proper,
Black felt Harlan not only "ignores it completely" but "mistakes the factors
to be weighed." What is at stake is not only the governmental interest and
Barenblatt's individual interest in a private "right of silence," but the broader
public "interest of the people as a whole in being able to join organizations,
advocate causes and make political 'mistakes' without later being subjected
to governmental penalties for having dared to think for themselves. . . . It
is this right, the right to err politically, which keeps us strong as a Nation."
Such insensitive balancing is "a mere play on words," and changes the First
Amendment to say that

> "Congress shall pass no law abridging freedom of speech . . . unless Con-
> gress and the Supreme Court reach the joint conclusion that on balance
> the interest of the Government in stifling these freedoms is greater than
> the interest of the people in having them exercised." This is closely akin
> to the notion that neither the First Amendment nor any other provision
> of the Bill of Rights should be enforced unless the Court believes it is
> *reasonable* to do so. Not only does this violate the genius of our *written*
> Constitution, but runs expressly counter to the injunction to Court and
> Congress made by Madison when he introduced the Bill of Rights. . . .
> Unless we return to this view of our judicial function, unless we once
> again accept the notion that the Bill of Rights means what it says and that
> this Court must enforce that meaning, I am of the opinion that our great
> charter of liberty will be more honored in the breach than in the obser-
> vance. . . .

Black concluded:

> Ultimately all questions in this case really boil down to one—whether we
> as a people will try fearfully and futilely to preserve democracy by adopting
> totalitarian methods, or whether in accordance with our traditions and
> our Constitution we will have the confidence and courage to be free.

"The thought kept recurring," one courtroom observer told Black, "that
I was listening to a peer of Thomas Jefferson. The history of the founding

of our Republic suddenly came alive." To Alexander Meiklejohn, the grand old man of free speech, the opinion stated "the issue of political freedom in the form in which, sooner or later, it must be decided." Black replied: "I would like very much to have a good long talk with you about constitutional liberties."

In late 1959 they met again, for the second time (after fourteen years), for dinner and discussion at Black's house. Their harmony of view on the need for unfettered speech in the realm of public affairs was so great as to need no elaboration, but their disagreements, although relatively minor, could not be ignored. Meiklejohn thought libel and obscenity were "private" speech not protected by the First Amendment. At present Black believed this to be true only in regard to libel. Obscenity was different. He was working on a concurrence to the Court's reversal on December 15 of a conviction for possessing a book later found to be obscene: "I read 'no law . . . abridging' to mean *no law abridging*." The First Amendment "has thus fixed its own value on freedom of speech and press by putting these freedoms wholly 'beyond the reach' of *federal* power to abridge. . . . While it is 'obscenity and indecency' before us today, the experience of mankind— both ancient and modern—shows that this type of elastic phrase can, and most likely, will be synonymous with the political and maybe with the religious unorthodoxy of tomorrow. Censorship is the deadly enemy of freedom and progress. The plain language of the Constitution forbids it. I protest against the Judiciary giving it a foothold here." And he listed several statements by Jefferson and Madison indicating that they may have held the view that Frankfurter, in another concurrence, called "doctrinaire absolutism."[2]

Black took little more than a month preparing his NYU speech. He drafted it as carefully as he wrote any opinion. He spoke with Madison biographer Irving Brant about the accuracy of the transcription of the speeches in the first Congress when Madison introduced the Bill of Rights. His former clerks Louis Oberdorfer and Charles Reich worked on his speech, as did John Calhoun, a law school classmate of Hugo, Jr.'s, and former clerk to Justice Reed who had struck up a friendship with Black and happened to be in town. In all, ten full drafts were produced. Reich furnished several of the later ones; Black amended all. "The Judge told us Charlie helped him, then read it out loud in his inflection and with that dramatic intonation of his," his clerk John McNulty recalled. "When he did that, it was hard to disagree." The final version did not reflect any doctrinal changes or progression of views, but was distinctive for its simple eloquence and a profound faith in humanity and a democratic citizenry.

Black and Elizabeth spent several days in New York, visiting friends and JoJo, and dining and going to the theater with the Cahns. Cahn had earlier cleared with the justice the guest list for the pre-speech dinner. Black crossed off the name of Roger Baldwin, the principal organizer of the American Civil Liberties Union. He had reason to dislike Baldwin, who had publicly criticized his Senate investigation into public utilities lobbying, his appointment, and his opinion in the Japanese internment cases during World War Two; but it was the tone of Baldwin's criticism, as well as his haughty manner on the few occasions they met, that Black resented. Before the speech Black was very nervous, speaking faster than normal, jittery in his mannerisms and pacing more than normal. But once it began, he was his usual relaxed self, spicing his remarks with humor and banter.

In the manner of an experienced teacher, Black first spoke of different views of the Bill of Rights. Some people, he noted, regard even the most unequivocal constitutional commands as mere admonitions; "all constitutional problems are questions of reasonableness, proximity, and degree." This approach, which "comes close to the English doctrine of legislative omnipotence," he could not accept:

> It is my belief that there *are* "absolutes" in our Bill of Rights, and that they were put there by men who knew what words meant, and meant their prohibitions to be "absolute." The whole history and background of the Constitution and the Bill of Rights, as I understand it, belies the assumption or conclusion that our ultimate constitutional freedoms are no more than our English ancestors had when they came to this new land to get new freedom. The historical and practical purposes of a Bill of Rights, the very use of a written constitution, indigenous to America, the language the framers used, the kind of three-department government they took pains to set up, all point to the creation of a government which was denied all power to do some things under any and all circumstances, and all power to do other things except in the manner prescribed.

Black went through the Bill of Rights in reverse order. In each amendment he found a core of absolute protection, certain defined areas in which the federal government simply cannot act. Once a classification is made whether particular conduct fits within the rule, that rule is unconditional.

He reached the First Amendment. It is "composed of plain words, easily understood." Like Madison's original proposals, it is nothing "less than absolute." It lists the areas that government is barred from entering. Yet

Congress may think otherwise, and a judge may attempt to follow suit. Black applied the balancing concept in a "wholly imaginary opinion of Judge X."* Under it, he said, his voice dripping with sarcasm, the government "could always claim it needed more power," especially in emergencies. Legislative supremacy rules again. "Congress may do anything that courts believe to be reasonable." This was not the constitutional intent: the "document settles the conflict" in case of varying claims. "Our Constitution," Black told the packed audience, "with its absolute guarantees of individual rights, is the best hope for the aspirations of freedom which men share everywhere. . . . It is old but not all old things are bad. The evils it guards against" are timeless.

> Since the earliest days philosophers have dreamed of a country where the mind and spirit of man would be free; where there would be no limits to inquiry; where men would be free to explore the unknown and to challenge the most deeply rooted beliefs and principles. Our First Amendment was a bold effort to adopt this principle—to establish a country with no legal restrictions of any kind upon the subjects people could investigate, discuss and deny. The Framers knew, better perhaps than we do today, the risks they were taking. They knew that free speech might be the friend of change and revolution. But they also knew that it is always the deadliest enemy of tyranny. With this knowledge they still believed that the ultimate happiness and security of a nation lies in its ability to explore, to change, to grow and ceaselessly to adapt itself to new knowledge born of inquiry free from any kind of governmental control over the mind and spirit of man. Loyalty comes from love of good government, not fear of a bad one.

The impact of such an inspiring peroration was immediate and enormous. Black did not know or care about the copyright, the royalties, or even his honorarium (even though he put it in the bank when he received it). He was "vitally interested" in having his views discussed publicly, even by those who opposed them—and "no doubt there are many." He expected "a whole outcropping of hostile criticism." What is surprising is that it did not come earlier. For everything Black said he had written before, scattered in bits and pieces throughout his opinions and infrequent public remarks of the past decade and more. His speech was a distillation of that thinking, and with the scaffolding of a formal address it made a potent impact. It was

---

* " 'Judge X' is wholly a creature of the imagination. I think that his opinion could well be written by anyone who fully subscribes to the 'balancing' methods of deciding constitutional questions" (HLB to Vernon Patrick, 3/7/60).

"considerably at odds with the Harvard line and of those who subscribe to it," he told Alfred Knopf. "Harvard has a powerful influence in shaping legal and constitutional views throughout the country."

Alexander Bickel taught at Yale Law School but subscribed to "the Harvard line." In an article bursting with cynicism and misunderstanding, he accused Black of wholesale wrongs. "Does not Justice Black so circum-scribe his subject as to obliterate it, does not he exclude all the difficulties that matter, leaving himself with the proposition, which it would be foolish to deny, that when everybody is agreed, all agree?" Bickel asked. He ques-tioned "the utility of illusions and of the justification for creating them." Such an illusion "can . . . breed free-ranging government by the judiciary" that "is incompatible on principle with democratic institutions, and in prac-tice . . . will not be tolerated."

A damning accusation indeed. But "it is, of course, too much to hope that anyone will discuss different opinions others hold without getting more or less personal in what is said," Black observed to John Frank. His friends rushed to his defense. Fred Rodell sent an "open letter," really a broadside against Bickel, to the *New Republic,* which gave Black information about the article, since he had not, and would not, read it. "I must confess that Professor Bickel's article has not tended to give me apoplexy or anything like that," he told Rodell. "If my memory serves me correctly, I have been previously attacked by men of equal importance to the Professor." Indeed, he told Meiklejohn, "I can well imagine what Professor Bickel would say. He was Justice Frankfurter's clerk and at present time his intimate friend and advisor," spending the year in Washington. The result of this is that he largely reflects Felix's views. I respect those views very much but prefer to hear them discussed by the man who originates the concepts." These were reverberating in Justice Douglas's ears when he wrote *New Republic* publisher Gilbert Harrison:

> The Bickel article raises a point of more than passing importance. [He] is a talented man and undoubtedly will have contributions to make in many fields, except those that pertain to the work of the Court. There he is not a reporter, but an out-and-out propagandist. I am one of the first to believe in the full expression of all ideas, those with which I disagree as well as those of which I approve. And I certainly do no think that any magazine, let alone the *New Republic,* should be wedded to one school of thought.
>   The Court deals with very large, important, provocative issues. But I do earnestly and deeply believe that . . . Bickel is disqualified to tell the readers of the *New Republic* what are the merits or demerits of the various

positions taken by various members of this Court. While that school of thought, which he represents on your staff, should be heard, it was for me sad that the *New Republic,* instead of offering a debate *pro* and *con* on Justice Black's views, should come down on him so heavily—taking sides on this basic issue of constitutional interpretation. Justice Black, after all, represents the great liberal tradition, to which even the *New Republic* owes its existence.[3]

The next year, 1961, Charles L. Black, Jr., of Yale Law School (and no relation to Justice Black) assayed a sophisticiated defense of the justice's use of "absolutes." Twenty years earlier, Justice Black recalled, "Walton Hamilton told me I should take Charles Black as a law clerk before he had taken any law course." Recently he had enjoyed an article of Black's. "Perhaps before too long I shall be citing some of his writings myself," the justice wrote a friend. "He does write well." Every judge knows in his soul, Charles Black asserted, that free speech cannot be completely unrestricted, but there is value in putting it that way—as unrestricted—regardless. "You realize *I* cannot agree with that," Justice Black commented.

Black's speech came after Judge Learned Hand's mention of "absolutes" in an address nearly two years earlier, which was still echoing throughout the legal world. Hand spoke of his teachers at Harvard Law School in the late nineteenth century who "asked no quarter of absolutes and they gave none," and he admonished his audience to "go ye and do likewise." These were "fine rhetoric statements . . . ," Black wrote Columbia law professor Milton Handler in 1963.

> I admired Judge Hand and think he had few superiors in eloquent graphic expressions. This does not mean that I agreed with all of them, and certainly I would not agree to the implications of the rhetorical statements in his Harvard address. They, however, fit his philosophy that the Bill of Rights contains admonitions rather than definite, unequivocal prohibitions against the exercise of certain powers. My belief is that if judges are charged with no more responsibility than to treat the Bill of Rights as admonitions, the Bill of Rights is not worth the struggle which brought it into existence. "Absolute" power in the hands of one or many is synonymous with dictators; and "absolute" prohibition against the exercise of power in certain fields is quite the contrary.

Harvard Law School dean Erwin Griswold picked Black's birthday in 1963 to rebuke his beliefs vigorously. Black always appreciated Griswold's directness and Griswold was nothing if not direct now. Absolutes "are likely to be phantoms, eluding our grasps," he said in a speech. Dealing with words is the most basic part of judging, but under the "Fundamentalist Theologist" approach the judge "looks at one phrase only; he blinds himself to everything else." It is "a delusive way to certainty . . . reason is abandoned." Griswold entitled his lecture "Absolute Is in the Dark."

The lambasting did not disturb Black. He never viewed matters one-sidedly when it came to Griswold, whom he called "a fine man, a useful citizen, and, I think, a thorough-going patriot." "As you can guess," the justice wrote, "I disagree with most of the constitutional principles you advocated. . . . As a matter of fact, you could not possibly think my con-stitutional philosophy is any more dangerous than I think is the [one] you expressed." But "my admiration for you—and my respect for your sturdy integrity—are such that I am compelled to admit that your championship of your views causes me to hope that maybe they are not as dangerous as I still believe they are."[4]

The thrust of most American thinking starting in the late nineteenth century had been to slay the dragon of the absolute. "Damn great Empires! including that of the Absolute," said William James. By the mid-twentieth century that task had been achieved. After the horrors of totalitarianism had been dethroned in World War Two, it was no longer possible to mount a non-religious-based defense of absolutes. Indeed, merely asserting absolutes raised the hackles of commentators more than almost anything else could. Black knew this—he could not even pretend otherwise—but his instinct, reading and ruminations combined to convince him he was merely following the framers' intentions. Except for rare exceptions,* Black would make unlimited free speech the rule unless a valid textual objection interfered.

Calling the First Amendment an "absolute" served several important goals for Black. He could emphasize its positive features while limiting the speech that government could restrain; his approach demanded that terms (such as "abridge" and "freedom of speech") had to be defined—which he would do—and these definitions thereafter bound judges. Judicial discretion would be severely curtailed. The word "absolute" admittedly has broad phil-

---

* The classic example is publication of troop movements in time of (constitutionally declared) "war"; on another level, a witness who lies under oath has no constitutional immunity from prosecution, even though the perjury is pure speech. But the Constitution itself makes something "absolute"—four times in one alone: Article I, section 9 says that "No Bill of Attainder or ex post facto Law shall be passed." No one has ever argued that the framers, meticulous draftsmen that they were, did not mean what they wrote there.

osophical implications, with which Black did not fully agree. But these did not prevent Justices Jackson and Frankfurter from using the word in religious cases. This freedom, Jackson wrote, "was set forth in absolute terms, and its strength is its rigidity." And Frankfurter pointed to "the need for absolute separation" and noted that "the basic Constitutional principle of absolute Separation was violated. . . . Separation means separation, not something less." (Does the shoe feel different on the other foot?)[5]

Nevertheless, why did Black choose the word "absolute"? He told a story about a senator, Irving Brant reported, "who said that when he wanted to accomplish something, he introduced two bills, the one he wanted passed, and another that made the first one seem conservative." In the same way Black wanted to circulate his draft opinions to the other justices as quickly as possible "so they're arguing on *our* grounds"; after he received their comments, he said, "Let's get something to the printer tomorrow." Clever persons of power and purpose would find it that much more difficult to twist his language, based on what he perceived as unconditional prohibitions, toward results they found more congenial. Using "absolutes" was a rhetorical tactic that had the great advantage of making the text the starting point for discussion. Each word has a fixed meaning, Black came to believe. This had changed from 1947, when he wrote in the *Adamson* case, "Since words can have many meanings, interpretation obviously may result in contraction or extension of the original purpose of a constitutional provision. . . ." When it served his end, the Constitution to Black meant what it read—literally. And the First Amendment was given such categorical wording because of the overriding principle it embodied: when free discussion of public affairs is stifled, the philosophical foundation on which a representative democracy rests is undermined.[6]

*   *   *

"The gong has just sounded and Court is out for the term!" Black wrote Fred Rodell in late June 1960. He congratulated Rodell on his style and unusual restraint in a recent *New York Times Magazine* article. Rodell had laid out the opposing Black and Frankfurter views while arguing for an expansive interpretation of the Bill of Rights. The next week, Harvard law professor Louis L. Jaffe replied. "He did not, as so many partisans do," Black told Rodell, "cast personal reflection against those of us who entertain the views he so strongly opposes. I cannot make this same statement about all the members of the Harvard faculty although I wish I could. It seems quite out of place to me for teachers who are supposed to be scholars to attempt to support their views by attributing bad motives or something of the kind to the spokesmen of other views that they criticize. People need not be scholars at all to argue that way."

Black spent the summer in his usual manner, playing tennis and reading his usual fare of the classics, history and law. One of the books was *Government Under Law*, a collection of addresses at Harvard a few years earlier, on the bicentennial of John Marshall. "The implication of each of these articles, unless that of Father Snee is an exception," Black thought, "is that each provision of the Constitution, affirmative or prohibitive, should be measured by the Court on the basis of its 'due process' reasonableness." He had just finished the book when he received a note from Bill Douglas that "on the First Amendment" he should look at a book review by Bickel in the *New Republic*. Black did. It "expresses very much the philosophy which was a central theme of all the discussions at Harvard . . . ," he told Douglas. Quickly he read the book itself, *Legacy of Suppression: Freedom of Speech and Press in Early American History*, by Brandeis University dean and historian Leonard W. Levy.

The combined effect of the two volumes was immediate and terrifying to Black: they "raised disquieting questions about the constitutional future of the United States," he wrote a former clerk. "These seem to be a part of a well organized, carefully planned advocacy of a philosophy which reduces all of the Constitution's affirmations and prohibitions to a rather lowly standard of reasonableness as determined by judges. Whether this is good for a country or not, I am unable to persuade myself up to now that it is what our Constitution meant."

Levy's "revisionist interpretation" struck at the heart of Black's theory that the framers of the First Amendment had a broad understanding of freedom of speech. Levy argued that they had not intended to abolish seditious libel, which made criminal *any* criticism of government, whether true or false, and that only during debates over the Sedition Act of 1798 did writers abandon seditious libel and create a truly libertarian theory of a free press. In 1941 Black had first expressed "the generally accepted historical belief that 'one of the objects of the Revolution was to get rid of the English common law on liberty of speech and of the press.' . . . No purpose in ratifying the Bill of Rights was clearer than that of securing for the people of the United States much greater freedom of religion, expression, assembly, and petition than the people of Great Britain had ever enjoyed." A decade later he claimed, "But the First Amendment repudiated seditious libel. . . . Unless I misread history. . . ."[7] Levy asserted that Black and many others had misread history and, by implication, distorted it for their own libertarian ends. Of course, Black's historical interpretations had been challenged before, but earlier criticism was largely aimed at his belief that the Fourteenth Amendment directly incorporated the Bill of Rights to the states.

The First Amendment was something else. Chipping away at Black's interpretation meant not only some personal repudiation but, more important, damaging the very core of a democratic society. He read Levy's book "with unusual care" and "many parts of it more than once," and "spent a large part of the summer" perusing its sources, Black later noted. Not knowing this, Cahn favorably reviewed the book in the *New York Herald Tribune* and sent the review to Black.[8] Black's reply went through three drafts. The final draft and his next two letters rank among the most vehement and impassioned letters he ever wrote.

The book "strikes one of the most devastating blows ever directed against civil liberty in America," Black said at first. It was "absolutely necessary that someone expose what I consider to be as fallacies, unless the First Amendment becomes less than a tinkling cymbal" or simply "a futile admonition." Levy's book

will give aid and comfort to every person in the country who desires to leave Congress and the states free to punish people under the old English seditious libel label. . . . If seditious libel is permitted in this country . . . I see no obstacle to imprisoning and punishing people here exactly as they were punished in England and in the Colonies before the First Amendment was adopted. I am perfectly willing to admit that Alexander Hamilton, numerous Federalists, and others, probably thought and hoped that the First Amendment could be utilized in such a way as to prosecute people for seditious libel. It seems to me, however, that the facts upon which Dean Levy relies to draw such inferences point precisely in the other direction. . . . I was particularly impressed with the many conclusions that [he] drew from negative premises, that is, from statements of this nature: "While this man talked or wrote in broad, rhetorical language about liberty of speech, press and religion, it must be noticed that he never did specifically and unequivocally express a desire wholly to bar prosecutions for seditious libel." From the many instances cited by Dean Levy of prosecution of people for seditious libel in this country and in England, I draw the inference, quite contrary to [his], that the First Amendment was adopted to bar such prosecutions then and thereafter. . . .

My own basic disagreement with Dean Levy is that I think the First Amendment was intended to give us a "Legacy of Liberty" and not, as he says, a "Legacy of Suppression." . . . I can only say that his book can be most helpful to those who want to leave the way open in this country for

Congress to abridge speech, press, religion and assembly wherever the
Congress and this Court believe that such abridgement is sufficiently necessary in the public interest.

"Unfortunately, . . . those to whom he credits with having given him assistance largely, if not wholly, belong to the school that believes the First
Amendment to be little more than an admonition." Indeed, the first person
Levy had thanked was Frankfurter, who felt privately, however, that Levy
was "very creative and not necessarily very scholarly" in the book. Black
did not know this, and so it was, two days later, that he told Cahn that
Levy's conclusions "will for a long time supply material" to those who favor
a restricted meaning. "If Congress does have power to prosecute for 'seditious
libel' under some circumstances, there is no method that I can conceive of
to put an effective limitation on the boundaries of that power."[9]

Legacy of Suppression remained on Black's mind. It was, he said, "a deliberate
attempt to undermine the First Amendment." Then in 1963 Levy wrote
Black for permission to reprint the Madison Lecture at NYU in a collection
of essays while lavishly praising Black as a judge but not as a historian. "You
rightly assume," Black replied, "that my historical interpretation of the times
about which you write is different from yours. . . . It may well be, as you
suggest, that I have sometimes attributed to Jefferson or Madison positions
and intentions that they did not actually have. My view, however, is that
neither you nor I can *know this.* Words are ambiguous and positions taken
at one time in a man's life may not be consistently followed in every word
uttered thereafter. My own hope and belief is that if you continue to study
the history behind the First Amendment, with a completely open mind
[here Black removed "(if that is possible)" from the final draft], you will
[Black added "as I have"] find ample support for your own "cherished convictions and presuppositions"—a consummation, I think, devoutly to be
wished by those who believe in individual freedom."[10]

The historian dips into the bucket shop of history in an attempt to capture
a pattern, to elucidate a theme, from the variegated mass of materials he
retrieves. History is impressions and incidents, perceptions as well as "facts,"
on paper or not. A train of events, sometimes not seemingly connected,
can take on a life of its own. And to snatch a brittle literalness from an

overflowing, always imprecise past is folly. What is fetched is often the result of what is being looked for. Black was far from alone in unconsciously reading what he wanted into compromises and inconclusive results. The concept of seditious libel was still in state constitutions and hung in the American air while the First Congress considered the Bill of Rights. Not once during those two months was a single voice raised to assert that the First Amendment excluded it. To Black this was of paramount, overriding importance. He treated ideas "as ignorant persons do cherries," as James Russell Lowell said about abolitionist leaders. "They think them unwholesome unless they are swallowed stones and all."[11] The First Amendment swallowed the concept of seditious libel, and to Hugo Black the First Amendment, utterly vital as it was to the country, could not be digested piecemeal. He swallowed it whole.

CHAPTER 34

THE FIRST AMENDMENT
WITH PASSION

E VEN BEFORE THE 1960 TERM BEGAN, Black knew it would be arduous. "More cases of great importance" were on the docket than during any other year since he joined the Court, he told a former clerk. "I can assure you that I am enjoying good health and happiness but I do not anticipate a year in which I shall have to rarely dissent." By the end of the fall First Amendment cases overshadowed all others on the Court's calendar. "Unfortunately," Black wrote Charles Reich, "I am afraid there is considerable education needed . . . if the people are to learn that there is a decided support for changing the name of the 'Bill of Rights' to the 'Bill of Admonitions.' " He could as well have been talking about the Court. In nearly all major free speech cases the justices divided the same way: Frankfurter, Clark, Harlan, Whittaker and Stewart to uphold the restriction; Black, Douglas, Warren and Brennan to strike it down as a violation of the First Amendment.

At the center of the struggle stood Stewart. Patient and tolerant, a thoughtful Ohio Republican in the mold of Robert A. Taft, an old family friend, he took everything and everyone with a grain of salt. He was very proud of having been editor-in-chief of the *Yale Daily News,* and had almost become a journalist. And now "he felt very much on the spot," recalled his law clerk Jerold Israel. "He was feeling his way on the Court, testing the currents. A couple of years later he most likely would have voted differently." The other justices regularly in the majority would not have. Frankfurter was their captain and strongman. He and Harlan gave them an intellectually safe harbor. That port was secure but under incessant attack by civil libertarian forces led by Black. Whether a case concerned a Communist or a miscreant, the same "basic principles of freedom that are responsible for this

Nation's greatness apply," Black wrote in one dissent. "Those principles are embodied for all who care to see in our Bill of Rights. . . . Liberty, to be secure for any, must be secure for all—even for the most miserable merchants of hated and unpopular ideas." "I have your letter . . . ," Black told a former clerk, "and hope you are not 'too hopeful' as to changes that may yet occur."

The case in which he wrote this dissent came down on Black's seventy-fifth birthday. "You have in every way earned a Diamond Jubilee," Chief Justice Warren told him. "Being on the Court with you has been the most stimulating portion of my career," said Tom Clark. The *Washington Post* saluted him "as a free man and as a dauntless champion of freedom." Hugo and Elizabeth cried upon reading Fred Rodell's praise that "this man is meant for the ages." But the most surprising tribute, and the one Black appreciated the most, came from the *Shades Valley Sun,* a newspaper "with a thoroughly Southern outlook" published outside Birmingham, in posh Mountain Brook, Alabama:

> Hugo Black is still moved by those first affections and recollections that belong to a time before the noisy years engulfed him. It is a profound pity that a man with his yearning for the homely aspects of his youth and earlier manhood should be shut out of these gifts. . . . But he should not be shut out of appreciation of his intellectual power, the rich fruitage of a widely ranging mind, and of an unquenchable zest for ascertaining truth as he sees it. . . . From later generations, even in his own South, Hugo Black may receive the compensation of being understood.
>
> Meanwhile, we can at least be seemly in our salutation to a man of five and seventy. . . . With him, [age] is not an affliction, but rather a challenge. Like Tennyson's Ulysses, he may not now have the strength that once moved earth and heaven, but that which he is he is, "strong in will to strive, to seek, to find, and not to yield."[1]

The tributes were wonderful—another vote on the Court would have been better. George Anastaplo's case showed this best. After a distinguished military record in World War Two and finishing at the top of his class at the University of Chicago Law School, he passed the Illinois bar examination and appeared in November 1950 before the State Bar Committee on Character and Fitness. He was a gentle, reserved scholar, but with an iron backbone, so his answer to a question on a personal history form asking him to name the fundamental principles underlying the Constitution was in character: he listed the separation of powers, the Bill of Rights and the right of

revolution. Jefferson in the Declaration of Independence had expressed the
prototypical Enlightenment creed "that whenever any form of government
becomes destructive of these ends"—of life, liberty, and the pursuit of happiness—"it is the right of the people to alter or to abolish it. . . ." Committee members, apparently unaware of this, were alarmed; McCarthyism
had become part of the English language earlier that year. The inevitable
question was asked: "Are you a member of the Communist Party?" Anastaplo
refused to answer since political affiliation was not relevant to the committee's
function; the question violated his constitutional rights, he claimed. The
Illinois courts upheld the committee and he was denied admission to
the bar. He took his case to the Supreme Court, receiving permission to
argue it himself.*

Black emerged uncharacteristically depressed from the December 1960
conference at which the justices considered this and two other bar cases.
"I'm not going to write a dissent this time," he said. "I've written enough
on these." Besides, Anastaplo "is too stubborn for his own good. This whole
thing is a little silly on his part." In March 1961, on a Friday afternoon,
Harlan circulated majority opinions. "Harlan lacks fiber," Grenville Clark,
a founder of Harlan's old law firm, wrote of one of his recent efforts. These
opinions were no different: all displayed a former prominent corporate practitioner's deference to the legal establishment and its disdain for plaintiffs'
lawyers. Black put the opinions in his briefcase.[3]

On Monday morning, stirred to action, he came in with a single dictated
dissent for the three cases. But his clerk, George Saunders, convinced him
that each case merited separate treatment. "I took the poetry the Judge had
dictated and spread it around," Saunders said. Black did not object. On his
own, Saunders went through the record in the Anastaplo case. Now Black
was emotionally involved. In March and April he wrote eight drafts. The
case "is so touching to him," Elizabeth wrote his children, "that when he
reads quotes from the man's reply in question, tears flow down his cheeks."
He and his clerks went through the final draft in his study at home in one

---

* To make ends meet during his appeals, Anastaplo drove a taxi in Chicago. One day he
picked up Joseph H. Daily, an astonished justice of the state's supreme court, who wrote
the majority decision in his first appeal.
  Daily: "You should answer and get admitted. You're not a Communist, are you."
  Anastaplo: "But, Mr. Daily, that is not the point."
  Daily: "No, it's not the point. But you should answer."
  Anastaplo: "It's not a question of Communism."
  Daily: "Well, you should answer anyway. No one ever thought you were a Communist."
(Anastaplo, The Constitutionalist [Dallas, 1971], 338–40; originally emphasized).

long session lasting until after midnight.* Saunders served as scribe. "To get anything into the Judge's opinions," observed his co-clerk Lawrence Wallace, "you had to hear his voice, listen with your inner ear to what he was saying. We got into his wavelength." After "balancing" the various interests involved, Harlan had written that Anastaplo "holds the key to admission in his own hands." Black thought Anastaplo had long ago unlocked the door:

> The effects of the Court's "balancing" here is that any state may now reject an applicant for admission to the bar if he believes in the Declaration of Independence as strongly as Anastaplo and if he is willing to sacrifice his career and his means of livelihood in defense of the freedoms of the First Amendment. But the men who founded this country and wrote our Bill of Rights were strangers neither to a belief in the "right of revolution" nor to the urgency of the need to be free from the control of government with regard to political beliefs and associations. . . . This country's freedom was won by men who, whether they believed in it or not, certainly practiced revolution in the Revolutionary War.
>
> . . . The record clearly shows that conflict resulted, not from any fear on Anastaplo's part to divulge his own political activities, but from a sincere, and in my judgment correct, conviction that the preservation of this country's freedom depends upon adherence to our Bill of Rights. The very most that can fairly be said against Anastaplo's position in this matter is that he took too much of the responsibility of preserving that freedom upon himself.
>
> . . . It is such men as these who have most greatly honored the profession of the law—men like Malsherbes, who, at the cost of his own life and the lives of his family, sprang unafraid to the defense of Louis XVI against the fanatical leaders of the Revolutionary government of France—men like Charles Evans Hughes, Sr., later Mr. Chief Justice Hughes, who stood up for the constitutional rights of socialists to be socialists and public officials despite the threats and clamorous protests of self-proclaimed superpatriots—men like Charles Evans Hughes, Jr., and John W. Davis, who, while against everything for which the Communists stood, strongly advised the Congress in 1948 that it would be unconstitutional to pass the law then proposed to outlaw the Communist Party—men like Lord Erskine, James Otis, Clarence Darrow, and the multitude of others who have dared to speak in defense of causes and clients without regard to personal danger to themselves. The legal profession will lose much of its nobility and its glory if it is not constantly replenished with lawyers like these. To force the bar to

---

* "Your father is working very hard now every night, and has girded his loins to battle," Elizabeth wrote Black's children. "He goes to the office early, works hard all day, and usually while we are waiting on the dinner bell he reads me a draft of one of his dissents. After dinner we come back into the study . . . and he writes on one of his yellow pads until he gets so exhausted he has to go to bed" (ESB to HLB, Jr., SFB and JBP 3/23/61, JBP papers).

become a group of thoroughly orthodox, time-serving, government-fearing individuals is to humiliate and degrade it.

But that is the present trend, not only in the legal profession but in almost every walk of life. Too many men are being driven to become government-fearing and time-serving because the government is being permitted to strike out at those who are fearless enough to think as they please and say what they think. This trend must be halted if we are to keep faith with the founders of our Nation and pass on to the future generations of Americans the great heritage of freedom which they sacrificed so much to leave to us. The choice is clear to me. If we are to pass on that great heritage of freedom, we must return to the original language of the Bill of Rights.

His ending continues to resonate: "We must not be afraid to be free."

George Anastaplo "retired" from the "practice" of law by filing a petition for rehearing with the Supreme Court, which was denied. Over the next ten years he and Black corresponded periodically. Each exchange began with Anastaplo's sending the justice a copy of one of his writings; Black invariably replied that he enjoyed it. "He comes very close to embodying Black's idea of what a lawyer should be," Harry Kalven, Jr., later noted. "Maybe there is no need for you to do so," Black wrote Anastaplo in 1969, "but I take great pride in the course you have followed since your case in Illinois and at this Court. You have acted with great dignity and have, in my judgment, established the fact that you are not destined to be the great extremist which some people thought you were sure to become. I have long thought and still believe that you have the capacity to make a highly useful citizen of this country." Black's "obvious influence" remained as Anastaplo became a teacher and one of the most prolific scholars in the nation.[2]

Black wrote dissents in seven major free speech cases that the Court decided by a 5–4 vote in 1961. The mere mention of the First Amendment always made him lunge for it like a drunk diving for a jigger of whiskey, but even by his standards these dissents were vigorous, spirited and powerful. He condemned the "so-called 'balancing' test" more incisively and for a longer time than any judge ever has, as just a "high-sounding slogan" under which the government can "justify almost any action [it] may wish to take to suppress First Amendment freedoms." The test resembled the old story of the thrifty butcher who weighed his own thumb with every pound of meat sold. "The men who drafted our Bill of Rights did all the 'balancing' that was to be done in this field." Black would have applied the speech-conduct test he had been long urging. The framers, he wrote in one dissent, gave the government "the fullest power to prosecute overt actions in violation of valid laws but withheld any power to punish people for nothing more than advocacy of their views."

Historical analogies studded his opinions as much as legal analyses. He culled them from his reading, or his clerks found them. "He loved them," recalled George Saunders. "He would say, 'even back then, they didn't do this' or 'that's why we left England, fought a war and wrote a constitution.' " To Black history served as much as a precedent as any of the Court's prior rulings. It was alive; the present was merely the cutting edge of the past. He had a stable full of martyrs and dissidents, and he was the casting director, bringing them out as needed. One half expected Jefferson or John Lilburne to walk through the door. Black marched a parade of horribles from English history before the reader, such as a 1593 English law that destroyed all dissenting religious sects and forced all people to become members of the established church.

He asserted historical episodes that gave sanction to his beliefs as if they were immutable truths. But in no way could history be as irrefutable or as one-sided as Black liked to believe. He tried to hold up the framers of the Constitution as patriots of unblemished principle who wrought an almost divine document, not one filled with compromises necessary for passage by ambitious politicos with human frailties. Mention of historical incidents and the framers also enabled him to dramatize his dissents. Perhaps he could then persuade more readers, if not the majority of the Court. "Frequently, in a Black dissent," noted Anthony Lewis, "there is an air of his standing alone against a hostile world—the despairing tone of one who has often fought against long odds."[3]

Black had developed such strong views on language that he could easily have been by himself in almost every case. In *Anastaplo* and *Konigsberg* (the second bar admissions case that term) he pressured Warren and Brennan to go along with him, even though he cited his own former dissents which they had not joined. "It's hard to swallow," they complained. Brennan in particular, despite his deep admiration of Anastaplo, may not have fully agreed with what Black wrote; some formulations were not what he preferred. "You have immortalized George Anastaplo," he told Black. But he and Warren gulped their objections. And now Black did the same thing with some of Warren's opinions.

At his urging, when the Court in 1961 upheld "blue laws" variously forbidding sales on Sundays, Warren altered his test of "establishment" of religion and omitted any qualification of Black's language in the 1947 school busing case.[4] Black wanted to keep the liberal bloc together and was very proud of it. ("I know we're going to lose," Douglas said, "but we're going to make them write and write some more until they crack.") The liberals all got along fine in every way (although Douglas occasionally got peeved at Warren). Black and Brennan were spending much time together socially— he persuaded Brennan to join the Army-Navy Club—and their wives were warm friends. He saw Brennan as the next generation of leadership on the liberal side. "Bill is my heir," he said. But he was very aggravated when someone who usually did what he considered the right thing did the wrong thing and left his reservation. So when Warren wrote the Court's opinion in a tax case, and Brennan joined it (joking to his clerks that it should begin with "Be it enacted," so much did it seem like a statute), Black had to get his feelings out of his system.

The decision, he felt, was bad enough—it allowed for the duplication of punishment in a tax prosecution for what was essentially a single crime— but it overruled a 1946 opinion by Frank Murphy, and that Black did not like. In the privacy of his office Black said that Warren's appointment was just a political payoff. But they worked together as smoothly as any two members of an institution could. (Off the Court they were friendly, but not really close.) Black believed Warren had the right instincts, and that his own job was to provide the scholarship and analysis to back them up. He did this by persuading Warren to change his opinions.[5]

*   *   *

The Court was as polarized intellectually as it had ever been. Frankfurter's camp believed the Court should enter a conflict in which another branch of government had already acted only to maintain harmony within the federal system. It made no difference whether personal liberties might be infringed or claimed economic rights were at stake. The view from the Black barracks exalted this precise distinction as inherent in democracy. Both the wording and import of the Bill of Rights demanded that courts act upon them. The whole debate boiled down to a scale of values, of diverging choices between competing ends. When forced to choose, Frankfurter picked order. Black preferred liberty.

The relationship between the two protagonists had changed again. The aging process had soured and hardened Frankfurter's feelings toward Black.

His fear and distrust of Hugo now reached "something approaching para-
noia," according to one of his clerks, Daniel Mayer. "He had the darkest
and deepest suspicions about Black." Black was "lawless and concerned with
his hidden agenda. He will always try to work something in," Felix said.
Hugo fascinated, intrigued and frustrated him. Underlying it all, however,
was a bottomless intellectual respect. "Hugo Black is absolutely brilliant,
one of the most brilliant legal minds in the United States," Frankfurter said.
"So I've got to be especially sharp for him."

Black's attitude toward Frankfurter was light-years away from Felix's
toward him. He never let a clerk criticize Felix and always defended him.
"I've seen worse on the Court," Hugo said. He was more concerned with
his own business than talking about Felix. They worked together on certain
cases, but it was not always easy. Black badly wanted a unanimous Court
for his 1961 opinion overturning Maryland's religious oath test for public
officeholders. "The Judge had a wonderful time because it involved a history
lesson," recalled his clerk Lawrence Wallace. He quickly dictated a draft
that listed and quoted from several of Frankfurter's opinions. "It's clear Justice
Black drafted this with you in mind," Warren told him. "I've read it very
carefully," Frankfurter replied. "He is the craftiest man ever to sit on this
Court and I'm not going to join it." Frankfurter and Harlan concurred only
in the result.

Such was what Justice Brennan meant when he referred to "some of the
molten material beneath the surface." Frankfurter "closely monitored the
tenor of Harlan's opinions" and "attempted to mold Harlan's jurisprudence
to the subtleties of his thinking," Harlan's biographer has written. So when
Black delivered a dissent to a Harlan opinion, he looked straight at Frankfurter while denouncing the "so-called balancing theory." His tone was
sarcastic.[6]

In April 1961 the Fund for the Republic asked Black to be the guest of honor
at a dinner in early June. Black agreed, and unsuccessfully tried to talk the
sponsors out of having Robert Hutchins deliver a talk on his accomplishments
on the Court. Like Black, Hutchins tried to bring lessons from the classics
to bear on civil liberties. But Black had the same mixed feelings about
Hutchins that he did about many liberals, and often spoke about him to
Edward Levi, who served under Hutchins at the University of Chicago and
was one of his successors as its president. "For years Black usually brought
Hutchins up," Levi recalled. "He approved in general of what Hutchins was

doing. But he said, 'Hutchins is an elitist. It won't help if he doesn't reach the people.' " Hutchins certainly reached his audience at the dinner. "If we explore the Black country," he said, "the world of Justice Black's dissenting opinions, we see that if we lived there we should be living in a different atmosphere. . . . What would be unconstitutional would be limitations or inhibitions on learning. . . . This is the essential content and spirit of its constitution."

Black spoke last. It went the same way every time he made an impromptu speech. He'd meander around at first, getting himself warmed up. Then the words flowed as if he were a preacher who had worked all week preparing his sermon. Black paid tribute to Hutchins's "great contributions to our democratic society." He came "not to speak but to listen. I have no pessimism. I am not afraid of people with silly ideas of converting this country to one which would no longer allow itself to be on a solid basis. I subscribe to the belief that where differences are stifled, freedom and liberty cannot be secured."

Having four solid votes on the Court helped him keep his optimism. In April 1961 Black went to Harvard to speak to the Southern Club. Erwin Griswold's touching introduction left the normally stolid dean on the verge of tears.* Then Black stood up, Elizabeth wrote Hugo's children, "and all the students stood and gave him an enthusiastic standing ovation that must have lasted about five minutes. The Judge was greatly affected and tears came into his eyes, his lips quivered, and it took him a few minutes to be able to speak. He had such a struggle that I felt sorry for him, and I greatly wished that he could laugh off praise as easily as he can criticism. However, he soon regained his composure." He appealed for them to become "lawyers in the great tradition." And he spoke about their common roots. "There are no finer people on earth than Southerners. Their only fault" is that they "are too prone to believe in ancestor worship." He hoped the students who came from Alabama would go back there. It was "a good place even though you'll find there, as in every state of the Union, men and women who are not tolerant, who are not gentle and kind. I trust the American people myself. . . . I congratulate you, all of you. I wish I were in your place. I can tell you from experience that it's a great world. Here's hope and strength and love to those who give hope and strength and love." He closed with a

---

* The same thing happened the year before at the *Harvard Law Review* banquet, recalled John French (int.), who soon clerked for Frankfurter. Griswold was "visibly choked emotionally when he introduced Black."

poem from Virgil that "again made him emotional, and his voice quivered as he read it," Elizabeth noted. "The next day—Sunday—Hugo told me he wanted to go to church. We went to the First Unitarian Church."

Black returned home to finish a lesson in history and civic virtue. Frankfurter, who even before World War Two wanted to deny freedom of speech to Communists ("enough is enough") on the grounds that they were a "Fifth Column" and "not loyal citizens," upheld the registration provisions of the Subversive Activities Control Act. Such a law constitutes "a baseless insult to the patriotism of our people," Black wrote in dissent. Frustrated though he was, he closed his dissent on an upbeat:

> I would reverse this case and leave the Communists free to advocate their beliefs in proletarian dictatorship publicly and openly among the people of this country with full confidence that the people will remain loyal to any democratic government truly dedicated to freedom and justice—the kind of government which some of us still think of as being "the last best hope of earth."[7]

After the term, he felt a deep disillusionment. "I am beginning to wonder more and more," he wrote his former clerk Nicholas Johnson in October 1961, "whether very many people believe in free speech for views they are against. . . . Not even all people who boast about their belief in a bill of rights can stand up under fire in the support of the rights of unpopular people or causes. And of course such a difficult course can only be followed by people who themselves appreciate the value of freedom and who know that suppression of the views of some jeopardizes the freedom of all." Black urged "the formation of an association of young law school professors dedicated to studying, publicizing and working for the freedoms the First Amendment was designed to secure. The right words at the right time can undoubtedly have great effect. "As time goes on . . . ," Black had written in a draft of this letter, "I am more persuaded that one of the worst blows struck against free speech in this country" was Justice Holmes's "cryptic" statement about "shouting fire in a crowded theater." "It is used everywhere to justify [restricting] First Amendment freedoms."[*]

---

[*] Like so many other people, Black got the quotation wrong. In *Schenck v. U.S.* (1919), Holmes wrote, "The most stringent protection of free speech would not protect a man in *falsely* shouting fire in a theater *and causing a panic*" (emphasis added).

That, Black believed, was the undeniable conclusion of Frankfurter and many of the legion of academics and journalists whom Felix strove to bring under his wing to spread his version of the Court's proper role. Black read what Paul Freund, Wallace Mendelson and Anthony Lewis, among others, wrote, and it rankled him. "Is Mr. Lewis an expert on 'legal craftsmanship'?" he scrawled next to Lewis's label of a Harlan opinion in an August 1961 article on the Court's "new lineup." "Not true," Black noted about several statements in Mendelson's 1961 book, *Justices Black and Frankfurter: Conflict on the Court.* (Mendelson, who taught government at the University of Texas, had been a Frankfurter law student and later served as his privately funded research assistant at the Court during the 1953 term.) "Mount Sinai speaking! but untruthfully." But "here he is correct for once"—about the First Amendment. Freund "all along here is assuming we should and do decide on constitutionality by weighing values, not by interpreting the language of the constitution," Black complained in marginal comments in Freund's 1960 volume, *The Supreme Court of the United States.* "He has not made the real textual arguments" to support civil liberties. What these authors shared was a deep attachment to Harvard Law School and the intellectual restraint it stood for on the issues that mattered most to Black. "It would be good for Harvard to get a few professors who have some fresh ideas," Black soon wrote a former clerk who was offered a job there.[8]

*   *   *

In October 1961 Edmond Cahn told Black he had suggested to the American Jewish Congress that it honor the justice's approaching twenty-fifth anniversary on the Court. Black's typical reluctance to accept institutional honors did not put Cahn off. He got himself invited to dinner and told Hugo that the idea of a "public interview" had arisen. (Cahn had proposed it.) He simply planned to raise the standard objections to Black's constitutional philosophy so Hugo could refute them. Black accepted because no preparation would be necessary. It would be a pleasant couple of days in New York. He had agreed to deliver the Carpentier Lectures at Columbia University at some point but he hadn't done any real work on them. "Too many speeches," he complained. "All I want to do is write and work."

Cahn opened the April 14, 1962, interview by asking why Black asserted in his Madison Lecture at NYU that "there *are* 'absolutes' in our Bill of Rights." "The really basic reason why I believe that 'no law' means no law," the justice answered, is "that I took an obligation to support and defend the Constitution as I understand it. And being a rather backward country fellow,

I understand it to mean what the words say. Gesticulations apart, I know of no way in the world to communicate ideas except by words." Government could preserve itself only by "leaving people with the utmost freedom to think and to hope and to talk and to dream if they want to dream." Cahn then asked: "Do you make an exception in freedom of speech and press for the law of defamation? That is, are you willing to allow people to sue for damages when they are subjected to libel or slander?"

> JUSTICE BLACK: My view of the First Amendment, as originally ratified, is that it said Congress should pass none of these kinds of laws. As written at that time, the Amendment applied only to Congress. I have no doubt myself that the provision, as written and adopted, intended that there should be no libel or defamation law in the United States under the United States Government, just absolutely none as far as I am concerned. . . .
>
> My belief is that the First Amendment was made applicable to the states by the Fourteenth. I do not hesitate, so far as my own view is concerned, as to what should be and what I hope will sometime be the constitutional doctrine that just as it was not intended to authorize damage suits for mere words as distinguished from conduct as far as the Federal Government is concerned, the same rule should apply to the states. . . .
>
> I believe with Jefferson that it is time enough for government to step in to regulate people when they *do* something, not when they *say* something, and I do not believe myself that there is *any* halfway ground if you enforce the protections of the First Amendment.

This response startled Cahn. Six years earlier, based on his conversations with Black, he had written: "Certainly Justice Black has not contended that the sponsors of the First Amendment expected it to end civil actions for defamation. I understand he would freely grant the existence of this 'exception.' " Now Black had changed his position. He had stopped just short of doing so in a 1959 obscenity case. And in 1961 he had written: "The freest interchange of ideas about all public matters . . . , of course, means the interchange of *any* ideas. . . ." His clerks were not surprised; they had heard this before. "It wouldn't bother me," Black now said, "if there were no libel or slander laws. They infringe on free speech." This was simply an extension of his thinking, but no other judge or commentator had ever taken such a position before, and none has since. Black had never said this in an opinion, nor would he ever. It was too far out and it wouldn't get any votes. Afterward Cahn asked him when he expected courts to accept his position. "Never," Black answered.

Why, then, would he speak at some length about it and even mention

seditious libel and "political libel suits" in Alabama? The Alabama Supreme
Court was considering a case of seditious libel against the *New York Times.*
The paper's chances of winning there ranged between zero and none, and
it would likely appeal to the United States Supreme Court. By forcefully
rejecting the principle of any libel laws, Black was also declaring that any
seditious libel law (which, he said, "is nothing in the world except the
prosecution of people who are on the wrong side politically") was unconstitutional. That would certainly be one of the *Times'* central points on
appeal. Black could test the waters to see if the idea would float. If some
people thought he went too far, he could always pull back and say that the
First Amendment protected all speech about public affairs. He would not
get much of an argument, and would achieve his goal of purging the law of
the detestable seditious libel.

Concluding the interview, Black summarized his conception of the
judge's role in cases arising under the First Amendment and the Bill of
Rights:

> I am for the First Amendment from the first word to the last. . . . I believe
> it means what it says. . . . I have never been shaken in the faith that the
> American people are the kind of people and have the kind of loyalty to
> their government that we need not fear the talk of Communists. Let them
> talk! In the American way, we will answer them.

The interview was a rousing success. The criticism Black expected was,
surprisingly, not at all vituperative. Indeed it was almost understanding in
tone and invariably respectful. He had long ago gained the admiration of
all but his bitterest enemies. Many in the press and the legal profession
strongly disagreed with his position on libel; few otherwise openly objected.
But the *Saint Louis Post-Dispatch* spoke for many people when it said that
those who differed "owe the nation a more precise explanation of where
government can invade rights that the First Amendment gives to the people."

Libertarians were ecstatic. Black was "our boy."[9] But on the Supreme
Court he still needed one more vote to convert his minority views into
majority doctrine. The search for it preoccupied him. How could he get it?

VI

THE COURT YEARS,
1962–1971

CHAPTER 35

TRIUMPH

THE SUPREME COURT took a needed collective breath in the fall of 1961. The cases did not produce much controversy or tension—with one exception: a challenge to the Tennessee legislative districting law. A statute passed in 1901 still determined the composition of the state assembly, despite the state constitutional requirement of reapportionment every ten years. As in many states, representation was wildly disproportionate. A legislator from an urban district represented fifteen times as many people as one from a rural area. The subject was a political question, beyond judicial remedy, the Court had said in 1946 over Black's dissent, and it had refused to hear any further challenges.

The justices in April 1961 divided evenly on whether the matter was within the jurisdiction of the federal courts: Warren, Black, Douglas and Brennan thought yes while Frankfurter, Clark, Harlan and Whittaker said no. Stewart was undecided. "I'll be the sixth vote for jurisdiction but not the fifth," Whittaker said. That set Frankfurter off like an alarm clock. "Felix really berated him," Black said later. He talked for four and a half hours, going to the shelves to get cases, reading from them, powerfully arguing that *Colegrove v. Green* (his 1946 opinion) had been correct, and looking directly at Whittaker the whole time. After a while Black had enough and walked out. The justices agreed to put the case over to the next term.

One day after reargument in October 1961, Frankfurter circulated a lengthy memorandum arguing that this was not a case in which a state had denied Negroes, Jews or redheads a vote or given them only a small fraction of one. Next to this Black scrawled: "But it is a case in which a state has given persons—not only Negroes or Jews—¼ or 1/40th of a vote. . . . The

517

legislature and government have administered the [state constitution] provision with an unequal hand." At conference the expected comments were made. But the justices were waiting to hear from Stewart. When he said that the malapportionment in this case was so extreme it could not have a rational basis, that made the vote five to four.

Warren waited ten days, as opposed to the usual three or four, before assigning the opinion in *Baker v. Carr*. He did not want to write and talked it over with Black and Douglas while Black also discussed it several times with Stewart. Black and Douglas urged Warren to assign it to Brennan, because it would then be easier to get Stewart to go along. Warren did, and Brennan hugged the middle of the majority in holding that apportionment was a justiciable matter for federal courts and that they could provide relief. *Colegrove*, one of the edifices in Frankfurter's juristic crown, was rejected.[1]

Frankfurter's pounding of Whittaker took its toll. Overwhelmed by the work, way over his head intellectually, Whittaker suffered a nervous breakdown. "Certainly Frankfurter was a major factor in causing it," said Whittaker's son. He spent most of March 1962 at Walter Reed Hospital and retired at the end of the month, just after *Baker* came down. To replace him President John F. Kennedy named Deputy Attorney General Byron R. White. "Jack thought he'd be a great liberal," said his old friend Harvey Poe, co-director with White of Citizens for Kennedy in 1960. "But Byron has a quirky streak. He likes it that nobody really knows him or his views. He enjoys being individualistic." Frankfurter should have retired when he suffered his heart attack, Warren thought, since "he wasn't up to the job any more." And, Warren later said, he protested bitterly, louder and longer and more vehemently in *Baker* than in any other case since Warren came on the Court. On April 5, 1962, while sitting at his desk at the Court ten days after the decision, Felix Frankfurter suffered a stroke. Black was shocked and deeply concerned. "I am very happy to learn that you are getting better every day," he wrote Felix, who couldn't talk or walk. ". . . I hope you will not let Court business disturb you. In this way you can get back sooner and continue your long and highly useful public service." Hugo was only repeating what he had always felt.

In early August, Felix went to see Hugo at home. They talked in Felix's car. He asked many questions about Hugo's children, "expressing the deepest kind of interest," because they were also Josephine's children, Hugo wrote them. Frankfurter hoped to return to the Court but did not show much improvement, and Warren, afraid of the effect his indisposition was having on cases and wanting a more liberal justice, tried to persuade him to retire.

He did, on August 28, 1962. "We're going to miss you on the Court because we need you," Hugo soon told him. "When some of my friends say to me 'things will be easier on the Court now,' I tell them they couldn't be more wrong." Somewhat more accurately, Black wrote a former clerk: "While I think [Felix's] constitutional philosophy cannot possibly bring about adequate protection of the liberties safeguarded by the Bill of Rights, I think he has done a fine job on the whole. Of course we both know he is a brilliant man. He loves this country and the Supreme Court very much, indeed."[2]

Hugo remained attentive to Felix, visiting him regularly. He congratulated Felix for receiving the lifetime service award of the American Bar Association. "No one is as competent as you to assess the worth of my work on and for the Court," Felix replied. Hugo remained on his mind. "He said Black was so able that he could have done much more, gotten more majorities, but that he didn't because he wanted more to move the Court than to moderate his position," recalled David Ginsburg. Their last exchange came in December 1964. A dissent of Hugo's, upholding a conviction in a sit-in case, stirred Felix to tell him of "my pride in you." Their agreement "was not surprising," Hugo replied.

> More than a quarter of a century's close association in the Supreme Court's exacting intellectual activities has enabled both of us, I suspect, to anticipate with reasonable accuracy the basic position both are likely to take on questions that importantly involve the public welfare and tranquility. Our differences, which have been many, have rarely been over the ultimate end desired, but rather have related to the means that were most likely to achieve the end we both envisioned. Our years together, and these differences, have but added to the respect and admiration that I had for *Professor* Frankfurter even before I knew him—his love of country, steadfast devotion to what he believes to be right, and to his wisdom. Feeling this way you can understand what I mean by saying to you it "was good to get your letter."

When Felix's condition worsened, Hugo took only JoJo to see him. "It was moving," she recalled. "Justice Frankfurter was dying and Daddy knew it." He wept when he learned, from a newspaper, of Felix's death in February 1965, as he was driving home from Florida. For his tribute in that most fitting of places, the *Harvard Law Review*, Hugo reviewed their correspondence. Their differences were more over means than ends, he noted. Felix was "a formidable adversary" who "thrived on argument. . . . My initial respect and friendship for Felix survived all differences of opinion, in fact grew with the years. . . ."

Harvard Law School has reason to be proud of Professor Frankfurter. American lawyers have reason to be proud of Lawyer Frankfurter. The Supreme Court has reason to be proud of Mr. Justice Frankfurter. The United States has reason to be proud of Felix Frankfurter, who came to this country as an idealistic immigrant and for the rest of his life gave to it the fullest measure of loving, intelligent, effective service. I am happy to have had the opportunity and good fortune to have served with him for twenty-three years and seven months; to argue with him; to agree with him; to disagree with him; and to live a large part of my life in the light of his brilliant intellect, his buoyant spirit and his unashamed patriotism. This was a man. We need more like him.

After drafting it, Hugo said: "Well, now that I have written about my deep and sincere friendship for Felix, I feel free to write my views on how mistaken his views were." Hugo had been doing that since shortly after Felix came on the Court, and once he had retired, the Court began doing it.[3]

*   *   *

Frankfurter's replacement by Arthur J. Goldberg, Kennedy's secretary of labor, was one of the turning points in modern Supreme Court history. For the first time in nearly twenty years a majority of five justices was ready to press vigorously for the strong protection of the Bill of Rights. The Court could now defend the claims of those upon whom the law acts. In *Baker v. Carr* the Court had not discussed the question of standards. The justices wanted state and lower federal courts to deal with them. But in conference the next year Douglas said the measure should be "one man, one vote." In his opinion for the Court this became "one person, one vote": the catchy new standard was quickly applied. Both houses of a state legislature must be apportioned to reflect "approximate equality," Warren held in 1964. At the same time Black extended the principle to congressional districts. "As nearly as practicable one man's vote in a congressional election is to be worth as much as another's," he wrote for seven justices. The framers intended each citizen to have an equal vote in choosing representatives.

The New York State Board of Regents, a governmental agency, had composed and recommended, but not required, for use in public schools at the start of each day a twenty-two-word prayer: "Almighty God, we acknowledge our dependence upon Thee, and we beg Thy blessings upon us, our parents, our teachers and our Country." Five parents of children attending a New Hyde Park, Long Island (New York) public school objected that the prayer violated separation of church and state as well as freedom of religion, and brought suit. Black longed to hear the case but feared the Court would decide it wrong. "I want to know what these guys do before I vote to take it," he said. Their seven-to-two vote to hear it relieved him. He worked himself up before the April 6, 1962, conference—the case went to the whole purpose of why we have a constitution. The prayer patently violated the First Amendment, he told his colleagues. All seven justices sitting agreed, except Stewart, who passed. Black told Warren, when they discussed opinion assignments afterward, that he wanted to write the majority opinion. When Warren left, Black smiled and told his clerks he was writing it.

A more formally irreligious man would have been hard to find. Black had long since drifted away from organized religion. Even though he never quite felt there was a hereafter, he and Elizabeth sometimes went to services at the All Souls Unitarian Church. "Hugo says he's going to hold on to Dr. Howlett because he's his closest connection to God," she wrote in her diary. (Duncan Howlett, the minister, was the successor to Hugo's friend Powell Davies.) In 1964 Black contributed $100 to All Souls "to be used in such of its activities as it sees fit," he wrote. "It is a pleasure to be able to do this." Soon Hugo said, "I can't exactly believe and I can't exactly not believe."

"People had been tortured, their ears lopped off, and sometimes their tongues cut or their eyes gouged out, all in the name of religion," Hugo told Elizabeth while working on the case. He advocated religious diversity because "when one religion gets predominance, they [sic] immediately try to suppress others." That was what he feared about the Catholic Church. His dislike culminated in reading Paul Blanshard's outspokenly anti-Catholic tracts. Theology never interested Black even though he knew the Bible well since childhood. But his belief in man's unending struggle against the perversities of his own nature, which only one's will could overcome, strongly resembled modern Christian realism. Black was imbued with Protestantism's strongly individualistic character. If democracy is Protestantism in its secular form and relevant to the present age, he viewed his main task on the Court as protecting the people's impulses from state intrusion and compulsion in any form.

That was his goal in writing the opinion. But first he read, starting with the Book of Common Prayer and John Bunyan, both of which he reread. "The Judge had religious references on his fingertips," recalled his clerk George Saunders. "He read them and told me to go to the library to get more. We split these. I served as the traffic cop. If I thought a book were worthwhile, I'd give it to him and he'd take it home. If I didn't think so, we'd talk whether he should read it. But he landed up reading everything I took out." After a few weeks, Black felt ready to dictate a draft declaring that the regents' prayer violated the First Amendment's establishment of religion clause based on the Court's past decisions, and he added some historical observations to round out the opinion. (He kept *The Pilgrim's Progress* on his desk throughout.) The cumulative effect of his reading was apparent by the time of the fourth draft in late May. It contained as much historical discussion as legal analysis. In a fifth draft, dated June 1, Saunders added some more history, and in a sixth, a footnote that gave some hint as to the opinion's outer limits.* This came in response to Justice Stewart's sole dissent, in which he perceived no establishment of religion in "letting those who want to say a prayer say it."

Black's published opinion, except for the opening statement of facts, is almost completely an excursion into the history of church-state relations in England and America in the sixteenth, seventeenth and eighteenth centuries. The framers, he concluded, intended to prohibit all establishments of religion like the regents' prayer program: there can be "no doubt that [the] daily invocation of God's blessings . . . is a religious activity. . . . It is no part of the business of government to compose official prayers for any group of the American people to recite as a part of a religious program carried on by the government." The result should have been obvious ever since the Court first held that the establishment clause applied to the states. Perhaps that was why Black did not cite one substantive case supporting his points.

When delivering the opinion, he leaned forward, resting his arms on the bench, and read with considerable emotion. He gave a brief résumé of the case, then paused, grasped his paper more firmly and, "his voice deeper and with the faintest tremble" (noted one reporter), said that New York had "adopted a practice wholly inconsistent with the Establishment clause." No one who heard Black could doubt his sincerity. The First Amendment, he continued, expressed the framers' belief that religion "is too personal, too sacred, too holy to permit its 'unhallowed perversion' by a civil magis-

---

* There is of course nothing in the decision reached here that is inconsistent with the fact that school children and others are officially encouraged to express love for our country by reciting historical documents such as the Declaration of Independence which contain references to the Deity or by singing officially espoused anthems which include the composer's profession of faith in a Supreme Being, or with the fact that there are many manifestations in our public life of belief in God. [372 U.S. at 435 n.21.]

trate." Again, "his voice trembled with emotion," wrote one observer, "as he paused over 'too personal, too sacred, too holy.' " He pointed out it did not mean that songs with the word "God" could not be sung. And he added extemporaneously, "The prayer of each man from his soul must be his and his alone."[4]

The hurricane of protest unleashed, from politicians and prelates alike, both surprised and pained the justices. President Kennedy's quick and strong support defused some of this vitriol, but fifty-odd bills to overturn the decision were nevertheless introduced in the House of Representatives. Justice Clark soon defended the Court publicly. The Constitution, he told the American Bar Association, provides "that both state and federal governments shall take no part respecting the establishment of religion or prohibiting the free exercise thereof. 'No' means 'No.' That was all the Court decided." Reading this, Black had to chuckle at its familiar sound.

As quickly as the opinion was released, the phone in Black's chambers started ringing without a stop. And more than one thousand letters tumbled in. He answered the "nice" ones, but not those that abused the Court or its decision.* It was a "real education" to read them, he thought. While most letters coming from Protestants were approving, "the biggest percentage of group approval have come from Baptists, Jews and Quakers. These letters indicate to me that it would practically require a miracle to secure a vote by the people of the United States favorable to changing the First Amendment," as some congressmen in their fury wanted. Many people wrote to say they changed their minds about the decision once they read it; often this was after he sent it to them. But in Alabama only the intervention of his old political friend Harwell Davis saved him from further criticism. "Don't come down too hard on Black. He's a good guy," Davis told several Birmingham preachers, and they didn't. A letter to his niece Hazel Davis, three days after the most controversial decision Black ever wrote, summed up his feelings:

> The basic premise of the First Amendment is that people must be left to
> say their prayers in their own way, and to their own God, without express

---

* One exception was a dispatch from a woman who condemned him to hell, without a hearing, he said. If she would go to the library, as he was sure she didn't have it in her house, and ask for a book called the Bible, he replied, she could read where it said, "Pray in your own closet" (HLB, Memoirs, 95).

or explicit coercion from any political office holder. There are not many
people with religion and intelligence who will think this constitutional
principle wrong on mature second thought. To those who think prayer
must be recited parrot-like in public places in order to be effective, the
sixth chapter of Matthew, 1 to 19, might be reflected upon, particularly
verses 5 through 8.

Seventy Baptist ministers, concerned about the Court's religious opinions,
visited Black in May 1964. They sat on the floor of the conference room,
questioning him and telling him about the enmity some of their congre-
gations felt toward the Court. He hoped people would not lose their religious
convictions, for religious people conceived the Constitution, he said. Educate
your people but basically "just let 'em talk."[5]

The day of the prayer opinion, as soon as the Court was seated and the crier
had bellowed "God save the United States and this honorable Court," Solicitor General Archibald Cox stood up. Black was completing his twenty-
fifth term, "a rare event in the Court's history," he noted, and he wished
to "mention Mr. Justice Black's extraordinarily great contributions . . . to
the country, to the law and to the Court." Chief Justice Warren responded
briefly. "This is, indeed, a significant event in the life of the Court." Only
sixteen previous justices had served as long, "and none with greater fidelity
or singleness of purpose." Justice Black's "unflagging devotion has been to
the Constitution of the United States." It was "with affectionate regard"
that the Court recorded his service in its proceedings, the only time this
has been done. Black, surprised, sank back in his chair expressionless.

When the next term started in October 1962, he looked ahead and
back. "Why do you stop me at thirty-five? My health is still good," he told
John Frank, who had suggested Black might serve another ten years. Indeed,
"Twenty-five years do not seem nearly so long in retrospect as they do when
looking forward," he wrote another clerk. "The events of my appointment
seem to be about as vivid now as they were when they took place." His law
clerks threw a party for him. Afterward, Black wrote his first clerk, Buddy
Cooper:

You are the only clerk who stayed with me three years. Those three years
were my first and helped to shape the direction of all the years after them.
During those three years, we fought together, worked together and wrote
together. At the 25th anniversary dinner Judge Skelly Wright [recently

appointed to the federal appeals court in Washington] read, with considerable emotion, the closing part of *Chambers v. Florida*. I explained to those here at that time the difficulty I had always had in reading those closing words without emotion. You can understand.[6]*

*   *   *

In his first term Black held for the Court that in federal criminal trials an indigent defendant was entitled to a court-appointed lawyer. Defense counsel was necessary "to complete the court." It was a simple thought—that a lawyer for a poor defendant was as important as the prosecutor and judge—but Black could not persuade his colleagues to expand the principle. In *Betts v. Brady* in 1942 the justices explicitly rejected his call for the right to counsel in all serious state criminal cases. Instead, in a series of cases they took a defendant's "special circumstances" into account and looked to such factors as his age, education, mental condition and the complexity of the crime. Despite the growth of legal aid, the court often remained incomplete.

In 1956 the Court took a step to fill it up. Black firmly established the right of an indigent defendant to an effective hearing on appeal by holding, for a sharply divided Court, that a state must furnish a free transcript to an appellant in a noncapital case. "There can be no equal justice where the kind of trial a man gets depends on the amount of money he has," he wrote. By the end of the 1950s the Court had not upheld a single state conviction against a claim of special circumstances, yet *Betts* remained on the books. So Black changed tactics. By now, as his former clerks became seasoned and established in their practices, he had a ready pool of talent to draw on. In several instances when an appropriate pauper's case arose from an area (other than Alabama) in which one of those clerks lived, the Court appointed that clerk as counsel. (He was the first justice to have his clerks thus appointed in even an irregular way.) None of these cases challenged *Betts* directly; but perhaps its fringes could be eliminated, he thought, until he had the votes to overturn it completely in the proper case.

Even before the 1961 term began, the Court, including Frankfurter, determined to find that case. A defendant claimed his Florida conviction was invalid because, even though he could not afford a lawyer, he had not

---

* "I would still rank *Chambers v. Florida* very high among decisions expressing my constitutional views," Black had recently written. "This is not merely because of the emotional appeal evoked by the manner in which those young Negroes were treated, but because my views about due process later amplified in my *Adamson* dissent and many other cases were all pretty accurately foreshadowed by what I said in *Chambers*" (to Irving Dilliard dated 7/25/63, but the contents clearly indicate 1962).

been offered one. "I'd meet *Betts* and overrule it," Black declared at conference on February 25, 1962. Frankfurter disagreed, simply wanting to base a reversal on *Betts*. Douglas, Brennan and Whittaker supported Black; Clark, Harlan and Stewart approved Frankfurter's approach; undecided was Warren, who favored scrapping *Betts* but was reluctant to do so by only a bare majority. But Frankfurter had written Brennan, "I think I'm prepared in view of the change of climate and of legislation to spell out my view of due process and overrule Betts and Brady," even if not in this "unsavory" case.

The Court, in an opinion by Brennan that came down after Whittaker retired and Frankfurter had his stroke, reversed the conviction based on *Betts*. Although he joined Brennan's opinion, Black wrote a concurrence stressing *Betts*'s "basic failure as a constitutional guide." It was now time to hold that defendants in *all* criminal cases were entitled to counsel. He did not want, he told Brennan, to leave the impression "that the right to a lawyer under state law depends entirely upon a 'shock the conscience' due process concept." He opposed this "stretching-contracting meaning of 'due process' " as strongly as ever. Any repudiation of *Betts* would be "wholly incomplete . . . if it is at the cost of leaving as the only standard . . . that of the accordion-like meaning of due process. . . ." Unless he wrote, Black stated in another note to Brennan, the "accordion followers" would cite this case "as a plain holding that accepts that concept. . . . That philosophy, I think, more and more leaves this country no bill of rights except as doled out by this Court."

Clarence Earl Gideon was indicted for breaking and entering, in a poolroom in Panama City, Florida, with intent to commit a crime. The trial judge refused his request for a lawyer. Forced to conduct his own defense, he was convicted; and this was confirmed on appeal. He then sent the Supreme Court a petition, scrawled in pencil in his childlike handwriting on lined prison sheets, claiming he had been denied due process because he had been denied counsel. The justices decided in June 1962 to hear Gideon's case and appointed Abe Fortas to represent him. Counsel were specifically requested to discuss: "Should this Court's holding in *Betts v. Brady* be reconsidered?" Fortas argued the case masterfully, and the justices voted unanimously in January 1963 to reverse Gideon's conviction and to overrule *Betts*. Appropriately, Warren assigned the opinion to Black. He drafted it in Miami, where, as usual, he spent most of the Court's winter recess.

"I decided to write this way instead of dictating because I wanted to use many quotes from Betts, Powell and Palko," Black noted when he mailed the opinion to Washington. *Powell v. Alabama* was the leading case besides *Betts* on the right to counsel, and *Palko v. Connecticut* was Cardozo's classic formulation of the selective (or piecemeal) incorporation of the Bill of Rights into the Fourteenth Amendment, which Black had been castigating for more than twenty years now. Nevertheless, in this and two later drafts Black approvingly used its necessarily imprecise rhetoric. He had his clerk Dick Howard take the first draft to Brennan with this note:

> On study and after reflection I decided the thing to do was to meet the "absorption" idea that you have head on. There is no intimation in that I have written of an en masse application of the Bill of Rights to the States, something that can be made wholly clear if you wish, by a footnote or otherwise. I . . . cannot now imagine that there is anything in the draft that will bother you. Maybe Potter will not go along, but so far as you, Bill Douglas, the Chief and I are concerned, I cannot think of a legitimate way we can escape something like I have written. Of course we could use some weasel words but it seems to me that the time has come to spell out what we really think in this field. Whether through the 14th Amendment as a whole or the due process alone, as I understand your view it is that in line with the Palko view those Bill of Rights provisions control states that are "fundamental" or some language like that.

"I could not be more enthusiastic about your proposed opinion . . . ," Brennan replied. "I think it's exactly right." He particularly welcomed the opinion's brevity. (As published, it was only ten pages long.) Black agreed to add some thoughts on "the important necessity for counsel in our adversary system of Justice," and Howard drafted a page.

"This doesn't read like your *Adamson*" (Black's 1947 case advocating the total application of the Bill of Rights to the states), Brennan said when Black returned to Washington. "Well yes," Black replied. "It is different because we're in the majority now." But Hugo wanted as many votes as possible and he sent the draft to Justices Stewart, White and Goldberg for their reactions before circulating it generally. They all agreed. Douglas, remembering the battles over *Betts*, noted, "This is a fine opinion and I am glad I lived long enough to see it come down." He, Clark and Harlan said they would each write separately, and concurred at least in the result. That did not disturb Black, because now that he had the votes, the result—more than the theory of a decision—was the important thing.[7]

Black's life reads like a study in the struggle between the ideal and the possible. This is an underappreciated aspect of him, given his insistence on

principle. The best feasible outcome was his goal. He considered opinions
for the Court victories, battles already won, and by this point in his life he
didn't even care who wrote them. But dissents were the future. He had a
distaste for values notable only for their nobility, and wouldn't say much if
one raised them. "I'm not going to let any wild-eyed hypothetical interfere
with my theory," he said. He didn't pick fights when he was hopelessly
outgunned and outmanned. "What is practicable must often control what
is pure theory," Jefferson wrote. Black underlined it. When he had a majority,
he would do anything to keep his troops in line. "Sometimes I have to use
words to hold my court," he later said with a smile. "They're just semantics.
They mean nothing to me." In *Gideon* he used the due process approach,
which he otherwise despised. "Hugo knows exactly what he's doing here,"
Brennan said. The framers of the Constitution did not intend to give in-
digents charged with crime a constitutional right to counsel at public expense: they aimed more broadly, to guarantee a defendant a fair trial. For
this the right to counsel was required. Black was applying old general principles to modern particulars unforeseen when the document was drafted.
(Could he have been doing what he continually criticized Frankfurter for
doing?)

The Court, Black wrote, accepted the assumption of *Betts* that a provision of the Bill of Rights that is "fundamental and essential to a fair trial"
is binding on the states through the Fourteenth Amendment. "The right
to the aid of counsel is of this fundamental character. . . . Any person hauled
into court, who is too poor to hire a lawyer, cannot be assured a fair trial
unless counsel is provided for him. This seems to us to be an obvious truth"—
short, sweet and simple.

On March 18, 1963, Black smiled and chatted cheerfully as he drove
in to work with his clerk, as he often did when a clerk lived nearby. When
Warren called on him on the bench, he leaned forward and spoke in an
almost folksy way, reading sections of his opinion. Happiness, contentment,
gratification filled his voice. "When *Betts v. Brady* was decided," he said a
few weeks later, "I never thought I'd live to see it overruled." (Anthony
Lewis inscribed *Gideon's Trumpet*, his moving account of the case, "For Mr.
Justice Black, who first heard the sound of the trumpet.") "*Gideon* was real
exuberance," said Dick Howard. "It was a classic incorporation case. The
Judge knew he was summing up thirty years of cases, knitting up in this
area. It gave him special pleasure." ("Hello, or should I say, congratulations!"
Lewis said to Elizabeth as she left the courtroom.) It was indeed a moment
of supreme satisfaction, one of the highlights of Black's years on the Court.[8]

....

Black's emphasis in *Gideon* almost made him seem an apostle of the "living Constitution," adapting the document to new conditions, as Frankfurter had always championed. And, just before the opinion appeared, "Mr. Justice Black and the Living Constitution" was the title of an appreciative article in the *Harvard Law Review* by his former clerk Charles Reich, now teaching at Yale Law School. It had to surprise Black to read of his "method of construing provisions of the Bill of Rights in the light of current problems." But Black looked upon Reich with "parental pride" and wrote:

> Last night I spent about two hours reading an article of yours on a subject which is not wholly without interest to me. The first thing I thought about, however, was how very, very much work you had put into that article. Quite a number of people have already told me what a magnificent job they thought you had done. . . . I agreed with them. That is not to say, as you would know from our many controversies over points of law while you were my clerk and since, that I necessarily agree with every word you wrote. Your article would not have been *your* article, however, and it would not have pleased me as much had you not revealed here and there just a wee bit of the Reich as well as the Black philosophy. . . . Of course, you know that I apreciate the work you have put into the article largely because I appreciate you.

Privately, however, Black told his clerks that Reich had skewed his philosophy: "He doesn't understand me at all."

At the same time a volume of Black's civil liberties opinions appeared. Alfred Knopf put the idea to Black in 1959. Of course Hugo wouldn't mind; "The only suggestion I would make . . . is perhaps that you would lose money because you could not sell enough." Knopf thought Irving Dilliard would be the "best man" to select and edit the opinions, and Black agreed. He had long liked and admired Dilliard, who had recently stepped down as editorial page editor of the *Saint Louis Post-Dispatch*. A devoted civil libertarian and the first editorial writer (indeed the first journalist at all) who specialized in legal affairs, Dilliard had written numerous editorials and articles praising Black and the Court, and had sent many of them to him.

"The glory that is Hugo LaFayette Black," Dilliard exulted as he worked on the book. But Black felt Knopf published *One Man's Stand for Freedom* "more largely because of your friendship for me than on account of any hope of financial return. As for myself I sincerely hope that the publication may help at least to give people a keener appreciation of our Constitution and

Bill of Rights." ("About the only thing I can say about those opinions," he wrote a friend, "is that they represent a lot of hard work.") Knopf insisted his interest stemmed "not so much from my friendship for you as from my admiration for you. Good deeds do not always go unrewarded. . . ." The book received wide attention, selling over 10,000 copies, and spread Black's beliefs to even more people.

Black was at ease. "He was riding high and winning cases," said Dick Howard, who clerked for him in the 1962 and 1963 terms. "He had boundless good humor. He talked about 'shock the conscience' a lot and loved to fight the old fights with Felix. It made him happier if the clerk would supply the references. He used them as a child would tell favorite horror stories. But he dismissed the critics. There was a detachment toward them."[9] Serene, however, Hugo Black could not be, not as long as there were cases to be won.

Applying the Bill of Rights to the states was still his cause. Throughout the 1960s almost every one of its major guarantees relating to the criminal process was so applied. The Court achieved this result by finding each individual guarantee fundamental, one by one, rather than incorporating them in one fell swoop, as Black preferred. He spoke for the Court in only one of the cases as he and Warren evenly spread these assignments, and he used the same test of "fundamental" rights untied to any specific constitutional language. But the destination was more important to him than the route by which he reached it. As he wrote in a 1968 concurrence, "I am very happy to support this selective process." The outcome was "the big thing" the Court had done in recent years, he said in 1967, quickly adding that he was not claiming "sole credit."

Equally important was keeping the courts out of passing on economic and social legislation. "Under the system of government created by our Constitution, it is up to legislatures, not courts, to decide on the wisdom and utility of legislation," Black wrote in 1963 in upholding Kansas's right to limit the practice of debt collection to lawyers. ". . . Whether the legislature takes for its textbook Adam Smith, Herbert Spencer, Lord Keynes, or some other is no concern of ours. The Kansas debt adjusting statute may be wise or unwise. But relief, if any be needed, lies not with us but with the body constituted to pass laws for the State of Kansas."

Black hoped the case would eradicate substantive due process. His first draft decisively rejected the "meaning of due process [that] allows courts to strike down statutes which they believe to be 'unreasonable.' " But Goldberg found troubling "its many references to the idea that it is no longer this Court's function to pass upon the 'reasonableness' of a state's economic legislation." Thinking of possible extreme cases, he asked Black to remove six references to (un)reasonableness which Hugo had inserted for emphasis. "I agree to some of these changes with great regret but not to all," Black lamented on Goldberg's letter after deleting them. "With the changes, however, we fail to administer the final fatal blow to the idea that this Court can overrule a legislature's belief of reasonableness."[10]

*   *   *

One piece of business remained from the time Frankfurter was still on the Court. Arizona had filed suit back in 1952, asking the Court to decide how much water in the Colorado River that it shared with California it had the right to use. (Nevada and Colorado later became parties.) At issue was whether the federal government, through the secretary of the interior, or the states should determine the allotment of waters coming through the irrigation canals that are fed by the federal dams. After extensive oral argument, Black (presiding since Warren, having been governor of California when Arizona brought suit, disqualified himself) assigned the case to Frankfurter, who had asserted in a lengthy memorandum before argument that the federal government should control the rights and had told Hugo he'd like to write the opinion. He circulated an opinion in late March 1962; two weeks later he suffered his stroke.

The Court held the case until the next term and then heard more extended argument. The justices by a 5-to-3 vote agreed to follow the broad outline of Frankfurter's opinion; Black took it over. "It was a walk down memory lane for him," said Dick Howard. "He talked about the debates in the Senate when the Boulder dam act was passed in 1928." Essentially he rewrote the principal part of Frankfurter's draft in his own words. It came to fifty-two pages, his longest opinion. In late March he sent a draft to Clark, Brennan, White and Goldberg, the other majority justices. All called it "magnificent."

On June 3, 1963, the Court announced its decision. Black read his opinion. Harlan read his, a partial dissent which Douglas and Stewart joined. And Douglas read his dissent. From the beginning of the case he had been in his quiet way unusually animated. He wrote two memos about it the year before, at least one more than normal. In the first, after missing the conference at which the case was discussed, because of an out of town engagement he would not change, he noted: "This matter of water rights in the Western States is too important—far too important—for Congress ever to trust to the discretion of the Secretary of the Interior." The states, the government closest to the people, should decide it. The United States had no more committed environmentalist than Douglas; a lyric strain ran through his writings, not just his several books on mountains and the wilderness. It all came to the fore as he read his opinion. Talking was the devout conservationist, the westerner fearful of government regulation, the former administrator who had firsthand knowledge of how agencies could foul things up.

"His face, always ruddy, flushed, and his voice began to bristle," James Clayton wrote. The decision, Douglas said, "has made the dream of the federal bureaucracy come true by granting it, for the first time, the life-and-death power of dispensation of water rights. . . . The present case will, I think, be marked as the baldest attempt by judges in modern times to spin their own philosophy into the fabric of the law in derogation of the will of the legislature." Black sat expressionless, staring forward, as Douglas said that the result was "lost in 52 pages of words." His sharp words and tone were unlike him. He was publicly angry as he had seldom been. There was obviously a cause for this outburst. Had anything happened between him and Black?[11]

Much had indeed happened. More than ever, frustration and disappointment could be heard in Black's voice whenever he intoned "Bill Douglas." Only a small part of his feelings came from Douglas's taking new positions Black thought were wrong. Black felt ashamed of Douglas's private behavior and, without being hostile, he estranged himself from Douglas except when necessary for Court business. By 1962 he had become very careful what he said about Douglas to his clerks, and wouldn't talk about him unless prompted, which was, naturally, rare. Douglas stopped speaking of Black to his friends and clerks for several years. "Personally, Black and I have never been very close," he even told an interviewer. ". . . It's more just happenstance, I think, that we have found generally some kinship, although [we] very often disagree on important matters." Douglas's generally slapdash opinions, with legal references recurrently taken from the briefs of the party in whose favor he decided, were often mailed in from airports when he was away delivering speeches or gathering material for a new book. "The reason Bill writes so many books," Black said, "is that he has to pay alimony." He lost interest in the Court: it had become just one of his jobs.

Meanwhile, his second marriage was unraveling. Although not separated from his wife, Mercedes, he moved out of their house in the summer of 1962, only to return whenever he felt like it. He lived part of the time at the Court, sleeping on a cot in his office and often eating at the Methodist Building a block away. Occasionally, when he picked up a woman around town or on his trips, he would bring her back to the Court for the night. At wit's end, trying to help a man who seemed to enjoy only hurting himself, Mercedes asked for Black's help. Hugo wanted them to remain married, for their sake and the Court's. He spoke to Douglas and asked Sidney Davis, Douglas's close friend (and Black's former clerk) to whom Mercedes also had confided, to speak to him. Douglas was annoyed at Black's concern. Once during this period, he was in the hospital. Black found out and visited him. His first words were "What are you doing here?"

Black always thought Douglas was an authentic genius. He continually marveled at how Douglas sat on the bench, writing a book, an article or letters (sometimes licking stamps to put on envelopes), then raised his head to ask an acute question. "His mind has two separate tracks," observed an astonished Black. Only Hugo could influence Douglas, tell him when he should not do something for his or the Court's sake. And they could still work together in startling unison. In February 1963 the Court discussed in conference a case arising under the 1934 Bankruptcy Act. "That's how I wrote it," said Douglas, who had indeed written the relevant section. "And that's how I got it through the Senate," continued Black, who had indeed taken a role. The Court went along. Next week: "I did not know until late afternoon that this is your birthday. Here are my greetings to you and best wishes for many years to come. This would be a very lonesome place without you. As ever, Bill Douglas."[12]

*   *   *

Justice Brennan's opinion in *New York Times v. Sullivan* is one of the enduring landmarks of constitutional law. All speech about public affairs was protected, he held—government and its actions and officers could be mercilessly lambasted, with the sole exception that an official charged with misconduct could recover damages for injury to his reputation only if the offending statement was known to be false or was made with "reckless disregard of whether it was false or not." The case arose from facts in which Black took a special interest.

An advertisement in the *Times* soliciting funds for civil rights causes charged that Martin Luther King, Jr.'s, arrest in Montgomery was part of a campaign to destroy his advocacy of civil rights in the South. L. B. Sullivan, the Montgomery city commissioner, whose duties included supervising the police department, sued for libel in a state court, claiming the allegations defamed him personally.* The *Times* had trouble obtaining counsel to represent it in Alabama. The newspaper asked Hugo, Jr. At first he agreed, even though his participation would have meant that its staunchest supporter on the Court would have to disqualify himself if the case reached it. Nevertheless he requested his fee in advance. The paper refused, as he knew it would. After obtaining able counsel, the *Times* unsurprisingly lost in state courts as the jury awarded Sullivan $500,000. The case was one of eleven libel claims, totaling $5,600,000, pending against the *Times* in Alabama when it reached the Supreme Court in 1964. The libel suits were instituted to prevent the national press from reporting on the civil rights movement in the South.

In Clay County during Black's youth there had been few secrets. People spoke their minds and, he felt, were the better for it. During his career, he received every type of criticism imaginable. About nearly all of it was philosophical, even though no one who heard Black castigate journalists such as Arthur Krock of the *New York Times* or David Lawrence of *U.S. News and World Report* would say he enjoyed it. But such criticism was both an incident and the strength of a democratic society. "Criticism is all in a day's work for anyone in public life," he told Hazel Davis. "Of course, one of the weaknesses of relying on criticism to improve conditions generally is that most critics know practically nothing at all about the subject they discuss." In Sidney Smith's essay "Fallacies of Anti-Reformers," one of Black's favorite essays in the *Harvard Classics*, he underlined "Soldiers expect to be shot at; public men must expect to be attacked, and sometimes unjustly."

So, during oral argument in January 1964, Black pressed the *Times'* lawyer, Columbia law professor Herbert Wechsler, to concede that the Montgomery jury had good reason to find that the advertisement was an attack on Sullivan. "My father always had five reasons for anything he did," Sterling Black noted. Here Justice Black had at least three: he wanted to force the Court to confront Wechsler's broader argument; to treat this case as if it arose from a direct attack on a public official; and to have the Court hold that the First Amendment protected such an attack. At conference the Court unanimously agreed to overrule the Alabama verdict. Black acknowl-

---

* The advertisement claimed that "Southern violators" in Montgomery had expelled King's student followers from college, ringed the campus with armed police, padlocked the dining hall "to starve them into submission," bombed King's home, assaulted him, and arrested him seven times for dubious offenses.

edged his views were "so far" from the Court's. "If there's anything clear to me, it is that in public affairs" the First Amendment "was intended to foreclose any kind of proceedings which would deter full and open discussion." It "permits any type of discussion, including false." Harlan disagreed, saying that the "public interest in discussion" weighed against "the private right not to be defamed"—the old balancing test. Brennan summed up the Court's consensus: the First Amendment requires "clear and convincing evidence" of every element when a public official brings a libel suit. "None of these charges amounts to this and we could reverse just on the ground this wasn't defamation." Warren assigned the opinion to Brennan.

"We consider this case against the background of a profound national commitment to the principle that debate on public issues should be uninhibited, robust, and wide-open, and that it may well include vehement, caustic, and sometimes unpleasantly sharp attacks on government and public officials," Brennan wrote. The advertisement clearly qualified for constitutional protection. This reversed more than a century of libel law. Brennan also declared unconstitutional the 1798 Sedition Act, which "first crystallized a national awareness of the central meaning of the First Amendment." The decision exalted the citizen to his rightful place as both the governed and governor, the ruler and critic of government. "You have done a great service to the freedoms of the First Amendment," Black wrote Brennan.

> For your opinion I believe will inevitably lead to a later holding that people have complete immunity from having to pay damages for criticism of Government or its officials in the performance of their public duties. Most inventions even of legal principles come out of urgent needs. The need to protect speech in this area is so great that it will be recognized and acted upon sooner or later. The rationalization for it is not important; the result is what counts, and your opinion I think will be the point from which this result will be achieved.

"Doesn't this take care of everything you want?" Black's clerk asked him. "I'm going to write something for the record," he replied. "This is a great victory." For his concurring opinion Black drew on his irrefutable knowledge of Alabama and its juries, his dry wit and his brutal realism. His first words put the verdict in perspective: "I concur in reversing this half-million-dollar judgment. . . ." The hostility to desegregation in Montgomery, he wrote, "has sometimes extended itself to persons who favor desegregation, particularly to so-called 'outside agitators,' a term which can be made to fit papers like the Times, which is published in New York. . . . Viewed realistically, this record lends support to an inference that instead of being damaged Commissioner Sullivan's political, social, and financial prestige has likely been enhanced by the Times's publication."

Yet Black saw a danger in Brennan's doctrine of "actual malice." Even as Brennan carefully defined it,* malice was "an elusive, abstract concept, hard to prove and hard to disprove," providing "at best an evanescent protection." The Constitution "has dealt with this deadly danger to the press in the only way possible . . . by granting the press an absolute immunity for criticism of the way public officials do their public duty." More than in most other opinions he worked on the words for dramatic effect. He concluded:

> This Nation, I suspect, can live in peace without libel suits based on public discussions of public affairs and public officials. . . . An unconditional right to say what one pleases about public affairs is what I consider to be the minimum guarantee of the First Amendment. I regret that the Court has stopped short of this holding indispensable to preserve our free press from destruction.

It was an occasion for dancing in the streets, said Alexander Meiklejohn, whose philosophy animated the opinion. When he had recently been awarded the Presidential Medal of Freedom at the White House, Warren, Black, Douglas and Goldberg rushed up to congratulate him. He died later that year at the age of ninety-two, and in January 1965 Black spoke at a memorial meeting in Washington of a man he met fewer than ten times, including several occasions on which they played tennis at Black's house. This was the first time he had left one of the Court's conferences, Black told the group. But he could not resist coming,

> to express my appreciation, my admiration, and indeed my affection for a man who fought so valiantly—so gently in language but so firmly in conviction for his belief that if this country is to remain free, the minds, the tongues, and the pens of people must not be shackled. [He] agreed with the idea that I certainly have, that those who love this country should not be afraid of what people may hear or what they may say about public affairs. Fear is bad enough in any field but in none is it more dangerous than in the area of freedom of expression. . . . His epitaph could well be that which the historian, Diogenes Laertius, composed for an ancient and aged phi-

---

* "The knowledge that [the statement] was false or with reckless disregard of whether it was false or not," which was a far cry from the dictionary definition of "ill will."

losopher: "We have buried Polemo, laid here by that fatal scourge of wasted strength. Yet not Polemo but merely his body, which on his way to the stars he left to moulder in the ground."[13]

*   *   *

"A happy man," Black called himself. He was winning on those things he held dearest, in an era of good feelings in the marble palace. Personal relations were much smoother without Frankfurter's presence; there was no petty backbiting and the decibel level was perceptibly lower. No voices had been raised in conference for three years, Warren said in October 1965. That just happened to be the period since Felix left. "He had absolutely not a particle of rancor . . . about any public official," Robert Warner noted after interviewing Black about Frank Murphy. Hugo's appearance was striking: "bright, sparkling, twinkling eyes, ruddy, healthy complexion; firm hand clasp; a picture of great vitality, and certainly not of age or senility. He spoke very vigorously" and conveyed "the feeling of warmth, informality and old-fashionedness. . . ."

It all came through in a cover story (with portrait) on him in, of all places, *Time.* The article "very much pleased" Hugo, "particularly because it had no barbs aimed at the Court or its work. I think it was good for such an article to come out at this time." Already he had seen more of his dissents turned into doctrine than any other justice, *Time* noted. Hugo Black "has lived to see the 'Warren Court,' as it is known out of respect for its Chief Justice, more accurately called the 'Black Court' after its chief philosopher."[14]

CHAPTER 36

OVERTAKEN BY
EVENTS

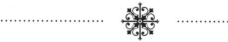

RACE WAS AN INESCAPABLE PART of Hugo Black's career. It could hardly have been otherwise for a southern liberal. Equality of opportunity for all people had always been his lodestar. When he hit his stride in the Senate, he achieved it in necessarily roundabout ways. On the Court, as the legal revolution for racial equality gained momentum, he saw, read and heard painful reports about the racial situation in Alabama.

Segregation was poisoning life there. Politicians outdid one another in praising its cause. Few people felt its mindless sting more than Hugo, Jr. Some friendly politicians gave him advance notice they were going to say bad things about his father. But there was no such warning when he and his family were threatened on the telephone, and only the interference of a client friend kept him from being burned in effigy on his own lawn. By the summer of 1957 he was thinking of leaving his hometown. His father "thoroughly" understood. Soon even short trips there were no longer possible because they would only cause trouble: the justice would be "treated like a leper." After the city closed its recreational facilities rather than integrate them, Hugo, Jr., had no place to play tennis, since the two country clubs wouldn't let a labor lawyer join. Then an opposing lawyer tried to make an issue of him in a case in which he wasn't even involved—his partners were arguing it. But when Hugo III was picked on and made fun of in school, it became just a matter of where and when Hugo, Jr., would move. Black only advised Hugo, Jr., that his and his family's happiness came first, "even at a great financial sacrifice." He wrote Sterling, "I am inclined to believe he did the right thing in leaving Birmingham." Hugo, Jr., moved to Miami in

538

1962. When he told his father how many lawyers he found there, the response was reassuring: "There is always room at the top."

Birmingham was simmering. Soon the lid came off. Police surveillance, wiretappings and mail interceptions were commonplace. "Fear and hatred" stalked Birmingham streets, *New York Times* reporter Harrison Salisbury wrote in 1960, comparing the city to Stalinist Russia, which he had covered. The next year, Edward R. Murrow equated it to Nazi Germany. Television showed police dogs attacking peaceful marchers and fire hoses thrashing at them in spring 1963. Bombs flew and tear gas filled the air, Governor George C. Wallace promised segregation "forever" and "Bombingham" commissioner of public safety Eugene (Bull) Connor yelled his head off. The lack of a natural aristocracy or a leadership group with humanitarian values enabled this rabble-rouser to fill the vacuum in "the Johannesburg of America," the largest segregated city in the country. *

Yet even as the old guard was making its most resistant stand, other voices were being heard. The *Alabama Law Review* ran an admiring article on Black and his law clerks by Daniel Meador, a former clerk and Selma native. Black thought it was "a good advertisement for the Court. [It] will give people an idea of the common everyday things that go on in the Court." Much to the consternation of the state's legal hierarchy, the article hit a responsive chord among younger lawyers. It was one of the few sources of favorable information about Black in Alabama. The University of Alabama library refused to buy a copy of *One Man's Stand for Freedom*. And the issue of *Time* with Black on the cover was not available in Montgomery.

But Hugo Black had a coterie of devoted friends and followers in Alabama. Ben Ray, Black's assistant prosecutor before World War One and stalwart political supporter since, regularly sent along political news. He had kept to his progressive beliefs: "You are one of those rare persons in our native state," Hugo told him. Thirty-seven Birmingham lawyers signed a birthday letter in 1964, expressing their "personal conviction of the great service you have rendered the Nation and the Constitution." Black was touched. "It is quite thrilling to me, not for myself however, but for Birmingham, to have so many sign the letter," he told Vernon Patrick, the former clerk who had organized the effort. "It indicates to me that there

* Debating whether or not to urge compliance with a federal court decision to integrate city recreational facilities, the Birmingham Bar Association finally voted in December 1961 to take no position. That was better than the state government under Governor John Patterson (1959–1962), when it searched for mechanisms to contravene court orders that it didn't approve (Virginia Hamilton, *Alabama: A History* (New York, 1977), 141; Patterson int.).

are many others there besides you and David [Vann, another clerk] who are willing to move along with the times towards a better society." Vann had just led the successful effort to change the city's government from a commission to a mayor-council form, with the intended result of removing Bull Connor, who had assumed the responsibilities of mayor, from office. ("Can it be that Birmingham would defeat His Honor, the Mayor, after such long, distinguished and humane public services he has rendered?" Black wrote.)

Those efforts helped restore a smidgen of common sense. *Birmingham News* editorial page editor E. L. (Red) Holland, Jr., wrote in an editorial that Black "undoubtedly is the most misunderstood Alabamian of all times. . . . It is something of a shame in the native state he has loved so few voices dare rise in some word of honorable recognition of his judicial stature." Given the feelings in Alabama, Black felt Holland was "rather courageous. . . . It is most encouraging to know that a man like that is editor of the *News* because it indicates that there is going to be one editorial voice heard in the South which does not wholly follow the orthodox and conventional ideas which satisfy most people." Ever so gradually and begrudgingly, in steps that could be measured in millimeters, progress was beginning. As Black put it in 1965, "More and more people are beginning to realize that Alabama is a member of the Union and that this is a fine thing for Alabama. My guess is that many political officeholders will soon be compelled to take note of this change in the sentiment of their state."

One official who never hid his esteem for Black was former governor Jim Folsom. Black "is the greatest man ever to walk the clay hills of Clay County or to gaze on the marble monument of Abraham Lincoln," he said. That was not the wisest remark a candidate for Democratic national commiteeman from Alabama could say. But, then, Folsom's political acumen left something to be desired. "It is a great tragedy about Jim Folsom," Black wrote in 1965. "On the whole he has perhaps had sounder basic governmental views than any of the candidates for governor during the last quarter century. He has lacked something, however (I cannot say what), that he needed to make these sound views a part of the laws of Alabama."[1] That something, as Black knew, was judgment; few people had more of it than he did. Perhaps if Alabama's leaders had had even a bit in the early 1960s, the state would have been spared some of the unrelieved turmoil it went through.

*   *   *

Against this backdrop Black and the Court considered a series of direct action (often called "sit-in") cases from 1960 to 1966. They raised the issue of whether a state could use its power to help a private owner to discriminate against Negroes. A major problem was that the equal protection clause did not reach purely private discrimination. The First Amendment right of assembly clashed directly with the right of property; the demand for civil rights challenged the need for preservation of public order.

From the beginning Black believed the Constitution did not govern in this area. "I remember nigras had to come in the back door of my Pappy's store," he told the Court's clerks at lunch in late 1960. "They had no constitutional right to come in any place they wanted." This was shortly before Black, speaking for the Court, reversed the conviction of a Negro passenger on an interstate bus who had refused to leave that part of the bus station restaurant reserved for white people after being told to do so, in violation of state law. All the justices unconditionally endorsed the notion that any facilities that served interstate passengers could not discriminate. The Interstate Commerce Act so provided, and on it, not on any constitutional justification, Black based his opinion.

The first sit-in had taken place earlier in 1960, in Greensboro, North Carolina. "Black recognized what was coming," his clerk George Saunders recalled, "and he didn't like it."* In March 1961 his former clerk Luther Hill paid him a visit after arguing a case. "He got started on sit-in cases," Hill recalled. "He was adamant, arguing that we have a system of private property in this country." That summer Black wrote in the margin of a book, "The 1st Amendment protects speech, not confrontation." Sit-in cases came regularly to the Court now. In conference in November 1962 he stated, "We have a system of private ownership of property."

> I see nothing in the Constitution which says an owner can't tell people he doesn't want to get out. Therefore, he can call the police to help protect that right. If the right is in the owner, then certainly he can call the police and the law must enforce his right. There's a difference between a home and a store. A store owner as a home owner has a right to say who can come on his premises and how long they can stay. If he has that right, he cannot be helpless to call the police. I have no difficulty in sustaining a state or federal law that merchants must serve everyone despite [one's] color. I will meet this basic point on the merits. I'd have to look closely to find if there's anything which says the owner can't tell people he doesn't want

---

* "The Supreme Court forbids discrimination in bus-stop restaurants," columnist Fletcher Knebel noted. "It's a new legal doctrine: Everyone has an equal right to risk ptomaine poisoning" (WS, 12/6/60, in Walter Wyatt to HLB, 12/7/60; Wyatt was the Court's reporter of decisions).

to get out. I see nothing in the Constitution which says this. Therefore, he can call the police to help protect that right. The Constitution, taken without legislation, doesn't prevent this. I have no difficulty in sustaining a state or federal law that merchants must serve everyone despite color. But when the state wants the owner to do it, the burden is on the state.

This remained Black's view throughout the sit-in cases. Nearly all involved trespass or breach of the peace statutes. In 1962 and 1963 a deeply divided Court rested its decisions on narrow grounds, avoiding the central issue until forced to do so.

In June 1963 the Court considered two petitions. One asked the justices to eradicate a sweeping temporary injunction issued by a Mississippi state court in a case of street demonstrations that "tied up traffic" and caused "fights" and "riots." "These street parades should be stopped," Black said in conference, according to a Douglas memorandum, and the Court "should not raise a hand to interfere in any way." The racial situation was "getting more and more acute"; he predicted "many outbreaks" during the summer. He repeated his belief that "it was time to clamp down on the Negroes." Douglas, Goldberg and (although "somewhat lightly") Brennan spoke strongly the other way, but all the justices voted to deny the petition.

The other case involved Negro youths arrested while trying to attend a religious revival billed as open to the public but in fact open only to whites. It was "high-time the Court handed down a decision against the Negroes," Black said. This was a "flagrant" case of Negroes invading a church. "Nothing" was "sacrosanct" if they would go so far. Refusing to hear the case would serve a "healthy purpose." All except Douglas agreed.[2]

Physical protest never appealed to Black. Direct action, such as sit-ins, intentionally violated society's necessity to maintain order, he felt. Public disorder threatened the fabric of democracy. If demonstrations disturbed him, mobs scared him. "He talked about them, said they take off by themselves, that their chemistry can't be trusted because it's unknown," recalled Louis Oberdorfer. " 'Something unleashes a mob and it's transformed by electricity,' he said." His attitude was formed partly in response to the French Revolution. He strongly opposed the March on Washington in August 1963, predicting wrongly that it would turn into a huge riot.

"You better tell your friend Martin Luther King to stop marching," Black told Virginia Durr afterward. She did. King replied, "I'm sorry, Mrs. Durr.

I greatly respect Justice Black, but we must march. I have to get fear out of these Negroes. They've been scared for three hundred years and they must get rid of fear before they'll ever be able to do anything. Marching is the only way to do that." Black felt that King's practice of civil disobedience could result in anarchy across the nation. "Marches lead to violence," he said, "and are not the way our system is supposed to work." Time and again he argued that the state had authority to take over an area. He knew the southern temperament—few knew it better. He had seen mob violence at first hand in the Klan. He had predicted it would happen after *Brown* and he urgently wanted to thwart it now.

Black liked a certain orderliness to his life. He was very conscious of the security of his person, and viewed anyone coming uninvited to his house almost as a bodily assault against which one was entitled to protection. Law was the great savior. "The day after Fidel Castro came into power in 1959, he came into the clerks' room, sat catty cornered on the desk and flipped the newspaper to me," noted Guido Calabresi, who was in that room. "It was open to the page where the Castro article was. He said, 'They're just as bad as those who came before,' took the paper from me and walked right out. That's why he couldn't abide the Nuremberg trials. They were lawless. He preferred what happened to Mussolini because that can be dealt with." The security that law provided was one of the primary reasons Black believed that anything with a legal content should be made as clear as possible. His search for simple doctrine—easily understood and binding on judges, the people, and electoral and legislative process alike—more than reflected his background in elective politics: it epitomized his judicial philosophy.

He was so worked up about the sit-in cases that while they were pending he mentioned them to someone outside the Court or his extended legal family. Rarely had he done this. "We had a long talk," recalled Norman Dorsen, who had clerked for Justice Harlan. "He hinted, the drift of what he was saying was that he was on the other side from the liberals. He spoke of his father's country store, that he could serve whomever he wanted. He was very emotional about it." Soon came the annual dinner Harlan's clerks gave for him. Usually it ended with Harlan's giving a dull report on the Court, with such scintillating insights as that the health of the justices was fine and "we're up to date in our work." This time was different. "Things are very troublesome at the Court," Harlan said. "We're going through a very bad period. I'm very concerned. If it weren't for Justice Black, things would be in much worse shape. Justice Black has been a rock. He is saving the Court. Some men are institutional men, who care about the institution, and Black is one of them." Harlan used the phrase several times, to his audience's wonderment. "Everyone was so amazed he was so candid," noted Dorsen. "He never before spoke like this."³ Soon the reason was apparent.

*   *   *

Bell v. Maryland involved a dozen Negroes who sat down at a lunch counter in a Baltimore department store and didn't get up when asked. They were arrested and convicted of violating the state trespass law. From the beginning Black planned to affirm. He was impassioned in the two conferences in October 1963, in which this and three related cases were discussed. Once again he said that he believed his "pappy" would have had the right to decide whom he would or would not serve in his store. State laws could make it "lawful for the owner to ask [a customer] to leave. I don't think the Constitution forbids the owner of a store to keep people out. . . . I deny that people have a constitutional right to trespass or stay on property over the owner's protest." Such treatment, Goldberg remarked, amounts to an "indicia of slavery." "I think it is an indicia of slavery to make me associate with people I do not want to associate with," Black replied. Neither *Marsh v. Alabama,* a 1946 case that held that a "company town" could not ban distribution of religious literature, or *Shelley v. Kraemer,* which two years later rendered restrictive covenants unenforceable in court, was relevant, he said; but if they were regarded as governing, "I would overrule them." Since he had written *Marsh,* that would have meant Hugo Black would have overruled himself, a most unlikely prospect.

Whence this seemingly new concern for private property? It was always there but so masked it could hardly be seen; Black's concern for civil liberties overwhelmed it. But even in *Marsh* he balanced: "Ownership does not always mean absolute dominion," he wrote. "The more an owner, for his advantage, opens his property for use by the public in general, the more do his rights become circumscribed by the statutory and constitutional rights of those who use it." He evaluated property rights in terms of their underlying function. But now Black tipped the scale the other way, and his rhetoric on behalf of his new preference was typically combative. He erected property rights as an unqualifiable principle, as an end unto themselves, even when the property was open to the public. He had always been careful to qualify his broad assertions of First Amendment rights; occasionally his bombastic emphasis overpowered his qualifications; now the stipulations took equal place with his assertions.

Four other justices—Clark, Harlan, Stewart and White—went along with Black's position in the sit-in case and he assigned the Court's opinion to himself. "It would betray our whole plan for law and order," Black wrote in the first draft, to say that a citizen cannot summon police because of personal prejudices.

> We hold that [section 1 of] the Fourteenth Amendment* does not bar Maryland from enforcing its trespass laws so long as it does not do so with an evil eye and a prejudiced heart and hand. We do not believe that the amendment was written or designed to interfere with a property owner's right to choose his social or business associates, so long as he does not run counter to a valid state or federal regulation. . . . This Court has done much in carrying out its solemn duty to protect people from discrimination. It is destined to do more as cases and controversies involving racial questions are brought before it. The case before us does not involve the power of the Congress to pass a law compelling privately owned businesses to trade with all if they trade with any. We express no views as to such a law. We simply decline to construe the Fourteenth Amendment as embodying such a drastic change in what has until very recently been accepted by all as the right of a man who owns a business to run the business in his own way so long as some valid regulatory statute does not tell him to do otherwise. If free enterprise means anything, it means that. . . . It would overturn the whole history of this country to take away a man's property or any part of it except by taking it for a public use and paying him just compensation as the law provides.

This draft was circulated March 5. Congress was considering the civil rights bill, which was why some members of the Court's majority wanted to release the opinion as quickly as possible. The minority vociferously disagreed. Warren and Brennan had early expressed their fear that affirming the convictions might cripple the bill's prospects. The dissenters would do their utmost, Brennan said, to delay the decision in the hope that Congress would pass it or that some member of the majority would change his vote. (They felt, as Elizabeth noted in her diary, that "Hugo's enormous prestige would work adversely on the bill's passage.")

In April, Warren, Douglas, Brennan and Goldberg all circulated dissents. Goldberg's was especially adamant, comparing Black's opinion to the ill-starred Dred Scott case, which helped to bring on the Civil War, and referring to it as a veiled "apologia" to racism. Black did not rise to the bait. In a footnote in his next draft he simply noted his regret at Goldberg's

* ". . . nor shall any State deprive any person of life, liberty or property, without due process of law. . . ."

"inflammatory" reference. Black also demolished Goldberg's claim that the Fourteenth Amendment, of itself, was intended to prohibit discrimination by privately owned businesses. "Supreme Court Justices are not very good at historical analysis," Goldberg later said with a laugh. "They're not historians, and even the best historians differ. In *Bell* we became amateur historians and we were not very good at it." He admitted Black had the better of the historical argument. "When Hugo was in agreement, he was a sober brother," Goldberg continued. "When he was in disagreement, he was a terrible and vigorous adversary. He was a gut fighter. It took much independence to stand up to him."

Brennan had it. He told Black the case could not come down on May 4, as Hugo had planned, since he would revise his opinion to meet Black's new points. Brennan issued a new draft the next day. The Senate was in the midst of its longest filibuster ever, over the public accommodations section of the civil rights bill, and his colleagues, Brennan charged, "unnecessarily create the risk of a 'self-inflicted wound.' " Clark had earlier told Goldberg that the majority was "absolutely solid and indestructible." But since Black feared that the infighting was making Stewart "nervous and edgy," he conferred frequently with Stewart in order to hold his vote. Stewart stayed with him, and Black softened the opinion to mollify the minority's fear it might damage the civil rights bill. "The case does not involve the constitutionality of any proposed state or federal legislation requiring restaurant owners to serve people without regard to color," the opinion now began. But Brennan changed his draft to make Maryland law the basis for reversing the convictions. "I was so concerned that if we came down with *Bell* on constitutional grounds, it would kill the civil rights act," he later said. "Hugo was just beside himself with me on that. He came in storming saying 'You can't do that!' "

But to everyone's surprise Brennan's change in his draft gained Clark's vote. At conference on May 15 he immediately asked that cases be heard again since he now thought Brennan was correct, as he had told Black before the conference began. The discussion, one justice noted, was "exceedingly tense"; Black and Clark said hardly anything. Hugo felt Clark had betrayed him, that he had committed his vote in October. He liked Clark very much but didn't really respect him. Clark's pogo-stick-like unpredictability angered every justice at one time or another; nearly every term he changed his vote in important cases.

The Court was now at an impasse since Douglas continued to vote to reverse but only on the ground that the convictions violated the Fourteenth

Amendment. Clark based a draft on that ground: "The character of the state's multifold involvement makes it responsible for the discrimination here." At the same time he said he still preferred that Brennan's opinion speak for the Court. Whether or not Clark's draft was simply a tactic to assure a majority for Brennan's, Stewart changed his vote to join Brennan, who now commanded a secure majority.

Black revised his dissent. The Maryland statute was "directed not against what petitioners said but against what they did—remaining on the premises of another after having been warned to leave, conduct which states have traditionally prohibited in this country. And none of our prior cases has held that a person's right to freedom of expression carries with it a right to force a private property owner to furnish his property as a platform to criticize the property owner's use of that property." He could not "appreciate the fairness or justice of holding the present generation of Marylanders responsible for what their ancestors did in other days. . . . The Fourteenth Amendment is 'color blind,' in the sense that it outlaws all state laws which discriminate merely on account of color." Upon this basis *Brown v. Board of Education* had been decided. But there Black stopped. *

> The right to freedom of expression is a right to express views—not a right to force other people to supply a platform or a pulpit. . . . The experience of ages points to the inexorable fact that people are frequently stirred to violence when property which the law recognizes as theirs is forcibly invaded or occupied by others. Trespass laws are born of this experience. . . . The Constitution does not confer upon any group the right to substitute rule by force for rule by law. . . . At times the rule of law seems too slow to some for the settlement of their grievances. But it is the plan our Nation has chosen to preserve both "Liberty" and equality for all. On that plan we have put our trust and staked our future. This constitutional rule of law has served us well. Maryland's trespass law does not depart from it. Nor shall we.

The decision came down June 22, 1964. Black, joined only by Harlan and White, dissented, delivering his dissent almost like a campaign speech. If Black's had been the majority opinion, the constitutionality of sit-ins and

---

* "Our position," Black wrote, "is that the Constitution of itself does not prohibit discrimination by those who sell goods and services. There is of course a crucial difference between the argument—which we do make—that the Constitution itself does not prohibit private sellers of goods or services from choosing their own customers, and the argument—which we do not make—that the Constitution affirmatively creates a right to discriminate which neither state nor federal legislation could impair."

peaceful demonstrations would have been seriously in doubt—but only for a short time. On July 2 the Civil Rights Act of 1964 became law. It prohibited racial discrimination in restaurants and other public accommodations, an intent Black wholeheartedly shared. The goal of the sit-in demonstrators had been elevated to the law of the land.[4]

*   *   *

The political branches, in Black's view, shared responsibility for the prevention of lawlessness. "The streets are not now and never have been the proper place to administer justice," he wrote, dissenting from the Court's 1965 reversal of a conviction for picketing near a courthouse. "Use of the streets for such purposes has always proved disastrous to individual liberty in the long run, whatever fleeting benefits may have appeared to have been achieved. And minority groups, I venture to suggest, are the ones who always have suffered and always will suffer most when street multitudes are allowed to substitute their pressures for the less glamorous but more dependable and temperate processes of the law. Experience demonstrates that it is not a far step from what to many seems the earnest, honest, patriotic, kind-spirited multitude of today, to the fanatical, threatening, lawless mob of tomorrow." He was already visualizing those throngs.

In February 1966 the Court overturned breach of the peace convictions against Negro youths who staged a "sit-down" (as Black called it) in a small public library in Louisiana to protest segregated library services. Black ringingly denounced the majority's assumption that such behavior should be measured by the same standards as conduct occurring in the streets. His dissent bristled: the petitioners were treated with "every courtesy and granted every consideration," they got complete service, no discrimination was involved, they came simply to stage a protest. "It is high time to challenge the assumption in which too many people have too long acquiesced," Black wrote, "that groups that think they have been mistreated or that have actually been mistreated have a constitutional right to use the public's streets, buildings, and property to protest whatever, wherever, whenever they want, without regard to whom such conduct may disturb." Inviting protesting groups to take the law in their own hands was undermining the rule of law:

> I am deeply troubled with the fear that powerful private groups throughout the Nation will read the Court's action, as I do—that is, as granting them a license to invade the tranquility and beauty of our libraries whenever they have a quarrel with some state policy which may or may not exist. It

is an unhappy circumstance in my judgment that the group which, more than any other has needed a government of equal laws and equal justice, is now encouraged to believe that the best way for it to advance its cause, which is a worthy one, is by taking the law into its own hands from place to place and from time to time. Governments like ours were formed to substitute the rule of law for the rule of force. . . . But I say once more that the crowd moved by noble ideals today can become the mob ruled by hate and passion and greed and violence tomorrow. If we ever doubted that, we know it now. The peaceful songs of love can become as stirring and provocative as the Marseillaise did in the days when a noble revolution gave way to rule by successive mobs until chaos set in. The holding in this case today makes it more necessary than ever that we stop and look more closely at where we are going.

In a draft he had originally accused the Court's majority of bias against the South, but omitted it. (Abe Fortas, who wrote the opinion, hailed from Memphis, Tennessee, which borders Mississippi.) A "somewhat saddened" Warren told Fortas that Black's opinion "does not represent the better part of his nature."

Black's voice rose and fell, and he shook his finger at the audience as he delivered his dissent. Fortas's opinion, he charged, would lead "misguided" civil rights demonstrators to think that they would be "automatically turned loose, so long as whatever they do has something to do with race." The First Amendment did not protect "psalm-singing" demonstrators because their actions constituted conduct, not speech. "Government must protect itself," he later insisted when talking about *Brown* and *Cox.* "The official who allows sit-ins should be thrown out of office. That librarian should have been fired." Permitting a library to be used for nonreading purposes was to Black the same as going through a church with an ax. Civil rights advocates acting outside the bounds of law threatened the very existence of democracy, which he considered an ordered way of protecting people's rights.

Soon he gained a majority for his position. Negro college students were arrested for trespassing on the grounds of the Tallahassee, Florida, county jail, where they had been protesting the arrest of other students, who had been demonstrating against racial segregation in local movie theaters. The Court considered the case in October 1966. In conference Black said he thought the sheriff had acted correctly in arresting the trespassers, since they were "on the grounds of the jail and tried to get in" and the sheriff was the legal custodian of the jail and its grounds. The next month, Black wrote the majority opinion, affirming the convictions. "Singing, clapping and dancing" demonstrators did not have "a constitutional right to stay on

the property, over the jail custodian's objections," simply because it seemed
an appropriate place for a protest. An argument that holds otherwise, he
continued, "has as its major unarticulated premise the assumption that people
who want to propagandize protests or laws have a constitutional right to do
so however and wherever they please. Nothing in the Constitution of the
United States prevents Florida from evenhanded enforcement of its general
trespass statute against those refusing to obey the sheriff's order to remove
themselves from what amounted to the curtilage of the jailhouse. The state,
no less than a private owner of property, has power to preserve the property
under its control for the use to which it is lawfully dedicated."[5]

Hugo Black was an old-fashioned liberal who believed in equal opportunity,
then stopped. The civil rights movement, he felt, had won what it wanted
and needed when the legal impediments to segregation had been removed.
"Hugo, like me," explained Clifford Durr, and few understood Black better,
"was a desegregationist, not an integrationist. We wanted to get rid of racial
barriers, not set up new ones that gave anyone an unfair advantage." That
was the whole purpose behind Brown. It was "not just a matter of Negroes,
but other groups getting their rights too," Black said. He feared the establishment of a "split-level system of justice, one for Negroes, one for whites,"
he told a former clerk. "I haven't spent my life working for that." The rights
of people as people, not as members of any supposedly special group, concerned him. "Unfortunately, there are some who think that Negroes should
have special privileges under the law." Constitutional safeguards are not
selective. They must protect everybody, or eventually they won't protect
anyone.

The aftermath of Brown saw a rampant lawlessness, reminiscent of the
frontier, sweeping the South. In the direct action cases Black was responding
to the imperative of the return to legal processes. He believed in orderly,
traditional channels of change; anything done outside them is by definition
extralegal and fraught with the most serious consequences. He abhorred
violence above all and would do anything in his power to prevent even the
merest possibility of its occurrence. And when he looked around, he saw a
leadership vacuum in the South; the few mediating figures he saw were much
younger than he, and he did not know them. He did not expect the South
to change. "The racial problem won't be solved in my lifetime or yours,"
he said in 1961. "It won't be solved until there's intermarriage."

Black "is having his problems with racial decisions," Warren told Drew

Pearson just before the library sit-in case came down. Soon he was saying with a chuckle, "Hugo just wants to be buried in Alabama." Brennan repeated this remark to friends. The continuance of democracy, so Black's unspoken message seemingly went, depended on upholding public order statutes. He made no attempt to invoke the "balancing" test he had established to examine if these laws indirectly affected speech. He simply accepted public order statutes at face value, fearing that to rule otherwise would result in government by mob. This was far from the Black who in 1951 labeled a decision sanctioning police action to silence a speaker "a long step toward totalitarian authority."[6] No longer was he giving freedom to address public matters priority over appeals for public convenience and civic order. He meticulously explained each vote, as he gave to these laws the respect he had always given to First Amendment rights themselves. Formerly he had treated dissenters as heroes indispensable to progress, who helped the country live up to its highest aspirations. Now he disparaged protest groups and their leaders: he considered them ambitious, misinformed, dangerous agitators. A very different Black was focusing on constitutional limitations of a very different sort.

CHAPTER 37

CONTINUITY AND CHANGE

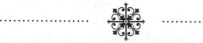

THE DYNAMICS on the Court had shifted by 1965. The past few years had seen a sea change in the law. Black recognized the reality that the Court, having turned issues that he had started into law, would eventually move on to other things. Egalitarianism and political liberalism were guiding most justices; if the other institutions of government were not filling the people's social needs, the Court would. It was a conception of the Court's role Black accepted only uneasily now. The composition of the new majority alone meant that he wrote fewer majority opinions and that these were in less important cases.

"Absolute Liberties not subject to Government or other control," Black marked in John Stuart Mill's *On Liberty*. He usually found them directly, or at least directly inferable, in the text of the Constitution. Chasing Frankfurter's ghost, he was still railing against the use of "fairness" in opinions; still accusing his brethren of reading their own views into decisions (through the contract clause now as well the due process clause); still zealously protecting the interests of plaintiffs in jury trials and procedural matters; still basing decisions on specific constitutional language; still supporting the Fifth Amendment as staunchly as ever. "The Constitution there," he told Harlan, "carves out a type of evidence *absolutely* forbidden." The First Amendment remained the center of Black's constitutional universe. He continued to uphold it against claims of libel.* And he and Justice Douglas dissented in

---

* After one such case, *St. Amant v. Thompson* (1968), Pennsylvania congressman Lawrence Williams wrote each justice to denounce the decision. "I am not nearly so sure that you are right in prophesying that this opinion will discourage good men from running for public

552

every case where the Court prohibited the dissemination of allegedly "ob-scene" material.

The rawness of life in Clay County had surrounded Black as a child. People daily saw others in various states of dress and undress. He liked to say that after the stuff passed behind the barn nothing else could surprise him; it remained his idea of "obscenity." No one who knew him ever recalled his using even the most faintly profane language. His view as to what was appropriate fare for mixed company approached the Victorian: he found the play *How to Succeed at Business Without Really Trying* offensive.

In 1957 the Court (through Justice Brennan, who became its de facto spokesman in these matters) defined obscenity as "utterly without redeeming social importance." Two years later, after six and one-half justices (Warren sent his clerks) saw the movie version of D. H. Lawrence's novel *Lady Chatterley's Lover*, the Court ruled that government could not interfere with a film's exhibition simply because it disapproved of the idea expressed (adultery in this instance). Justice Harlan, concurring, specifically noted that he had reviewed the film. Black underlined that, turned the page of Harlan's draft over and wrote his own concurrence. Slightly revised, it presented the essence of his views in a field that the Court has continually found intractable:

> My belief is that this Court is about the most inappropriate Supreme Board of Censors that could be found. So far as I know, judges possess no special expertise providing exceptional competency to set standards and to super-vise the private morals of the nation. In addition, the justices of this Court seem especially unsuited to make the kind of value judgments—as to what movies are good and bad for local communities—which [Frankfurter's and Harlan's] concurring opinions seem to require. . . . Under these circum-stances, each member of the Court must exercise his own judgment as to how bad a picture is, a judgment which is ultimately based at least in large part on his own standard of what is immoral. The end result of such decisions seems to me to be a purely personal determination by individual justices as to whether a particular picture viewed is too bad to allow it to be seen by the public. Such an individualized determination cannot be guided by reasonably fixed and certain standards. . . . This uncertainty cannot easily be reckoned with the rule of law which our constitution envisages.

If people can be arrested for "obscenity," a demagogue could call his critics "obscene" and arrest them. That is just what happened, Black said, citing

---

office," Black replied. "I am confident, for illustration, that it will not keep you from running next time." Williams immediately told Black he had just announced for reelection.

Tacitus, in Rome under Caesar Augustus, when the law of treason was grossly expanded, under the guise of legislation, to protect ethics and morality. Despite the difficulties, the middle-aged and elderly men trained in law on the Court—but never Black—solemnly assessed the 'evidence.' They "think they're invested with the God-like power of looking at it and tell what's obscene," he said in 1968. They were trying to identify something that has thus far in human history escaped precise definition. It would have been easier to nail jello to the wall. By the end of the decade the Court effectively threw up its hands, * and most material called "obscene" by those who didn't want it available to others was freely available.[1]

*   *   *

To Black, the Fourth Amendment presented problems of interpretation as did no other constitutional provision. It is the only place in the Constitution where "reasonable" is mentioned, he said, emphasizing the word as he read the amendment to his clerks. "I have a duty as a judge to determine what reasonable is and I will do it." Balancing is required, he admitted, but he never identified the factors to be considered and weighed. The result was that Black construed the Fourth Amendment more restrictively than any other justice in modern times. He was the only justice who upheld wire-tapping *without* a warrant. Almost invariably he approved extensive warrantless searches conducted incidental to arrest. Similarly, he went further than any other justice in sanctioning warrantless searches of automobiles on probable cause as determined by police. If this went against his continual goal of reducing judicial discretion, the language, he claimed, and only the language, caused it. But behind the language is history. And this historically minded judge completely avoided discussion of the amendment's rich historical background. Here lay the basis for a libertarian field day, but Black purposely ignored it. (Apparently he bought no books about the amendment, and read relatively little on it.) He became fixated with its wording, not with its significance.

By the late 1950s he "was having unending trouble coming to a position he liked and could defend," recalled Guido Calabresi, who clerked in 1958.

---

* Douglas later gave one reason. "With considerable glee" he explained to his friend Harry Ashmore "why his venerable brethren had so much more difficulty agreeing on a definition of pornography any more precise than Justice Potter Stewart's insistence that he knew it when he saw it. 'The legal test,' he said, 'is whether the material arouses a prurient response in the beholder. The older we get, the freer the speech' " (Ashmore, "Doubling the Standard," *Virginia Quar. Rev.* 62 [Winter 1986]).

The language suggested balancing, but no, said Black, it simply means greater absention; judges should not second-guess police actions. More frequently, he almost indicated that his approach was a way to protect the absoluteness of the First Amendment, as if in contrast. He gave the impression that the Fourth Amendment's reasonableness requirement underscored the literalness of the other amendments, which he felt were much more important.

Mapp v. Ohio came to the Court as a straightforward obscenity case in 1961. Police officers had heard that a wanted person was hiding in a Cleveland home. The owner refused to admit them without a search warrant, but they forced their way inside and found not the person but "obscene" material. She was convicted for its possession. All the justices agreed that the vagueness of the Ohio obscenity statute violated the First Amendment. But Douglas gave *Wolf v. Colorado*, a 1949 Frankfurter opinion that held that the "core" of the Fourth Amendment applied to the states without stating how, as another ground for reversal. Warren and Brennan went along with Douglas, and Clark indicated at least tentative approval. Just after leaving the conference room, Clark said to Black and Brennan that this would be a good case in which to apply the Fourth Amendment to the states. This left Black as the pivotal vote. He agreed to overrule *Wolf*, as long as it did not require the states to apply the exclusionary rule barring the use of illegally obtained evidence at trial, noting that he still had difficulty doing so based on the Fourth Amendment alone. When Warren suggested that he write the opinion, Black replied, "I don't want to. Somebody else should." Clark was assigned *Mapp*.

Warren, Douglas and Brennan together soon went to see Black. He caved in, and agreed that *Wolf* should be overruled and that the Fourth Amendment should be applied to the states—a move that would radically transform the American criminal justice system. He approved the draft Clark sent to members of the majority but wanted it based more on cases. Clark did this. None of his changes raised "insuperable barriers," Black told him after reading his circulated draft. "I think they add life that contributes to clarity and persuasiveness. Your discussion of 'privacy' is so limited that it does not justify a belief that you are using it as a synonym for the 4th Amendment." They conferred at length several times in Black's office, going over the opinion word by word until he was satisfied. His belief in muting controversy whenever possible to gain a Court majority made the task easier.

At the same time Black's clerk George Saunders was trying to convince him that since he was changing his mind from *Wolf*, he ought to write a concurrence explaining why. "Not a bad idea," Black said; "write it." Saunders did. Black then took the draft and dictated the same ideas in his own words. The Fourth and Fifth amendments "throw great light on" and "run almost into each other," the Court had said in *Boyd v. U.S.* in 1886. The Fourth's underlying principles rather than its precise text concerned the Court there. Black called the case "precise" and "intelligent" now, and he tracked its analysis. Both amendments were entitled to "a liberal rather than a niggardly interpretation." When "considered together . . . a constitutional basis emerges which not only justifies but actually requires the exclusionary rule." He had rejected this argument in *Wolf*, but its "force" had recently become more "compelling." State courts now had to exclude illegally seized evidence.

Black nonetheless remained troubled. Clark's draft asserted that "the Fourth Amendment's *right of privacy* has been declared enforceable against the states through the due process clause of the Fourteenth." This, Black wrote him, "makes it necessary for me to say that my agreement depends upon my understanding that you read *Wolf* as having held, and that we are holding here, that the Fourth Amendment *as a whole* is applicable to the states and not some imaginary and unknown fragment designated as the 'right of privacy.' " Black grudgingly went along with Clark's change: "The right of privacy embodied in the Fourth Amendment is enforceable against the states, and . . . the right to be secure against rude invasions of privacy by state officers is, therefore, constitutional in origin.[2]

A notion of privacy has seemed implicit in the Fourth Amendment to everyone who has considered it—but never to Black. He pounced on any draft opinion that chanced to mention it. At his suggestion Clark changed "Fourth Amendment's right of privacy" to "[its] protection from unreasonable searches and seizures" in a 1963 opinion. " 'Privacy' is not in my judgment the test under the 4th" Amendment, Black wrote on one of Brennan's drafts the next year. He could have added "or any other amendment."

For years, in a series of cases and off-Court writings, Douglas had advanced a constitutional right of privacy. His efforts were exceptionally cogent and compelling (perhaps because they spoke so directly to his personal needs). A 1952 dissent, Black told him, was "one of the best pieces of writing you have ever done." "I regret that my own constitutional ideas prevent my agreeing with you." Yet he joined a 1959 Douglas dissent on privacy on which Douglas worked atypically hard; when that happened, which wasn't too often, Black might say, "Bill really cares about this case," and that could be enough for his vote. (It also didn't hurt that Frankfurter wrote the majority opinion, and that Warren and Brennan joined Douglas's opinion.)

At the same time as *Mapp* in 1961, the Court decided *Poe v. Ullman*. A Connecticut law prohibited the use of contraceptives and claimed that its general criminal accessory statute prevented the giving of medical advice for their use. Since Connecticut authorities had not enforced the law, the Court dismissed suits brought by three plaintiffs challenging it. Douglas vigorously dissented, upholding the patient's right of privacy. "It emanates from the totality of the constitutional scheme under which we live," he wrote. Black was deeply disturbed.

The Connecticut Planned Parenthood League soon opened a clinic in New Haven. Its director and medical adviser were amiably arrested and convicted, as they had expected and wished, in state courts. Justice Brennan had earlier suggested to New York University law professor Norman Redlich that the Ninth Amendment might be used to declare the law unconstitutional. Redlich wrote an article expressly for this purpose. When the Court considered the case in conference in April 1965, Black said, as opposed to four years earlier, that he found no First Amendment issue involved. "The right of association is for me a right of assembly and the right of husband and wife to assemble in bed is a new right of assembly to me." (If so, much human behavior indeed has been unconstitutional.) Only Potter Stewart agreed with him that a state could enact such a law. Douglas's opinion for the Court in *Griswold v. Connecticut* plowed new ground. "Specific guarantees in the Bill of Rights have penumbras, formed by emanations from those guarantees that help give them life and substance," he wrote. "Various guarantees create zones of privacy." Born was the constitutional right of privacy.[3]

Black later called his dissent "the most difficult I have ever had to write. I found that law abhorrent, just viciously evil, but not unconstitutional." His clerk drafted a dissent, from which he dictated a new version, responding to concurring opinions as they were circulated. Themes that would increasingly appear in his opinions dominated. The First Amendment does not protect defendants who admittedly helped others to break the law, he noted. More important, "it belittles [the Fourth Amendment] to talk about it as though it protects nothing but 'privacy' . . . a broad, abstract and ambiguous concept. . . . I like my privacy as well as the next one, but I am nevertheless compelled to admit that government has a right to invade it unless prohibited by some specific constitutional provision." He impugned the whole idea of the "living Constitution." Amendments are the only permissible method of changing the document. It "was good for our Fathers, and being somewhat old-fashioned I must add it is good enough for me." He even quoted Learned Hand, to the unstated effect that the Court was becoming "a bevy of Platonic Guardians" ruling the country.

The use of the Ninth Amendment he found especially galling, calling its application "a recent discovery." Yet as far back as 1951 Black had used it in a draft of a concurring opinion. Now he thought it utterly subjective and open-ended. "I have had entirely too much trouble through the years with the broad interpretation of the due process clause to welcome a discussion along the same lines about the Ninth Amendment," he later told Redlich. "Even religions split in Griswold," Black said in 1970. "I dissented because of three reasons: one, privacy; two, due process–natural law, judges shouldn't have that power; and three, the literalness of the constitution. What they wanted wasn't in there."

Black disparaged the constitutional right of privacy with all the ardor that he had denounced First Amendment balancing. He was forever critical of "penumbra," thinking it almost as dangerous as Frankfurter's "shock the conscience."* "How could Bill possibly come up with that?" he wondered. This, he felt, was but another species of the substantive due process the Old Court used in its attempt to derail the New Deal: the same philosophy could come back to haunt a new generation. "The notion of privacy just protects the substance of rights under the guise of privacy," he said. "People fought and fought for what the majority shall not do. Then they sat down to write a constitution. It's an anti-majoritarian document and must be clear and precise."[4]

The Fourth Amendment was outside Black's milieu. Because the Constitution turned it into a test of reasonableness, he became oriented toward precedent in this area. That gave him the certainty he wanted. But not even certainty could account for his lone dissent to the Court's 1967 decision

---

* In a 1968 speech Black said with a chuckle that the Court "found some penumbras and emanations from various parts of the Bill of Rights to make a right of privacy. I don't know about penumbras or emanations" (NYT, 3/22/68).

overthrowing New York's wiretapping statute on privacy grounds. Oblivious to the dangers of uncontrolled wiretapping, Black stressed the petitioner's "obvious guilt." He rebuked the Court for even invoking the Fourth Amendment, since it does not "speak in clear and unambiguous prohibitions or commands." The Court was playing "sleight-of-hand tricks." The right of privacy, "like a chameleon, has a different color for every thing." Wiretapping did not bother Black. He started with the notion that "it can't be against the law to overhear what someone is saying. If someone is talking loudly enough to be heard," he told his clerks—that is, unless one is talking to oneself—"that can be used against him. When I talk on the phone, I know the operator will be listening in. That's why you have to be careful." Electronic eavesdropping (or wiretapping) was similar to the hated general warrants out of which the American Revolution sprang in that it allowed a discreet surveillance. This would naturally resonate on Black's historical beliefs. So he got around the problem by claiming that eavesdropping was merely listening outside a structure to conversations inside—a definition at least a century out of date.

He was much more argumentative than analytical in privacy and Fourth Amendment cases, and admitted he was "out of synch" with the Court. When a clerk gave him a substantial memo on a search and seizure case, he said, "You don't need to go into such length and detail. Keep it down to a page or two in these cases. If there's anything there, Brennan and that crowd will find it." His opinions now frequently started with detailed descriptions of the violation. "More crime, more crime. Won't it ever stop? We have to do something," he often said to Elizabeth in the morning while reading the newspaper. The Court was "coddling criminals," he told his clerks, and felt that both it and he were responsible. "We've gone too far. We're too indulgent." So many criminals "getting away on technicalities" worried Black. "We should let the police do their job." And starting in the mid-1960s, as the crime rate in offenses against persons soared, he began writing more in these cases and less in white-collar crime cases. How the suspect was caught was not as important as giving him a fair trial. "Bringing guilty criminals to book," Black wrote in 1968, was "far more crucial" than "giving defendants every possible assistance in their attempts to invoke an evidentiary rule which itself can result in the exclusion of highly relevant evidence." He never granted the profound meaning gathered within the Fourth Amendment's words.[5]

....

Hugo Black always kept continual ideological warfare in perspective. His family remained his anchor. His best times were spent at home with them. It was there in June 1959 that JoJo married Mario Pesaresi, a New Jersey psychiatrist. Few things could have made him happier. In his eyes his "little girl," like her mother, could do no wrong, and her three children gave him immense joy. His relationship with Sterling continued to be very different. After working as a lawyer for the Atomic Energy Commission in Los Alamos, New Mexico, Sterling was elected to the state senate in 1960. "For some unaccountable reason he seems to be inclined towards politics," Black wrote his niece Hazel Davis. It was hard, he told his son, for him to guess which would be better for Sterling—to win or lose. He believed the latter.

Black thought that Sterling, because of his hearing problem and because "he has always been rather timid and diffident about his own attitudes and activities," should continue as a backroom lawyer in a secure job not requiring much public contact, so he could provide for his large family. Serving in the legislature, as Sterling did through 1968, meant that his practice would suffer financially. But despite his pride in Sterling's staunchly liberal and civil libertarian positions, he told Sterling, "It is much better not to hold public office if one cannot be wholly and completely independent." He raised his concerns in long letters that Sterling answered point by point. Occasionally, he and Elizabeth visited. Once, after speaking in Los Alamos, Black made a point to say to Sterling, "I *almost* remembered to tell them I had a son in the state senate." Later Sterling, having noted that Earl Warren had administered the oath to his son who had been newly elected to a judgeship in California, asked his father to do the same after he won re-election. Black refused.

Hugo, Jr.'s, situation contrasted. His private practice in Miami quickly flourished. And not only did he and his family continue to spend a few weeks in Alexandria each summer, but they saw much of Hugo and Elizabeth during the winters, in Florida. Black felt that Hugo, Jr., would succeed him as head of the family. "This is my beloved son, in whom I am well pleased," he crowed to a Miami legal group.[6]

*   *   *

Into the early 1960s Black seemed like a physical marvel. He continued to outwork clerks one third his age. An article in *World Tennis* magazine called him "one of the finest doubles players in official Washington."[*] Then, in

---

[*] Once Elizabeth complained that it was not polite to keep lobbing over the head of a retired

the summer of 1962, at the age of seventy-six, he had a heart scare. His electrocardiogram during his annual examination in early July deviated from past readings. "The doctors told me to go right ahead and live a normal life," he wrote Sterling, except "not to press too hard": no outside work during the Court term and no more singles in tennis. His basic routine remained the same. He was wiry, ate sparingly, walked up the steps at the Court instead of using the elevator and took his testosterone shots faithfully. Starting in late 1964, however, he tired more easily; there were days when it seemed he wouldn't get through them. He began to take notice of age as never before. In 1963 he underlined a quotation by Justice Holmes at seventy-nine: "But I am gradually reconciling myself to the inevitable . . . "; and three years later: "As he advanced in years, not only did Jefferson's unfamiliarity with current legal developments increase, but the incessant drudgery of answering letters exhausted his strength and patience." (Black's own letters grew noticeably shorter while still retaining much of their pithiness.)

He was reading markedly less ("our cases mostly"), and with more difficulty. It took him a full day in March 1965 to finish a mere three-hundred-page book on William Howard Taft as chief justice. Six months later he placed his last order with a book dealer. In March 1966 his fear that he had cataracts was confirmed. He needed bright lights and a magnifying glass to read; Elizabeth read certiorari notes to him and other sources for him.

She was the reason why he whistled as he walked up the Court steps. He wanted Harold Laski's widow Frida to meet her: "You would then understand why she has made these latter years of my life so happy, and I am confident you will have the same feeling of affection for her that you had for Josephine." "I have been much happier and I think I have been much healthier since I married," he told a cousin in 1960. "Of course this may just be the reflection of an old man who wants to feel that he is as youthful as his younger wife." He was twenty-two years older than Elizabeth and could not keep up with her. "She wants to go to every invitation we get," he complained. "You told me this was one of the fringe benefits if I married you," she said. His offer of the glamorous life was coming home to haunt him.

As Elizabeth's confidence grew, so did her social ambitions. She beamed when a guest at a party said, "Elizabeth, you have become a person in your own right." At some point during the mid-1960s she gained a form of equality

---

military man who had an artificial leg. "But they're winning," Hugo answered (BPH, 4/28/78).

in her marriage. Hugo stopped fighting all the time. No longer did he have to win every argument at home or always have everything go his way. He also depended more on her physically and emotionally, now. Often she sat up watching television in the study until well after midnight while he wrote opinions. Her mere presence gave him support. She looked up to him completely; his life was hers. "At first," she later said, "I was slightly in awe of him. Soon I realized his place in history." In mid-1964 she started to keep a diary "because he was a great man and I wanted a record of his greatness." He did not stop her. "He was hard to live with," she granted, then paused. "He was just eccentric." Yet she loved him and savored their life together.

An operation on one eye, in January 1967, substantially restored lost vision. But Hugo found it difficult to write with a pencil; Earl Warren led him from the conference room so that he wouldn't trip; and only a superb workhorse of a clerk, Stephen Susman, saved him during this term. "The Judge would give me an opinion to write, for the Court or in dissent, and tell me the result he wanted," Susman recalled, "but no guidance, just, 'Go look at this opinion.' It was usually a past opinion of his." Susman produced opinions that did Black proud. For the first time his clerks started to draft opinions on a regular basis (as did the clerks for all the other justices except Douglas). Near the end of each previous term Black had let his clerks write a first draft of an obscure case for their own enjoyment; he then took it and made it into his own. But starting in the 1964 term the clerks drafted the bulk of the opinions, with Black saving what he considered the more important cases for himself. ("I used to write all my opinions," he told them. "I finally realized I could do this. Now you fellows need the practice.") And as the Court departed increasingly from his philosophy, and as he dissented more, the scaffolding of his opinions changed. He largely stopped citing historical works and law review articles; in the 1965 term these appeared in only one opinion.

Yet Black continued to be notably active. When Earl Warren asked Hugo to join him in Geneva in July 1967 at the World Peace Through Law conference, Hugo accepted with alacrity. An American judge in attendance wrote of his speech:

> But perhaps the most dramatic, the most forceful, and best communicated appeal of any of those who preceded him, was by our own Mr. Justice Black. Justice Black, a very frail man, approaching 80, if not already, spoke for

20 minutes without a single note of paper or manuscript. His pungent remarks about his own personal fears for the future of the world, for the survival of mankind, "of you here today and myself . . . ," so interspersed with references from the pages of past and current history, so scrupulously delivered, left his audience spellbound with piercing, poignant emotion.

Then on to London, where the House of Lords was debating an abortion bill. Hugo leaned forward, listening intently and seemingly staring at a speaker advocating its passage. He was staring at a miniskirted Lady Lord. "My, she has good legs," he whispered to Elizabeth.

When they returned after a month, having also gone to Greece, Rome and Paris, Hugo was exhausted. A short hospital stay revived him before his second eye operation. It was not as successful as the first and, despite contact lenses (he sometimes used glasses instead for reading), his vision was never the same. The operations took their toll. "He is not the spry, determined tennis player of a year ago," noted Virginia Hamilton, who saw him that September, "but an old man who finds it difficult to rise and greet a visitor." His doctors told him he had failed a good bit since the operations because he had not gotten his daily exercise. On the bench during the next term, he sometimes sat back with his mouth open, asleep. He started asking more questions, and more vigorously than ever, as if to make sure he would stay awake. Often he looked weak, pale and frail—no longer the driving force he had been.[8]

*   *   *

A changing Court necessarily meant changing relationships. By the mid-1960s Douglas had alienated himself from the Court. One draft opinion had a note about a cocktail party he had been to the night before; he once appeared at the Court with lipstick on his collar. By now Black was resigned to accepting Douglas as he was, as different from everybody else as he was gifted. ("Old lover boy is the most brilliant man on the Court," noted Earl Warren.) Brennan had replaced Black as the most influential justice. As Brennan knew better than anybody else when he wrote opinions, often at Black's suggestion and admittedly influenced in part by him,* turning Black dissents into law, the Court in the 1960s was Hugo Black writ large. Brennan was much like Black in his heyday, working the halls, going to each office

---

* "Hugo influenced me in extending the Bill of Rights against the states," Brennan said (int.). "It was not an inconsiderable amount even though we still disagreed. You just can't ignore his position. He really made me think the whole thing through."

to talk over opinions, trying to switch votes or get changes in opinions or, better yet, of votes. Black didn't like this, because he was starting to lose cases as well as energy.

His feeling for Brennan came through in different ways. After the 1964 sit-in cases, he told Brennan that despite their disagreement he was "proud of" the way Brennan fought. Then there was the time near the end of a term, when pressure is great and patience often short, that Brennan told Black quite sharply over the phone that at some point in writing an opinion the end is reached. Black had been stalling, trying to persuade an undecided colleague. Soon after the conversation, Black went to see Brennan and suggested he leave the building. "This place can become like a pressure cooker and it can beat the strongest of men. You should get out of here and forget it for a few days." Brennan accepted the advice. Black was growing close to Potter Stewart. Under Stewart's reserve was a character that engendered trust. "Potter's coming along," he would say upon returning from his frequent visits to Stewart, who was thirty years younger. "He's going to be a great Justice." What he meant was that Stewart was agreeing with him more. (In 1964 Hugo "jokingly, but with great sincerity," an interviewer wrote afterward, said "that his criterion for judging whether an opinion of a fellow Justice was good or bad, was whether it agreed with his own.)

Black was perfectly friendly with Arthur Goldberg without fancying him at all. His aggressiveness, personally and intellectually, put Hugo off somewhat; he found Goldberg abrasive and arrogant. "He's another of those guys who says something is just because he says it is," Black said. He came to the Court with "the idea of doing the right thing." "I told him, 'We're here to apply the law.' " Black regarded Goldberg, and to some extent Brennan, as apostates, and that upset him, for he liked apostles: Brennan and Goldberg, he felt, would not stop until they achieved their social goals.

Goldberg resembled northern liberals whom Black had always distrusted; the cultural gulf between them and him was too large to be bridged. In 1963 Edmond Cahn told Black that "a certain civil liberties organization" (the Emergency Civil Liberties Committee) was debating whether to submit a brief opposing the claim of Mississippi governor Ross Barnett, who had willfully disobeyed a court order to admit James Meredith as the first Negro student at the University of Mississippi, that a defendant accused of contempt is entitled to a jury trial. This "simply confirms a suspicion long entertained by me that many libertarians are in favor of liberty for others unless those others harbor views obnoxious to the libertarians," Black replied. The American Civil Liberties Union submitted a brief supporting Barnett's claim. The

Court did not agree; Black and Goldberg, joined by Warren and Douglas, strongly dissented. Shortly after the case came down the next year, Norman Dorsen, a young NYU law professor just getting involved in civil liberties work (which would culminate in his being president of the ACLU), who had written its brief, visited Black at the Court. Black spoke about the "illiberalism of liberals."[9] He meant it as a friendly warning.

In a 1966 "lecture," according to a Warren biography, Black denied that Warren deserved credit for the constitutional revolution that the Court was executing. The supposed statement was correct in the large sense: a majority of justices working together in one of history's fortunate moments warranted the honor. The press distorted his remark, Black allegedly told Warren, who laughed and said, "Look, Hugo, you can't unring a bell."* But no one had ever heard such a comment, even privately, from Black, and Warren well knew the standard, if transparent, line public figures regularly used to half deny something when it serves them; he had used it himself. Seemingly endless references to the "Warren Court" galled Black enormously, and this came when he was having problems with his eyes. Soon he bragged to Thurman Arnold, Jr., "Do you realize how much I've done on the Court?" His frustration had run over.

Warren well understood and appreciated Black's feelings. "He didn't talk about it being called the 'Warren Court,'" said Justice Brennan. "He knew what Hugo was saying and thought that naming the Court after the Chief was inappropriate." For the first time Warren indicated that Black's stubbornness grated on him. "Hugo never changes his mind about anything, even things he did fifty years ago." Warren laughed as he said it, but he had never said it before. Black always expressed his admiration for Warren personally. "The Chief," he said, "was just what we needed so badly when he was appointed—someone with his instincts, not a traditional corporate law type." He noted how hard Warren worked, that he stayed up much of the night before conference to review cases. Their instinctive understanding of their complementary abilities and positions made the Court stronger and contributed to their lasting renown. Each knew when and how far to push a certain viewpoint. Warren unfailingly treated Black with deference and when he talked about him in chambers, it was always "Hugo" and with a special affection. "I love that man of yours!" he told Elizabeth many times.

* This author has found no such "lecture" or statement by Black in 1966 or any other year.

Hugo wanted to pay tribute to Warren in open court on his seventy-fifth birthday in March 1966, but Warren vetoed the idea. "Nothing in the past thirteen years has given me more pleasure and satisfaction than my association with you," Warren soon told him. "That association has really made them rewarding years for me."

Warren's mind worked like a dull knife, not a razor. He wasn't the type to reflect much, he admitted. Who won was more important than what the opinion said. He knew his limitations: his clerks wrote almost all his opinions, under his guidance and direction. Sometimes he took his clerks along, to supply references and to address doctrine, when he went to discuss cases with other justices. He instinctively understood what was at stake in the cases—what was significant and why—but "didn't think or care about his intellectual processes," observed several of his clerks. When one gave him a seven-page memo on an important case, he read it and said, "I'm not interested in this as a den of themes on both sides." Black showed his mastery of understatement when, after serving fourteen terms with Warren, he said, "I wish he knew a little more law." The camaraderie between them had lessened by then even though they still worked well together. Warren felt Black was becoming more rigid and doctrinaire. "The Chief," observed one of his clerks, "gave the distinct impression they had been very close and were now moving away from each other.[10]

*   *   *

Arthur Goldberg's resignation from the Court in 1965 was likely the biggest personal blunder by a public figure in American history. He found the Court too isolating and not as interesting as he had hoped. Johnson had tried a few times earlier to get Goldberg off the Court so that he could appoint his old friend and adviser Abe Fortas. And shortly after the death of United Nations ambassador Adlai Stevenson, he called Goldberg, who was meeting in his office with Warren and Black. They knew just why LBJ was calling and several times said, "Tell him no." But Johnson said, "Arthur, you're the only man who can bring peace to Vietnam and the man who does that will be the next man to sit in my seat." He knew, and Black also knew, that Goldberg wanted to be president (even if his chances were nil). "Arthur's great flaw was his ego," noted his longime friend David Feller. "Once you told him that he's the only man in the world able to do something, he believed it. LBJ knew that. He was really laying it on and Arthur kept saying, 'Yes, Mr. President,' and Warren and Black kept on saying, 'Tell him no.' It went on like that, Arthur said. When he got off the phone, he told them,

'I couldn't say no to the President.' He had just agreed to leave the Court and felt he couldn't back out. He told me how upset they were. He said LBJ just talked him into it."

Fortas took Goldberg's seat. Fortas was a brilliant lawyer and superb corporate counselor, a devout believer in social justice, a compassionate friend and a tough customer with a side, in the words of Charles Reich who worked for him at his law firm, "as dark as the far side of the moon." He could "render a great service on the Court," Black told Douglas. But a strain between them existed from the beginning. It was not just the overt signs of Fortas's intimacy with Johnson—such as the private line to the White House in his office (no one was allowed to interrupt him when they were talking)—that irritated Black, but that this link prevented Fortas from giving his all to the Court and that Fortas intended to keep it this way.

Black quickly realized that Fortas was the most able new justice since at least Frankfurter more than twenty-five years earlier. In one early obscure case Fortas's draft dissent persuaded two justices to switch from Black's majority draft. Fortas's became the Court's opinion, and Black was forced to dissent. On the surface he "took this in stride," Black's clerk Drayton Nabers recalled. His anger came out when he characterized Fortas's position from the bench so harshly that Harlan asked Fortas whether he realized he was "describing all that." The next month, February 1966, Black lambasted Fortas's opinion for the Court from the bench in the Louisiana library sit-in case. Yet four days later he wrote Hugo a flowery letter on his eightieth birthday.[11] Never again would Fortas write that way.

Black remained as fierce an advocate and fiery a protagonist as ever, but his causes were different. He even found considerations injecting themselves to the full exercise of "the cherished right of people in a country like ours to vote." In 1966 the Court unanimously upheld the 1965 Voting Rights Act, except for Black, who concurred and dissented. The requirement that states with a record of voting rights abuses must submit proposed changes in their election laws to the federal government for "preclearance," he wrote, inevitably creates the effect that states are "little more than conquered provinces" (the same phrase he used about the South in his 1935 Senate filibuster against the antilynching bill). In a 1969 case he made things more explicit: "This is reminiscent of old Reconstruction days when soldiers controlled the South and when those states were compelled to make reports to military commanders of what they did." Black was advancing a classic "states' rights" argument. His constitutional justification was federalism, a factor that had previously not loomed large in his mind.

In such pronouncements some people thought they saw "a new Black" emerging, one in whom a conservatism of a different type was central. Their observation was largely right. At times his new outlook was disturbing indeed. "Is there any indication how many times the [white] victim consented with Nigra men?" Black asked the defendant's lawyer in a rape case in 1966. Such a question was new. Of what relevance was this? Why did he do it? Where was this coming from?

He first started carrying a Government Printing Office issue of the Constitution around with him in the late 1940s. A decade later, he wouldn't go anywhere without his dog-eared, almost frazzled and all-marked-up copy in his coat jacket. "Let's see what it says," he would say during a disscussion at lunch and reach for it as one would for a pack of cigarettes; he also did so on the bench. In the office it was always within ready reach. "He would read it out loud and get worked up as though this decided everything," recalled a clerk. Of course it was a prop, just for show, completely unnecessary, since he had memorized the Constitution. It was also a manifest symbol of his commitment to the document—there could be no better one for a Supreme Court justice. But now he was looking for answers largely within its four corners.

His reformist zeal had sharply abated. "As the years go on . . . ," he wrote a grandniece in college, "you will find it is good to be cautious before you get out too far along any line. While it is true that all things that are old and accepted are not necessarily good, it is also true that they are not necessarily bad. . . . You always need to think very carefully before making too great a break with the past." Also his shoptalk was different. Now he spoke more about the limitations on the Court than about its powers. It was not "a day-by-day Constitutional Convention," he said. To Black the Court was no longer an engine of reform—sometimes even when the claims in the cases were essential for the democratic process to reach its full potential.

In 1966 the Court invalidated a Virginia requirement that a $1.50 tax be paid as a condition of voting. When the case was first considered in February 1965, the justices agreed to uphold the tax in a per curiam opinion until Goldberg circulated a vigorous draft dissent; Warren and Douglas joined it. A memorandum by Black led the Court to hear the case again the next term. He then led the opposition. "This is a tax," he said at conference in January 1966, "and not necessarily a discrimination. I don't doubt Congress can get rid of this under section 2 [of the Fifteenth Amendment], but the

Court can't. I don't think it comes within the classification [reached by] equal protection." At conference he voted with misgivings to overturn the tax.

Voting was a "fundamental right" in light of the Court's precedents, Douglas wrote for the Court. "Notions of what constitutes equal treatment for purposes of the equal protection Clause *do* change." On March 15 Black drafted a concurrence, calling the "right to vote" in either state or federal elections "equally basic and precious." Overnight Black changed his mind. "The Federal Constitution had not been amended" since the decision of two cases (one in 1937, the other in 1951) supporting his view. "Whatever may be our personal opinions," he wrote in his first draft, "history is on the side of rationality of the state's poll tax policy. The Colonies had property qualifications for voting and so have some of the states since the Constitution was adopted, all the way up to this very date." His opinion went through five drafts in five days. He objected to using the equal protection clause as the due process clause had been used, as "a blank check to alter the meaning of the Constitution as written," he wrote in the final version. Black wanted to limit it solely to reach racial discrimination.

His switch annoyed Earl Warren and put Douglas in the unhappy position of responding to Black's arguments. "Our conclusion . . . ," Douglas added, "is founded not on what we think governmental policy should be, but on what the equal protection clause requires." Five other justices agreed; only Black, Harlan and Stewart dissented. When delivering the opinion, Elizabeth noted in her diary, "Hugo was determined not to be charged with 'shaking with anger,' " as the press had reported the month before. "And so he talked with a half-smile on his face and without the usual passion, though now and then it would creep in at the turn of a phrase. It was a matter he felt very strongly on—not just the demise of the poll tax, but of Bill's splitting with him and 'writing new law' by construing it under the equal protection clause. Bill had pushed Hugo unmercifully on this case all week and Hugo was relieved after it came down."

They went at it again in December 1966, after the Georgia legislature, under federal court order to reapportion itself, was preparing to elect a governor according to a provision in the state constitution giving it that power when no gubernatorial candidate receives a majority of the vote. Black and Douglas virtually debated the case through opposing counsel at argument; Black pounced on other justices' leading questions. He wrote for five justices, over four strong dissents. "This Court, *this* Court, this *Court*," he said—three times in all—when announcing his opinion, "is not allowed to

write laws. We are here to interpret only!" The original judicial champion
of reapportionment was accepting the argument that a malapportioned legislature can frustrate the apparent will of the people.[12]

Flashes of the old Black burst through occasionally. "It's really a magnificent opinion," Brennan told him about one 1967 effort, overruling a
decade-old precedent. But the Court in these years was crossing a seam in
history, a dividing line to a new era; and Black not only would not join it,
he led the revolt against it. For the first time in his life he was seriously out
of joint with his times. He had been steering the charge in one direction
and was now rebelling against the logical extension of his own views. The
openness, the flexibility, the receptivity to new ideas that had so typified
him were now quickly atrophying. The surprising thing is that becoming a
prisoner of his philosophy, not its servant, didn't bother him.

"Hugo changed, the man changed, right in front of us," noted Justice
Brennan. "It was so evident. We talked about it much, the Chief and Bill
Douglas probably more than anyone else. Bill especially was really hurt. We
lost our fifth vote," Brennan continued, his voice rising. "Those of us who
cared for him certainly felt sad. We were afraid it would hurt him in history
and in academia." In early 1966 Earl Warren observed: "Black has hardened
and gotten old. It's a different Black now.[13]*

---

* "Hugo of today is not Hugo of five years ago," Brennan said in early 1968 (Drew Pearson
  int. with WJB, Pearson papers).

THE LEGEND

B<small>Y THE</small> <small>MID</small>-1960s Hugo Black had gained lasting recognition as one of the handful of truly great Supreme Court justices. Ranking the justices has never been one of the favorite indoor games of most Americans, but those who played it placed Black in the highest tier. This was not surprising: he had led the redirection of American law toward the protection of the individual. What was surprising was the source of some of the new admiration.

Felix Frankfurter's death released his "boys" from the grip of what Fred Rodell had called "those velvet claws." It started after Felix suffered his stroke. No longer clashing and vying for dominance with Hugo, he let one and all know how deeply Hugo's concern touched him. Felix's acolytes started writing and saying things about Hugo's personal qualities that they would never have done (at least they never did) while Felix was active. They knew about these admirable traits all along but ignored them. Now that Hugo's change of views bridged much of the doctrinal gap, and the afterglow of Felix's pyrotechnics faded (in John Hart Ely's phrase), they suddenly appreciated Hugo's worth as a human being, instead of remaining fixated on his supposed "lawlessness." These Frankfurter devotees became leading voices in the ideologically diverse chorus praising Hugo.

Black was now "one of the great men of his generation" and "a master advocate" to Wallace Mendelson. "Magnificent in great age," Alexander Bickel characterized him in 1969. The most notable encomium came from Paul Freund: "He is without doubt the most influential of the many strong figures who have sat during the thirty years that have passed in his Justiceship. He has exhibited to a singular degree an intense moral commitment, concentrated through the focus of an unwavering vision, and brought to bear with immense prowess." "Of all the men in power in the New Deal," Tom Corcoran told Black in 1962, "you have had what will be historically the greatest because you have wielded yours from a strategic position for so long." By 1967 only seven other justices had served as long as Black; and of these Marshall, Holmes and Brandeis had the most enduring influence. But that was before the constitutional revolution of recent years which, in broad terms, had made Black's views those of the Court. As Judge Charles E. Wyzanski, Jr., said in 1966: "A historian writing 100 years from now would probably conclude that Justice Black had the greatest impact on the Supreme Court and on constitutional law in this country of any justice on the Court to date except Chief Justice Marshall."

Tributes were coming Black's way at every turn. After receiving honorary degrees in 1941, 1954 and 1955, he declined any further degrees or awards. "Basically," he explained, "I presume my reason is that I think it is the duty of a Supreme Court Associate Justice to perform his duties the best he can and that doing this gives him as much honor as he is entitled to receive." In more lasting form Stephen Strickland, a young Alabamian serving as the head of the White House fellows under Lyndon Johnson, edited a volume of sympathetic essays on Black. "While I appreciate what everyone wrote in that book," the justice wrote a former clerk, "I must say that there are some few statements with which I would have difficulty myself. At any rate, Steve did a good job in exciting the public to some extent about his book."[1]

Even Alabama joined in tribute. Buddy Cooper, Black's first clerk and always his biggest booster in the state, spearheaded a quiet effort to honor him in Birmingham. No hall was available for such purpose, so Cooper booked the Hillcrest Country Club, a Jewish establishment, for July 1966. Over one hundred people were quietly invited, but word inevitably got out and, perhaps predictably, the Birmingham Bar Association's governing board voted against asking him to speak. Black bounced from friend to friend he hadn't seen in years, pumping hands with abandon, engaging in animated conversation. "Why, he's back down here running for the Senate again," observed his old supporter Abe Berkowitz. Then for more than an hour and a half he re-minisced while proclaiming his happiness ("I'm not mad at anybody"), en-tertained, philosophized and even lectured a little. "I yield to no man in my love for the South. But I also love all my country. . . . The American dream calls for a society in which every individual shall live as a free man. . . . We look forward to a world in which men everywhere shall be entitled to walk upright, to enjoy full individual freedom, and to live in peace." It was Hugo's first visit to Alabama in over six years. He visited relatives and old friends, paid respects at cemeteries, sang old songs, returned to his roots. A start had been made.

Black was surprised and gratified that the South was changing. "Brotherly love" would be needed to solve the race problem; the South had much to teach the North in this regard. Even so, he wrote a grandnephew who grew up in south Alabama:

> I hope you can do some part of your college work outside the particular section in which you have been reared. This will subject you to ideas and habits quite new to you, broadening your intellectual horizons. People in each section of our great nation tend to have their ideas fashioned by their own immediate environments—that is they become provincial in their thinking. A man with a good education shakes off this habit, learns that no one person, group, or section has a monopoly on knowledge or truth, and then has a chance to live a wiser and a happier life. In this connection you might get some good thoughts from the story of the cavemen which you can find in Plato's *Republic*, Book VII.

Alabama remained mired in the past longer than any other state. True change did not come until the late 1960s at the earliest, only in part because of the presence of that gifted demagogue George Wallace—"the greatest danger in the state's history," Black called him. But a new generation was rising, and it warmed Black's heart that both the Alabama and Birmingham bar associations wanted to honor him in 1968. "Agree with him or not," James E. (Red) Clark, the president of the state bar, said later, "Hugo Black was the greatest lawyer and the greatest man ever to come from Alabama. He deserved all the tributes we could give him." So Clark, whose wife had long been close friends with Elizabeth, well understood Hugo's response: "I have in my home a very strong advocate for my going to all the places in Alabama to which I am invited. . . . Since I am rather fond of that lady and want to keep her in good humor, I shall probably have to be constrained to accept your invitation, although two speeches within three months in one state is a little more than I had contemplated.[2]

Circulating around Birmingham for a while was a line some fine wit had come up with. Hugo, Jr., also picked it up and used it to introduce his father to speak in Miami. It spoke to Black's predicament in his adopted native city:

Hugo Black used to go around in white robes, scaring black people. Now he goes around in black robes, scaring white people.

"Not riches, as some say, but honour is the delight of men when they are old and useless," Black had long ago underlined in Thucydides' funeral speech for Pericles. These tributes were a great tonic for him. With less to look forward to, he yearned for public recognition of what he had done. The Birmingham Bar Association, keeping to form, noted in a press release that some of his recent opinions had a "characteristic 'Southern' posture" and that he was increasingly "aligned with the more conservative justices" such as Harlan and Stewart. A federal judge and leading lawyers met Black at the airport on May 3, 1968, and a police escort squired him downtown, where he saw a growing skyline. (No skyscraper had been built in Birmingham between 1927 and 1962; this was a city where a reporter wrote, "Progress came once more to downtown Birmingham today with the opening of a gleaming new parking lot.")

How different it was from the times Black came quietly at night to see Hugo, Jr. "I'm glad to be home again," he told a reporter. But Black gave no "conservative" speech. Virtually equating the Supreme Court with the Constitution, he said, "I don't want to live under a government that can kick me around without my rights in court." The Bill of Rights "is one of the greatest things in the Constitution. They had to put it in because of protest from southern states. When you hear people insulting the Constitution of the United States, tell them 'that's my Constitution. I'm a southerner.'" He was conspicuously conciliatory. "I thought you were almost too kind to your old enemies," Virginia Durr told him, "but you simply heaped coals of fire on the head and killed them with kindness." The meeting was "excellent," Black replied.

It seems to me that the sentiment in Birmingham is greatly improved. I must confess that getting back home after so long an absence and seeing many of my old friends and the sons of my old friends, and missing others, gave me a nostalgic feeling that was perhaps manifested in what I said.

As one looks back over the years, however, past differences which seemed so all-important at the time they existed, somehow get smoothed out and put in the position of relativity [sic] that they should really occupy. I presume the reason it sounded like I was forgiving was that I was. As a matter of fact, as I reflected on the past I could not think of any Birmingham lawyer as an enemy. Time has permitted me to realize that those I thought were the worst had some good qualities. . . . I sincerely hope that what I said may have made some people think just a little more of their national government.

In July 1968 the state bar honored him. Riots, demonstrations, strikes and other controversies are nothing new, he told the group at its annual meeting, displaying a copy of a 1934 Alabama newspaper. He referred to the one man—one vote reapportionment case: "How many votes would you want your opponent to have?" And he brought the house down with his remarks that "any judge who won't interpret the Constitution according to his best intellectual judgment isn't worth his salt and ought not to be a judge" and "I am just old fashioned enough to believe that the Constitution of the United States means exactly what it says." His hands shaking, tears rolling down his cheeks, he closed by reading from William Cullen Bryant's poem "Thanatopsis":

> So live, that when the summons comes to join
> The unnumerable caravan which moves
> To that mysterious realm, where each shall take
> His chamber in the silent halls of death.
> Thou go not, like the quarry-slave at night,
> Scourged to his dungeon, but, sustained and soothed
> By an unfaltering trust, approach thy grave,
> Like one who wraps the drapery of his couch
> About him and lies down to pleasant dreams.[3]

*   *   *

Black never cottoned to any of the Kennedys: they were just too different. He deplored Joseph Kennedy because of his pro-Nazi stance before World War Two. (When John Frank told Black that John J. Burns, who had reviewed his book on Black in 1949, had been a close associate of Kennedy's, Black replied, "I should regret to think that either of these two gentlemen thought too highly of me.") Nor, visiting the sins of the father on the son, did Black particularly like John Kennedy. As a senator, Kennedy had introduced a bill depriving defendants of jury trials in certain types of contempt cases. "They're saying this guy is a liberal," Black remarked. "I could understand someone being a liberal all along introducing a bill like this, perhaps for political reasons. They'd be wrong but I could understand that. But this guy hasn't really done anything yet. Whatever he is, he is no liberal." Black favored Adlai Stevenson for the presidency in 1960.*

The Court was in conference on November 22, 1963, when word came that Kennedy had been shot in Dallas. One week later, the new president, Lyndon Johnson, persuaded Warren to head a commission to investigate the assassination. Warren returned to the Court to tell the justices. Black, Harlan and Brennan said he was wrong in accepting. Black cited Chief Justice Stone's criticism of Robert Jackson for taking a leave from the Court to serve as Nuremberg prosecutor. Only Goldberg did not disapprove. "I don't approve of it either," Warren said tearfully, "but circumstances were such that I couldn't refuse." The next year, after the commission's report was released, Black tried to give the impression that the Warren Commission was an unfortunate necessity: " 'This is different. It's so important for the confidence of the people.' But the way he said it," recalled his clerk James North, "it seemed he was trying to talk himself into believing it." He could not quite say justices should do nothing other than sit as justices, for he had done many other things himself; but those were occasional chores, nothing like the formal post Warren assumed. Black thought justices should not undertake any other official duties while on the Court.[4]

Black had long admired Johnson's remarkable ability as a political operator. He overlooked some of Johnson's mannerisms, for they believed in much the same things. As a congressional assistant in the mid-1930s, Johnson played up to Black, once driving him home from the Senate and asking repeated questions about his economic views, trying to soak him for information. Black knew such techniques well, having used some of them himself years before. Soon House Speaker Sam Rayburn was telling Johnson "quite often," recalled Lady Bird Johnson, "that Senator Black was very smart and shrewd. He usually didn't talk much about the Senate but he did about Senator Black." Hugo and Josephine began seeing Lyndon and the charming Lady Bird at parties, usually at the Durrs', who were close friends of the Johnsons. The guests generally included Bill Douglas, Abe Fortas and Lowell Mellett and their wives, and Tom Corcoran and Ben Cohen. "It was an intellectual group," Lady Bird said, "loaded on the liberal side and young.

---

* Black also simply did not like Robert Kennedy, even aside from his father and his working for Senator Joseph McCarthy. Kennedy lunched with the justices' law clerks in 1961. "He was so nervous," recalled one of Black's clerks, "saying, 'I'm with all these guys who are all so smart.' " Then he wrote an article in *Esquire* about the lunch, claiming how confident he was. "The Judge didn't like that sort of thing" (Saunders int.). And knowing what her father's reaction would be, JoJo never told him of Robert Kennedy's advances toward her when they were in Iran with Justice Douglas.

There was always good conversation." After Johnson's 1948 election to the Senate, where he became minority leader in four years and majority leader two years later, an unprecedented accomplishment, Black heard much about him from Lister Hill. He was duly impressed.

"I do not believe Lyndon Johnson would make a bad President," Black told Virginia Durr in 1959. "He has many fine qualities." The next spring, when Kennedy and Johnson were the leading candidates for the Democratic presidential nomination, Elizabeth said, reflecting Hugo's views, "We think well of Lyndon Johnson." Johnson, he felt, would be "a formidable candidate, although being from the South is probably a considerable handicap for him." After the Kennedy-Johnson ticket was elected, many people in Washington ignored and scorned Johnson. He found Black's always extended hand of friendship even more welcome, and he and Lady Bird occasionally came over to the Blacks for an informal meal and relaxed conversation. (Sometimes Lady Bird played bridge with Hugo and Elizabeth.) Each time after dinner, as Hugo took them into the kitchen so they could tell Lizzie Mae how good the corn bread or the turnip greens were, Lady Bird said to herself, "Only a Southerner . . ."

This common bond was never far from the surface. "Since Fate for some reason hard to understand decreed that there was to be a new President," Black wrote Johnson shortly after Kennedy's assassination, "I am happy that the new one is a Southerner, and that you are that Southerner. I knew before you so earnestly and eloquently said it that you would give this country your *best*. With Lady Bird to help I am confident that your 'best' will cause history to write your name high among the special group of American Presidents illustrious because of their humanity, courage, wisdom, and integrity." Johnson's ascension reaffirmed Black's conviction that "Republican" was a synonym for rapscallion. Thus he wrote LBJ in early 1965: "It was therefore no surprise to me that in 1964 you were elected President despite the political handicap that had helped to close the doors of the White House to southerners for more than a century. In accomplishing this you performed a great service to the south and to the Nation as a whole.

Johnson had felt the same way about Black for thirty years. "Here is a southerner," he told Lady Bird, "with a type of mind who could compete with the brightest minds in the nation. He could outHarvard the Harvards and beat the politicians at politics." "Lyndon thought the Justice could do it all," she said. And now he showered praise on Black. To a laudatory birthday letter ("you have, as your colleagues like to say, placed the 'Black brand' on many historic advances in America's progress"), he added by hand,

"And I need not remind you that I have been the recipient and beneficiary of your courage and wisdom." Above all, Lyndon Johnson never forgot Black's role in his election to the Senate in 1948.[5]

Noting Black's eightieth birthday in the newspaper in 1966, Johnson threw a small party in the family quarters on twenty-four hours' notice. He inscribed a watercolor portrait of himself "To Hugo Black, 80 years young and every one of them fighting for the people." Lady Bird Johnson called it "one of the warmest and happiest evenings in the White House. He is a man whose friendship we've treasured for more than twenty-five years." Black saw Johnson several times over the next few months. They had an off-the-record meeting on May 21, 1966. "He wants to discuss the judicial conference from which he has recently returned in the 5th Circuit," a presidential assistant noted. This was a likely cover: Johnson would soon make five appointments to the Fifth Circuit, including one from Alabama.

Five days later, Hugo and Elizabeth had a dinner for the justices and the Johnsons. It was a most congenial crowd. Black, Douglas, Clark and Fortas had known LBJ for years, Warren for not as long but still well, and White had been a prominent member of the Kennedy administration. "Sometimes we'd get into a car," said Brennan, "and go over to the White House for a drink late in the afternoon. Tom Clark set it up." And this dinner, Lady Bird wrote in her diary, "was so casual and friendly, such a feeling that we were at home."

Like anybody who knew Lister Hill, Johnson knew that he and Black had been close friends. When he heard they hadn't spoken in a while, he had them and their wives to a small dinner in the White House. They stayed late reminiscing. Even aside from politics, Hugo's relationship with Lister was never the same after he "broke" with Lister for Lister's sake in the mid-1950s. It could not be, and soon they saw each other "most infrequently," as Hugo later noted. Each time Lister was restrained. Hugo understood this, and he sympathized with Lister's predicament on racial issues. "Lister doesn't believe in what he's doing. He has to do it," Hugo told Elizabeth. (Hill admitted this after he retired.) And in 1964 Hugo said with a smile: "Alabama has a tradition of great senators." He became more serious: "Lister and Sparkman couldn't stay up there politically otherwise." But basically the relationship declined because, as Elizabeth noted, "Henrietta did not want to see another wife in Josephine's place." She resented (and was jealous of) Elizabeth, conveyed the definite impression she looked down on her and deliberately snubbed her more than once. This so annoyed Black that he did not speak to Hill about supporting Buddy Cooper for a federal judgeship in Birmingham in 1961.[6]

In 1967 Johnson honored Black's thirty years on the Court with a gala party for almost one hundred guests in the State Dining Room. Black took Spencer and Lizzie Mae with him. All the justices, some Fifth Circuit judges, the Alabama senators, many of Black's family and friends, most of his clerks and some journalists were there; Tom Corcoran played his accordion. Johnson had to go to Germany to attend Chancellor Konrad Adenauer's funeral, so Vice President Hubert Humphrey stepped in. Black had few greater admirers than this former Minnesota senator. They likely met through Lister Hill and saw each other quite often at dinners at Martin Agronsky's (after which Black would always say, "Hubert talks too much"). But here, for once, Humphrey was concise, saying Black stood for the people nobody else was for. Then Hugo spoke. He talked about his years in Washington, about his feeling for his fellow senators and justices, and the changes he had seen. "Never did I wish more ardently that we'd had a tape recording . . . ," Lady Bird Johnson wrote. "There was a web of silence in the State Dining Room and a communion between all of the guests. It was a long speech but we would have all liked more." No other justice has ever been feted in this way, much less twice.

"Dear Lyndon," Hugo wrote on December 15, 1967, "Christmas and New Year's evoke memories of what has happened during the past twelve months. My reflections bring vividly to mind your kind and generous action in inviting my family and friends to a reception in honor of my thirty years' service as an Associate Justice. It was good to have an opportunity to see so many of the people I love under circumstances so pleasant. We, of course, greatly missed you but Lady Bird was as always magnificent. Her graciousness and charm made the party a complete success. . . . I cannot thank you enough for the reception. . . . Sincerely your friend, Hugo."

He had mellowed. To his former clerk Charles Reich, who refused to attend because of Johnson's Vietnam policy, Black said: "I am inclined to think that at 25 or so or at your age I might have felt very much as you do about a situation of this kind. Years, however, bring changes in emotions and emphasis and it seems wholly appropriate for me now to have had this reception at the White House although I am not and never have been a friend of the Vietnam war."[7]

. . . .

Black adamantly recoiled against American involvement in Vietnam nearly from the beginning. "It's immoral," he said in early 1964. "Our national interest isn't involved and the domino theory is silly. They all like it now but in a little while they'll call it Johnson's war and nobody's going to like it. It's going to ruin Lyndon. He could be the greatest president we've ever had but when those bodybags come back they'll ruin him." He brought the subject up often: "What a horrible mistake for the country and a political mistake for Lyndon." Political considerations were never far from Black's mind. "If Lyndon doesn't stop that war, he'll never be re-elected President," he said in Spring 1966. "Those silver caskets will be big trouble." Who would the other candidates be? "There's an election going on in California soon, and I hope Pat Brown wins. I know him and like him, he's a Democrat. But there's a movie actor running out there and he might make it to the White House."

Black resolved to do what he could to prevent what he considered that catastrophe. He spoke to Johnson's assistants. In June 1965 he told Douglass Cater, an Alabamian with whom he had long been friends, how "sad and wrong" the American presence in Vietnam was; and in August (to Jack Valenti), how wars often cause presidents to be defeated. In between came Arthur Goldberg's resignation. So overriding was ending the "war" to Black that as much as he did not want Goldberg to leave the Court, the search for peace was inestimably more urgent. He considered discussing the matter with Johnson but decided not to. It won't help, he said. But he also didn't want to threaten his friendship and the good times they, and especially Elizabeth, were having, even if Lady Bird Johnson has said, "it would have made no difference to us whatever the Justice might have said." And what he was saying was that "Vietnam is the worst thing that has ever happened to this country": "It's insanity." *

Johnson's Great Society represented the fruition of many programs Black had proposed in the Senate, the culmination of his hopes and dreams. Nearly as important, his affection for Lady Bird was an important reason he liked Lyndon so much. To Black she epitomized womanhood, and not just southern womanhood. She and Elizabeth got along splendidly; and Elizabeth relished

---

* Despite his views on American involvement in Vietnam, Black refused to be the fourth vote (besides Douglas, Brennan and Stewart, and Harlan on one occasion) to hear claims that it was not a "war." "That's very far out," he said. "It's a political question and the Court would be powerless to enforce its decision" (Price, Harmon ints.).

Lyndon's stock question, "Did he beat you yesterday? At tennis, I mean."
In 1968 Black told an interviewer for the Johnson Library:

> I don't know how much he's read [which was Black's way of saying John-
> son didn't read much]. He has a higher love, and [an] excellent mind by
> nature. . . . He's learned government from the practical standpoint. It's
> not theoretical and he believes in a consensus perhaps more than I do.
> Maybe I'd fight quicker than he would, I don't know [which meant that
> Black would]. But one thing [for] sure, I wouldn't fight any harder. Nobody
> can fight any harder than he does. I have the greatest faith in his honesty
> and his integrity and his ability. He has ability. He has far more ability
> than many college professors and presidents or many names with honorable
> degrees after them. He's learned government from the bottom, and he's
> just valuable.
>
> That doesn't mean I agree with all he's done. I don't. Some things
> I'm much against that he's very strongly for. But that's all right. He's for
> them, and I recognize that he's honest. And he's giving it all he has. And
> I couldn't say anything about him—I couldn't stop talking to you about
> him without saying that I think the greatest good fortune that ever came
> into his life came when he married his wife. She is grand. She's a great
> person. She can lead people. She's honest. She helped him. And I think
> she loves him very devotedly. And she's been an asset to him that nobody
> can exaggerate. As you see, I place him very highly.[8]

*   *   *

William C. Warren, dean of Columbia Law School, first approached Black
about delivering the Carpentier Lectures in the fall of 1956. "He always said
they'd take too much time to prepare," Warren recalled, "and switch the
conversation. I liked him so much I almost didn't mind." To his clerks Black
talked about the lectures too often for them to be something he shouldn't
do. "I have just about decided" to give them, he said in June 1959, only to
change his mind the next month: "I do not want to be in a rush. Deadlines
are not conducive to clear and mature thought." So it went. He intended
to do it but wasn't in much of a hurry. Elizabeth, however, kept after him.
And in the summer of 1966, spurred by the memorandum he wrote in *Time
v. Hill,* which persuaded the Court to switch from Abe Fortas's proposed
majority opinion, he worked on them.

Commentators, meanwhile, were increasingly remarking that Black was
reaching seemingly different results from a few years earlier. Archibald Cox
had, Harry Kalven soon would, and several conservative journalists mistakenly thought they saw a latter-day convert to their persuasion. But the inquiry
that goaded Black came from Henry Steele Commager. Black considered

Commager "a practical pragmatic historian who is not easily influenced by people or prejudice" and who had "rendered some fine service through the years by discussing basic liberties in a clear and forthright manner." In January 1967 he asked Black whether his opinion in the recent sit-in case *Adderley v. Florida* "represents a modification or a retreat" from his earlier views. "I am unaware" of any variation, Black replied; and in his next letter: "Try as hard as I can, I have discovered that it is difficult to write so as to get my own views clearly understood." Each letter atypically went through several drafts; Black was getting tired of hearing people say he changed.

"A number of people," he soon told Warren, "have been writing about my views in a way that causes me now to want to express those views for myself." Because of his cataract operations Black did not work on the lectures until the fall of 1967. He asked his clerks for cases his critics said he would now supposedly decide differently. "Whenever we came up with some," recalled Stephen Schulhofer, "he would always distinguish them. He was pretty agile in doing so." He assigned the other clerk, Joseph Price, to work nearly full time on the lectures and even took Price with him to Florida for three weeks. By year's end he said the lectures would be ready for delivery the following spring. "It's the hardest thing I ever wrote," he noted. He felt like he was lifting a veil of secrecy.[9]

The demand for tickets was so great that Columbia had to move the lectures to a larger auditorium. Hugo wore a necklace microphone as he delivered his remarks. (On a day between lectures he lunched with the *New York Times* editorial board. He told Elizabeth "to look pretty but act dumb, and I think I succeeded in the latter," she noted. To the journalists' astonishment he said the Court "could survive" a few promotions of judges from lower courts to the Court.) He received standing ovations at the beginning and end of each of the three lectures, and applause rippled throughout.

Drawing liberally from his favorite sources—history and his own past cases—Black painted with broad strokes indeed. He spoke of the role of courts under the Constitution, due process and the First Amendment. "Language and history" are "the crucial factors . . . in interpreting the Constitution." This separated him from those people who wanted the Court to be a leader in fostering social change: "I say I have known a different court from the one today. What has occurred may occur again." Soft phrases about the "living Constitution" have a "siren-like appeal." But they did not penetrate his intellectual skin: he trotted out his old Senate speeches about excesses under the due process clause. ("I didn't find anything in them that I could disagree with," he told a friend. "Of course, I might have purified the language some.") And he repeated that government must guard speech but need not provide a platform for it. Our system does not require that officials "will act in response to pre-emptory demands of the leaders of tramping, singing, shouting, angry groups controlled by men who, among their virtues, have the ordinary amount of competing ambitions common to mankind. . . . Government by clamorous and demanding groups is very far removed from government by the people's choice at the ballot box." Once again, he drew the line between "freedom to believe in and advocate a doctrine and freedom to engage in conduct violative of law."

Emotionally, he closed expressing his "deep respect and boundless admiration and love for our Constitution and the men who drafted it."

> My experiences with and for our government have filled my heart with gratitude and devotion to the Constitution which made my public life possible. That Constitution is my legal bible; its plan of our government is my plan and its destiny my destiny. I cherish every word of it, from the first to the last, and I personally deplore even the slightest deviation from its least important commands. I have thoroughly enjoyed my small part in trying to preserve our Constitution with the earnest desire that it may meet the fondest hope of its creators, which was to keep this nation strong and great through countless ages.

The crowd stood and cheered and cheered as the tears rolled down Hugo's cheeks.

"Your correspondence to me, along with Dean Warren's constant prodding," Black soon told Henry Commager, "had something to do with my decision to give the lectures." Alfred Knopf happily published them with minimal changes under the title A Constitutional Faith. The reviews were invariably respectful. As Jon Waltz wrote in the Washington Post, "Readers will know that they have come face-to-face with a man who, throughout a long and consequential life, has employed his powers for no purpose other than the advancement of this nation's founders."[10] Few people would dare to cavil at such a testament by the grand old man of the American Constitution.

*   *   *

Martin Agronsky first approached Black for a television interview in 1957. "I just thought it would be a wonderful idea to have someone so eloquent and such a part of history on TV," Agronsky said. Then, in early 1964, "I really started working on him. I saw him every few weeks. At first he utterly refused. 'It's the wrong thing to do,' he said. 'What would my colleagues think?' Black felt that only a judge's opinions spoke for him." Agronsky relayed Black's objections to CBS News president Fred Friendly. "He can't do that," Friendly said. "Let's have dinner. I'll take care of him." By meal's end, having heard Friendly's appeal about how useful it would be to future students to view him on tape, Black softened a little; at least he didn't say no. (Later Friendly told Agronsky, "Really charming guy but really stubborn.")

The idea sat quiescent for a while. Agronsky asked Elizabeth to "work on him a bit." She tried; Hugo didn't appreciate it. "I'm thinking about it," he told Friendly and David Ginsburg, whom Friendly had asked to speak to Black. That was progress. When Friendly joined public television in the summer of 1968, he again approached Black. "I'm still thinking about CBS" came the reply. Finally, in August 1968 Black unexpectedly told Agronsky he had spoken to Earl Warren and Douglas, and they wouldn't mind if he did the interview. Respect for the Court was at a low ebb: conservatives were attacking it relentlessly, and Richard Nixon, the Republican presidential candidate, was trying to arouse "the peace forces as against the criminal forces" in the country. He promised that if elected, he would appoint only "strict constructionists" to the Court. "He's talking about you and me," Douglas jokingly told Black, who laughed and said, "I don't think so." Nixon's was the reaction to the Court's decisions Black feared, and to counter it he accepted Agronsky's offer.

Black and Agronsky talked about possible interview subjects. "I'd raise one and he often said, 'well, I've written about it,' " Agronsky recalled. "Even about cases he said, 'you shouldn't evaluate them after they're written.' And he stayed away from politics. Sometimes he'd say, 'I'm tired,' and send me away. After we did a practice run, he said he decided not to do it and went into the whole thing about judges only writing opinions. I told him about 'your place in history. When you're gone, I want to have your record.' That helped some. I pointed out how valuable his Columbia lectures were. 'That's a teacher talking to students,' he said. 'I'm speaking at a university.' He felt a Supreme Court Justice shouldn't be revealed on camera." Hugo, Jr., came to Washington on business. His father told him about the verbal agreement he had with CBS, allowing him to review the recording for accuracy and any misstatements or to withhold permission for the broadcast entirely. Get it in writing, the son said. The justice did. (It's good to have a lawyer in the family.)

They filmed it in Black's study at home. The CBS News hierarchy insisted that Eric Sevareid join Agronsky in questioning Black, claiming that the show would be livelier with two people. Black very reluctantly went along. One of the subjects they asked about was the Klan. "I did it because it mattered," Agronsky said. "You couldn't do a public TV show without it. If Black didn't talk about it, I thought we shouldn't run the show." Black interrupted his questioners more when discussing this than any other subject; he was defensive and evasive. Why did you belong? Agronsky asked. "Just joined it to—it was one of those organizations," answered Black. ". . . I joined many. I wanted to meet people and I did and a large number of the lawyers belonged to them, all of them." Upon reviewing the tape, Black recalled his 1937 statement that he would not address the question publicly again and insisted that his comments be deleted. It turned out that producer Burton Benjamin had already eliminated them.

The program was originally scheduled for a half hour, for which three hours were shot. Benjamin called CBS News president Richard Salant from the airport on his way back to New York. "This interview is electrifying," he said. "It must be an hour." Black called Agronsky again to say how distressed he was and what a mistake he made. "I told him it was the best thing I had ever done, and it was," Agronsky recalled. "I had to keep reassuring him. He resisted from beginning to end. He was just wonderful to be with and a great man but the most difficult guy I ever had to deal with. [11]

The broadcast depicted a judge doctrinaire only in his fidelity to the Constitution. To those who claimed this was purposely ambiguous, that the document compelled interpretation, Black tried to show otherwise. He had long felt that a Supreme Court justice did not have to be a lawyer: "The legal profession could use a breath of fresh air," he once said. But when he now suggested Walter Lippmann as an example of a nonlawyer who would be a good justice, that was a bone to the intellectuals. Black would have more likely preferred Walter Reuther. Agronsky brought up accusations that the Court's decisions restricted police and aided criminals:

> BLACK: Well, the Court didn't do it. . . . The Constitution-makers did it. They were the ones that put in no man should be compelled to convict himself. . . . I don't see how anybody could deny that the Constitution says absolutely and in words that nobody can deny, in the Fifth Amendment, that "no person be compelled in a criminal case, to be a witness

against himself." And so, when they say the Court did it, that's just a little
wrong. The Constitution did it.

AGRONSKY: Mr. Justice, do you think that those decisions have made
it more difficult for the police to combat crime?

BLACK: Certainly. Why shouldn't they? What were they written for? Why
did they write the Bill of Rights? They practically all relate to the way
cases shall be tried. And practically all of them make it more difficult to
convict people of crime. . . . They were written to make it more difficult.
And what the Court does is try to follow what they wrote, and say you've
got to try people in this way. . . . They were, every one, intended to make
it more difficult before the doors of a prison closed on a man because of
his trial.

AGRONSKY: You're all for that?

BLACK: Yes, I'm for it. I'm for it. I'm for the Bill of Rights. I'm not saying,
now, that I would write every one in the exact language they have written
them. But I'll try to enforce them in the exact language they were written. . . . I think when those men met in Philadelphia, they had behind
them knowledge of a long series of oppression in Europe. They knew about
people getting their tongue torn out, their ears clipped off. Having to fight,
fight, fight. I think they wanted to get away from that. . . . This Constitution . . . is, to me, the best document that has ever been written to
control a government. . . . It's failed at various times and in various localities. But it's done mighty well, compared with other nations of the
world. . . . I think this country has lived because of its Constitution and
its laws and its ideals of liberty and equality and freedom.

The words rolled out, thirty years of certitude behind them. He picked up
a volume of cases beside him and read, with mounting emotion, the closing
of *Chambers v. Florida*. By the end ("this constitutional shield, deliberately
planned and inscribed for the benefit of every human being, subject to our
Constitution . . ."), the camera showed him wiping away tears.

Hugo and Elizabeth watched the program at Agronsky's house as a favor to
his wife, who was suffering from cancer. Also on at the same time was a
Brigitte Bardot movie, whose banning in Dallas the Court had recently
overturned. The resulting publicity, Black told a friend, would add to her
audience and perhaps leave few people to watch his interview. So at dinner
Agronsky said, deadpan, that two television sets were available. "One is for
Mr. Justice Black to watch his program. The other set is for the nine of us."

The next day, Bill Douglas said it was "excellent. Maybe you will make
Cary Grant move over!" Potter Stewart called it "just fine. You did a great

deal of good for the Court, for the Constitution, and for the country."
(Hugo's old constitutents in Birmingham could not discover this: its CBS
affiliate did not run the show.) Commentators nationwide were nearly unanimous in their approval, and the program won an Emmy as the best cultural
documentary of the year. "It was the best interview ever on TV," said Fred
Friendly, who had seen as many as anybody since his days with Edward R.
Murrow. *

The voluminous praise dispelled Black's misgivings. At the Court's next
conference he went on at length about how much he enjoyed the interview
and how many letters of praise he was receiving. "We let the old man talk,"
Douglas grumbled afterward. "We figured, if it made him happy, why not?"
The 1,500 letters Black received "convinced" him that he had made no
mistake. Its reception was "a great pleasure for me." Hugo had not become
a folk hero—that is rare even among monumental figures. More fitting, as
Max Lerner noted, was "a near-reverence with which lawyer and layman
alike now regard him." All people had to admit what Elizabeth wrote of the
accolades: "Some may say that he may be wrong in some of his views but
all agree he is a warm, great, and good man, and a patriot to his country
and its Constitution."[12]

---

* Since Black had often referred to his copy of the Constitution during the show, CBS
announced at the end that it would mail one to any person who requested one. Over 128,000
copies were sent (Burton Benjamin to HLB, 6/2/69).

CHAPTER 39

IN THE SUNSET

Starting in the mid-1960s, Black's already warm friendship with John Harlan deepened. They were a study in opposites—the latter-day populist and the quintessential Wall Street litigator with a patrician mien—and neither lost the perspective which he brought to the Court. Black often remarked that he would not worry about giving power to judges if they were all like Harlan. "John Harlan," he said, "is one of the few people who convince me that there is such a thing as a good Republican." At whatever they did, Hugo Black and John Harlan were true pros. What brought them together from the beginning were their qualities as human beings, their integrity and decency, and their devotion to the institution. In early 1964 Harlan had suddenly gone almost blind from cataracts; yet, if anything, the quality of his work improved to rank among the highest in the Court's history. His illegible 1970 birthday greeting brought tears to Hugo's eyes.

They talked daily during these years, saw each other most days they were at the Court together and dined regularly. When Hugo and Elizabeth went to the Harlans', protocol dictated that Hugo as the ranking guest leave first; he would drive around the block so others could depart, then return to continue visiting. A common sight at the Court was to see them—Harlan, tall, gaunt and stooped, and Black, now no more than five feet seven after shrinking over two inches in 1966—walking down the hall, on their way to the bench or to conference, their arms around each other, Black trying with great animation to convince Harlan to join him in a case.

Black was dissenting now more than ever. He was losing the marked sense of knowing when not to write. His opinions were more heated and abrasive, often with a new essayistic structure. For support he (or his clerks, who wrote most of them) frequently cited his old opinions. No longer was he the artist, painting with strong, confident strokes for an unfolding future. He was now working largely on the surface, and much from memory. And that memory was less reliable.

"That's not like Uncle Hugo," Black's cousins remarked among themselves after he forgot some important incidents in family history when visiting Alabama in 1966. At the same time he also confused candidates for a federal judgeship when he had been senator. But no one really thought anything of it. "Court work is harder now," he told a former clerk in September 1967. "My mind isn't as quick." Then, in the spring of 1968, at least as early as that March, Black had transitory (or "mini") strokes. He wrote an inquirer about a point he had made "in a dissent I wrote a few years ago in *Feldman v. United States*." That case came down in 1944. And several times toward the end of the term Douglas noted that in conference "Black made unexpected remarks that don't make any sense."

Affected was Black's ability to reason by analogy, the basis of legal analysis. The First Amendment permits peaceful picketing in a privately owned shopping center which serves "clearly [as] the functional equivalent of a 'business block,' " Justice Thurgood Marshall held for the Court in May 1968. This was an extension of Black's reasoning in the 1946 company town case (*Marsh v. Alabama*).* Marshall had his clerk talk to Black. "Black absolutely would not buy Marshall's proposition," recalled the clerk, Peter Lockwood. "He said, 'people live in company towns and they don't live in shopping centers. It's different.' " The Court "completely misreads *Marsh* . . . ," Black claimed in dissent. "The Constitution recognizes and supports the concept of private ownership of property. . . . *Marsh* was never intended to apply to this kind of situation." Title, Black now seemed to be saying, should control First Amendment rights.[1]

*   *   *

Black grew suspicious of Abe Fortas shortly after Fortas joined the Court. Real ill feelings developed after Fortas circulated his majority opinion in the Louisiana library sit-in case in 1966. Black blamed Fortas for his not being able to persuade the Court. Fortas accused Black of racism: "Look, Hugo was in the Klan and now he's coming to the aid of southern white wom-

---

* Black had asserted in *Marsh* that since the operation of facilities in a company town "is essentially a public function, it is subject to state regulation."

anhood," the librarians who served the five Negro petitioners. A pattern began. When Fortas wrote for the Court, Black would only join in the result. Why? "Just because Justice Fortas is writing," Black's clerks said, reflecting the unspoken voice of their boss.

Time v. Hill pitted freedom of the press against the right of privacy. The Hill family sued *Life* magazine for invasion of privacy and portraying them in a false light for reporting on the opening of a play, *The Desperate Hours*, which had been based on their experiences as hostages. The report failed to distinguish between truth and fiction in the play, the Hills claimed. Representing them was Richard Nixon, who by common agreement did an excellent job in April 1966. "Newspapers have the right to report and criticize plays," Black told the justices in conference. But the Court voted 6–3 in favor of the Hills, with Black, Douglas and White dissenting. Warren assigned the opinion to Fortas, who circulated his revised draft on June 20, less than a week before the scheduled end of the term. He assailed the press, and called the constitutional right to privacy "a basic right."

Black marked every one of Fortas's twenty pages. "The right to be let alone" is a "popular idea but not embodied in any constitutional provision." "Peeping Tom [is] not in the Constitution." At the next conference, the justices agreed to hear the case again. Black denounced Fortas's draft as "the worst First Amendment opinion since *Beauharnais*" (the 1952 case upholding a group libel statute). "I'll need all summer to write a dissent," he said. "It'll be the best of my life." He lobbied colleagues and worked on a memorandum which he hoped would be the basis of a new Court opinion.

"Hugo didn't seek to sell views that didn't sell," Brennan later said. "He was a patient listener. He had a way of delaying to marshal arguments to change others' views." The day before reargument in October 1966, Black circulated his memorandum. Fortas went to Black to demand an apology because Hugo had deliberately parodied his colorful writing style. More important to Black, the justices changed their decision. "The subject of the . . . article, the opening of a new play linked to an actual incident," Justice Brennan wrote for the Court, "is a matter of public interest" and therefore constitutionally protected. Black's memorandum had personalized his dispute with Fortas beyond redemption. For the next several years the tension between them was the only source of true friction on the Court.[2]

. . . .

In June 1967 Tom Clark retired from the Court so that his son Ramsey could be named attorney general without any conflict of interest. Johnson appointed Solicitor General Marshall to be the first Negro on the Court. "I hold the character and ability of Mr. Marshall in high esteem," Black had written in 1952. When Marshall was appointed a federal appellate judge in 1962, Black told him "how happy I am that you are there and to congratulate the nation on having a man of such ability, integrity and patriotism." A few years later, Black and historian Irving Brant were discussing who might next be appointed to the Court. Brant raised Marshall's name. "Without saying a word," he recalled, "Black got a book from the shelves. He showed me Marshall's brief supporting a petition for rehearing in *Beauharnais*. 'Any man who writes that deserves to be on this Court,' he said." Marshall asked Black to give him the oath. "His swearing-in was a historical event in the Court," Black later told a Gideon's official, "and I was happy to contribute to it."[3]

*   *   *

The cases on the Court's calendar reflected the social changes that transformed the country during the 1960s. Black did not approve of many of them, but he had never lost his youthful optimism. Black's son Sterling, endowed with his father's low threshold of outrage, actively participated in the politics of the 1960s. But as the decade wore on, this increasingly angered Black. In 1968, as the leading liberal in New Mexico, Sterling was a delegate to the Democratic National Convention supporting insurgent Senator Eugene McCarthy and then lost in the Democratic primary for Congress. Black was happy only that Sterling lost. "If you want to go ahead and change the world, then try," said the man who had tried to change so much. "You won't do it."

In February 1969 the Court held that high school students could not be forbidden to wear black armbands to school as a protest against American involvement in Vietnam. Such symbolic speech was constitutionally protected, Fortas wrote in *Tinker v. Des Moines School District*. Black insisted the Court was wrong both as a matter of law and policy. The Court should affirm the lower court "on a broad ground, as broad as possible," he said in conference. "The schools are in great trouble. Children need discipline— the country is going to ruin because of it. This is no First Amendment problem. The question is whether the rule is reasonable."

"We had mammoth arguments at his desk, at lunch," recalled one of his clerks, "or he'd wander into our room just to tell us we're wrong." He spoke about it frequently to Elizabeth: "I think I'll start out, 'There are 3,465,999 schools in this country and the Court is today taking direct supervision over them,' or, 'It is a fine thing America is going to the moon* because the Supreme Court will have extended jurisdiction.' " The brethren, she noted, were in various stages of shock as he delivered his blistering dissent from the bench.

> If the time has come when pupils of state-supported schools, kindergartens, grammar schools, or high schools, can defy and flout orders to keep their minds on their own schoolwork, it is the beginning of a new revolutionary era of permissiveness in this country fostered by the judiciary. . . . One does not need to be a prophet or the son of a prophet to know that after the Court's holding today some students in Iowa schools and indeed in all schools will be ready, able, and willing to defy their teachers on practically all orders. This is the more unfortunate for these schools are already running loose, conducting break-ins, sit-ins, lie-ins, and smash-ins. . . . It is nothing but wishful thinking to imagine that young, immature students will not soon believe it is their right to control the schools rather than the right of the states that collect the taxes to hire the teachers for the benefit of the pupils.

"Uncontrolled and uncontrollable liberty," Black wrote, "is an enemy to domestic peace." (Upon reading this, an astonished Fortas scribbled in the margin, "Hugo Black!!") "Old Hugo really got hung up in his jock strap on that one," Earl Warren said.

Why this outpouring, this vicious harangue? After the Court had heard argument, Sterling, Jr., was suspended from high school for helping to write and distribute an underground newspaper which called the administration " 'brutal, vicious,' and 'finkos.' " He was "sorry" to learn this, Black wrote Sterling, Jr.'s, mother, Charlotte, but "personally I think the school has done exactly right and I would not myself consider any law suit against the school for doing its duty. The time has come in this country when it must be known that children cannot run the school which they attend at government expense." Sterling, Sr., who had founded and was then the vice president of the New Mexico branch of the American Civil Liberties Union (ACLU), told his father that he was thinking of taking the matter to court if the school board ruled against Sterling, Jr. Black told his son, "If the case reaches the Court, I will disqualify myself not only in it but in every other

* The first astronauts to orbit the moon went up two days later.

case in which the ACLU takes any part, no matter how small." Whether or not he was trying to chasten Sterling for his actions, Black wrote his opinion with Sterling's children directly in mind.

"Anyone has a right to be proud of children these days if those children do not succumb to the evil practices of the times," he noted in 1967. "I find it difficult to believe that students from the kindergarten on through college have a constitutional right to use the schools for advertising their political views," he wrote Charles Reich. ". . . There are some things in our society that relate to activities that are not exclusively controlled by constitutional provisions." Even the First Amendment rights of college students on campus could be limited. "I lean to the belief that it would be best for those in charge of the schools to establish the rules for the students to follow," Black told Charles Alan Wright. "Also, while I believe that the level of intelligence of college students would enable them to make mature judgments superior to that of high school students, I still did not intend for my dissent in *Tinker* to be limited to grade school or high school students."[4]

*   *   *

Until recently, Black had read the constitutional text with the spirit which gave it life. He held up the Bill of Rights like the Holy Grail, trying to impart accuracy and trustworthiness to admittedly slippery language. Now he viewed it as if it presented a jurisprudence of certainty and the First Amendment as if it were a literal Gospel instead of a living charter for a society full of contradictions. He was pursuing a quest, usually without documentation now, for a past that could not be recaptured. This fundamentalism cramped his approach toward individual rights. Justice Black stood his constitutional ground when the rights asserted rested squarely on specific constitutional provisions; but where he could not find an express constitutional base, he was unwilling to look for one.

Chief Justice Warren toned down his language to keep Black's vote in a 1966 case because it referred to the right to marry, which the Constitution does not mention. Similarly, Brennan charged in 1970, Black opposed busing because the word "bus" is not in the Constitution. He had been the foremost advocate on the Court of treating a juvenile defendant like an adult. "Whether or not he's a juvenile, he's being restrained of his liberty," the justice told his colleagues in a 1967 case. "Thus, he's entitled to all the guarantees" of the Bill of Rights. But not in 1970: reviewing a criminal juvenile proceeding, Black could not now find in "the words" of the Constitution that "proof beyond a reasonable doubt" is needed for conviction, and he dissented. "Whatever I've written to suggest it was, I depart [from] now and say [there is] no constitutional requirement." In the mid-1960s he took to calling the due process clause the "shoot the works" clause. Justice Brennan recalled how Black was "frightened to death" that if the Court intervened more, it "might end up with the same kind of business that led to the Nine Old Men" and the Court-packing struggle.

Black's Constitution had become all anchor and no sail, all umbra and no penumbra. As he aged and his tendons shrank, so did the joints in his Constitution lose their elasticity. He refused to exercise them and they became almost calcified. He had formerly aspired to determine the soul of a document intended to endure for ages to come and to perceive its values in order to apply them to contemporary problems. Now he was trying to fit cubes into round holes: only he, and no one else, thought it could be done.

The Court held in 1970 that welfare recipients must be granted a hearing before termination of their benefits. "I think the procedures are okay so long as later there is a full hearing," Black said at conference. Welfare payments are a "gratuity," not "property" protected by the "words" of the due process clause. In 1964 Reich had written a seminal article that traced the emergence of government as a major source of wealth as it poured forth "money, services, contracts, franchises and licenses," and that claimed these warranted protection similar to that previously given traditional property rights. Black liked the article "very much," he told Reich. "You found a new approach to a subject which I believe needs discussion very much." But now Black in dissent expressed deep apprehensions about the ability of the judicial system to handle the new cases that would arise. For the first time he mentioned the Court's expanding caseload in opinions. He had never complained about it, always accepting it as part of the job. But now it meant more work. . . .

"If I had been younger, well—," he told Hugo, Jr. He now spent some evenings watching movies on television with Elizabeth (and rooted for the heroes) or fell asleep early. And he was dependent on her for so many things, from putting in his contact lenses to doing background reading for an article he wrote and helping choose law clerks to driving him around after a minor accident near the Court in March 1968 in which he hit a parked car. He became increasingly affectionate toward Elizabeth. "He always comes back to the theme of how lucky he is to have found me for his twilight years, how he can sail on into the sunset," she wrote. "He worried about being old," said Martin Agronsky. "It bugged him a lot and he got more emotional.

He had a lot of problems with having a younger wife. He thought some other guy would also find her attractive and was terribly jealous of anyone near her."

His behavior sometimes became bizarre. The other justices sat embarrassed on the bench in March 1967 as Black kept a lawyer arguing a case well beyond the allotted time by repeatedly demanding that the attorney agree with his view of the case. In June 1968 they looked edgy as he spent over ten minutes describing in detail the facts of an interracial rape case. At first he planned to dissent in a 1969 case striking down a one-year residency requirement before an applicant could qualify for welfare benefits. Then he recalled a 1948 opinion of his which spoke broadly about the right of people to reside where they wished, so he joined Brennan's majority opinion. Soon Black changed his mind again. When his law clerks told him he had agreed to Brennan's opinion, he said he did not remember that and dissented.

On the surface little of this was apparent. His light drawl remained intact. So, on most days, did his rolling half-walk, half-run—he moved surprisingly rapidly for his age even if he looked frail—and his thinking still overflowed with historical allusions. He seemed like an institution at the right hand of Chief Justices. His white hair was almost gone, "his expression fixed and blank, yet watchful . . . ," wrote John Medelman.

> It offers nothing, it implies nothing . . . Beneath this facial impassivity Justice Black sits badly. His foot taps; one hand punches the other; he tilts forward and then folds back; his body seems eager to rise and move something with his muscles. Then, when he begins to speak, that bodily energy pours into his face; its warmth melts off twenty of his years. His blue eyes—his whole visage—gleam with a tough good humor which suddenly and openly transmits to a gleaming anger, or to scorn. . . . Privately, he is mild and cheery—'so free of malice it seems he must be shamming.' . . .[5]

He always had a ready smile or joke, and he still whistled his way down the Court's marble corridors to work.

*   *   *

"As soon as Hugo retires, I'll be happy to follow," Earl Warren liked to say, then chuckle. But while Black showed no indication of leaving, intermittent angina pains led Warren to tell Lyndon Johnson in June 1968 that he would retire "effective at your pleasure." Johnson accepted Warren's decision "effective at such time as a successor is qualified." Why this unusual arrangement? Publicly Warren said that a vacancy would result in a "vacuum" in the chief justice's administrative work. But in that instance the senior associate justice assumes that responsibility until the post is filled, as Black did after the deaths of Harlan Stone and Fred Vinson. Warren felt, however, that Black's health would not permit him to function even temporarily as head of the Court. So by ambiguously phrasing his plan to retire, he made certain Black would not become acting chief justice and avoided embarrassing Hugo publicly.

Johnson quickly nominated Fortas for the chief justiceship. Black advised Fortas not to accept it because the opposition could stall his confirmation in the Senate. Did Hugo's intuitive political sense tell him this? Or was it because of his continuing antipathy toward Fortas? His actions gave different answers. Fortas's work habits disturbed Black from the beginning. He could never forgive Fortas for being a part-time justice, helping Johnson prosecute the Vietnam War. Singularly in Fortas's case, that and his brusque manner were more important to Black than his particular views. Such was Black's animus toward Fortas that, according to Douglas, in August 1968 Hugo called Lister Hill, whom he had not spoken to in a year, to urge Lister to vote to continue debate and thus keep the full Senate from voting on the nomination. Hill, who had been on the fence, agreed.

Warren's unusual retirement arrangement set in motion a series of events unprecedented in Supreme Court history. Johnson withdrew Fortas's nomination at Fortas's request in October 1968 after the Senate would not bring it to a vote. In May 1969 the Court was shaken to its foundation. *Life,* with the cooperation of the Nixon administration, revealed that in his first term on the Court Fortas had accepted $20,000, only to return it later, as the first of what were to be annual payments for life from a foundation dealing with racial relations and other social welfare issues established by imprisoned stock manipulator Louis Wolfson.

Fortas, disregarding continuing animosities, called for Black's advice. Hugo said that "for the good of the Court *he* would resign," Elizabeth wrote after he and Fortas met for almost two hours. He did not believe Fortas had committed an impeachable or criminal act, and urged him to reveal all evidence. Fortas did that at a conference on Tuesday, May 13, at which he indicated he would resign. Black returned to his office ashen-faced. "I don't think Abe had any criminal intent," he said. At home he told Elizabeth, "Abe just made a terrible error in judgment." Fortas resigned two days later. "Like you," Black wrote Virginia Durr, an old friend of Fortas's, "we have a terrible sense of sorrow about what has happened to Abe. It is a great tragedy and I am wholly unable to explain it." Nixon had gotten one liberal off the Court. Would there be others?

The week following Fortas's resignation, Nixon nominated Warren E. Burger of the federal appellate court in Washington for chief justice. He was easily confirmed in early June, at the same time that the Court was celebrating Warren's upcoming retirement with two parties within two weeks. Black gave the toast at one and served as the master of ceremonies at the other. It was a time of nostalgia. "Through our years of service together," Black wrote for the Court in a formal letter to Warren, "we have been constantly impressed by your patriotism and your unswerving devotion to liberty and justice." Soon he told a correspondent, "As I read history, the 'Warren Court,' I believe, will hold in future annals of this nation's record a high position." Black felt this deeply. Warren had long admitted privately that he was primarily a disciple of Black's. Unspoken was the thought that an era was coming to an end.

Black continued to play tennis at the insistence of his cardiologist. Then on July 18, 1969, after volleying with Elizabeth for fifteen minutes, he wobbled off the court. The doctor hospitalized him for four days of bed rest and observation. Hugo had suffered a minor stroke, a slight clot in a very small blood vessel of the brain, resulting in a partial loss of memory. He was fully aware of what had happened and his speech did not change. The doctor said he had about a 90 percent chance of completely recovering his normal memory, but there was no way to tell whether the impairment was such that he should retire. "But what would I do?" Hugo kept on asking. He had "about decided to quit" when the doctor told him that he could not say whether it would shorten his life if he stayed on; he thought Hugo should continue for one more year, then retire. Thereafter Hugo wavered in his decision. His mind was becoming clearer, but still Elizabeth, if no one else, noticed that he struggled for details of stories he told at parties. Soon, without chasing the shots much anymore, he was back playing tennis, a knobby-kneed, scrawny-looking figure on the court.[6]

For the other court, to replace Fortas president Nixon nominated first South Carolina federal appellate judge Clement F. Haynesworth, Jr., a respected conservative, and then G. Harrold Carswell, a Florida federal judge who gave mediocrity an exalted status. The Senate rejected both nominations. Black told Elizabeth that the present Senate would never confirm a southerner. Nixon's third choice, federal appellate judge Harry

Blackmun of Minnesota, was fully qualified and the Senate rushed to confirm him in May 1970. The Court had gone without a ninth justice for
over a year.

*   *   *

Sitting at the center of the bench was a man of self-aggrandizing tendencies
who strutted around like a peacock and acted like the anointed. Warren
Burger wanted a carpet from his chambers to the bench. More chief housekeeper than chief justice, he regularly went around the building checking
on the potted palms. Black complained that Burger's interest in adminis-
tering the federal courts kept him from writing opinions. Some colleagues
called Burger "the least prepared member of the Court." He never commanded their respect. This led to a vacuum. In earlier years Black would
have easily filled it. But he just didn't have the energy to fight anymore. He
limited his complaints about Burger's antics (such as assigning the majority
opinion even when voting with the minority) to telling his secretary about
them after returning from conference. Only Black's opinions spoke for him
now. No longer did this born proselytizer lobby his colleagues. "He just
circulated his opinions," observed his clerk John Harmon, of whom he grew
especially fond. "His position was his position." His was the pivotal vote
when the Court in December 1970 upheld the power of Congress to lower
the voting age to eighteen in federal, but not state or local, elections. He
made no attempt to secure a consensus in a case ripe for one.

Burger had been enamored of Black since coming to the Court, treating
him with absolute deference and respect, and often coming to talk and lunch
with him. The day before Hugo's birthday in 1970, Burger stated in open
court: "This Court commonly does not take note of birthdays of justices,
but our brother, Justice Hugo Black, is a very uncommon man." He praised
Black's record and added, "In short, happy birthday, sir. And, I may add,
I am authorized by the Court to say this is unanimous. . . ."[7]

*   *   *

A new generation was fueling new social movements. "The convictions of
young people are right," Black said, but they should be *doing* something
about the problems surrounding them, not just singing songs.* He refused

---

* "Hang your sensibilities!" William James wrote and Black underlined in Ralph Barton Perry's
biography. "Stop your sniveling complaints, and your equally sniveling raptures! Leave off
your general emotional tom-foolery, and get to work like men!" This was read at Black's
funeral.

to drive through the Georgetown section of Washington in the summer of 1970 because of "all those young men with long hair." But he just teased clerks who had long hair; he never complained: he was too dependent on them now. In 1970 as student unrest continued, Charles Reich published a best-selling book, *The Greening of America*. He bluntly disparaged classically conservative and traditional liberal values while striving to identify a set of new self-styled radical ones for society. Black thought it all absurd. "I do not agree," he wrote in the margin. The American dream "is not yet destroyed." His attention petered out less than halfway through, as it did with so many books he now read.

Reich's views symbolized new issues coming to the Court in which Black had little interest or sympathy. Capital punishment had never fazed him. When Arthur Goldberg, dissenting from a 1963 petition for certiorari, claimed it was cruel and unusual punishment in violation of the Eighth Amendment, Black scoffed. He wrote but removed from an 1969 opinion: "As to the contentions that imposition of the death penalty for common-law robbery is cruel and unusual punishment in violation of the Fourteenth Amendment and that to permit a jury to inflict the death penalty without any standards denies due process, he would reject them on the ground that they are frivolous." The death penalty was simply a legislative decision to deal with a criminal problem, Black thought. And he would have been the most vociferous opponent of *Roe v. Wade*, the Court's 1973 decision that due process permits a right to abortion. Black flatly opposed any constitiutional recognition of such a right during conference in a 1971 case.[8]

*   *   *

There have been three great partnerships in American history: Jefferson and Madison, Holmes and Brandeis, and Black and Douglas. Hugo inscribed a copy of *A Constitutional Faith* "To my good friend Bill Douglas, my close-working colleague for nearly thirty years, a genius in his own right, a man of indomitable courage, unexcelled energy and to whom I am indebted for his contribution to the formulation of many of the constitutional principles expressed in this book." They worked instinctively as a team. "We can read each other's mind," Douglas said. When a matter came up at conference, they "would sort of look at each other and pass back and forth who would respond and who would do the drafting on this or that particular issue." This changed only somewhat in the early 1960s as Douglas started raising the ceiling of the Constitution's civil liberties guarantees while Black was equally concerned with reinforcing their foundation.

Black still remained Douglas's emotional connection to the Court. "The Roosevelt of the Court in this century," Douglas once called Hugo, and he was disappointed when the *Harvard Law Review* in 1967 asked Harlan, not him, to write a short article celebrating Black's thirty years on the Court. "Hugo's not fighting anymore," Douglas said in 1969. "He's praising all those sons of bitches who have hated him his whole life.' " Black missed his former easy friendship with Douglas and often talked wistfully about the old days together. He "almost had a stroke," noted Frances Lamb when Douglas married his third wife, Joanie, who walked out on him after six months of marriage. And when Douglas married his next and last wife, Cathy, Hugo, by now immune, simply said, "Bill, why don't you keep your pants zipped up?"

"Like any long relationship Hugo's and Bill's had its ups and downs," said Cathleen Douglas Stone, Douglas's widow, "but the underlying love never changed. Bill felt much more strongly about Hugo than he wrote." "I am having labor pains—very severe—," Hugo told him while drafting a 1964 tribute honoring Douglas's twenty-five years on the bench. He took refuge in noting their "such frequent agreement." They had been through the wars together, the cold war and the hot ones against Frankfurter and Jackson. Nothing—nothing, absolutely nothing—could break the bond between Hugo Black and Bill Douglas.

In May 1969 Deputy Attorney General Richard Kleindienst asked Hugo, Jr., his college roommate, how the justice would feel if the Nixon administration attempted to impeach Douglas. Now he immediately called his father. "You tell them not to try," Black said. "I'll defend Bill in the Senate." Hugo, Jr., told this to Kleindienst but the administration was not deterred. The grounds for the impeachment attempt would never be made precise. Nor could they, for it was Douglas's opinions (and his lifestyle) that the administration objected to. "The present political hubbub about him will get exactly nowhere," Black wrote in May 1970. The effort failed through a combination of shrewd strategy on the part of Douglas's lawyers, friends on Capitol Hill, an absurdly weak case pressed chiefly by House Republicans and, not least, subtle pressure on Nixon from Burger that the time had come to stop ripping down the Court's reputation.

One night that spring, Bill and Cathy Douglas were having their usual predinner drink. He was usually expansive at that hour but this evening he was quiet. She asked what was wrong. He explained that the Court had been sitting that day and Hugo had passed him a note. It read:

Dear Bill: If they try to impeach you, I'll resign and be your lawyer. I have one more hard trial left in me. Hugo.[9]

*   *   *

He remained a "canny, lovable manipulator . . . ever the politician, ever the Senator still," said Justice Harry Blackmun. The Nixon administration joined Mississippi authorities in urging yet another delay in meaningful desegregation of the state's schools. This infuriated Black. He had long wanted an "end date" for any desegregation plan and viewed Nixon's tactics as nothing more than another cynical plank in his "southern strategy." In September 1969, acting as circuit justice, he refused to approve a delay in the submission of plans to desegregate Mississippi's schools granted by the court of appeals. "This long denial of constitutional rights is due in large part to the phrase 'with all deliberate speed.' I would do away with that phrase completely." He would never again join an opinion using it, Black said at conference the next month when the whole Court considered the case. The Court should not even prepare an opinion, but simply issue a brief, sharply worded order rejecting any further delay and demanding immediate desegregation.

"If anybody writes, I dissent." There was silence around the table. "It made us almost numb," Brennan recalled. Several asked Black how he would enforce the order. He refused to discuss it. "You do what you want and I'm going ahead."

He drafted a dissent. "The time has passed for promises and plans to desegregate," Black wrote, and included almost verbatim an order composed by Brennan he would have the Court issue. The duty of courts, he noted in a cover letter, "is to extirpate all racial discrimination from our system of public schools NOW." Four other justices, including an outraged Harlan ("you don't give in to blackmail," he said), also circulated opinions. Eventually, only a unanimous Court agreed to an unsigned opinion. The justices had capitulated; Black had won every major point. Most importantly, "all deliberate speed" was "no longer constitutionally permissible, and busing was established as a tool for desegregating a public school system.

Black's views hardened by the next year. Convinced that busing to achieve racial balance would trigger massive resistance in the South, he wanted to limit the power of federal judges to order it. Violence may result and white parents would enroll their children in private schools, he said. At oral argument in October 1970 he lashed out at those he said would "try to change the lives of the people around the country" by busing children to faraway schools and imposing racial quotas. Courts should only correct "plain discrimination on account of race," but not try "to change the lives of people around the country. . . . I don't like this trying to condemn a whole way of living. You want to haul people miles and miles in order to get an equal ratio in the schools. It's a pretty big job to assign to us, isn't it? How can you rearrange the whole country?" A fortnight later, he wrote a friend, "My father walked five miles to get to his nearest neighborhood school."

Black would not go along with any opinion that explicitly approved mandatory busing, as the Court by late March 1971 was on the verge of approving. Then he reconsidered. A dissent would only comfort and encourage segregationists, and result in an even stronger Court opinion. Burger slightly modified that opinion while keeping fully intact its thrust of upholding the authority of federal courts to use necessary means to assure meaningful desegregation. Black decided to join.[10]

*   *   *

As always, his interest was sparked when the First Amendment was involved. "Views and beliefs are immune from bar association inquisitions designed to lay a foundation for barring an application from the practice of law," Black wrote for the Court in March 1971, announcing the Court's judgment in *Baird v. State Bar of Arizona.* It "is not a matter of grace, but of right for one who is qualified by his learning and his moral character." But now for every point there was a counterpoint. A young war protester, Paul Cohen, had been sentenced to thirty days in jail for disturbing the peace by wearing a jacket with the words "Fuck the Draft" inscribed on the back while walking through a courthouse. Black insisted that the Court summarily reverse the conviction without even holding oral argument. Overnight he reversed his position. He was not deviating at all from his views, he told the justices at conference, but this was "conduct," not "speech." Picketing a courthouse was illegal conduct. People could not "tramp up and down the streets by the thousands" and threaten others. What this had to do with the case, Black did not explain.

"I could anticipate Hugo in every First Amendment case," Justice Brennan later said. "You knew where he stood. He never hid it under a bushel." Asked if Black's position in Cohen's case surprised him, he replied, "Yes. I didn't expect it. That was a different Hugo." Black had been increasingly erratic, testy and belligerent since his stroke. He had always been emotional but the self-control with which his emotion had warred—a struggle central to his success—had deteriorated. He dictated vehement letters and kept them in his drawer for a couple of days. "Do you really want to send those?" his secretary asked. "Probably not," he replied, and he didn't. He had good days and bad days. At times his memory, focus and sharpness were all seemingly gone, he'd be crotchety, and one would almost ache for him. At other times an unsuspecting observer could think he was an older version of the same Hugo, as alert if not as spry as ever. He'd be very chipper in the morning when a law clerk picked him up at home. (He had not been coming to the Court daily now for several years.) But by late afternoon he usually got sleepy and dozed in his chair. JoJo gave him some psychiatry books to read. He earnestly tried to understand them, but couldn't. "I can't do it anymore," he told her. "I'm too old."

Starting with his sixtieth birthday, Black's clerks threw him a party in Washington every five years. In 1971 the affair was held at the Federal City Club, and nearly all of his forty-five former clerks were present. His physical condition alarmed those who had not seen him recently. The senior clerk, Buddy Cooper, presided and read a letter by President Nixon, part of which was handwritten. Barney Whatley sent a gift. Each year on their respective birthdays he and Hugo joked as only lifelong friends could, about who should listen to whom considering Barney's "seniority" of four months. His gift was presented: a wig and a letter about Hugo's bald plate and his 1969 decision that courts should keep out of controversies involving the length of schoolchildren's hair. Hugo tried the wig on. But uppermost in his mind were his clerks.

Black's feeling toward them was a satisfied teacher's feeling about his best students. Almost as much as his sons, they represented his personal investment in the future. He felt paternal pride as they progressed in their law practices, in government (three became federal judges and two turned down appointments) or in academia. Each of "the young men who are practically members of my family," he once wrote, had "a secure place in my affections." And he proceeded to tell them this in an unusual way. "The Judge wanted to talk about the best of Justice Black," recalled Guido Calabresi. "And he started reciting phrases from opinions. The older clerks looked startled. In each instance it was what the clerks had suggested in the opinions, not what the Judge had contributed. What he was saying, to make us feel good, is that we were the best of Justice Black."[11] They returned to the house, where Elizabeth took a picture of each clerk with Hugo in the study. Several clerks left wondering how many more reunions there would be.

. . . .

"I want to get things straight," Black said about the Fourth Amendment's exclusionary rule, barring the use of illegally obtained evidence at trial. It "bothered the Justice tremendously every day," noted his clerk John Harmon. By 1971 "he was ready to abandon it." Black would have converted the Fourth Amendment's limitation on government into grant of power: it "provides a constitutional means by which the Government can act to obtain evidence to be used in criminal prosecutions. The people are obliged to yield to a proper exercise of authority under that Amendment." Not even this relegation of the Fourth Amendment to a lowly position in the hierarchy of constitutional safeguards satisfied Black. "It is not my final statement on the Fourth Amendment," he said, only his latest one, which put him all over the interpretive map on the exclusionary rule. He did, however, expect it to be his final opinion of the term. In the volume of the United States Reports in which it appeared, he had thus far written only two other opinions.

In late March 1971 he started having acute pain in his left ear and a chronic headache over his eye and in the back of his head. Aspirin did not help. He found it more difficult to concentrate. His short-term memory was waning. He would latch onto some event of long ago and reminisce. In conference he began to stumble badly, becoming tired and confused, and unable to remember which case was being discussed. But he bitterly rejected Burger's suggestion that the conferences end a little earlier to accommodate him. Burger told courtroom guards that Black might be stricken while sitting on the bench and requested that one of them "keep an eye" on him.

A new crankiness appeared. Black gave each judge a nickname. Douglas, Brennan and Marshall, who usually voted together, were the "Three Musketeers"; Harry Blackmun, for some reason, was "Harry James." He complained about the pressures of time. No one "can understand how much of my time is taken up with this job," he told Virginia Durr. "Usually I am up to 11 or 11:30 at night and also work in the daytime. Just simple time off to write a letter amounts to a great deal to me."

In early May Black made his annual speech to the Fifth Circuit. He quoted Socrates' last comment: "We go our separate ways, you to live, and I to die. Which is best, God only knows."* For forty-five minutes he reaf-

---

* Before the speech, Hugo, Jr., told his father he would swing his stopwatch back and forth if he talked too long. At that, Elizabeth noted, the justice "bit off his head" and said, "you

firmed his faith in the country and its people and his love for the Constitution. Thurgood Marshall was in the audience, he noted. "Forty years ago," Black said, "some people would have considered it sacrilege to have a Negro on the Supreme Court. But brains and intelligence cannot be measured by the color of a man's skin, his religion or his political leanings." Late in the month, he returned feebly from conference, his face drained of color, his lips almost blue, his body shivering from a severe chill and running a high fever. His knees buckled as he leaned on his secretary. He recovered, but was weaker and the headaches worsened. The almost constant pain, and not knowing what was causing it, tortured him. But the Court's longevity record was within sight and Black determined to break it.[12]

CLOSING THE CIRCLE

Character is fate, the Greeks believed. "Hugo has gotten purer as he has gotten older," his old Birmingham political friend Ben Ray noted in the mid-1960s. The years had erased some of the hard, partisan edge; but it could never be completely removed. Hugo still had the continuing general wish that Democrats should win all elections. "I wish I could take charge of the Democratic party in Alabama now," he said in 1969. "I think I could straighten things out." He started to spend time with young Alabama journalists, especially Ray Jenkins, editorial page editor of the (Montgomery) *Alabama Journal*, and Brandt Ayers, who succeeded his father, Harry, as the publisher of the *Anniston Star*. Their combination of liberalism, courage and an Alabama base appealed to Black as few other things could.

Much of his heart had never left Alabama. Northern prejudice played a role in antagonism toward southern judges and politicians, he still thought. "I think there are few people in or out of the South that really know how very much Southerners did contribute both to our Articles of Confederation and to our Constitution." He had been trumpeting this theme for several years as a way of rebutting southern criticism of the Court. Without southerners "there would have been no Constitution," he told a 1967 University of Georgia law school audience. He wanted "lawyers who are not only proud Georgians, but proud Americans who get the same thrill from the 'Star Spangled Banner' that they do from 'Dixie.' " He ended his speech with a

***

don't understand. Old age is nostalgic and different from youth. If I make my mistakes, then let me make them" (HLB, *Memoirs*, 262).

favorite line from Benjamin H. Hill, a prominent Georgian of the Civil War era:

> There was a South of slavery and secession—that South is dead.
> There is a South of union and freedom—that South, thank God, is living, breathing, growing every hour.

In 1968 Lister Hill retired after forty-five years in Congress. "My first thought on leaving the United States Senate in 1937," Black wrote him in January 1969, "was that you should be my successor and I did what I could to make that thought come true. I have never regretted that I did this. I do regret that you are no longer a United States Senator from Alabama but hope that your influence and your voice will still be used to help the people of our native state restore and keep Alabama true to its highest traditions."[13]

Black embraced those younger judges who were trying to maintain the best part of that heritage while fostering a new order bringing the South into the national mainstream. In Alabama that meant Frank Johnson, Jr. He came to Washington in 1959 to discuss with Black whether he should hold George Wallace, then a state judge, in contempt for having refused to turn over to the U.S. Civil Rights Commission voting files Wallace had ordered impounded, ostensibly for a grand jury investigation. Black talked Johnson out of jailing Wallace. After losing the recent gubernatorial primary, Wallace promised never to be "out-niggered again." He wanted to be locked up. That would make him a martyr, Black told Johnson. It would be an open door and give time for the forces of resistance to brew. He told the other justices that they should rely on Johnson's understanding in a 1969 school desegregation case. Johnson's "patience and wisdom are written for all to see and read" in the case's record, Black wrote for the Court. He mentioned Johnson by name six times, using laudatory adjectives, a rare tribute to a lower court judge.

Black's main contact with the Fifth Circuit's judges and their business came during its annual spring conference. Throughout the 1950s, this was held in New Orleans, where J. Skelly Wright, the local federal judge, met Black at the airport and escorted him about. Black felt that Wright, who was being vilified and ostracized for ordering the integration of the public schools in his native city, represented "America at its best." Wright ranked

Black with John Marshall as the two greatest justices. ("You rate me entirely too high," Black replied, "but as Judge McCord [Leon McCord of the Fifth Circuit in Montgomery] used to say at the end of his favorite story, 'that's the way I like it.' ") "Black took to Skelly because Skelly worshipped him, thought he was the greatest thing that ever happened to this country," said Martin Agronsky. In 1962 this quiet man of swift intelligence and a burning sense of injustice was appointed to the federal appellate court in Washington and became one of the most staunchly liberal judges in the country. Hugo and Skelly, neither a shining example of sartorial splendor, shopped for clothes together; Elizabeth and Helen Wright were also close friends. Both couples saw each other frequently, celebrating birthdays, anniversaries and other occasions together.

Each year Black delivered a dramatic, inspirational speech on the Constitution. It was the conference's highlight. His only notes were in his head but "he held people spellbound," noted Judge John Brown. "He always thrilled most of us." "A judge, a real judge," Black said in 1967,

> stands above the clamor of the multitude and puts his gaze on the great charter of the multitude and will fight for it even to the end. I've been coming to see you for many years—how many more I cannot know. I . . . have passed over the crest, over the brow of the hill. I hope I have learned more tolerance, more friendship, more about the love of human kindness during those thirty years.
>
> Now I am far beyond the crest. I look over into the glowing rays of the sunset. . . . They do not frighten me. . . . I hope you'll think of me as one who tried always to be—really to be—a judge. For I think there is no higher calling for an American citizen than to be a judge.[14]

Chief Justice Burger accepted the Alabama Bar Association's invitation to speak in Birmingham in July 1970 and asked Black to introduce him. Black easily agreed; it would be "his salute to Alabama," Elizabeth noted. At the same time, Hugo wrote an Alabama friend, "in order to get [Burger] to visit" the association "we agreed to go down with him. . . ." When they arrived in Birmingham, Howell Heflin, Tom Heflin's nephew and newly elected as Alabama chief justice, told Elizabeth that the whole affair was in Hugo's honor. It was the first they had heard about it. "Hugo seemed taken unawares at first but soon relaxed," she wrote. On the way to the hotel they did a double take upon passing a billboard that read: "Welcome Chief Justice Burger and Justice Hugo Black." At the hotel hundreds of people were turned away; scalpers were enjoying a field day.

"This is a man of old-fashioned virtues," Burger told five hundred Alabama lawyers as well as Governor Albert P. Brewer. "He believes in our country, he believes in our Constitution, and he believes free people must protect the system of ordered liberty." They lifted their glasses in tribute, then stood and applauded. Hugo rose hesitantly, nodded and smiled slightly as the ovation, a reporter wrote, grew to "thunderous proportions." "The sweetest music that ever comes to the ears of a public man is the applause of the people," said Champ Clark, Speaker of the House in the early twentieth century. And these lawyers were Hugo's people. He had known them, their parents and their children, all his life. He had struggled with them against their common adversaries at home and fought for them in Washington.

There was silence as he started to talk. He was happy for the homage and happy for Alabama, he said. The state had come a long way. It was a metaphor for the changes taking place—in voting rights, public accommodations, educational opportunity—in the South. Burger had tears in his eyes when he came up to the podium to embrace Black afterward. "That's his due," observed Francis Hare, Birmingham's leading plaintiffs' lawyer. Adulation had replaced abuse. The senator had finally returned home.[15]

*   *   *

"I still sometimes have fleeting ideas about writing my memoirs," Black told Alfred Knopf in 1956. "I lose enthusiasm about it however when I read some of the prejudiced memoirs that are written. Perhaps it will be impossible for me to write anything without being as prejudiced as all the others." In 1963 he underlined Holmes's comment, "I am insisting to myself that I have outlived duty and have a right to be idle. I greatly enjoy being so. The writing of recollections and reflections I abhor." Black had a compassionate, deeply ingrained reluctance to commit to paper an unkind thought even about longtime enemies. An honest memoir meant telling many things: that wouldn't be fair to this gentleman of the old school to whom, moreover, introspection was not a strong point.

Yet he never quite lost the idea. Elizabeth and Hugo, Jr., were pushing it and in May 1968 he began, crying as he completed the preface. He worked

on the memoirs sporadically over the next few years. Looking inward somewhat, advanced age, a declining condition and a general mellowing led
him to soften his views of his father. By the summer of 1970 he had completed
twelve chapters, up to his marriage to Josephine, with the intention of adding
several more, then publishing it. Published in 1986, the memoirs remain
charming reading, full of details available nowhere else, but without revealing
insights or any self-examination and in places purposely dissembling. An
autobiography, he told Harry Golden after reading Golden's and as he was
working on his own, should tell readers "the good and the bad about your
life, with equal lucidity and frankness . . . but it is a difficult and almost
impossible thing to do." In Black's case it was unimaginable.

The publication in 1956 of Alpheus T. Mason's biography of Harlan
Stone brought to the fore the issue of the use of justices' papers—votes and
comments in conference, drafts of opinions and correspondence about cases
and other Court doings. Black replied to a query from Edmond Cahn:

> I have long doubted the wisdom of publishing communications that were
> confidential when prepared. I have never thought that the diaries or mem-
> oranda of public men containing their contemporary personal impressions
> could be anything but one-sided. This I believe to be true, however fair a
> diarist might try to be. From this general view you can surmise how I feel
> about publishing private confidential communications and memoranda ac-
> cumulated by Supreme Court Justices during their terms of office. All of
> us know that incidents that may loom high at the time they occur are
> frequently forgotten in a very short time because of their triviality. Then,
> too, one-sided writings leave wrong impressions when published long after
> they are jotted down. I am inclined to think that public officials can be
> better judged by their public utterances than by their private correspon-
> dence, memoranda, and diaries. There are particular reasons which I need
> not further elaborate why I think that this Court is not benefitted by digging
> up old confidential papers and publishing them. I know this view is some-
> what at odds with the general practice of many people, but I have long
> felt this way.

Such books are "awful," he said. "They pick up a particular thing,
somebody's statement, and the other guys can't respond. They only stir up
bad feelings and misconceptions." But his objections went deeper. "Matters
which were confidential when they took place . . . should remain immune
from historical speculations," Black stated in 1963. He had already told his
clerks that he would destroy his court papers, stressing that they exalted

backstage maneuvering and pushed important issues off to the side. Nor did he "think much" of "private letters being turned over to governmental agencies for any purpose anyone wants to utilize private correspondence," he wrote Virginia Durr after the Alabama archives approached her for her correspondence as a way, she thought, of getting Black's letters. ". . . If I were in your position I would think a long time before I complied with such a request." ("You don't seem to want to pay the price of fame," she told him, "but you are so famous that anything connected with you is of interest to historians and will continue to be. . . .")

He realized he would have to make a decision about the disposition of his papers. Since they dealt with "national activities," he told C. J. (Jack) Coley, head of the Alabama archives, in 1966, "it might be best for them to be handled by a national institution." The idea of leaving "those that I preserve" at the Library of Congress had "much impressed" Black. He often discussed the matter with Elizabeth and his devoted secretary Frances Lamb. "I am not sure that I shall leave my conference papers where anyone else can read them after I leave the Court," he informed one researcher after reading how he had changed his mind in the 1946 reapportionment case.

Then came a lengthy correspondence starting in April 1970 with University of Kentucky political scientist S. Sidney Ulmer, who wanted to quote from a letter of Black's he found in Justice Burton's papers. Black preferred that the letter not be published: Ulmer made a reference instead. "I do not believe that such so-called 'historical sources,' " such as justices' notes about conference and their inter-court memoranda, "are reliable for basic uses in connection with the opinions of people." They "may frequently leave a false impression of history." After exchanging sixteen letters over six months, Black had had enough. It was, Elizabeth said later, "the final nail in the coffin." "I don't think I'm going to keep my Court papers," Black told an interviewer (the author) the next week. A few days later he wrote the University of Alabama Law School, which was establishing a Hugo Black Room: "So far as my old papers are concerned, many of them will be destroyed, particularly those reporting what occurred in the conferences of the Court. These conferences have been held in secret and I am of the opinion that history will not lose too much by destroying them."

He went through his papers, Court and non-Court, marking letters with his family and removing numerous documents he considered too sensitive, such as his correspondence with the FBI and his files on Lyndon Johnson's 1948 case and the segregation cases. But it was too big a job, certainly at this stage of his life, to do thoroughly, and much remained that earlier he might have destroyed: many sarcastic, derogatory letters he wrote other justices, especially Douglas, about "my brother Frankfurter" were left untouched, at least for now. He deplored Frankfurter's notes saying nasty things about other people or Felix's clerks' revealing confidential matters which Hugo felt should not have been revealed. Black had no desire for posthumous revenge. That, he thought, was a low blow. He had a desire to further his point of view, as expressed in his opinions.[16]

*   *   *

While Black naturally hoped history would do him justice, he was too busy working to get what he wanted done to make sure it would. He took his ideas far more seriously than he took himself, especially as he aged. Despite a healthy ego (which he never denied having), he sought little personal glorification. For years before and after his 1949 book about Black, John Frank gathered information for an eventual, larger volume. "Usually when he comes to see me," Black noted in 1961, "he expresses the fear that he may die first, in which event he says the public would be deprived of his great biography!" Black wanted Frank to write the later book, feeling that Frank knew his mind better than any other clerk. But he did not believe in authorized biographies.

By 1970 numerous prospective biographers were cropping up, especially in Alabama. He thought "some of them are terribly over-estimating the possibility of the success of a biography" about him. His position, he told Hazel Davis, "is that I do not want to stand in anyone's way who wants to write nor do I agree to give them information for a book." He was always available to serious students of his career, his stock of stories at the ready. He enjoyed the many interviews he granted, reminiscing about his pre-Court experiences rather than himself, and rare was the questioner with the courage to pierce that formidable exterior by asking a question that cut too personally, especially about the Klan. One reporter, interviewing him for a future obituary, asked him to interpret a remark he once made about Frankfurter. The justice was evasive. "Can you imagine the effrontery trying to read something into what I said?" Black said later.

"What is said about me has long since ceased to disturb me or even interest me very much," he told Arthur Goldberg in 1964.[*] Now, more

---

[*] HLB had earlier underlined Jefferson's comment, "To glide unnoticed through a silent execution of duty, is the only avocation which becomes me, and it is the sincere desire of my heart" (Malone, *Jefferson*, 213, in HLB Books).

than ever, he was thanking those in the cheering sections. "I want to congratulate you on a statement closer to my views than any heretofore published," he told one scholar who had delivered a paper on him. And he thanked a reviewer of A *Constitutional Faith* "for what I consider to be a full and fair explanation of the views I have been trying to advocate since I became an Associate Justice of the Court."[17] They were cheering the magnificence of the man fully as much as the opinions.

CHAPTER 40

THE GRAND FINALE

On Sunday, June 13, 1971, the *New York Times* printed long excerpts from a secret, forty-seven-volume history of American involvement in Vietnam prepared by the Defense Department—the Pentagon Papers. Black was pleased to see an exposé of the whole long, sordid story, he said after reading about it in the next day's *Washington Post*. After a second installment appeared that day in the *Times*, the Nixon administration moved to stop further publication. For the first time, the American government was trying to use the courts to censor news before it was printed. Further dissemination, it claimed, would cause "immediate and irreparable harm" to the national security. The government also sought to stop the *Post*'s version of the papers, which was published on June 18.

Black was stunned. "They're actually stopping it. What's happened to the idea of prior restraint?" he said before returning to the neurologist who could find no further reason for his headaches except calcium deposits in the blood vessels; he gave Black vitamins and painkillers, and told him the headaches would wear off. "Just like Republicans," Black said afterward. "I'm not surprised. What else could you expect?" All his old foes had come together: Republicans, Nixon, those who opposed genuine freedom of the press. Black had always been horribly suspicious of Nixon. "Any man could grow in office," Black said of the man he sometimes called "Tricky Dick." "But I never liked him since the Checkers speech," back in 1952.

Nor had Black ever quite forgiven the press for the way he was treated in the aftermath of his appointment to the Court. "Hugo is still somewhat bitter, though in a way philosophical" about it, Drew Pearson noted in 1952 (adding, "However, Hugo says that the press has got to be protected just the same"); the feeling was at least partly responsible for his tight-lipped attitude toward the press thereafter. Moreover, rich Republicans controlled the press, Black claimed. He retained the attitude of many politicians in liking reporters more than their editors, many of whom he distrusted, thinking they changed what their reporters submitted. The aims of the press suffer from the sensationalism inherent in selling newspapers, he said, referring to his Senate experiences with the Hearst papers. He became fond of James Reston, the *Times'* longtime Washington columnist, and respected him as a journalist. But he never forgot *Times* publisher Arthur Hays Sulzberger's animus against him. "It was impossible for me to say anything on any subject that would permit him [a reporter] to write an article that the *Times* would publish," Black noted in 1967. "Sometimes it seems to me that people value the *New York Times* too highly."[1]

The federal courts acted with unusual alacrity in the Pentagon Papers case. On June 23 the courts of appeals in both New York and Washington ruled—in New York against the *Times* and in Washington for the *Post*. The restraining orders preventing publication (limited in the case of the *Post*), however, remained in effect. Near noon the next day, the *Times* asked the Supreme Court to hear the case as soon as possible and to lift the restraint; the *Post* filed the same requests. The case rejuvenated Black, firing him up as nothing else could. His spirits were buoyed, as they used to be. All the old excitement of a case that *had* to be won was there. He geared himself up, coming earlier into the Court. This had been the way he relished cases. But he was concerned. Douglas, Brennan and Marshall, he knew, would join him. Burger, Harlan and Blackmun would be opposed. That left Stewart and White for the fifth vote. He didn't hold out much hope for White. Stewart, then, was the key. He thought Stewart was having a problem with matters of degree; Black talked with him about it. "Potter always wonders when enough is enough," he said. Black was not certain how the case would come out. He was only sure that his headaches had lessened.

The justices met on Friday, June 25, to consider the applications. Until then they had discussed the case informally. Their consensus was that it might be best simply to refuse to hear it, but only if both appellate courts decided in the newspapers' favor. "I was never too fond of injunctions against newspapers," Black said at dinner one night during this period. Even if national security were involved? Elizabeth asked. "Well, I never did see how it hurts national security for someone to tell the American people that their government lied to them," he replied. His position was as certain as that there would be a tomorrow. Douglas, who had left for Washington State for the summer, phoned in his view. Brennan and Marshall would have dismissed the case and vacated the restraints against the newspapers without oral argument. Burger, Harlan, White and Blackmun wanted to set the case for argument the next week. (Burger strongly opposed making public the desires of those who agreed with Black, but they wanted their views on record.) Stewart wished to have oral argument the next morning while keeping the stays in effect; that is what the Court decided.

The upper echelon of much of the government was undergoing one of its periodic "security" manias. This time the cause was not hunting "Communists," but secrecy. Parts of all four lower court proceedings were held in closed session; the fixation affected each trial and appeal. The "top spook" of the National Security Agency, his bodyguard at his side with guns visible in holsters, visited *Times* management in another location in New York by clandestine agreement. Armed guards took the record in the case, including a complete copy of the secret study, to the Supreme Court the evening before argument. It was placed in the conference room. Burger, whose chauffeur carried a gun and who by his actions tried so hard to make himself part of the administration, decreed that only justices could enter. Security guards, not armed, stood at the door. All the justices except Black looked at the material. *

It took Erwin Griswold, the imperturbable solicitor general, to cut through some of the government's obsession. He worked almost through the night preparing its brief. Government agents initially would not permit his secretary to type it since she wasn't "cleared." But because otherwise there would not have been a brief, they finally relented. But they would not allow the *Post*'s lawyer to have a copy, as required by the Court's rules. That, an FBI security guard said, "is giving it to the enemy," and he seized it from the lawyer. It was a theater of the absurd, with potentially disastrous consequences for self-government.

Black was disappointed in Griswold for arguing the case. He had tried unsuccessfully to work out a compromise within the government and, as he said later, "It was not my favorite type of case." Yale law professor Alexander Bickel, of all people, argued for the *Times*. Proudly he had just proclaimed himself "not a First Amendment voluptuary." Afterward Black said, "It's

* Even Douglas, despite his wholeheartedly sharing Black's First Amendment views. He had been so deeply involved in the antiwar movement that Bill Moyers, who had been Lyndon Johnson's righthand man in the White House, suggested that he go to Hanoi in 1966 to test North Vietnam's willingness to negotiate (memorandum for the President 1/28/66, LBJL). Douglas likely looked at the documents for curiosity's sake.

too bad the *Times* couldn't find someone who believes in the First Amendment."[2] Both Bickel and Griswold aimed their argument at Stewart and White. Bickel specifically stated he was not arguing against prior restraint in all instances.

It was a tremendously emotional time for the Court. Feelings had not run as high since the Steel Seizure, Rosenberg and school segregation cases nearly twenty years earlier. Over 1,500 people competed for the 174 seats in the courtroom. During the tense oral argument on June 26, 1971, Griswold admitted not knowing "what the alternative is" to making the federal courts a censorship board in such a matter.

BLACK (quietly): The First Amendment might be. [general laughter]

Griswold's responses, which Black reproduced in his opinion, then took on an *Alice in Wonderland* quality:

GRISWOLD: Now, Mr. Justice Black, your construction of [the First Amendment] is well known, and I certainly respect it. You say that "no law" means "no law," and that should be obvious.
BLACK: I rather thought that.
GRISWOLD: And I can only say, Mr. Justice, that to me it is equally obvious that "no law" does not mean "no law," and I would seek to persuade the Court that that is true. . . . There are other parts of the Constitution which grant powers and responsibilities to the Executive; and . . . the First Amendment was not intended to make it impossible for the Executive to function, or to protect the security of the United States.

Black leaned back, a quizzical smile on his face.

The justices went into conference immediately after argument. They were still split: Black, Douglas, Brennan and Marshall for the newspapers; Burger, Harlan and Blackmun for the government; and Stewart and White undecided. Now Stewart, who had been troubled by the government's case from the beginning, said that it had not met the burden of proof that publication of the documents would cause immediate and irreparable harm, and that the newspapers could publish them. The discussion was continuing when one of Black's clerks heard over the radio that the government had obtained a temporary restraining order against the *Saint Louis Post-Dispatch,* which had also printed the papers; other newspapers were also getting copies of the Pentagon Papers. Any further injunctions against the *Times* and *Post* would now be futile; much of the metropolitan press could not be enjoined. This was communicated to the justices. White quickly announced he would also vote for the newspapers. That made six votes. The majority agreed to issue a one-paragraph per curiam opinion that Brennan had prepared beforehand; and each justice went ahead, writing his own opinion.

Douglas, having returned to Washington for the argument, flew back to Washington State the next day after having completed his opinion while his colleagues were still working on theirs. It declared the hostilities in Vietnam to be unconstitutional. Black objected, Douglas was contacted, the opinion was revised and Black joined it, as Douglas joined his.

With no other cases left, Black got right to work. He thought this was the most important First Amendment opinion of his career. "Never did he work harder or more earnestly than on the *Pentagon Papers* case," his secretary Frances Lamb noted. "The mental anxiety he suffered about this potential threat, as he regarded it, to the freedom of the press was apparently more excruciating than the physical pain." He turned it off to write his opinion, staying up past midnight.

One of his passages was "Paramount among the responsibilities of a free press is the duty to prevent any part of the government from deceiving the people and tricking them into a war where young Americans will be murdered on the battlefield." He went to bed, then woke up within an hour and talked to Elizabeth about his opinion, as he often had. "How would it be if I said that the press should be left free to prevent presidents from sending American boys to foreign lands to be murdered?" She thought it was too strong; he turned off the light. At 4 A.M., he turned it on again. "How would it be if I said, 'send American boys to die of foreign fevers and foreign shot and shell'?" She liked it and the substitution was made. The line was an adaptation from the southern ballad "I Am a Good Old Rebel"—Yankees dying from "Southern fever, and Southern steel and shot"—long a favorite of Hugo's, which he used to sing for fun with his sons and then clerks, but then quit singing after George Wallace started fighting integration.

All three clerks reviewed Black's draft, honing, toning and sharpening it. At his secretary's suggestion, he omitted that the injunctions were a "wanton" breach of the First Amendment; "flagrant, indefensible, and continuing" would suffice. Black spent most waking minutes polishing this lesson on the history and meaning of the First Amendment. He was going to make it as lucid and as tight as possible. Prior restraints were an execration in a democracy. On Wednesday afternoon, June 30, the opinions were ready.

The government, the per curiam opinion stated very simply, directly and positively, had not met the "heavy burden of showing justification for the imposition of such a [prior] restraint." No other opinion in the case, no other First Amendment opinion of Black's except possibly *Anastaplo,* and only a small handful ever, matched the power, simplicity and eloquence of his concurrence.

"I believe that every moment's continuance of the injunctions against these newspapers amounts to a flagrant, indefensible, and continuing violation of the First Amendment." He scolded those justices who suggested "that the publication of news may sometimes be enjoined. Such a holding would make a shambles of the First Amendment. . . . The Solicitor General argues . . . that the general powers of the Government adopted in the original Constitution should be interpreted to limit and restrict the specific and emphatic guarantees of the Bill of Rights adopted later. I can imagine no greater perversion of history." Black reached the heart of the matter. Into it he packed a lifetime of thought and study, of reading and reflection, of passionate conviction:

In the First Amendment the Founding Fathers gave the free press the protection it must have to fulfill its essential role in our democracy. The press was to serve the governed, not the governors. The Government's power to censor the press was abolished so that the press would remain forever free to censure the Government. The press was protected so that it could bare the secrets of government and inform the people. Only a free and unrestrained press can effectively expose deception in government. And paramount among the responsibilities of a free press is the duty to prevent any part of the government from deceiving the people and sending them off to distant lands to die of foreign fevers and foreign shot and shell. In my view, far from deserving condemnation for their courageous reporting, the New York Times, the Washington Post, and other newspapers should be commended for serving the purpose that the Founding Fathers saw so clearly. In revealing the workings of government that led to the Vietnam war, the newspapers nobly did precisely that which the Founders hoped and trusted they would do.

. . . To find that the President has "inherent power" to halt the publication of news by resort to the courts would wipe out the First Amendment and destroy the fundamental liberty and security of the very people the Government hopes to make "secure." . . . The word "security" is a broad, vague generality whose contours should not be invoked to abrogate the fundamental law embodied in the First Amendment. The guarding of military and diplomatic secrets at the expense of informed representative government provides no real security for our Republic.

The nation survived the publication of the Pentagon Papers; indeed it became stronger as a result. Without such cases and without judges willing to affirm the commands of the First Amendment,* the sounds of hobnailed boots might well be heard marching in the night. After the decision was announced, Chief Justice Burger rose, turned to Justice Black, took him by the elbow, and smiled. Black smiled back as Burger helped him down the steps first. They walked through the scarlet drapes that were parted for their exit from the bench. Elizabeth said, "Honey, if this is your swan song it's a good one." He agreed he could be proud of this opinion.[3]

*   *   *

The headaches returned, more often and stronger than before. It showed in Black's eyes. He never had any real desire to retire, as long as he was physically capable. When he joined the Court, Justice Sutherland practically had to be led around. "That'll never happen to me," Black vowed. "I'll know when to retire." "I'll have to be carried out feet first," he said in 1957; and in 1961, "I'll stay as long as I can write a first draft." After his heart scare in 1962, he mentioned retirement indirectly. "One of the hardest things you have to do up here," he told four former clerks individually, "is to know when to leave. If you stay too long, you impose terrible burdens on your colleagues. I ask you to tell me when that is." Black never mentioned it to the clerks again. "I just want to spend my working years on the Court," he said in 1967, and the next year he told a clerk, "I'll stay as long as I can. But I won't be here forever."

Warren's 1968 announcement that he would retire led Black to ponder retirement himself. "Hugo has always said he didn't mind retiring," Elizabeth noted June 16, 1968, "but that was belied tonight when he said in an anguished voice, 'But what will I do!' " He rejected all the possibilities she mentioned. One week later he said he "won't be a part of a mass retirement." He did not want to think about it. "As yet I have not had any reason to change my mind," he soon tersely wrote John Frank, "and at present do not contemplate leaving the Court." He told his old friend George Reynolds, "I'll stay on until my next to last breath."[4] There were cases to be won, and a record to be set.

Black wanted very much to break the longevity record (even though,

---

* "I wouldn't do away with the First and Fifth Amendments," Black said in 1970 (int.). "We can get along without the other amendments. I have trouble picking out which of the first eight amendments has primacy except for the First Amendment."

Elizabeth recalled, "he did not talk about it much just as he did not talk about many things which he felt very strongly"). In December 1970 Irving Dilliard, who kept track of such things, told him he was approaching the record. Black knew he was, but now had his secretary look it up. Thereafter he kept on his desk a small card noting the exact dates of the two justices, John Marshall and Stephen Field, who had served longer than he thus far. By the time the 1971 term would start, he would need less than six months to break the record, and on March 2, 1972, he would pass Stephen Field, who retired in 1897.

"During the last year," Black told a visitor in October 1970, "my wife has wanted me to quit the Court, to be together more so we could go places and do things. But I feel pretty good except for my eyes. Last week I fell down on the stairs because I couldn't see them. My wife says that maybe we should sell the house, but I don't want to." By March 1971 even Black began to doubt he could continue much longer. "How long after [the next few months] I shall hold on," he told Tom Corcoran's son David, "no one knows—not even I." The night before the Pentagon Papers case was argued, he had to be helped down the steps as he left a restaurant after dinner.[5]

He spent four days in the Bethesda Naval Medical Center in mid-July and was listless the rest of the month. He had lost fifteen pounds and his voice was an octave higher due to weakness. In early August new medication (prednisone) gave him a momentary lift; his spirits bounced back. He told his new clerks that he was glad to have three southerners for what would probably be his last year on the Court. "Probably?" uttered an aghast Elizabeth. Hugo laughed. When he did not continue regaining his strength, he called Louis Oberdorfer. He had long been a regular part of Black's life. Hugo enormously respected Oberdorfer's judgment and showered plaudits on him as he rarely did on anyone. He deeply hoped Lou, a "wonderful," a "grand person," would be appointed to a judgeship. (Oberdorfer was appointed to the federal bench in 1977.) As the years passed, Black phoned him regularly and Oberdorfer was frequently at the house. Now he became almost as central to Black as Elizabeth.

For parts of four days he and Oberdorfer talked. Black was paranoid about the future, expressing fears of governmental collapse; Nixon was preparing a military coup, he said. "Anything can happen here. We have small groups fragmenting the government. There may not be a 1972 election—a dictator might take over." Such thinking is not unusual in stroke victims who remain active, Black's neurologist has noted. When they spoke about the justice's plans, Oberdorfer recalled, "he kept on equivocating, one way and then the other." Then Black said, "If I were younger and healthier, I would stay on the Court and fight it out, but I can't see well and my memory is not as good. If I can't measure up, then I should get off the Court." He was adamant. Oberdorfer, emotionally torn but hoping to convince him to step down, drafted a letter of resignation. Black signed it, leaving the date open. "This will protect the Court," he said. The next morning, August 27, very weak and depressed, he reentered the hospital. "I'm not going there to die, am I?"

He didn't want visitors. * The doctors had diagnosed his condition as temporal arteritis, an inflamation of the blood vessels. Ever since his brother Orlando had died of arteritis in 1917; the word had frightened him. He had an "I give up" attitude and refused to believe he would get better. "I'm going to die," he said. The doctors told him no, but he shook his head and insisted he would. He stared at the lights on the wall, traced a circle with his finger and said he wished they would stop twirling, medically a certain indication of more serious problems to come. Elizabeth and Hugo, Jr., who had come up from Miami, were shaken.

In the adjoining room, as he was at the Court, was John Harlan, who was undergoing tests for recurring back pains. He was running his chambers from his hospital bed, and often came in to perk Black up. He had no luck: Hugo didn't want to see his best friend and told Elizabeth to stop him from coming in. "John Harlan can't see a thing," Black said. "He ought to get off the Court too." (Black always ignored Harlan's earlier remark that perhaps both of them had stayed on too long.) Thoughts of imminent death haunted both old men, but Harlan put them off when he was around the Blacks. They had been his family the last few years as his wife suffered from Alzheimer's disease. When Sterling came, Elizabeth sent his wife, Nancy, a psychologist, in to see Harlan. She talked to him and held his hand for an hour. "My life has been all work," he said, crying. "I've gotten all my satisfaction and enjoyment through it. I've never felt loved."[6]

*   *   *

Almost from the moment Black went into the hospital, his major concern was to have his Court papers, or at least his conference notes, burned. "As

* President Nixon wanted to visit, but Hugo, Jr., begged off by saying his father could not be moved to a more secure area in the hospital.

I have indicated to you on several occasions," he wrote Frances Lamb on September 1, "I do not believe that my personal notes on and for Court conferences should be left in the official files or made public. I have decided that the best thing to do is to burn them as Justice Roberts did. Nobody can get any history out of them that is worthwhile. Please burn them at your earliest convenience and advise me that you have done so." He ordered Hugo, Jr., to do it. Hugo, Jr., feeling he had no choice, stalled, hoping his father's condition would improve, but it continued to deteriorate. Once the appropriate papers were determined, Spencer tried to burn them in the fireplace at the house, but a neighbor complained about the ashes (Virginia had a law prohibiting open burning). So Hugo, Jr., and JoJo took the material to Elizabeth's son's home in Maryland, where historic ashes ("Operation Frustrate the Historians," they called it) filled a rainy sky. Hugo, Jr., told his father he had burned all the papers when he purposely had not. He just couldn't bring himself to destroy correspondence among the justices and drafts of opinions.

With his papers taken care of, Black turned his thoughts to a successor. For years he had wanted Frank Johnson in his place. Several times he had told Elizabeth, "Frank would make a good Justice. He has all the qualifications." Black asked Burger to sound out Nixon. Nixon agreed, and had Attorney General John Mitchell start an investigation. "You're going to be appointed to the Supreme Court," Burger told Johnson, whom he had known since the mid-1950s. "I just thought you ought to know before the newspeople descended on you." Nixon was planning to submit the nomination to the Senate when three Alabama congressmen, all Republicans like Johnson, heard about it. William Dickinson of Montgomery, John Buchanan of Birmingham* and Jack Edwards of Mobile (three of the five Republicans who were elected on Barry Goldwater's coattails when he swept the state in 1964) decided that Johnson's appointment "would ruin us politically" in Alabama. They asked Mitchell "not to do it." (Several years later Dickinson told Johnson, "If I had to do it over again today, I wouldn't do it. We made a mistake and I want to apologize.")[7] The nation was the loser.

*   *   *

When Black showed no improvement in the hospital, his family wanted him to retire. The only chance for any recovery, the doctors said, was to increase

---

* Buchanan, the son of a conservative Birmingham minister whom Black knew, later became head of the outspokenly liberal organization People for the American Way.

his dosage of prednisone even though this would heighten the chance of a stroke, already an elevated possibility. The dosage was increased, but Black made no progress. Finally, on September 15, Hugo, Jr., said, "Daddy, we all want you to get off the Court now." He had spoken with Chief Justice Burger, who had indicated he was willing to let Black serve until he broke the longevity record. But Black replied, "I can't serve." Elizabeth typed in the date on the retirement letter.

On September 17, 1971, after serving thirty-four years and one month on the Supreme Court, Hugo Black retired. He had Hugo, Jr., first give a copy of his retirement letter to Earl Warren. ("Daddy always called him 'the Chief'— he loved him—while Burger was just 'Burger,' " said Hugo, Jr.) Black's messenger, Spencer Campbell, delivered the original to the White House.

John Harlan retired on September 23 after learning he had cancer. He delayed his announcement for a week to avoid detracting from the accolades and attention Black would receive and Harlan wanted him to receive. "He is one of the all-time greats of our Court," Harlan told Hugo, Jr. ". . . Nobody's judgment ever exceeded his—his is just the best."

Black did not know about this; after another stroke, he had lapsed into a coma. The tributes poured in, also too late for Hugo to know about them. Warren Burger called him "a rare and remarkable man." His old friend Max Lerner, who had stood by him so loyally after his appointment, ended an affectionate column with "The Hugo I remember will live forever in the Court opinions the young will devour." But the tributes Hugo would have appreciated the most came from home: the Alabama House of Representatives passed a resolution honoring him, as later did the Alabama and Birmingham bar associations, the latter memorializing "its most distinguished former member."

The family did not want to use extraordinary measures to prolong Black's life. He just lay waiting for the end. It came as swiftly as he wanted, early on September 25. Just before, JoJo went in to see him. She touched his head. Onto his cheek was falling a single tear for a life he loved.

Earl Warren said all that had to be said. "A great man has passed away."[8]

*   *   *

Hugo, Jr., JoJo, Elizabeth's son, Fred, and Justices Brennan and White went to Gawler's Funeral Home, the most prominent in Washington, for a coffin. More than thirty coffins "were lined up like used cars," JoJo recalled. "We didn't want an expensive one. We all knew how Daddy felt about it." She asked to see the least expensive one. The mortician showed a box with embossed gray cloth for $165, moved quickly to others costing more, then proudly pointed to a mahogany one selling for $4,000. "A justice should be buried only in this," he said. "What's underneath the cloth of the cheapest one?" JoJo asked. "Pine," the mortician replied; "$250, $750, they all look pretty much alike," White noted. "Let's look underneath." He picked them up, examined them, and stated, "We think Justice Black would like the one that costs the least." The mortician objected—his clients usually exited in grandeur—but the group went over to the pine one.

"We're going to bury him in this," White said. "Let's pull this stuff." He started ripping the cloth off as the mortician protested, "oh no, you can't do that." The others joined in, furiously pulling off the glued fabric. It was their catharsis. They saw a plain pine casket with knotholes in it. White asked if the wood could be polished and the holes filled. JoJo said she would pay for this. The cloth was soaked off, the coffin sanded down, the pock marks and the nail holes shaved. It remained looking unfinished. "You couldn't get it simpler," recalled Joseph Hagan, Gawler's president. "That was how the family wanted it. We've never done it before or since." (Gawler's has been in business since 1850.) "I got him what he wanted," JoJo said. "We knew what statement my father wanted to make."

One thousand persons attended the brief and simple services, impressive and homey like the man himself. Much of official Washington was present; for a blip of time the business of government stalled. At the door pocket-size, Government Printing Office copies of the Constitution were free for the taking; several copies were in the suit pocket of the deceased. Members of the Supreme Court police force carried the coffin into Washington Cathedral. Past and present justices served as honorary pallbearers, walking slowly behind the coffin under high gothic arches. Only John Harlan was not present; his doctor ordered him not to attend. The pine knots, the markings on the wood, and the joinery on the corners and sides of the coffin showed clearly as it sat on a perch of royal purple velour. Its stark simplicity looked strangely out of place in the magnificent cathedral, a last dissent by the boy from Clay County, Alabama.

The organist played "Swing Low, Sweet Chariot," one of Black's favorite hymns, and the congregation sang "Rock of Ages." The dean of the cathedral, the Reverand Francis B. Sayre, Jr., read the deceased's favorite biblical passage, from I Corinthians 13. As the military held the flag over the coffin, a Unitarian minister, the Reverand Duncan Howlett, read passages from books he had chosen in Black's study—Aeschylus, Diogenes, Cicero, Jefferson, William James, Edith Hamilton, and Virgil's song about life and death, which Black had said he wanted read at his funeral.* He did not know Black's philosophy well and some of the quotations were at variance with it. But no one could disagree with the excerpts from the opinions that Hugo, Jr., had chosen for him, *Everson* and *Barenblatt* (and the Madison Lecture at New York University), as well as that trinity that will live through the ages—*Chambers, Anastaplo* and Pentagon Papers.

One of the listeners, unexpectedly, was President Nixon. "He didn't especially want to go," his aide William Safire later wrote, but two other assistants, Leonard Garment and Richard Moore, persuaded him. He and Attorney General John Mitchell sat impassively as Black was eulogized for his faith in man. Looking right at Nixon, the minister spoke about "so-called 'strict constructionists' who substituted principles laid down by latter-day jurists for the decrees of the Constitution itself."[9]

He closed with the standard refrain "We will not see his like again." For the first, perhaps the only, time in those eighty-five years since Hugo Black came into the world on that cold, rainy Saturday morning screaming—undoubtedly at some injustice—there were no dissents.

---

* "Let the sweet muses lead to their soft retreats. . . . At my funeral let no token of sorrow be seen, no pompous mockery of woe. Crown me with chaplets; strew flowers on my grave, and let my friends erect no vain memorial, to tell where my remains are lodged." The minister mistakenly attributed this to Tacitus.

OF HUGO AND ME

In 1967 I was one of the young devouring Hugo Black's opinions. I first came across them in a course on civil liberties taught by Professor Walter E. Volkomer at Hunter College. Both their conclusions and their raw power captivated me. The next year, while I was searching for a topic for an independent study project, Volkomer, who had already noted my interest in writing, suggested Black. How this former member of the Ku Klux Klan could be such an ardent civil libertarian had already intrigued me. The Franklin D. Roosevelt Library at Hyde Park granted me special permission to do research. The paper I wrote, on Black and the Japanese internment cases, was not publishable, but I was hooked. What began as a curiosity became a frequent preoccupation and then, admittedly, an obsession. The long journey started.

I wrote to Justice Black in 1969, began corresponding with some of his clerks and interviewing those who lived close by. Since his papers were not available, I approached Lenore Cahn, widow of his close friend Edmond Cahn, to look at Edmond's. This afforded my first feel of Black's mind. A small National Endowment for the Humanities stipend enabled me to spend part of the summer of 1970 reading manuscript collections in the Library of Congress. That October I interviewed Black. "The justice didn't come in today," his secretary Frances Lamb told me in his chambers, "and wondered if you could come to his home." Could I! He met me at the door wearing a suit and slippers, his handshake firm, his eyes direct. We talked for over six hours about many subjects, ranging from his ancestors to his wife Elizabeth's wanting him to retire, upon which he immediately said, "Don't print that." I haven't, until now. Only rarely since have I discussed the "shock the conscience" test of due process while eating a grilled cheese sandwich. The strongest remaining impressions are the intensity of his convictions and the equal firmness of his cordiality. Soon, after checking with him, his daughter Josephine Pesaresi, who lived in New Jersey, agreed to see me. "Why not?" she said. "It's his life, not mine."

After his death, I spoke several times with Elizabeth Black at their house, marking the beginnings of a warm friendship, before spending the summer of 1972, the first following his death, in Alabama. Clifford and Virginia Durr (his first wife's sister) kindly offered to put me up at their country home outside Montgomery. When I got there, on July 4, cars from six states were parked on the lawn. Virginia was holding court, a veritable latter-day, southern Eleanor Roosevelt. Cliff was quieter, and thoughtful. After everyone left, her first words to me were, "You know you have an appointment tomorrow with Judge Rives." I had not known, but was glad I did. Hugo Black was fresh in the memories of most of the people I met on that initial trip to Alabama. His first cousin, Harlan Martin, sat straight-backed in a chair in his Birmingham home, reminiscing about Clay County, their family and the 1926 Senate race; and Crampton Harris would not let me leave his office, motioning me with gnarled fingers to stay seated. "I'm having more fun talking about Hugo than practicing law," he said. Elizabeth's friends from the clerk's office at the federal court took me to lunch at the Joy Young restaurant; on the way to one of its curtained areas I saw Harris eating alone. Most of the people I then spoke to (as well as many since) are now, alas, dead. I returned to Alabama only once over the next several years. But I continued to interview and research on Black whenever possible. I was at the Library of Congress the first morning his extensive papers opened in 1974. On the way into the reading room I ran into Elizabeth. For the only time in the nearly two decades I knew her, she did not smile when seeing me. Her beloved Hugo was passing into "history" and, despite her fondness of me, it was not a pleasant thought for her.

Not until after the publication of my book *Banned Films*, on the history of movie censorship, in 1982 could I devote myself full-time to a book on Justice Black. I was planning to write a book on another subject before I got to the biography. I figured time was on my side. But my agent Carl Brandt quickly dissuaded me. "You'll never really be happy until you do this," he said. It didn't take long to realize he was right. A quick check reconfirmed that no one else was planning to write a complete book. So I began in earnest. The Black family never in any way authorized the book, but cooperated fully, and more. After checking with Elizabeth, some people spoke freely to me; JoJo suggested and opened other doors; and Hugo, Jr., gave me several important leads. Writing a comprehensive biography of a major historical figure like Black is not a task I would suggest for the faint of heart or the weakly determined: perseverance and sheer doggedness are necessities. Black's papers in the Library of Congress alone come to 512 boxes. I went through them piece by piece in the winter and spring of 1985. That was only the beginning. Eventually, after combing my way through hundreds of collections of his colleagues, opponents and friends in both public and private hands, I constructed and climbed (and now have the problem of storing) a paper mountain.

I packed copies of Black's Supreme Court files in my car and used them for the basis of many interviews I did on a cross-country trip of eighteen months in 1985 and 1986. It was a once-in-a-lifetime opportunity, and I used it to meet anyone who had some connection to Black's life or even to that of a colleague, several hundred people in all. The complexities of Black's personality revealed themselves as I continued my interviews. I returned east to attend the unprecedented ceremony at the Supreme Court releasing the stamp honoring Black's centennial, the idea for which I conceived; Congress passed the bill, which I helped draft, declaring the day in his honor. I lived in Birmingham for eight months, making that my base in Alabama. Ultimately I did research at upwards of one hundred institutions, saw many times that number of manuscript collections, and interviewed in thirty-three states. Some people I interviewed several times over a short period; with others I had many discussions over the years; and with a few, especially members of the Black family and a few close friends and clerks, it has virtually seemed like one long conversation of over twenty years. I have conducted well over one thousand interviews and briefly questioned many hundreds more. The total probably comes to well over two thousand people. Scores of these people had never been interviewed before.

The settings were varied. While most interviews took place at a person's office or, occasionally, over a meal, others were at Park Avenue and Georgetown homes or rustic country stores. There was the early chance meeting on the square in Ashland with an old man who poked his cane at me while recalling ten-year-old Hugo playing baseball (he was a third baseman). While driving in the Mellow Valley area below Ashland (not far from the remains of the house in which Black was born, near what local residents call Seven Forks), I saw a couple walking alongside the road and stopped to ask if they knew anyone who might know something about Black. That got the gentleman started about how Hugo successfully defended his uncle on a murder

charge. Then he asked me to help plant some seeds on his farm. Of course
I did.

The two most unforgettable interviews came with Hugh Rozelle and
Bill Rozelle, who were cousins. Hugh briefly lived with his uncle Hugo while
working in the Senate during the New Deal; later he became an Alabama
legislator and circuit judge. We met in his law office in Atmore, in South
Alabama, one Saturday morning at 10 o'clock. Through lunch and then
dinner with his wife, and into the evening, we talked. At 10 P.M. she started
calling to ask when he would come home. She gave up at midnight. By 1
A.M. we figured it was time to call it a day (or night), but continued talking
over the roofs of our cars. The next Saturday we mercifully called a halt at
7 P.M.

I saw Bill Rozelle in Talladega, down the winding road from Ashland.
Ten years younger than Hugo, he knew of the Blacks only by reputation in
his childhood but came to know Hugo slightly in the Klan. But he was a
good friend of Hugo's friend Chum Smelley and well remembered Hugo's
defending Chum in 1927. While talking about this, he wondered when
Chum died. "Let's go to the cemetery and find out," he said. We went and
for the only time in my life I pushed aside overgrown weeds around graves.
We found Smelley's tombstone; I dutifully took down the date as he chatted
more about Chum. I thanked him for his help and we exchanged goodbyes
and started to drive away. Suddenly he stopped his car, got out, strode
purposefully toward me and asked, "How old do you think I am?" "Not a
day over seventy-five," I said, knowing he was quite a bit older. "Ninety,"
he replied, as he got back into his car.

The journey has now been completed. Hugo Black has been a marvelous
teacher. Through him I learned much about law, history, politics and, as
he would have wanted most of all, about life.

My heart overflows with gratitude. My debts are manifold. I thank the John
Simon Guggenheim Foundation for awarding me a Fellowship. Justice William J. Brennan, Jr., Arthur M. Schlesinger, Jr., and Norman Redlich
graciously wrote the necessary letters of recommendation. I am grateful to
Mrs. Louise Schweitzer, acting in the spirit of her late husband Louis, who
underwrote several civil libertarian ventures, for having the Louis Schweitzer
Charitable Trust give me a grant; and also to the Lyndon Baines Johnson
Foundation for its award of a grant in aid. The following kindly found time
to read the manuscript in full or in part: Judge Richard S. Arnold, Judge

Guido Calabresi, Jesse Choper, William Cohen, Sam Daniels, Norman Dorsen, John Hart Ely, Wayne Flynt, John P. Frank, George C. Freeman, Jr., Robert A. Girard, Eugene Gressman, David Haber, Alonzo Hamby, William H. Harbaugh, John M. Harmon, Judge Frank M. Johnson, Jr., John G. Kester, Diane McWhorter, Jeffrey B. Morris, Judge Louis F. Oberdorfer, Robert M. O'Neil, Paul Pruitt, Norman Redlich, Donald A. Ritchie, George L. Saunders, Jr., William R. Snell, Lawrence Wallace, Calvin Woodard and Hugo Black's children. Their comments greatly improved the final product and they are absolved for any errors that remain, for which I alone am responsible.

In a special category are Hugo Black's law clerks, an extraordinary group of fifty-two men (the one woman, Margaret Corcoran, is deceased). They spoke to me with a frankness and understanding that reflected their affection for "the Judge." More than one cried as he reminisced. They gave me information available no place else and my debt to them is large indeed.

Librarians, curators and archivists across the country, hundreds altogether—too many handmaidens of history to name—brought me materials. I thank them all, especially Marvin Y. Whiting of the Birmingham Public Library, as well as the many people who secured access to these collections for me where necessary and gave me permission to quote from them. Additionally, I am grateful to the dozens of people who gave me information or leads, shared research or otherwise made materials available to me: Nils Anderson, Jr., Donald Bacon, Chester Bandman, Jr., and Marjorie Bandman Kahn, Jack Bass, Aline Berman, Michael Bernick, the late Paul Block, Jr., William Block, John R. Block and William Block, Jr. (the sons and grandsons of Paul Block, who so kindly opened the resources of the *Pittsburgh Post-Gazette* and *Toledo Blade*), Walter Brower, Jr., William Brower, Howard Buschman, Jr., Lenore Cahn, A. K. Callahan, Carleton Chapman, Aline Benjamin, Dr. William Brannan, Alexander Charns, Blair Clark, William Cohen, Geoffrey Cowan, Irving Dilliard (continually), Father Richard E. Donohue, Peter Fishbein, John P. Frank, Lee Marvin Fraser, George Freeman, Jr., Richard Friedman, Faustine Hill, Helen Hoyt, Ray Jenkins, Ingrid Jewell Jones, Marian Brown Kinney, Rae Sprigle Kurland, Diane McWhorter, Mayer Newfield, Luvie Pearson and Jack Anderson, Claude Pepper, Helen Wright Pickering, Peter Prescott, Ronald Radosh, Norman Redlich, H. Gerald Reynolds, the late Fred Rodell and Janet Rodell, Bryce Rucker, the late Art Seidenbaum, William Snell, Stephen P. Strickland (who gave me appreciated early encouragement), Peter Teachout, Miriam Beard Vagts, Thomas Walker, Connie Kaiser Williams and a *Newsweek* employee who made its file on Black available; and in Hugo Black's family: his widow, Elizabeth Black, his children Hugo Black, Jr., Sterling Black and Josephine Black Pesaresi, and Charlotte Black, Helen Garrett Byrnes, Robert Davis, the late Fred DeMeritte, Virginia and the late Clifford Durr, Evelyn Hail Pringle, Bette Davis Salinas, Robert Smith, Thomas Toland and Dorothy Pruet Tristram. I also thank the many people, especially in Alabama, who ransacked attics, family archives and memorabilia for anything which might be of use to me. If I have inadvertently omitted any other people, it is an error of the mind, not the heart.

In 1985 Norman Redlich, then dean of New York University School of Law, appointed me Research Scholar, which has aided me immeasurably in writing this book; I deeply appreciate his confidence in me. His successor, John Sexton, kindly continued the appointment and his interest. For many years Irving Dilliard has been a staunch and spirited friend. Many other friends and relatives, of mine and Hugo Black's, both put me up and put up with me several times. During most days over the past several years, I have spoken with Diane McWhorter (whose definitive book on the history of Birmingham will be published shortly), swapping information and talking about friends and past personages in her native city. Behind me from the very beginning in every way, in this and many other things, has been John P. Frank; he has never once failed me. He is a master of the art of friendship. I treasure his and count it as one of the joys of my life. I greatly regret, of course, that Elizabeth Black is not here to see this book to which she contributed so much. Justice Brennan and the late Judge J. Skelly Wright long inspired me and many others, and magnificently continued the tradition of the friend whom Judge Wright called "my mentor." Carl Brandt, my agent, has been a mainstay throughout. His shrewd advice and good cheer (along with a friendly whip) kept me going through some murky moments. Simon Michael Bessie, my publisher, makes his authors his friends. His enthusiasm, wise counsel and sense of craft have buoyed me. To both of these consummate gentlemen and peerless professionals I owe much indeed. There simply are none better.

I have difficulty finding the right words to credit Josephine Black Pesaresi adequately: that this book would not exist without her is only the beginning. She started as a "source" and turned into a dear friend. Both the telephone company and I profited from my innumerable conversations with her and her brothers. From the first, Hugo Black, Jr., has been characteristically gracious and cooperative, saying, "I may disagree violently with what you write but it's your book." He has kept his promise while wondering what else "Boswell" has found out about his father and his family. So has his brother Sterling. We talked many times, even while climbing the Sandia Mountains outside Albuquerque; few things can equal discussing the First Amendment at ten thousand feet to clear one's mind, although the beer at the summit comes close. My parents, Sydney and Shirley Newman, have always guided and supported me. More recently, my wife, Ricki, and our children, Peter and Beth, make everything worthwhile.

Brooklyn
Manhattan
Birmingham
Riverdale, N.Y.
1968–1994

SOURCE NOTES

CONSIDERATIONS OF SPACE as well as traditional standards of accuracy have guided me in documentation. I have tried to keep additional substantive information in the notes to a minimum whenever possible. References are given at the head of the notes for each chapter, or in the notes themselves, or are otherwise stated in the text, for most quotations and for curious, debatable or relatively obscure items for which an inquiring reader might want to know the source. I have not documented the fact that Franklin D. Roosevelt was elected President in 1932 or that Pearl Harbor Day was December 7, 1941. The Basic Source List gives those sources other than manuscript collections that I have used most frequently and, almost without exception, in more than one chapter. References to works on this list are by author's last name and short title. For works by more than one author, only the first author's name is mentioned in the source notes.

I have sharply limited the interviews cited in the notes because listing all of them would be unwieldy. Instead I have listed separately the names of persons I have interviewed or otherwise spoken with who have enhanced my understanding. Generally I have tried to cite only direct quotations. Often I was given the same information by many people and it would serve no purpose to list each of their names for the same facts. With many of these people I had several interviews; with some, as has been noted, many discussions over the years. The "average" interview lasted one to one and one-half hours. Some were conducted by telephone toward the end of the project, when I was writing and could not travel as much. One interview was conducted off-the-record. A handful of people asked that their names not be mentioned in connection with part of their remarks; I have, naturally, honored those requests. The accumulated information from these discussions has obviously been a major, and indispensable, source.

In a separate category, and equally vital, are the thoughts of Hugo Black's children. These ideas far exceed the number of citations and are incorporated indirectly throughout.

I have also listed the manuscript collections which I have consulted, both in public repositories and in private hands. These are essential yet must be used with great care, for like interviews, they cannot and do not tell the whole story and must be checked against each other as well as against other sources.

Citations to Supreme Court cases decided by opinion are noted by case name and date; these are readily available in college, university and law libraries, and many have been otherwise widely reprinted. Citations to Supreme Court cases decided without opinion and to lower court opinions are given in full. "Sou." means the Southern reporter, cases emanating from southern states. Legal citations are in traditional form: for example, *Brown v. Board of Education,* 347 U.S. 483 (1954), means that the Supreme Court decided the case in 1954 and that the opinions (in this instance only one) begin at page 483 of volume 347 of the *United States Reports,* the official volumes of the Court's decisions. Citations to periodicals and journals are given in concise formats; abbreviations used are listed in the next section. As for documents, if no source is listed, which occurs at least as often as not, then that document comes from HLBLC (Black's papers in the Library of Congress). Occasionally, if it is not clear where a particular item is from, I have inserted "HLBLC" to avoid possible confusion.

This system is necessary because to document every single item fully, as I originally did, would have more than tripled the length of the notes and made them more than half as long as the already lengthy text. Confining the notes almost exclusively to quotations and to statements of fact or description whose source is not standard or self-evident seemed the best solution. I wish here to thank all those persons, by no means limited to those listed here, whose research and writing on Hugo Black and related subjects have influenced me and blazed trails that have greatly eased my task.

ABBREVIATIONS FOR SOURCES FREQUENTLY CITED

ADAH	Alabama Department of Archives and History, Montgomery, Ala.
ALS	Albert Lee Smith
AP	Associated Press
AS	*Ashland Standard*
BES	*Baltimore Evening Sun*
BAH	*Birmingham Age-Herald*
BL	*Birmingham Ledger*
BN	*Birmingham News*
BNAH	*Birmingham News, Age-Herald*
BP	*Birmingham Post*
BPL	Birmingham (Alabama) Public Library
CB	Charlotte Black
CCAC	*Clay County Advocate*
CCAN	*Clay County Advance*
CEH	Charles Evans Hughes
CJD	Clifford J. Durr
COHP	Columbia Oral History Project, Columbia University
conv. (s)	conversation(s)
CR	*Congressional Record*
CSM	*Christian Science Monitor*
CT	*Chicago Tribune*
DAB	*Dictionary of American Biography*
DP	*Denver Post*
EC	Edmond Cahn
ESB	Elizabeth Seay Black
EW	Earl Warren
FDR	Franklin D. Roosevelt
FDRL	Franklin D. Roosevelt Library, Hyde Park, N.Y.
FF	Felix Frankfurter
FFLC	Felix Frankfurter papers, Library of Congress
FFHLS	Felix Frankfurter papers, Harvard Law School Library
FR	Fred Rodell
FV	Fred Vinson
HER	Hugh E. Rozelle

635

HLB	Hugo L. Black
HLB, Jr.	Hugo L. Black, Jr.
HLBLC	Hugo L. Black papers, Library of Congress
HST	Harry S Truman
HSTL	Harry S Truman Library, Independence, Mo.
int. (s)	interview(s)
JBP	Josephine Black Pesaresi
JFB	Josephine Foster Black
JMH	John M. Harlan
JPF	John P. Frank
LAT	*Los Angeles Times*
LBJ	Lyndon B. Johnson
LBJL	Lyndon B. Johnson Library, Austin, Tex.
LC	Library of Congress
MA	*Montgomery Advertiser*
MR	*Mobile Register*
NYHT	*New York Herald Tribune*
NYP	*New York Post*
NYT	*New York Times*
OH	Oral History (Project)
PP	*Pittsburgh Press*
PPA	*People's Party Advocate*
PPG	*Pittsburgh Post-Gazette*
RHJ	Robert H. Jackson
ROHO	Regional Oral History Office
SFB	Sterling F. Black
St. L P-D	*St. Louis Post-Dispatch*
SC	(Tuscaloosa, Ala.) *Southern Courier*, 7/27-28/68
TC	Tom Clark
TB	*Toledo Blade*
TNB	*Toledo News-Bee*
UA	University of Alabama
UA remarks	Remarks at University of Alabama HLB centennial symposium, March 17–18, 1986 (author's notes)
UAB	University of Alabama at Birmingham
UC	University of California
UK	University of Kentucky
UM	University of Michigan
VFD	Virginia Foster Durr
VH	Virginia Hamilton
WJB	William J. Brennan, Jr.
WDN	*Washington Daily News*
WOD	William O. Douglas

WODM	Conversations between Justice William O. Douglas and Professor Walter F. Murphy, taped during 1961–1963, Seeley G. Mudd Manuscript Library, Princeton University
WP	*Washington Post*
WR	Wiley Rutledge
WS	*Washington (Eve.) Star*
WT	*Washington Times*

MANUSCRIPT COLLECTIONS

This list includes only those collections which are cited in more than one chapter.

William Bankhead papers, ADAH
Burton Benjamin papers, State Historical Society of Wisconsin
Charlotte Black papers, privately held
Elizabeth S. Black papers, privately held
Hugo L. Black Books, UA Law School
Hugo L. Black papers, LC
William E. Borah papers, LC
Irving Brant papers, LC
Walter J. Brower papers, privately held
Eleanor Bumgardner papers, UM
Harold H. Burton papers, LC
Edmond Cahn papers, New York University Law School
Hattie Caraway papers, University of Arkansas
Raymond Clapper papers, LC
Grenville Clark papers, Dartmouth College
Tom Clark papers, Tarleton Law Library, University of Texas
Thomas G. Corcoran papers, LC
Homer Cummings papers, University of Virginia
William O. Douglas papers, LC
Clifford J. Durr papers, ADAH
Virginia Foster Durr papers, ADAH
Jerome Frank papers, Yale University
Felix Frankfurter papers, HLSL
Felix Frankfurter papers, LC
George C. Freeman, Jr., papers, privately held
Eugene Gressman papers, UM
Virginia Hamilton papers, BPL
John Marshall Harlan papers, Princeton University
E. Palmer Hoyt papers, privately held
Harold L. Ickes papers, LC
Robert H. Jackson papers, LC
Joseph P. Lash papers, FDRL
Max Lerner papers, Yale University
Raymond Moley papers, Hoover Institution
Henry Morgenthau diary, FDRL
Frank Murphy papers, UM
Newsweek files, *Newsweek*, New York City

Drew Pearson papers, LBJL
Claude Pepper diary, in his possession when I looked at it, now in his papers at Florida State
　University
Josephine Black Pesaresi papers (including those of Josephine Foster Black), privately held
Stanley F. Reed OHP, UK
Stanley F. Reed papers, UK
Fred Rodell papers, Haverford College
Fred Rodell private papers, privately held
Wiley B. Rutledge papers, LC
Grace Black Smith papers, privately held
Ray Sprigle papers, privately held
Harlan F. Stone papers, LC
Dorothy Pruet Tristram papers, privately held
Fred M. Vinson OHP, UK
Fred Vinson papers, UK
Earl Warren papers, LC
J. J. Willett papers, Stanford University

INTERVIEWS

Eve Adams, James Adler, Martin Agronsky, Carl Allen, Cleveland Allen, Jr., Jane Allen, Maryon Allen, Judge Clarence Allgood, Joseph Alsop, William Alsup, George Anastaplo, Lee Anderson, Nils Anderson, Jr., Neosha Anglin, Douglas Arant, Thomas Arbitage, Charles Ares, Frances Arnold, John C. Arnold, Jr., Cleveland Allen, Jr., Judge Richard S. Arnold, Thurman Arnold, Jr., Brandt Ayers, Annie Badham, Mary Jim Smathers Bagley, George Lewis Bailes, Jr., Frank Bainbridge, Jr., Mildred Bainbridge, Joseph Barbash, Edwin W. Barnett, Stephen Barnett, Wayne Barnett, Adrienne Barth, Jacques Barzun, Jack Bass, Robert Basseches, Roderick Beddow, Jr., Gould Beech, Irving Beiman, Aline Berman, Paul Bender, George Bentley, Michael Bernick, Simon Michael Bessie, Eugene Beyer, Scott Bice, Alexander M. Bickel, Ann Black, Charlotte Black, Elizabeth S. Black, Hugo L. Black, Hugo L. Black, Jr., Hugo L. Black III, John T. (Jay) Black, Nancy Black, Sterling Black, Paul Block, Jr., William R. Block, John R. Block, Fred Bodecker, Bennett Boskey, Lee C. Bradley, Jr., Dr. William Brannan, Irving Brant, Judge Howard Bratton, Justice William J. Brennan, Jr., Paul Brest, Murray Bring, Patrick Brock, Richard A. Brock, Mrs. William E. Brock, Jr., Walter J. Brower, Jr., William Brower, Edmund G. (Pat) Brown, Sr., Judge John R. Brown, Herbert Brownell, Bessie Black Bruce, Mary Virginia Fadely Buck, Chief Justice Warren E. Burger, Samuel Burr, Howard C. Buschman, Jr., Pierce Butler III, Helen Garrett Byrnes, Lenore Cahn, David Cairns, Judge Guido Calabresi, Mamie Helen Campbell, Jared Carter, Walter Chaffee, Jr., Carleton Chapman, Marquis Childs, Jesse Choper, Warren Christopher, David Clark, James E. Clark, Leigh Clark, Ramsey Clark, Robert Emmet Clark, Justice Tom Clark, Orville Clayton, Pauline Clayton, Melford O. Cleveland, Clark M. Clifford, Gladys Coates, Betty Maury Cobb, Nicholas Cobbs, Benjamin V. Cohen, Jerome Cohen, Sheldon Cohen, William Cohen, Robert Cole, John J. Coleman, Jr., C. J. (Jack) Coley, Jerome (Buddy) Cooper, Betty Copeland, Thomas G. Corcoran, Thomas G. Corcoran, Jr., Vern Countryman, Geoffrey Cowan, Lucille Cowherd, Donald Cronin, Donald Cronson, Geoffrey Cowan, James Crafts, Charles B. Crow, Jr., Mattie Lou Teague Crow, David Currie, Charles E. Danforth, Jr., Ann Butt Daniel, Clifton Daniel, Sam Daniels, C. Girard Davidson, James T. Dawkins, L. A. Davis, Robert J. Davis, Sidney Davis, Tillie Davis, Fred DeMeritte, Elizabeth Dempsey, William H. Dempsey, Jr., Calvin DeWitt, John L. DeWitt III, John W. Dewitt, William DeWitt, Irving Dilliard, Marvin Dinsmore, Chris Dixie, Betsy Robinson Dobell, Terri Dobell, Robert J. Donovan, Norman Dorsen, H. L. Dozier, Earl Dudley, Ronnie Dugger, Clifford J. Durr, Virginia Foster Durr.

Robert Edington, Mercedes Douglas Eichholz, Peter Ehrenhaft, George Elsey, John Hart Ely, Marvin Engel, Ben Erdreich, Robert Esdale, Betty Davis Eshelman, Charles Fairman, Jerome Falk, James Fargason, Mary Fargason, Creekmore Fath, Mildred Black Faucett, John Fawcett, Floyd Feeney, David Feller, Martha A. Field, Sidney Fine, Peter Fishbein, Raymond Fisher, Fred Fishman, Bill Fite, C. C. Fite, A. Key Foster, Dr. Lay M. Fox, John P. Frank, Lorraine Frank, Marc Franklin, Robert Frazer, James Free, George C. Freeman, Jr., Ira Freeman, Lee Freeman, John French, Paul Freund, George Frey, Stephen J. Friedman, Fred Friendly, Ralph Frohsin, Sr., Clifford Fulford, James Gaither, J. Browder Garber, Lucien Gardner, Jr., Warner Gardner, Murray Gartner, R. James George, Jr., Adele Fort Ghisalbert,

White E. Gibson, Jr., John Gillon, David Ginsburg, Robert Girard, Judge John Godbold, Justice Arthur J. Goldberg, Herbert F. Goodrich, Jr., Richard Goodwin, Henry Graff, Monte Gray, Jr., Cooper Green, Eugene Gressman, Thomas Grey, Erwin N. Griswold, Isaac Groner, Harvey Grossman, Judge Hobart Grooms, Gerald Gunther, Judge Robert Gwin, David Haber, Cecil F. Hackney, Lucy Durr Hackney, Joseph Hagan, Roscoe Hagan, Margaret Toland Hail, A. B. Hale, James Hale, Claude E. Hamilton, Jr., Dagmar Hamilton, Irene Hamilton, J. W. (Bill) Hamilton, Jr., Larry Hammond, Milton Handler, Francis (Brother) Hare, Jr., June Dawkins Hargrove, John Harmon, Crampton Harris, Crampton Harris, Jr., Jack Harris, Charles Harrison, Gilbert Harrison, John M. Harrison, Alan Hart, Mrs. Carl Hatch, Robert Hearin, William J. Hearin, William Randolph Hearst, Jr., Senator Howell Heflin, Louis Henkin, Matthew Herold, Henry Hess, Jr., Ira Michael Heyman, Faustine M. Hill, Lister Hill, Luther L. Hill, Jr., Judge Truman Hobbs, Roscoe B. Hogan, Jr., Thad Holt, Charles Horowitz, Charles Horsky, A. E. Dick Howard, J. Woodford Howard, Jr., Milo Howard, Helen Hoyt, Henrietta Hill Hubbard, Edward Huddleston, Thomas Huey, Mabel Hughes, Maxwell Isenberg, Jerold Israel, William E. Jackson, Marie Jemison, Virginia Parrish Jamison, Eliot Janeway, Elizabeth Janeway, Marie Jemison, Ray Jenkins, Judge Frank M. Johnson, Jr., John W. Johnson, Jr., Lady Bird Johnson, Nicholas Johnson, Philip Johnson, Joseph F. Johnston, Paul Johnston, Ingrid Jewell Jones, G. Ernest Jones, Hugh E. Jones, William K. Jones, William Joslin, Marjorie Bandman Kahn, Howard Kalodner, John Kaplan, Andrew L. Kaufman, Edward Keane, Arthur J. Keefe, John Keker, John G. Kester, James Kilsheimer III, Snyder (Jed) King, Marian Brown Kinney, Richard Kleindienst, Thomas Klitgaard, Herman Kogan, Marilew Kogan, Alan Kohn, John Peter Kohn, Adrien Kragen, Douglas Kranwinkle, Philip Kurland.

Frances Lamb, Robert Lasky, Leonard Leiman, Marx Leva, Max Lerner, Howard Leshnick, Edward H. Levi, Daniel Levitt, Herbert Monte Levy, Herman Liebert, William T. Lifland, Hans Linde, Helen Linde, Hugh Locke, Jr., Peter Lockwood, James Loken, Ephraim London, Peter Low, Charles F. Luce, Louis Lusky, Judge Seybourne Lynne, Ann Durr Lyon, Walter Lyon, Dennis Lyons, Judge Daniel T. McCall, Jr., Patricia McCarren, Robert McCaw, Donald McDonald, Carl McFarland, Nicholas McGrath, John K. McNulty, George H. Mandy, William H. Mandy, Sr., Keith Mann, Bayless Manning, Eugene Marsh, James Marsh, Charlotte Martin, Harlan Martin, John Andrew Martin, Lucy Harris Martin, Jewel Massey, Alpheus T. Mason, Daniel Mayers, Daniel J. Meador, Bianca Meiklejohn, Donald Meiklejohn, Kenneth Meiklejohn, Wallace Mendelson, Paul Meyer, James E. Mills, Walter L. Mims, Jessica Mitford, Robert Mnookin, Carter Monasco, Bernard (Barney) Mongahan, Bill Monroe, Dan Moody, Jr., Graham Moody, Annie Haynes Moore, Mary Knox Moore, John Morrow, Sam Moskow, Robert Mull, J. Sanford Mullins III, Walter F. Murphy, Reese Murray, Jr., Drayton Nabers, Jeffrey Nagin, Philip Neal, Mayer Newfield, Judge Jon Newman, Sherman Nichols, Judge Eugene Nickerson, Roy Nolen, Jr., Judge William Norris, James North, Judge Louis Oberdorfer, J. Orlando Ogle, Covey T. Oliver, William Oliver, Camper O'Neil, Robert O'Neil, Michael Osborn, Nancy Huddleston Packer, John M. G. Parker, Jr., Virginia (Tilla) Durr Parker, Covert (Pete) Parnell, Claire Parsons, William Partlow, Vernon Patrick, Judge John Patterson, James Paul, Luvie Pearson, Ruth Street Pedigo, Claude Pepper, Josephine Black Pesaresi, Mario Pesaresi, Earl Pettus, Jr., Harlan B. Phillips, John Pickering, Mary Pierson, Richard Pizitz, Harvey Poe, Judge Sam C. Pointer, Jr., Earl Pollack, Judge Louis Pollak, Lucas (Scott) Power, Joseph Price, Lucy Prichard, Evelyn Hail Pringle, Clarence Pruet, Sr., Clarence Pruet, Jr., Mary Pruet, Esther Wood Quantock, James T. Ragland, Mary Ray, John Daniel Reaves, Norman Redlich, Charles Reed, Charles Reich, Charlotte Reid, Judge Gerard Reilly, James Reston, George Reynolds, Lee M. Rhoads, Charles Rickershauser, Audrey Rozelle Riddle, Russell Riggs, Judge Richard T. Rives, Marjory McGahey Roberts, John W. Robinson, Majorie DeWitt Robinson, Ruby Robinson, Fred Rodell, Janet Rodell, David Rogers, James Roosevelt, David Rosenbloom, Albert Rosenthal, Stuart Ross, Eugene Rostow, John Rothermel, Albert Lee

Rozelle, Hugh Rozelle, William M. Rozelle, Ernest Rubinstein, Neal Rutledge, James Ryan.

William H. Sadler, Jr., Richard Salant, Bette Davis Salinas, Terrance Sandalow, Cynthia Sartain, George L. Saunders, Jr., Norbert Schlei, Arthur Schlesinger, Jr., Benno Schmidt, Jr., Stephen Schulhofer, Evan Schwab, Murray Schwartz, Robert M. Scott, Vern Scott, William D. Scruggs, Carl Seneker II, Julia Sparkman Shepard, Richard Sherwood, Howard Shirley, Jr., Victor Sholis, Joseph Shuman, Larry Simon, Donald Simpson, Henry Simpson, James Simpson, Jr., Thomas E. Skinner, Marshall (Pop) Small, Albert Lee Smith, Sr., Albert Lee Smith, Jr., Grace Black Smith, Frances Boykin Smith, Gregory L. Smith, Hardy B. Smith, Michael Smith, Robert J. Smith, Sylvester Smith, Jr., Jerry Snider, Stanley Soderland, Judge Gus Solomon, Ormond Somerville, Stanley Sparrow, Robert Spearman, Gustave Speth, Clarke Stallworth, Veenie Stephenson, Robert Stern, Samuel Stern, Richard Steuer, Richard Stewart, Preble Stolz, Cathleen Douglas Stone, Michael Straight, Peter Strauss, Stephen P. Strickland, Judge William Sullivan, Stephen Susman, Peter Taft, Ralph Tanner, Robert Tate, Judge Daniel Thomas, Thomas A. Thrift, Ellen Schneider Thum, Michael Tigar, Bunyan Toland, Charles Toland, Thomas Toland, Bertha Tonkin, Mary Tortorici, George Treister, Jane Treister, Dorothy Pruet Tristram, Ray Troubh, Florey Tucker, Horace Turner III, David J. Vann, David Waggoner, C. Richard Walker, Lawrence Wallace, Lucyle Black Wallace, Harold Ward, Paul W. Ward, Tom Ward, Jr., Earl Warren, Jr., William C. Warren, John Weaver, Herbert Wechsler, Nancy F. Wechsler, Horace Wilkinson Weissinger, Joseph Wershba, Peter Westen, Alfred Whatley, William Whatley, Burton Wheeler, Frank S. White III, Mary Gardner White, Kent Whittaker, Clarence Wiley, Jr., Joseph Wiley, Percy Williams, Charles Wilson, Jr., Whit Windham, Payson Wolff, Paul Wolkin, W. H. Woolverton, Jr., Frank Wozencraft, Charles Alan Wright, Judge J. Skelly Wright, Tinsley Yarbrough, Kenneth Ziffrin, Peter Zimroth, Sidney Zion.

BASIC SOURCE LIST

Abell, Tyler, ed. *Drew Pearson, Diaries, 1949–1959* (N.Y., 1974).

Aikman, Duncan. "Justice Black: A Man of Two Personalities," *New York Times Magazine*, 8/22/37.

Alsop, Joseph, and Turner Catledge. *The 168 Days* (Garden City, N.Y., 1938).

Alsop, Joseph, with Adam Platt. *"I've Seen the Best of It": Memoirs* (N.Y., 1992).

AP release, "Black's Road to the Supreme Court," [about 8/14/37], found in Sprigle papers.

Atkins, Leah Rawls. *The Valley and the Hills: An Illustrated History of Birmingham and Jefferson County* (Woodland Hills, Calif., 1981).

Ball, Howard. *The Warren Court's Conceptions of Democracy: An Evaluation of the Supreme Court's Apportionment Opinions* (Rutherford, N.J., 1971).

Ball, Howard, and Cooper, Philip J. *Of Power and Right: Hugo Black, William O. Douglas, and America's Constitutional Revolution* (N.Y., 1992).

Bass, Jack. *Taming the Storm: The Life and Times of Judge Frank M. Johnson, Jr., and the South's Struggle Over Civil Rights* (N.Y., 1993).

———. *Unlikely Heroes* (N.Y., 1981).

Berman, Daniel M. "The Political Philosophy of Hugo L. Black" (Ph.D. dissertation, Rutgers University, 1957).

Bernstein, Irving. *The Lean Years: A History of the American Worker, 1920–1933* (Boston, 1960).

Bickel, Alexander M. *The Least Dangerous Branch* (Indianapolis, 1962).

Billington, Joy. "The Justice Blacks—Affectionate Respect," *Washington Star*, 7/5/70.

Black, Elizabeth S. "Hugo Black, The Magnificent Rebel," 9 *Southwestern University Law Review* 889 (1977).

———. The Magnificent Rebel (unpublished manuscript).

———. Unpublished diaries, 1964–1971.

Black, Hugo, Jr. *My Father: A Remembrance* (N.Y., 1975).

Black, Hugo L. *A Constitutional Faith* (N.Y., 1968).

———. "The Bill of Rights," 35 New York Univ. Law Rev. 865 (1960).

———. "Justice Black and the Bill of Rights," CBS News Special, broadcast 12/3/68.

———. "The Lawyer and Individual Freedom," 21 *Tennessee Law Review* 461 (1950).

Black, Hugo L., and Elizabeth Black. *Mr. Justice and Mrs. Black: The Memoirs of Hugo L. Black and Elizabeth Black* (N.Y., 1986).

Blum, John Morton, ed. *The Price of Vision: The Diary of Henry A. Wallace 1942–1946* (Boston, 1973).

Branch, Taylor. *Parting the Waters: America in the King Years, 1954–63* (N.Y., 1988).

Brant, Irving. *The Bill of Rights* (N.Y., 1967, Mentor paper ed.).

Bresler, Horace J. "Hugo Black—Champ Turned Judge," manuscript [1946], HLBLC.

Brown, Dorothy M. *Mabel Walker Willebrandt* (Knoxville, Tenn., 1984).

Bunche, Ralph. *The Political Status of the Negro in the Age of FDR* (Chic., 1973).

Burke, Robert E., ed. *The Diary Letters of Hiram Johnson, 1917–1945* (N.Y., 1983), 7 vols.

Cahn, Edmond. "The Firstness of the First Amendment," 65 *Yale Law Journal* 464 (1956).

Cahn, Edmond. *The Moral Decision* (Bloomington, Ind., 1955).
———. *The Predicament of Democratic Man* (N.Y., 1961).
———. *The Sense of Injustice* (N.Y., 1949).
Calabresi, Guido. *A Common Law for the Age of Statutes* (Cambridge, Mass., 1982).
Catledge, Turner. Book review, 47 *Tulane Law Review* 1214 (1973).
Chalmers, David. *Hooded Americanism* (Garden City, N.Y., 1965).
Childers, James Saxon. "Hugo Black, Always an Alabamian," *Birmingham News*, 1/31/37.
Childs, Marquis. *Witness to Power* (N.Y., 1975).
———. "Stone on Black," *Birmingham News*, 6/14/46, *St. Louis Post-Dispatch*, 6/15/46.
Clayton, James E. *The Making of Justice: The Supreme Court in Action* (N.Y., 1964).
Clifford, Clark, with Richard Holbrooke. *Counsel to the President: A Memoir* (N.Y., 1991).
Cohen, William, and David J. Danelski. *Constitutional Law—Civil Liberty and Individual Rights* (Westbury, N.Y., 3rd ed., 1994).
Confessions of the Law Clerks—Extracted for the 80th Birthday of Mr. Justice Black—February 27, 1966.
Cooper, Jerome A. "Mr. Justice Hugo L. Black: Footnotes to a Great Case," 24 *Alabama Law Review* 1 (1971).
———. "Mr. Justice Hugo LaFayette Black of Alabama (1886–1971)," 33 *Alabama Lawyer* 22 (1972).
Cruickshank, George M. *A History of Birmingham and Its Environs* (Chic., 1920).
Curtis, Charles P. *It's Your Law* (Cambridge, Mass., 1954).
———. *Law as Large as Life* (N.Y., 1959).
Davis, Hazel Black. *Uncle Hugo: An Intimate Portrait of Mr. Justice Black* (Amarillo, Tex., 1965).
Davis, Kenneth S. *FDR: The New Deal Years, 1933–1937—A History* (N.Y., 1986).
"The Deliberations of the Justices in Deciding the Sit-in Cases of June 22, 1964. From the files of Justice Black, compiled by A. E. Dick Howard and John G. Kester, Law Clerks," HLBLC.
de Grazia, Edward, and Roger K. Newman. *Banned Films: Movies, Censors and the First Amendment* (N.Y., 1982).
Dilliard, Irving, ed. *One Man's Stand for Freedom: Mr. Justice Black and the Bill of Rights* (N.Y., 1963).
Donovan, Robert J. *Conflict and Crisis: The Presidency of Harry S Truman, 1945–1948* (N.Y., 1977).
Douglas, William O. *Go East, Young Man: The Early Years* (N.Y., 1974).
———. *The Court Years, 1939–1975* (N.Y., 1980).
Dunne, Gerald T. *Hugo Black and the Judicial Revolution* (N.Y., 1977).
Durr, Clifford J. "Hugo L. Black: A Personal Appraisal," 6 *Georgia Law Review* 1 (1971).
Durr, Virginia Foster. "Interview with Virginia Durr on Hugo Black, May 14, 1981," ESB papers.
———. *Outside the Magic Circle: The Autobiography of Virginia Foster Durr*, edited by Hollinger F. Barnard (University, Ala., 1985).
Ehrlichman, John. *Witness to Power: The Nixon Years* (N.Y., 1992, Pocket ed.).
Farley, James A. *Jim Farley's Story: The Roosevelt Years* (N.Y., 1948).
Ferrell, Robert H., ed. *Off the Record: The Private Papers of Harry S Truman* (N.Y., 1980).
Fine, Sidney. *Frank Murphy: The Washington Years* (Ann Arbor, Mich., 1984).
Frank, John P. "Hugo L. Black: Free Speech and the Declaration of Independence," 1977 *University of Illinois Law Forum.*
———. "Hugo L. Black Funeral, 9/29/71," copy in author's possession.
———. "Hugo Black: Little Man's Lawyer," *Progressive*, 4/1/46.

————. *Mr. Justice Black—The Man and His Opinions* (N.Y., 1949).

Freedman, Max, ed. *Roosevelt and Frankfurter: Their Correspondence, 1928–1945* (Boston, 1967).

Freund, Paul A. "Memo of Conversation with Justice Black at his chambers, 7/16/68, at 2 p.m.," given to author by Richard Friedman.

————. *On Law and Justice* (Cambridge, Mass., 1968).

————. *The Supreme Court of the United States* (Cleveland, 1961).

Freyer, Tony, ed. *Justice Hugo Black and Modern America* (University, Ala., 1990).

Friendly, Fred W., and Martha J. H. Elliott. *The Constitution: That Delicate Balance* (N.Y., 1984).

Gerhart, Eugene C. *America's Advocate: Robert H. Jackson* (Indianapolis, 1958).

Grafton, Carl, and Anne Permaloff. *Big Mules and Branchheads: James E. Folsom and Political Power in Alabama* (Athens, Ga., 1985).

Griswold, Erwin N. "Griswold—ABA Dinner Speaker," *Stanford Lawyer* (winter 1972–73).

————. *Ould Fields, New Corne: The Personal Memoirs of a Twentieth Century Lawyer* (St. Paul, Minn., 1992).

Hackney, Sheldon. *Populism to Progressivism in Alabama* (Princeton, 1969).

Hamilton, Edith. *The Greek Way* (N.Y., 1942).

Hamilton, Virginia Van de Veer. *Hugo Black: The Alabama Years* (Baton Rouge, La., 1972).

————. *Lister Hill: Statesman for the South* (Chapel Hill, N.C., 1987).

————. "The Senate Career of Hugo L. Black" (Ph.D. dissertation, University of Alabama, 1968).

Harbaugh, William H. *Lawyer's Lawyer: The Life of John W. Davis* (N.Y., 1973).

Harper, Fowler V. *Justice Rutledge and the Bright Constellation* (Indianapolis, 1965).

Harris, Carl V. *Political Power in Birmingham, 1871–1921* (Knoxville, Tenn., 1977).

Hendrix, William. "Mr. Justice Black," *True Story Magazine*, 2/38.

Hofstadter, Richard. *The American Political Tradition* (N.Y., 1948).

Howard, J. Woodford, Jr. *Mr. Justice Murphy: A Political Biography* (Princeton, 1968).

Howe, Mark DeW., ed. *Holmes–Laski Letters: The Correspondence of Mr. Justice Holmes and Harold J. Laski, 1916–1935*, abridged by Alger Hiss (N.Y., 1963).

Huff, Martin. "Interview with the Hon. Hugo L. Black . . . , by Martin Huff, Alexandria, Virginia, 1/29/70," HLBLC.

Hunnicutt, Benjamin Kline. *Work Without End: Abandoning Shorter Hours for the Right to Work* (Phila., 1988).

Hutchinson, Dennis J. "The Black–Jackson Feud," 1988 *Supreme Court Review*.

————. "Unanimity and Desegregation: Decisionmaking in the Supreme Court, 1948–1958," 68 *Georgetown Law Journal* 1 (1979).

Huthmacher, J. Joseph. *Senator Robert F. Wagner and the Rise of Urban Liberalism* (N.Y., 1968).

Ickes, Harold L. *The Secret Diaries of Harold L. Ickes* (N.Y., 1954), 3 vols.

Jackson, Kenneth T. *The Ku Klux Klan in the City 1915–1930* (N.Y., 1967).

Jackson, Robert H. *The Struggle for Judicial Supremacy* (N.Y., 1941).

Jackson, Walter A. *Gunnar Myrdal and America's Conscience: Social Engineering and Racial Liberalism, 1938–1987* (Chapel Hill, N. Car., 1990).

Janeway, Eliot. "Douglas Revisited: Braintrusting Social Change," *Washington Star*, 12/21/75.

Josephson, Matthew. *Sidney Hillman: Statesman of American Labor* (Garden City, N.Y., 1952).

Kalman, Laura. *Abe Fortas: A Biography* (New Haven, 1990).

Kluger, Richard. *Simple Justice* (N.Y., 1976).

Landynski, Jacob. "In Search of Justice Black's Fourth Amendment," 45 *Fordham Law Review* 453 (1976).

Lash, Joseph P. *Dealers and Dreamers: A New Look at the New Deal* (N.Y., 1988).

Lerner, Max. *Ideas Are Weapons: The History and Uses of Ideas* (N.Y., 1939).
———. "I Remember Hugo," *New York Post,* 9/22/71.
Lewis, Anthony, "Justice Black at 75: Still the Dissenter," *New York Times Magazine,* 2/26/61.
Lilienthal, David E. *Journals,* vol. 1, *The TVA Years, 1939–1945* (N.Y., 1964).
Louchheim, Katie, ed. *The Making of the New Deal: The Insiders Speak* (Cambridge, Mass., 1983).
Malone, Dumas. *Jefferson and the Rights of Man* (Boston, 1951).
Mason, Alpheus T. *Harlan Fiske Stone: Pillar of the Law* (N.Y., 1956).
———. *Security Through Freedom: American Political Thought and Practice* (Ithaca, N.Y., 1955).
Meador, Daniel J. *Mr. Justice Black and His Books* (Charlottesville, Va., 1974).
Mendelson, Wallace. *Justice Black and Frankfurter: Conflict in the Court* (Chic., 1961).
Miller, Merle. *Ike The Soldier: As They Knew Him* (N.Y., 1987).
Murphy, Bruce Allen. *The Brandeis/Frankfurter Connection* (N.Y., 1982).
———. *Fortas: The Rise and Ruin of a Supreme Court Justice* (N.Y., 1988).
Murphy, Walter F., James E. Fleming and William F. Harris II. *American Constitutional Interpretation* (Mineola, N.Y., 1986).
Niznik, Monica Lynne. "Thomas G. Corcoran: The Public Service of Franklin Roosevelt's 'Tommy the Cork' " (Ph.D. dissertation, University of Notre Dame, 1981).
O'Brien, David J. *Storm Center: The Supreme Court in American Politics* (N.Y., 1986; 2nd ed., 1990; 3rd ed., 1993).
Patterson, James T. *Congressional Conservatism and the New Deal* (Lexington, Ken., 1967).
Pepper, Claude D., with Hayes Gorey. *Pepper—Eyewitness to a Century* (San Diego, 1987).
Perkins, Frances. *The Roosevelt I Knew* (N.Y., 1946).
Pollack, Jack Harrison. *Earl Warren: The Judge Who Changed America* (Englewood Cliffs, N.J., 1979).
Pruden, Durward. "The Opposition of the Press to the Ascension of Hugo Black to the Supreme Court of the United States" (Ph.D. dissertation, New York University, 1945).
Pusey, Merlo. *Charles Evans Hughes* (N.Y., 1951).
Reich, Charles. *The Sorcerer of Bolinas Reef* (N.Y., 1976).
Rodell, Fred. "Justice Hugo Black," *American Mercury,* 8/44.
Rucker, Bryce. Interviews with Clifford J. Durr, 1967–70.
Safire, William. *Before the Fall: An Inside View of the Pre-Watergate White House* (N.Y., 1977).
Salisbury, Harrison E. *Without Fear or Favor: An Uncompromising Look at "The New York Times"* (N.Y., 1980).
Schlesinger, Arthur M. *In Retrospect: The History of a Historian* (N.Y., 1963).
Schlesinger, Arthur M., Jr. *The Coming of the New Deal* (Boston, 1959).
———. *The Crisis of the Old Order* (Boston, 1957).
———. *The Politics of Upheaval* (Boston, 1960).
Schwartz, Bernard. *The Ascent of Pragmatism: The Burger Court in Action* (Reading, Mass., 1990).
———. *Super Chief: Earl Warren and His Supreme Court* (N.Y., 1983).
———. *The Unpublished Opinions of the Burger Court* (N.Y., 1990).
———. *The Unpublished Opinions of the Warren Court* (N.Y., 1985).
Sholis, Victor. "One Young Man, Hugo Black—A Country Boy's Rise," *Chicago Sun-Times,* 8/18–20, 22–24/37.
Silverstein, Mark. *Constitutional Faiths: Felix Frankfurter, Hugo Black and the Process of Judicial Decision Making* (Ithaca, N.Y., 1984).
Simon, James F. *Independent Journey: The Life of William O. Douglas* (N.Y., 1980).
Sims, George E. *The Little Man's Big Friend: James E. Folsom in Alabama Politics, 1946–1958* (Tuscaloosa, Ala., 1985).

Smith, Richard Norton. *Thomas E. Dewey and His Times* (N.Y., 1982).

Snell, William R. Interviews with James Esdale, 6/67, copy in author's possession.

———. *The Ku Klux Klan in Jefferson County, Alabama, 1916–1930* (M.A. thesis, Stanford University, 1967).

Stallworth, Clarke. "Hugo Black: The Boy and the Man," *Birmingham News*, 2/22/76.

Stewart, Kenneth. "Black: Serene storm-center," *PM*, 7/5/47.

Strickland, Stephen P., ed. *Hugo Black and the Supreme Court: A Symposium* (Indianapolis, 1967).

Swain, Martha H. *Pat Harrison: The New Deal Years* (Jackson, Miss., 1978).

Tindall, George Brown. *The Emergence of the New South, 1913–1945* (Baton Rouge, La., 1967).

Tushnet, Mark. *Making Civil Rights Law: Thurgood Marshall and the Supreme Court, 1936–1961* (N.Y., 1994).

———. "What Really Happened in *Brown v. Board of Education*," 91 *Columbia Law Review* 1867 (1991).

Urofsky, Melvin I., ed. *The Douglas Letters: Selections from the Private Papers of Justice William O. Douglas* (Bethesda, Md., 1987).

Warner, Robert M. "A Report by Robert M. Warner on Interviews with Justices Hugo Black and William O. Douglas, 10/21 and 22/64," Michigan Historical Collections, UM.

Warren, Earl. *The Memoirs of Chief Justice Earl Warren* (Garden City, N.Y., 1977).

Weaver, John D. *Warren: The Man, The Court, The Era* (Boston, 1967).

White, Walter. *A Man Called White: The Autobiography of Walter White* (N.Y., 1948).

Woodward, Bob, and Scott Armstrong. *The Brethren: Inside the Supreme Court* (N.Y., 1979).

Woodward, C. Vann. *The Strange Career of Jim Crow* (N.Y., 1974).

Wyzanski, Charles E., Jr. *Whereas—A Judge's Premises* (Boston, 1965).

Yarbrough, Tinsley E. *John Marshall Harlan: Great Dissenter of the Warren Court* (N.Y., 1992).

———. *Mr. Justice Black and His Critics* (Durham, N.C., 1988).

Zimmern, Alfred. *The Greek Commonwealth: Politics and Economics in Fifth Century Athens* (Oxford, Eng., 1931).

Zion, Sidney. Interview with Hugo Black for *New York Times* obituary, May 1967.

NOTES

Chapter 1

SOURCES: HLB, *Memoirs*; HLB, "Reminiscences," 18 *Ala. Law Rev.* 3 (1965); HLB, Jr., *Father*; Childers , "Black"; Davis, *Uncle*; Frank, *Black*; Hamilton, *Black*; Hendrix, "Justice"; Pruden, "Opposition"; Paul M. Pruitt, Jr., *Joseph C. Manning, Alabama Populist: A Rebel Against the Solid South* (Ph.D. dissertation, College of William and Mary, 1980); Stallworth, "Black"; Stewart, "Serene"; and HLB to Irving Dilliard 7/25/62. Interviews: HER, Harlan Martin.

1. ESB to Ethel and JMH 8/22/68, JMH papers (Little Della death). Name: Family Bible in possession of Mildred Black Faucett.

2. Tolands: "Orlando E. Black" in Joel C. DuBose, ed., *Notable Men of Alabama* (Atlanta, 1904), I, 409; HLB to HER 10/4/44; to Hazel Davis 9/27/65; to Robert E. Clark 7/21/53; to Robert E. Sherwood 5/30/45; "Thomas L. Toland" in *The Goodspeed Biographical and Historical Memoirs of Southern Arkansas* (Chic., 1889); *Ala. Journal* 7/4/60 (James and Della Toland); John Francis Williamson Toland, "A History of the Toland Family" (1902); "Black and Toland" and other information in Smith papers; information also provided by Faustine M. Hill, Robert Toland and Evelyn Pringle; Harlan Martin, Thomas Toland, HER, Pedigo ints.

3. "Information on Black Family History—From Thomas Noell, Clerk of Court, Oglethorpe County, Georgia," JBP papers (oh Lordy); Columbus M. Black Confederate Army Records, HLBLC. Faet and Civil War: HLB to Hazel Davis 2/28/71; NYP 9/11/43; undated CCAN article in HLB scrapbook (close up). Settle in Harlan: JBP papers (land so poor).

4. Henry Pelham Martin (HLB's first cousin), *A History of Politics in Clay County During the Period of Populism From 1888 to 1896*, (M.A. thesis, UA, 1936), 1–3, ch. 3; CCAN 4/13,22/1892; PPA 3/2/1894 (grand mission), 2/9/94 (true religion), 3/9/1894 (still insist). Whatley: Martin, 43; Hackney, *Populism*, 49; CCAN 9/7/1894; PPA 2/2/1894; William Warren Rogers, *The One-Gallused Rebellion: Agrarianism in Alabama, 1865–1896* (Baton Rouge, La., 1970), 233. Michael Manning: Martin, 47, 67–8; Rogers, 237–41; CCAN 6/15/1894.

5. Lucille Griffith, *Alabama: A Documentary History to 1900*, rev. and enlarged ed. (Univ., Ala., 1972), 566 (no free high schools); HLB to L.D. Patterson 2/20/69 (most beloved). Ashland College: AS 5/24/01; PPA 8/17/1899; HLB to George P. Viegelmann 4/5/71 (no more than); Camel int. (heated; her mother was a classmate of HLB's). Evans: Tom Nichols, *Rugged Summit* (San Marcos, Tex., [1967]), 452; Hiram Martin Evans, Lt. CSA, 22nd Infantry Div., 1841–1928, Cecil E. Evans papers, Southwest Texas State Univ.; PPG 9/15/37 (young gentlemen). Whatley: DP 1/30/50; William Whatley int. (desperate).

6. House: Mildred Black Faucett, "Boyhood Home of Justice Hugo Lafayette Black, Ashland, Alabama," privately printed pamphlet (1975); CCAN 10/27/1893 (property), 1/19,26/

1894; Clay County Tax Assessment for Pruet and Pruet, 1901, Tristram papers (stock of other store); Pruet, Sr., int. (credit business).

7. Manning, *From Five to Twenty-Five: His Earlier Life as Recalled by Joseph Columbus Manning* (N.Y., 1929), 66 (handful). Faet's activities: No. IO (12/19/1877), Commissions, Clay County, v. 13 (1868–1882), p. 4, ADAH (justice of peace); *Ashland News* 7/12/1878 (election inspector); CCAN 2/3/1894 (councilman), 2/6/1894 (board of trustees), 12/6/1895 (takes in exposition), 4/2/1897 (charter); PPA 11/16/1897 (railroad).

8. This section is drawn from many interviews with HLB's children, family and friends; and Ernest Jones, *The Life and Work of Sigmund Freud*, ed. and abridged by Lionel Trilling and Steven Marcus (London, 1961), 6. After Little Della had been buried, the other children mourned that they had neglected her; they imagined that if they had only spent more time with her she might have lived. And, although they never believed that they did, they showered their time on Hugo.

9. Herbert Shelton [Robert Lee Black], *The Deserter* (Talledega, Ala., 1900); HLB to Hazel Davis 2/26/71 (position sound); HLB to Hudson Strode 9/15/59 (felt for long time); HLB to Edna Street Barnes 11/14/62 (tragic); HLB, "Lawyer" (every generation fought). I base the statements on Clay County and the Civil War on a reading of all county newspapers from 1875 to 1907.

10. HLB, Pruet (books) ints., BN 8/13/37 *(Wandering Jew)*; HLB to JPF 1/20/48 (Merriwell); Barney Whatley, remarks at Cumberland School of Law, Birmingham 2/26/76 (pitch pennies).

11. Sims murder: PPA 8/21/1896, 2/19/1897; CCAN 9/3/1897; WOD, *Go East*, 451 (share-cropper). Trials: BN 9/5/35 (what next); ESB int. with Whatley, ESB papers (attending sessions, entertainment). HLB to JPF 1/20/48 (attended, expected).

12. PPA 4/9/1900 (Pelham brilliant), 9/27/1900 (conversed, preacher); AS 9/27/1900 (businesses); HLB to Howard S. Muse, Jr., 9/8/65 (largest); Estate of W. L. Black, Deceased, M. A. Black, Administratrix, Clay County Courthouse (the author added up the items). Turnipseed: Emma McCord Lee to HLB 1/14/58 (classmate, correctly stating the year of the incident); Durr, "Black." Lee was one of the organizers of the Ashland Young Men's Democratic Club and succeeded Faet Black on the city council; he was also secretary of the Baptist and its Sunday school.

13. AS 1/19/03 (test), 2/6/1903 (failed); HLB to Denson N. Franklin 4/17/67 (Goodwater). Mules: NYP 5/4/55; HLB to William Pickens 7/16/45 (sleeping). Pelham death: Pruet, Sr., Thomas Toland ints. HLB, biographical statement 4/29/43 (decided); Birmingham Medical College, Schedule of Lectures, Clinics and Laboratory Work, Session 1903–1904, Jefferson County Medical Archives, Birmingham.

14. James B. Sellers, "History of the University of Alabama," II, 8, 200 (Thorington story), W. Stanley Hode Collection, UA; SC; UA catalog 1904–1905 (room and board); Timothy Walker, *Introduction to American Law* (11th ed., rev. by Clement Bates) (Boston, 1905), 67. The 1904–05 and 1905–06 catalogs note the prescribed courses. First-year courses were: the law of persons—personal property (including sales) and domestic relations; contracts; torts, bailments and carriers; constitutional and international law; and mercantile law. And in the second year: evidence; corporations; real estate (real property); equity jurisprudence and procedure; and the law of crimes and punishment.

15. 1905–06 catalog; *The Crimson White* 11/1/04 (debate), 9/26/05 (secretary and treasurer); HLB to Charles D. Butts, 1/18/71 (tobacco); *St. L P-D* 8/21/67 (tennis); *The Corolla* (UA Law School), 1905 and 1906; *BAH* 5/30/06 (degree).

16. Martin, Annie Moore ints.; Rucker int. with CJD; *BN* 5/31/61 (object of pity); State Auditor files, ADAH (bond); HLB to Dilliard 7/13/62 (debts owed Faet); HLB to HLB, Jr. 4/27/50 (income). Leaving Ashland: *AS* 8/31/07; "Hugo L. Black. Biographical Data," supplied by U.S. Supreme Court, 1970 (not too unhappy); HLB, biographical statement (rather a relief); *WS* 2/27/34 (best way); *SC* (heard mourning); *BP* 8/13/37 (friends offered). The only time HLB appeared in court in Ashland was when he was appointed to defend an indigent charged with murder. Quickly he realized that his client would likely be found guilty and sentenced to death; and he did not want to start his legal career in this manner. At Hugo's request the judge appointed a co-counsel, Edgar L. Whatley. Hugo and Whatley made an agreement with the prosecutor to accept a guilty plea with life imprisonment, in which the judge acquiesced: *State v. Henry Fields*, undated (probably late 1906), State Motion Docket, v. 1, Clay County Courthouse.

Chapter 2

sources: HLB, *Memoirs*; HLB, Jr., *Father*; Childers, "Black"; Hamilton, *Black*; Harris, *Power*; Pruden, "Opposition"; Stallworth, "Black."

1. Malcolm C. McMillan, *Yesterday's Birmingham* (Miami, 1975), 75 (murder capital); Wayne Flynt, "Dissent in Zion: Alabama Baptists and Social Issues, 1900–1914," *Jour. South. Hist.*, v. 35 (1969), 523; Flynt, "Religion in the Urban South: The Divided Religious Mind of Birmingham, 1900–1930," *Ala. Rev.*, v. 30 (1977), 108; Woodward, *Jim Crow*, 7, 100 (laws); HLB to Robert Lee Black 11/13/07, Smith papers (pretty busy); *SC* (pig case).

2. HLB to HLB, Jr. 7/16/53 (largely). Beck: *Southern Israelite*, [about early 1938], HLBLC; *Cruickshank*, I, 302; Rabbi Ferdinand M. Isserman, sermon, "The Radio Address of Justice Hugo L. Black," 10/8/37, Corcoran papers; HLB int. (best friend). Strike: George R. Leighton, "Birmingham, Alabama: The City of Perpetual Promise," *Harper's* 8/37; Frank S. White III int.; Hackney, *Populism*, 175; Lerner, *Ideas*, 255. Tuggle Institute: *BAH* 11/17/08; Atkins, *Valley*, 100.

3. Norton case: Sholis, "Young," 8/19/37; Samuel T. Dew to HLB 7/13/62 (foreman); *Sloss-Sheffield Steel & Iron Co. v. Norton*, 49 Sou. 1038 (1909); Rucker int. with CJD; SFB (pretty rough), William Whatley (mean-looking) ints.; JPF, "Black: Little" (ambulance chasing).

4. *BAH* 4/11/11 (talked with lawyer); *BAH* 4/12–13/11, 8/20/12; *BN* 4/13/11, 12/11/11 (Orne). Mandy on HLB: *BAH* 1/23/12, 4/16/12, 9/17/12 (face immobile), and the following undated articles by Mandy HLB collected in a scrapbook, HLBLC: "The Official Court Smiler" (shade of skin), "A Dry Land Diver" and "Judge Black Has Scare About His Heart Action." *BAH* 1/26/12 (opium), 4/6/12 (lowered fine), 8/20/12 (everybody seated); *NYT* 8/15/37 (Mose Roden), 9/15/37 (furnace collector). 130 cases: *BAH* 5/17,20/12, 8/20/12.

5. *BAH* 8/31/12 (police commissioner), 3/14/12 (loan shark case); Berman, "Philosophy," 7; HLB to SFB 5/2/45 (punishment policy); Rodell, "Black" (drunken Negro); MA 10/30/55 (got to thinking). Mandy articles: *BAH* 1/25/12, 2/14/12, 8/29/12, 9/9,19,24,25,29/12, and others in HLB scrapbook; Mandy int. (gave start); *BN* 10/18/12 (valuable experience); *BAH* 10/23/12 (abandonment).

6. HLB to Harry Golden 10/5/66 (background); Mandy, "Judge Black Once Liked Eggs" in HLB scrapbook (banquet); Fred Larkin to HLB 11/20/65 (lumberman); HLB to Alfred A. Knopf 9/16/52; *Newsweek* files (grasp); Rodell, "Black" (grasp, made up mind); ESB int. (offer).

7. HLB to HLB, Jr. 4/27/50 (took long time); *Hobson-Starnes Coal Co. v. Alabama Coal & Coke Co.*, 66 Sou. 622 (1914); *Jaspar* (Ala.)*Mountain Eagle* 12/17/13 (press notice); HLB to Evans C. Johnson 5/7/52 (do not think possible), 5/29/52 (memory blank); Johnson to VH [about 12/70]; VH papers (Hewitt); HLB to James J. Vickrey, Jr. 4/6/65 (vote for Underwood); BAH 9/27/13 (candidacy).

8. Campaign: BAH 4/5/14; "Young Men's Club for Hugo Black for Solicitor," HLBLC; VH int. with ALS, VH papers (cards). Sadler int. Welch and Brower: BN 11/30/14; BAH 12/2/14; NYP 12/24/48. HLB's political importance was confirmed when he was assigned to sit as a judge under an Alabama law that allowed for the appointment of a lawyer to act as one in certain instances; *Birmingham Railway, Light & Power Co. v. Hass*, 67 Sou. 504 (1914).

Chapter 3

SOURCES: HLB, Memoirs; HLB, Jr., *Father*; Frank, *Black*; Hamilton, *Black*; Harris, *Power*; Stallworth, "Black."

1. Fee system: HLB to Henry Ellenbogen 10/21/68. BAH 3/6,9/15, 5/6/15, 9/26/15; Rives int. (food allowance). Talk of impeachment: BAH 5/6/15, 9/6,8,12,29/15; TNB 8/13/37; BL 2/23/17.

2. Cases: BAH 3/6,10,11,18,24/15; *State ex rel. Black v. Delaye*, 68 Sou. 993 (1915). Near beer: BAH 5/23/15, 9/18/15. Federal court: BAH 9/5,6,7/16, 10/1,3,13/16.

3. Grand jury report: BN 9/18/15 (quote), 10/12,14/15; BAH 9/18,22,26,28/15, 10/1,12,21 (matters exaggerated)/15; *Bessemer Weekly* 9/25/15 (there are ways), 10/2/15. Goolsby case: BL 4/16/16; BAH 10/15,21–3/15; HLB to JPF 12/4/48. Capital punishment: BAH 6/25/15, 9/28/15.

4. Girard: Patterson int.; HLB to Clarke Stallworth, 5/20/66 (convicted everybody); *Wilson v. State*, 71 Sou. 115 (1916); *Martin v. State*, 71 Sou. 693 (1916); BAH 8/20/16; Pruden, "Opposition," 75. Whatley trial: Alfred Whatley, William Whatley ints.; BAH 6/22/16 (fit of anger); *People v. Whatley* file, Colorado State Archives, Denver (judge's charge); *Leadville* (Colo.) *Herald-Democrat, Carbonate Weekly Chronicle* (Leadville), *Summit County* (Colo.) *Jour.*, DP, *Rocky Mountain* (Denver) *Jour.* 6–7/16.

5. Prosecutors: BAH 11/3/16 (exception), 5/16/17. HLB–Tate: BAH 11/3/16, 1/17,20,21,30/ 17, 2/14,21/17, 5/12/13/17 (sued); *State ex rel. Gaston v. Black*, 74 Sou. 387 (1917). Resignation: Berman, "Philosophy," 11 (do not feel); BAH 7/15/17 (depends upon). Aikman, "Black" (gone wrong); BAH 6/22/17, 7/14/17 (every office); BN 7/15/17; BL 8/13/17.

6. Army: Sholis, "Young," 8/18/37; HLB to SFB 11/6/43. Headquarters Eighth Division, Extract 4/2/18, HLBLC; NYT 10/2/37; George W. Yancey to Walter S. Brower 11/18/18, Brower papers (appeared to knock); HLB to Frank E. Driscoll 8/9/66. Orlando Toland: HER, Charles Toland ints.; Huff int. with HLB (pirated, ease out); HLB to Thomas Hart Kennedy 2/17/69; *San Francisco Recorder* 8/29/38. Practice: Cruickshank, *Birmingham*, I,

218 (leading lawyers). HLB's partners were Basil Manly Allen, former head of the state Knights of Pythias; John W. Altman, a leading labor lawyer; and Arthur B. Foster.

7. ALS, ESB (Zelda), Hail (Eugenia), VFD (meeting JFB, join angels). Dr. Foster: Minutes of Session 4/4/09, South Highland Presbyterian Church, Birmingham files; Virginia Foster [Durr], "The Emancipation of Pure, White, Southern Womenhood," *New South* (v. 26, winter 1971, enthusiasms). JFB: *BP* 8/19/37; VFD, COHP (never said much); Anne Firor Scott, *The Southern Lady—From Pedestal to Politics, 1830–1930* (Chic., 1970), 168–9; FF to Harold J. Laski 11/12/48, FFLC (no love letter); VFD to Paul and Isabel Johnston 11/16/61, Paul Johnston papers, BPL (natural friends). Young Bolshevik: Joseph Johnston, Paul Johnston, VFD ints. Marriage: *BAH* 2/23/21 (conspicuous interest). Large wedding: ESB int. with VFD; VFD, *Outside*, 46. Marry above: Thomas Toland, Cooper ints.

Chapter 4

SOURCES: HLB, Jr., *Father*; Frank, *Black*; Hamilton, *Black*. Interview: Crampton Harris.

1. ALS (bluffed), Windham (turf), Hammond (in eye), JBP (aptitude test), SFB (doing your job) ints.; FR, ch. 3 ("Hugo Black: Justice for the Ages") of proposed book on Supreme Court, FR private papers (mildness); HLB to HLB, Jr. 3/21/47 (foreswear adjectives, originally emphasized), 2/2/50 (master of himself); Sholis, "Young," 8/20/37 (no sympathy). HLB represented a few small businesses and some small unions, among which were Herman Beck's food company, a Chinese restaurant, a local carpenters group and the Brotherhood of Railroad Trainmen; and he often acted as special attorney for the United Mine Workers.

2. *Newsweek* files (seizes point); Gillon, Monasco ints. Best cross-examiner: Leigh Clark, Grooms. Hare (relating view of his father), Joseph Johnston, Lucius Gardner, Jr., Gillon and Windham, indeed all lawyers who witnessed Black in action, agree as to this.

3. Transcript, *Miniard v. Hines*, Circuit Court of Jefferson County 10/8/19, HLBLC (HLB at trial); Records and Briefs, ADAH (jury award); *Hines v. Miniard*, 86 Sou. 23 (1920), 94 Sou. 302 (1922). HLB–Percy: Abe Berkowitz to HLB 10/8/64; HLB to Berkowitz 10/13/64. Ego: Joseph Johnston, Skinner ints.

4. Ellenburg case: Records and Briefs, 57 ($14,500), 60, ADAH ($20,000); Saunders int., relating story by Richard Rives (judge-jury); *Birmingham Belt Railroad Co. v. Ellenburg*, 104 Sou. 269 (1924, first appeal). HLB appealed to the United States Supreme Court, his first contact with that body, which refused to hear the case; 269 U.S. 529 (1925). Then came a second Alabama appeal: 111 Sou. 219 (1926). HLB, Jr., *Father*, 49–50, incorrectly states Borden Burr: the lawyer was Cocke. Millonas case: Complaint, 17 (counsel persisted), 21 (man discharged), *Millonas v. U.S. Fidelity & Guaranty Co. of Baltimore*, ADAH; *U.S. Fidelity & Guaranty Co. v. Millonas*, 89 Sou. 732 (1921). *Southern Railroad Co. v. Dickson*, 100 Sou. 665 (1924, practical way); Pettus int. (good month's work).

5. Clark int. Woman in building: ESB to Ethel and JMH 2/12/68, JMH papers. A breakdown of the 108 cases in which the Alabama appellate courts wrote opinions shows the nature of Black's practice: over half—53—involved torts (largely injuries); insurance (mainly fire and life), 11; domestic relations, 9; criminal, 9; contracts, 8; property, 4; wills, 3; agency, 2; bills and notes, 1.

6. HLB to HLB, Jr. 10/26/56 (chief reason); Hare, Patrick (defendants' lawyers), Gibson ints. Case against Spain: Frank E. Spain to VH 8/7/72, VH papers; Gillon (Spain's partner) int. Damage suit lawyer: Bradley, Arant, ALS ints. "Damage suit lawyer" was the phrase of contempt to many corporate lawyers in Birmingham's class-conscious bar in the 1920s.

7. VH int. with Hugh Locke, VH papers (give up); Grooms, Luce (draw jury), Thrift (without his friends), Oberdorfer (poison jury), HER (in jury box) ints.

8. BN 4/29/24, in Arthur F. Howington, "John Barley Corn Subdued: The Enforcement of Prohibition in Alabama," Ala. Rev., v. 23 (7/70, ring); MR 11/23/23 (seized); BN 12/19,20/23 (indicted). Relieved of duty: OH int. with Harwell G. Davis by F. W. Helmbold and Arthur L. Walker 28–33, Samford Univ. Library; Edward Boykin, Everything's Made for Love in This Man's World: Vignettes from the Life of Frank W. Boykin (Mobile, Ala., 1973), 61.

9. OH int. with Davis, 33 (straight as string); Brown, 63; BN 4/2,14,29/24, 5/8,10,22/24; Boykin, Everything, 61–2, 77; Monasco int. (right from wrong); J. L. LeFlore to Roy Wilkins 8/12/37, NAACP papers (niggers); Harry H. Smith to H. V. Kaltenborn 6/11/46, RHJ papers; VH int. with Esdale, VH papers; Sholis, "Young" 8/19/37. Boykin and telegram: Patrick, Vann, Gregory Smith, Hardy Smith ints.; Francis H. Hare, My Learned Friends ([Birmingham], 1976), 93.

10. Huff int. with HLB (judge friend of miner, also Lewis case); minutes of meeting 10/31/23, and notes on rear of Constitution and By-Laws of the Alabama Prison Reform Association, Statewide Campaign Committee for the Abolishment of the Convict Contract System papers, BPL (president); BAH 12/28/23 (HLB to Brandon). Lewis case: Lewis v. Roberts (1925); Strickland, Black, xxiv–xxv; Harris, Paul Ward ints., Ward to HLB 3/31/67.

11. ALS int.; Annie Foster to Virginia Foster 3/5,21/23, VFD papers (living with Fosters); JBP papers (application). Jefferson: CJD, "Black"; VFD int. Sunday school class: Grooms (class member), Thrift (drinking or womanizing), Lee Anderson (do good) ints.; First Baptist Church sermon, no date, HLBLC (religion vital part). HLB was also the head of the church's buildings committee.

12. Alan Barth to VH 6/6/72 (happiest time); Annie Lee Watson (whose husband Lawson was one of HLB's students) to VH 4/3/68 (teaching course), both VH papers; Ingrid Jewell, "Hugo Black After 22 Years on Bench," PPG 3/2/59 (fun); BN 8/12/24 (Hanson remarks), 7/27/86 (Birmingham jurics); tax returns, HLBLC (income); VII, "Senate," 34 (lawyers' incomes); HLB OH, LBJL (judgeships); ESB to Mary Tortorici 4/68, JBP papers (drop in income); CJD, "Black" (partners admitted); Joseph Johnston, ALS (politics), HLB, Jr. (total worth) ints. Property: the agreements and other papers are in HLBLC.

Chapter 5

sources: BAH, BN and BP, for the period August–October 1921, which on the whole admirably covered the entire sordid affair; and the trial transcript and other records which St. Paul's Church kindly made available to me. Other sources include Pruden, Opposition, 96–102; Vincent J. Scozarri, Father James E. Coyle: Priest and Citizen (M.A. thesis, Notre Dame Seminary of New Orleans, 1963); Paul M. Pruitt, Jr., "The Killing of Father Coyle: Private Tragedy, Public Shame," Alabama Heritage (Fall 1993, no. 30); William E. Fort to Joseph B. Keenan 10/18/37, and Fort, Memorandum for Keenan 10/19/37; Edward T. Leech,

"Black's Career," *New York World-Telegram* 6/18/46; *PP* 10/2/37 (editorial written by Leech who in the 1920s was the editor of the BP); Snell, *Klan,* 22–23; Snell ints. with James Esdale; *Alabama* 10/11/37; Ray Sprigle, "Murder Makes a Senator," *PPG* 8/6/49; "Re: Hugo L. Black appointments, etc.," and Notes, Sprigle papers; J. Fisher Rothermel to VH 1/23/67, VH papers; scrapbook, 7–8/37, Royal Copeland papers, UM; and ints. with HLB, Jr., Buck, Mamie Helen Campbell, Cooper, Danforth, Foster, Lucien Gardner, Jr., Gillon, Harris, Joseph F. Johnston, HER and Stephenson.

1. Charles Sweeney, "Bigotry Turns to Murder," *Nation* 8/31/21; Leech, "Black's Career," *New York World-Telegram* 6/18/46; Atkins, *Valley,* 132.

2. Leech, "Black's Career."

3. "Evidence which constitutes part of the main case," Judge Fort wrote later, "cannot be put on by the state after the defendant has rested his case, because that would be starting the case over and would allow the defendant to put on new testimony which might prolong the case indefinitely." In the opening part of the trial he called this rule to the lawyers' attention and said it would "be strictly carried out, unless either side had witnesses which could not be reached by subpoena or other processes of law before the main testimony was completed." But the prosecution "had reserved this man for later use in the hope that the court might allow to put him on": Fort to Keenan 10/18/37.

4. *Alabama* 10/11/37; *Kloran—Knights of the Ku Klux Klan* (5th ed.) (Atlanta, 1916), 13–14.

5. Jurors: Snell int. with Esdale; VH int. with Esdale, VH papers. Hand signals: Oberdorfer, Huey ints.

6. Rothermel to VH 1/23/67.

7. Sprigle, "Murder Makes a Senator," and *PPG* 8/21/37, 9/28/37; Alabama Bar Association Code of Ethics, Canon 10.

8. Rothermel to VH 1/23/67.

Chapter 6

SOURCES: Snell, *Klan;* and his articles "Fiery Crosses in the Roaring Twenties: Activities of the Revised Klan in Alabama, 1915–1930," *Ala. Rev.,* v. 23 (10/70); and "Masked Men in the Magic City: Activities of the Revised Klan in Birmingham, 1916–1940," *Ala. Hist. Quar.,* v. 34 (fall and winter 1972).

1. "A Defense of the Ku Klux Klan," *Literary Digest* 1/20/23 (absolutely American); Knights of the Ku Klux Klan, "At the Threshold: Fundamentals of Citizenship" (about 1924), Ku Klux Klan papers, State Hist. Scty. of Colorado (America safe for Americans); Hiram Evans, "The Klan's Fight for Americanism," *North Amer. Rev.,* v. 223 (3–5/26) (real indictment).

2. Michael A. Breedlove, "Progressivism and Nativism: The Race for the Presidency of the City Commission of Birmingham, Alabama in 1917," *Jour. Birmingham Hist. Scty.,* v. 6 (7/80); Snell int. with Esdale (city workers); Monaghan int. (Baptist Hospital); Chalmers, *Hooded,* 78 (Frost).

3. *PP* 10/2/37 (Klan occurences in Birmingham); *BN* 12/19/71 (requirements quote). Esdale and membership: *BN* 10/31/26; VH (VH papers) and Snell ints. with Esdale; Jackson,

Klan, 82 (Shirley). In 1919 Esdale as president of the Elks rapidly increased that group's membership.

4. *BN* 9/12/23 (proceedings); Snell int. with Esdale (membership estimates); *BN* 12/19/71 (largest); Lerner, *Ideas*, 256 (political behavior); Thrift int. (law abiding organization, relating conv. with M. B. Grace, who was present); Evans, "Klan's Fight" (Jews as problem); Jackson, *Klan*, 82 (powerful); Re: Hugo L. Black appointments, etc., Sprigle papers (Harris replacing Brower). On August 8, 1924 Brower was appointed Klan Giant, an honorary office bestowed on former Exalted Cyclops in good standing: appointment paper in Brower papers. Bandman: Mark Cowett, *Birmingham's Rabbi: Morris Newfield and Alabama, 1895–1940* (Univ., Ala., 1986), 136; Newfield to Jacob Billikopf 9/23/37, HLBLC; information supplied by Marjorie Bandman Kahn and Chester Bandman, Jr.

5. ESB (couple of meetings), Annie Moore (uniform) ints.; Hamner Cobbs to Ray Jenkins 8/67, MA files (Greensboro); VH int. with George Bentley, VH papers (West Blocton); MA, MR 11/4/65 (hood and mask). Toledo: *TB* 9/15/37; *TNB* 9/22/24; *Toledo Times* 9/23/24.

6. *PPG* 9/13/37 (swear); Imperial Wizard William J. Simmons in *Hearings before the Committee on Rules. The Ku Klux Klan*, House of Representatives, 67th Cong., 1st Sess., 1921, p. 98 (ritual); *Kloran—Knights of the Ku Klux Klan* (5th ed.) (Atlanta, no date), 28–39 (worthy aliens).
   In the mid-1920s George Frey was an active Klansman who shared a law office with Esdale. For many years he saved "Klan stationery with Jim Esdale's name, Mr. Frey's and Black's printed on it as Klan officers," recalled his longtime secretary Mary Pierson, who threw it out after his death (int.). And Birmingham congressman George Huddleston "knew Black was an officer in the Klan," said his daughter Nancy Huddleston Packer (int.). The only mention of Black's role in the Klan this writer has seen was written by a former *BP* editor when Black was appointed to the Supreme Court. It reads in full: "He was no inoffensive dupe of clever leaders—he was one of the leaders"; "Black's Confession," *PP* 10/2/37. The 1924 *Klansman's Manual* stated: "The Kladd is the conductor of the Klan. He shall conduct candidates for naturalization . . .": *Klansman's Manual* ([Atlanta], 1924), 63; see also *Kloran*, 4; and *Constitution and Laws of the Knights of the Ku Klux Klan* (Atlanta, 1930), 38. "I was one of a group of more than 200 initiated into the Klan in 1925 at a meeting which was addressed by Hugo Black," Travis McGahey, a Birmingham physician, said in 1949; *BP* 9/22/49. "I was initiated by Hugo Black"; *BAH* 9/21/49, MA 9/22/49. McGahey's quarter-century-old recollection was apparently off by one year. According to the Alabama Klan's thorough historian, William R. Snell, in 1925 the Klan did not have any mass initiations, at least any reported ones, in the Birmingham area where McGahey lived. Over four thousand Klansmen were initiated in Birmingham on June 27, 1924, and a thousand more on that October 15; in 1925 such ceremonies took place only outside Birmingham.

7. Mattie Crow (Ashville), Byrnes, Pauline Clayton, HLB, Jr., Agronsky, Lamb ints.; J. S. Conwell telegram to HLB 10/1/37 (Burr); Dunne, *Black*, 105–06 (old law partner); *NYT* 9/26/71 (obituary); Jackson, *Myrdal*, 126; Huff int. with HLB (interviewer late in life); Paul Ward (told reporter), Arnold (told law clerk), HLB (Herman Bck). Last part of section based on SFB, Haber, Girard, Luce, Feeney, Choper, Harold Ward, McNulty ints.; diary 10/20/37, Keating papers (told friend). Hollis Black in Klan: Thrift, Gillon, Lucien Gardner ints.

8. *Civitan Magazine* 5/45 (Civitan); HLB (Moose, Praetorian insurance cheap), Marilew Kogan (why join), Keefe (join for votes), Alan Kohn (would have joined too), HLB (made friends in organizations) ints.; Dunne, *Black*, 112 (voting machinery); Herman Beck to William E. W. Yerby 8/10/25 (Knights of Pythias Supreme Representative). HLB joined the Pythians, the night before he left Ashland for Birmingham, largely because his brother Orlando was a member and he knew he had to meet people in Birmingham; unedited transcript, 1968 CBS int., Benjamin papers. Masons: HLB to Fred Larkins 7/6/62; Larkins to George E. Sokolsky 7/3/62. He didn't join the Elks because they served liquor; HLB to SFB 9/10/62, CB papers.

Chapter 7

SOURCES: Dunne, *Black*; Frank, *Black*; Hamilton, *Black*; PPG 8–9/37; Snell, *Klan*; Snell int. with Esdale; Harlan Martin, HER ints.

1. *NYT* 6/30/24 (denunciation of Klan); VH int. with HLB, VH papers (rumors); Underwood to Henry R. Howze 4/6/25, in Evans C. Johnson, *Oscar W. Underwood: The Development of a National Statesman, 1894–1915* (Ph.D. dissertation, Univ. of North Carolina, 1953, 411; not disposed); BN 6/7/25 (friends of HLB). Years later, Underwood's colleague William E. Borah wrote that Underwood retired "because, as he said, he could not be elected in opposition to the Klan . . ."; Borah to Isaac H. Levy 10/25/37, Borah papers.

2. Shape campaign: BN 7/1/25; *NYT* 7/2/25. VH int. with Esdale, VH papers (Esdale on HLB). Bar association: Harris int. (also getting money); Irving Beiman, "Birmingham: Steel Giant with a Glass Jaw" in Robert S. Allen, ed., *Our Fair City* (N.Y., 1947), 102. By March 1926 Harris was former Cyclops.

3. HLB to Herman Beck 8/24/25; Rodell, "Black" (Bankhead); Sholis, "Young," 8/22/37 (introducing HLB); Childers, "Black" (each town); HLB to Roy W. Kimbrough 3/27/61 (no other candidate); Carl Elliott, Sr., with Michael D'Orso, *The Cost of Courage: The Journey of an American Congressman* (N.Y., 1992), 34–5; VH ints. with Esdale (boys sprinkled around) and Charles Harrison (ain't lost), VH papers. Until now HLB had been making a "personal canvass" of the state which would become a "speaking tour"; statement 2/25/26.

4. BP 2/8/26 (youthful); Conal Furay, *The Grass-Roots Mind in America: The American Sense of Absolutes* (N.Y., 1977), 25. Sparkman: I have combined his comments in Dedication Ceremonies for Hugo L. Black Room [1978], Special Collections, UA Law School; and ESB to Mary Tortorici 1/23/69, JMH papers. Stallworth: BPH 4/21/65; Stallworth int.

5. Ashland speech: flyer, "Principles Advocated by Hugo Black, Candidate for United States Senate"; BN 3/21/26 (Crampton Harris drafted part of this speech), 8/4/26 (imperialists); V. O. Key, Jr., *Southern Politics in State and Nation* (N.Y., 1949), 37–41 (friends and neighbors); BP 7/8/26 (question), 8/3/26 (Will Bankhead), 4/22/32 (complained); Sholis, "Young," 8/20/37 (half amount); TB 8/19/37 (damage suit lawyer, warming up); Berman, "Philosophy," 21 (his clients); MA 6/12/26 (Kilby-Bankhead debates); *Ex parte Blackburn*, 85 Sou. 495 (1920), and *Blackburn v. Moore*, 89 Sou. 745 (1921; both HLB–Bankhead in court); CR 8/18/37, 9219 (no bitterness). The BP, which supported Kilby, would not even run Black's ads; Harris int.

6. BAH 1/4/26 (common people); Ashland speech (sunlight of justice); Robert Frazer int. (mingle); BN 8/4/26 (Bankhead father's son); HLB to Nathan J. Siegel 4/24/50 (primary

held when announced); Grover Hall, "Alabama Editor, Who Never Cast Vote for Black, Describes Him," *BES* 8/13/37 (Bankhead to family; he also told this to Musgrove: Kimbrough to HLB 7/29/26).

7. VH int. with Harrison, VH papers; "Principles Advocated" (Patterson letter); *Ala. Christian* [Methodist] *Advocate* 7/29/26 (kind of prohibitionist); HLB to L. D. Patterson 3/15/61 (article); *Mobile Post* 5/18/28. Conventions: HLB to C. B. Smith 8/29/62; M. M. Wood to David J. Davis 7/27/26, in "Principles."

8. *London Daily Express* 9/16/37 (Evans quote); MA 4/2/26 (money spent); VH ints. with Esdale (Esdale quote) and Ben Ray (rejected), both VH papers; *NYT* 8/9/26 (attack Smith); BN 8/3/26 (drinking liquor). National Klan: BN 7/23/26, 8/8/26. Danger of liquor: Berman, "Philosophy," 22.

9. VH int. with Locke, VH papers; *NYT* 8/12/26 (posted and mentioned); James J. Curtis to William B. Bankhead 2/1/30, William Bankhead papers (at Klaverns); BAH 8/5–8/26; *PPG, TB* 8/22/37 (official document); Sholis, "Young," 8/22/37 (Davis); Hamner Cobbs to Ray Jenkins 9/15/67, MA files (young Kilby worker); VH, *Hill,* 72 (Graves). Mayfield reported $1,242 in expenses; Musgrove $4,183; and Kilby $9,763: MA 8/19,17,22/26. Alabama law allowed candidates to report their total expenditures *before* the primary was over. An example of volunteers was Albert Lee Smith's letting his thirty insurance agents take off the week before the primary to work for HLB. The case in which HLB was upheld on appeal was *Porter v. Porter,* 112 Sou. 646 (1926).

10. *Alabama Official and Statistical Record* (1927), 406–07; Harris int.; Bunche, *Political,* 383; BN 8/15/26, 10/31/26 (never meddle); MA 8/13/26; BAH 8/15/26 (Esdale boasting), 10/31/26 (never meddle); Richard T. Rives to author 6/14/73 (state officers); Charles N. Feidelson, "Alabama's Super Government," *Nation* 9/28/27 (Klan-controlled state). Paid poll tax: HER, William Rozelle ints.

11. SFB int. (pull, laziness); HLB to Arthur S. Curtis 4/1/69 (ceased trial); partnership returns and financial records, HLBLC. Last case: *American Surety Co. v. Pryor,* 115 Sou. 176 (1927); BP 8/13/37; Frank Bainbridge, Jr., int. (too good); *NYT* 8/15/37 (courthouse wag). "Upon going to the Senate, I discontinued the practice of law," HLB wrote Jerome Frank, 12/14/36, one year after his involvement in his last case. *Farrar v. Pure Milk Company* was filed 9/11/26 in Jefferson County Circuit Court, No. 43362: a car hit an eleven-year-old and he suffered a fractured skull; HLB sued for $50,000 and settled for $3,000 (Curtis to HLB [about 3/23/69]).

12. Quantock int. (pregnancy); HLB to JPF 1/20/48 (reading). The caption to one of the photographs in HLB, Jr.'s, *My Father,* says, "My mother, Josephine, with Sterling and myself. Mother is pregnant with Jo-Jo." This was not possible at the time: In the picture the boys look to be under one and about three years old respectively. Since Sterling was born in September 1924, Hugo, Jr., in April 1922 and JoJo in October 1933, it was taken in about early summer 1925—just as the campaign was starting.

13. Chapman (businessmen; his father was one of these), John Robinson (shoot Ware; Smelley told this to him), Tucker, Dozier (pretty good buddies: "Chum later beat a guy up for criticizing Black. He sent Hugo a turkey every Thanksgiving. And Black wrote him every Christmas through World War Two. Black once sent Chum a citron. He was always a country boy at heart") ints.; *Ware v. State,* 108 Sou. 645 (1926, holding that the trial judge had committed errors of sufficient weight to justify a new trial); HLB, "The Majesty of the Law," *The Civitan,* v. 9 (8/27, Maine); JPF, "Little" (Lane). The

main sources for this section besides those mentioned above are: an unpublished 1985 essay, "Hugo Black's Last Case: A Critical Event in the Life of Associate Justice Hugo Black (1886–1971)" by Dr. Carleton Chapman, a Talladega native to whom I am indebted for his kind assistance concerning this episode; *Talladega Daily Home* 12/8/24–11/15/27; and ints. with Freeman, Sullivan, Vern Scott and William Rozelle.

Chapter 8

SOURCES: HLB, Jr., *Father*; Frank, *Black*; Hamilton, *Black*.

1. HLB OH, LBJL (Coolidge); *NYT* 12/12/26 (bundle of activity); Wheeler int. Reading: HLB (Senate library), ALS (trying to use) ints.; Meador, *Black*, 2–3 (Durant); Catledge, book review (press wag).

2. Bruce: CR 8687–91 (5/15/28, no apology), 8815 (5/16/28, HLB–Bruce); WP 9/16/37 (Kluxer); *Newsweek* files (honor of Dixie); HLB, Jr., *Father*, 80 (maintained reserve).

3. CR 5/15/28, 8687 (line washed away); 5/15/28, 8815 (Negroes to vote); 5/25/29, 1903 (radio speech). HLB to C. H. Billingsley 10/16/28 (wrote during 1928 campaign); Thomas Toland int. (told cousin); HLB to M. S. Parrish 11/20/29 (marriage of Negro and white). Reapportionment: CR 5/15/29, 4243; 5/24/29, 1846.

4. Operation: Beech (plowing), Quantock ints.; MR 6/7/29. Obscenity regulation: BAH 3/19/30 (interest in exhibits); CR 10/11/29, 4468–9.

5. HLB to James P. Dee 11/28/49 (HLB later wrote); CR 4/3/30, 6438 (praise); HLB to Horace Turner 9/27/28 (causes injured); BN 4/8/30 (HLB–Pierce, alleged bribe), 4/23/32 (opening blast); Preston J. Hubbard, *Origins of the TVA: The Muscle Shoals Controversy, 1920–1932* (Nashville, Tenn., 1961), 262, 293; Frazer int.

6. CR 2/1/30, 3584 (Norris pointed out); HLB to Hugh E. Jones 6/28/62 (opposition); *United Mine Workers v. Red Jacket Consolidated Coal & Coke Co.*, 18 F.2d (4th Cir. 1927); Huff int. with HLB; HLB OH, LBJL; Freund, "Memo" (better judge); AP, "Black's Road" (remained for time, hit stride).

7. James B. Sellers, *The Prohibition Movement in Alabama* (Chapel Hill, N.C., 1943), 199; HLB to Claude A. Swanson 9/19/28 (Smith's views); HLB to William C. McAdoo 7/16/28 (Republicans carry state); Dunne, *Black*, 135 (encouraging violations); HLB to Ed Nixon 2/23/28 (execute laws); VH int. with HLB, VH papers (Walsh as choice); WS 10/1/37 (senator asks about Klan); Cecil Hackney int. (Klan infiltrator). Klan membership: BN, BAH 11/23/30. HLB had typed all reports on Smith and prohibition in the *NYT* back to 1918.

8. VH ints. with HLB (no choice), Locke (lead campaign), VH papers; HLB to Rev. Bob Jones 10/11/28; HLB to Claude Swanson 9/19/28 (leadership); HLB to M. M. Striplin 10/4/28 (wrote publisher); Hugh Locke, Jr., int. (torn); HLB telegram 8/25/28, in response to the MA's query whether he would support the Democratic ticket "despite prohibition and immigration views"; HLB to JPF 12/4/48 (hostility). "The probability is that I would be removed from all the committees on which I am serving, if I did not support the Democratic ticket"; HLB to James F. Hester 9/27/28. Better serve ticket: Grover C. Hall to Arthur Krock 10/7/37, Krock papers, Princeton. HLB wrote many letters along these lines and others, such as that his speaking would only solidify the opposition and might encourage the formation of a strong Republican Party.

9. Berton Dulce and Edward J. Richter, *Religion and the Presidency* (N.Y., 1962), 86–7; Tindall, *Emergence*, 245 (Roman hierarchy); Ralph M. Tanner, *James Thomas Heflin: United States Senator, 1920–1931* (Ph.D. dissertation, UA, 1967), 174–5 (William Bankhead reported), 194 (like him); Neal R. Pierce, *The Book of America: Inside Fifty States Today* (N.Y., 1983), 449 (Mobile Bay); Thrift int. (creaking of oars); BN 12/22/29 (violated election laws); *Wilkinson v. Henry*, 128 Sou. 362 (1930). Democratic vote: NYT 1/19/28; Cal Ledbetter, Jr., "Joe T. Robinson and the Presidential Campaign of 1928," *Arkansas Hist. Quar.*, v. 45 (summer 1986).

10. Tanner, *Heflin*, 194 (admitted), 228 (no defense in Washington); HLB to Winnie Childre 11/4/70 (confessed); BN 10/8/30 (told Montgomery crowd), 8/3/30 (regular party candidate); HLB to Curry S. Goodwin 12/4/30, William Bankhead papers (would defend Alabama); diary 3/17/32, Caraway papers (bantam cock); and CR: 1/29/31, 3472–73 (resolution, deny right of federal government [see HLB letter to BN 5/24/31]); 4/23/32, 8770–79 (accusing Republicans); 4/26/32, 8918–45 (combination). Fair election: CR 1/15/31, 2241; BN 1/16/31.

Chapter 9

SOURCES: Frank, *Black*; Hamilton, *Black*.

1. Claude G. Bowers, *Jefferson and Hamilton: The Struggle for Democracy in America* (Boston, 1925), vii; Bowers, *The Tragic Era: The Revolution After Lincoln* (N.Y., 1929); HLB to Crampton Harris 6/13/30. CR: 1/31/29, 2519 (scholarly senator); 3/9/36, 3436 (Jefferson's writings, published in 1829); 2/8/32, 3516 (agree). HLB called Bowers "that matchless and superb Democrat, that glorious upholder of the standards of Jackson and Jefferson and the great Democrats of the ages"; CR 2/16/32, 4044.

2. Diary 12/15/31, Caraway papers (waxed eloquent); BAH 12/16/31 (public works); BN, BAH 12/19/31 (re-election); Bernstein, *Lean*, 317 (Birmingham hard hit); Fred Greenbaum, *Fighting Progressive: A Biography of Edward P. Costigan* (Wash., D.C., 1971), 126 (ending subsidies); Federal Aid for Unemployment Relief, Hearings before the Committee on Manufactures, 72nd Cong., 1st Sess. (1932), 239–40 (Huddleston); CR 3318 (2/3/32, twitted HLB), 3516–24 (2/8/32, trust states); Paul Y. Anderson, "Democracy at Work," *Nation* 3/2/32 (became hysterical); Patrick J. Maney, *"Young Bob" La Follette: A Biography of Robert M. La Follette, Jr., 1895–1953* (Columbia, Mo., 1978), 99 (trickery).

3. "Montgomery—Confederate Reunion," reprinted in BN 6/17/31 (Confederate veterans speech); HLB to Mayme Hatley 3/20/32 (ask ladies; written by HLB's assistant Hugh Grant, who harbored deep anti-Negro feelings); MA 4/2/32 (discuss case); HLB, "Memorial Speech, Auditorium, Birmingham," [1931] (country is Christian). He told another Montgomery group: "Subject to God's laws, man rules the world, and the kind of rulership depends upon the kind of thoughts that abide in his mind"; "As a Man Thinketh," speech to Judge Leon McCord's Bible Class, Montgomery, 1931. HLB was an Inspector in the Alabama Division of the Sons of Confederate Veterans; *Confederate Veteran*, v. 36 (11/27), 396.

4. BP 4/26/32 (straddle, arid dry), BN 4/30/32 (duty to state); HLB to William E. Fort 4/2/32 (check welcomed: the case was *Benefit Association of Railway Employees v. Armbruster*, 116 Sou. 164 [1927]: HLB handled the trial; a later appeal extended the case

(129 Sou. 78 [1930]); VH int. with Locke, VH papers (glad). Kilby's charges, *BP* 5/1/32, appeared, first, as "paid political advertisements" by Birmingham businessmen in the *Pickens County* (Ala.) *Herald* and, then, in other country newspapers. "Governor Kilby apparently did not have the courage to sign" the ads, Black noted; to J. J. Willett 4/17/32, Willett papers. "I may have to do a little advertising," HLB wrote ALS 3/14/32. "While I shall spend very little under any circumstances, I shall probably be forced to spend a thousand or two dollars."

5. VFD, *Outside,* 81 (man as angry); HLB to J. J. Willett 4/17/32, Willett papers (going too far; Willett brought the matter to HLB's attention in a letter of 4/15/32); Harris int.; Schlesinger, *Crisis,* 227 (nepotism): even the revered George Norris hired his son-in-law as his longtime chief assistant, and the wife of House Speaker John Garner served as his secretary for most of his career. And at least four other Alabama legislators followed the practice; *Lafayette* (Ala.) *Sun* 4/13/32.

6. BN 5/4/32 (exhibition of strength), 5/9/32 (Kilby charged), 5/17/32 (referendum); ESB int. (failed); MA 5/21/32 (Klan); Willett to HLB 4/20/32, Willett papers (Kilby spending money); VFD, *Outside,* 84; BN 6/5/32 (Black sulk); HLB comments on Johnston-Kilby advertisement, [about 6/7/32]; Harris int. The vote in the primary was: Black, 92,930; Kilby, 57,875; Burns, 15,528; and Anderton, 9,467; and in the runoff primary: Black, 103,453; Kilby, 74,039. When prohibition was repealed in 1933, Black received less than half a dozen letters from Alabama about his two votes, one for and one against repeal.

7. Bonus marchers: *NYT* 7/30/32 (wholly unnecessary); *Fort Payne* (Ala.) *Journal* 8/17/32 (babies). Birmingham property: Lafayette R. Hanna to HLB, ALS, David S. Meyer and William P. Engel 9/29/32; draft of HLB to Hanna 10/1/32; ALS to HLB 10/5/32 (Frank thinks); HLB to Frank E. Spain 10/8/32 (attitude of insurance company). "This company knows that this property is worth more than the amount of the mortgage indebtedness," Black's draft to Hanna continued. "The company has also been informed of the reason why payments were not carried on." He still managed to close the letter "with kind personal regards." Ray Sprigle of the PPG learned about this whole episode at the time of Black's nomination to the Supreme Court, including the fact that a Birmingham lawyer then sent a copy of Black's letter to Spain to the American Bar Association; and wrote a memorandum about it which is in his papers.

8. HLB, Jr., int. (back to Birmingham); Stallworth, "Black Champions Little Man," *Columbus* (Ga.) *Ledger-Enquirer* 3/6/66 (I changed); HLB to J. R. Hobbs 12/29/32 (greatest problems of government). William Fort was one of the very few people Hugo told about his decision to be a true leader, in a letter which has not survived; see Fort to HLB 12/28/32.

Chapter 10

SOURCES: Frank, *Black;* Hamilton, *Black;* Hunicutt, *Work;* Schlesinger, *Coming.*

1. Aikman, "Black" (crime decreasing); Charles A. and Mary R. Beard, *The Rise of American Civilization* (N.Y., 1927), 694 (table of acquisition); HLB to JPF 1/20/48 (read everything, recalling that G. D. H. Cole had written several books on the minimum wage law in England); CR 1/25/32, 2632 (individual initiative); HLB OH, LBJL (England ahead, wild).

2. Josephson, *Hillman,* 354–5 (AFL unions); Frank Freidel, *Franklin D. Roosevelt: Launching the New Deal* (Boston, 1973), 418 (technology); Davis, *FDR,* 97 (wages dropped); Catledge, book review (worst hit); Bernstein, *Lean,* 319 (Birmingham coal miner), 483 (Brook-

ings economists); HLB to JPF 1/20/48 (several reasons); HLB to Elizabeth Brandeis 7/22/55 (wrote bill, agreed); VH, *Senate*, 165 (win labor support); Schlesinger, *Crisis*, 3–4 (Green).

3. HLB to FDR 3/10/33, FDRL (notified FDR); Davis, *Uncle*, 50; HLB OH, LBJL (six months); *NYT* 3/31/33 (constitution final, Perkins tell committee); Perkins, *Roosevelt*, 193–95; Raymond Moley, *The First New Deal* (N.Y., 1966), 284 (neither); journal 3/19/36, Moley papers (unwise); HLB to Alfred Knopf 9/29/52 (first time see FDR). "Changing conditions, however, bring about different applications of the present constitution," HLB wrote H. C. Nixon 2/15/33.

4. VH, *Senate*, 167–8 (opponents); *NYT* 4/7/33 (exemptions and amendment); Huthmacher, *Wagner*, 144 (FDR asked HLB); William E. Leuchtenburg, *Franklin D. Roosevelt and the New Deal 1932–1940* (N.Y., 1963), 56 (passed bill); diary 4/6/33, Keating papers (Rainey); HLB to Irving Dilliard 7/13/62 (FDR opposed); HLB to John M. Gizzi 1/16/70 (HLB opposed); VH int. with HLB (immigration amendment), VH papers. FDR and Perkins: Perkins, *Roosevelt*, 198; Freidel, *Launching*, 420; HLB to Alfred Knopf 9/29/52; Rexford G. Tugwell, *The Democratic Roosevelt: A Biography of Franklin D. Roosevelt* (Balt., 1969), 283–84 n. Even some New Deal economists thought the bill would make business "unprofitable"; Steven Fraser, *Labor Will Rule: Sidney Hillman and the Rise of American Labor* (N.Y., 1991), 286.

5. Diary 5/7/33 (amend bill), 5/19/33 (kept hands off, wanted HLB to handle), Keating papers; HLB OH, LBJL (HLB recollection). NRA and prediction; CR 6/8/33, 5284 (transfer lawmaking power); HLB to Knopf 9/29/52. Initially HLB hoped that the NRA's purposes would fulfill those of his thirty-hour bill. "I actually refused to offer the [amended] measure for consideration"; HLB to Irving Dilliard 7/13/62.

6. Charles A. Madison, *Leaders and Liberals* (N.Y., 1961), 370 (blocked); Michael Osborn and Joseph Riggs, *"Mr. Mac": William P. MacCracken, Jr., on Aviation, Law, Optometry* (Memphis, 1970), 180 (Robinson); *NYT* 5/2/33 (Merchant Marine), 6/11/33 (staff); BP 12/4/33 (summer); *Labor* 10/3/33 (pulse); *Newsweek* 11/11/33.

7. David D. Lee, "Senator Black's Investigation of the Airmail, 1933–1934," *Historian*, v. 53 (Spring 1991), 423 (Lewis, Hearst); Thomas T. Spencer, "The Air Mail Controversy of 1934," *Mid-America*, v. 62 (10/80), 161 (three holding companies); HLB, "Those U.S. Mail Contracts," speech over NBC 1/24/34 (government operating air transport); Raymond Clapper, "Hugo Black: Nemesis of Subsidy Spoilsmen," *Rev. of Reviews* 4/34; *NYT* 1/27/34 (limit), 2/10/34 (Jurney); Osborn, *"Mr. Mac,"* 157 (MacCracken friendship), 181–83, viii (HLB-MacCracken discussions), 166–67, 183; *Jurney v. MacCracken* (1935). Farley: Farley, *Story*, 42; Farley to HLB 8/31/67. For years, except for a brief moment in late 1951, HLB and MacCracken had no contact. Then in 1969, shortly after giving an interview for "Mr. Mac," HLB appeared, unannounced and uninvited, at the MacCracken's fiftieth anniversary party in Washington. No one knew how he found out about it, recalled Osborn (int.). He wanted to rectify and clarify things. MacCracken, touched, said, "He's reaching out after all these years."

8. Press Conference no. 92, 1/26/34, FDRL; Brown, *Willebrandt*, 200 (Farley cancelled); James T. Williams, Jr., COHP; *NYT* 3/8/34 (FDR to Foulois and proposal); HLB to David J. Davis 4/20/34 (cannot tell); Karl Crowley to Carlton Putnam 5/29/45 (supermen of lobbyists), HLBLC; HLB to FDR 6/18/35, FDRL (final report). Canceling the air mail contracts, HLB later wrote, "was the only way at the time to unscramble the mess the contracts

were in and to let some of the powers in the industry have their chance to continue the work they had begun"; HLB to Thomas Hart Kennedy 2/17/69.

Chapter 11

SOURCES: VFD, *Outside.*

1. HLB to Charles E. Wyzanski, Jr. 3/8/48 (comfortable); HLB to Grover C. Hall, Jr. 1/23/56 (inadequate; "I could not afford to pay the subscriptions for various papers while I was in the Senate"); *Alabama Great Southern Railway Co. v. Norrell,* 143 Sou. 904 (1932, wrongful death); HLB to Eloise Stewart 10/12/32 (conscience of court); Brief and Argument on Motion for Rehearing, 6, 7, 9 (motion for rehearing); Joseph Johnston int. Bank: George Pegram to John Y. G. Walker 8/30/37, HLBLC (Pegram was a Birmingham lawyer when this happened); *BP* 9/16/37 (one of the other directors of the defunct bank was HLB's friend, department store owner Louis Pizitz). Friends who referred cases to HLB included William Fort and W. C. Dalrymple. *Sharp v. Shannon,* Circuit Court of Jefferson County, No. 20473, lasted until 9/35: Fort's firm handled it; for its early stages, see 118 Sou. 173 (1928).

2. Hugh Grant to HLB 8/13/32 (supplementing salary); Dr. James A. Becton to HLB 2/16/32 (mental disorder); CJD to HLB 2/20/32 (did not tell her); VFD, "A Touch of Rue" in Studs Terkel, *Hard Times* (N.Y., 1970), 461. HLB and Durr split the cost of the earlier institutionalization; CJD to HLB 2/20/32. Bennett case: HLB, Brief Opposing Petition for Certiorari, *Birmingham Belt Railroad Co. v. Bennett* (1933), at 2, 21; HLB to W. C. Dalrymple 10/10/33 (more than ever convinced).

3. Bagley int. (JFB-Mrs. Coolidge); Louchheim, *Making,* 303 (Lady Bird Johnson); Frances S. Copeland, "Prelude" to *The Good Guest,* Royal S. Copeland papers, UM (see *BN* 12/20/36); Anna Graham in *BP* 5/8/29 (yesterday passed where you lived).

4. Mary Knox Moore int.; BN, A-H 7/7/35; JFB diary 9/30/32 (found place in attic), 10/3/32 (wrote short story), 10/4/32 (Mary sick), and commonplace book (which was actually HLB's official Senate diary), 5/31/30 (lord), 3/28/30 (individual based).

5. HER int.; Demitri F. Papolos and Janice Papolos, *Overcoming Depression* (N.Y., 1987), 44, 71–2; JFB, in 1933 calendar book for 11/14–16/33, but written about 10/20–25/33, JBP papers (to baby yet unborn). "It was because [Josephine] had some kind of an antipathy to [her] name that she deliberately conceived giving little Josephine the nickname of 'JoJo' "; HLB to SFB 3/25/54, CB papers.

Chapter 12

SOURCES: Frank, *Black;* William A. Gregory and Rennard Strickland, "Hugo Black's Congressional Investigation of Lobbying and the Public Utilities Holding Company Act: A Historical View of the Power Trust, New Deal Politics, and Regulatory Propaganda," 29 *Oklahoma Law Rev.* 543 (1976); Hamilton, *Black;* D. B. Hardeman and Donald C. Bacon, *Rayburn—A Biography* (Austin, 1987), ch. 5; Lash, *Dealers;* Arnold Markoe, *The Black Committee: A Study of the Senate Investigation of the Public Utility Holding Company Lobby* (Ph.D. dissertation, New York Univ., 1972); *NYT;* Schlesinger, *Politics;* Senate Special Committee to Investigate Lobbying Activities, *Hearings,* 74th Cong., 1st Sess. (1935).

1. FDR press conference 6/28/35 (mobilization). Messages: Philip J. Funigiello, *Toward a National Power Policy: The New Deal and the Electric Utility Industry, 1933–1941* (Pittsburgh, 1973), 100 (Wheeler refused); Wheeler (went to HLB), Cole (Minton) ints.; HLB to David H. Corcoran 2/28/68 (suggestion); *Newsweek* files (reporter wrote, Gibson and vote, most will allow himself): CR 6/11/35, 9045 (no more sympathy), 9046 (bloodsucking); 7/11/35, 11003 (any other matter).

2. CR 9/25/29, 3948 (represent interests, communist ideas); *NYT* 9/26/29 (mask); *U.S. News* 6/14/37 (inquiry); Kenneth G. Crawford, *The Pressure Boys: The Inside Story of Lobbying in America* (N.Y., 1939), 3 (5000 lobbyists); 74th Cong., 2nd Sess., H.R. 11633 (House bill). 1935 proposal: CR 4/4/35, 4983; Karl Schriftgiesser, *The Lobbyists: The Art and Business of Influencing Lawmakers* (Boston, 1951), 73; James Deakin, *The Lobbyists* (Wash., D.C., 1966), 76 (conference rejection).

3. *Time* 7/22/35 (boys of press); diary 7/16/35, Keating papers (revelation). Elmer: *Newsweek* 7/27/35; *Time* 7/29/35.

4. HLB, "Inside a Senate Investigation," *Harper's* 2/36 (estimate).

5. CR 8/9/35, 12772 (sordid group). Hopson search: Schriftgiesser, *Lobbyists*, 72; Thomas L. Stokes, *Chips Off My Shoulder* (Princeton, 1940), 341–2. O'Connor: Patterson, *Conservatism*, 53. Caucus room and next search: *Literary Digest* 8/17/35 (Allen). Hopson appearances: CR 8/15/35, 13077, 13199–200.

6. Frank Freidel, *Franklin D. Roosevelt—A Rendezvous with Destiny* (Boston, 1990), 169 (bill). FDR and records: Schriftgiesser, *Lobbyists*, 72; Henry Morgenthau, Jr., Diary, 7/24/35, FDRL.

7. Paul C. Yates to HLB 9/25/35 (dragnet subpoena); Cole int. (Minton); H. Y. Saint to HLB 3/13/36 (task). CT 2/10/36, and on 3/7/36 (cartoon): "Why doesn't Mr. Black include that organization [the Klan] in his investigations? Probably because it elected him in Alabama and he knows too much about it."

8. CR 3/5/36, 3330 (judge issuing injunction; no senator noted disagreement); HLB, "Burned Evidence Smokes Out Liberty League," speech over NBC 3/9/36 (radio speech). Strawn argument: Bill of Complaint, *Strawn v. Western Union*, No. 60814 (Sup. Ct. D.C. 1936) and "Note to Washington Correspondents," (3/2/26), both in James Ford Bell papers, Minnesota Hist. Society; *NYT* 3/3/36. Restraining order: CT 3/5/36.

9. Hearst telegram quoted in HLB to Western Union Telegraph Comp. and T. B. Kingsbury 3/18/36; HLB to T. D. Samford 3/23/36 (controversy); HLB to John A. Carroll 5/25/36 (wrote lawyer); HLB to Samuel Morris 5/13/36 (another correspondent); *NYH-T* 3/14, 15/36 (telegram in Congress); Rives int.; *Hearst v. Black*, 87 F.2d 68 (C.A.D.C. 1936, Groner); Moley, journal 5/2–3/36, Moley papers (long discourse).

10. Benjamin Cohen int.; HLB, "Inside Investigation" (no power on earth, press complaints); *NYH-T* 3/5/36 (Lippmann); HLB to Wyzanski 2/28/49 (no witness can truthfully say), 3/8/49 (surprised); Norman Redlich to HLB 1/17/66 (thirty years later); HLB to Seba Eldridge 3/23/36 (ACLU); HLB to Charles A. Madison 2/20/59 (browbeat), 3/31/59 (Hopson).

11. Sholis, "Young," 8/23/37 (face wrapped in smile); James M. Landis, COHP; *Newsweek* files (newspaperman wrote); HLB to Madison 3/31/59 (Gadsden and Hopson); *Newsweek* 3/14/36 (shaking hands); Aikman, "Black" ("good day"); Paul Ward int. (reporters' feelings). Preparation: HER int. Best investigator: *Newsweek* files; Ward, Childs ints.

12. *BN* 9/5/35 (eyes sparkle); *Newsweek* 3/14/36 (knows answers); Wheeler int. (invaluable); Dunne, *Black*, 62 (CT); D. Clayton Brown, *Electricity for Rural America: The Fight for REA* (Westport, Conn., 1980), 11 (Alabama Power Company); VFD, COHP.

Chapter 13

SOURCES: HLB, Jr., *Father*; Frank, *Black*; Hamilton, *Black*.

1. CJD, "Black" winning people over); Stanley Reed to HLB 1/5/55, relating story by Louis Brownlow, who was present (Robinson on HLB); John Peter Kohn int. (Long's mind); CR 2/7/35, 1667 (HLB-Long on corporations); Davis, *Uncle*, 58 (study people). "I Am a Good Old Rebel" (which HLB called "The Rebel Song") continued: "I'm glad we fit agin 'em and I only wish we'd won,—And I don't axe no parton for anything I've done"; and ended: "And I don't axe no pardon for what I was or am. I won't be reconstructed and I just don't give a damn!"

2. SFB int.; Horace J. Bresler, "Hugo Black—Champ Turned Judge," [about 1946], HLBLC (Senate restaurant). Long filibuster: *NYH-T* 6/13/35; T. Harry Williams, *Huey Long* (N.Y., 1969), 833–35; Franklin L. Burdette, *Filibustering in the Senate* (Princeton, 1940), 3–5, 182–87.

3. Pepper, Wheeler ints.; Hollis O. Black to Mrs. T. B. Andrews 5/18/36 (assistant wrote). Staff: Cobb, Quantock, Rhoads ints.

4. Alsop int.; *Newsweek* files (willing to talk); *WP* 3/15/36 (fwottle fweedom); ESB to Mary Tortorici 4/68, JBP papers (Catledge); HLB to William Hendrix 10/24/35 (*NY Daily News*). Merchandisers: see James Ragland, "Merchandisers of the First Amendment: Freedom and Responsibility of the Press in the Age of Roosevelt, 1933–1940," *Georgia Rev.*, v. 16 (1962), 366, which HLB considered "a fine job"; to Ragland 11/12/62.

5. CJD int.; *NYP* 11/24/75. In early 1937 Josephine wrote a poem entitled "Pain":

> Your face is cold and your eyes are bleak
> Your nails are blue, and your nostrils reek
> With fumes that foil and foul and seek
> To shatter my soul to its own defeat.
>
> You close your ears to my anguished plea
> You shut your eyes and refuse to see
> My tortured limbs and this struggling me
> Who strives and strains—oh just to be!

6. Undated clipping, JBP papers (love affair); SFB int. (hardest, running away, Goldsmith). HLB was also physically rough with the boys, hitting them when he felt they needed it, even well into their teens. He liked to tell the press that the family went for rides in their Ford; but, according to Sterling Black, that happened rarely, if at all. They would ride to a picnic in the Ford but not just take a ride: that would be a waste of time.

7. HLB to JPF 1/20/48 (list); Lilienthal, *Journals*, 68 (desk piled high); Catledge, book review (books under arm); Wheeler int.; CR 2/8/32, 3519 (Fleming); Aikman, "Black" (Aristotle); HLB to Neil O. Davis 7/26/66 (subject chosen; HLB inscribed Dilliard, *Stand*).

8. CR 4/29/35, 6520–34 (Senate speech); White, *Man*, 169 (FDR statement); Woodward, *Thinking Back: The Perils of Writing History* (N.Y., 1986), 87 (Jim Crow); Woodward, *Jim Crow*, 116, 118 (ordinances); HLB to Charles R. Bell, Jr. 5/10/37, Bell papers, Samford Univ. (proceed successfully). On the antilynching issue, see George C. Rable, "The South and the Politics of Antilynching Legislation, 1920–1949," *Jour. South. Hist.*, v. 51 (1985), 201, which lists other sources; and for Norris's doubts, Richard Lowitt, *George W. Norris: The Triumph of a Progressive, 1933–1944* (Urbana, Ill., 1978), 226. Rable notes HLB's "carelessly ignoring the historical record" (210).

9. Monasco int. (fast friends); HLB to Bankhead 11/8/35 (friendship); BN 10/28/35 (lawyers campaigning); HLB to Bankhead 11/4,8/35 (Davis); Bankhead to HLB 11/2/35 (widely known); HLB to Henry J. Willingham 11/11/35 (almost all instances, originally emphasized). Bankhead supporting Davis: Bankhead to HLB 11/6,11/35; HLB to Bankhead 11/8/35.

Chapter 14

SOURCES: Alsop, *Days*; Irving Bernstein, *A Caring Society: The New Deal, the Workers and the Great Depression* (Boston, 1985); Elizabeth Brandeis, "Organized Labor and Protective Labor Legislation" in Milton Derber and Edwin Young, eds., *Labor and the New Deal* (Madison, Wisc., 1957); James M. Burns, *Congress On Trial: The Legislative Process and the Administrative State* (N.Y., 1949).

1. HLB to Farley 8/10/36 (Alabama); Dunne, *Black*, 165 (touring); Rhoads, Durr (educate Alabamians), Beech ints.; MA 9/15/37 (rain); Grover Hall to HLB 6/29/36 (grade A company). Campaigning: *Detroit News* 3/31/37 (safe for Republicans); *Springfield* (Mo.) *Leader & Press* 1/9/36 (Jackson Day banquet), 1/10/36 (held spellbound); HLB to James Farley 6/10/36 (glad to talk). Good old days: see HLB to Norman Thomas 7/17/37.

2. Lilienthal, *Journals*, 64 (La Follette invitation); *Memphis Commercial Appeal* 10/11/36 (left Iowa): *Rockford* (Ill.) *Morning Star* 10/13/36 (Republican Party, Du Ponts); HLB to FDR 10/18/36, FDRL; PP (terming Hearst a war promoter), *York* (Pa.) *Gazette & Daily*, both 10/28/36; *Ala. Herald* 11/13/36 (HLB to reporter); Ralph Hurst, "Alabama's Hugo Black," BN, A-H 11/12/36 (talk for 1940); Pepper DeMerritte (HLB–Corcoran–Cohen) ints. The states HLB visited were Minnesota, Missouri, Oklahoma, Nebraska, Iowa, Illinois, Indiana, Ohio, West Virginia, Pennsylvania and New York; HLBLC (also number of speeches). "I have been of the opinion all the time that if the proper effort had been made, President Roosevelt could have carried Vermont"; HLB to Graham Wilson 11/28/36.

3. *U.S. v. Butler* (1936, Stone dissent); BN 1/18/36 (five men rule); *Hearings on S. 2176 before the Senate Judiciary Committee, 74th Cong., 1st Sess.* (1935, justices appearing); William E. Leuchtenburg, "The Origins of Franklin D. Roosevelt's 'Court-Packing' Plan," 1965 *Supreme Court Rev.* 347 (strange things). Reading: HLB to W. H. Woolverton 3/18/37 (real study), 3/27/37 (Bill of Rights, judges determining); to Olivia O'Neal Rouzer 3/17/37; to W. C. Bentley 3/18/37. Federalist charges: to Rouzer; to Roy W. Kimbrough 7/17/37; to David P. Anderson 3/17/37 (writers of constitution, imperative duty); to John Temple Graves 2/15/37 (clearer); to Jelks Cabiness 3/18/37 (trained and influenced); CR 3/25/37, A639 (human rights); HLB to H. C. Green 3/17/37 (constitution written by framers).

4. Schlesinger, *Retrospect*, 125 (genes); *NYT* 2/6/37 (favor plan); HLB to Bentley 3/18/37 (jeopardizing Constitution); HLB to Woolverton 3/18/37 (theory of government); "Rendezvous with Democracy: The Memoirs of 'Tommy the Cork,' " Corcoran papers; Sylvester Smith, Jr. (lay low; he headed the ABA's effort in Washington), Wheeler ints.; CR 2/17/37, 1288, 1292; it was actually for eighteen years that the federal income tax was unconstitutional—from 1895, when the Supreme Court so ruled in *Pollock v. Farmers' Loan & Trust Co.*, to 1913, when the Sixteenth Amendment, which was designed to circumvent *Pollock*, was ratified). HLB had suggested to Roosevelt (1/28/37) that the Supreme Court be separated into two divisions, with the chief justice sitting with each division; in constitutional cases the whole Court would sit. "Two or more" justices would have to be added since "the present number" is "wholly inadequate to give [appeals] the attention their importance deserves." "We seem to have been thinking along the same or else parallel lines!" FDR replied 2/6/37.

5. CR: 2/24/37, A306 (HLB radio address); 3/25/37, 3574 (HLB New York speech 3/24/37); 2/17/37, 1294 (incapable of definition); 3/25/37, A636 (rights of human beings) HLB int. (supported president); *WS* 8/13/37 (zealous supporter); *BP* 8/13/37 (never did anything); Farley, *Story*, 78–9 (smoke out). Country was young: *WS* 8/15/37; *BP* 8/16/37. Newspapers: *NYT* 3/15,25/37 (speeches); the first radio address was given on 2/11/37 (see CR 2/15/37, 224). For letters to editor, see CR 7/28/37, 7745–47.

6. Gene L. Mason, *Hugo Black and the United States Senate* (M.A. thesis, Univ. of Kansas, 1964), 170–81; HLB, "The Shorter Work Week and Work Day," *Annals of the American Academy of Political and Social Science*, 186 (3/36). *NYT, BN* 1/22/37 (FDR–HLB discuss).

7. Corcoran-Cohen: George E. Paulsen, "Ghost of the NRA: Drafting National Wage and Hour Legislation in 1937," *Soc. Sci. Quar.*, v. 67 (1986), 241; Lash, *Dealers*, 335–37. HLB not liking draft: Louchheim, *Making*, 172; Rhoads int. (also markup sessions). Reunite party: Hunnicut, *Work*, 243–44; Perkins, *Roosevelt*, 256. FDR message: S. 2475, 75th Cong., 1st Sess., introduced 5/24/37; *NYT* 5/24/37; AP dispatch in MR 5/24/37. Since Congress had not enacted the administration's whole program and courts had denied government the right to regulate earnings and working conditions, labor felt that its only recourse was "the bayonet and the gun." HLB said to enthusiastic applause at an American Labor Party rally in New York City; *NYT* 3/31/37.

8. *U.S. News* 6/14/37 (NRA official), Josephson, *Hillman*, 443 (labor). Unless labor rallied to its support, the bill may be shelved for this session of Congress, HLB warned; *WDN* 6/14/37. After each committee session, either HLB or his assistant Lee Rhoads would brief the press.

9. Diary 8/1/37, Cummings papers (froth); Patterson, *Conservatism*, 149 (Bailey); diary 7/27/37, Pepper papers; HLB OH, LBJL (Bilbo); Louchheim, *Making*, 113 (Fireside Chat). On southern reaction to the bill, see Tindall, *Emergence*, 533–34; Swain, *Harrison*, 163–65; MA 7/5/37. FDR not wanting bill: ESB int. with Corcoran, ESB papers; see Niznick, "Corcoran," 313, 315. Roosevelt "was at first reserved in his support of a minimum-wage bill," despite the 1936 Democratic platform; Josephson, *Hillman*, 443, based on ints. with participants. Corcoran had to barter with senators on the basis of both Court-packing and working hours. And while HLB as a Robinson lieutenant tested colleagues' sentiments on the one, he had to pressure for and shepherd the other one through almost on his own. For, once it was submitted, FDR's assistance was distinctly limited.

10. HLB–Corcoran: *WS* 6/8/37; *NYT* 6/6/37; HLB to Corcoran, ca. 6/7/37, Corcoran papers. HLB argument: CR 6/15/37, A1479 (National Radio Forum speech over NBC 6/7/37,

discussed in *WS* 6/8/37); CBS address ("The Shorter Work Week and Work Day")
5/26/37; "Should There Be Federal Control of Wages and Hours?" NBC Town Meeting
of the Air 7/15/37 (from Charlottesville); letter to *NYT* 7/25/37. HLB to John Temple
Graves 7/3/37; Graves used the essence of this letter in his 7/15/37 *BAH* column. Human
intelligence, HLB had earlier told Graves, was not adequate to "really fair fixing" of either
prices or wages—"not even a shoe merchant" could fairly set the price of shoes—and
that he merely wished to limit the supply of labor by restricting working hours in order
that there might be a "real working of supply and demand" in fixing labor's price; Graves
to HLB 7/1/37.

11. *WS* 8/15/37 (personally, seldom stopped, hair); HLB to Louise P. Floyd 7/1/37 (so engaged);
ESB int. with Corcoran, ESB papers; *CR* 7/8/37, 6894 (new bill; see *NYT* 7/9/37).
Exemptions: see Robert S. Allen, "Washington Sweatshop," *Nation* 7/17/37; Huthmacher,
Wagner, 246–47. At one committee conference Claude Pepper noted, "I battled Black,
La Follette, Cohen and Sidney Hillman, [John L.] Lewis's lieutenant, to make the be-
ginning of the bill moderate and gradually to extend it. Hillman wants 25 to 60 cents
per hour—in discretion of board; I [want] 25 to 40 cents. That's all we can get over in
Florida now": Pepper diary 6/30/37.

12. *CR* 7/31/37, 7872 (Smith), 7946–51 (should thank God). Smith pictured living conditions as "so kindly that it takes only fifty cents a day . . . to enable one to live comfortably and reasonably" in the South, and spoke of "the splendid gifts of God to the
South." The bill was finally passed in June 1938 after many more compromises, but it
placed an ironclad floor under wages and a ceiling above hours.

Chapter 15

SOURCES: Frank, *Black*; Hamilton, *Black*.

1. HLB to J. B. Wadsworth 7/3/37 (platform); *MA* 7/22/37 (manufacturer); Barney Whatley
to HLB 2/20/37; *BAH* 6/1/37 (attorney general story; two months later, it remained alive:
Tuscaloosa News editorial 8/9/37); *MA* 8/9/37 (cotton prices); *BN* 7/18/37 (extremist);
Green, Rives ints.; *BP* 8/16/37 (talk about Civil War). Opposing candidates: *BP* 7/1/37;
Decatur (Ala.) *Daily* 7/13/37; *BN* 7/14/37. HLB–Hill: VH, *Hill*, 61–2; Hill, Paul Ward,
Claude Hamilton, HLB, Jr., ints. 1938 campaign: SFB, HLB, Jr., Hill ints.; Hill verified
his conv. with HLB.

2. *Wiregrass* (Headland, Ala.) *Farmer* 7/8,22/37; *MA* 7/24/37 (Mullin's observation); *BP*, *MA*
7/24/37; *Alabama Journal* 7/22/37 (HLB's response, also reprinted in many Alabama newspapers); HLB to Crow 8/4/37, John Bankhead papers, ADAH (pleasure); HLB to James J.
Willett, Sr. 7/23/37, Willett papers (platform); Hamilton int. (no worries about reelection); P. O. Davis to HLB 5/1/67 (biggest majority); HLB to John C. Walters 7/13/37
(Muscle Shoals). "Too much learning has made him mad," claimed the *Pickens County
Herald* (7/22/37); but "I did not have the slightest question but what my record in the Senate would be approved by the people of Alabama" (HLB to George Bondurant 8/26/37).

3. HLB to Joseph Lyons 7/22/37; to George Pegram 7/22/37 (*Mobile Press-Register*: "This is a
stale theme in Mobile" and "no longer makes any impression," Lyons replied, 7/27/37);
HLB to C. W. Rittenour 7/21/37 (hiring lobbyists); HLB to Walter McAdory 7/19/37

(Ala. Power Co.); HLB to John Temple Graves 7/19/37; James M. Landis COHP (HLB–Lewis).

4. Childers, "Black" (beyond state boundaries); HLB to Willett 2/1/36, Willett papers (understand sadness); NYT 5/21/37 (Civilian Conservation Corps). Education bill: NYT 3/14/37 (radio speech); Sen. Report No. 217, 75th Cong., 1st Sess., Comm. on Educ. and Labor, No. 933, v. 2; MA 6/2/48, citing 1938 CR (Borah); White, Man, 177–8 (education is answer). Although the bill reached the floor in both the House and the Senate, Black and Harrison decided not to try to push the Senate to a final vote: Swain, Harrison, 210–14. It took a full generation for the first similarly comprehensive federal aid to education in modern times to be approved. HLB later noted that he and Houston "worked together in trying to get agreements among various groups in support of" the bill. "The friendship we formed then continued until his death. He was a fine man and a great lawyer": HLB to Frances H. Williams 11/13/57.

5. BAH 7/5/34 (health of nation). Medical insurance: NYT 1/6/35, 6/20/35; Schlesinger, Coming, 307; Huthmacher, Wagner, 263; CR 1/7/35, 142, and 6/10/37, 5517; U.S. Senate, Committee on Labor and Public Welfare, 100th Anniversary, 1869–1969, Sen. Doc. No. 90-108 (1970), 54 (postponed), 63 (cooperate); WT 10/1/37 (HLB's physician). The senator "most effective in rationalizing the Social Security bill to his fellow members was Senator Black. . . . Time and again he would restate the point under discussion in more meaningful [language] for the other members of the committee . . ."; Joseph Harris in Social Security Project, II, COHP.

6. Alsop, Days, 300-01 (anomaly, radical); WP 8/22/37 (strove for); AP release, "Black's Road," (revolution); Aikman, "Black" (break up combinations); CR 6/14/34, 11438–39, 11442–44 (Tugwell); Pearson papers (Byrd, originally emphasized). "Tugwell is a theorist," Black said years later (int.). "His head is in the clouds. He has no realism. He's not at all practical, never was."

7. Aikman, "Black" (address Senate); Landis, COHP (except for accent); BP 8/18/37 (colleague's three hour speech; the speaker was Arthur Vandenburg of Michigan); Roosevelt int.; Cooper, "Black, Alabama" (Davis). WOD: Go East, 279–80; WODM, 57.

8. Grover Hall, "Alabama Editor, Who Never Cast Vote for Black, Describes Him," BES 8/13/37; Aikman, "Black" (physiognomist's delight); HLB to Henry C. Ferrell, Jr. 8/21/61 (Swanson); Claude Hamilton int. (optimistic); John Bankhead to FDR 8/13/37, FDRL (evangelic progressive).

Chapter 16

SOURCES: Alsop, Days; Dunne, Black; Frank, Black; Hamilton, Black; William E. Leuchtenburg, "A Klansman Joins the Court: The Appointment of Hugo L. Black," 41 Univ. of Chi. Law Rev. 1 (1973).

1. Leuchtenburg, "FDR's Court-Packing Plan: A Second Life, A Second Death," 1985 Duke Law Jour. 673, 683–686 (consequences); NYT 7/28/37 (appointment after adjournment); Reed OH, UK (searched); Reed, COHP (canvassed); McFarland int. (Cummings and appointment); memorandum in re Supreme Court 8/3/37, FDRL (list of names: omitted, undoubtedly because of his age, sixty-five, was the most notable federal judge, Learned Hand); Lash, Dealers, 311 (Corcoran–FF).

2. Unidentified newspaper article 9/28/37, HLBLC (fearing); William H. Smathers to FDR 8/12/37, FDRL (gathering); Paul Ward int. (1/37; La Follette told Ward this); HLB to Robert T. Simpson, Jr. 5/29/37 (wrote inquirer).

3. HLB, SFB, Frances Arnold ints.; Jim C. Smith to HLB 8/12/37 (dull); Alsop, "I've Seen," 111 (refuge). Would take Court: HLB int. "I was not absolutely certain in the beginning," he told a friend; HLB to John W. Altman 8/26/37 (see BAH 8/13/37).

4. Huthmacher, Wagner, 239 (debate); NYT 8/13/37 (opponents); Life 8/23/37 (dinner).

5. Corcoran, Roosevelt, HLB (meeting with FDR) ints.; diary 8/14/37, Clapper papers (Richberg). HLB told FDR that he was looking forward to his reelection campaign "with considerable pleasure"; HLB to P. O. Davis 5/4/67.

6. Lilienthal, Journals, 69 (background); Wilma Dykeman and James Stokely, Seeds of Southern Change: The Life of Will Alexander (Chic., 1962), 307 (our part of country); Farley, Story, 97–8 (morning talk); McFarland int. (FDR–Cummings). Senate: WT 8/12/37; CR 8/12/37, 8732 (Ashurst). Robert Jackson, then an assistant attorney general, might have also known about the appointment. He later said that before it was announced, he saw FDR who told him, "I'm going to name Black for two reasons: the Supreme Court will puke and half the Senate will puke, and neither can do a damn thing about it"; Marsh int.

7. NYT 8/13/37 (1888, constitutional bar; "a majority of the senators expressed no real concern over the question, BAH 8/13/37, based on a talk with HLB); AP release 8/12/37 (Barkley); Wheeler int. (conservatives skeptical); diary 8/12/37, Keating papers (picked devil); Phila. Record 8/13/37 (kick in face); BAH 8/13/37 (lunch); FDR to FF 8/12/37, FDRL. (discombobulated); WS 8/13/37 (Glass). Earlier, when Glass heard a bystander call the appointment a great victory for the common people, he roared, "They must be God damn common!" Newsweek 8/21/37.

8. Farley, Story, 98 (have to take); "Nomination of Hon. Hugo L. Black for Associate Justice of the Supreme Court of the United States, United States Senate, Subcommittee of the Committee on the Judiciary, Washington, D.C., Friday, August 13, 1937," HLBLC; WDN 8/13/37; WP 8/14/37 (also no comment); BN 8/15/37 (northern publisher); William R. Castle to William Borah 8/13/37, Borah papers (Republican national committee); LAT 8/14/37 (anything found).

9. Walter White to Max Lowenthal 8/19/37, FFLC (personally had confidence); diary 8/16/37, Pepper papers (get hard-boiled); Amer. Bar Ass'n Jour. 9/37 (eligibility); MR 8/17/37 (Dieterich–Burke); New York Sun 8/16/37 (most powerful organization); Wash. Herald 8/15/37 (Senate leaders agreed).

10. CR 8/17/37, 9070 (Copeland quote), 9073 (unnamed person); MR 8/17/37 (insult); Phila. Record 8/18/37 (stony silence); Irving Brant to FF 9/23/37, FFLC (make statement, Borah, let callers understand); HLB, draft of radio address [9/29/37], Corcoran papers (telling Borah).

11. Brant to FF (also to Justice Harlan Stone) 9/23/37 (committee decided); CR 8/17/37, 9098 (Borah); Phila. Record, 8/18/37 (Connally; CR 8/17/37, 9087–88, does not include the reference to the park bench); diary 8/17/37, Keating papers (Catholics and opponents); WS 8/18/37 (congratulate); diary 8/17/37, Pepper papers (Halsey's office); HLB to Homer T. Bone 11/30/44 (depression); Ickes, Diaries, II, 196 (royalists). Southerners: HER, Frazer ints.; St. Louis Star-Times 8/13/37.

12. Grover Hall to HLB 8/12/37 (sensation); Rives (drafting announcement; also Rives to HLB 8/16/37), Hill, HER (Dixie Graves) ints.; MR 8/21/37 (good senator). Lister Hill (int.) confirmed Rives's entire account: "That's exactly what happened."

13. HLB, "Statement to be appended," 4/8/68 (to correct for posterity; the article was Virginia Van Der Veer [Hamilton], "I Nominate Hugo L. Black . . . ," Amer. Heritage 4/68); James Roosevelt int.; Chalmers, Hooded, 258 (replace Copeland); Wash. Herald 8/20/37 (smiling); HLB to Ray Jenkins 2/2/65 (anxious moments); Lilienthal, Journals, 69 (going to take oath); NYT 8/20/37 (Levitt). Copeland-Hearst: Chalmers, Hooded, 217, 271; and Jackson, Klux, 194. On FDR and the Georgia Klan, see Frank Freidel, Franklin D. Roosevelt: The Triumph (Boston, 1956), 276–77; Chalmers, 306–07; Robert W. Horton in WDN 9/15/37.

14. Resignation: HLB to Graves, Graves to HLB 8/19/37, and Graves, draft of statement [8/19/37], Edwin A. Halsey papers, LC. Took oath: WS 8/20/37. Europe: Whatley to HLB 8/14/37 (Clay County style); HLB to Henry H. Balch 9/26/32 (cost in 1932). Cash: HLB and Whatley family ints. Colorado trip: John Gillon, Alfred Whatley ints. Gillon's law partner, and HLB's good Birmingham friend, Frank Spain also happened to be vacationing there with his wife, and both couples golfed together. Each morning at breakfast Spain, who knew full well Hugo's affiliation with the Klan, took the newspaper, open to the page of hushed rumors of it, over to him and asked, "Where is Senator Black?": Spain to VH 8/7/72, VH papers.

15. Rhoads int. (jobs); W. J.Worthington to HLB 8/17/37 (man representing BN); HLB to L. N. Duncan 8/26/37 (sail for Europe); Time 8/23/37(new robe). Secretary: Quantock, HER, Cobb (young Catholic secretary), Ann Daniel (another assistant) ints. Alabama Democratic Executive Committee records contain no such indication as HLB claimed; ADAH.

Chapter 17

SOURCES: Dunne, Black; CJD, "Black"; Frank, Black, Hamilton, Black; Lerner, Ideas; Leuchtenburg, "Klansman."

1. Paul Block, Jr., Shuman, Paul Johnston ints.; Clarksburg (W. Va.) Telegram 8/23/38 (pick up paper); "Story Related by Cooper Green, Postmaster of Birmingham," [early 10/37] (fee); Green to CJD 10/16/37, CJD papers (Klansmen). Sprigle-Esdale: PPG 7/31/49; Alvin Rosensweet, "Ray Sprigle" (1975), PPG files; Rae Sprigle Kurland int.

2. Shuman (tobacco), Paul Block, Jr. (not paying) ints.; In re Esdale, 173 Sou. 55 (1937, disbarment); PPG 7/31/49 (Esdale quotes, helpful); Clarksburg Telegram 8/23/38 (HLB never paying); Ray Sprigle to Agnes Sprigle 8/23/37, Sprigle papers (hotel); VH to Robert Gallagher 8/8/67, VH papers (vague answer). Disbarment: records and briefs, In re Esdale, ADAH; BP 12/20/35; BAH 12/21/35. Sprigle wrote two articles, on the Klan's role in the 1926 senate race and on the Father Coyle murder trials, but they made nary a ripple; PPG and Toledo Blade (which Block also owned), 8/22,24/37.

3. A. W. Brazelton [?] to Hollis Black 8/27/37 (mug), enclosed in Hollis Black to HLB 8/30/37 ("Nothing of any special interest has occurred since you left," added Hollis); NYT 9/13/37 (calling hotel, also Catholic groups); diary 10/20/37, Keating papers (Hearst reporter). Paris: NYH-T 9/9/37; JFB diary 9/18/37 (rest). Investigation: WDN, BP

9/14/37; John W. McCormack to Henry F. Ashurst 8/13/37, Senate Judiciary Committee files, National Archives (also Catholic groups); *WP* 9/17/37 (Wheeler). Catholic groups: *WT* 9/16/37; David J. O'Brien, *American Catholics and Social Reform* (N.Y., 1968), 74. Impeachment: Pepper (shocking thing), HLB (how could they) ints. Birmingham newspapers carried only excerpts from the series.

4. *NYT* 9/14/37 (Cummings), 9/15/37 (no further comment); *WS* 9/23/37 (Norris); *WDN* 9/13/37, *BP* 9/14/37 (both Bankhead); Frazer int. (Hill); Morganthau diaries, 9/20/37 (LeHand); "Notes," Corcoran papers (opinion divided); Mary W. (Molly) Dewson, "An Aid to the End" (autobiographical memoir), II, 226–7, Dewson papers, FDRL (disturbed look); *WP* 9/21/37 (stalling). FDR anger: Paul Ward int., relaying Corcoran's belief; John Gunther, *Roosevelt in Retrospect: A Profile in History* (N.Y., 1950), 48.

5. JFB diary 9/13/37 (Ward phoning and ugly stories), 9/14/37; Ward (right people, HLB comments, reporters took turns, lunches, talk with HLB which was, apparently, on Friday, 9/17, HLB's fifth night in London), HLB (sign) ints.; *NYT* 9/14/37 (reporter), 9/15/37 (asking questions), 9/24/37 (Klandestinely); Ward to HLB 9/13/37 (lunches); *Wash. Herald* 9/14/37 (leaving London, also not seeing reporter); *CT* 9/18/37 (sailing); Corcoran, "Autobiographical Notes" 7/5/80, Lash papers; Lash, *Dealers*, 312. Ireland: Ward int. and telephone message to HLB 9/17/37; *CSM* 9/16/37. "Black would talk for hours about what happened in England after he was appointed," said Arthur John Keefe (int.). "He must have told me this story ten times. But to his dying day he wouldn't talk about all the persecution he was under. He couldn't admit it."

6. *WP* 9/21/37 (Franklyn Waltman column quoting Ashurst, CR); Mundelein to FDR 9/25/37, FDRL; Paul Johnston, HER, Beech ints.; *PPG* 8/6/49 (affadavits); "Green Story" (reporter). Spellman: Alden Whitman, *Come to Judgment* (N.Y., 1980), 58 (favorite bishop); Robert I. Gannon, S.J., *The Cardinal Spellman Story* (N.Y., 1963), 197 (only answer). Ryan int.: *Indiana Catholic and Record* 9/24/37 (the publicity is in FDRL); see Francis L. Broderick, *Right Reverend New Dealer: John A. Ryan* (N.Y., 1964), 233.

7. Ickes, *Diaries*, II, 216 (FDR suggestion); HLB telegrams to Thomas Woodward, [9/25, 27/37]; Woodward telegram to HLB 9/26/37; VH to Gallagher 9/12/67, VH papers (word from FDR, relating int. with HLB; this was his retrospective version of Corcoran's call to him in London); *WS* 9/30/37 (want and come along, back to Block); *PPG*, *CSM* 9/30/37 (reception); *Norfolk Ledger-Dispatch*, AP release 9/29/37; *WP* 9/30/37. Mylander nevertheless sent the Sprigle articles on 9/30 to HLB, who naturally found them useful in preparing his speech. Cabin and after: CJD int. (driving).

8. Harris, Hamilton, CJD, Alsop ints. (see Alsop, "*I've Seen*," 111); HLB, *Memoirs*, 230 (childhood membership); Alsop in *NYH-T* 10/2/37 (by dinner); [HLB], "very rough" draft, and draft, "ECH [E. Crampton Harris] marked" (revisions), both Corcoran papers; Farley, *Story*, 99 (terrible); Corcoran papers and CJD int. (Corcoran and Cohen draft). Chickening out: Lash, *Dealers*, 312; Corcoran recollections in Lash papers; Tom Corcoran's statement about the Klan 7/14/81, ESB papers.

9. Hamilton int.; *Life* 10/11/37 (picture). Speech: *WP*, *WS*, *WDN*, *BAH*, 10/2/37. Audience: *Time* 10/11/37. The networks, with a stake in the number, estimated 50 million (*Newsweek* 10/11/37); while the Gallup organization estimate of 20.6 million seems rather low: Amer. Inst. of Public Opinion (AIPO) release 10/23/37, FDRL. The speech was reprinted in almost every newspaper in the country.

10. *PPG* 8/6/49 (ain't way); Paul Block to Grenville Clark 10/1/37, Grenville Clark papers;

Alabama 10/11/37 (Sprigle in Birmingham, Williams); Scripps-Howard editorial: *NY World-Telegram, WDN, PP* and other papers 10/2/37; *NYT* 10/2/37 (Wheeler); VH to Gallagher 9/12/67, VH papers (pointing); *WP* 10/2/37 (open car); Farley, *Story,* 100 (grand job): *WT* 10/1/37); Leigh Clark, Windham ints. Public opinion: *BN* 10/3/37 (before speech); AIPO releases 10/2,23/37, FDRL. Sprigle did write one further article, on the Father Coyle trial (*PPG* 9/29/37), and he had pictures taken of Coyle's grave to use if needed. But once Black admitted his Klan membership, he saw no reason.

11. HLB to Hugh Grant 10/26/37 (nothing but fight); MA 10/6/37; Davis, *Uncle,* 31–2.

12. Greenbaum, COHP; CJD, Beech ints.; Greenbaum to CJD 2/8/38 (leaning on him); answer of defendants, *Block v. The Nation,* draft of 3/30/38 (Greenbaum's response), both HLBLC; Pruden, "Opposition," 318–319 (joke and price; his sources were HLB and Crampton Harris: Pruden int.). Hearst and Block: Hearst, William Block, Paul Block, Jr.; John M. Harrison, *The Blade of Toledo: The First 150 Years,* (Toledo, 1985), 209–10, 255; Ferdinand Lundberg, *Imperial Hearst: A Social Biography* (N.Y., 1936), 180–181, 330–331; W. A. Swanberg, *Citizen Hearst* (N.Y., 1960), 484–85; Oliver Knight, "Paul Block" in *DAB,* supp. 3 (1973). 1926: MA 9/2/26; Paul Anderson, letter to editor (American Newspaper) *Guide Reporter* 5/9/38.

Chapter 18

SOURCE: Cooper, "Footnotes."

1. ESB int. with VFD (exit). Demonstrators: *CSM* 10/4/37; HLB int.; HLB to Malcolm Williamson 7/26/66. Notice: *London Times* 9/23/37; *NYT* 9/24/37. Monaghan: Monaghan int.; see "The Road Not Taken," *Fortune* 7/1/75. Cooper int. (appointment and meeting). Cardozo visits: HLB int.; unidentified newspaper article (UP release) 10/5/37, HLBLC. Brandeis: Schlesinger, *Retrospect,* 125 (well-qualified). Meeting Brandeis: HLB to Billikopf 11/30/44; *NYH-T,* 10/2/37. HLB had his choice of chambers because even after the Court building was completed in 1935, all the justices continued to work at home, using the marble palace only to hold conferences and sessions and for ceremonial purposes.

2. Courtroom: *WS, WDN* 10/4/37; *WP, WDN, Wash. Herald, WT, CSM* 10/5/37; Butler int. JFB: Benjamin V. Cohen to FF, 10/11/37, Cohen papers, LC: Lash, *Dealers,* 312. Louchheim, *Making,* 71 (World's Fair); Fred Friendly, *Minnesota Rag* (N.Y., 1981), 104 (CEH-HLB); *Newsweek* 10/18/37 (at home). Motions: *Ex parte Levitt, Ex parte Kelly;* see *NYT* 10/12/37; *BN* 10/11/37; *Newsweek* 10/18/37.

3. ESB int. with VFD (death threats and war college); Cooper to HLB, 10/12/64 (time); Ann Daniel int. (calling Judge); *WS* 10/25/37 (house); HLB to Lister Hill 10/22/37 (work); diary 10/20/37, Keating papers (NYT); CJD to Thomas Corcoran, [probably late 10/37], FDRL (wanting to see FDR).

4. Primary: HLB to Arthur Sartain 10/14/37 (busy, originally emphasized); diary 10/20/37 (corporations), 11/1/37 (utilities), Keating papers; Hill, Cooper (Rushton) ints.; HLB to Luther Patrick 10/20/37 (noise); *LAT* 11/20/37 (Patrick poem). Gridiron Club: *WT* 12/12/37; Robert Sherrill, "The Twilight of the Gridiron Club," *WP Potomac Magazine,* 5/5/74 (stalking out); Riggs int. (fifteen years). Clan: *WT* 1/21/38; Claude Hamilton int.

5. Cooper, HLB, Lusky (law school standards) ints.; diary 2/13/38, Clapper papers (deter-

mination); unidentified newspaper article 10/5/37, HLBLC (Roberts); WODM, 139 (admire Stone).

6. *McCart v. Indianapolis Water Co.* (1938); Stone to CEH 12/30/37, in Mason, *Stone,* 468 (troubled); Corcoran int. (Cohen and Corcoran clerks; Stone saved an unmarked newspaper clipping implying this); *Connecticut General Life Insurance Corp. v. Johnson* (1938, history of amendment; HLB's emphasis); *Santa Clara County v. Southern Pacific Railroad* (1886, persons); CJD to mother 11/3/37, CJD papers (not binding).

7. Lusky (startle, HLB's mind), Cooper (grammar books, Stone seeing HLB) ints.; Stone to FF 2/8/38, FFLC (know HLB well; FF's 2/13/38 response was noncommittal); HLB to Ben F. Ray 2/7/38 (dissent and disagreement); John Medelman to HLB 9/12/67 (learning to write); Walton H. Hamilton, "Mr. Justice Black's First Year," *New Republic* 6/8/38 (arguments); *WDN* 2/13/38 (Broun). Meals: Cooper in *Confessions;* Ann Daniel, Claude Hamilton (arrive) ints. Brandeis told FF that he had never seen anyone work as hard as Black; Calabresi int.

8. Lusky, Cooper ints.; *U.S. v. Carolene Products Co.* (1938), which merely applied to United States law generally the rule of *West Coast Hotel Co. v. Parrish* (1937) which in turn had upheld a state minimum wage law and interred *Lochner;* Stone to HLB 4/22/38, Stone papers (hold statute unconstitutional); Zion int. with HLB (why I came on Court). *Erie* was the other part of the day's revolution. Justice Brandeis ruled that federal courts must honor state law, whether declared by the legislature or the courts, in such diversity of citizenship cases.

9. WODM, 140 (gossipy, HLB got impression); *St. L P-D* 1/22/38; Childs, COHP (national reading); Childs, "Stone" (protest); Childs, "The Supreme Court Today," *Harper's* 5/38; Childs, *Witness,* 38 (letting off steam); *Wash. Herald* 5/12/38 (no hand; see Mason, *Stone,* 472–76), 5/13/38 (HLB wasting energies); HLB to Irving Brant 5/20/38 (not disturbed); diary 5/11/38, Clapper papers (plot); HLB (Stone swore), Childs (intent, admitted to HLB) ints.; *Montgomery Journal* [mid 5/38], enclosed with Harry T. Hartwell to HLB 5/20/38 (CEH's regard); ESB, *Rebel,* ch. 7 (great institution); Freund, "Memo" (lifeblood).

10. Diary 5/11/38, Clapper papers (Brandeis); Alexander M. Bickel, *The Unpublished Opinions of Mr. Justice Brandeis* (Cambridge, Mass., 1957), 18 (group action); FF to HLB 8/13/37 (articles), 10/26/37 (books); FF to LDB 5/20/38, FFLC; Graves, *Roanoke* (Va.) *Times* 8/6/58, quoted in *CR* 8/8/58, A7146 (this was in 8/38); Hamilton, "Black's First Year" (fresh air). Brandeis defended Stone's actions toward HLB: Brandeis to FF, 2/11/38, FFLC; also in Melvin I. Urofsky and David W. Levy, eds., *"Half Brother, Half Son": The Letters of Louis D. Brandeis to Felix Frankfurter* (Norman, Okla., 1991), 608.

Chapter 19

SOURCES: Fine, *Murphy;* Mason, *Stone.*

1. HLB to Laski 2/7/39; Cooper int. (describing things); *Polk Co. v. Glover* (determine necessity); William T. Gossett, "The Human Side of Chief Justice Hughes." 59 *Amer. Bar Assoc. Jour.* (1973, sorry to disappoint); FF, *Of Law and Life and Other Things That Matter* (Philip B. Kurland, ed., Cambridge, Mass., 1965), 28 (Professor Frankfurter); WOD, "Judges, Juries and Bureaucrats," speech at Univ. of New Hampshire 10/29/59; Freund, "Memo" (CEH as presiding officer, none like him, follow first line); Luther Hill

(correctly stated), Claude Hamilton (CEH and Christmas tree) ints. Inhale page: WOD, *Court*, 216; Oscar Ewing OH, HSTL, 54.

2. Docket book, WOD papers (hearing case: the vote was 4–3, with Stone and McReynolds also voting to deny, while CEH was not recorded and Butler was ill); JPF to HLB 11/15/ 51 (fearing wrong decision); WODM, 130 (merits); HLB, Cooper ints.; FF to JFB 2/12/40, JBP papers (enduring utterances); John A. Ryan, "Due Process and Mr. Justice Black," *Catholic World* 4/40; *NYT* 2/14/40; Charles A. Beard, *The Republic* (N.Y., 1943), 239; FDR press conference 2/13/40, FDRL. HLB noted by hand on his final circulation that the case was scheduled to come down 2/5.

3. HLB draft in *Schneider v. Irvington* (1939); observations of Chief Justice Hughes, No. 690, OT 1939, FM papers (like skittish horse); JPF, book review, 32 *J. Legal Educ.* 432 (1982, fall of France opinion); *Minersville School Board v. Gobitis* (1940); Brant, *Bill*, 511 (rush of work, notify Stone); Friendly, *Constitution*, 115 (support FF); Sidney Zion conv. (knew wrong); WODM, 48–9; Cooper int. (due process; HLB took detailed notes from Rodney Mott's treatise, *Due Process of Law*, at this time). FF statement: Freund, "Charles Evans Hughes as Chief Justice," 81 *Harv. Law Rev.* 4 (1967); WOD int., FM OHP, UM. Vote: docket book, WOD papers. Assigning opinion: Dilliard int. (immigrant; he had talked with WOD).

4. FM notes 3/30/40, Gressman papers (Murphy); David J. Danelski, "The Role of the Chief Justice" in Walter F. Murphy and C. Herman Pritchett, eds., *Courts, Judges and Politics* (N.Y., 1961, voting); Janeway int. (in awe). Visits to Roberts: Cooper int.; WOD, *Court*, 32; Roberts to FF 8/28/40, FFHLS. Return, 11/40, in *Milk Wagon Drivers' Union v. Lake Valley Co.* (1940, returns of election); Roberts to HLB 7/15/42 (dishes of talk). *Milk Wagon* (1941 picketing case; FF wrote Court's opinion; "banned" is from injunction).

5. Diary 1/21/38, Lilienthal papers, Princeton (importance of court); HLB to WOD 9/15/41, WOD papers (last word); FM notes 6/2/41, Gressman papers (health); HLB to CEH 6/3/41, CEH papers, LC (four years); HLB to Hugh E. Jones 6/28/62 (wonderful lawyer); HLB int. Powell: quoted in FF to Stone 3/17/39, FFHLS; Dilliard int.

6. Book orders, HLBLC (received 6/10/39; HLB especially marked A *Fragment on Government*, 216–24, 240 in HLB Books); Howard, *Murphy*, 269 (ping-pong); TC conv.; FF inscription 10/27/39, in HLB Books; MacLeish to author 9/9/74; FF to Laski 12/19/39, FFLC (greatest possible respect); FF to HLB 1/10/41 (something more important).

7. Notes, *U.S. v. Bethlehem Steel*, FM papers; *U.S. v. Bethlehem Steel* (1942). Letter: Isenberg int.; Frank, *Black*, 205. In 1949 FF wrote: "Legislation is needed which will effectively meet the social obligations of occupational disease" (*Urie v. Thompson*).

8. "Affirm—maybe pass," Murphy recorded for FF; No. 19. O.T. 1940, FM papers, which notes CEH's statement; FF draft opinion of court, Reed papers (freedom of public expression, HLB comments); HLB *Bridges* draft dissent no. 1, repeated almost exactly in draft no. 2 in the 1940 term; HLB notes 7/17/41 (scratch pad); *Bridges v. California* (1941). "Public judgment alone to restrain licentiousness of the press," HLB noted in the margin of a collection of Jefferson's writings, Saul Padover, *The Jefferson Democracy* (N.Y., 1939), which FF gave to him, inscribing it on 5/17/39 "For Hon. Hugo L. Black, a true apostle of Jefferson with the warmest regards of his co-worker, Felix Frankfurter"; HLB Books.

9. HLB int.; JPF to HLB 12/3/49 (understand); FF to CEH 3/1/41, FFLC (400 decisions); HLB draft dissent no. 2, 1940 term (English judges); Jerome Frank, "The Place of the Expert in a Democratic Society" in Barbara Frank Kristein, ed., *A Man's Reach: The*

Selected Writings of Judge Jerome Frank (N.Y., 1965; 1944 speech, went far to dissipate; see Frank to HLB 12/22/41); *NYT* 10/16/43 (attire). "I told Felix to stop using big words that the average lawyer can't understand without going to the dictionary, but he wouldn't listen," Black said later; Skinner int.

10. *Chic., Burlington and Quincy R.R. v. Chic.* (1897); *Gitlow v. N.Y.* (1925); HLB int. (loving Cardozo); Cooper, "Footnotes" (difficulty); FF to HLB 10/31/39, FFLC (FF asking); *Chambers*, 309 U.S. at 235–36 n. 8 (current), n. 9 (footnote). "I was new on the Court," HLB said in 1958 about *Palko*. "In conference Butler made a wonderful statement why this was wrong. It was so good that here was this railroad lawyer saying this while the great Cardozo was on the other side. He didn't convince me but he seemed so full of moderation and common sense and decency. I think that if Butler had written an opinion I would have had to go along." [Calabresi int.]

11. FM papers (HLB-FF at 4/42 conference); *Betts v. Brady* (1942); *Johnson v. Zerbst* (1938, first term); FF to HLB 11/13/43, FFLC (materials). The "fundamental" label came in *Powell v. Alabama* (1932).

12. 1940 case: *Avery v. Alabama. Jones v. Opelika* (1942, see different question) was the HLB, WOD and Murphy dissent. FF: FF, *Mr. Justice Holmes and the Supreme Court* (Cambridge, Mass., 1961), 76 (Holmes philosophy; original ed. 1938); FF to Stone 5/27/40 (agree with distinction), in Mason, *Security* 217 (put in at FF's request; Mason int.); FM conference notes, *Jones v. Opelika*, 1941 term (different question), *Martin v. Struthers*, 1942 term, both FM papers (community barred); HLB draft, no date, FM papers (limits dissemination); JPF int. (persuaded he was wrong).

13. WODM, 51–52 (separated from FF). This falling-out slowly began in the latter days of Hughes's chief justiceship. I base the statement on the Court's conferences on reading all surviving conference notes; see J. Woodford Howard, Jr., "Justice Murphy: The Freshman Years," 18 *Vanderbilt Law Rev.* 473 (1965).

14. Sam Daniels (HLB's clerk), Isenberg ints.; Prichard, book review, *WP Book World* 10/26/75 (personalized); *WP* 10/28/60 (reliable diaries). *Bridges:* written on *Bridges* draft, FFHLS (going mad), which FF repeated for twenty years (FF to JMH 5/19/61, FFLC). On the other, similar remarks, see Harry N. Hirsch, *The Enigma of Felix Frankfurter* (N.Y., 1981), 146–47. At about this time Brandeis told his old friend Stephen Wise that the world will recognize Black as "one of our great jurists and liberals"; Edmund I. Kaufman to HLB 9/28/45. One of FF's greatest admirers, Paul Freund, wrote: "Recoiling from what he regarded as the freewheeling proclivities of certain colleagues, [FF] perhaps leaned backwards in a more conservative posture than would normally have been comfortable for him"; *Proceedings of Mass. Hist. Scty.* 32 (1975).

Chapter 20

SOURCES: Frank, *Black*; Meador, *Black*

1. Jonathan Daniels, *White House Witness, 1942–1945* (Garden City, N.Y., 1975), 28 (feeling of pleasantness); H. J. Haskell, *This Was Cicero: Modern Politics in a Roman Toga* (N.Y., 1942), 74 (jurymen of good sense underlined); HLB to James Rice 1/25/43 (little new); Livy, *The History of Rome* (George Baker trans., 1914), I, 475 (FDR), V, 70 (Pearl Harbor); in HLB Books; Dixie int. (*War and Peace*); HLB to Hudson Strode 7/21/41, Strode papers, UA; HLB; HLB, Southern Conference for Human Welfare speech 11/23/38.

2. HLB int. (Lerner); HLB to Lerner 10/8/43, Lerner papers (Holmes); HLB to HLB, Jr. 10/17/44 (understanding), 11/30/44 (style), 1/12/45 (food for thought). Montaigne, "Of the Institute and Education of Children" in *Harvard Classics*, v. 32, p. 65; George Hellman, *Benjamin N. Cardozo: American Judge* (N.Y., 1940), 130, 139; both HLB Books. In Montaigne HLB also underlined: "It is a natural, simple, and unaffected speech that I love . . ." and "unaccustomed quaint words, proceedeth of a scholastical and childish ambition"; at 65, 66. He had "just one suggestion to all of the present-day philosophers: that they drop the professional jargon of their trade, stop writing for experts, and seek a wider audience by simplifying their terms"; *NYP* 9/11/43.

3. Marx Leva, UA remarks (fifties); Sidney Davis (tennis the menace) in *Confessions*; Salant int.; Carroll Kilpatrick in *BN* 7/14/42 (unknown player); HLB to HLB, Jr. 4/8/43 (practice), 9/18/44 (bragging), 1/17/46 (embarrassed); HLB to HLB, Jr., and SFB 11/2/44 (frightened). Wallace: JBP int.; *NYP* 9/11/43; Wallace, COHP, 1332, 1385, 1530.

4. Fath, Pepper, Hubbard, Smathers (also store), SFB, Irene Hamilton ints.; JPF to A. Powell Davies 12/9/51 (JFB addressing HLB); Hill to Roy Nolen 6/13/42, Hill papers, UA (living with Blacks); *Wash. Times-Herald* 3/27/39, and WS 5/7/39 (American Univ.); JFB diary, 2/23/39 (ominous note) 3/1/39 (edge of razor); HLB to Hazel Davis 3/26/64 (wife told me); WS 11/8/40 (operation); HLB to Barney Whatley 2/21/41. Further tests: JFB diary 3/15/39; diary 3/24/39, Keating papers. Institutionalized: Salinas, Smathers ints.

5. "Proposal I sent to Claude Hamilton, Saturday, April 9, 1938" (originally emphasized); Scottsboro: Allan Knight Chalmers, *They Shall Be Free* (Garden City, N.Y., 1951), 134, 166–67; Hill int.; HLB to JFB 9/17/45 (federal judges); Bass, *Unlikely*, 324–25 (since 1937). James Goodman, *Stories of Scottsboro* (N.Y., 1994), 317. Black's continuing political involvement was common knowledge in Alabama political circles. James Simpson, Hill's 1944 primary opponent, knew of his calls to probate judges and former supporters and contributors; Henry Simpson int. Two aspirants for federal judgeships, Tom Ward and James Rice, wrote HLB asking for his support. Clarence Mullins, who received the Birmingham post in 1943, thanked him for helping him.

6. Reynolds, Dixie (detective stories), Roosevelt, Alsop (Corcoran suggestion), Janeway (may have to run), Monasco (HLB spoke to people) ints.; Pepper, *Eyewitness*, 91 (predicted); JFB diary 6/28/39 (Lee, recounting 6/25/39 dinner), 7/14/39 (FDR lunch); *NY H-T* 8/10/39; diary 4/20/40, Pepper papers (FDR run); WODM, 295–96 (Corcoran and others); Fine, *Murphy*, 193 (Klan); HLB to FDR 7/25/40, and FDR to HLB 9/6/40, FDRL; Robert S. Allen to HLB 10/19/40.

7. Byrnes int. (HLB, Jr., and SFB); WS 10/20/42 (volunteering); CJD to Nancy Lyon 12/5/58, CJD papers (justice and mercy); VFD, *Outside*, 145; JBP papers (yearly depressions); JFB diary, about 1944. Mamie Eisenhower: HLB, Jr., int.; in his book he states without further elaboration that "the wife of a future President" came to Josephine (169). JFB and Mrs. Eisenhower took a Spanish class together during the war.

8. Thomas Corcoran, Jr. (contact), HLB, Jr., SFB (Corcoran) ints.; JFB diary notes 7–8/44 (testosterone). Solicitor General: Niznick, "Corcoran," 524–534; Murphy, *Brandeis–Frankfurter*, 192–193; Lash, *Dealers*, 448–51. Black strongly supported Corcoran for Solicitor General; HLB to FDR 9/10/41, FDRL. Corcoran had access to all sorts of people and political money. It is intriguing to try to figure out which financial sources he might have tapped for a Black campaign. Would Corcoran's good friend (and client) Joseph P. Kennedy, who would have been among the first he approached and was not among Black's favorite people but would have bankrolled any Douglas campaign with pleasure (they served on the

SEC together), have contributed to a Roosevelt-Black ticket? Other Corcoran sources included companies and individuals he represented in the munitions and drug industries.

9. HLB to HLB, Jr. and SFB 11/2/44 (golf); HLB to HLB, Jr. 1/18/45 (ten years); WS 9/25/44 (mother's death); JFB diary, [early 1945] (aimlessness); HLB to JFB 8/24/45 (chewing gum), 8/31/45 (homesick), 8/15/45 (quietness), JBP papers; Smathers int. (gorilla); JFB draft, "The Psychological Menopause" (early 1946), JBP papers. I have combined HLB to JFB 8/4,19/45 (insistence; emphasis in originals), 7/27/45 (cooking), 8/23/45 (De Gaulle). The next night, De Gaulle "did smile once, but I was unable to find what provoked it"; HLB to JFB 8/25/45.

Chapter 21

1. SFB, Price (Hitler), Pepper (Lend Lease draft) ints.; Sherman Minton to HLB [late 2/42] (apprehensions); HLB to WOD 6/11/41, WOD papers (general situation); Ickes, *Diaries*, III, 661 (Pearl Harbor); HLB to JFB 12/8/41; Cooper int. (sons of bitches). Preparedness: HLB to FDR 5/19/40, FDRL; Ickes unpublished diary, 4406, 4474–75, Ickes papers; CJD and VFD OH, tape no. 2, 16–17, LBJL; diary 6/18/40, Pepper papers.

2. Treister int. (fearful); Fine, *Murphy*, 409; Pearson papers (Birmingham investigation); BN, A-H 7/12/42 (rally); John Morton Blum, *V Was for Victory* (N.Y., 1976), 159 (Jap's a Jap); T. H. Watson, *Righteous Pilgrim: The Life and Times of Harold L. Ickes, 1874–1952* (N.Y., 1990), 791 (President authorized); Ronald Steel, *Walter Lippmann and the American Century* (Boston, 1980), 394 (concentration camps); HLB, "Win the War" speech delivered in Raleigh, North Carolina, 7/14/42, in CR, 7/15/42, A2751.Amelia Roberts Fry, "The Warren Tapes: Oral History and the Supreme Court," 1982 *Sup. Ct. Hist. Scty. Yearbook*, notes two submarines in San Luis Obispo and one in San Diego, all "verified in Coast Guard records"; while Earl Warren, California attorney general before being elected governor in 1942, mentions the former as well as two others in his *Memoirs*, 145–46. When Stone in conference stated "concentration camp," none of his colleagues disagreed; Fine, *Murphy*, 438.

3. Conference notes, FM papers (Stone suggestion), WOD papers (evacuation); *Hirabayashi v. U.S.* (1943); FF to Stone 6/4/43, FFLC (Nisei), confirmed in WODM, 161; undated statement, HLBLC (own views). HLB–DeWitt: HLB, Jr., SFB, John L. DeWitt III ints.

4. Peter Irons, *Justice at War: The Story of the Japanese American Internment Cases* (N.Y., 1983), 74 (living conditions); Weaver, *Warren*, 109 (EW quote); conference notes, Reed and WOD papers; *De Funis v. Oregon* (1974, thirty years later); Eugene Gressman to FM 10/24/44, Bumgardner papers (hopping mad); JPF (upset toward Stone, no avail), Cleveland (reservations), Sidney Davis (confining opinion) ints.; WODM 164 (very much discussed); HLB typewritten draft (separate situations), draft 11/8/44 (racial prejudice); RHJ draft 11/30/44, WOD papers (military power and order).

5. Stone contact and total exclusion: Irons, 344–45; Fine, *Murphy*, 452; HLB to WOD, n.d., in WOD, *Court*, 35 (complete satisfaction); Davis int. (military necessity); WODM, 164 (reluctance); HLB typewritten draft, n.d. (immediately suspect); *Korematsu v. U.S.* (1944); Murphy, *American*, 62–72. WOD's later regret: WOD, *Court*, 280; WODM, 359.

6. HLB to Lawrence Drasin 1/19/56 (slight differences); NYT 9/26/71 (1967); Davis int.

Chapter 22

SOURCES: Fine, *Murphy;* Harper, *Rutledge;* Howard, *Murphy;* Janeway, "Douglas"; Mason, *Stone;* WODM.

1. Nickerson (Stone and FF), JPF (HLB-WOD), Buschman (happy to serve), Roosevelt ints.; Ernest Cuneo to WOD 8/12/68, WOD papers (Murphy quote); JPF int. (HLB-WOD); FR, "The Supreme Court Today," *Progressive* 10/4/43 (thinks with heart); Ickes, *Diaries,* III, 417, 425 (coveted); Pusey, *Hughes,* II, 787–88 (invaluable). I base my observation on the conference discussion on reading all available conference notes.

2. Gerhart, *Jackson,* 241 (HLB–RHJ at first); Ickes unpublished diary, 6062–63 (RHJ praise of HLB), 6674 (no longer liberal), 7595 (temporary), Ickes papers. Tax case: *Helvering v. Griffiths* (1943); Mendelson, *Conflict,* 33, in HLB Books (1961). Possibility of resigning: Ickes diary, 8477–78, 9439, 9475. FF and enemies: Lash int. with Louis Henkin, Lash papers; Hand, COHP. RHJ even chided HLB in a case in which he (RHJ) did not participate (*U.S. v. Bethlehem*), and "often had biting things to say about Black" after returning from conference, recalled Philip Neal, his clerk in 1943 and 1944 (RHJ to WOD 2/9/42, WOD papers; Neal int.).

3. Docket book, WOD papers (incorrect); WOD memorandum to Stone, 1/5/44 Stone papers (January 3); *Federal Power Commission v. Hope Natural Gas Co.* (rate-making case); returns in *Helvering v. Sabine Trans. Co.* (1943, naked and exposed); *Cochran v. Kansas* (1942); JPF to HLB 5/29/68 (evenings). Case could come down: Gressman int. "Good opinion! See [several pages] for carping and ill-natured comments. Do as you damn please about them," Roberts wrote about HLB's 1942 opinion in *Ex parte Kawato.* "Roberts told Black that Murphy was leaking, not Douglas, and that Black had to choose between Murphy, his ally, and Roberts, his friend, and he chose his ally." So Black, Douglas and Rutledge told John Frank (int.) the story.

4. *Smith v. Allright* (1944, Roberts dissent); HLB to SFB 2/25/44 (differences, familiar with Court history); HLB to HLB Jr. 1/11/44 (rift).

5. HLB opinion: draft 2/26/45 (proposed release date; next proposed release date was 4/3; *U.S. v. South-Eastern Underwriters Association* (1944); "Mr. Justice Black" [6/44], Jerome Frank papers (holler head off); Gerhart, *Jackson,* 493 n. 80 (Pearson prediction); diary 2/25/66, Pearson papers (transcript); Luce int. (Stone-clerks).

6. Dick Howard, who had been a Rhodes Scholar at Oxford, inscribing *Journeys Through Foreign Lands* (1963) in HLB Books; Redlich int. (too long; the case was *Abington v. Schempp* [1963]); Joseph Goldstein, *The Intelligible Constitution* (N.Y., 1992), 112 (momma); WS 5/16/54 (judicial sins); HLB to JMH, no date, JMH papers (unintelligible, about *Konigsberg v. Calif.* [1957]); ESB to HLB, Jr., SFB and JPB 12/18/59 in ESB, *Rebel* (sits at desk).

7. McNulty int. (wanted someone); HLB to Nicholas Johnson 10/10/60 (bound to make man); HLB to EC 12/13/57, EC papers (person who gives greatest promise). Most of HLB's clerks felt he did not need a clerk: as several said, "he had almost total recall, of cases and almost anything else."

8. Ernest Cuneo to WOD 8/12/68, WOD papers (heil; Murphy told this to Cuneo, who noted that his "voice was like a boy reciting how the school bully was whipped. . . . I

think he said Mr. Justice Black was equally definitive"); Cooper, Beyer (imitate HLB) ints.

9. WOD never wanted to be candidate: "Statement" (WOD's answers to his own questions), attached to WOD to E. Palmer Hoyt (publisher of *The* [Portland] *Oregonian*) 7/12/44, Hoyt papers. He repeated this on many occasions: Urofsky, *Douglas*, 215–16; WOD to Stone 7/12/44, Stone papers. Haber int. (no justice should do that); WOD to HLB 7/23/41 (nothing but opportunity).

10. *United Public Workers v. Mitchell* (1947, legislation muzzling); conference notes, no. 804, O.T. 45, FM papers (Reed quote); Edward N. Beiser, "The Misread Milestone: *Colegrove v. Green*," *N.Y. State Bar Jour.* 8/67 (WOD quote); Haber int. (clerks ganging up, egalitarianism); *Colegrove v. Green* (1946; FF opinion); Yarbrough, "Justice Black and Equal Protection," 9 *Southwestern Univ. Law Rev.* 899 (1977; Whig planters); Anthony Lewis, "Mr. Justice Black," *NYT* 9/20/71 (crazy). Another contemporary example of Black's political essence is *McDonald v. Commissioner*, a 1944 tax case in which the Court upheld not allowing a judge to deduct campaign expenses. This was incorrect "unless our democratic philosophy is wrong . . . ," he wrote in dissent. "Without monetary rewards office-holding would necessarily be limited to one class only—the independently wealthy."

11. FM, conference notes, no. 114, O.T. 1945, FM papers, which also records FF as saying: "I am inclined to Black's interpretation. A company town: it is private in same [way] a house is private. Here you have political community operating as such"; *Marsh v. Alabama* (1946); Haber int. (dropping idea); *Associated Press v. U.S.* (1945); FF to HLB, n.d., 1945 term (Jefferson). "Yes sir," FF noted on the return of HLB's opinion in *Marsh*, which did not prevent him from submitting a concurring opinion. In a 1943 opinion HLB had written of the right to distribute literature and "the right to receive it"; *Martin v. Struthers*.

Chapter 23

SOURCES: "Summaries of Conversations (Thomas G. Corcoran)," FBI wiretaps of Corcoran's office telephone, June 1, 1945–May 1947, HSTL; Frank, *Black*; Gerhart, *Jackson*; Hutchinson, "Feud"; WODM; Edwin M. Yoder, Jr., "Black vs. Jackson": A Study in Judicial Enmity" in *The Making of a Whig—And Other Essays in Self-Definition* (Wash., D.C., 1990).

1. Irving Brant to Luther Ely Smith 6/5/46 (slowing down), Brant to Alpheus T. Mason 7/22/51 (conservative), both Brant papers. Dinner: *WS* 3/3/45, 4/2/45. Max Lerner had recently asked Jackson to speak at an upcoming National Citizens Political Action Committee dinner. "Regret impossibility [to] attend January 31 [1946] meeting . . . ," Jackson cabled. "Wish I could be there . . ."; Lerner to RHJ 12/17/45; RHJ to Lerner 12/18/45, HLBLC.

2. Reed to Stone 3/12/45 (Reed changing mind); FM to RHJ [probably 4/6/45] (delaying case); RHJ to FM and FM response on bottom [probably 4/6 or 4/7/45] (accommodating others), all RHJ papers; Eugene Nickerson to HLB 6/11/46 (legislative history irrelevant); Howard, *Murphy*, 392 (quoting out of context); HLB to members of conference 5/5/45 (different version). Vote: docket books, Reed, WOD papers; conference notes, FM papers. Jackson drafting Act: Lash, *Dealers*, 335–36, 341; Louchheim, *Making*, 86. *Jewell Ridge Coal Company v. Local No. 6167, United Mine Workers* (1945); previous year's case: *Tennessee Coal Co. v. Muscoda Local* (1944). On rushing opinions: for FF see *N.B.C. v. U.S.* (1943); Stone, *In re Yamashita* (1946); and FM, *S.E.C. v. Chenery Corp.* (1947).

No contemporaneous evidence exists for RHJ's later claim that only Stone's "vigorous" protest prevented the decision from coming down before negotiations ended; memorandum 5/46, RHJ papers.

3. Gartner (approving HLB sitting, RHJ in conference; also noting "Jackson had a desperate sense of independence"), Brant (WR), Girard (HLB on RHJ) ints.; HLB to Stone 6/11/45; Reed OH, FV OHP, UK; HLB to Robert Girard 9/23/60 (new votes; originally emphasized); HLB to HLB, Jr. 10/2/44 (getting angry); WS 5/16/46 (HLB reacted); NYT 6/11/46 (according to RHJ); Jewell Ridge, 325 U.S. at 897 (denied rehearing).

4. HLB to Jesse B. Hearin 4/16/45 (faces of people); diary 4/14/45, Pepper papers (dining); Rucker int. with CJD (big enough); Roberts to FF [about 9/44], FFHLS (guess). Goodrich: Wolkin, Goodrich, Herbert Wechsler, Burton clerks ints. HLB to JFB 9/17/45, JBP papers (insisted); HST inscription in HSTL (originally emphasized). "Wanted Minton on Supreme Court," HST wrote of HLB's visit; HSTL. If HST were to appoint a Republican, Black would have preferred Vermont Senator Warren Austin; Corcoran-HLB conv. 8/30/45, FBI wiretaps. Goodrich told the story of his near appointment to his law clerks, nearly all of whom went on to clerk for Burton, who was the Circuit Justice on which Goodrich sat. So certain did it seem that he had already started to look for a house in Washington. If he had been in Burton's place, the Supreme Court would have been decidedly more efficient and its opinions more liberal.

5. HST to Bess Truman 7/26/35, in Ferrell, ed., Dear Bess: The Letters from Harry to Bess Truman, 1910–1959 (N.Y., 1983), 374 (people's friends); HST to HLB 11/20/40 (to see you); HST to Oscar L. Chapman 4/3/45, HLBLC (country); Corcoran–Brant conv. 9/10/45, FBI wiretaps (best man). Truman investigation: Reynolds (praise), HLB, Jr. (HST at house) ints.; Blum, Wallace, 616 (excellent work). HLB to JFB 8/23/45, JBP papers (HST's conduct).

6. Luther Hill (mistake; "it made a travesty of the judicial system," HLB added), Pepper (nervous), Gardner (shocking) ints.; Wyzanski, Whereas, 188, 190 in HLB Books; HLB to JFB 8/26/45, JBP papers (Jackson's Court; "(?)" is in original).

7. Arthur T. Vanderbilt II, Changing Law: A Biography of Arthur T. Vanderbilt (New Brunswick, N.J.), 1976), 216 n.66; Ferrell, Truman, 64 (good man); HST to RHJ 5/1/46, HSTL (outstanding job); Clifford (successor), Freeman (WOD better one) ints.; JPF to HLB 11/12/49 (anything on earth); Pepper, HER ints.; Hill to William C. Taylor 4/30/46; John Bankhead to Taylor 5/1/46, both HLBLC; HLB to Minton 6/14/46. Nominating for chief justice: Corcoran–Mrs. Stanley Reed conv. 4/30/46; FBI wiretaps; Francis Shea to RHJ 5/17/46, RHJ papers. Not a candidate: HLB to Irving Engel, to Sidney Davis (also future course), both 4/29/46.

8. Corcoran–Ernest Cuneo conv. 4/28/46; Corcoran-Hill, WOD, Reed convs. 4/30/46, 5/5/46; Corcoran–James H. Rowe ["'Rowan"] conv. 5/2/46 (Rowe's contacts), all FBI wiretaps; Pearson column, WP 4/24/46 (two members); Ickes unpub. diaries, 9475 (retiring year before); JPF to FR 5/25/46, FR private papers (Hannegan assuring visitor); Reed OH, FV OHP, UK (Reed wanting chief justiceship; he referred to it several times); HLB to JPF 12/4/48 (either satisfactory, unfortunate); WP 5/4/46 (no hurry).

9. WS 5/16/46 (Fleeson column); White House telephone logs 5/17/46 (talk to WOD), 5/23,29, 31/46 (Rosenman), HSTL; Cooper, ed., "Sincerely your friend" . . . Hugo L. Black: Letters of Mr. Justice Hugo L. Black to Jerome A. Cooper (Univ., Ala., 1973), 4 (prevented RHJ's appointment); Shea to RHJ 5/17/46, RHJ papers. "Bill Douglas went to Truman," HLB

told Hugo, Jr. (int.). Except for Hill's visit and Douglas's call to Truman, White House records, necessarily incomplete, contain no indication of any justice or possible "representative" thereof seeing or calling the president or any staff member from the time Stone died until the beginning of the Court's next term. But Fleeson's column served Black's purpose of making certain Jackson would not be nominated.

10. TC OH, HSTL, 52, 54; Clifford, *Counsel*, 72 (poker companion); TGC–Pearson conv. 5/4/46, FBI wiretaps (not too interested); Eben Ayers diary 12/2/47, HSTL (Vinson knew); Clifford int. (serve, rather doubt); LBJ on CBS program on HST 12/26/72 (HST–FV conv., author's notes).

11. HER (shot from hip), JPF (pissmire, no response) ints.; Harper, *Rutledge*, 315; Eugene Gressman to Lady [Eleanor Bumgardner] 6/17/46, Bumgardner papers (thoroughly disgusted, last thing, never say anything); Reed to FF 7/8/46, FFLC; Sidney Davis to WOD 6/30/46, WOD papers (right thing); RHJ to FF 6/19/46 (step); Francis Biddle to FF 12/10/62 (admired Bob), both FFLC; Ferrell, *Bess*, 525 (haywire).

12. Robert S. Allen to HLB 6/11/46; Minton to HLB 6/12/46; HLB to Minton 6/14/46 (same thoughts recurred in several letters at the time); JPF int. (corner); JPF, "Disqualification of Judges," 56 *Yale Law Jour.* 605 (1947); HST to Bess Truman 6/22/46, in Ferrell, *Bess*, 528; HLB to JPF 5/11/48 (small event); Lamb (nothing), Wozencraft (understand) ints.; HLB to Cooper 6/20/46 in Cooper, "*Sincerely*." Minton's reference is to *U.S. v. Butler* (1936), which declared the New Deal's AAA farm program unconstitutional; Pepper, a lifelong friend of Roberts, had recommended to Herbert Hoover his appointment to the Court: Pearson column 6/21/46.

Chapter 24

1. HLB (study), JPF (FF invented) ints. The lost article was likely Louis Boudin, "Truth and Fiction about the Fourteenth Amendment," 16 *New York Univ. Law. Quar. Rev.* 19 (1938).

2. *Malinski v. N.Y.* (coerced confession case); HLB to court 3/23/45 (broad judicial power); Arthur S. Miller and Jeffrey H. Bowman, " 'Slow Dance on the Killing Ground': The *Willie Francis* Case Revisited," 38 *DePaul Law Rev.* 1 (1983); HLB on Reed return 12/17/46 (disagreed); WOD to Reed 12/20/46 (switched); Reed draft 1/2/47 (HLB decided to note concurrence, all Reed papers; HLB draft 1/3/47 (ample historical support).

3. Conference: docket book, Burton papers; conference notes, WOD, FM papers; Fine, *Murphy*, 501–02 (did not vote); HLB int. (think it is); Zion int. with HLB (if I didn't find); CR (3/29/37, 2828 (no charge against integrity); *Adamson v. California* (1947). "Everybody else called it either one or the other so I just put a dash in between and called it due-process-natural-law"; HLB int. (see U.S. 332 at 90).

4. Oberdorfer (scholarship), Henkin (trying to change world) ints.; *Adamson*, 332 U.S. at 67–68; FF to HLB 11/13/43, FFLC (twenty years).

5. Fairman, "Does the Fourteenth Amendment Incorporate the Bill of Rights? The Original Understanding," 2 *Stanford Law Rev.* 5 (1949); HLB to JPF 1/10/50 (originally emphasized); Feeney (FF got Fairman), HLB (Harvard job) int.; HLB to Charles P. Curtis 4/6/59 (Fairman's arguments). Fairman was then teaching at Stanford; he moved to Harvard in 1955. "Warren Christopher, the editor in chief of the *Stanford Law Review*, suggested that I write it," he said (int.). "I wrote it as straight as I could." When it appeared the next year,

Christopher was clerking for Douglas. Neither he nor Black mentioned it, "but Frankfurter did, saying how very good it was," Christopher recalled (int.).

6. *Rochin v. California* (1952); FF to Vinson 11/29/51 (kind of instrument), FFHLS; Silverstein, *Faiths*, 161 (puke); FF draft, *Rochin*, 12/4/51; Vann (FF nicest guys), Daniels (gangster trial) ints.; planned *Rochin* concurrence, HLBLC (rounded periods, originally emphasized).

7. North (read proceedings), HLB (history one-sided) ints.; Freund, *Supreme*, 46; *Bickel, Least*, 102 (HLB read it in 1966), both in HLB Books; *Duncan v. Louisiana* (originally emphasized; the opinion as published is largely HLB's clerk's second draft).

Chapter 25

sources: Fine, *Murphy;* Landynski, *Search;* Note, "The 'Released Time' Cases Revisited: A Study of Group Decisionmaking by the Supreme Court," 83 *Yale Law Jour.* 1202 (1974).

1. *Everson* conference: conference notes, FM papers (also Burton and RHJ switch); FF to JMH 1/12/65, JMH papers (FF due process remark); HLB–WR drafts: HLBLC; Harper, *Rutledge*, 348; Charles A. Beard, *The Republic* (N.Y., 1943), 165, in HLB Books (marked); HLB to Clarence Mullins 11/11/43 (great book); Cohen, *Constitutional*, 627–28. The image of a wall was old. Roger Williams, who established the colony of Rhode Island early in the seventeenth century, wrote of a *"wall of separation* between the garden of the church and the wilderness of the world" which would shield the church from the state; quoted in Leonard W. Levy, *The Establishment Clause: Religion and the First Amendment* (N.Y., 1986), 184. (originally emphasized). Jefferson made it part of the American heritage when he spoke of "a wall of separation between church and state": he sought to protect the state from the church.

2. Brant to WR 3/11/47, Brant papers; Hobbs (RHJ would have), Oberdorfer (victory) ints.; Freund, "Memo" (verge); HLB to Lerner 3/11/49, Lerner papers. HLB wrote a disappointed ex-clerk: "I suggest you read it again, however, and see if the majority opinion did not give 'weight to the basically religious nature of Catholic education.' The majority opinion did not treat bus transportation as synonymous with education nor did it consider bus transportation as of a 'basically religious nature' ": to Charles Luce 4/2/47.

3. *McCollum v. Board of Education;* HLB to Burton 1/6/48; FF to WR 1/28/48, WR papers (FF draft opinion); FF memorandum for conference 2/11/48 (delete references); HLB memorandum for conference 2/12/48 (just been handed memorandum); HLB to WR and Burton 2/12/48 (agree on basis of *Everson*); Allen Drury, *A Senate Journal 1943–1945* (N.Y., 1963), 32 (look upon world); HLB draft 3/3/48 (removing).

4. HLB to Lerner 3/1/49; Levy, *Establishment*, xv; HER int. (Toland). "Get volume 1" was written on Peter Masten Dunne to HLB 9/25/47; Dunne, a history professor at University of San Francisco, castigated his opinion in *Everson.* Black "was personally assailed by Catholics, by fundamentalists, by preachers and by politicians," noted his clerk. "The most violent and spiteful letters evoked in him only pity and sympathy for the writers. The Judge would chuckle as he read the blasts from the politicians, many of whom were his personal friends. He knew which ones were using the Court as a whipping boy in their election campaigns": William Joslin in *Confessions*.

5. Gressman int. (HLB–RHJ conv.); WODM, 223 (took HLB on); Donovan, *Conflict*, 28 (fuzzy-minded); HLB to JPF 1/2/47 (new Chief).

6. Agronsky (FF), Ares (WOD), Gressman (FM–HLB), Haber (HLB on WR), Hobbs (not talk much), Joslin (disappointment in FF), ints.; Mac Asbill, Jr., OH, 4, Reed OH (Reed on HLB); Melvin I. Urofsky, "Getting the Job Done: William O. Douglas and Collegiality in the Supreme Court" in Stephen L. Wasby, ed., *"He Shall Not Pass This Way Again": The Legacy of William O. Douglas* (Pittsburgh, 1990), 42 (lowest form); Arthur M. Schlesinger, Jr., "The Supreme Court: 1947," *Fortune* 1/47; Jerome Frank to Schlesinger 1/22/47, Frank papers. Law clerks to all justices joked that Black's clerk got more out of Douglas than even his own clerk because Douglas grunted twice to him in the hall. Black recommended Schlesinger's *Age of Jackson* to several people at the time. "Judge in accord with views. Likes to talk with him" is noted of Schlesinger in a card file in HLBLC.

7. WOD to HLB, HLB to WOD 5/7/48, WOD papers (the case was *Parker v. Ill.*); *Saia v. N.Y.* (1948; sound truck dissent); *Kovacs v. Cooper* (1949; "basic premise" quote; HLB indicated that he would accept a reasonably drawn ordinance limiting the time, place and volume of public speaking devices, but could not agree to what he saw as absolute prohibition); docket books, Reed, WOD papers (5–4 vote); return, 2/5/49 (FF); WR to HLB 3/10/49 (hard to get around); *Giboney v. Empire Ice & Storage Co.* (1949; Frank's handwriting is on the drafts he reviewed).

8. *Friedman v. Schwellenbach* (1947, reasonable doubt); *Feldman v. U.S.* (1944, flat prohibition, ordinary criminals, surprising); conference notes, *Goldstein v. U.S.* (1942, remarks in conference); HLB, *Memoirs*, 38 (soldiers); *U.S. v. Wallace & Tiernan Co.* (1949, extraordinary sanction); *Felix Frankfurter Reminisces*, Harlan B. Phillips, ed. (N.Y., 1960), 49 (FF passion on fourth amendment); conference notes, *Harris v. N.Y.* (1947), FM papers (nuts about it); HLB handwritten draft (wisdom of rule); JPF, "The United States Supreme Court, 1948–49," 17 *Univ. of Chic. Law Rev.* 1, 35 (1949). *Wolf* conference: docket books, Reed, WOD papers; *Wolf v. Colorado* (1949).

9. James William Moore quoted in Harold Chesnin and Geoffrey C. Hazard, Jr., "Chancery Procedure and the Seventh Amendment: Jury Trial of Issues in Equity Cases Before 1791," 83 *Yale Law Jour.* 999 (1974, jury trial like rock music); HLB to John R. Brown 6/28/62 (outside boundary); *Southern Pacific Co. v. Arizona* (1945); *Hood & Sons v. Du Mond* (1949, Siamese twins); *Lincoln Fed. Labor Union v. Northwestern Iron & Metal Co.* (1949, deliberately discarded); *Morgan v. Virginia* (1946, state law requiring segregation).

10. Paul Porter OH, LBJL (legal talent); motion for stay, *Johnson v. Stevenson*, Mildred Steagall papers, LBJL (Fortas); HLB OH, LBJL (dozen years); Hobbs, HLB, Jr. (stole), Moody (Moody felt) ints.; Marshall McNeil, "How Fortas Gave LBJ His Start," *WDN* 8/3/65 (granting stay). HLB's order: *Johnson v. Stevenson*, 9/29/48, FV papers. Court upholding stay: *Johnson v. Stevenson* (1948, supplemental motion for stay submitted by Johnson denied; and motion by Stevenson to vacate Black's order and to dismiss proceedings denied); *Stevenson v. Johnson* (1949, certiorari denied). HLB also permitted six Washington reporters for Texas newspapers to be present at the argument.

11. Kalman, *Fortas*, 202 (Rauh); Ronnie Dugger, *The Politician: The Drive for Power from the Frontier to the Master of the Senate* (N.Y., 1982), 336–37 (HLB denying Rayburn); Robert Dallek, *Lone Star Rising: Lyndon Johnson and His Times, 1908–1960* (N.Y., 1991), 341 (Clark); James Reston, Jr., *The Lone Star: The Life of John Connally* (N.Y., 1989), 154 (Truman). Porter, one of the guests, said that LBJ concluded: "That is not really the reason for this birthday party. But it sure as God is the reason I am giving it"; Porter OH, 16. But many of those present recall it differently.

Chapter 26

SOURCE: HLB, Jr., *Father*.

1. HLB to Hill 11/14/46; Hill int.; Ray Jenkins, "Hitting' the Comeback Trail with Alabama's Big Jim," *NYT* 5/4/74 (greatest man); HLB to Folsom 1/29/47. Chinese art story: New Orleans newspaper, [spring 1947], HLBLC. HLB amended this to "ancient Chinese art. And these days I'm not so sure that's a safe subject": *BN* (7/50), HLB file, BPL.

2. HLB to Freda Kirchwey 12/28/44; HLB to Horace Bresler 7/19/45 (UN conference); Blum, *Wallace*, 536–37 (Alsop dinner), 615–17 (Cohen, straight for war, voted right); HLB to Homer Bone 9/5/46; Reynolds int. (Hiroshima); HLB to Charles A. Madison 12/9/65 (Wallace poor politician). Los Angeles speech: *LAT, WS* 6/23/45, reprinted in *CR* 7/19/45, A3814; HLB sent a copy of the speech to Truman. "In spite of the fact that it is not an iron-clad guarantee against war," HLB wrote Barney Whatley 7/25/45, the United Nations charter "is a substantial move in that direction. It was because so many people were trying to undermine our efforts to obtain peace that I went to California to make the speech I did. . . . I grew weary of having pessimists constantly exclaim that we must get ready for a war with Russia. I do not want to get ready for a war with any country in the world again."

3. HLB to HLB, Jr. 3/2/46 (own belief); HLB OH, LBJL (pretty high); HLB to Edward B. Pedlow 6/5/52 (high principles). Durr: HLB to editor, *Nation* 4/18/66 [also *CR* 4/28/66, A2309] (one of best men, fight for Senate confirmation); CJD, "Black" (mindlessly cruel); John A. Salmond, *The Conscience of a Lawyer: Clifford J. Durr and American Civil Liberties, 1899–1975* (Tuscaloosa, Ala., 1990), 117–21; CJD to Saul Carson 1/24/66 (regrets); to HST 11/30/55 (tear country); to HST 11/30/55 (not happy), all CFD papers; CFD int. (take ball away); HSTL (HST calling HLB); CFD to HLB 3/10/66 (purpose). Amend program: CFD to Irving Brant, 3/20/63 CFD papers; CJD to HLB. HLB–CFD: CFD int. Durr saw Truman at HST's request.

4. HLB to CJD 3/1/66, enclosing draft of letter to *Nation* (greatness of character); *Nation* 4/18/66 (came out); HLB to Lawrence G. Wallace 11/15/61 (makes fights); Parker int. (martyr). Black's letter came in response to a *Nation* editorial which, upon congratulating Durr on receiving a civil liberties award, also stated, "Durr's career came to an end when he boldly quoted the Constitution to Harry Truman . . ."; 2/21/66. "I wanted to concur in the good things it said about you and wanted also, at the same time, to straighten out the editor about you and Harry Truman," HLB wrote CJD. He meant the letter "as a memorial of my high regard for both of you": draft of HLB to CFD 3/10/66. Truman likewise noted his "high regard for Cliff Durr" when Black sent him this draft for his comments; HST to HLB 3/24/66.

5. Hobbs, Wozencraft (justices and politics), ESB (Eisenhower) ints. Dinner for Douglases: Frances Arnold, HLB family ints. Going to Alabama: VH int. with Locke, VH papers; Ray, Nolen and Locke ints. Presidency: Allgood (Hill on HLB), Clifford (Truman lacked confidence; see Clifford, *Counsel*, 188) ints. Clifford said this shortly after David McCullough had written that Truman had decided to run "by late autumn 1947"; *Truman* (N.Y., 1992), 586. The Speaker of the Alabama House of Representatives wrote Truman: "I think we will be able to control the situation and send a Truman delegation to the Convention"; William M. Beck to Truman 2/13/48, HSTL. On McCorvey, see Grafton, *Folsom*, 54.

6. Diary 5/14/48, Pepper papers (all against Truman; "Not a word favorable to Truman was

heard": Pepper, *Eyewitness*, 159); Hobbs (happy), HST, Jr. (discussed race with HST) ints.; HLB to Minton 12/13/48 (heard HST talk); HLB to HST 11/4/48, HSTL (grand victory, originally emphasized); HST to HLB 11/9/48 (want to see you); HLB to Pedlow 11/8/48 (what happened other day); HLB to Irving Engel 11/22/48 (illness); HLB to HLB, Jr. 11/8/48 (weak-kneed Democrats).

7. JBP int. (never felt same); HLB to Luce 12/15/50 (mistake to go to Korea); HLB to David Vann 2/15/51 (some hope); HLB to JPF 4/17/51 (relieving MacArthur); Robert W. Barnett OH, 37–38, HSTL. "I wouldn't have fought in Korea"; unedited transcript, 1968 CBS int., Benjamin papers.

8. JPB (Miami), CJD (done everything), Haber (see how good), Cooper (do anything) ints.; JBP papers (constant headaches); JFB to HLB, Jr. [about 1944], (conscious of forces); HLB to ALS 12/13/45 (not erased debt); Smith to HLB 12/19/45 (restructuring).

9. HLB to SFB 4/11/44 (pretty gay experience), 1/25/45 (Chandler), to HLB, Jr. 1/25/45 (association with people); HLB family ints. (HLB drinking); HLB to SFB 1/25/45 (Chandler). New York trip: Zion int. with HLB (originally emphasized). Florida dinner: George W. Healy, Jr., *A Life On Deadline* (Gretna, La., 1976), 178; Healy, "Hugo Black Laughed," *New Orleans Times-Picayune* 9/28/71. Funeral: Bennett Cerf, "Laughter—The Best Medicine: A Selection of Stories by Bennett Cerf," *Reader's Digest* 2/48. Tennis: Bresler, "Champ" (more time); HLB to Luce 9/19/45 (find out), 12/27/45 (tonic); HLB to Austin Rice 5/7/52 (endurance); JBP int. (Budge); HLB to sons 6/7/50 (going strong). Of his sons' defeating him, he noted, "I am looking forward with no pleasure to the day that event occurs"; HLB to SFB 5/13/50.

10. HLB to HLB, Jr. 2/28/45 (so-called intellectuals), 10/12/45 (inviting career), 3/1/49 (aspires to lead), 11/6/46 (more work), 11/20/45 (inclination to brood), 3/21/45 (slave to desires), 2/15/51 (useful in career), 3/12/51 (Cicero); Haber int. (Alabama friend and Oxford); HLB to Richard T. Rives 9/10/48 (Yale training); HLB to W. R. Withers 1/10/50 (welcome ideas); HLB to Charles Luce 12/29/48 (tendency). I am indebted to David McCullough's discussion of Theodore Roosevelt's asthma, strikingly parallel to Hugo, Jr.'s, situation except in its severity, in his *Mornings on Horseback* (N.Y., 1981), ch. 4 ("A Disease of the Direst Suffering"). Hugo, Jr. "will go back to Yale quite a different young man from the one who was compelled to come home at the end of the last session on account of asthma," HLB wrote Fred Rodell 10/8/47.

11. HLB to HLB, Jr. 11/29/49 (narrow views), 2/2/50 (best lawyer), 4/1/50 (speech), 10/24/49 (helping Hill), 2/6/50 (hot discussion), 4/8/43 (candidate after war), 5/13/50 (economic issues, best preparation).

12. JBP int. (popular); HLB to Edward H. Levi 3/4/71 (graduate of Sweet Briar). JoJo party: WP 6/20/51; *Chic. Sun-Times* 6/17/51; Ruth Montgomery column, undated, in Bumgardner papers; HLB to SFD 4/11/44. Josephine was visiting Sterling at the time. "I still think it would have been better for her to go to some place like Sweet Briar," HLB wrote when JoJo was a junior; HLB to VFD 10/28/53.

Chapter 27

1. Fine, *Murphy*, 582 (RHJ doggerel); JPF, book review, 19 *Georgia Law Rev.* 777 1985 (right reason); David Caute, *The Great Fear* (N.Y., 1978), 28 (internal security); WOD to HLB

8/15/49 (gnawing away). HLB wrote a short tribute to Murphy ["Mr. Justice Murphy," 48 *Mich. Law Rev.* 739 (1950)], which he found "a little difficult because I cannot say so many of the things I would like to"; HLB to JPF 11/2/49.

2. Abell, *Pearson*, 75 (old, retire); Simon, *Douglas*, 281 (WOD live). FM–WR: Bumgardner, "Re Frank Murphy," Bumgardner papers: *WDN* 9/15/49, which also reported that en route to Murphy's funeral, a lawyer stopped Rutledge to say, "Please keep in mind. I want to take the Justice's place." Rutledge replied: "I wish I could arrange that with the undertaker." Rejecting FM–WR: JPF, *Marble Palace: The Supreme Court in American Life* (N.Y., 1958), 190. Results: JPF, "Supreme Court, 1949–50"; Irving Dilliard, "Change on the Supreme Court: An Instance Appraised" in Ronald K. L. Collins, ed., *Constitutional Government in America* (Durham, N. C., 1980). Small docket: JPF, "The United States Supreme Court, 1950–1951," 19 *Univ. of Chic. Law Rev.* 165, 166 (1951). Dilliard, *St. L. P-D* editorial page editor and already a longtime perceptive Supreme Court watcher, was the first to note this development publicly, in an 10/23/49 editorial, "Something to Watch." He sent it to HLB, who replied, "Naturally I found it interesting," which, coming from a Supreme Court justice, meant agreement; HLB to Dilliard 11/2/49.

3. Sherman Minton, book review, 24 *Indiana Law Jour.* 299 (1949, Fourteenth Amendment); HLB to Minton 11/3/49 (early effort; the case was *Commissioner v. Connelly* [1949]); David N. Atkinson, *Mr. Justice Minton and the Supreme Court, 1949–1956* (Ph.D. dissertation, Univ. of Iowa, 1969), 67 (hidebound), 108 (Shay talk); HLB to Carl A. Hatch 10/24/49, CB papers (grand fellow); Paul int. (baseball antitrust case); HLB to JPF 11/17/49 (information).

4. Wozencraft int. (man of the people); WOD to HLB 10/20/49. Whatley arranged: Whatley to HLB 1/9/50; see Alva A. Swain, "Under the Capitol Dome," *Rocky Mountain News* (Denver) 2/1/50. WS 7/5/51 (Declaration of Independence; HLB saved this article); Fred J. Cook, *The Nightmare Decade* (N.Y., 1971), 20 (three-year-old girl); *Dennis v. U.S.* (1950). Perlman: Wozencraft in *Confessions*; JPF, "Supreme Court, 1949–50."

5. JBP int. (always right); *American Communications Association v. Douds* (1950); HLB to Truman Hobbs 2/14/51 (people get frightened); HLB, "Lawyer" (obsession); HLB to JPF 3/13/51 (stifle views); written on final opinion in *Feiner v. N.Y.* (1951, ingenuity of policeman); *Breard v. Alexandria* (1951, hobbling of ideas); *Breard* draft opinion (new philosophy).

6. Michael Belknap, *Cold War Political Justice: The Smith Act, The Communist Party, and American Civil Liberties* (Westport, Conn. 1977), 80–82 (prosecution has no proof); conference notes, 12/9/50, WOD papers.

7. Luther Hill, Treister ints.; *Joint Anti-Fascist Refugee Committee v. McGrath* (1951; concurring opinion). So thankful was Black for popular support that when two editors, Dilliard of the *St.L. P-D* and James A. Wechsler of the *NYP*, sent him their editorials (the only other major newspaper backing his position was the *Louisville Courier-Journal*), he addressed each editor as "My dear Mr. . . . ," which he did very infrequently.

8. Oberdorfer and Cleveland ints. (framers); HLB to HLB, Jr. 6/12/51 (very happy). Besides his usual rereading of ancient classics, HLB found Werner Jaeger's multi-volume *Paideia: The Ideals of Greek Culture* "absorbingly interesting"; HLB to EC 7/22/51, who had sent the books to him.

9. JFB to SFB Thursday [12/6/51], CB papers (get west); HLB family ints. After JFB death: Daniels, Cooper, Berman (went to death), Cahn, Oberdorfer (leaving Court) ints. HLB

to Max Lerner 3/12/52, Lerner papers; to Sterling J. Foster 3/18/52; to Hazel Davis 3/14/52 in Davis, *Uncle*, 38; to Jesse B. Hearin 3/8/52 (apartment); to Austin Rice 5/7/52.

Chapter 28

1. *Harisiades v. Shaughnessy* (1952; deportation of Italian); *Shaughnessy v. U.S. ex rel. Mezei* (1953); Cleveland and Ares ints.; Cleveland UA remarks. Eventually, Mezei was admitted to the country; Glendon Schubert, *Dispassionate Justice: A Synthesis of the Judicial Opinions of Robert H. Jackson* (Indianapolis, 1969), 212.

2. Meiklejohn, *Free Speech and Its Relation to Self-Government* (Chic., 1948), reprinted with a minor change as *Political Freedom: The Constitutional Powers of the People* (N.Y., 1960); *Adler v. Bd. of Educ.* (1952, quite a different policy; emphasis added); *Carlson v. Landon* (1952, belief that we must have freedom of speech; emphasis added); Burton to FF 1/11/52, Reed papers (shifted to majority); *Beauharnais v. Illinois* (1952; emphasis added); Cleveland int. and letter to author 8/15/73 (absolutes and table); HLB to Charles P. Curtis 10/21/52 (open the area; the article was "Ethics in the Law," 4 *Stanford Law Rev.* 477 (1952); *Wiemann v. Updegraff* (1952, test oath). The origins of the speech-conduct distinction are enmeshed in the rich threads of Enlightenment thought. Jefferson apparently first explicitly employed it in 1776, the same year Bentham (almost) did. Others who wrote as Jefferson did, and whom Black also read before he went on the Court, included Tacitus and Montesquieu.

3. Daniels (hat), Cleveland (move in, cold, anniversary), Reich (move in) ints.; Reich, *Sorcerer*, 24 (drink or smoke; HLB had stopped smoking a few years earlier), 23–25 (portrait); Reich in *Confessions* (car roof); Vann, UA remarks (newspapers).

4. Cleveland to HLB 11/12/53; HLB to JPF 11/26/52 (library; Frank initiated the effort and chose to volumes); HLB to T. L. Tolan, Jr. 1/14/53 (Jefferson); HLB to Harry A. Iseberg 1/5/53 (Stevenson); Abell, *Pearson*, 235; HLB to Hazel Davis 7/1/53 (Sterling's job); Pepper, *Eyewitness*, 225; Cleveland int. (tomorrow). "I had long been one of his most ardent admirers," HLB wrote after Stevenson's death, "and have always felt that our nation would have been much better had he been elected President at the time he ran"; to Otto Kerner 7/26/65.

5. Harbaugh, *Davis* 463 (Davis told justices), 478 (Perlman); *Youngstown Sheet & Tube Co. v. Sawyer* (1952); WODM, 260–65 (vote); JPF, "The United States Supreme Court: 1951–1952," 20 *Univ. of Chic. Law Rev.* 1, 12 (1952, FF from bench); HLB to Truman Hobbs 8/12/52 (consistent); Robert J. Donovan, *Tumultuous Years: The Presidency of Harry S. Truman, 1949–1953* (N.Y., 1982), 386 (Vinson advice); HST to WOD 7/9/52 (not sent), HSTL (crazy decision); memo for president, 6/5/52, HSTL (HLB call Truman; on which HST noted: "6:30, Monday, June 9. Hugo Black is giving a party for the Court. I promised to go"); WOD, *Go East*, 450 (Truman gracious); WOD on "About Harry Truman," ABC news program 1/73 (bourbon good). Best lawyers: many ints. and HLB, CBS int. Wonder: Joseph Dorfman to HLB 7/29/52; Dorfman to HLB 8/12/52.

6. *Zorach v. Clauson* (1952). Sparkman: Cooper, Hubbard ints. HLB to WOD 5/19/53 (surely: the Court could not reach agreement and when the case was decided the next term FF wrote the majority opinion denying the claims; *Maryland Casualty Co. v. Cushing* [1954]).

7. Phillips (lazy), Pollack (no chief justice), HER (Truman's appointments) ints.; Kluger,

Simple, 585 (made no bones). "See this," Truman once said, pointing to a phone beside his bed, as he was escorting Irving Dilliard (int.) through the White House living quarters. "I pick it up and it rings in Fred Vinson's bedroom. We talk every night"; also see *NYT* 9/9/53. Vinson's familiarity continued with the next occupant of 1600 Pennsylvania Avenue, Dwight Eisenhower, whom he had known since the early 1930s. Asked why Truman's Court appointments were not distinguished, Clark Clifford replied (int.), "I don't know. They were his weakness. He placed great emphasis on knowing a man and trusting a man. He felt comfortable knowing an appointee personally and working with him. But that doesn't explain it. I just don't know."

8. Marsh (class), Cromson (polish), Cleveland (best RHJ felt), HLB (shook hands), Phillips (Cropley ceremony), Calabresi (some people), HER (just get together) ints.; Hutchinson, "Black" (HLB treats with respect). Animosities gone: ints. with RHJ's and all of HLB's clerks of the period. Shortly before joining the Court, RHJ had explicitly upheld the idea that First Amendment rights occupy a 'preferred position'; Jackson, *Struggle*, 285.

9. HLB to Sam Daniels 4/3/53 (mint julep), 6/22/53 (foot still bothers); Daniels int. (lost great deal) int. HLB explained to Daniels 1/12/53, why he preferred Daniels' house rather than a hotel: "Your closeness to the Coral Gables tennis courts is what a more learned person would call the piece de resistance."

10. Rosenberg case in lower courts: Ronald Radosh and Joyce Milton, *The Rosenberg File: A Search for the Truth* (N.Y., 1983), 277–81; Vern Countryman, "Out, Damn Spot: Judge Kaufman and the Rosenberg Case," *New Republic* 10/8/77; Michael E. Parrish, "Cold War Justice: The Supreme Court and the Rosenbergs," *Amer. Hist. Rev.* v. 83 (1977). Louis Nizer, *The Implosion Conspiracy* (N.Y., 1973), 430 (left word); WODM, 320–25, upon which I have drawn throughout this section. Hospital: Radosh, 400; HLB to SFB 6/3/53, CB papers.

11. Brownell int. (hot under collar, didn't authorize); Parrish, "Cold War Justice," 835 (full court: Judge Kaufman was the FBI's source, having received the information from one of the prosecutors, J. Edward Lumbard, who heard it from Brownell); WODM, 220–23 (granting stay); *Ex parte Quirin* (1942, Stone convening court); Ball, *Power*, 146 and 344 n. 60, quoting FBI files (Brownell aware). Conference: notes, TC papers (take matter up); HLB to JPF 11/26/52.

12. *Rosenberg*, 346 U.S. at 300 (HLB opinion); Dunne, *Black*, 294, quoting HLB int. with Daniel Berman (Rosenbergs guilty); Childs, *Witness*, 48; Robert L. Stern to FV 6/19/53, FV papers; JBP int. (crying). Laundry van: Ryan, Cleveland ints. Sometime after seven o'clock, Farmer and an associate, Gloria Agrin, went to HLB's home in Alexandria and pounded on the door. No one answered. HLB gone to hospital: Radosh, *Rosenberg*, 415. HLB revised WOD's brief first draft of the stay he granted; WOD then rewrote and expanded the opinion.

13. HLB, Jr. (home phone wiretapping), Agronsky (Hoover) ints.; Vann in *Confessions* (deciding cases). Ernst: HLB, Jr., int.; Michael Bessie conv. On Ernst, see Harrison E. Salisbury, "The Strange Correspondence of Morris Ernst and John Edgar Hoover, 1939–1964," *Nation* 12/1/84; and Roger K. Newman, "Morris L. Ernst," *DAB* (suppl. 10), 1994.

Chapter 29

SOURCES: Hutchinson, "Unanimity"; Schwartz, *Super* and *Unpublished Warren*; Tushnet, *Making Civil Rights Law* and "What Really Happened in *Brown*"; Warren, *Memoirs*.

1. Reich, "Foreword: Mr. Justice Black as One Who Saw the Future," 9 *Southwestern Univ. Law Rev.* 845 (1977, drive to White House); *Weaver*, 55 (HST–EW); John P. McEnery OH, 5, HSTL (took over Democrats); EW, "Home Again," 39 *Jour. of State Bar of Cal.* 75 (1963, also CR 10/21/63, 19848; headed straight for HLB); Vann in *Confessions* (Aristotle); HLB to HLB, Jr. and SFB 10/15/53 (new Chief).

2. Some significance: I have combined the three sources in which Bunche's int. with HLB appears: Jackson, *Myrdal*, 125–26; Bunche research memoranda used for preparation of Myrdal, *An American Dilemma*, in Special Collections, UA Law School; and Bunch, *Political*, 383. Haber (no way; the interstate commerce case was *Morgan v. Virginia* [1946]); Cooper (blood in streets), Hobbs (assault) ints.; *Shelley v. Kraemer* (1948, restrictive covenants). A third case (*Henderson v. U.S.*) involved segregated dining car service on interstate trains; Burton wrote the opinion for a unanimous Court.

3. Conference notes, Clark, WOD, Burton papers; diary 4/15/50, under date of 4/4/50 (cases were argued on that and previous day), Burton papers (relinquished assignment); FV papers (would join *McLaurin*). Vinson assigned cases to himself and changed mind: docket books, WOD, Reed papers; assignment lists, TC papers. HLB did "not state he would go *now* beyond separate and equal," Burton noted, and he reversed "on the statute." "This is written in beautiful style and I sincerely hope it can obtain a unanimous approval," Black wrote on his return of Vinson's opinion in *Sweatt*. "Certainly I shall say nothing unless someone writes in a way that impels me to express separate views. Full Court acceptance of this and the McLaurin opinions would add force to our holdings"; 5/18/50, FV papers.

4. JPF, "The United States Supreme Court: 1949–50," 18 *Univ. of Chic. Law Rev.* 1 (1950, Alabama legislature); ESB (tomatoes thrown), Sam Daniels (matter of discretion; the case was *Bagsby v. Trustees of Pleasant Grove Independent School Dist.* [1951]) ints.; *Grafton*, 132 (Alabama brief); HLB to Francis Hare 6/28/50 (Ala. Bar Assn. meeting; this came shortly after some members of the Tennessee bar walked out when Black addressed them that June: Thad Holt OH, UAB OHP); HLB to HLB, Jr. 6/28/50 (high emotions), 3/19/52 (no means sure); HLB, Jr., to HLB 3/16/52 (senator's affection); Clark OH, FV OHP, UK 9–11 (all of us, originally emphasized);

5. Cleveland int. (not going to hold); conference notes, TC papers. "I don't understand this problem about discrimination," Jackson said while working on a case involving it in the mid-1940s. "In Jamestown [New York, his hometown] we had no problem. The one Negro family went to the same theater and the same schools as the rest of us, and didn't complain" (Gartner int.).

6. TC notes (don't vote); Paul int. (kept views to self). FF questions: HLB willing, on WOD on FF to conference, 5/27/53 (majority agreed; the questions are in 345 U.S. at 972–73); HLB to conference 6/13/53 (political uses).

7. WOD conference notes (basic premise); WODM, 277 (getting nine); TC OH, FV OHP, 4 (HLB responsible); HLB to HLB, Jr. 4/7/54 (wholly impossible); Vann (never said anything), Reich (you boys) ints.; Clayton, *Making*, 158 (Princeton). Seat to Walter White: White to HLB 10/16/53; HLB to White 10/19/53. HLB told the Court's clerk:

"It seems to me that this man has a very good claim to get in if we have any places at all. No one else has asked me and if I have a seat I am perfectly willing for him to have it."

8. *Bolling v. Sharpe* (1954); Vann, UA remarks (best part); Reich int. (steer); Davis, *Uncle,* 40 (loneliness); HLB to SFB 11/23/53, CB papers (cold weather). Both Lee and Hattie died in early 1954; Hugo's sisters Ora and Daisy died in 1949 and 1947 respectively.

9. HLB to JPF 3/31/54; Vann int. (pick); HLB to Melford Cleveland 3/18/54 (Fox speeches). *Maryland Casualty Co. v. Cushing* (1954) was the twelve-page opinion and his most interesting one of the term; to help pass time while writing it, he repeatedly went to the dictionary to look up words.

10. Vann (Secret Service), Jackson (makes sense) ints.; HLB to Cahn 11/22/60 (my decision); Harbaugh, *Davis,* 516 (inevitability); Vann in *Confessions* (first of many).

11. Vann, UA remarks (no indication); Vann (added unanimously, Alabama, are you sure), Straight (very long time) ints.; Katie Louchheim, *By the Political Sea* (Garden City, N.Y., 1970), 64 (tree of liberalism); *NYT* 12/27/84 (only so much); WOD conference notes (more than bare bones).

12. Conference notes, EW, Burton papers, FFLC; WODM, 286–91; *Brown v. Board of Education* (1955). The justices, except for Warren, kept the clerks out of *Brown II* as they had in the main case. All deliberate speed: HLB (wasn't happy), Girard (one of worst things), WJB (several times) ints.

13. Letter to editor, MA 11/8/55 (criticism); BPH 4/24/57 (lawyer arguing; the case was *West Point Grocery Co. v. Opelika*); WOD, *Go East,* 451 (law school class); MA 3/17/57 (Folsom); Allgood and Tortorici (chest protector), Kinney (Harris), HER (relatives, Fink), Rives ints. Country club: William Brower, Lynne, Packer ints. HLB, Jr.: HLB, Jr.; HLB to HLB, Jr. 12/1/54 (easy to understand); Rives int. (when HLB said).

14. Bass, *Unlikely,* 17 (Marshall), 58–77 (bus boycott cases); Rives (nomination), Calabresi (Russell) ints.; HLB, Jr., "Richard Taylor Rives 1895–1982," 44 *Ala. Lawyer* 59 (1983, noting that "Justice Black repeatedly said that perhaps his most important gift to his country was his input on his appointment of Dick Rives to the Fifth Circuit"); Taylor Branch, *Parting the Waters: America in the King Years 1954-63* (N.Y., 1988), 139. Rives's son, Richard, Jr., was going to clerk for Black after graduation from law school in 1950 but was killed in a 1949 automobile accident; Rives int.

15. Rives (opposition), Brown (photographed) ints.; Sims, *Folsom,* 183–84 (legislature); MA 3/17/57 (rumor); HER, Patterson ints. (HLB's remains; resolutions condemning).

16. VH, *Hill,* 211–12 (expressions); Hubbard (HLB–Hill), Freeman (stay in office), Packer (motives) ints. Richard Rives, whom Hill (int.) called "my best friend since the fourth grade," similarly knew his feelings, as did close Washington friends like Claude Pepper (int.), Tom Corcoran and Drew Pearson. "At the height of massive resistance, Hill could only visit Dick Rives in secret. [They] dare not be seen in public." (Ray Jenkins, "Lister Hill," BES 12/29/84) Luther Hill, Lister's nephew, who clerked for Black in 1950 and dined with his uncle every Sunday, recalled (int.): "Lister usually talked about what he was doing politically. He often discussed the race issue. He said, 'I've never tried to be a Tom Tom [Heflin]. I'm doing more good for people staying here than if I went out front on the race issue.' He didn't believe what he was saying about race, he had to say it. He knew it and it didn't bother him at all. He had made up his mind that was what he was going to do. He felt about race like Black did. They didn't really differ on anything."

Chapter 30

SOURCES: Meador, *Black*

1. JBP (books as friends with bodies), HLB clerks (*Greek Way*), Gressman (Aristotle) ints.; HLB to Katharine McBride 7/23/65 (great thinkers); Hamilton, *Greek*, 184 (human mind and nature); 66 (brush aside; not underlined), 75 (clarity; "watchwords" was not underlined), in HLB Books; HLB to HLB, Jr. 2/15/51 (Cicero, Xenophon), 4/17/51 (similarity); to Charles Reich 6/10/68 (Tacitus); Meador, UA remarks (clerks' room); HLB to JPF 10/3/62 (favorite author), after reading his review of James William Moore's *Federal Practice*: "The general spirit of the entire work is one of practical justice" (50 *Calif. Law Rev.* 582 [1962]). Black underlined "practical justice," originally Aristotle's phrase, and wrote "OK" in the margin. In a copy of Hamilton's book bought in the early 1950s HLB marked numerous passages dealing with tragedy and suffering; HLB Books, JBP int. "The first week I was clerking," recalled George Freeman (int.), "the Judge asked if I read Tacitus, Thucydides and *The Greek Way*. He said, 'They have a lot to do with some of the cases we're considering this term. Go buy them so you have your own copies because I want you to have them.' " He made another clerk read Tacitus before any law books; Calabresi in *Confessions*.

2. JBP int. (learning Greek); *Johnson v. Eisentrager* (1950 dissent); HLB to Alfred Knopf 2/1/43 (observation after reading Haskell); HLB, speech at Einstein Memorial Meeting, Town Hall, New York 5/15/55. In 1954 he called for college courses "on our ancient liberties, a discussion of that part of the Constitution that has to do with personal liberty. I would like to see colleges teach citizenship and history in relation to why this government of ours has the principles it has. Very few people seem to know. At least very few people act on the basis of such knowledge, if they have it. If the schools will begin to teach the people in plain everyday language why we have the country we have—and that we should not live in fear—they will have performed a service and will give this nation a long life": WS 5/16/54; this was the day before the school segregation case.

3. Thucydides, *The Peloponnesian War*, underlined in EC, *Moral*, 177, in HLB Books (Pericles' Funeral Oration); Zoltan Haraszti, *John Adams and the Idea of Progress* (Cambridge, Mass., 1952), 110 in HLB Books; Hamilton quoted in Edwin S. Gaustad, *A Religious History of America* (N.Y., 1974), 272. "Black once explained that you had to look for people's real motives—not what they said, or even what they might convince themselves, but the reasons behind the reasons," wrote *Washington Post* cartoonist Herbert Block; *Herblock: A Cartoonist's Life* (N.Y., 1993), 120. Thucydides' quotation was one of HLB's favorites, which he often read and occasionally used in speeches. He also underlined it in *Thucydides, Translated Into English* (Oxford, Eng., 1900), I, 129–30 (Benjamin Jowett, trans., sec. ed. rev.); and in Zimmern, *Greek*, 204; both HLB Books.

4. HLB to Mitchell Franklin 3/7/60 (difficult reading); HLB to EC 3/16/59 (Dewey's works); JBP (Russell, habits, novels), Luther Hill (summer reading, Macauley in *Joint Anti-Fascist Refugee Committee v. McGrath* [1951]) ints. "Personally, I do not think you would go wrong if you would get all the rest of Dewey's books," he told a former clerk. "I think that probably all of them would be helpful although I am not sure that it would be worthwhile to read his book on logic" (which Black had read in 1942): HLB to Melford Cleveland 3/18/54. "I can think of no person whose work and life have made a greater impression on this era than Dr. Dewey's"; HLB to William H. Kilpatrick 4/12/54. Later he served as an honorary member of the Committee for the Observation of Dewey's Centenary.

5. HLB, Jr. (historical hero), ESB (looking like Jefferson) ints.; HLB to Edward Dumbauld 5/20/66 (written about Jefferson); Malone, *Jefferson,* 232 (anybody's feelings), 370 (boldness), 365 (personal friendships), in HLB Books; WOD conference notes 10/12/56, WOD papers; *Yates v. U.S.* (1957).

6. Meador (pored), JBP (recommended), Freeman (stop), Poe (Louis Oberdorfer, who had clerked for HLB in 1946, introduced them), Feeney (two weeks) ints.; HLB to Don T. Udall 5/11/59 (general ideas; he was referring to John Udall, a predecessor of Udall's and an ideological precursor of the Levellers); HLB to William W. Adams 9/1/61 (enact laws); HLB, "Bill," reprinted in Dilliard, *Stand.* HLB had the Supreme Court library route directly to him any new books on English constitutional history; Saunders int. "Whenever I came home from college after that, he would always teach me about the Levellers," JoJo recalled. Her course was American Political Thought, taught by John Roche, and the textbook in which the selection from the Levellers was found, the first one in the book, was Alpheus T. Mason's *Free Government in the Making* (1949). HLB regularly read from his children's books.

7. JBP int. (Hoffer, Durant, Montaigne); Will and Ariel Durant, A *Dual Autobiography* (N.Y., 1977), 301, 303 (Durant in Florida); HLB to Sandburg 8/18/49 (*Remembrance Rock*; HLB and Sandburg apparently met only once, in early 1962: HLB to Harry Golden 2/1/62); Knopf unpublished memoir, 451 (best friends); Knopf to HLB 5/8/39 (Curtis article); HLB to Knopf 5/17/39 (Knopf to Washington); Lerner to Knopf 6/8/43, 10/11/45, 4/22/47, Lerner papers (Lerner proceeding); HLB to Knopf 5/6/47 (JPF); Susan Sheehan int. with ESB. Mencken suggesting book: Mencken to Knopf 5/15/39, in Guy J. Forgue, ed., *Letters of H.L. Mencken* (N.Y., 1961), 435; Knopf, "H.L. Mencken: A Memoir" in John Dorsey, ed., *On Mencken* (N.Y., 1980), 307–8. HLB-Knopf-Lerner: Lerner to HLB 5/25/39, Lerner papers; also Knopf to HLB 5/20/42. Peter Prescott provided Knopf's unpublished memoir, Sheehan's interview and other materials.

8. HLB to Knopf 2/21/61 (Camus), 6/19/63 (Dabbs's *Southern Heritage,* originally emphasized; sent then even though published in 1959). "You have done a very fine job in presenting the southern attitude with a critical, nonetheless affectionate, understanding," HLB wrote Dobbs 6/19/63. Knopf sent almost anything he published dealing with the South. HLB found Kenneth Stampp's *The Peculiar Institution* "so informative and interesting that I shall not put it aside until I finish it. [He] has a message which he gives in plain understandable English. Quite naturally the book is slanted in accordance with his own feelings—that is, against exploitation of one group of people by other groups of people. I do not see, however, where anyone could have done a fairer job who entertained any views at all, and a discussion of slavery coming from one wholly neutral on the subject would doubtlessly be rather boring. . . .": to Knopf 9/26/56.

   Wholly different was Black's response to Wilfred Binkley's *American Political Parties:* "I cannot say it is objectively written. It is a little difficult for me to accept the hypothesis that Mark Hanna and McKinley were the two outstanding friends of the laboring men and that the present Republican Party and its philosophical predecessors have, when defeated, been the victim of that Party's basic hostility to control of the country by big business and Wall Street financiers. One unfamiliar with American history would finish this book with the distinct impression that most of the militant crusading for the right has been done by those who oppose the Party of Jefferson, Cleveland and the later Roosevelt. One might also be impressed by a subtle argument that even though an election was stolen from Tilden, nevertheless it was justified because persons qualified to vote in the Southern States had been kept away from the polls." [HLB to Knopf 10/2/43]

"Before I reached his discussion of Reconstruction, I had become so certain that he was writing from the standpoint of a deep-rooted conviction against the traditional Democratic Party that I consulted Who's Who, in which he had classified himself as a Republican. When I reached the language in which he referred with hushed reverence to those who had visited the birthplace of the Republican Party and had stood at that hallowed spot with bowed heads, I could not refrain from the belief that it was highly probable that he was one of that reverential group." [HLB to Knopf 10/9/43]

9. HLB to Saul Padover 6/14/71; HLB to HLB, Jr. 2/8/54 (Thomas's *Abraham Lincoln: A Biography* [1952], one of the many books John Frank sent him over the years); Gettysburg, underlined in Zimmern, *Greek*, 206, in HLB Books; HLB to Nicholas Johnson 1/11/62 (Andrew Johnson); HLB to Knopf 10/9/43 (read all he found; grave); Schlesinger conv. HLB-Brant: HLB telegram to Irving Brant 11/15/61; EC to HLB 11/16/61. At HLB's request Padover promptly sent another, also inscribed copy in 1971. A close friend of Cahn, he sent the book to HLB upon publication in 1962. HLB thanked him profusely and read extensively from it to the annual Fifth Circuit judicial conference; HLB to Padover 5/15/62, and to Meador 6/28/62. Schlesinger's *The Politics of Hope* was "a series of essays breathing hope into the ideas of Democracy as a continuing process suffering its ups and downs," HLB wrote inside the book 7/1/63; HLB Books. He also read and enjoyed several others of Schlesinger's books.

10. Beard to HLB 10/16/43 (watch that man); HLB, "Foreward" to Howard K. Beale, ed., *Charles A. Beard: An Appraisal* (Lexington, Ky., 1954), xi; Richard Hofstadter, *The Progressive Historians: Turner, Beard and Parrington* (N.Y., 1969, Vintage ed.), 316 (vendetta). "[Charles] and I had innumerable conversations about you from our first meeting at the Cosmos Club when you sat between us and you gave me intense satisfaction by letting me know you had read one of my favorite historians, Samuel Dill," Mary Beard wrote HLB 9/15/48, after Charles's death.

11. HLB to Charles E. Wyzanski, Jr. 6/2/61 (Curtis); HLB, *Memoirs*, 108 (Taft). "I have thoroughly enjoyed *For the Defense*," HLB wrote Stryker 7/18/47, who sent him a copy. "The fact that you have written the life of a lawyer in such a way that a layman can appreciate it is quite a tribute to you. . . . Every lawyer, particularly those who try cases, would do well to read what you tell about Erskine." In June 1957 HLB read four more books about Erskine which his former clerk David Vann sent. "Erskine, in my estimation, is one of the world's great lawyers," he wrote Vann 6/26/57. "He stood for fine principles of liberty when it amounted to something to do so."

12. HLB to JPF 4/6/62 (Lincoln), 8/28/62 (interesting). After JPF published *American Law: The Case for Radical Reform*, HLB wrote him (10/3/69): "You are a marvel! How a man can take care of a big law practice like you do and write a book comparable in scope, I imagine, to a miniature edition of Blackstone's Commentaries is beyond my comprehension. [I] know that it will compare favorably with "Walker's American Law" which I studied in the University of Alabama Law School in 1904–6. [It] will create so much discussion that it will serve a wonderful purpose. There is no doubt but that the laws of this country need a more realistic treatment than they have been given in a long time and I think you are to be congratulated for having said the things that will cause people to review the law as it is and as it functions. I congratulate you on writing the book."

13. Jerome Frank in *NYT Book Review* 12/18/49; EC, *Sense*, 13–14 (originally emphasized), in HLB Books; HLB, "About Edmond Cahn," 39 *New York Univ. Law Rev.* 207 (1964,

about *Sense*); JBP (New York trips, Kaye, defensiveness), Davis (HLB as philosopher), Lamb (EC letters), EC (HLB-EC), HLB (agree, great friend), ESB (understood, also HLB-EC) ints.; 65 *Yale Law Jour.* 464 (1956, Firstness); HLB, "Foreword" to Lenore L. Cahn, ed., *Confronting Injustice: The Edmond Cahn Reader* (Boston, 1966), xi; draft to introduction to *Confronting* (top of list); JBP int. (psychiatry books). HLB had tears in his eyes after reading his other tribute to Cahn, "About," to Elizabeth; HLB, *Memoirs*, 97. On Cahn, see Roger K. Newman, "Edmond Cahn," *DAB*, suppl. 7; and *Hugo Black and Edmond Cahn: A Philosophical Friendship* (M.A. thesis, Univ. of Virginia, 1976).

When Black told Cahn, "Maybe I shall break my rule after all," about giving a blurb for a 1954 volume, *Supreme Court and Supreme Law*, which Cahn edited and to which he contributed an essay, Cahn wrote Jerome Frank, "I feel like writing [him] that the value of virginity consists in the losing of it, but abstained because I've noticed he sometimes laughs when you and I wouldn't and sometimes looks shocked when we would be in stitches." "No," replied Frank, "don't try your virginity image. He's too virginal": HLB to Cahn 11/17/53; Cahn to Frank 11/24/53, Frank to Cahn 11/27/53, both Frank papers.

Chapter 31

SOURCES: ESB, *Rebel*; HLB, *Memoirs*; HLB, Jr., *Father*.

1. Harold Ward int. (picking clerks); HLB to Daniel Berman 10/24/55 (event); HLB to Hazel Davis 1/17/56, in Davis, *Uncle*, 56 (prefer to lament); HLB to Charles Luce 3/9/56 (grinding away); HLB to Alfred Knopf 3/20/56 (reached point); Meador, *Black*, 27 (DAB); Hofstadter, *Tradition*, 32 (underlined) in HLB Books.

2. HLB to children 10/26/54 ($3,000); JBP, Ward (trips to Florida) ints.; HLB to VFD 3/2/56 (her plan); HLB to JPF 9/4/56 (birth of baby and dissent); Grover Hall, Jr., to HLB 10/21/63. Leonard Lyons in *NYP* 5/4/55 says that HLB got a ticket for going in the wrong direction in Rock Creek Park and that it was Justice Douglas who was stopped by a cop; Black told WOD this at dinner. But Hugo Jr. insists this happened to his father, and certainly it is consistent with everything else about his driving.

3. HLB to JPF 6/22/56 (miss them), 9/4/56 (rather of opinion); HLB to Joseph D. Shane 11/27/59 (tennis at noon). JPF (doldrums), Brownell (HLB meeting Eisenhower), ESB (dined), Meador (limited ability) ints.; Merle Miller, *Ike The Soldier: As They Knew Him* (N.Y., 1987), 307 (charitable); HLB OH, LBJL (nice man).

4. Zimmern, *Greek*, 124 in HLB Books (Thucydides); Vann, UA remarks (steak); HLB to VFD 12/5/58 (marriage license); HLB to John Gilbert Harlan 10/7/68 (two drafts, another woman); JBP (parties), Coates, Tortorici, Packer, Patrick ints.; HLB, Jr., to HLB 2/24/56 (all I can gather); *Richmond* (Va.) *News-Leader* 3/14/86 (gray ghost).

5. BPH 9/13/57 (things happened); JPF, "Mr. Justice Black: A Biographical Appreciation," 65 *Yale Law Jour.* 454 (1956, bridge); Freeman in *Confessions* and *Richmond* (Va.) *Times-Dispatch* 12/12/71 (dancing).

6. HLB to JPF 8/12/57 (tennis); Lorraine Frank int. (happier); HLB to HLB, Jr., 8/21/57 (necessary to see her).

7. WP 9/13/57 (order). Present at the wedding were JoJo, Hugo, Jr., Elizabeth's mother, her son Fred and his wife Janice, Maggie Bryan (who had accompanied Elizabeth to buy a

wedding dress), Neosha Anglin (a young neighbor and friend of HLB's), Cleveland, and Lizzie Mae, the housekeeper-cook who kept HLB going on a daily basis, and her brother, Spencer, his messenger. Otherwise, except for Willie Koontz, a former Reed clerk who helped Cleveland procure the marriage license, no one knew—not even Justice Clark, with whom HLB had taken a steam bath at the Court the day before and whom he had seen that very morning: Mary and Tom Clark to ESB and HLB 9/12/57.

8. ESB cold and hungry: ESB, Cahn ints.; Billington, *Black,* Inferences: JPF to HLB 9/13/ 57; HLB to JPF 9/19/57. Tortorici int. (calling him Hugo); ESB to Donald and Mary Frost 3/15/58 (writing letters). HLB at night: Oberdorfer, HER ints. The tray was presented to Hugo and Elizabeth during Chief Justice Warren's party for the Court, which was a train trip to Philadelphia to attend the Army-Navy football game in late November 1957. The inscription was Tom Clark's idea, and the justices and their wives "roared with laughter" as Elizabeth read it aloud. "They were as pleased as teenagers who had just played a joke on someone," she wrote later.

9. Dinners and friends: Frances Arnold, Pearson, Hill ints. ESB int. (tennis).

Chapter 32

1. Harold Ward int.; JPF to HLB 10/14/55 (unusual qualifications); HLB to JPF 1/10/57 (great head). HLB–EW assigning opinions: HLB clerks, WJB (not too much secret) ints.; ESB, *Rebel* (lasting thing; her published diary is replete with such instances). Herbert Brownell, who knew Warren well, believed that Black was responsible for "much of Warren's increasing liberalism. . . . He learned a lot from Black," who "carefully tutored him in his views on the Fourteenth Amendment"; Brownell with John P. Burke, *Advising Ike: The Memoirs of Attorney General Herbert Brownell* (Lawrence, Kan., 1993), 173–74. During Warren's last term, HLB told his clerks before conference, "why don't you boys look at this list and see what you want to work on"; Schulhofer int.

2. Freund, *Law,* 221; Luce, Calabresi (how position put), Girard (last night), Saunders (start) ints.; David Clark in *Confessions* (mind nimble); Cahn, *Sense,* 94, in HLB Books. HLB underlined Dumas Malone's remark about Jefferson, that "the road to knowledge begins with doubt"; Malone, *Jefferson,* 84, in HLB Books.

3. Reich, *Sorcerer,* 24; Zimmern, *Greek,* 135, in HLB Books; HLB to HLB, Jr., 10/26/56 (like new justice); Feeney (doesn't know), Calabresi (time spent) ints.; Hart's article was "The Time Chart of the Justices," 73 *Harv. Law Rev.* 84 (1959). Changed results: see FF's dissent in *Ferguson v. Moore-McCormick Lines* (1956). The sole exception to HLB's supporting workers' claims came in a case where the plaintiff on the witness stand virtually repudiated his own claim; *Herdeman v. Pennsylvania R.R.* (1957). Black read much satire over the years; in March 1953 he ordered Juvenal, *Satires of Persius, Sulpicia and Lucilius.*

4. Nicholas Johnson (Ike nice fellow), WJB (helpful, needed something, gung ho do, dry), Fishbein (mistake) ints.; Schwartz, *Super,* 293 (reaffirm duty); WJB draft (no delay), TC notes re draft opinion (punch), both 9/17/58, TC papers; Ball, *Power,* 182 (cut throat); HLB and WJB draft opinion 10/6/58, FFLC (not be accepted); HLB, comments on WJB drafts 9/22/58 (new paragraph); Schwartz, 303 (JMH satirical opinion); *Cooper v. Aaron* (1958). The first draft of the Court's opinion stated at the head, "Mr. Justice Brennan delivered the opinion of the Court"; Opinions of Mr. Justice Brennan—October Term,

1958, in Fishbein's possession. HLB was as secretive about *Cooper* as he had been about *Brown,* not letting his clerks in on anything. But "all deliberate speed" remained on his mind and throughout the term he kept referring to it; Calabresi int.

5. Freeman (waste), Calabresi (worked on dissent), Girard (worked harder), Meador, Wallace (talk to WOD), Ginsburg ints. HLB to WOD 1/6/55 (fond of Mildred; this came when WOD went on a delayed honeymoon after marrying Mercedes Davidson in 10/54); WOD to HLB 8/24/54 (journey); WOD to FR 4/19/56, FR papers (hardest thing); HLB Books (dedicated). WOD inscribed his 1954 volume, *An Almanac of Liberty,* "For Hugo L. Black with great admiration and affection"; HLB called it "a great contribution to the cause of civil liberties" (HLB Books; to JPF 11/15/54).

6. I have combined HLB to JPF 12/11/53, 1/7/54, 3/8/54; WOD to HLB, (early 1954, FF's candidate); Rostow (repair relations), Calabresi (great law school) ints.; Rostow to HLB 10/12/55 (James; Rostow later said it was Leviticus: Rostow to HLB 3/11/65); HLB to JPF 11/26/52 (stone wall), 12/22/52 (great credit); HLB to Griswold 3/18/54 (continuation of free government). Griswold's speeches were published as a book, *The Fifth Amendment Today* (Cambridge, Mass., 1954).

7. HLBLC (lawyer as legalist); HLB to Sam Daniels 10/18/60 (more knowledge); HLB to Harrison J. Goldin 10/20/60 (case system); HLB to FR 10/20/60, FR papers HLB to Henry M. Holland, Jr. 2/17/64 (judges decide cases); Plato, *Laws* 645a, quoted in EC, *Sense,* 105; Aristotle, *Nichomachean Ethics* 1179b et seq. (education). Cahn: HLB to Lenore Cahn 2/23/65 (read all Cahn's writings).

8. *Green v. U.S.* (1958, trial by jury); FF to Whittaker 11/25/57, (11/57 conference); Whittaker to FF 11/29/57 (shock conscience), both FFHLS; Schwartz, *Super,* 322–23 (10/58 conference); *Bartkus v. Illinois* (1959, sovereigns); Calabresi (bell, first example, St. Augustine, destroy, HLB re Stewart, FF, WJB), Lamb (sick), Alan Kohn (Whittaker) ints.; EC to HLB 4/3/57, 3/31/59, which repeat HLB's point on "technical justice"; Clayton, *Making,* 216 (8 to 1). TC recorded HLB as saying at the 1958 conference in *Green:* "May be too large a step that here the instigation was by federal and [fifth] amendment prevents it. However policy of federal government is not to permit its agencies to prosecute twice even in state. I can reach it by shock process [?]": conference notes, TC papers.

9. Calabresi (brightest man), Freund ("the good Lord gave Hugo Black more brains than it gave any other man on this Court") ints.; Louchheim, *Making,* 70 (best brain); Jerome Frank to HLB 8/8/54 quotes FF telling Hand that HLB has "the naturally best mind on the Court"; FF memorandum 1/25/61, FFLC (told Warren); HLB note, FFLC (hope nothing); HLB int. (rules). Shahn got the idea for the painting after his friend Irving Dilliard said he was editing a book of Black's civil liberties opinions; the picture appeared in 1969: Dilliard int.

10. Lewis, "Black" (concerns Bill of Rights); Saunders (1961), Ward (differences with FF), Girard (code), ESB (scream), Snyder (Clark, who told him this), Reich (1954), Lamb (1958) ints.; Lash int. with HLB, Jr., Lash papers (fellows in law schools); Aristotle, *Rhetoric* (Ellis trans.), 10 n. 22 (logic), 61 n. 11 (species), in HLB Books (HLB's underlining). ESB later asked WOD whether Hugo or Felix got the most upset. "I think it was kind of mutual," he answered, "but Hugo had better control of his emotions then Felix had of his. . . . Sometimes after conference, Hugo was very tense and would come

in to my office and say, 'sometimes I think our friend Felix is trying to drive me up the wall' "; ESB, *Rebel*.

11. Girard int. (constitutional system); Hand's statement came in *The Bill of Rights* (Cambridge, Mass., 1958). In developing HLB's views on man and life, I have been helped by and drawn upon George Freeman, Jr., in *Richmond* (Va.) *Times-Dispatch* 12/1/71; and Freeman int.

Chapter 33

1. HLB to EC 7/8/59 (somewhat of dilemma), 12/31/59 (change subject); EC memorandum to Dean [Russell N.] Niles 9/3/59, Madison Lecture files, NYU Law School (every persuasive device); ESB int.

2. *Speiser v. Randall* (1958); *Barenblatt v. U.S.* (1959, originally emphasized; recent opinion was *Watkins v. U.S.* [1957]); Charles Luce to HLB 6/9/59 (thought recurring); Meiklejohn to HLB 7/5/59 (issue of political freedom); HLB to Meiklejohn 7/8/59 (have talk); *Smith v. California* (1959, originally emphasized). "I cannot think of how I came up with the direct-indirect test," Calabresi recalled (int.). "None of my teachers ever mentioned it. The Judge and I discussed the case at length and I may have sensed this was what he was getting at," which is what a law clerk is supposed to do.

3. McNulty int. Dinner: EC papers; London int.; HLB, "Bill," 35 *New York Univ. Law Rev.* 865 (1960; originally emphasized), reprinted in Dilliard, *Stand*; HLB to EC 2/24/60 (vitally interested); to John Fischer 3/15/60 (opposite views); to Alfred Knopf 3/15/60 (at odds); Bickel, "Mr. Justice Black: The Unobvious Meaning of Plain Words," *New Republic* 3/14/60; HLB to JPF 3/23/60 (too much to hope); FR to *New Republic* (about 3/21/60; HLB to FR 3/20/60 (confess no apoplexy, and continuing: ". . . Now to something more important"); HLB to Meiklejohn 4/22/60 (well imagine); WOD to Gilbert A. Harrison 3/22/60, WOD papers (Bickel article raises point).

   In 1966 Black finally did read what Bickel had written, as part of his 1962 book, *The Least Dangerous Branch*, in which he incorporated his article. Black's markings, not surprisingly, included: "I did not do that," "no," "false," "cheap satire," "this is an implication of deceit by me," and "his due process formula does what he most condemns": 87, 90, 97, 95, 93, in HLB Books. Black underlined "free-ranging 'activist' government by the judiciary . . . is incompatible with democratic institutions," and wrote alongside: "I agree to this and his due process formula does what he most condones" (93). "I agree but doubt that he does," he noted about Bickel's "attitude springing from illusion" (96). "I am not interested in receiving any honorarium at all . . . ," HLB told Cahn 2/24/60. "I shall never accept an honorarium for discussing matters of this kind, and I want the University to feel perfectly free to send me no honorarium." But when law school dean Russell Niles sent the honorarium to Black ten days later, Black thanked him; HLB to Niles 3/5/60, NYU Law School.

4. Charles L. Black, Jr., "Mr. Justice Black, the Supreme Court, and the Bill of Rights," *Harper's* 2/61; HLB to Calabresi 6/27/60 (Hamilton; this sentence makes little sense: what likely happened is that Hamilton had suggested his student Black as a clerk to HLB in 1943); HLB to Daniel Berman 6/9/60 (write well); Calabresi, *Common*, 181 (realize; originally emphasized); HLB to Milton Handler 5/13/63 (Hand); Griswold, "Absolute is in the Dark," 8 *Utah Law Rev.* 167 (1963); HLB to EC 3/5/63 (fine man).

5. Ralph Barton Perry, *The Thought and Character of William James* (Cambridge, 1948), 248; see 265–66. In a 1961 draft opinion Black wrote: "whether so in science or not, there are some absolutes in the law . . ."; draft of dissent in *Braden v. U.S.* In 1968 he contrasted law with science, which "naturally shows a changing world where it is impossible to know enough to talk in absolutes. The law, however, intends for some formulas to be absolutes": HLB to Floyd Feeney 12/17/68. Religious cases: RHJ in *Everson v. Board of Education* (1947); FF in *McCollum v. Board of Education* (1948). RHJ had earlier written: "Religious activities which concern only members of the faith are and ought to be free—as nearly absolutely free as anything can be"; *Prince v. Massachusetts* (1944). And in 1952, after still another religious case (*Zorach v. Clauson*), FF didn't peep in response when RHJ told him, as has been noted, that the Court should apply separation of church and state "as an absolute."

6. Harold Ward (our grounds), Luce (something to printer) ints.; Irving Brant, "Hugo Black: A Man Who Honors Liberalism," *PM* 4/3/45 (senator). Archibald Cox has written: "Surely some virtually absolute restraints upon the ways we pursue even the worthiest objectives . . . furnish the best, perhaps the only, hope for man. . . . I speak of these ["fundamental liberties such as the Bill of Rights declares"] as 'virtually absolute' because philosophers can pose examples calling for exceptions, chiefly in closed, authoritarian societies far removed from our conditions": "Ends," *NYT Mag.* 5/19/74. Absolutes in law, Guido Calabresi has noted, "serve to preserve, nominally untouched and subject only to slow change, great aspirations, ideals in conflict; and they keep us from foolhardy action where wrong results really matter"; Calabresi, *Common*, 179.

7. HLB to FR 6/27/60 (gong); WOD to HLB 7/18/60 (look at Bickel review, which appeared in *New Republic* 7/28/60); HLB to WOD 7/28/60 (implication, expresses philosophy); HLB to Robert Girard 8/4/60 (advocacy of a philosophy); Levy, *Legacy of Suppression* (Cambridge, Mass., 1960), vii; *Bridges v. California* (1941); *Beauharnais v. Illinois* (1952). *NYT Mag.* articles: FR, "Crux of the Court Hullabaloo," 5/29/60; Jaffe, "The Court Debated—Another View," 6/5/60. Father Snee refers to Joseph M. Snee, S.J., "Leviathan at the Bar of Justice" in Arthur E. Sutherland, ed., *Government Under Law* (Cambridge, Mass., 1955), 91.

8. HLB to Charles Reich 10/10/60 (unusual care); to EC 10/19/60, marked "not sent" (many of sources; by my count, HLB read at least fourteen of Levy's sources); *NYHT Book Rev.* 10/16/60. Black's marginal notations in *Legacy of Suppression* were extensive. When Levy wrote, "They had defended religious rather than political speech," HLB noted, "falacious distinction." (145) On another page (189): "This fallacy exploded by this statement" and "No! as shown by parenthetical statement." On 215: "His usual weak inference drawn from negatives" and "Why was it necessary to shout that the language meant what it seemed to mean? Besides Madison explained it to Congress." "I find no evidence that Madison was reluctant" to frame a Bill of Rights. (226) "Calls clamor for Bill of Rights a 'smokescreen.' " (227) "Another negative inference." (233) "More attenuated inferences!" (234) And "Now gets down to impliedly disowning inferences from the 'possible'?" (234; all in HLB Books).

9. HLB to EC 10/19/60 ("1st draft, not used"; "futile admonition" comes from a second draft of the same day, simply marked "not used"), 10/24/60 (long quote), 10/26/60 (boundaries of power); Kurland int. (creative).

10. Levy to HLB 9/24/63 (permission); HLB to Levy 10/14/63 (rightly assume, originally emphasized; the first draft is dated 10/7/63). In 1985 Levy revised himself, publishing a

new edition of *Legacy*, now neutrally titled *The Emergence of a Free Press*. Freedom of speech and of the press defined by the First Amendment, he admitted, may have absorbed new limitations on the law of seditious libel. Even so, he concluded that the First Amendment was adopted to exist alongside the common law legacy of seditious libel and did not repudiate it. That did not happen until 1798, when the debates over the sedition act transformed American libertarian thought. Black would have thought Levy's new views an improvement that would still leave the people's right to speak and write freely at the whim of the judges who chanced to be on the Court at the time: the First Amendment's glorious mandate would still be at risk.

11. Brant, *Bill*, 225–31 (single voice); Hofstadter, *Tradition*, 143 (Lowell).

Chapter 34

1. HLB to John McNulty 10/10/60 (cases of importance); HLB to Reich 11/4/60 (education needed); HLB to Nicholas Johnson 3/6/61 (have letter); Israel int. (Stewart). *Wilkinson v. U.S.* (1961, basic principles); "Black, 75th birthday," Bumgardner papers (EW); TC to HLB 2/27/61, TC papers (being on Court); WP 2/27/61; FR, "A Sprig of Laurel for Hugo Black at 75," 10 *Amer. Univ. Law Rev.* 1 (1961). Black's old friend Charles Feidelson, long an editor of the *BAH*, wrote the *Shades Valley* editorial (3/2/61). It took "courage enough to write," HLB said in thanking him, 3/28/61.

2. Wallace (dictated dissent, hear voice), Saunders (written enough) ints.; Grenville Clark to Louis Lusky 11/17/60, Grenville Clark papers (lacks fiber, referring to *Uphaus v. Wyman* [1960]); ESB to HLB, Jr., SFB and JBP 3/23/61, JBP papers (touching); *In re Anastaplo* (1961; the Court had initially refused to hear it in 1955 [348 U.S. 496; HLB and WOD dissenting]); Kalven, *A Worthy Tradition: Freedom of Speech in America*, edited by Jamie Kalven (N.Y., 1988), 574 (comes close); HLB to Anastaplo 9/2/69 (no need); Anastaplo, *The Constitutionalist: Notes on the First Amendment* (Dallas, 1971), xii. As one of Anastaplo's teachers, C. Herman Pritchett, wrote, "As W. C. Fields might have said, any man who is kicked out of Russia, Greece and the Illinois bar can't be all bad"; book review, 60 *Calif. Law Rev.* 1476 (1972).

3. *Wilkinson v. U.S.* (1961, slogan); *Scales v. U.S.* (1961, justify action); *Konigsberg v. State Bar* (1961, drafted Bill of Rights); *Communist Party v. Subversive Activities Control Board* (1961, fullest power, 1593 English law); Saunders int. (loved them); Lewis, "Black" (standing alone). "The creation of 'tests' by which speech is left unprotected under certain circumstances," HLB continued in *Konigsberg*, "is a standing invitation to abridge it."

4. Saunders (hard to swallow), Wallace (WJB, immortalized) ints. HLB never gave any thought to writing in the Sunday Closing cases. He scrawled comments all over Warren's draft distinguishing between laws with a religious purpose and those with a secular purpose (general welfare laws, HLB called them) even if they were originally religiously motivated. "Black is raising a lot of trouble," EW said, and sent the clerk who drafted it, Jesse Choper, to talk to him. "You're using what the dissenters in *Everson* said," Black told Choper, referring to his 1947 school busing case. "There was no bending him," Choper recalled. "He said he reread *Everson* and he still agrees with it"; Choper int. Warren's revisions met HLB's objections: he changed the test of an "establishment" of religion from whether regulation operated "predominately" to support religion to whether the legislation does or does not aid it; Schwartz, *Super*, 380–81.

5. Arnold (know lose [WOD told this to WJB], enacted), Lamb (pay-off) ints. WJB next generation: Saunders (heir), Kester ints. Tax case: *James v. U.S.* (1961; HLB, joined by WOD, concurred in part and dissented in part to EW's judgment of the court). HLB joined Warren's comprehensive dissent in *Times Film Corp. v. Chicago*, a 1961 movie censorship case, but only after atypically allowing his clerk to negotiate with Warren's clerk to make changes that satisfied Black; Wallace int.

6. Mayers (FF "talked in chambers all the time about the nefarious scheme of Black's Four-teenth Amendment"), French (brilliant), Wallace (seen worse), Choper (craftiest) ints.; WJB to FR 5/3/61, FR papers (surface); Yarbrough, *Harlan*, 124, 127 (FF–JMH); FR to HLB 4/28/61 (HLB looking at FF; the opinion was *Konigsberg*); *Torcaso v. Watkins* (1961, Maryland case).

7. Levi int. (Hutchins as elitist); Robert M. Hutchins, "Dissenting Opinion as a Creative Art," *Saturday Rev.* 8/12/61; HLB to Hutchins 6/14/61 (tribute to Hutchins); WS 6/2/61 (came to listen). Southern Club talk: Anthony Lewis, "Mr. Justice Black," *NYT* 9/20/71; Freund, "The First Amendment: Freedom of Religion" in Hamilton, ed., *Hugo Black and the Bill of Rights* (Univ., Ala., 1978); ESB to HLB, Jr., SFB and JBP 4/20/61 in ESB, *Rebel* (students stood); *Communist Party* (baseless insult); David Halberstam, *The Powers That Be* (N.Y., 1979), 172–73 (FF on Communists).

8. HLB to Nicholas Johnson (beginning to wonder), and draft (time goes on), both 10/5/61; Lewis, "A New Lineup on the Supreme Court," *The Reporter* 8/17/61 (originally under-lined); Mendelson, *Conflict* 28 (his idol), 46 (correct for once), 119 (plainly, Mt. Sinai), 124 (deeply humilitarian). Not true: 30, 41 (also similar comments at 40, 59, 119, 121). Freund, *Supreme*, 44, 76, all HLB Books; HLB to Robert Girard 9/28/62 (fresh ideas); the job he was offered was as a visiting professor). Mendelson did research for FF's speeches and on the decree in the segregation cases during the 1953 term; the Ford Foundation paid his salary in an arrangement that apparently remains unprecedented: Mendelson int.

9. ESB int. (complained); HLB and EC, "Justice Black and First Amendment 'Absolutes': A Public Interview," 37 *New York Univ. Law Rev.* 562 (1962), reprinted in Dilliard, *Stand*, 467 (originally emphasized); EC, "The Firstness of the First Amendment," 65 *Yale Law Jour.* (1956) 464 (six years earlier); *Smith v. California*, 361 U.S. at 157–58 n. 2 (obscenity case); *Communist Party* (1961, freest interchange; HLB's emphasis); *St. L P-D* 6/17/62; Leon Green to EC 6/6/62, EC papers (our boy). Cahn asked: Irving Brant, "Edmond Cahn and American Constitutional History," 40 *New York Univ. Law Rev.* 218 (1965); Brant int. Not even Douglas took HLB's position on libel: "It would take, however, considerable persuasion to indicate that the adoption of the Fourteenth Amendment deprives the states of something that was as historic as libel and slander. Because they have been in existence from the very beginning": WODM, 269 (shortly after HLB–Cahn int.).

Chapter 35

sources: ESB, *Rebel*; HLB, *Memoirs*; HLB, Jr., *Father*.

1. Arnold (sixth vote), Saunders (berated) ints.; FF memorandum, *Baker v. Carr* 10/10/61, at 30, 31 (HLB scrawl); assignment sheet 10/23/61 (ten days); WODM, 147–48 (WJB assignment). Put case over: Saunders int.; FF to Stewart 5/1/61, FFHLS. HLB's comment was written next to "the discrimination relied on is the deprivation of what appellants conceive to be their proportionate share of political influence."

2. Whittaker, Poe, Bring (up to job), Dilliard (FF protested) ints.; HLB to FF 4/19/62, FFLC (happy to learn); HLB to HLB, Jr. 8/10/62 (deepest interest); diary 8/5/63, Pearson papers (persuade); Paul Freund, remarks on CBS Reports program on the Court 2/20/63, quoted in Fred Friendly to HLB 2/7/63 (miss you; on the bottom of which HLB wrote, "While I cannot vouch for the precise words quoted above, they represent my views, and I have certainly expressed them to Felix and others many times and I reiterate them now. Miami, Fla., 2/9/63"); HLB to Robert Girard 9/28/62. EW was careful to say that no one on the Court "asked" FF to retire; Pearson diary 8/23/[66].

3. Ginsburg, JBP ints.; FF to HLB 8/16/63 (no one as competent), 12/15/64 (pride; the case was *Hamm v. Rock Hill,* which came down the day before); HLB to FF 12/22/64 (quarter of century; originally underlined); HLB, "Mr. Justice Frankfurter," 78 *Harv. Law Rev.* 1521 (1965).

4. Ball, *Warren,* 143 (one man, one vote); *Gray v. Sanders* (1963, WOD opinion: one person, one vote); *Reynolds v. Sims* (1964 EW opinion); *Wesberry v. Sanders* (1964 HLB opinion); Saunders int. (want to know); HLB to Richard F. Gardner 12/11/64 ($100); *Engel v. Vitale* (1962); "A Little Decision Day Color," *Newsweek* files (delivering opinion); *NYT* 6/26/62 (prayer of each man). Voice trembled: Clayton, *Making,* 21; David L. Gray, *The Supreme Court and the News Media* (Evanston, Ill., 1968), 40–41.

5. Clayton, *Making,* 4–5 (Clark); Eshelman (Davis) int.; HLB to Nicholas Johnson 8/27/62 (education), HLB to Saunders 8/29/62 (biggest percentage); HLB to Hazel Davis 6/28/62 (basic premise); *NYT* 7/15/63 (White). Baptist ministers: Connie Mauney, "Justice Black and First Amendment Freedoms: Thirty-Four Influential Years," 35 *Emporia State Resarch Studies* (fall 1986).

6. Tribute: 370 U.S. iv–v; *NYT* 6/26/62; HLB to JPF 7/5/62; HLB to Girard 9/28/62 (25 years); to Jerome Cooper 11/12/62. "Mr. Cox is an extremely able lawyer and I think did a great job as Solicitor General," HLB wrote after Cox left the post; to Edward Born 4/4/66.

7. Nathan Lewin, "A Response to Goldberg and Bickel: Helping the Court with Its Work," *New Republic* 3/3/73 (before 1961 term); Schwartz, *Super,* 408–10; *Johnson v. Zerbst* (1938, complete courts; *Griffin v. Illinois* (1956; effective hearing): thereafter, seven of HLB's clerks, in addition to Claude Pepper, were appointed as counsel by the Court in right to counsel cases. *Gideon v. Wainwright* (1962; should holding be reconsidered), 1963 (Howard's page appears at 372 U.S. at 344): HLB to Frances Lamb, dated 1/19/63, but he misdated it and meant 1/29/63 (write this way); HLB to WJB 2/1/63 (on study); WJB to HLB 2/4/63 (more enthusiastic); "on back of opinion in No. 62," (necessity for counsel); O'Neil int. (read like *Adamson,* knew exactly); HLB note 2/11/63 (sent draft to justices); WOD comment on HLB draft 2/14/63 (fine job).

8. Choper (hypothetical), O'Neil (Hugo knows), Howard (real exuberance) ints.; Hofstadter, *Tradition,* 44 (quoting Jefferson), in HLB Books; Yarbrough, *Black,* 229 (using words); Clayton, *Making,* 230 (smiled and chatted); Anthony Lewis, *Gideon's Trumpet* (N.Y., 1964), 187–88 (reading opinion), 192 (never thought); Lewis inscription (HLB Books; after which came: "With the affection and admiration of Abe Fortas—to whom Hugo Black has always been a chief inspiration").

9. Reich, "Mr. Justice Black and the Living Constitution," 76 *Harv. Law Rev.* 673 (1963); HLB to Reich 2/20/63 (last night; originally emphasized); Howard int. (doesn't understand); Knopf to HLB 7/23/59 (best man), 2/21/63 (admiration); HLB to Knopf 7/23/59

(suggestion), 2/20/63 (friendship); Dilliard to Knopf 5/24/61, Knopf papers, Univ. of Texas (glory that is HLB); HLB to Irving M. Engel 2/2/65 (only thing).

10. *Duncan v. Louisiana* (1968, happy to support); VH to Robert Gallagher 9/12/67, VH papers (big thing); *Ferguson v. Skrupa* (1963); Goldberg to HLB 4/18/63 (many references). "Fundamental": see *Pointer v. Texas* (1965).

11. PPG 6/4/63 (oral argument); FF memorandum 1/8/62 (142 pages); assignment list 1/26/62 (HLB assignment); FF draft 3/22/62 (circulating opinion); Howard int. (down memory lane); WJB, Goldberg to HLB 4/1/63; White to HLB 4/2/63 (Clark apparently made no written response; HLB sent it to them 3/29/63); WOD memoranda 1/30/62, 2/1/62; *Arizona v. California* (1963).

12. WODM, 57 (never close); John McNulty (alimony), ESB (WOD mind), O'Neil (bankruptcy case: *Wolf v. Weinstein* [1963]) ints.; WOD to HLB 2/27/63 (birthday). WOD delivering opinion: Clayton, *Making*, 252; *NYT*, 6/4/63. Moving out: WP 4/12/63; Simon, *Douglas*, 372. Living at Court: Murphy conv. (also hardly mention, HLB–WOD–Mercedes, first words); Carter int. (also bringing women to Court). The night the water rights case came down, Hugo laughingly told Elizabeth about Douglas's dissent, "Oh, I think he has always considered himself an authority on matters like that in the West and he resents my poaching on his territory."

13. HLB to Hazel Davis 1/18/61 (criticism); *Harvard Classics*, v. 27, p. 251, in HLB Books (soldiers); SFB, Kester (clerk), Kenneth Meiklejohn (tennis) ints.; Lewis, *Make No Law: The Sullivan Case and the First Amendment* (N.Y., 1991), 133–34 (three), 175 (great service); conference notes, TC papers; Schwartz, *Super*, 532–33 (consensus); Harry Kalven, Jr., "The New York Times Case: A Note on 'The Central Meaning of the First Amendment,'" 1964 *Supreme Court Rev.* 191 (Meiklejohn on dancing in streets); HLB tribute to Meiklejohn at the Capitol, 1/15/65, partly reprinted in "Homage to Alexander Meiklejohn, Champion of the First Amendment," 12 *Rights* (1965, nos. 1&2), 10; Meiklejohn to WOD 1/28/64, Meiklejohn papers, State Hist. Scty. of Wisconsin (rushed up). "I have always viewed personal attacks as incident to my work"; HLB to Charles Groves Haines 7/2/46.

14. Rodell ints. with justices, FR private papers (no voices raised); Warner, "Report" (absolutely); HLB to McNulty 10/19/64 (pleased); *Time* 10/9/64 (Black Court).

Chapter 36

SOURCES: HLB, *Memoirs*; HLB, Jr., *Father*; *Deliberations*; A. E. Dick Howard, "Mr. Justice Black: The Negro Protest Movement and the Rule of Law," 53 *Virginia Law Rev.* 1030 (1967); Schwartz, *Super*.

1. HLB, Jr., to HLB 8/18/57 (thought of leaving); HLB to HLB, Jr. 8/21/57 (thoroughly); HLB to Jerome Cooper 11/3/61 (sacrifice); VH, *Alabama: A History* (N.Y., 1977), 141 (recreational facilities); HLB to SFB 12/21/61, CB papers; VH int. with Cooper, VH papers (responsive chord); HLB to VFD 10/19/64 (UA library, *Time*); HLB to Daniel Meador 3/13/63 (good advertisement); Abe Berkowitz et al. to HLB 3/18/64 (Birmingham lawyers); HLB to Vernon Patrick 4/10/64, 6/5/64 (courageous); HLB to Ben Ray 6/27/62; "Justice Black and His State," BN 5/24/64 (misunderstood); HLB to Edward B. Rozelle 3/4/65 (more and more people); BPH 12/5/67 (greatest man); HLB to Ray Jenkins 9/7/65 (tragedy).

Birmingham even filled the holes in a public golf course with concrete to defy integration.

2. Choper int. (remember nigras); *Boynton v. Virginia* (1960, first case); Saunders, Hill (the case was *Smith v. Bennett*, argued 3/28/61) ints.; WOD memoranda 6/18/63, in Urofsky, *Douglas*, 169–71 (parades should be stopped, concerning *Salter v. City of Jackson* [1963]; high time, concerning *Ford v. Tennessee* [1964]); Freund, *Supreme*, 48, in HLB Books (1st amendment protects speech). November 1962 conference: I have combined conference notes in the TC, EW, WJB and WOD papers. (Schwartz uses the WJB papers without attribution throughout *Super.*)

3. Oberdorfer, VFD, Calabresi, Dorsen ints.; Dorsen to author 5/16/86 (JMH).

4. HLB to brethren (TC, JMH, Stewart and White) 3/5/64, JMH papers (Congress); Goldberg, UA remarks (justices not very good, when Hugo in agreement); Goldberg int. (HLB had better); Schwartz, *Unpublished Warren*, 187 (unnecessarily create); Ball, *Power*, 168 (Hugo beside himself). ESB, likely using Hugo's word, wrote in her diary that Clark "deserted" him. HLB also explicitly balanced in *Martin v. City of Struthers* (1943).

5. *Cox v. Louisiana* (1965, courthouse protest case; streets are not now); *Brown v. Louisiana* (1965, library protest case; TC, JMH and Stewart joined his opinion); WP 2/24/66 (delivering opinion); HLB int. (government must protect itself); Ball, *Power*, 165 (sheriff acted correctly), 166 (major unarticulated premise); EW to Fortas 1/12/66, EW papers, (somewhat saddened).

6. Kester (civil rights movement), CJD, Sidney Davis (split-level system), Calabresi (racial problem) ints.; HLB to Louis Lusky 7/11/68 (unfortunately); diary 2/7/66, Pearson papers (having problems); Graff conv. (WJB to friends); *Feiner v. N.Y.* (1951, long step).

Chapter 37

SOURCES: Ball, *Power*; HLB, *Memoirs*; Schwartz, *Super.*

1. Mill, *Three Essays: On Liberty; Representative Government; The Subjection of Women* (London, 1933), 214–15 (absolute liberties), in HLB Books; JBP int. (behind barn); *Roth v. U.S.* (1957, utterly without); *Kingsley International Pictures Corp. v. Regents* (1959, *Lady Chatterley's Lover* case); unedited transcript, 1968 CBS int., Benjamin papers (God-like power). Tacitus: *Time* 10/9/64; Freeman int. HLB bought this edition of Mill on 11/18/ 65; he first read "On Liberty" at least forty years earlier.

2. Calabresi (protect First Amendment), Wallace (HLB reply to EW), Saunders (based on cases) ints.; Friendly, *Constitution*, 189–210; TC typed draft 4/[22]/61, HLBLC; TC typed draft 4/25/61 ("TCC draft after OK from HLB, 4/27/61"); HLB to TC [about 5/2/61] (barriers), both TC papers; *Mapp*, 367 U.S. at 666 (HLB on *Boyd*); HLB to TC 6/15/ 61 (right of privacy, HLB's emphasis).

3. Protection: HLB, written on TC recirculation (draft no. 5), [about 5/1/63], "new draft with latest suggestions of Black, J., as per your discussion with his clerks," TC papers, incorporated in 374 U.S. at 32 (protection from). Test under 4th amendment: written on WJB circulation 5/1/64, *Malloy v. Hogan*, p. 5 (HLB softened this in a memorandum to WJB 5/12/64). WJB changed a quotation in the text of his opinion from *Wolf* to *Mapp*, simply citing *Wolf* in a footnote; see 378 U.S. at 6.

4. HLB draft 5/13/65 (dictated version); HLB to Redlich 6/26/68 (too much trouble); William

Dempsey (most difficult), Redlich (WJB suggestion; the article was Redlich, "Are There 'Certain Rights . . . Retained by the People'?" 37 *New York Univ. Law Rev.* 787 [1962], HLB (religions split), Price (come up with that), Saunders (notion of privacy) ints. 1951: George Treister to HLB 2/1/51; the draft using the Ninth Amendment in *Joint Anti-Fascist Refugee v. McGrath* does not survive.

5. Harmon (can't be against law), Susman (too far), Price (technicalities), Schulhofer (out of synch, clerk memo), ESB ints.; *Berger v. N.Y.* (1967, obvious guilt, sleight-of-hand, chameleon); *Simmons v. U.S.* (1968, criminals to book). "He said the Wall Street crowd was big on the Fourth Amendment but on the Fifth," noted Schulhofer. As he had thirty years earlier, "he gave the impression it was a class issue."

6. HLB to Hazel Davis 7/17/62 (unaccountable reason, independent); HLB to CJD 3/29/60 (latter); HLB to JBP 11/10/60, JBP papers (timid); SFB int. (oath).

7. C. Alfonso Smith, "The First Ten in Washington," *World Tennis* 4/63 (finest players); HLB to SFB 9/5/62, JBP papers, and 9/10/62, CB papers, *WS* 2/27/66 (cases mostly); Lamb (invitation), ESB (awe), HER (hard to live with) ints.; HLB to Frida Laski 3/9/61; HLB to Alma Black [about 3/3/60], (cousin); Howe, *Holmes-Laski*, I, 210, in HLB books (reconciling self); Edward Dumbauld, "Thomas Jefferson and Pennsylvania Courts," 37 *Penn. Bar Assoc. Quar.* (3/66), 236 (Jefferson).

8. Susman, Harmon (you fellows) ints.; Neil N. Bernstein, "The Supreme Court and Secondary Source Material: 1965 Term," 57 *Georgetown Law Jour.* 55 (1968); Raymond Pace Alexander in "The Legal Intelligencer" (Phila.) 9/18/67, quoted in Frances Lamb to JMH 9/29/67, JMH papers (most dramatic); VH to Robert Gallagher 9/12/67, VH papers (tennis player, doctors). London: Billington, *Blacks*; ESB int. One week after the August operation HLB saw Lyndon Johnson off-the-record; LBJL. HLB allowed a clerk to write the first draft of the majority opinion in *U.S. v. Von's Grocery* (1966), an important antitrust case.

9. North (lipstick; this was in between WOD's marriages), Sam Moskow (loverboy), Price (right thing), Kester (another of guys) ints.; *U.S. v. Barnett* (1964, Mississippi case); EC to HLB 5/13/63; HLB to EC 5/17/63; Norman Dorsen to HLB 5/20/64 (illiberalism). WJB: *In Memoriam, Honorable Hugo LaFayette Black—Proceedings of the Bar and Officers of the Supreme Court of the United States* 4/18/72, 78. (pressure cooker); WJB int. (accepted advice). Stewart: North int. (coming along); Warner, "Report" (great sincerity). The Blacks and the Goldbergs long enjoyed a family friendship. Not only had Josephine Black and Dorothy Goldberg painted together nearly every day for two years, but Goldberg had encouraged Hugo, Jr., to go into labor law and later, when secretary of labor, offered him a position in the Labor Department, which he turned down.

10. Thurman Arnold, Jr., WJB, Schmidt (Hugo never changes mind), Price (just what we needed, knew more law), EW clerks (talk with HLB, clerks wrote opinions), Simon (den of themes: the case was *Penn-Central* [1968]), Ziffrin (gave impression) ints.; EW to HLB 3/28/66 (pleasure). Wanting to pay tribute: HLB to WOD 3/21/66. Warren read the briefs carefully to gain the import of controlling precedents, but only if absolutely necessary would he look at the precedents themselves; Bring int. He had a real grasp of issues, said James Roosevelt (int.), who knew him well for over twenty-five years, "but he was limited. If he were President, he would have to study awfully hard to understand the situation in Europe or Russia, for example, and I'm not sure he would understand any of the intricacies or finer points. He wasn't lazy but just not theoretically inclined. He liked things pretty much pat and dry, and to deal with them as they are, not as they might be because of

others' actions. He was charming and a wonderfully smooth politician, but not much of a thinker or someone who liked to ponder with those inevitable problems."

11. Feller (Goldberg–LBJ), HLB (Goldberg wanted presidency), Reich, Nabers (took in stride) ints.; Kalman, *Fortas*, 321 (JMH asked); Fortas to HLB 2/27/66; HLB to WOD 8/3/65). Obscure case: *U.S. v. Yazell* (1966): HLB draft for Court, recirculated 11/2/65; Fortas draft dissent, circulated 11/30/65.

12. *Louisiana v. U.S.* (1965, cherished right); *South Carolina v. Katzenbach* (1966, preclearance); *Allen v. State Board of Elections* (1969, dissenting opinion, Reconstruction); HLB to Marilyn Black 3/11/66 (grandniece); HLB to Reich 6/28/65 (day-by-day); Girard int. (read out loud). Rape case: *Giles v. Maryland* (1967); Susman int. Virginia poll tax: Yarbrough, *Black*, 229; Schwartz, "More Unpublished Warren Court Opinions," 1986 *Supreme Court Rev.* 317 (conference remarks); *Harper v. Virginia Board of Elections* (1966, notions change; originally emphasized); HLB typed (first) draft, 3/16/66; Ziffrin int. (annoyed EW); WOD to conference, 3/22/66 (responding). 1966 Georgia case (*Fortson v. Morris*): NYT 12/14/66 (argument).

13. WJB (also WJB to author 9/8/76), Choper (hardened) ints.; WJB to HLB [about 4/21/67] (magnificent opinion, about *Afroyim v. Rusk*, holding that the Fourteenth Amendment denied Congress authority to strip Americans of citizenship without their consent.).

Chapter 38

SOURCES: HLB, *Memoirs*.

1. FR to *New Republic* about 3/21/60 (velvet claws); Ely, *Democracy and Distrust: A Theory of Judicial Review* (Cambridge, Mass., 1980), 3; Mendelson, "Hugo Black and Judicial Discretion," 85 *Pol. Sci. Quar.* 17 (1970); Bickel, *The Supreme Court and the Idea of Progress* (N.Y., 1970), 39; Freund, *Law*, 222 (echoed by Philip Kurland, book review, *Chic. Sun-Times* 11/3/68); Corcoran to HLB 7/13/62; George C. Freeman, Jr., to John Wessells 4/22/66, Freeman papers (Wyzanski comment); HLB to Robert E. L. Strider 3/12/65 (assume reason; thus HLB turned down honorary degrees from Harvard, Yale and Columbia, among other institutions); HLB to John McNulty 7/3/68 (Strickland, *Black*).

2. VH int. with Cooper, VH papers (Cooper); MA 7/7/66 (word got out); NYT 5/11/68 (bar association); Susman (gratified), ESB (Wallace) ints.; Freund, "Memo" (brotherly love); HLB to Edward Rozelle 8/30/65 (grandnephew); Cooper, "Footnotes" (reminisced); BN 7/17/66 (not mad). Bar invitations: James Clark int.; HLB to Clark 11/6/67 (have in home). Plato's famous parable about how people deceive themselves by looking at shadows instead of substance, was one of Black's favorites and he liked to suggest it especially to southerners: he thought it typified the south before integration.

3. NYT 5/11/68 (white and black robes, Birmingham bar); *Thucydides Translated Into English* (Benjamin Jowett trans.) (London, 1900, 2nd ed., rev.), I, 125, in HLB Books; Charles Morgan, Jr., *A Time to Speak* (N.Y., 1964), 6 (reporter on progress); BN 5/4/68 (speech), 5/6/68 (home); VFD to HLB 5/8/68; HLB to VFD 5/10/68. State bar speech: SC (Bryant); ESB to Ethel and JMH 8/22/68, JMH papers; A. K. Callahan to author 3/17/89; BPH 7/20/68 (votes). Miami: *Miami Herald* 2/23/68; HLB, Jr., *Father*, 105. The wit apparently was Maurice Rogers, a Birmingham lawyer who used it while writing the *Dallas Morning News* in 1964, calling Black's nephew, John Andrew Martin, a Birmingham native prac-

ticing law in Dallas, a communist for having written the *BN* praising Black; *BN* 6/9/64; Martin int.

4. Calabresi int. (John Kennedy); HLB to Cyril Pruet 2/20/61 (Stevenson). Frank book: HLB to JPF 4/5/49; Burns, review, 35 *Amer. Bar Assn. Jour.* 213 (1949). Warren Commission: North int. EW acceptance: Pearson int. with WJB; Pearson, "The 'Chief,' " unpublished manuscript, both Pearson papers.

5. Lady Bird Johnson, Meador (ESB said) ints.; HLB to VFD; 7/8/59 (do not believe); HLB to JPF 10/9/59 (formidable); HLB to LBJ 12/3/63 (Fate; originally emphasized), 3/7/65; LBJ to HLB 2/27/65 (birthday letter; "Hugo read [it] aloud," Elizabeth noted, "and before he finished his voice broke a little and his eyes were moist"). Johnsons coming to Blacks: DeMeritte, Lady Bird Johnson ints.; Lady Bird Johnson, *A White House Diary* (N.Y., 1970), 513–14 (after dinner).

6. Lady Bird Johnson to Lucyle Taylor 3/31/66, LBJL (warmest evenings); LBJL (meeting, assistant noted); WJB (take car to White House), Lady Bird Johnson (reading from unpublished part of her diaries) ints.; Bess Abell to LBJ 2/28/66, LBJL (small party). Hill: HLB to John Bestor Robertson, Jr., 7/23/62 (most infrequently); ESB (Lister doesn't believe, another wife), North (tradition), Hubbard (White House dinner) ints. Cooper and judgeship (early 1961): ESB, Cooper ints. Hill admission: Ray Jenkins, "Lister Hill," *BES* 12/29/84; MA 8/21/77. The LBJ Library has no record of the Blacks and Hills at dinner. Most likely, according to Mrs. Johnson (int.), "Lyndon had Jack Valenti call Lister and the Justice to come over. It would be just like Lyndon to do that."

7. Lady Bird Johnson (party), Meador, Agronsky (HLB–Humphrey) ints.; Johnson, *Diary,* 513–14; HLB to Charles Reich 5/2/67. In his will HLB left $1500 to Lizzie Mae, who was indispensable to his daily functioning, and $1000 to Spencer.

8. Vietnam: Kester, Nabers, Price, Lady Bird Johnson, Oberdorfer ints.; Vardaman remarks UA (movie actor); HLB OH, LBJL (don't know how much).

9. William Warren, Schulhofer, Agronsky (hardest) ints.; HLB to JPF 6/11/59; HLB to William Warren 7/23/59; HLB to EC 12/5/58, EC papers; Commager to HLB 12/11/66; HLB to Commager 1/9/67, 1/24/67 (try as hard); HLB to William Warren 1/17/67 (number of people). Thought saw convert: Cox, "Foreward: Constitutional Adjudication and the Promotion of Human Rights," 80 *Harv. Law Rev.* 91 (1966); Kalven, "Upon Rereading Mr. Justice Black on the First Amendment," 14 *U.C.L.A. Law Rev.* 428 (1967).

10. HLB, *Faith,* 8 (language and history), 11 (known different court), 21 (appeal), 56 (freedom to believe), 63 (will act, government by groups), 67–68 (experiences); HLB to Commager 4/4/68; Jon R. Waltz, book review, *WP* 10/27/68. Find anything: H. Brandt Ayers, "Clay County forgets a son," *Anniston* (Ala.) *Star* 3/9/86; Ayers int. HLB sent the lectures to Commager inscribed: "To Prof. Henry Steele Commager with admiration and appreciation for the great public service he has rendered."

11. Agronsky, Friendly, Strickland ints.; ESB, "Hugo Black: A Memorial Portrait," *Yearbook 1982, Sup. Ct. Hist. Scty.*; Stephen Strickland to ESB 10/11/76; transcript, CBS Reports, "Mr. Justice Douglas," 9/6/72 (HLB–WOD); HLB, Jr., *Father,* 244 (Nixon's reaction); HLB CBS int., unedited transcript, 78–79, Benjamin papers (just joined Klan); Liva Baker, *Miranda: Crime, Law and Politics* (N.Y., 1983), 251 (electrifying).

12. JPF, "Funeral" (favor to wife); *BN* 12/5/68 (Agronsky); WOD to HLB [12/2/68], (excellent); Potter Stewart to HLB 12/4/68 (fine); Friendly (best ever), Westen (old man

talk) ints.; HLB to Benjamin 4/16/70 (convinced); Max Lerner, "The Man From Ala-bama," *NYP* 12/5/68 (reverence). Justice not lawyer: Saunders, Ragland; Abell (HLB told him this in 1958) ints. The CBS interview is reprinted in 9 *Southwestern Univ. Law Rev.* 937 (1977).

Chapter 39

SOURCES: HLB, *Memoirs;* HLB, Jr., *Father;* ESB, *Rebel;* Schwartz, *Ascent, Super, Swann's Way: The School Busing Case and the Supreme Court* (N.Y., 1986); Woodward, *Brethren*

1. Yarbrough, *Harlan,* xii (good Republican), 138 (protocol), 333 (birthday greeting); Bran-nan (mini-strokes; he was HLB's neurologist), Meador (work harder), Seneker (WOD), Lockwood (not buy proposition) ints.; HLB to Norman Redlich 3/29/68 (dissent few years ago); *Amalgamated Food Employees v. Logan Valley Plaza* (1968). HLB and Harlan even had their clerks join the other justice for lunch and dinner; McCaw int.

2. *Brown v. Louisiana* (1966, library sit-in case); Levitt (Klan, need all summer), Rosenbloom (Fortas writing) ints.; Fortas draft opinion, *Time v. Hill,* recirculated 6/14/66, and HLB comments on it (has relation to public information); WJB, UA remarks (seek to sell views); HLB memorandum, *Time v. Hill,* 10/17/66 (use of weighing process); *Time, Inc. v. Hill* (1967). It did not help Black's feelings toward Fortas that at the very time Fortas circulated his draft he proposed adding to another opinion he was writing for the Court that Black's position in dissent partly "ignores the truth (stated in a different context) that 'Governments like ours were formed to substitute the rule of law for the rule of force' [citing an earlier HLB dissent]. I would add that the rule of law equally was substituted for the rule of deceit": Fortas memorandum 6/17/66, re *Dennis v. U.S.*

3. HLB to Linwood G. Koger 11/12/52 (hold character), HLB to Marshall 11/8/62 (how happy); Brant int. (got book); HLB to Robert A. Bailey 10/27/67 (historical event). HLB had also given Marshall the oath in the White House when he became Solicitor General in August 1965; ESB to Ethel and JMH 9/1/67, JMH papers.

4. Schulhofer (mammoth arguments), Meyer (jock strap) ints.; *Tinker v. Des Moines School District* (1969); Cohen, *Constitutional,* 521–22 (quoting WOD conference; notes); Kal-man, *Fortas,* 290 (Fortas); HLB to John McNulty 4/26/67 (proud of children); HLB to Reich 6/24/69 (difficult to believe); HLB to Charles Alan Wright 8/27/69 (lean to belief). SFB, Jr.: HLB to CB 12/13/68 (sorry to learn); ESB unpublished diary 12/23/68. On 5/23/66 HLB wrote Wright, a Yale Law School classmate of Hugo, Jr.'s, "A number of years ago, I reached the conclusion that you were performing a very fine public service both in the classroom and in your public work outside the classroom. As a matter of fact I have mentioned to several people that I hope the Government will sometime have the benefit of your services as a judge."

5. Removed from first draft by HLB in *Frank v. U.S.* (1969, dissent; constitution does not contain); BES 3/24/67 (the case was *Thorpe v. Housing Authority of Durham;* HLB joined the Court's per curiam opinion); Earl Dudley (3/68; *Bumper v. North*), Agronsky ints.; John Medelman, "Do you swear to tell the truth, the whole truth, and nothing but the truth, Justice Black? He does," *Esquire* 6/68; *Goldberg v. Kelly* (1970, deep apprehension); HLB to Reich 6/23/64 (like article): "Lawyers and doctors in particular, I think, need to give this matter more consideration than they ever have in the past. And it is too much to hope, I believe, that lawyers' associations themselves can be expected to protect the

rights of individual lawyers the same as they would be protected under a 'law of the land' procedure." Reich had inscribed a copy of the article "For HLB, from whose dissents this article grew"; "The New Property," 73 *Yale Law Jour.* 733 (1964). HLB mentioned the Court's expanding caseload in dissents starting in 1968, even in pauper's and habeas corpus cases.

6. Gaither (happy to follow), ESB, Lamb ints.; NYT 6/27/68 (LBJ reply); Murphy, *Fortas*, 524–25 (on fence); HLB to VFD 5/27/69 (sense of sorrow); HLB to B.C. Mann 9/22/69 (read history); WS 9/19/71 (disciple of HLB).

7. O'Brien, *Storm*, (1986 ed.); Harmon int. 1970 birthday: 397 U.S. v; Burger to justices [except HLB], 1/23/70, JMH papers. Occasionally Burger discussed the assignment of opinions with HLB, as Warren had, and when in the majority, HLB had his choice of opinions to write; ESB unpublished diary 11/18/69; Harmon int.

8. Parker (convictions of young), Anne Black (long hair), Harmon (tease) ints.; Reich, *The Greening of America* (N.Y., 1970), 21, in HLB Books. Capital punishment: Kester (Goldberg petition in *Rudolph v. Alabama*), Price (legislative decision) ints. Abortion: Harmon int.; Yarbrough, *Harlan*, 313–14 (*U.S. v. Vuitch*). 1969 opinion: HLB to JMH 5/28/69, JMH papers, concerning *Boykin v. Alabama*.

9. HLB inscription of *Constitutional Faith* to WOD 10/19/68 (genius); Ball, *Power*, 6 (look at each other); Seneker (Harvard tribute), Price (HLB clerks), Arbitage (FDR), Cooper (not fighting), Lamb (almost stroke), Bring (pants zipped), Stone (long relationship), HLB, Jr. (possible WOD impeachment) ints.; HLB to WOD [1964], (labor pains); HLB to FR 5/13/70 (hub-bub). Burger pressure: William Safire, *Before the Fall: An Inside View of the Pre-Watergate White House* (N.Y., 1977, paper ed.), 345; Ehrlichman, 110. Note: Stone, Powe ints. HLB repeated his remark to Justice Brennan and Marx Leva, his second clerk and long a good friend of Douglas's, but not to Elizabeth. "Hugo was serious," Brennan said: ESB, Leva, WJB ints. HLB's article was "William Orville Douglas," 73 *Yale Law Jour.* 915 (1964).

10. Ball, *Power*, 78 (Blackmun); *Alexander v. Holmes County* (1969, in chambers; no excuse); WJB (numb), Mnookin (blackmail) ints.; HLB to justices 10/26/69 (extirpate); HLB draft dissent [10/26/69]; *Alexander v. Holmes County* (1969); MA 10/14/70 (oral argument; the case was *Swann v. Charlotte-Mecklenburg* [1971]); HLB to Harry Golden 10/26/70 (father walked).

11. *Baird v. State Bar of Arizona* (1971); *Cohen v. California* (1971, JMH opinion); WJB, Lamb (letters), Calabresi ints.; *Karr v. Schmidt* (1971, in chambers; hair decision). Young men: I have combined HLB to Sam Daniels and Neal Rutledge 10/14/57; and to Eleanor Reich Brussel 3/12/63. Nixon added by hand to a formal complimentary letter: "As I have told many of my fellow lawyers, you were the sharpest questioner of all when I appeared before the Court!": ESB, *Rebel*.

12. Harmon (also nicknames), Speth (nicknames) ints.; *Coolidge v. New Hampshire* (1971); HLB to VFD 2/26/71; Frances Lamb, "Prelude to Death," 9/25/73 (eye). HLB had developed an infected eye and ear in Florida in February 1971.

13. ALS (purer; to whom Ray told this), John Black (take charge) ints.; Anthony Lewis, "In Search of Jimmy Carter," NYT 5/31/76 (northern prejudice); HLB to John Fischer 6/24/64 (southern contribution); HLB, "There is a South of Union and Freedom," 2 *Georgia Law Rev.* 10 (1967; HLB had quoted this poem in several speeches; it also appears in William H. Skaggs, *The Southern Oligarchy* [N.Y., 1924], 424, which HLB ordered in

10/40 and read shortly thereafter, but likely first read it much earlier); HLB to Lister Hill 1/4/69.

14. Johnson holding Wallace in contempt: Bass, *Taming*, 185–96; Saunders int. (he clerked in 1959–60 for Richard Rives, who sat in the same building as Johnson); *U.S. v. Montgomery County Bd. of Education* (1969). Wright: Michael S. Bernick, "The Unusual Odyssey of J. Skelly Wright," 7 *Hastings Con. Law Quar.* 971 (1978, New Orleans); Wright, Agronsky (worshipped) ints.; HLB to Donald Edgar 7/8/59 (American at best); HLB to Helen and Skelly Wright 3/1/61 (McCord); Ruth Bader Ginsburg, "In Memoriam: Judge J. Skelly Wright," 57 *Geo. Wash. Univ. Law Rev.* 1034 (1989) (clothes; they went to T. I. Swartz and Sons in Baltimore, from whom HLB bought his suits for many years). Brown int. (thrilled). I have pieced together the 1967 speech from the following: *Ala. Jour.*, 5/13, 27/67; Bass, *Unlikely*, 324; *Atlanta Constitution* 9/27/71; and an incomplete transcript "from minutes as taken by Helen Randall, secretary," given to me by ESB.

15. BN 7/17/70 (Burger and invitation); *BPH* 2/27/76 (salute, happy for homage); HLB to C. J. Coley 7/6/70 (go with Burger); *NYT* 7/19/70 (tribute); Clarence C. Dill, "Congress— Impressions Before and After Going," speech 11/3/54, Dill papers, Eastern Wash. Hist. Scty. (music); Hare int. (due).

16. HLB to Knopf 3/20/56; Howe, *Holmes-Laski*, II, 393, in HLB books (Holmes; HLB also noted the page on the inside back cover); HLB to Golden 9/23/69; HLB to EC 11/1/56; Patrick (awful), ESB, HLB. Lamb (brother FF), Saunders (confidential matters: HLB specifically referred to Philip Kurland's derogatory remarks on Murphy and Vinson; book review, 22 *Univ. of Chic. Law Rev.* 297 [1954]) ints.; HLB to Walter F. Murphy 9/4/63 (remain immune); HLB to VFD 12/8/65 (think much); VFD to HLB 1/17/66 (seem to want); HLB to C. J. Coley 11/21/66 (national activities); *BPH* 2/27/76 (unfair inferences); HLB to Howard Ball 1/21/69 (not sure); Lamb comments on HLB to S. Sidney Ulmer 5/4/70 (prefer letter not published) 5/15/70 (thought for some time, serve history better); HLB to Ulmer 9/29/70 (so-called sources); HLB to Thomas L. Jones 11/3/70 (old papers). Ulmer wrote about the correspondence in "Bricolage and Assorted Thoughts on Working in the Papers of Supreme Court Justices," 35 *Jour. of Politics* 286 (1973).

17. HLB to Hazel Davis 10/24/61 (JPF); HLB to VFD 2/26/71 (over-estimating); to Hazel Davis 2/26/71; Schulhofer int. (effrontery); HLB to Goldberg 4/23/64, in *Deliberations*; HLB to Tinsley E. Yarbrough 10/13/70 (congratulate; the paper was eventually published as "Mr. Justice Black an Legal Positivism," 57 *Virginia Law Rev.* 375 [1971]); HLB to Allen Sultan 10/13/70, whose review appeared in 47 *Jour. Urban Law* 579 (1970).

Chapter 40

sources: ESB, *Rebel*; HLB, *Memoirs*; HLB, Jr., *Father*; Frances Lamb, "Prelude to Death" (1973, privately printed); Woodward, *Brethren*.

1. Abell, *Pearson*, 235 (press protected); Parker (Checkers), Harmon (prior restraint) ints.; Seth Goldslager to FR 11/17/70, FR private papers (aims of press suffer); ESB to VFD 6/16/71, copy in author's possession (neurologist); HLB to Charles A. Bane 7/28/67 (impossible to say anything).

2. Harmon (never too fond, too bad *Times*), Griswold (type of case, compromise) ints.; 403 U.S. 942 (certiorari granted); Sanford J. Ungar, *The Papers and the Papers: An Account of*

the *Legal and Political Battle over the Pentagon Papers* (N.Y., 1972), 162–63 (gun), 221–22; Salisbury, *Times*, 238. Government agent and lawyer: Griswold, "The Pentagon Papers Case: A Personal Footnote," *1984 Yearbook of Sup. Ct. Hist. Scty.*; Griswold, *Ould*, 303–8; "Griswold—ABA Dinner Speaker," *Stanford Lawyer* (winter 1972–73); Salisbury, 327–28.

3. *New York Times Co. v. U.S.* (1971, HLB-Griswold); Schwartz, *Ascent*, 161 (White announced); Ungar, *Papers*, 188–92 (St.L. P-D); Harmon int. (HLB objections); BN 7/1/71 (after decision). HLB kept a copy of "I Am a Good Old Rebel" in his desk drawer at home.

4. Cooper (vowed), Girard (1957), Feeney (1961), Freeman (hardest things), Price (as long as I can), Reynolds ints.; BPH 3/4/67 (1967); HLB to JPF 7/9/68. HLB told Freeman that he had asked the same thing of Oberdorfer "and two others of my clerks" without naming them.

5. HLB int. (during last year); HLB to Dilliard 12/7/70; HLB to David and Joan Corcoran 3/5/71; Milo Howard int. (stairs). Card on desk: Harmon int.; Lamb memorandum, "Stephen Johnson Field, Hugo L. Black," 7/15/71, prepared in response to JPF to Lamb 7/13/71.

6. HLB to Abe Berkowitz (wonderful), to Jerome Cooper (grand), both 5/25/64; Brannan (stroke victims), Nancy Black (die, JMH on life) ints.; *Ala. Jour.* 4/13/85 (going to die); diary 10/2/71, Pepper papers (system; Tom Corcoran told this to Pepper, noting JMH expressed the same fear). Step down: Oberdorfer, Parnell ints.

7. HLB to Lamb [9/1/71]: "If you have any questions about what are conference notes to be burned and what are not, and you are not able to consult with me, Hugo, Jr., will tell you what to do, which is to destroy them all"; HLB, Jr. ("when your father tells you to do something, you do it"), Gressman ints. (HLB, Jr., told), ESB (Johnson good justice) ints. Burger–Nixon: Bass, *Taming*, 276; Bass conv. "Virginia Durr told me that Black wanted me as his successor when he was very ill," Johnson later said (int.), "but I dismissed it as rumor." HLB had earlier expressed the wish that Skelly Wright be his successor; JPF int.

8. HLB, Jr. (EW), Brannan (doctors) ints.; *Miami Herald* 9/18/71 (Burger); Lerner, "I Remember Hugo," NYP 9/22/71; Cooper, "Alabama" (bar associations); JBP int. (EW); *Atlanta Constitution* 9/25/71 (Warren). The Alabama House resolution read: ". . . as Justice Black steps down from the bench for a well-desrved rest, the people of Alabama, through their legislature, pray that Providence will ever guide and sustain him, confident that history will regard Justice Black as one of the true giants of jurisprudence. . . ." Adopted on the last night of the session, it "initially was introduced as a House Joint Resolution," wrote Fred Gray, the black representative who had worked with Cliff Durr during the Montgomery bus boycott, "but when it became apparent that it was possible that the matter would never be brought up in the Senate, I introduced the identical resolution as a House Resolution"; Fred D. Gray to VFD 11/19/71, VFD papers; see Ala. House Journal, Regular Session, 1971, v. 5, p. 6059, 6451. Robert Edington of Mobile, an unabashed liberal and the son of HLB's law school friend David Edington, introduced it in the senate.

9. JPF, *Funeral*; Joseph Hagan int.; BN 9/29/71 (services); William Safire, "On Temper," NYT 8/23/73 (Nixon). Several days later, Elizabeth took the funeral register to John Harlan: he was the last person to sign it. For the sake of continuity, I have used some of the ideas and language in the introduction.

PERMISSIONS ACKNOWLEDGMENTS

Grateful acknowledgment is made to the following for permission to reprint previously published and unpublished material:

Alabama Department of Archives and History: Excerpts from Bankhead telegrams to Hugo Black, August 13, 17, 1937. The John H. Bankhead, Jr., papers. Reprinted by permission of the Alabama Department of Archives and History, Montgomery, Alabama.

The Baltimore Sun Company: Excerpt from "Alabama Editor, Who Never Cast Vote for Black, Describes Him" by Grover C. Hall, Jr. (*The Baltimore Sun*, August 13, 1937), copyright © 1936 by The Baltimore Sun Company. Reprinted by permission of The Baltimore Sun Company.

Bentley Historical Library: Excerpt of quote by Frances S. Copeland from the article "The Good Guest." Royal S. Copeland Papers, Box 23, Bentley Historical Library, University of Michigan. Reprinted by permission.

Melford O. Cleveland: Excerpt from a letter to Hugo Black, November 12, 1953. Reprinted by permission of Melford O. Cleveland.

The Estate of William O. Douglas: Excerpts used from the William O. Douglas papers reprinted by permission of Cathleen Douglas Stone.

Florida State University Libraries: Excerpts from Claude Pepper's diary (7/23/37; 8/16/37; 5/14/48). Reprinted by permission of the Mildred and Claude Pepper Library, Florida State University Libraries, Tallahassee, Florida.

New York University Law Review: Excerpts from Interview, Justice Black and First Amendment "Absolutes": A Public Interview, 37 N.Y.U.L. Review (1962). Reprinted by permission of the New York University Law Review.

Princeton University Libraries: Excerpts from the David E. Lilienthal papers and the John Marshall Harlen Papers. Seeley G. Mudd Manuscript Library, Department of Rare Books and Special Collections, Princeton University. Reprinted by permission of Princeton University Libraries.

Samford University Library: Excerpts from the J. J. Willett Papers, Special Collection, Samford University Library, Birmingham, Alabama. Reprinted by permission.

Hoover Institution/Stanford University: Excerpts from Raymond Moley's diary copyright © Stanford University. Raymond Moley Collection, Hoover Institution Archives, Stanford University. Reprinted by permission.

University of Arkansas: Excerpts from the Hattie Wyatt Caraway papers. The Special Collections Division, University of Arkansas Libraries, Fayetteville. Reprinted by permission.

University of Colorado at Boulder Libraries: Excerpt from the Edward Keating diaries. Edward Keating Papers, Archives, University of Colorado at Boulder Libraries. Reprinted by permission.

University of Virginia Library: Excerpt from the Homer Cummings Papers. Papers of Homer Cummings, (#9973), Manuscripts Division, Special Collections Department, University of Virginia Library. Reprinted by permission.

Yale University Library: Excerpts from Jerome Frank's letter to Arthur Schlesinger, Jr. (1/22/47) and Jerome Frank's letter to Hugo Black (8/18/54). Jerome Frank Papers, Manuscripts and Archives, Yale University Library. Reprinted by permission.

INDEX

Pizitz, Louis, 98
Planned Parenthood League, 557
Plato, 201, 286, 480, 705n2
Plessy v. Ferguson, 428
Poe, Harvey, 450, 518
Poe v. Ullman, 557
police court, 29–32
Politics of Hope (Schlesinger), 693n9
poll taxes, 115, 568–69
Polybius, 332n
populism, 6–7, 13
Porter, Paul, 374–75
postal policies, 161–66
Powell, Thomas Reed, 286, 367–68
Powell v. Alabama, 527
prayer in public schools, 520–24
precedent, Black's views on, 274
preferred freedoms doctrine, 295–96, 402,
    405
presidential elections:
  1928, 136–40
  1932, 151
  1936, 205–6, 207–8
  1940, 307–8
  1944, 308–9
  1948, 384–85
  1952, 415–16
  1964, 577
press, Black's attitude toward, 198, 414,
    613–14
press, freedom of: *see* speech and press,
    freedom of
Pretorians, 99
Price, Joseph, 582
Prichard, Edward, Jr., 483
Prince, Frank, 261
prior restraint, 613, 614–19
prisoners' rights, 39, 42–43
privacy rights, 296, 556–59
  press freedom and, 590
Progressive National Committee, 207
prohibition (Alabama), 39–42, 44–45
  Mobile whiskey ring, 63–65
prohibition (Birmingham), 31
prohibition (national), 146–47, 148, 152–
    53
property rights:
  sit-in cases and, 541–42, 544, 546, 547
  speech freedom and, 589
  welfare programs and, 594

Prudential Insurance Company, 150–51
Pruet, Clarence, 10, 12
psychiatry, 456
public utilities: *see* holding companies

racial relations:
  antilynching legislation, 201–3, 235–36,
    238
  in Clay County, 13–14
  education and, 225
  intermarriage issue, 129
  lynchings, 77
  see also civil rights movement; desegrega-
    tion; school desegregation; segrega-
    tion
Rainey, Henry, 159
Randolph, Maj. Innes, 195
Rankin, John, 182n
Rascob, John J., 185
rationality test, 276–77
Rauh, Joseph L., Jr., ix, 374n, 375
Ray, Ben, 383, 539, 605
Rayburn, Sam, 175, 375, 576
Reagan, Ronald, 580
"reasonableness" test, 480, 484, 498, 531
Red Jacket case, 135
Redlich, Norman, 557, 558
Reed, Stanley F., 215n, 282, 297, 306,
    320, 322, 333, 342
  antitrust law, 325
  appointment to Supreme Court, 273
  apportionment, 330
  Black's appointment to Supreme Court,
    233, 234, 237, 238
  on Black's opinions, 367
  chief justiceship, interest in, 343
  Court-packing plan, 213
  double jeopardy issue, 350, 351
  Jackson's public attack on Black, 346
  Japanese-Americans, internment of, 316
  labor law, 334
  libel law, 412
  religion, freedom of, 361, 364
  school desegregation, 429, 432, 434, 438
  self-incrimination issue, 352
  speech and press, freedom of, 290, 296,
    370
Reich, Charles, 414–15, 435, 436, 472–73,
    491, 502, 529, 567, 579, 593, 594,
    599

ABOUT THE AUTHOR

Roger K. Newman is Research Scholar at New York University School of Law. Born in Brooklyn, he was educated at Hunter College, the University of Virginia, New York University and the Cardozo Law School. He is co-author of *Banned Films,* a history of movie censorship, which was nominated for several awards. He has written for both popular and professional publications, has taught constitutional law at New York University, and was the recipient of a Guggenheim Fellowship. His interest in Hugo Black goes back twenty-five years, and for this book he traced Black's roots and career, moving to Alabama and Washington and traveling throughout the country. He lives in Riverdale, New York, with his wife, Ricki, and their two children.